RECOGNITION AND ENFORCEMENT OF NON-EU JUDGMENTS

This book examines the EU Member States' national rules on recognition and enforcement of Non-EU judgments.

Through its country report methodology, it explores the rules of 21 Member States in a structured manner. The emerging points of convergence – and divergence – form the basis of a detailed comparative report, which provides a unique overview of the current legal framework of recognition and enforcement of non-EU judgments across the European Union. This allows for (at least) three intriguing points of comparison: between the laws of the individual Member States; between the laws of the Member States and the legal framework applicable to EU judgments under the Brussels Ia Regulation; and between the laws of the Member States and the 2019 HCCH Judgments Convention.

This ambitious and unique work will be an indispensable reference for scholars, policymakers, and practitioners in the field of international commercial law.

Volume 41 in the series Studies in Private International Law

Studies in Private International Law

Recent titles in the series

Private International Law in Nigeria
Chukwuma Okoli and Richard Oppong

Planning the Future of Cross Border Families: A Path Through Coordination
Edited by Ilaria Viarengo and Francesca Villata

The Private International Law of Authentic Instruments
Jonathan Fitchen

The Hague Judgments Convention and Commonwealth Model Law: A Pragmatic Perspective
Abubakri Yekini

A Guide to Global Private International Law
Edited by Paul Beaumont and Jayne Holliday

Parental Child Abduction to Islamic Law Countries
Nazia Yaqub

The Application of Foreign Law in the British and German Courts
Alex Critchley

The HCCH 2019 Judgments Convention: Cornerstones, Prospects, Outlook
Edited by Matthias Weller, João Ribeiro-Bidaoui, Moritz Brinkmann and Nina Dethloff

Jurisdiction Over Non-EU Defendants: Should the Brussels Ia Regulation be Extended?
Edited by Tobias Lutzi, Ennio Piovesani and Dora Zgrabljić Rotar

Private International Law and Competition Litigation in a Global Context
Mihail Danov

Private International Law in Russia
Edited by Anton Asoskov, Daria Levina, and Milana Karayanidi

Private International Law in BRICS: Convergence, Divergence and Reciprocal Lessons
Edited by Stellina Jolly and Saloni Khanderia

Care Proceedings with an International Element: An Empirical Study
Maria Sofia Wright

Recognition and Enforcement of Non-EU Judgments
Edited by Tobias Lutzi, Ennio Piovesani and Dora Zgrabljić Rotar

Recognition and Enforcement of Non-EU Judgments

Edited by
Tobias Lutzi
Ennio Piovesani
and
Dora Zgrabljić Rotar

•HART•
OXFORD • LONDON • NEW YORK • NEW DELHI • SYDNEY

HART PUBLISHING

Bloomsbury Publishing Plc

Kemp House, Chawley Park, Cumnor Hill, Oxford, OX2 9PH, UK

1385 Broadway, New York, NY 10018, USA

Bloomsbury Publishing Ireland Limited, 29 Earlsfort Terrace, Dublin 2, D02 AY28, Ireland

HART PUBLISHING, the Hart/Stag logo, BLOOMSBURY and the Diana logo are trademarks of Bloomsbury Publishing Plc

First published in Great Britain 2026

A catalogue record for this book is available from the British Library.

A catalogue record for this book is available from the Library of Congress.

ISBN: HB: 978-1-50997-937-0
ePDF: 978-1-50997-939-4
ePub: 978-1-50997-938-7

Typeset by Compuscript Ltd, Shannon

FOREWORD

Few cases should be brought in any court without first considering whether a resulting judgment can be satisfied. In a world where relationships commonly cross borders, the satisfaction of a judgment often requires the ability to have that judgment recognised and enforced in the courts of a state other than the state of the court that has granted that judgment. This makes the law of judgment recognition a fundamental matter for transnational litigation practice, for the study of private international law, and for the future development of the law.

In the European Union (EU), the Brussels Ia Regulation has made the recognition and enforcement of judgments from the courts of other Member States a much more convenient and predictable matter than was the case before the existence of the Regulation and its predecessor Convention. Nearly 60 years of practice under those instruments has not, however, resulted in a uniform approach to the recognition and enforcement of judgments from courts outside the EU through either an EU instrument or harmonised Member State law.

Through a set of well-designed questions addressed by experts in 21 of the EU Member States, this book provides an accessible source for considering the law of judgments recognition in each of those Member States. Most importantly, it provides much more than that. The analytical compilation of the results of responses to the questionnaire created by the editors facilitates the practical and academic consideration of both the current state of the law across EU Member States and possibilities for development of the law to bring this element of private international law in those Member States to a more cohesive and coherent form.

In this book, the editors continue a process they began in their earlier book, *Jurisdiction Over Non-EU Defendants: Should the Brussels Ia Regulation be Extended?*. That book provided much of what Article 79 of the Brussels Ia Regulation required from the European Commission (originally due in 2020, but delivered in 2025) in the way of a review of the Brussels Ia Regulation, and, in particular, whether jurisdictional protections provided to defendants from other EU Member States should be extended to defendants from outside the EU. I suspect the first book was well read by Commission staff prior to completion of their 2025 report. Similarly, I hope this book will be studied within the Commission in order to consider whether the EU might adopt common rules for the recognition and enforcement of judgments from outside the EU. The Comparative Report, by compiling important data from the country reports, makes clear the importance of the question of jurisdiction in the court of origin to the requirements for recognition and enforcement in the courts of the 21 EU Member States surveyed. Thus, each of the two books adds value to the other.

The completion of the 2019 Hague Convention on the Recognition and Enforcement of Foreign Judgments in Civil or Commercial Matters, and its ratification by the EU on behalf of all Member States, has particular significance to the matters discussed in this volume, and that significance is incorporated into the questions, country reports and Comparative Report in ways that encourage additional study both in and beyond the EU of various factors involved in the law of judgment recognition. Notably, the discussion of the role of public policy, the basis of jurisdiction asserted in the court of origin, and reciprocity are raised in the questions and discussed here in a format and detail that adds significantly to any consideration of those important elements in a forward-looking legal system.

While the EU has joined the Hague Judgments Convention in an exercise of exclusive competence that makes the Convention effective in its Member States, the slow process of ratification and accession by other states (notably the United States) makes the proper approach to the further development of the law regarding the recognition and enforcement of judgments from non-EU courts in the courts of the Member States an open question. However one addresses that question, the material in this book advances the necessary analysis, making the process much easier. When that is added to the value to litigation practitioners of the information collected and presented here, the result is highly significant indeed.

I commend the editors and their contributors for the excellent work done through the auspices of the Young Research Network of the European Association of Private International Law. I commend to the reader this book as a welcome tool for practitioners, academics and government lawyers. And I look forward to the next product of the Young Research Network.

Ronald A Brand

SERIES EDITOR'S PREFACE

This book is a great example of something that is much better achieved by cooperation of a large team of experts rather than by a single scholar or even a small team of scholars. To give an accurate account of the recognition and enforcement of non-EU foreign judgments in the vast majority of EU Member States is best done, as it has been here, by recruiting experts from each of the Member States. The law discussed here is the national law of each of the 21 EU Member States included in the study on the recognition and enforcement of non-EU foreign judgments. Such recognition and enforcement is very varied in the absence of treaty relations from being almost non-existent in Sweden and the Netherlands, to rather restrictive in Ireland, to varying degrees of generosity in the other Member States analysed in this book. The editors of the book, in the overview given in chapter two, draw on the detailed findings in the following 21 chapters on each of the EU Member States covered in this book, to give us a much clearer understanding of the comparison of all the key nuances of the systems of recognition and enforcement of non-EU foreign judgments in those EU Member States. This will be a great help in enabling people with judgments in non-EU countries (or considering getting a judgment in a non-EU country) to know the likelihood of getting such a judgment recognised and enforced in any of the 21 EU Member States analysed in this book. It also greatly increases the understanding of scholars in this field as to the current law on recognition and enforcement of non-EU judgments in most of the EU Member States. This will enable a much more informed debate about whether the EU should at the next revision of the Brussels Ia Regulation extend the scope of that Regulation to cover the recognition and enforcement of non-EU judgments. This would be no easy task as the Member States cannot rely on the current premiss of the Brussels Ia Regulation in relation to non-EU States. Brussels Ia works on the basis that the direct rules of international jurisdiction are harmonised throughout the EU and therefore there is no need (apart from a few exceptional cases) to review the jurisdiction of the court that gave the judgment (because they should have been applying the same rules of jurisdiction) when deciding whether or not to recognise and enforce the judgment.

Of course, the premiss on which the Brussels Ia Regulation operates as a basis for not reviewing the jurisdiction of the court of origin discriminates against non-EU domiciliaries. In relation to non-EU domiciliaries the EU court of origin may apply exorbitant bases of jurisdiction, not permitted in relation to EU domiciliaries, and the courts in the other EU Member State where recognition and enforcement of the judgment is sought under the Brussels Ia Regulation are not allowed to review the exercise of jurisdiction by the court of origin in this type of case. There is a case in the next revision of Brussels I to limit the recognition and enforcement of EU judgments against non-EU domiciliaries when the basis of jurisdiction was exorbitant. This would finally show a mature approach by the EU to its treatment of this State nationals and businesses. However, this issue is not the subject matter of this book. It was a matter addressed, at least indirectly, in the sister book in the Series to this book which primarily considered tackling this issue by preventing the application of exorbitant bases of jurisdiction to non-EU domiciliaries (rather than allowing indirect jurisdictional control at the recognition and enforcement stage as I suggest here): see Tobias Lutzi, Ennio Piovesani and Dora Zgrabljić Rotar (eds) *Jurisdiction Over Non-EU Defendants: Should the Brussels Ia Regulation be Extended?* The solution suggested by some of the writers in the sister book would be very internationalist and welcomed by non-EU domiciliaries, but it is likely to be a step too far for the EU institutions who may want to preserve some exorbitant levers of jurisdiction for the courts of their Member States against non-EU domiciliaries while other major trading partners (including the UK and USA) keep exorbitant jurisdiction rules in place in relation to EU domiciliaries.

In relation to non-EU judgments there is of course no guarantee at all on which basis the foreign court exercised its jurisdiction whether the judgment relates to EU or non-EU domiciliaries. Therefore, a revised Brussels Ia dealing with recognition and enforcement of non-EU judgments would have to be based on an agreement by the EU legislature (the Council and European Parliament) as to what foreign bases of jurisdiction would be acceptable for this purpose. Furthermore, the Commission would need to be willing to make a Proposal to this effect which the Council and European Parliament by the appropriate majorities could agree on. Such a Proposal could be based on the Brussels Ia direct rules of jurisdiction but this would be very generous to non-EU States without any guarantee of reciprocity. It would be much more generous in terms of the acceptable rules of jurisdiction than the Hague Judgments Convention 2019 to which the EU is a Contracting Party. If the EU were to reduce the acceptable bases of jurisdiction to those in the Hague Judgments Convention 2019 it would make little political sense to unilaterally accept foreign non-EU judgments on that basis. The problem is that there would be no guarantee that non-EU States would recognise and enforce EU judgments on the same basis. Surely it would make more sense simply to remind non-EU States that they can become Contracting Parties to the Hague Judgments Convention 2019, gaining the benefits of getting their judgments recognised and enforced in the EU while accepting the requirement to recognise and enforce judgments from the national courts of EU Member States (apart from Denmark) on the same basis.

Whatever may happen at the next revision of Brussels Ia, which will take at least several years to come to fruition, the best way for non-EU States to ensure that their judgments are recognised and enforced throughout the EU is to become a Party to the Hague Judgments Convention 2019. By doing so they ensure that the minimum standards in that Convention apply to their judgments in all the Member States of the EU apart from Denmark. This immediately overcomes the very restrictive approaches in Sweden and the Netherlands and the rather restrictive approach in Ireland. It also makes it much easier to predict when a non-EU judgment will be enforced in all 27 EU Member States that are governed by the Judgments Convention as the Convention regime is transparent and cannot be changed unilaterally by States or by their courts. The Judgments Convention recently entered into force between the UK and the EU (which should generate some important case law) and it is to be hoped that many more

States will join Albania, the EU (covering 26 of its 27 Member States), Montenegro, Ukraine, UK, and Uruguay as Parties to the Convention.

The EU Member States that are missing from the book are Denmark, Estonia, Luxembourg, Portugal, Slovakia and Slovenia. Hopefully in a future edition of the book chapters on each of these States can be added.

This book is a very useful resource providing data that is not readily available elsewhere and will remain important even if every State in the world becomes a Party to the Hague Judgments Convention because that Convention is a floor and not a ceiling and preserves by Article 15 the possibility of getting a foreign judgment recognised under the national law on recognition and enforcement of foreign judgments. To decide which of the 21 EU Member States have rules on recognition and enforcement of foreign judgments which are, at least in some respects, more generous than the Hague Judgments Convention one can compare the rules set out in this book with the provisions of the Judgments Convention. The latter has been very well analysed in two earlier books in this Series: Abubakri Yekini, *The Hague Judgments Convention and Commonwealth Model Law: A Pragmatic Perspective*; and Matthias Weller, João Ribeiro-Bidaoui, Moritz Brinkmann and Nina Dethlof (eds) *The HCCH 2019 Judgments Convention: Cornerstones, Prospects, Outlook*.

Paul Beaumont FRSE
Professor of Private International Law
University of Stirling

PREFACE

In many ways, this volume may be regarded as a sequel to our 2023 volume, *Jurisdiction over Non-EU Defendants. Should the Brussels Ia Regulation be Extended?*. During our work on that book (and the underlying research project), it became abundantly evident that the distinction drawn by the Brussels Ia Regulation between EU and non-EU defendants for the purposes of jurisdiction is, in numerous respects, connected to the parallel distinction drawn between EU and non-EU judgments. Indeed, the exclusion of non-EU judgments from the Regulation's generous rules on recognition and enforcement (see Articles 36(1), 39) creates a second area in which the courts of the Member States continue to apply the Regulation and domestic law in parallel. With the recently adopted 2019 Hague Judgments Convention providing an particularly timely additional point of reference, the decision to follow up our work on jurisdiction with a consecutive research project on recognition and enforcement that would take a closer look at the national rules governing non-EU judgments was not a difficult one to reach.

Conducted, again, within the framework of the Young Research Network (YRN) of the European Association of Private International Law (EAPIL), the project attracted 30 national reporters, who were able to provide detailed information on 21 Member States. The comparative report that is published as chapter two of this book is testimony, above all else, to their expertise, diligence and continued commitment to the research project.

The project included a hybrid workshop at the University of Turin at the end of 2023 and a concluding conference at the offices of the Permanent Bureau of the Hague Conference on Private International Law (HCCH) a year later, providing the participants with the unique opportunity to discuss our findings in the very same room in which the 2019 Judgments Convention had been prepared, and with many of the people who are currently working on its successful adoption. We are deeply indebted to the EAPIL, the HCCH, and the Centre of International Legal Cooperation (CILC) for their support of the event, financial and otherwise. As more and more states are now considering to join the 2019 Judgments Convention, we hope that the detailed picture of the current treatment of non-EU judgments in the EU Member States painted by our book might prove helpful to some of them.

The production of this book would not have been possible without the ever-so-patient support of Sasha Jawed and Tom Adams at Hart Publishing, the diligent copy-editing by Vicki Hillyard or the excellent editorial assistance of Vivien Kleebauer and Rodas Mehari at the University of Augsburg. The editors would like to express their gratitude to them all.

Tobias Lutzi
Ennio Piovesani
Dora Zgrabljić Rotar

CONTENTS

LIST OF CONTRIBUTORS

Ivan Allegranti, Ph.D. Candidate at the University of Camerino

Karin Arnold, Senior Lecturer at the University of Tübingen

Tess Bens, Research Assistant at the University of Vienna

Katarzyna Bogdziewicz, Professor at Mykolas Romeris University

Ronald A Brand, Chancellor Mark A Nordenberg University Professor at the University of Pittsburgh

Claudia Cavicchioli, Lawyer, Linklaters

Ramona Cirlig, Lawyer, RC International Disputes

Paul Lorenz Eichmüller, University Assistant at the University of Vienna

Aleksandrs Fillers, Associated Professor at the Riga Graduate School of Law

Birgit van Houtert, Assistant Professor at Maastricht University

Yağmur Hortoğlu Grant, Lecturer at Maynooth University

Tena Hoško, Associate Professor at the University of Zagreb

Nicolas Kyriakides, Assistant Professor at the University of Nicosia

Ilia Lassin, PhD Candidate at Sofia University "St. Kliment Ohridski"

Eva Litina, Advisor, Ministry of Maritime Affairs and Insular Policy, Hellenic Republic

Tobias Lutzi, Junior Professor at the University of Augsburg

Radovan Malachta, Assistant professor at Masaryk University

Giedrius Ožiūnas, PhD Candidate at Mykolas Romeris University

Marco Pasqua, PhD Candidate at Università Cattolica del Sacro Cuore

Daniel-Florin Petrache, University Assistant at the University of Bucharest

Blas Piñar Guzmán, Lawyer, Belagua Abogados

Ennio Piovesani, Lawyer, Pistoia Bar Association

Patrik Provazník, Masaryk University

Ioannis Revolidis, Lecturer at the University of Malta

Konstantinos Rokas, Assistant Professor at the Aristotle University of Thessaloniki

Anna María Ruiz Martín, Lecturer at Open University of Catalonia

Dafina Sarbinova, Assistant Professor at Sofia University "St. Kliment Ohridski"

Erik Sinander, Senior Lecturer, University of Stockholm

Onerva-Aulikki Suhonen, Lecturer at the University of Eastern Finland Law School

Ferenc Szilágyi, Assistant Professor at Pázmány Péter Catholic University, Budapest

Leon Theimer, Lecturer and Research Fellow, Humboldt University of Berlin

Cedric Vanleenhove, Assistant Professor at Ghent University; Maître de conférences at HEC Management School, University of Liège

Anna Wysocka-Bar, Assistant Professor at Jagiellonian University in Krakow

Dora Zgrabljić Rotar, Associate Professor at the University of Zagreb

1

Questionnaire

Question 1. General Overview

Provide a *short* general overview of the national-autonomous rules[1] on the recognition and enforcement[2] of non-EU judgments[3] in civil and commercial matters.[4]

Question 2. Procedure

a) First describe the circumstances in which a judgment can be recognised and enforced:
   - Does recognition happen informally (ie within the context of other proceedings) or does it require a formal procedure (and if so, in what circumstances)?
   - Can the foreign decision itself be enforced or does enforcement (sometimes/always) require a domestic judgment? If it does, please clarify in what kind of proceedings (eg contentious/non-contentious) such a domestic judgment can be obtained and to which extent the foreign decision is taken into account there.

b) Then describe the procedural steps necessary for recognition and enforcement. Please address the following points, in the order you deem appropriate, and to the extent applicable: competent authorities; venue jurisdiction; the burden of proving the requirements for recognition and enforcement; the extent to which the requested decision may be reviewed on the merits; whether the decision granting or refusing recognition and/or enforcement can be appealed; whether the decision is binding for other courts.

[1] As a general guidance, you may refer to the role played by international treaties in force between your Member State and third states (other than treaties in force in all Member States, such as the Lugano Conventions, the HCCH 2005 Choice of Court Agreement Convention and the HCCH 2019 Judgments Convention), but only if they are of particular relevance.

[2] If recognition and enforcement are governed separately in your Member State, please mention this in your answer to this point, and detail the differences between the two cases in the following questions as appropriate.

[3] For the purposes of this questionnaire, the notion of 'judgment' is that of the HCCH 2019 Judgments Convention (Art 3(1)(b)), which however should include that of judicial settlements (Art 11).

[4] For the purposes of this questionnaire, the notion of 'civil and commercial' is that of the Brussels Ia Regulation (Art 1(1), including the matters excluded in Art 1(2) of the same Regulation, *with the exception of family law*.

Question 3. Requirements

List and describe the (positive and negative) requirements for recognition and enforcement. Please divide your answer into the following sub-paragraphs, to the extent applicable:

a) jurisdiction of the court of origin;[5]
b) finality and/or enforceability of the requested judgment in the country of origin;
c) irreconcilability with another judgment (*res iudicata*);
d) irreconcilability with pending proceedings (*lis pendens*);
e) specific requirements of due process (eg defendant's knowledge of the foreign proceedings; respect of the right of defence; appearance and declaration of default, etc);
f) public policy;
g) reciprocity;
h) other requirements.

Question 4. Documents to be Produced

List the documents to be produced and any possible requirement relating to the need of translations (including 'certified' translations) and of so-called 'legalisation'.

Question 5. Securities, Bonds and Deposits

Is the applicant required to provide securities, bonds or deposits?

[5] The answer to this point should not go so far as to 'replicate' the 3rd EAPIL Young Research Network's Project. It should explain only whether jurisdiction is a requirement and whether the existence of that requirement is assessed based on the rules on jurisdiction of the court of origin or of the requested court (and, in the latter case, the content of the relevant rules on jurisdiction, but without going into too much detail).

2

Comparative Report

Recognition and Enforcement of Non-EU Judgments in EU Member States

TOBIAS LUTZI, ENNIO PIOVESANI AND
DORA ZGRABLJIĆ ROTAR

This report has been compiled on the basis of the national reports published in chapter three. It also takes into account the results of a hybrid workshop held at the University of Turin in November 2023 and an on-site conference held at the Permanent Bureau of the Hague Conference of Private International Law (HCCH) in November 2024.

All references to national law have been verified by the respective national reporters, to whom the authors of this report wish to express their heartfelt gratitude.

The Comparative Report follows the same structure as the Questionnaire.[1]

Question 1. General Overview

While most elements of the domestic systems summarised in the answer to Question 1 will be analysed in more detail below, a number of interesting observations can already be drawn at this stage. In particular, it can be observed that recognition and enforcement of foreign judgments are governed by a complicated mosaic of international and domestic sources in all Member States. As for the latter, most Member States have adopted some form of general rules for judgments not covered by any international agreements, be it through codified rules or case law; in fact, even in the two Member States that have traditionally refused to give any effect to foreign judgments – The Netherlands and Sweden – limited exceptions have been developed by the courts.

[1] See above, ch 1.

International Sources

Several reporters have pointed out the practical importance of international instruments governing recognition and enforcement of foreign judgments in their Member States.[2] Indeed, all Member States appear to be bound by numerous international instruments, which govern a significant proportion of all foreign judgments.

Judgments from other EU Member States (including DENMARK)[3] are evidently governed by the Brussels Ia Regulation, which provides the most generous regime including automatic recognition and enforcement under Articles 36, 39 Brussels Ia, subject to the limited list of defences of Article 45 Brussels Ia.

The benefits of the Regulation are extended to judgments from SWITZERLAND, NORWAY and ICELAND, albeit on the terms of the original Brussels I Regulation: accordingly, enforcement still requires exequatur proceedings under Article 38(1) of the Lugano Convention. The same is true for the 2019 HCCH Judgments Convention (see Article 13(1) of the Convention), to which all EU Member States are parties, together with Ukraine, Uruguay, and the United Kingdom (since August 2025), as well as Albania and Montenegro (from March 2026).

Other multilateral treaties usually have similar effects but are limited to judgments in particular areas of law. Those treaties include the 2005 HCCH Choice of Court Convention,[4] the Convention on the Contract for the International Carriage of Goods by Road (CMR)[5] and the Convention concerning International Carriage by Rail (COTIF).[6]

In addition, virtually all Member States have entered into bilateral agreements, which usually accord some form of preferential treatment to judgments from other states as opposed to the otherwise applicable rules, while staying below the level of mobility accorded to decisions from other EU Member States under the Brussels Ia Regulation.

Although these different types of treaties are regularly implemented by the Member States through provisions similar, and often directly adjacent to, the 'purely' domestic rules on recognition and enforcement, the degree to which they vary and the fact that they are dictated more by what could be agreed upon at the international level than by any particular national approach to foreign judgments would make it a rather unproductive exercise to study those provisions more closely. Instead, the rest of this study will focus on the autonomous regimes that apply to any civil and commercial judgments that is not governed by any international agreement.

[2] See, eg, the Reports for → AUSTRIA, Question 1; → CYPRUS, Question 1; → CZECHIA, Question 1; → FINLAND, Question 1; → GREECE, Question 1; → POLAND, Question 1; → SPAIN, Question 1.

[3] By virtue of the Agreement of 19 October 2005 between the European Community and the Kingdom of Denmark on jurisdiction and the recognition and enforcement of judgments in civil and commercial matters [2005] OJ L 299/62, amended on 20 December 2012: OJ L 79/4.

[4] Convention on Choice of Court Agreements, 30 June 2005: Arts 8, 9.

[5] Convention on the Contract for the International Carriage of Goods by Road, 19 May 1956: Art 31(3), (4).

[6] Convention concerning International Carriage by Rail, 9 May 1980: Art 12(1).

Domestic Sources

As for these autonomous rules, the Member States can be readily sorted into one of two groups: while most Member States have long been allowing foreign judgments to be recognised and enforced under certain conditions, others traditionally refuse to attach any effect to such judgments. However, not a single Member State has maintained this latter position without at least some exceptions developed by its courts.

As for the Member States that are traditionally open to recognising and enforcing foreign judgments under certain conditions (see Question 3), the relevant rules can either be found in specific legislation on private international law (PIL), in general legislation on civil procedure, or even just in case law. For the Member States with codified rules, the split between legislation on PIL and general civil procedure law mirrors a similar split in the autonomous rules on international jurisdiction:[7] while many Member States have enacted specific legislation on international jurisdiction as part of a wider codification on PIL (which then also extends to recognition and enforcement), others derive both the rules on international jurisdiction over non-EU defendants and the rules on recognition and enforcement of non-EU judgments from their general laws on civil procedure. While some reporters have made statements as to the comparatively liberal or restrictive nature of their systems, these qualifications – if true – seem unrelated to how the domestic system is organised.[8]

Codified Rules		
Part of Private International Law	**Part of Civil Procedure Law**	**Case Law**
Belgium	Austria	Cyprus
Bulgaria	France[11]	Ireland
Croatia	Germany	The Netherlands
Czechia	Greece	sweden[13]
Hungary[9]	Latvia	
Italy	Lithuania	
Finland[10]	Malta	
	Poland	
	Romania	
	Spain[12]	

[7] See in more detail T Lutzi, E Piovesani and D Zgrabljić Rotar, 'Comparative Report' in T Lutzi, E Piovesani and D Zgrabljić Rotar (eds), *Jurisdiction over Non-EU Defendants* (Hart, 2023) 3–5.

[8] For instance, the reports for Austria and Finland mention the restrictive nature of their legal regimes (→ Austria, Question 1; → Finland, Question 2), while the French report underscores the liberal approach of French law (→ France, Question 3).

[9] The rules on exequatur are found in §§ 205–10 Judicial Enforcement Act of 1994: see → Hungary, Question 2.

[10] Finnish legislation is incomprehensive; some relevant provisions can also be found in civil procedure law.

[11] However, most specific requirements have been developed through case law.

[12] In Spain, the rules on recognition and enforcement of foreign judgments have been moved from domestic civil procedure law to a separate piece of legislation in 2015: see Act 29/2015 of 30 July on International Legal Cooperation in Civil Matters.

[13] Only available for decisions from a *forum prorogatum* since the Swedish Supreme Court's decision NJA 1973, 628. Not available even if the defendant submitted to the foreign jurisdiction.

Notion of Judgment

As stated in footnote 4 of the Questionnaire, this study focuses on judgments in the sense of Article 3(1)(b) of the HCCH 2019 Judgments Convention, ie

> any decision on the merits given by a court, whatever that decision may be called, including a decree or order, and a determination of costs or expenses of the proceedings by the court (including an officer of the court), provided that the determination relates to a decision on the merits which may be recognised or enforced under this Convention.

Yet, unlike the Convention (see Article 11), it does not exclude judicial settlements.

While reporters were not asked specifically to identify the extent to which the relevant rules in their Member State have a broader or – more importantly – smaller scope of application than the Convention, several reports have pointed out the broad definition of judgment under their own laws,[14] which often extends to decisions made by public authorities other than courts of law (but having a similar status in the country of origin)[15] and to judicial settlements.[16]

Question 2. Procedure

Despite the significant proportion of foreign judgments that benefit from a more or less uniform treatment across the Member States by virtue of the European and international instruments mentioned above, the domestic legal systems display a surprising variety regarding the conceptual approaches to recognition and enforcement of judgments that are not covered by such instruments. Even more interestingly, these systems converge with regard to the specific procedural steps that the judgment creditor needs to take.

Circumstances in which a Foreign Judgment can be Recognised and Enforced

The diversity in conceptual approaches is evidenced by the circumstances in which a judgment can be given effect in a legal system other than its country of origin. They range from purely informal recognition – ie any public authority or domestic court confronted with a question potentially affected by the foreign judgment makes its own determination as to its effect within those proceedings – to always formal – ie any effect of the judgment requires separate recognition proceedings.

[14] See, eg, → Belgium, Question 1; → Spain, Question 1.

[15] See, eg, Art 22(3)(1) of the Belgian Code of Private International Law; Art 66(3) of the Croatian Private International Law Act; Ministerial Report on the Italian Law 218/1995.

[16] See, eg, Art 122 of the Bulgarian PILC; Art 66(2) of the Croatian Private International Law Act; § 110 of the Hungarian PIL Code.

Recognition:			
is always informal	**is generally informal**		**is always formal**
	– but formal upon application	**– but formal for certain types of judgments**	
GERMANY[17] ITALY THE NETHERLANDS	AUSTRIA[18] BELGIUM BULGARIA CYPRUS CROATIA GREECE HUNGARY LATVIA[19] POLAND ROMANIA SPAIN	CZECHIA[20] FRANCE[21]	FINLAND IRELAND LITHUANIA MALTA SWEDEN[22]

Enforcement outside of the Brussels Ia Regulation is never purely informal or automatic. In fact, even the Lugano Convention and the 2019 HCCH Judgments Convention do not require automatic enforcement.[23] Instead, enforcement in all Member States requires a decision from a domestic court.

This decision can take two different forms, though, which rely on two almost completely different concepts. In the majority of Member States, the domestic court confirms the enforceability of the foreign judgment through so-called exequatur proceedings; on the basis of this declaration of enforceability, the foreign judgment itself can then be enforced.

In English common law, on the other hand, such enforcement was historically impossible because a foreign judgment could not be registered in England. This problem has been overcome for certain judgments through legislation (transposing European and international instruments) but persists for all other judgments. Accordingly, a judgment creditor needs to start new proceedings in England, in which they may then introduce the foreign judgment, either to use the debt created by the judgment as a cause of action[24] (only possible for money judgments) or to show that any substantive question is *res iudicata* (for non-money judgments).[25] The result is a new English judgment (often referred to as 'confirmation judgment' or 'merger judgment')

[17] But formal for certain status and family matters.

[18] Introduced in 1995 through the Enforcement Amendment Act 1995 (*Exekutionsordnungs-Novelle*).

[19] Formal recognition appears to be the default; informal recognition is accepted as an alternative option in scholarship.

[20] Informal recognition is primarily available for property matters and only if certain grounds for refusal recognition are not raised by the judgment debtor.

[21] Declaratory patrimonial judgments require formal recognition.

[22] This only applies to the limited number of cases in which recognition is possible at all.

[23] See Art 38(1) Lugano Convention; Art 4(1), 13(1) 2019 HCCH Judgments Convention.

[24] Sometimes referred to as '*actio judicati*'.

[25] See in more detail AV Dicey, JHC Morris, and L Collins, *The Conflict of Laws*, 16th edn (Sweet & Maxwell, 2023) paras 14R-012 (fn 95); 14-026M; 14-032.

that can be enforced in England. For historical reasons, the same mechanism applies in Ireland and Cyprus.[26] More surprisingly, a similar mechanism is also used in Sweden and the Netherlands, where the highest courts have overcome the traditional hostility towards enforcing foreign judgments in almost identical fashion.[27]

Enforcement:	
***of the foreign judgment* based on a declaration of enforceability after exequatur proceedings**	***of a domestic confirmation* judgment based on the judgment debt**
Austria Bulgaria Belgium Croatia Czechia Finland Germany Greece Hungary Italy Latvia Lithuania Poland Romania Spain	Cyprus Ireland The Netherlands Sweden[28]

Despite the fundamental differences between these two approaches, it has been noted by scholars that for practical purposes, the two types of enforcement 'closely resemble' each other.[29] Still, the conceptual difference has arguably played an important role in the European Court of Justice (CJEU)'s controversial decision in *J v H Limited*, in which the Court considered an English confirmation judgment to qualify itself for recognition and enforcement under the Brussels Ia Regulation.[30]

Procedural Steps

As for the practical steps that a party needs to take to have a judgment recognised (where recognition is not purely informal; see Question 1) or enforced, we notice that

[26] In Malta, such 'indirect' enforcement is possible but not necessary (→ Malta, Question 1).

[27] See the Dutch Supreme Court's decision in Hoge Raad, 26 September 2014, ECLI:NL:HR:2014:2838, *Gazprombank*, and the Swedish Supreme Court's decisions NJA 1949, 724 and NJA 1973, 628.

[28] Only available for decisions from a *forum prorogatum* since the Swedish Supreme Court's decision NJA 1973, 628. Not available even if the defendant submitted to the foreign jurisdiction.

[29] V Lazić and P Mankowski, *The Brussels I-Bis Regulation* (Edward Elgar Publishing, 2023) para 1.182.

[30] Case C-568/20 *H Limited*, ECLI:EU:C:2022:264; see T Lutzi, 'What remains of H Limited? Recognition and enforcement of non-EU judgments after Brexit' (2024) 20 *Journal of Private International Law* 651 for more detail.

despite many differences in detail, the legal systems of the Member States often resemble each other with regard to the broader lines.

As a rule of thumb, recognition (if subject to a formal procedure) can be requested by either party while enforcement naturally needs to be sought by the judgment creditor. In Member States requiring exequatur proceedings, the competent court is usually[31] the court of the defendant's habitual residence or domicile,[32] of the place of enforcement,[33] or a combination of them;[34] occasionally, a specific court is designated, such as the Sofia City Court in Bulgaria,[35] the Lithuanian Court of Appeal,[36] or the First Hall of the Civil Court in Malta.[37] By contrast, in Member States where foreign judgments are enforced through a new claim based on the judgment debt, the general rules on jurisdiction naturally apply.[38]

With the exception of Belgium[39] and Latvia,[40] the laws of all Member States provide for service to the judgment debtor before a decision on enforcement can be taken, allowing the debtor to challenge the application based on the lack of a requirement of, or existence of a defence to, enforcement (see Question 3).

While smaller details – such as the composition of the court, the requirements for legal representation, or the avenues for appeal – differ between the Member States, it is important to note that most of these differences persist even where international harmonisation of recognition and enforcement has been achieved.[41] In fact, even the Brussels Ia Regulation only contains a limited number of requirements for the enforcement of foreign judgments and leaves many procedural questions to the Member States.[42]

However, an exception needs to be made for the burden of proof. Regardless of whether specific rules on recognition and enforcement shift the burden of proof to the judgment creditor or debtor or whether it is subject to more general rules of civil procedure law, the question is intrinsically linked to the nature of these individual requirements. Moreover, it is also closely connected to the degree to which the requested court may itself review the conditions for recognition and enforcement of the foreign judgment. These points will thus be addressed together at the beginning of Question 3.

[31] In Poland, jurisdiction lies primarily with the district court that would be competent for the original dispute; subsidiarily, the Regional Court in Warsaw is competent: see Art 1148 § 1 of the Polish Code of Civil Procedure.

[32] See, eg, § 722(2) of the German ZPO; Art 905(1) of the Greek CCP.

[33] See Art 1103(1) of the Romanian RCCP; if the judgment creditor simultaneously seeks recognition and enforcement, the courts of the defendant's domicile are also competent.

[34] See, eg, Art 23 § 2 of the Belgian CPIL; Art 72(1) of the Croatian 2017 PILA; Art 43 of the French Code of Civil Procedure.

[35] See Art 119(1) of the Bulgarian PILC.

[36] See Art 811 of the Lithuanian COCP.

[37] See Art 826 of the Maltese COCP.

[38] See → Cyprus, Question 2 (with some qualifications); → The Netherlands, Question 2.

[39] Arts 23, 24 of the Belgian CPIL.

[40] Section 640 of the Latvian CPL.

[41] See eg Art 13(1) 2019 HCCH Judgments Convention.

[42] See Arts 40 et seq, 47 et seq and 51 et seq Brussels Ia.

Question 3. Requirements

Overview

The only condition for recognition and enforcement of the requested judgment that can be found in every single Member State is the compatibility with public policy. Still, in almost all Member States, recognition and enforcement of foreign judgments is subject to conditions related to: the jurisdiction of the court of origin;[43] the enforceability and/or finality of the requested judgment;[44] the respect for due process;[45] and the absence of irreconcilable judgments.[46] The condition related to the absence of parallel proceedings is also common in the Member States, whereas that related to the existence of reciprocity applies only in a few Member States. In a significant number of Member States, additional conditions exist; the most typical of these is the absence of fraud, while others are unique to one or very few Member States.

The conditions for recognition and enforcement of foreign judgments may be framed in either positive or negative terms.[47] In particular, the condition related to the enforceability and/or finality of the requested judgment is, in most Member States, framed as a positive requirement. The conditions related to the jurisdiction of the court of origin and reciprocity are in some Member States established as a positive requirement and in others as a ground for refusal. By contrast, the conditions related to due process, the irreconcilability of the requested judgment with other judgments, parallel proceedings, and public policy are, in most Member States, established as grounds for refusal. It should be noted that, in some Member States, the lack of finality and the existence of parallel proceedings, while serving as grounds for challenging recognition and enforcement, do not automatically lead to the refusal of the requested judgment, but to other consequences such as a suspension of the recognition and enforcement proceedings.

Although the distinction between positive requirements and grounds for refusal is either clear or easy to infer in many Member States,[48] it is either absent or difficult to establish in a significant number of others.[49] The existence or absence of the distinction appears to have implications for the allocation of the burden of proof and for the scope of the requested court's power and duty to assess the conditions for recognition

[43] But see → FINLAND, Question 3, a).

[44] But see → SWEDEN, Question 3, c).

[45] But see → IRELAND, Question 3, b).

[46] But see → AUSTRIA, Question 3, d), where irreconcilability of the requested judgment with another judgment is subsumed under public policy, and → SWEDEN, Question 3.

[47] In general terms, positive conditions can be understood as requirements that must exist for recognition and enforcement, while negative conditions can be understood as obstacles, ie grounds for refusing recognition and enforcement.

[48] See → AUSTRIA, Question 3; → BELGIUM, Question 3; → CROATIA, Question 3; → CZECHIA, Question 3; → HUNGARY, Question 3; → ITALY, Question 3; → ROMANIA, Question 3; and → SPAIN, Question 3.

[49] See → BULGARIA, Question 3; → CYPRUS, Question 3; → FINLAND, Question 3; → FRANCE, Question 3; → GREECE, Question 3; → IRELAND, Question 3; → MALTA, Question 3; → THE NETHERLANDS, Question 3; and → SWEDEN, Question 3; see also → GERMANY, Question 3; and → POLAND, Question 3, where all conditions are established as grounds for refusal; and see → LATVIA, Question 3, where the only positive requirement is that the requested judgment meets the definition of judgment eligible for recognition and enforcement.

and enforcement on its own initiative. In particular, in those Member States where the distinction exists or can easily be drawn, the burden of proof is often clearly divided: the judgment creditor must prove the existence of the positive requirements, while the judgment debtor bears the burden of alleging and proving the existence of the grounds for refusal.[50] In such Member States, the requested court's *ex officio* review is usually limited to some or all grounds for refusal.[51] By contrast, in those Member States where the distinction between positive requirements and grounds for refusal is absent or, at any rate, blurred, the judgment creditor must, in principle, prove that all conditions for recognition and enforcement are met, in accordance with the general rules (of civil procedural law) on the allocation of the burden of proof;[52] and the requested court's *ex officio* review extends to all such conditions.[53]

	Jurisdiction	Enforceability/ Finality	Res Iudicata	Lis Pendens	Due Process	Public Policy	Reciprocity	Other Requirements
AUSTRIA	P	P	–[54]	–	P/N[55]	N	N	–
BELGIUM	N	P	N	N	N	N	–	U
BULGARIA	U	U	U	U	U	U	U[56]	–
CROATIA	N	P	N	N	N	N	–	–
CYPRUS	U	U	U	–	U	U	–	U
CZECHIA	N	P	N	N	N	N	N	–
FINLAND	–	U	U	U	U	U	–	–
FRANCE	U	U	U	U	(U)[57]	U	–	U
GERMANY	N	N	N	N	N	N	N	N
GREECE	P	P	P	–	P	P	–	–
HUNGARY	P	P	N	N	N	N	P	–
IRELAND	U	U	U[58]	–	–	U	–	U

(continued)

[50] See → AUSTRIA, Questions 2, b); → CROATIA, Question 2, b); → CZECHIA, Question 2, b); and → ITALY, Question 2, b).

[51] See → BELGIUM, Question 2, b); → CROATIA, Question 2, b); and → CZECHIA, Question 2, b); but see → ROMANIA, Question 2, b), where, in principle, the *ex officio* judicial review is limited to positive requirements, and → AUSTRIA, Question 2, b); → HUNGARY, Question 2, b); and → ITALY, Question 2, b), where, as a general rule, the review in question extends to all conditions.

[52] See → CYPRUS, Question 2, b); → POLAND, Question 2, b); and → THE NETHERLANDS, Question 2, b).

[53] See → BULGARIA, Question 2, b); → FRANCE, Question 2, b); → GREECE, Question 2, b); → THE NETHERLANDS, Question 2, b); and → POLAND, Question 2, b). See also → GERMANY, Question 2, b), where all requirements are phrased negatively but will be reviewed *ex officio*, with the exception of the requirement of due process, which the defendant needs to invoke.

[54] Irreconcilability of the requested judgment with other judgment is subsumed under public policy. See → AUSTRIA, Question 3, c).

[55] Proper service of the document instituting the proceedings is established as a positive requirement, whereas violation of the right to be heard constitutes a ground for refusal. See → AUSTRIA, Question 3, e).

[56] The requirement applies only in matters of insolvency and in the 'niche situation related to the recognition and enforcement of arbitral awards stemming from non-signatory states to the New York Convention of 1958'. See → BULGARIA, Question 3, g).

[57] The respect of due process is subsumed under (procedural) public policy. See → FRANCE, Question 3, e).

[58] This requirement is not established by Irish Common Law, but rather by English Common Law, which is persuasive in Irish law. See → IRELAND, Question 3, c).

(Continued)

	Jurisdiction	Enforceability/ Finality	Res Iudicata	Lis Pendens	Due Process	Public Policy	Reciprocity	Other Requirements
ITALY	P	P	N	N	P	N	–	–
LATVIA	N	N	N	N	N	N	–	N
MALTA	P	P	N	N	N	N	–	N
THE NETHERLANDS	U	U	U	–	U	U	–	–
POLAND	N	N	N	N	N	N	–	–
ROMANIA	P	P	N	N	P	N	P	P
SPAIN	N	P	N	N	N	N	–	–
SWEDEN	U	–	–	–	U	U	–	–
P = positive requirement / N = negative requirement / U = unknown if positive or negative								

a) Jurisdiction of the Court of Origin

Recognition and enforcement of foreign judgments is subject to a condition related to the court of origin's jurisdiction in all Member States (arguably with the exception of FINLAND).[59]

As a preliminary condition, it is generally required that the dispute settled by the requested judgment does not fall within the exclusive jurisdiction of the requested state[60] under the national-autonomous rules on jurisdiction of the requested state,[61] Article 24 Brussels Ia Regulation,[62] or applicable international treaties.[63] POLAND appears to be the only Member State in which it is sufficient for the jurisdictional condition to be met, that the dispute settled by the requested judgment does not fall within POLISH exclusive jurisdiction.[64] In all other Member States, the assessment of the court of origin's jurisdiction extends beyond the issue of exclusive jurisdiction.

In fact, in a first group of Member States, it is further required that the court of origin did not rely on specific grounds of jurisdiction that are deemed – from the perspective of the requested state – to be exorbitant. In such Member States it is required that

[59] In Finnish law, no requirement of indirect jurisdiction is stipulated with regard to civil and commercial judgments; the requirement is common with regard to judgments in family matters, though. See → FINLAND, Question 3, a).

[60] This preliminary condition is expressly mentioned in the reports on → AUSTRIA, Question 3, a); → BELGIUM, Question 3, a); → BULGARIA, Question 3, a); → CROATIA, Question 3, a); → CYPRUS, Question 3, a); → CZECHIA, Question 3, a); → FRANCE, Question 3, a); and → POLAND, Question 3, a); see also → HUNGARY, Question 3, a); → ROMANIA, Question 3, a); and → SPAIN, Question 3, a). In general terms, the condition in question appears to be implied in those Member States adopting the mirror image approach (see → LATVIA, Question 3, a), described below in the text.

[61] See → BULGARIA, Question 3, a); → CZECHIA, Question 3, a); → HUNGARY, Question 3, a); and → POLAND, Question 3, a).

[62] See → BULGARIA, Question 3, a); and → BELGIUM, Question 3, a), where also Art 25 Brussels Ia Regulation is mentioned; see also → CROATIA, Question 3, a); and → CZECHIA, Question 3, a).

[63] See → CZECHIA, Question 3, a).

[64] See → POLAND, Question 3, a).

the court of origin did not assert jurisdiction solely based on the mere presence of the defendant or their assets in the state of origin,[65] or on the citizenship or registration of the claimant in the state of origin.[66] This assessment, as highlighted in the ROMANIAN report,[67] may require considering the rules of the state of origin based on which the court of origin established its jurisdiction.

However, the number of Member States that limit themselves to such a 'negative' test of the court of origin's jurisdiction (ie looking only at exorbitant and exclusive jurisdiction) is small.[68] In most Member States, the assessment of the court of origin's jurisdiction aims at ascertaining whether said court asserted jurisdiction based on an 'acceptable' ground.[69] What is considered acceptable varies from one Member State to another, and in this regard, at least three different approaches can be identified.

The first and most restrictive approach is that adopted in SWEDEN, where the only acceptable ground of jurisdiction for the purposes of recognition and enforcement is an exclusive choice-of-court agreement in favour of the court of origin.[70]

A second and more common approach – the so-called 'mirror image' approach – requires that the foreign judgment settles a dispute over which the court of origin would have had jurisdiction if the rules – or, more broadly, the principles – on jurisdiction in force in the requested state had been hypothetically applicable. Accordingly, the assessment underlying the mirror image approach is carried out against jurisdictional standards of the requested state,[71] whereas the rules on jurisdiction of the state of origin[72] – and whether the court of origin complied with the same[73] – are entirely irrelevant.[74]

Interestingly, BULGARIA is the only Member State where the mirror image approach is combined – in a somewhat sophisticated manner – with that specifically addressing the issue of exorbitant jurisdiction.[75] In that Member State it is required, on the one hand, that the court of origin has not asserted jurisdiction based on the exorbitant grounds

[65] See → BELGIUM, Question 3, a); and → CROATIA, Question 3, a); see also → ROMANIA, Question 3, a).
[66] See → BULGARIA, Question 3, a).
[67] See → ROMANIA, Question 3, a).
[68] See → BELGIUM, Question 3, a); → CROATIA, Question 3, a); and → ROMANIA, Question 3, a). For the sake of completeness, in CROATIA, Question 3, a), it is also required that the court of origin did not assert jurisdiction in contrast with the criteria enshrined in the protective rules of jurisdiction of the Brussels Ia Regulation.
[69] See → AUSTRIA, Question 3, a); → BULGARIA, Question 3, a); → CZECHIA, Question 3, a); → GERMANY, Question 3, a); → GREECE, Question 3, a); → HUNGARY, Question 3, a); → LATVIA, Question 3, a); → MALTA, Question 3, a); see also → CYPRUS, Question 3, a); → IRELAND, Question 3, a); and → ITALY, Question 3, a).
[70] See → SWEDEN, Question 3, a).
[71] The national reports on BULGARIA and CZECHIA specify that, the relevant rules on jurisdiction are not only those enshrined in national-autonomous law, but also in EU instruments (particularly, the Brussels Ia Regulation) and international treaties in force in the requested State, See → BULGARIA, Question 3, a), and → CZECHIA, Question 3, a).
[72] See → AUSTRIA, Question 3, a).
[73] See → GERMANY, Question 3, a).
[74] Incidentally, while the 'positive' assessment underlying the mirror image approach is broad, it is not necessarily more stringent than that limited to the issue of exorbitant jurisdiction. In fact, since the mirror image approach entails an assessment of the court of origin's jurisdiction against the jurisdictional standards of the requested state, where such standards are broad, if not exorbitant, the jurisdictional condition is rarely unmet. See → CYPRUS, Question 3, a), and → MALTA, Question 3, a).
[75] See → BULGARIA, Question 3, a).

of citizenship or registration of the claimant in the state of origin, which are, however, available grounds of (direct) jurisdiction under Article 4(1) of the BULGARIAN Private International Law Code (PILC). On the other hand, consistent with the mirror image approach, it is required that the court of origin would have had jurisdiction if BULGARIAN rules on jurisdiction (other than Article 4(1) PILC) had been hypothetically applicable.

An approach that appears to deviate only in form, but not in substance, from the mirror image approach is that adopted in FRANCE and SPAIN, where a sufficient connection between the dispute and the court of origin is required but deemed to exist when, in light of the rules on jurisdiction of the requested state, the court of origin would have had jurisdiction.[76]

Finally, a third approach, that appears to deviate, at least in spirit, from the mirror image approach, is that adopted in THE NETHERLANDS. While the mirror image approach may be based on the premise that there is an 'absence of an internationally uniform understanding of jurisdictional justice',[77] in THE NETHERLANDS there appears to be an effort to identify so-called internationally accepted grounds of jurisdiction: it is required that the court of origin asserted jurisdiction on a jurisdictional basis that relies on a broad international consensus.[78] IRISH law, too, limits indirect jurisdiction to certain broadly accepted grounds; following English precedent, the IRISH courts require that jurisdiction of the court of origin has been based on either presence, submission, or a contractual agreement.[79]

Finally, it is worth mentioning that differences among the Member States exist regarding the relevant point in time at which the jurisdictional requirement must be fulfilled. For instance, the jurisdictional requirement may be fulfilled at any point in time during the proceedings before the court of origin, up until the last oral hearing before such court;[80] when the requested judgment was rendered;[81] or, when the recognition and enforcement proceedings before the requested court are initiated.[82]

	Jurisdiction must not have been based on an Exorbitant Ground	**Jurisdiction must have been based on an 'Acceptable' Ground:**	
		Mirror Image Approach	**Other Approaches**
AUSTRIA		x	
BELGIUM	x		
BULGARIA	x	x	
CROATIA	x		
CYPRUS		x	

(continued)

[76] See → SPAIN, Question 3, a), and → FRANCE, Question 3, a), where, however, if the court of origin would not have had jurisdiction under French jurisdictional rules, the requested courts may still ascertain the existence of a sufficient connection in light of the specific circumstances of the case.
[77] See → GERMANY, Question 3, a).
[78] See → THE NETHERLANDS, Question 3, a).
[79] IRELAND, Question 3, a).
[80] See → GERMANY, Question 3, a).
[81] See → CROATIA, Question 3, a), with specific reference to the issue of exclusive jurisdiction.
[82] See → AUSTRIA, Question 3, a).

(Continued)

	Jurisdiction must not have been based on an Exorbitant Ground	Jurisdiction must have been based on an 'Acceptable' Ground:	
Czechia		x	
France		x	
Germany		x	
Greece		x	
Hungary		x	
Ireland		x	
Italy		x	
Latvia		x	
The Netherlands			x
Malta		x	
Romania	x		
Spain		x	
Sweden			
			x

b) Finality/Enforceability in the Country of Origin

A requirement related to the enforceability and/or finality of the requested judgment can be found in almost all Member States.[83] It is generally established as a positive requirement. The condition of enforceability may be kept distinct from that of finality.

Concerning the first condition, in most Member States, enforceability of the requested judgment in the state of origin is a requirement for recognition and/or enforcement.[84] Even if not expressly established as a condition, the possibility of enforcing the foreign judgment in the requested state generally presupposes its enforceability in the state of origin.[85] Only in Austria, France and Greece is the enforceability of the requested judgment in the state of origin sufficient,[86] whereas in all other Member States, finality is also required.

[83] But see → Sweden, Question 3, b), where no data on the existence of such condition seems to be available due to the limited number of foreign decisions qualifying for recognition and enforcement in Sweden.
[84] See → Austria, Question 3, b); → Belgium, Question 3, b); → Bulgaria, Question 3, b); → Croatia, Question 3, b); → Czechia, Question 3, b); → France, Question 3, b); → Greece, Question 3, b); → the Netherlands, Question 3, b); → Poland, Question 3, b); and → Sweden Question 3, b).
[85] In fact, 'it follows from logic that the possibility of subsequent enforcement of a foreign judgment … requires that it is also enforceable in the State of origin'. See → Latvia, Question 3, b).
[86] See → Austria, Question 3, b); → France, Question 3, b); → Greece, Question 3, b).

The notion of finality appears to be fairly uniform across Member States and refers to the stage at which the requested judgment is no longer subject to 'ordinary' means of recourse.[87] Only in CYPRUS and IRELAND, finality (and conclusiveness) is understood as the earlier stage where the requested judgment is no longer subject to means of recourse before the court of origin that rendered said judgment, regardless of whether the latter is or may be subject to appeal before higher courts of the state of origin. Although the notion of finality is generally established in accordance with the law of the requested state,[88] the unavailability of recourse against the requested judgment is assessed in light of the civil procedure rules of the state of origin.[89]

In some Member States, the absence of finality may render the requested judgment 'radically unsuitable' for recognition and enforcement, even if said judgment is enforceable in the state of origin.[90] In other Member States, the absence of finality may not automatically lead to refusal of recognition and enforcement, but rather, for instance, to a stay of the recognition and enforcement proceedings.[91]

Finally, it is worth anticipating that, in some Member States, a certificate from the state of origin may be required to 'confirm' the enforceability in the state of origin and finality of the requested decision[92] (→ see Question 4).

	Judgment can only be Enforced if it is:	
	Enforceable in the State of Origin	**Final**
AUSTRIA	x	
BELGIUM	x	x
BULGARIA	x	x
CROATIA	x	x
CYPRUS		x
CZECHIA	x	x
FINLAND	x	x
FRANCE	x	
GERMANY		x
GREECE	x	
HUNGARY		x

(continued)

[87] See → BELGIUM, Question 3, b), and → CZECHIA, Question 3, b). In some Member States, it is required that the requested judgment attained 'legal force', which generally corresponds to the stage where the judgment is no longer subject to ordinary means of recourse (see → HUNGARY, Question 3, b); → BULGARIA, Question 3, b); → GERMANY, Question 3, b); and → LATVIA, Question 3, b).

[88] See → CZECHIA, Question 3, b).

[89] See → BELGIUM, Question 3, b); → CZECHIA, Question 3, b); → LATVIA, Question 3, b); → MALTA, Question 3, b); and → POLAND, Question 3, b).

[90] See → ITALY, Question 3, b).

[91] See → IRELAND, Question 3, b); see also → CYPRUS, Question 3, b), and → THE NETHERLANDS, Question 3, b).

[92] See → AUSTRIA, Question 3, b); → BULGARIA, Question 3, b); → CZECHIA, Question 3, b); and → POLAND, Question 3, b); see also → CROATIA, Question 3, b).

(Continued)

	Judgment can only be Enforced if it is:	
	Enforceable in the State of Origin	**Final**
Italy		x
Latvia		x
Malta		x
Netherlands	x	x
Poland	x	x
Romania		x
Spain	x	x

c) *Res Iudicata*

The condition related to the absence of a judgment irreconcilable with the requested judgment can also be found, in some shape or form, in almost all Member States.[93] It is generally framed as a ground for refusal. This condition is, of course, closely linked to the fundamental principle of *res iudicata*[94] and may also be seen as a specific application of the condition of compatibility with public policy (→ see Question 3, f)).[95]

Generally, irreconcilability is established in accordance with the law of the requested state[96] and exists when two (or more) final judgments[97] have been rendered between the same parties and on the same matter.[98]

Most Member States address the issue of irreconcilability between the requested judgment and the 'domestic' judgment, but many also address that of irreconcilability between the requested judgment and a judgment from another foreign state that has been recognised and enforced in the requested state, or is amenable to recognition and enforcement therein.[99]

[93] But see → Austria, Question 3, d), where this condition is subsumed under that of compatibility with public policy, and → Sweden, Question 3, d), where any data on the existence of such condition is unavailable.

[94] See → Austria, Question 3, d), and → Germany, Question 3, c); see also → Italy, Question 3, d).

[95] See → Austria, Question 3, c); → Germany, Question 3, c); and → the Netherlands, Question 3, c).

[96] See → Croatia, Question 3, c), and → Malta, Question 3, c); but see → Germany, Question 3, c), where irreconcilability is defined based on relevant CJEU jurisprudence.

[97] See → Croatia, Question 3, c); → Czechia, Question 3, c); → Hungary, Question 3, c); and → Poland, Question 3, c); see → Belgium, Question 3, c), where the domestic judgment must be no longer 'appealable'; → Bulgaria, where reference is had to judgments 'entered into force'; Cyprus, Question 3, c), where finality is required by the Foreign Court Judgments (Recognition, Registration and Enforcement) Law (121(I)/2000) and bilateral treaties; → Greece, Question 3, c), where reference is had to a domestic 'final judgment not subject to appeal'; but see → the Netherlands, Question 3, c), where, on the on hand, finality is not a condition for recognition and enforcement, and, on the other hand, irreconcilability may exist irrespective of finality.

[98] See → Croatia, Question 3, c), and → Finland, Question 3, c); see also → Bulgaria, Question 3, c); → Cyprus, Question 3, c); → Czechia, Question 3, c); → Latvia, Question 3, c); → the Netherlands, Question 3, c); and → Poland Question 3, c).

[99] See → Belgium, Question 3, c); → Croatia, Question 3, c); → Cyprus, Question 3, d); → Czechia, Question 3, c); → France, Question 3, c); → Germany, Question 3, c); → Hungary, Question 3, c); → Latvia, Question 3, c); → the Netherlands, Question 3, c); → Poland, Question 3, c); and → Spain, Question 3, c).

The issue of irreconcilability between the requested judgment and a domestic judgment is solved through one of two approaches. The first solution is based on the principle of priority, although the specific points in time employed to establish priority vary from one Member State to another. In particular, while in most Member States, recognition and enforcement is refused if the domestic judgment was rendered earlier than the foreign judgment,[100] in other Member States, it may only be refused if the domestic judgment: became final before either the foreign judgment[101] or the application for recognition and enforcement;[102] or was rendered in proceedings instituted before the foreign proceedings.[103] The second solution for resolving the conflict between the requested and the domestic judgment disregards the principle of priority in favour of an 'egoistic' approach:[104] recognition and enforcement are refused regardless of which judgment was first in time.[105]

In turn, the issue of irreconcilability between foreign judgments is generally solved through the principle of priority. In most cases, the requested judgment may be refused recognition and enforcement if it was rendered[106] or became final[107] after the other foreign judgment. Only in two Member States, the Czechia and France, a 'first come, first served' approach applies: the requested judgment is refused if the other foreign judgment has already been recognised or enforced in the requested state.[108]

Irreconcilability between Requested Judgment and Domestic Judgment	
Principle of Priority	**Domestic Decision Trumps**
Austria	Belgium
Bulgaria	Croatia
Czechia	France
Finland	Germany
Hungary	Greece
Ireland	The Netherlands
Latvia	
Poland	
Spain	

d) *Lis Pendens*

In several Member States, the fact that the requested decision was issued in the context of foreign proceedings initiated after proceedings involving the same parties and the

[100] See → Austria, Question 3, c); → Hungary, Question 3, c); → Ireland, Question 3, c); → Latvia, Question 3, c); → Poland, Question 3, c), and → Spain, Question 3, c).

[101] See → Latvia, Question 3, c).

[102] See → Bulgaria, Question 3, c), and → Czechia, Question 3, c).

[103] See → Hungary, Question 3, c), and → Latvia, Question 3, c).

[104] See → Germany, Question 3, c).

[105] See → Belgium, Question 3, c); → Croatia, Question 3, c); and → Germany, Question 3, c); see also → France, Question 3, c); → Greece, Question 3, c); and → the Netherlands, Question 3, c).

[106] See → Belgium, Question 3, c); → Poland, Question 3, c); and → Spain, Question 3, c); see also → Hungary, Question 3, c); → Latvia, Question 3, c); and → the Netherlands Question 3, c).

[107] See → Germany, Question 3, c); → see also → Croatia, Question 3, c); Latvia, Question 3, c).

[108] See → Czechia, Question 3, c), and → France, Question 3, c).

same subject matter had already been pending before the courts of the requested state is either a ground for refusing recognition and enforcement[109] or a reason to stay the recognition and enforcement proceedings until the conclusion of the parallel proceeding before the courts of the requested state.[110] The latter solution is usually adopted in those Member States that follow an 'egoistic' approach to the irreconcilability between conflicting judgments (→ see Question 3, c)), ie one where even a later domestic judgment leads to the refusal of recognition and enforcement of an earlier incompatible foreign judgment. The reports on GERMANY and POLAND specify that the relevant time for assessing the pendency of the foreign parallel proceeding is determined based on the (procedural) law of the state of origin.[111]

e) Due Process

In all Member States, recognition and enforcement of foreign judgments are subject to requirements of due process, although their scope varies from one Member State to the other. FRANCE may be considered an exception as any requirement of due process is subsumed under (procedural) public policy in French law.[112] The common law of IRELAND could be considered another exception as the respect for due process in the foreign proceedings is not an established requirement there either. Still, a foreign judgment that contravenes principles of natural justice – typically understood as the right to be heard by an impartial tribunal – can be challenged by the defendant at the enforcement stage.[113]

In all other Member States, lack of due process is explicitly mentioned as a ground to refuse recognition and enforcement of a foreign judgment. It is usually understood as a violation of the right to be heard but may also, additionally, refer to a lack of judicial impartiality in the state of origin. Courts often apply the standards of Article 6(1) of the European Convention on Human Rights (ECHR), which guarantees the right to a fair trial for everyone.[114]

Even where it is acknowledged as a separate ground of refusal, the requirement of judicial impartiality does not seem to play a major role in practice. The right to be heard, on the other hand, has given rise to extensive case law in the different Member States, which usually focuses on the defendant's (in)ability to actively participate in the proceedings on the merits. It is therefore assessed on a case-by-case basis and *in concreto*.[115] It usually includes three specific requirements: that the defendant was properly served with a document initiating a claim; that the defendant was served in

[109] See → BELGIUM, Question 3, d); → BULGARIA, Question 3, d); → CZECHIA, Question 3, d); → GERMANY, Question 3, d); → ITALY, Question 3, d); → LATVIA, Question 3, d); → POLAND, Question 3, d); and → SPAIN, Question 3, d).

[110] See → CROATIA, Question 3, d); → FRANCE, Question 3, d); and → THE NETHERLANDS, Question 3, d); see also → HUNGARY, Question 3, d).

[111] See → GERMANY, Question 3, d), and → POLAND, Question 3, d).

[112] See → FRANCE, Question 3, e).

[113] See → IRELAND, Question 3, b).

[114] See J Erauw, *Internationaal Privaatrecht* (Kluwer, 2009) 282, para 208; and→ BELGIUM, Question 3, b).

[115] See → BELGIUM, Question 3, b); → BULGARIA, Question 3, b); → CZECHIA, Question 3, e); → HUNGARY, Question 3, b); → LATVIA, Question 3, b); → POLAND, Question 3, d); and → SPAIN, Question 3, b).

a timely manner; and that the defendant was given the possibility to familiarise themselves with the arguments on which the claim is based.

Despite the general consistency between the Member States on this point, differences can still be found. For instance, the relevant provision in CROATIA is based on, and interpreted in accordance with, Article 45(1)(b) of the Brussels Ia Regulation, while in AUSTRIA and GERMANY – as opposed to the Brussels Regime[116] – it is not necessary that the defendant has challenged the foreign judgment in the state of origin.[117] In BULGARIA, the right to be heard is considered violated if the foreign proceedings result in a judgment issued within a relatively short time after the deadline for serving notice to the defendant.[118]

In CYPRUS and MALTA, some requirements that would be considered as due process in other jurisdictions may fall under the specific ground of refusal of fraud (→ see Question 3, h)).[119]

	Right to be Heard	Judicial Impartiality
AUSTRIA	x	
BELGIUM	x	x
BULGARIA	x	
CROATIA	x	
CYPRUS	x	
CZECHIA	x	
FINLAND	x	x
FRANCE	x	x
GERMANY	x	
GREECE	x	
HUNGARY	x	
IRELAND	x	x
ITALY	x	
LATVIA	x	
THE NETHERLANDS	x	x

(continued)

[116] See Case C-420/07 *Apostolides*, ECLI:EU:C:2009:271. See also in more detail S Francq, 'Article 45' in U Magnus and P Mankowski (eds), *European Commentaries on Private International Law. Volume I – Brussels Ibis Regulation* (Otto Schmidt, 2016) paras 57–59b; Bundesgerichtshof, 2 December 1992 XII ZB 64/91 sub III.1.d).

[117] See → AUSTRIA, Question 3, e); → CROATIA, Question 3, e); → GERMANY, Question 3, e), sub 4).

[118] Sofia Appellate Court, 2 March 2021, Judgment No 115, commercial case No 2647/2020: see → BULGARIA, Question 3, b).

[119] According to Art 811(a) of the Maltese COCP, which via the reference in Art 827(1)(a) COCP is also applicable with regards to the recognition and enforcement of foreign judicial decisions, a foreign judgment will not be recognised and/or enforced in Malta where the judgment was obtained by fraud on the part of any of the parties to the prejudice of the other party: see → MALTA, Question 3, b).

(Continued)

	Right to be Heard	Judicial Impartiality
POLAND	x	
MALTA	x	
ROMANIA	x	
SPAIN	x	
SWEDEN	x	x

f) Public Policy

There is no Member State where a foreign judgment will be recognised or enforced if it is found to be contrary to the public policy of the requested state. The concept of public policy appears to be fundamentally consistent across the Member States.

The public policy objection is regularly emphasised to have an exceptional character; a mere contradiction to mandatory provisions of the law of the requested state is not sufficient. Some provisions of national laws of Member States include an explicit wording that emphasises a restrictive interpretation.[120] In THE NETHERLANDS, due to the absence of a 'manifestly contrary' requirement, it has been argued that the public policy exception may be more readily invoked in Dutch proceedings.[121] However, rulings by DUTCH lower courts show that a foreign judgment will still only be regarded as contrary to public policy in exceptional circumstances.[122]

The foreign decision must be contrary to the fundamental principles of the law of the requested state and, in most Member States, the case must have at least some connections to that legal system.[123] In FRANCE, substantive public policy is applied with varying degrees of intensity depending on the case's connections to FRANCE.[124] According to AUSTRIAN case law, in cases where a public policy violation stems from the breach of EU law, a connection to any EU Member State is sufficient.[125]

In many EU Member States, courts have ruled that punitive damages are contrary to public policy.[126] For instance, the GERMAN Bundesgerichtshof has famously held that a US judgment awarding 'exemplary and punitive damages' as a lump sum, in addition to material and immaterial damages, is 'obviously' incompatible with fundamental principles of German law.[127] Similarly, DUTCH courts have found that

[120] See → BELGIUM, Question 3, d);); CROATIA, Question 3, f); CZECHIA, Question 3, f);.

[121] See → NETHERLANDS, Question 3, c);.

[122] See Rechtbank Amsterdam, 29 June 2016, ECLI:NL:RBAMS:2016:5691, 4.17; Rechtbank Amsterdam, 25 Augustus 2021, ECLI:NL:RBAMS:2021:4730, 4.9; and see → NETHERLANDS, Question 3, c);.

[123] See → AUSTRIA Question 3, f); BELGIUM, Question 3, f); CROATIA, Question 3, f); → FRANCE, Question 3, f); GERMANY, Question 3, f); and → THE NETHERLANDS, Question 3, f).

[124] Cass Civ 1st Chamber, 17 April 1953, *Rivière*; Cass Civ 1st Chamber, 7 January 1964, *Munzer*; and see → FRANCE, Question 3, f).

[125] Oberster Gerichtshof, 6 March 2020, 18 OCg 7/19g, See → AUSTRIA Question 3, f).

[126] See in more detail T Lutzi, 'Dashed Hopes and Good Intentions. Changing Attitudes Towards Punitive Damages around the World' in T Lutzi (ed), *Who's Afraid of Punitive Damages?* (Mohr Siebeck, 2026), 1, 1–3.

[127] Bundesgerichtshof, 4 July 1992, IX ZR 149/91, BGHZ 118, 312, sub A.V.3. See → GERMANY, Question 3, f).

judgments awarding extraordinarily high damages – commonly known as punitive damages – are contrary to Dutch public policy.[128] The Polish Supreme Court has held that enforcing a foreign judgment granting punitive damages would be unacceptable, as it contradicts the principle, interpreted in accordance with the constitutional requirement of proportionality, whereby compensation is meant to redress actual damage and must not exceed it.[129]

In some Member States, courts have recently moved away from a blanket refusal to recognise and enforce foreign punitive damages awards. For instance, the French Cour de cassation has held that only foreign judgments awarding punitive damages that are disproportionate to the harm suffered, and to the contractual breach, violate public policy.[130] Similarly, the Italian Corte di cassazione has held, following reforms of its domestic law, that the recognition of a foreign judgment awarding punitive damages does not conflict with public policy, provided that it adheres to the imperatives of Article 25 of the Italian Constitution.[131] Austrian courts have not ruled conclusively on whether the prohibition of punitive damages is part of public policy so far.[132] However, certain obiter dicta seem to suggest that punitive damages may trigger the exception,[133] but only if the damages are actually unreasonable in the particular case – the mere fact that the damages are punitive in nature does not per se amount to a violation of public policy.[134]

g) Reciprocity

Reciprocity is a condition for the recognition and enforcement of foreign judgments in only a limited (and shrinking) number of Member States.[135] Where it is required, a foreign judgment will not be recognised and enforced if the State of origin does not grant reciprocal recognition and enforcement of judgments rendered in the requested state.

The condition of reciprocity aims to encourage 'non-cooperative' foreign states – ie foreign states with which no form of cooperation in the field of recognition and

[128] Dutch case law indicates that a judgment involving punitive damages will only be partially recognised and enforced with respect to the award of compensatory damages: see Rechtbank Midden-Nederland, 11 September 2019, ECLI:NL:RBMNE:2019:4310, 4.28–4.30; Hof 's-Hertogenbosch, 31 Augustus 2021, ECLI:GHSHE:2021:2699, 3.7.3–3.7.5, 3.9: and see → Netherlands, Question 3, f).

[129] Postanowienie Sądu Najwyższego z, 11 October 2013 r, sygnatura akt: I CSK 697/12, See → Poland, Question 3, e).

[130] Cass Civ 1st Chamber, 1 December 2010, No 09-13.303: 'although the principle of an award of punitive damages is not, in itself, contrary to public policy, that is not the case when the amount awarded is disproportionate in relation to the harm suffered and the debtor's breaches of contractual obligations'. See → France Question 3, f).

[131] Corte di Cassazione, Sezioni Unite, 5 July 2017, no 16601, (2017) Riv dir int priv proc 1049; see also → Italy Question 3, f).

[132] See → Austria Question 3, f).

[133] Oberster Gerichtshof, 15 May 2019, 18 OCg 6/18h; 22 March 2011, 3 Ob 38/11a; 21 November 2002, 2 Ob 273/02i. See → Austria Question 3, f).

[134] Oberster Gerichtshof, 22 March 2011, 3 Ob 38/11a. See → Austria Question 3, f).

[135] See → Austria, Question 3, g); → Bulgaria, Question 3, g), where, however, the condition of reciprocity applies residually to foreign judgments in matters of insolvency; → Czechia, Question 3, g); → Germany, Question 3, g); → Hungary, Question 3, g); and → Romania, Question 3, g); see also → Cyprus, Question 3, g); → Ireland, Question 3, g); and → Finland, Question 3, g).

enforcement of foreign judgment exists in the requested state – to grant recognition and enforcement of judgments of the requested state.[136] But the requirement is regularly criticised for targeting the 'wrong' subject (the judgment creditor rather than the non-cooperative state); for lacking empirical evidence of its effectiveness in encouraging non-cooperative states to recognise and enforce judgments from the requested state;[137] and for being too cumbersome to ascertain.[138] Even more critically, the requirement has also been considered incompatible with the fundamental right of access to justice. In light of these concerns, it has been repealed in a number of Member States.[139]

In those Member States where it still exists, the condition of reciprocity appears to have little practical relevance.[140] Indeed, as mentioned, the condition applies only with respect to judgments rendered in non-cooperative foreign states and, thus, residually, when recognition and enforcement of the requested state's judgments in the state of origin is not guaranteed by an international treaty (so-called 'diplomatic reciprocity').

Apart from the case of diplomatic reciprocity, reciprocity can also be established in other ways. In particular, the condition is generally considered met where 'factual reciprocity' exists – that is, where the judgments rendered in the requested state have been recognised and enforced in the state of origin, or where this appears possible in practice. Factual reciprocity can be distinguished from legislative reciprocity, which exists where the laws of the state of origin allow for the recognition and enforcement of judgments from the requested state. While factual and legislative reciprocity can be distinguished, the existence of the former appears to be closely connected to the latter. Indeed, although the existence of factual reciprocity may generally be proven by any type of evidence, a key role is played by the content of the law of the state of origin governing recognition and enforcement of foreign judgments.[141] As to the 'degree' of reciprocity required, the GERMAN report states that it is not necessary that the domestic and foreign law on recognition and enforcement be 'identical'; rather, it is sufficient that the recognition and enforcement of a GERMAN decision does not encounter 'significantly greater difficulties' than a foreign judgment would in GERMANY.[142]

In the context of the assessment of the condition of reciprocity, administrative authorities may be involved. In particular, the requested court may be allowed to consult the Ministry of Justice (of the requested state) regarding the existence of reciprocity with the given foreign state.[143] Typically, the Ministry's response is not binding but contributes, along with other evidence, to forming the requested court's

[136] See → GERMANY, Question 3, g).
[137] There is at least one piece of anecdotal evidence, though: see Coyle, 'Rethinking Judgments Reciprocity' (2014) 92 *North Carolina Law Review* 1131 ff.
[138] See → CROATIA, Question 3, g); → CZECHIA, Question 3, g); and → GERMANY, Question 3, g).
[139] See → BULGARIA, Question 3, g); → CROATIA, Question 3, g); → POLAND, Question 3, g); and → SPAIN, Question 3, g).
[140] But see → AUSTRIA, Question 3, g).
[141] See → CZECHIA, Question 3, g).
[142] See → GERMANY, Question 3, g).
[143] See → CZECHIA, Question 3, g); see also → CROATIA, Question 3, g).

opinion on the point. In other words, the responsibility for determining whether reciprocity exists remains with the requested court. By contrast, some Member States adopt an 'administrative model', where the Ministry plays a dominant role in the assessment of the condition of reciprocity.[144] This is the case of AUSTRIA, where, in principle, reciprocity exists – in addition to cases where diplomatic reciprocity is established – only if there is an ordinance from the Ministry of Foreign Affairs declaring the existence of reciprocity.[145] This administrative model is also followed in HUNGARY.[146]

Finally, it is worth anticipating that, in those Member States where the deposit of a security may be required in the context of applications for the recognition and enforcement of foreign judgments (or refusal thereof), such requirement may also be subject to the condition of reciprocity (→ see Question 5).

h) Other Requirements

In many Member States, in addition to the conditions described above, the recognition and enforcement of foreign judgments are subject to additional requirements, which vary considerably from one Member State to another.

CYPRUS, CZECHIA, BELGIUM, FRANCE, MALTA and ROMANIA share a common additional requirement in the form of fraud, which is generally considered a ground for refusal. However, the concept and scope of fraud are interpreted differently in these Member States.[147] In particular, in CYPRUS and MALTA, fraud is understood in a very broad sense, covering any deceptive conduct aimed at obtaining a favourable judgment. By contrast, in BELGIUM, FRANCE and ROMANIA, fraud is understood more narrowly as *fraude à la loi* (fraud against the law). In BELGIUM and ROMANIA, fraud against the law refers to cases where parties engage in deceptive practices to avoid the enforcement of non-disposable rights granted by the law that would have otherwise applied based on the relevant connecting factors. In FRANCE, following a doctrinal and judicial reinterpretation that has narrowed its scope,[148] fraud against the law (in the field of recognition and enforcement of foreign judgments) involves using artificial means to establish jurisdiction in a foreign country specifically to obtain a favourable judgment.

In any case, the burden of proof for fraud, including in its form of fraud against the law, is notably high, as it also requires the establishment of a subjective element: the intent to deceive.

[144] See → HUNGARY, Question 3, g).

[145] See → AUSTRIA, Question 3, g).

[146] See → HUNGARY, Question 3, g). The administrative model was once adopted also in → CZECHIA, Question 3, g).

[147] See → CYPRUS, Question 3, h); → BELGIUM, Question 3, h) → FRANCE, Question 3, h); → ROMANIA, Question 3, h); → MALTA, Question 3, e) n 1; CZECHIA, Question 3, f).

[148] See, in the wake of Cass Civ 1st Chamber, 20 February 2007, No 05-14.082, *Cornelissen*, P Mayer, V Heuzé and B Remy, *Droit international privé* (LGDJ, 2019) 391 ; and M-L Niboyet, 'L'abandon du contrôle de compétence législative indirecte' *Gazette du Palais* (3 May 2007) 2.

In Czechia, artificially establishing foreign jurisdiction to circumvent the application of the requested state's law is considered a violation of public policy and thus a ground for refusal of recognition and enforcement (→ see Question 3, f)).[149] Depending on the circumstances, this and similar cases of what is considered fraud in the Member States mentioned above may similarly be subsumed under the public policy defence of other Member States, too.

As mentioned before, the other additional requirements mentioned in the national reports are diverse and do not lend themselves easily to comparison. In general terms, though, the presence of such additional conditions often suggests a less welcoming stance towards foreign judgments. This is particularly true for Member States which, as additional requirements, allow the requested court to review whether the foreign court correctly determined the applicable law according to the requested State's conflict-of-law rules;[150] the validity of the foreign decision under the law of the state of origin;[151] or even the correct application of substantive law to the merits of the case.[152]

Question 4. Documents to be Produced

In almost all Member States, the party applying for recognition or enforcement of a foreign judgment needs to submit a set of highly similar documents. In some Member States, specific legal provisions guide applicants on the required documents, while in others, parties must rely on judicial practice and interpretation.[153]

Where the judgment creditor needs to apply for a declaration of enforceability (→ see Question 2), they usually must submit the original judgment along with a legalised translation into the language of the requested Member State. The Member States differ only slightly with regard to translation requirements. In Belgium and Hungary, a legalised translation is required only upon request by the court.[154] In The Netherlands, a translation is necessary only if the foreign judgment is not in English, German or French.[155] Malta requires a translation if the judgment is not in English or Maltese.[156] In Finland, the foreign judgment must be translated into Finnish or Swedish; however, in practice, courts often accept translations in English, French or German, especially in commercial cases.[157] In Germany, opinions vary: some

[149] See → Czechia, Question 3, f).
[150] See → Latvia, Question 3, g).
[151] See → Germany, Question 3, h) n 1, where the judgment must not be void under the law of the state of origin.
[152] See → Malta, Question 3, h), n 2.
[153] Such as Germany and Sweden.
[154] See → Belgium, Question 4; Hungary., Question 4.
[155] Art 2.16 of the National rules of procedure for civil summons cases at district courts (July 2025) (*Landelijk procesregelement voor civiele dagvaardingszaken bij de rechtbanken handel en kanton*). See → The Netherlands, Question 4.
[156] See → Malta, Question 4.
[157] R Koulu, *Kansainvälinen prosessioikeus pääpiirteittäin* (Talentum, 2003) 59–60. See → Finland, Question 4.

scholars argue that no translation is needed,[158] while others insist on the need for a translation[159] or even an official translation of the judgment title.[160]

Most Member States require proof that the judgment is final and enforceable in the State of origin (→ see Question 3, b)), and all Member States are rather flexible as to what qualifies as acceptable as the proof.

Some Member States also require proof that the document initiating the original proceedings was served to the respondent. While often a general requirement, many Member States only require such proof where recognition or enforcement of a default judgment are sought.[161]

Legalisation of the judgment to be recognised or enforced is only required in some Member States; but where it is, the procedures for legalisation vary considerably among the Member States. For instance, in FINLAND, legalisation is only required if the court questions the authenticity of the document, and failure to submit a legalised document may lead to the application's rejection.[162] Conversely, in BULGARIA, foreign judgments must undergo a formal legalisation process in accordance with the Rules for Legislations, Certifications and Translations of Documents and Other Papers (with the exception of foreign judgments falling under a bilateral treaty).[163]

	Certified Copy of the Decision	**Legalised Translation**	**Proof of Finality**	**Proof of Service to the Judgment Debtor:**			**Legalisation of the Decision**
				Always	**Only for Default Judgments**	**Never**	
AUSTRIA	x	x	x	x			
BELGIUM	x	Only if required by the court	x		x		x
BULGARIA	x	x	x			x	x
CROATIA	x	x	x			x	x[164]
CYPRUS	x	x	x		x		
CZECHIA	x	x	x			x	x
FINLAND	x	x[165]	x			x	x[166]
FRANCE	x	x		x			

(continued)

[158] Hüßtege, '§ 723 ZPO' in H Thomas and H Putzo (eds), *Zivilprozessordnung*, 45th edn (CH Beck, 2024) para 12a.

[159] U Spellenberg, '§ 107' in J von Staudinger (ed), *J. von Staudingers Kommentar zum Bürgerlichen Gesetzgebuch mit Einführungsgesetz und Nebengesetzen – Einführungsgesetz zum Bürgerlichen Gesetzbuche/IPR – Internationales Verfahrensrecht in Ehesachen 2* (Sellier/de Gruyter, 2016) para 181.

[160] Gottwald, '§ 722' in T Rauscher and W Krüger (eds), *Münchener Kommentar zur Zivilprozessordnung*, 6th edn (CH Beck, 2020) para 47.

[161] See in table below.

[162] See → FINLAND, Question 4.

[163] Promulgated in State Gazette No 73 of 12 September 1958, last amended in State Gazette No 31 of 7 April 2023. See → BULGARIA, Question 4.

[164] Recent amendments to the Private International Law Act have raised doubts as to whether legalisation is required for every foreign decision.

[165] Only if the foreign judgment is not in Finnish or Swedish and if the court did not grant an exemption.

[166] Only if the court did not grant an exemption.

(Continued)

	Certified Copy of the Decision	Legalised Translation	Proof of Finality	Proof of Service to the Judgment Debtor: Always	Only for Default Judgments	Never	Legalisation of the Decision
GERMANY	x	x	x	x			Only if required by the court
GREECE	x	x	x		x		
HUNGARY	x	Only if required by the court				x	x
IRELAND	x	x		x			x
ITALY	x	Only if required by the court				x	x
LATVIA	x	x	x		x		x
THE NETHERLANDS	x	x[167]				x	
POLAND	x	x	x		x		x[168]
MALTA	x	x[169]	x			x	
ROMANIA	x	x	x		x		x
SPAIN	x	x	x		x		x
SWEDEN	x	x				x	

Question 5. Securities, Bonds or Deposits

Only a few Member States – namely ITALY,[170] BULGARIA,[171] FINLAND,[172] FRANCE,[173] GREECE[174] and LATVIA[175] – do not require the provision of any type of security for the recognition and enforcement of third-country judgments. Although AUSTRIA technically does not impose such a requirement either, this is subject to an exception: if an appeal is lodged against the declaration of enforceability of a foreign judgment that is enforceable but not yet final in the state of origin, the requested court may, at its discretion, order the provision of a security until the judgment becomes final before enforcement may commence.[176]

[167] Only if the foreign judgment is not in English, German or French.
[168] Only for documents concerning the transfer of ownership of real property located in Poland.
[169] Only if the foreign judgment is not in English or Maltese.
[170] See → ITALY, Question 5.
[171] See → BULGARIA, Question 5.
[172] See → FINLAND, Question 5.
[173] See → FRANCE, Question 5.
[174] See → GREECE, Question 5.
[175] See → LATVIA, Question 5.
[176] § 411 (5) EO. See → AUSTRIA, Question 5.

All Member States that do require some form of security make exceptions in favour of international treaties under which no such security may be demanded. Interestingly, the exception contained in BELGIUM's Code of Civil Procedure has been held by the Belgian Constitutional Court to violate the principle of equality and non-discrimination.[177] As a result, the provision must now be interpreted to apply to any claimant, irrespective of nationality, who is domiciled or lives abroad and lacks sufficient assets in Belgium to cover the financial consequences of an unfavourable judgment.[178]

CROATIA and ROMANIA exempt the judgment creditor from providing security for costs in recognition and enforcement proceedings involving third-state judgments if the applicant is domiciled or seated in a country that recognises the decisions regarding court costs rendered in the requested state. In other words, an exemption applies where there is de facto reciprocity concerning cost-related judgments (→ see Question 3, h)). In CROATIA, the Ministry of Justice should, at the request of the competent court, provide information on whether the country of the claimant's domicile recognises the decisions of Croatian courts on costs.[179] In CZECHIA, the exemption is conditional upon the assurance of reciprocity,[180] which, as in other cases where the CZECH PILA refers to reciprocity, is a case of de facto reciprocity.[181] In ROMANIA, according to Article 2561(2) of the Civil Code, reciprocity is presumed.[182]

Finally, GERMANY and POLAND make an exception on security on costs in cases of recognition and enforcement of a third-state judgments if the claimant possesses real estate assets, or claims secured *in rem*, in the requested state that suffice to cover the costs of the proceedings.[183]

[177] Constitutional Court, 11 October 2018, n 135/2018. See → BELGIUM, Question 5.

[178] Court of Cassation, 10 March 2023, n C.22.0126.N. See → BELGIUM, Question 5.

[179] Art 61 of the 2017 PILA provides that Art 8 of the 2017 PILA should be applied accordingly, which leads to the conclusion that the Ministry of Justice is competent for providing the information on the recognition of decisions on costs. This view is supported in: H Sikirić, 'Zakon o međunarodnom privatnom pravu' (2018) 25 *Tradicionalno XXXIII. savjetovanje – Aktualnosti Hrvatskog zakonodavstva i pravne prakse, Godišnjak* 61, 126. See → CROATIA, Question 5.

[180] The requirement of reciprocity does not apply to nationals of the Member States of the European Union and other countries forming the European Economic Area: Section 10, second sentence, Czech PILA.

[181] Z Kučera and L Tichý, *Zákon o mezinárodním právu soukromém a procesním: Komentář* 274. See → CZECHIA, Question 5.

[182] See → ROMANIA, Question 5.

[183] See → GERMANY, Question 5; → POLAND, Question 5.

3

National Reports

Austria

PAUL LORENZ EICHMÜLLER

Question 1. General Overview

The Austrian domestic rules on recognition and enforcement are mainly set out in the Execution Act (*Exekutionsordnung*;[1] EO). Austrian civil procedure is fragmented insofar as the Jurisdiction Act (*Jurisdiktionsnorm*;[2] JN) covers the principal rules of when, by whom and under which conditions civil jurisdiction may be exercised, whereas the actual procedure of the court proceedings in civil and commercial matters is set out in the Civil Procedure Code (*Zivilprozessordnung*;[3] ZPO). Enforcement of the judgments resulting from proceedings according to the provisions of the JN and the ZPO is then regulated in the EO. As the EO is an act on enforcement, the focus of the rules thus lies on enforcement rather than recognition, the latter being seen rather as an addendum to the enforcement. Recognition differs from enforcement in particular in the aspect that it happens *ipso iure* if the requirements are fulfilled, whereas for enforcement, one has to seek a declaration of enforceability in Austria before one can proceed with the actual enforcement proceedings.[4]

In recent decades, the relevant provisions of the EO on recognition and enforcement of third-country judgments have undergone two major amendments. The first was the Enforcement Amendment Act 1995 (*Exekutionsordnungs-Novelle 1995*;[5] EO-Nov 1995) and happened in order to conform to the requirements set out by the Brussels and Lugano Conventions which Austria joined at that time.[6] While the substantive requirements for recognition and enforcement of third-country decisions were not changed by influence of the Brussels and the Lugano Regimes (and have not been until today), the procedure changed significantly under their influence: before the EO-Nov 1995, the enforceability of foreign judgments was assessed incidentally in the actual enforcement proceedings – with the effect that there was no binding decision on the enforceability and that it had to be assessed again in any

[1] RGBl Nr 79/1896 idF BGBl I Nr 77/2023.
[2] RGBl Nr 111/1895 idF BGBl I Nr 61/2022.
[3] RGBl Nr 113/1895 idF BGBl I Nr 148/2020.
[4] This already follows from the wording of § 415 EO; see also Oberster Gerichtshof, 14 September 2011, 6 Ob 96/11b.
[5] BGBl Nr 519/1995.
[6] Regierungsvorlage zur EO-Nov 1995 (195 der Beilagen zu den Stenographischen Protokollen des Nationalrates, XIX. GP, 35).

possible further enforcement proceedings brought later on. The EO-Nov 1995 then introduced independent *exequatur* proceedings resulting in a binding declaration of enforceability. These proceedings do not form part of the actual enforcement, but rather are a supplement to the foreign proceedings, extending the effects of the judgment to Austria.[7] The second amendment was the Enforcement Amendment Act 2016 (*Exekutionsordnungs-Novelle 2016*;[8] EO-Nov 2016). Although the substance of the rules remained largely the same, the rules on international enforcement that had previously been dispersed all over the EO were collected in §§ 403 et seq EO. They now form the third part of the EO and cover those specific rules for international enforcement which differ from the extensive purely national rules. In general, the domestic rules on recognition and enforcement of foreign decisions in Austria are highly restrictive in several aspects.[9]

In addition to these general provisions on international enforcement, bilateral treaties (among others with the UK,[10] Israel,[11] Liechtenstein,[12] Tunisia[13] and Turkey[14]) play an important role in Austria. Recently, the treaty with the UK has also received particular attention due to Brexit. Interestingly, it only applies to decisions from higher courts (Senior Courts in the UK; Regional Courts ('*Landesgerichte*') and upwards in Austria[15]); the decisions of other (lower) courts have to be enforced according to the rules of the EO. The large importance of bilateral treaties is not least the case, because the general rules on enforcement of foreign decisions are extremely restrictive and are thus only very rarely applied in practice.[16] This means that they are not subject to particular interest of scholars either, who rather focus on the European rules of recognition and enforcement.

In case a foreign judgment is not recognised, the entire proceedings have to be redone in Austria. There is not even a possibility to use the foreign judgment as

[7] Oberster Gerichtshof, 25 March 2004, 3 Ob 175/03m.

[8] BGBl I Nr 100/2016.

[9] See below, particularly in the fields of reciprocity (Question 3g)) and jurisdiction (Question 3a)).

[10] Vertrag zwischen der Republik Österreich und dem Vereinigten Königreich von Großbritannien und Nordirland über die gegenseitige Anerkennung und Vollstreckung gerichtlicher Entscheidungen in Zivil- und Handelssachen (1961), BGBl Nr 224/1962; this treaty was changed by Protokoll zur Abänderung des in Wien unterzeichneten Vertrages zwischen der Republik Österreich und dem Vereinigten Königreich von Großbritannien und Nordirland über die gegenseitige Anerkennung und Vollstreckung gerichtlicher Entscheidungen in Zivil- und Handelssachen (1970), BGBl Nr 453/1971.

[11] Vertrag zwischen der Republik Österreich und dem Staat Israel über die gegenseitige Anerkennung und Vollstreckung von gerichtlichen Entscheidungen auf dem Gebiet des Zivil- und Handelsrechts (1966), BGBl Nr 349/1968.

[12] Abkommen zwischen der Republik Österreich und dem Fürstentum Liechtenstein über die Anerkennung und Vollstreckung von gerichtlichen Entscheidungen, Schiedssprüchen, Vergleichen und öffentlichen Urkunden (1973), BGBl Nr 114/1975.

[13] Vertrag zwischen der Republik Österreich und der Tunesischen Republik über die Anerkennung und die Vollstreckung von gerichtlichen Entscheidungen und öffentlichen Urkunden auf dem Gebiet des Zivil- und Handelsrechts (1977), BGBl Nr 305/1980.

[14] Abkommen zwischen der Republik Österreich und der Republik Türkei über die Anerkennung und die Vollstreckung von gerichtlichen Entscheidungen und Vergleichen in Zivil- und Handelssachen (1989), BGBl Nr 571/1992.

[15] Art I(2) Austro-British Enforcement Treaty (n 10).

[16] J Höllwerth, '§ 407 EO' in A Deixler-Hübner (ed), *Exekutionsordnung: Kommentar*, 36th edn (LexisNexis, 2022) para 3.

evidence in the subsequent Austrian proceedings: Austrian rules on evidence are strict and according to them, judgments can only be used as documentary evidence that the foreign court decided in a particular way, not for the factual basis of this decision.[17] In addition, the principle of immediacy of the proceedings requires that all evidence for the foundation of the claim be taken by the deciding court.[18] Yet, § 281a ZPO makes a limited exception to this rule and allows for protocols or expert opinions from previous proceedings to be included in the subsequent proceedings, but only under specific conditions: in particular, the parties can object to the inclusion of the evidence, without needing to give a reason for this objection.[19] Exceptionally, the evidence from previous proceedings may be used in spite of an objection if it is no longer available, such as if a witness has in the meanwhile deceased.[20] In any case, the possibility of applying § 281a ZPO to evidence taken before third-country courts only exists if the foreign proceedings were equivalent in due process for the taking of evidence.[21]

Question 2. Procedure

a) Circumstances of Recognition and Enforcement

The enforcement of foreign decisions requires a declaration of enforceability in separate proceedings. On the other hand, the mere recognition of foreign decisions happens *ipso iure* if the requirements are met and can thus be determined incidentally in any proceedings.[22] Since an incidental assessment of the recognition does not have binding effect for future cases,[23] § 415 EO opens up the possibility for declaratory proceedings. By such proceedings, the recognition of a particular decision in Austria is determined with *res iudicata* effect. § 415 EO refers for these declaratory recognition proceedings to the preceding sections of the EO on enforcement. Thus, where this report talks about the (constitutive) declaration of enforceability, the provided information applies equally to the declaratory recognition proceedings.

Regarding specifically the declaratory recognition proceedings, it is very disputed in literature whether also the judgment debtor can apply for a binding declaration – in

[17] L Bittner, '§ 292 ZPO' in HW Fasching and A Konecny (eds), *Zivilprozessgesetze III/1*, 3rd edn (Manz, 2017) para 42.
[18] This follows *e contrario* from the provision of § 281a ZPO; see also W Rechberger, '§ 276 ZPO' in HW Fasching and A Konecny (eds), *Zivilprozessgesetze III/2*, 3rd edn (Manz, 2017) para 1.
[19] W Rechberger, '§ 281a ZPO' in HW Fasching and A Konecny (eds), *Zivilprozessgesetze III/1*, 3rd edn (Manz, 2017) para 9.
[20] W Rechberger and T Klicka, '§ 281a ZPO' in W Rechberger and T Klicka (eds), *Zivilprozessordnung*, 5th edn (Verlag Österreich, 2019) para 3.
[21] Rechberger (n 19) para 6.
[22] M Slonina, '§ 83 EO. Verfahren' in P Angst and P Oberhammer (eds), *Kommentar zur Exekutionsordnung EO*, 3rd edn (Manz, 2015) para 3.
[23] J Höllwerth, '§ 415 EO' in A Deixler-Hübner (ed), *Exekutionsordnung: Kommentar*, 36th edn (LexisNexis, 2022) para 10.

this case of the non-recognisability in Austria.[24] In light of the unclear wording[25] and for reasons of equality of arms between the parties, this procedural option should also be available to the obliged party in order to provide for effective protective measures. Yet, there is no conclusive case law.

b) Procedural Steps

The competent court for the declaration of enforceability is the district court ('*Bezirksgericht*')[26] at the domicile[27] of the judgment debtor.[28] The creditor trying to enforce the foreign judgment may, however, alternatively choose to apply for a declaration of enforceability at the court that is competent for the subsequent enforcement, which may lead to a large number of competent courts.[29] Which court is competent for the enforcement is determined by §§ 4–5c EO.[30]

In general, the proceedings start as unilateral proceedings that are held exclusively in writing.[31] The application may be combined with the application to start actual enforcement and neither of the two is sent to the opposing party at first, in order to guarantee a certain element of surprise so that the obliged party does not dissipate its assets.[32] In these initial, unilateral proceedings, the court has to investigate all requirements for a declaration of enforceability *ex officio*.[33] Possible grounds for the refusal of enforcement according to § 408 EO must be also be assessed by the court in this context.[34] The burden of substantiation (by documents) of the positive requirements is, however, nevertheless upon the applicant.[35] In any case, the court is limited to assessing the requirements for enforcement and is strictly prohibited from reviewing the case on the merits in any way.[36]

Once the court reaches a decision whether the requirements to issue a declaration of enforceability are met, it serves the order ('*Beschluss*') to both the applicant and the

[24] In favour of this possibility: Höllwerth (n 23) para 13; T Garber and C Koller, 'Vor § 79 EO' in P Angst and P Oberhammer (eds), *Kommentar zur Exekutionsordnung EO*, 3rd edn (Manz, 2015) para 567; opposing it: Slonina (n 22) para 4.

[25] § 415 EO talks about the open application for a 'declaration *whether* the act is enforceable' ('ob'), rather than the stricter 'declaration *that* the act is enforceable' ('dass') that would have been the obvious choice if a limitation to a positive declaration was intended.

[26] § 3 EO prescribes that generally, all matters relating to enforcement are in the competence of the district courts (*Bezirksgerichte*).

[27] Defined in the domestic sense of §§ 66 et seq JN; for this definition, see P Eichmüller, 'Austria' in T Lutzi, E Piovesani and D Zgrabljić Rotar (eds), *Jurisdiction Over Non-EU Defendants* (Hart, 2023) 33–34.

[28] § 409(1) EO.

[29] § 409(2) EO; see also M Slonina, '§ 82 EO. Zuständigkeit' in P Angst and P Oberhammer (eds), *Kommentar zur Exekutionsordnung EO*, 3rd edn (Manz, 2015) paras 6–7.

[30] J Höllwerth, '§ 409 EO' in A Deixler-Hübner (ed), *Exekutionsordnung: Kommentar*, 36th edn (LexisNexis, 2022) paras 5, 26. The reference in § 409(2) EO to §§ 18–19 EO (in which this issue was regulated previously) is a – yet uncorrected – drafting mistake.

[31] Oberster Gerichtshof, 26 September 2003, 3 Ob 142/03h.

[32] J Höllwerth, '§ 410 EO' in A Deixler-Hübner (ed), *Exekutionsordnung: Kommentar*, 36th edn (LexisNexis 2022) para 16.

[33] RIS-Justiz RS0114024.

[34] Höllwerth (n 34) para 17.

[35] Slonina (n 22) para 20.

[36] RIS-Justiz RS0002409.

obliged party. The latter is only now added to the proceedings, making them two-sided from this moment onwards. This order is subject to an appeal ('*Rekurs*'), in which the responding obliged party bears the burden of substantiating the negative requirements if it wants to resist enforcement.[37] The appeal is subject to the general provisions on appeals to orders in the ZPO.[38] However, § 411 EO sets out some specificities for enforcement proceedings: first, the time limit for appeal and the reply to it is set at four weeks[39] instead of the general two.[40] As the obliged party has not taken part in the proceedings until they receive the order, there is an additional four-week extension of this time limit for parties domiciled outside of Austria to allow for an overall assessment of the case, giving them a total of eight weeks to lodge their own appeal.[41] Another major difference to general civil procedure stemming from the particular nature of these proceedings is the fact that the obliged party may bring up new arguments and facts in their appeal.[42] This is contrary to the general principle in Austrian procedural law that only questions raised in the first instance may be brought as a ground for appeal.[43] However, once an appeal is lodged, all arguments must be brought in it or in the reply to the appeal. Otherwise, the parties are precluded from making those arguments (so-called 'maxim of eventuality').[44]

Appeals to such an appeal decision (so called '*Revisionsrekurs*', always decided by the Supreme Court) are subject to different rules. The time to bring such an appeal is always four weeks, even if the party is from a foreign country, as it already had the possibility to participate in the appeals proceedings and adequately prepare itself.[45] For the same reason, only the facts and arguments brought forward in the appeals proceedings may be relied upon in the *Revisionsrekurs*.[46] However, there still is one facilitation in comparison to ordinary *Revisionsrekurs* proceedings: normally, a further appeal to the Supreme Court is not possible where the court of second instance fully confirms the initial decision.[47] This rule is, however, inapplicable in proceedings for the declaration of enforceability, where also a confirming decision is subject to a further appeal.[48]

Question 3. Requirements

The principal requirements of enforceability in the country of origin and reciprocity are set out in § 406 EO, with additional requirements in § 407 EO. The grounds for the

[37] M Slonina, '§ 84c EO. Aufhebung und Abänderung der Vollstreckbarerklärung' in P Angst and P Oberhammer (eds), *Kommentar zur Exekutionsordnung EO*, 3rd edn (Manz, 2015) para 7.

[38] *cf* § 78(1) EO.

[39] § 411(1) EO.

[40] § 521(1) ZPO.

[41] § 411(2) 1 EO.

[42] See eg, Oberster Gerichtshof, 24 June 2021, 3 Ob 21/21s.

[43] H Pimmer, '§ 482 ZPO. Mündliche Berufungsverhandlung' in HW Fasching and A Konecny (eds), *Zivilprozessgesetze IV/1*, 3rd edn (Manz, 2019) paras 1–3.

[44] RIS-Justiz RS0120291.

[45] Höllwerth (n 16) in A Deixler-Hübner (ed), *Exekutionsordnung: Kommentar*, 36th edn (LexisNexis, 2022) para 27.

[46] Oberster Gerichtshof, 24 June 2021, 3 Ob 21/21s.

[47] § 528(2) 2 ZPO.

[48] § 411(4) EO; see also Oberster Gerichtshof, 4 November 2019, 3 Ob 141/19k; 19 November 2019, 3 Ob 206/19v.

refusal of recognition and enforcement which have to be brought forward by the other party are listed in § 408 EO.

a) Jurisdiction of the Court of Origin

As in many countries, foreign decisions are only recognised and enforced in Austria if the court of origin had a reasonable ground to exercise jurisdiction, as prescribed by § 407(1) EO. Yet, Austrian law opts for a very strict standard of assessing this fact. It requires that, in a mirrored application of the rules on Austrian jurisdiction,[49] the courts of the state of origin would hypothetically be competent to rule on the dispute, which is termed the '*Österreichische Jurisdiktionsformel*' in legal literature.[50] In this respect, it is important to note that only international jurisdiction is relevant in this assessment, not local territorial jurisdiction: if the application of Austrian jurisdictional rules leads to the jurisdiction of another than the deciding court within the state of origin, enforcement is still possible.[51] Similarly, if the court of origin violated its own rules on jurisdiction, that does not pose an obstacle to enforcement in Austria, as long as it complies with the hypothetical application of Austrian jurisdictional rules.[52] While the Austrian legal literature argues that the European rules on jurisdiction in the Brussels Ibis Regulation also need to be taken into account,[53] the Austrian Supreme Court consistently rules that only the domestic rules on jurisdiction (the JN) are relevant in this assessment.[54]

From a temporal perspective, this hypothetical jurisdiction does not need to exist at the time of the decision in the country of origin, but only at the time of 'the application for the *exequatur* proceedings'.[55] This is, however, criticised by some Austrian academics as an illicit form of retroactive application of a legal norm.[56] Yet, like with the requirement of reciprocity,[57] the better arguments speak for applying the rules at the time of the *exequatur* proceedings. The old case law might even be too restrictive, as it should not depend on the time of the initiation of the *exequatur* proceedings, but rather on the time of the decision. After all, the requirement of hypothetical jurisdiction is, paradoxically, not a jurisdictional provision that could be subject to a *perpetuatio fori*, but a substantive requirement for the granting of the declaration of enforceability that is generally assessed at the time of the decision.[58]

[49] For a summary of Austrian national jurisdictional rules, see Eichmüller (n 28) 31–44.

[50] Höllwerth (n 16) para 9.

[51] RIS-Justiz RS0002369; Oberster Gerichtshof, 23 September 2004, 6 Ob 170/04z; T Garber, '§ 80 EO' in P Angst and P Oberhammer (eds), *Kommentar zur Exekutionsordnung EO*, 3rd edn (Manz, 2015) para 10.

[52] RIS-Justiz RS0002369; F Matscher, 'Der Vorbehalt ausschließlicher Zuständigkeit im österreichischen Recht' (1979) *Juristische Blätter* 182, 184; Höllwerth (n 16) para 9; Garber (n 51) paras 8–9.

[53] M Neumayr and B Nunner-Krautgasser, *Exekutionsrecht*, 4th edn (Manz, 2018) 122; M Nademleinsky, *Internationales Scheidungsrecht* (Manz, 2014) para 73; T Garber, 'Zur Reichweite der österreichischen Jurisdiktionsformel' (2017) *Zeitschrift für Familien- und Erbrecht* 233, 235.

[54] RIS-Justiz RS0002369.

[55] Oberster Gerichtshof, 28 December 1915, Rv I 674/15.

[56] Garber (n 51) para 13, referring particularly to LV Heller, F Berger and L Stix (eds), *Kommentar zur Exekutionsordnung*, 4th edn (Manz, 1969) vol I, 773.

[57] See below Question 3 g).

[58] *cf* Oberster Gerichtshof, 26 April 2000, 3 Ob 258/99h.

b) Finality/Enforceability in the Country of Origin

Enforceability in the country of origin is expressly mentioned in the text of § 406 EO as a main requirement so that the Austrian court may issue a declaration of enforceability. First, the type of judicial act must, by its nature, be a base for enforcement proceedings in the country of origin,[59] yet it does not necessarily need to correspond to one of the types of acts amenable to enforcement in Austria.[60] It is thus irrelevant whether these acts were issued by a court, an administrative authority or even a notary.[61] Second, the judicial act must be enforceable *in concreto*.[62] This means in particular that it must be sufficiently definite,[63] yet measured according to the standards of the country of origin, not by possibly stricter Austrian domestic rules.[64] If necessary, the enforcement court might even have to supplement the initial decision to a certain extent.[65]

However, it is not necessary for the decision to have reached the stage of finality, as long as enforceability is given.[66] This is clear from the wording of § 407(3) EO, which stipulates that the decision must not 'be subject to an appeal that hinders enforceability'. This does not only extend to enforcement to obtain security for the claim (eg attachment of the assets without selling them). Even actual enforcement to settle the claim is possible if the appeal does not hinder enforcement in the country of origin.[67]

c) *Res Iudicata*

The issue of irreconcilability of the judgment that shall be enforced in Austria with other (Austrian or recognised foreign) decisions is – quite surprisingly – not discussed in Austrian literature. Similarly, there has not been any case law on this issue yet due to the very limited practical use of the domestic provisions on recognition and enforcement. It has to be noted that there is no explicit statutory provision mentioning such an irreconcilability as a ground for refusal of enforcement. However, a conflict with *res iudicata* can undoubtedly be a reason to invoke public policy and the enforcement of irreconcilable judgments can thus be effectively resisted. The Austrian Supreme Court has explicitly stated that *res iudicata* is one of the central concepts of Austrian procedural law.[68]

[59] Oberster Gerichtshof, 21 August 2003, 3 Ob 98/03p.

[60] J Höllwerth, '§ 403 EO' in A Deixler-Hübner (ed), *Exekutionsordnung: Kommentar*, 36th edn (LexisNexis, 2022) para 5; T Garber, '§ 79 EO' in P Angst and P Oberhammer (eds), *Kommentar zur Exekutionsordnung EO* 3rd edn (Manz, 2015) para 8. Those acts are laid out for Austria in § 1 EO.

[61] Garber (n 60) para 10.

[62] ibid, para 8.

[63] RIS-Justiz RS0117940.

[64] RIS-Justiz RS0118680; Neumayr and Nunner-Krautgasser (n 54) 119.

[65] On this issue see in detail Höllwerth (n 60) para 10.

[66] Oberster Gerichtshof, 24 May 2011, 3 Ob 65/11x; Garber (n 60) paras 8, 26; Neumayr and Nunner-Krautgasser (n 53) 118.

[67] § 407 Z 3 EO; Oberster Gerichtshof, 30 May 2006, 3 Ob 49/06m. Enforcing judgments that may later still be overturned is not particular to foreign decisions, as also national judgments may be enforced (to provide for collateral), before they have become final, *cf* §§ 370 and 371 EO.

[68] Oberster Gerichtshof, 24 January 2019, 6 Ob 3/19p.

As such, its violation is bound to trigger the public policy exception. Yet, it bears mentioning that – unlike under the Brussels Regime[69] – only prior irreconcilable judgments can lead to the refusal of enforcement, even if a later irreconcilable judgment stems from Austria. If the foreign judgment fulfils all of the other requirements for recognition in Austria, it is recognised *ipso iure*. Thus, it taints the proceedings that led to the later Austrian judgment with nullity due to being in violation of *res iudicata*.[70] In such a case, it would thus be the Austrian judgment that will not be enforced.

d) *Lis Pendens*

Pending proceedings on the same matter – whether in Austria or abroad – do not hinder the recognition or enforcement of foreign judgments in Austria. If a foreign decision is recognised, the *res iudicata* effect of the foreign decision is extended to the Austrian territory. This has the effect that pending proceedings in Austria need to be ended *ex officio* immediately, as the non-existence of a decision with *res iudicata* effect in the same matter is a general requirement for the admissibility of claims.[71] Should the court nevertheless decide on the subject matter in the second proceedings, the other party may bring an action for reconsideration of the second decision and thereby reopen the proceedings.[72]

e) Specific Requirements of Due Process

The requirement of adhering to due process in the original proceedings is not uniformly regulated in Austrian enforcement law. The only part of due process that is explicitly mentioned is the right to be heard, which is set out in a twofold manner: on the one hand, § 407(2) EO establishes the positive requirement that the respondent in the original proceedings must have received the document which instituted the proceedings. In this document, the respondent must at least be informed about the extent of the claim and its basis.[73] Whether further documents in the foreign proceedings after the initial one were served on the respondent is, however, irrelevant – even if the claim is extended in one of them.[74] Similarly, the service of the decision that is being enforced does not matter for this requirement.[75] As it is a positive requirement, proper service of the initial document must be assessed by the court independently and *ex officio*; in this assessment, the enforcement court is not bound by the findings of the court of origin.[76] Whether the defects in the service of the initial

[69] *cf* Art 45 (1) (d) Brussels Ibis Regulation.

[70] The Austrian judgment should thus never have been issued, the reasoning behind it is the same as described in the section on *lis pendens*, see above Question 3 d).

[71] T Klicka, '§ 411 ZPO. Rechtskraft des Urteils' in HW Fasching and A Konecny (eds), *Zivilprozessgesetze III/2*, 3rd edn (Manz, 2017) para 134.

[72] ibid, para 135.

[73] Garber (n 51) para 17.

[74] ibid para 18. However, the failure of the service of these documents might lead to a ground for refusal of enforcement according to § 408(1) EO.

[75] Höllwerth (n 16) para 17.

[76] Oberster Gerichtshof, 29 August 2019, 3 Ob 91/19g; Garber (n 51) para 24; Höllwerth (n 16) para 25.

document might have been cured at a later point in time (in particular by joining the proceedings and acting accordingly) has to be determined by the rules of the country where the service was effected in order to allow for a uniform assessment of this question.[77]

On the other hand, § 408(1) EO deals with the right to be heard on a different level – as a ground for the refusal of enforcement (ie a negative requirement). It allows for a refusal in cases in which the respondent was unable to participate in the original proceedings due to procedural irregularities. This ground is broader than the positive requirement just mentioned: eg, where the initial document was delivered, but too late to allow for an appropriate defence, the respondent can refuse the enforcement in Austria.[78] It is important to note that in order to rely on this ground for refusal, it is – as opposed to the Brussels Regime[79] – not necessary to become active in the state of origin and lodge appeals there.[80] Other violations of due process can – while not explicitly mentioned – also be brought forward under § 408 EO, as it comprises a general check of *procedural* public policy.[81] The Austrian Supreme Court generally emphasises, however, that the procedural *ordre public* is only to be applied exceptionally and thus in cases where 'an overall assessment shows that procedural fundamental rights of one party have been curtailed in an unbearable way',[82] and thus, one cannot speak of orderly proceedings in their entirety.[83] As opposed to the service of the initial document (§ 407(2) EO), the grounds for refusal pursuant to § 408(1) EO must be invoked and proven by the party resisting enforcement.[84]

Particular cases that are discussed in Austrian literature are, for example: the service of initial documents in a language that is unknown to the respondent and that they were not required to understand (as the language of their country of nationality or of the country where service of the document took place);[85] under certain circumstances also the exclusion of a party from the proceedings in a common law country if they are in contempt of court;[86] lack of impartiality and independence of the deciding court;[87] unequal treatment of the parties;[88] fraud in the original proceedings;[89] or a decision that entirely lacks reasoning.[90]

[77] Höllwerth (n 16) para 21.

[78] T Garber, '§ 81 EO. Versagungsgründe' in P Angst and P Oberhammer (eds), *Kommentar zur Exekutionsordnung EO*, 3rd edn (Manz, 2015) para 4; J Höllwerth, '§ 408 EO' in A Deixler-Hübner (ed), *Exekutionsordnung: Kommentar*, 36th edn (LexisNexis, 2022) para 4.

[79] Case C-420/07 *Meletis Apostolides v David Charles Orams and Linda Elizabeth Orams*. See also in more detail S Francq, 'Article 45' in U Magnus and P Mankowski (eds), *European Commentaries on Private International Law. Volume I – Brussels Ibis Regulation* (Otto Schmidt, 2016) paras 57–59b.

[80] Garber (n 78) para 8.

[81] Höllwerth (n 78) paras 3 and 7; Garber (n 78) para 16.

[82] eg Oberster Gerichtshof, 20 February 2019, 3 Ob 251/18k; id., 20 November 2001, 3 Ob 250/01p.

[83] Höllwerth (n 78) para 7.

[84] RIS-Justiz RS0125461; Höllwerth (n 78) para 10.

[85] Which is even deemed an invalid service and thus falls under § 407(2) EO, see RIS-Justiz RS0110260; RIS-Justiz RS0110261; F Mohr, H Pimmer and B Schneider, '§ 407 EO' in *Exekutionsordnung – EO*, 17th edn (Manz, 2021) 717.

[86] Oberster Gerichtshof, 30 September 2009, 3 Ob 161/09m.

[87] Garber (n 78) para 16.

[88] ibid.

[89] Höllwerth (n 78) para 8.

[90] This will not be the case if a supplementary document can prove the reasoning behind the decision. See Höllwerth (n 78) para 9.

f) Public Policy

Other than the procedural *ordre public*,[91] the Austrian Enforcement Act also provides for the refusal of enforcement for reasons of substantive public policy in § 408(3) EO. Also in its substantive form, the public policy objection should have an exceptional character, a mere contradiction to mandatory provisions of Austrian law is far from enough.[92] In order to constitute a violation, the decision need not only be incompatible with fundamental principles of the Austrian legal order,[93] but the case must also have sufficient connection to Austria.[94] In the past, it was held that public policy is the same in a national[95] and in an international context, the 'sufficient connection test' only determining whether public policy can be invoked at all.[96] However, the Austrian Supreme Court has recently ruled that the content of public policy is also subject to 'relativity', depending on how close the connection to Austria is.[97] In cases where the public policy violation is based on a deviation from common principles of European law, a connection to any EU Member State is sufficient.[98]

Cases which were considered incompatible with Austrian public policy include: the denial of a claim after the significant (legislative) shortening of an existing limitation period without transitional arrangements;[99] damages awarded for a broken betrothal;[100] discrimination on the basis of race or religion;[101] claims based on contracts that were concluded under duress or by fraud;[102] or (effective) interest of more than 100 per cent per annum.[103] Regarding punitive damages, the Austrian courts have not ruled conclusively on whether their prohibition is part of public policy so far. However, certain obiter dicta seem to suggest that punitive damages may trigger the exception;[104] yet, only if the damages are actually unreasonable in the particular case – the mere fact that the damages are punitive in nature does not per se amount to a violation of public policy.[105]

More specifically, § 408(2) EO sets out that one cannot enforce actions that are in Austria either impermissible (eg, against criminal law) or generally not enforceable (eg, betrothals, where parties cannot be forced into marriage).[106] Although this is listed as a separate ground for refusal, it is in fact only a specific sub-case of a public policy violation.[107]

[91] See above Question 3 e).
[92] RIS-Justiz RS0110743.
[93] RIS-Justiz RS0074428.
[94] Oberster Gerichtshof, 13 September 2000, 4 Ob 199/00v; 12 October 2011, 3 Ob 186/11s.
[95] In these contexts, public policy can become relevant as a ground for setting aside an arbitral award pursuant to § 611(2)8 ZPO.
[96] Höllwerth (n 78) para 14.
[97] Oberster Gerichtshof, 6 March 2020, 18 OCg 7/19g; 29 January 2019, 2 Ob 170/18s; 12 October 2011, 3 Ob 186/11s.
[98] Oberster Gerichtshof, 6 March 2020, 18 OCg 7/19g.
[99] Oberster Gerichtshof, 26 February 1958, 6 Ob 7/58.
[100] Oberster Gerichtshof, 14 June 1899, GlUNF 642.
[101] Oberster Gerichtshof, 10 July 1986, 7 Ob 600/86.
[102] Garber (n 78) para 15.
[103] Oberster Gerichtshof, 26 January 2005.
[104] Oberster Gerichtshof, 15 May 2019, 18 OCg 6/18h; 22 March 2011, 3 Ob 38/11a; 21 November 2002, 2 Ob 273/02i.
[105] Oberster Gerichtshof, 22 March 2011, 3 Ob 38/11a.
[106] Garber (n 78) para 9.
[107] ibid.

Unlike the other grounds for refusal of enforcement, public policy can be invoked by the court of its own motion if and when the violation in question does not only touch upon interests of the party but also upon those of the state.[108]

g) Reciprocity

Arguably the most restraining (and therefore notorious) requirement for the enforcement of foreign decisions in Austria is reciprocity of enforcement with the country of origin. This requirement has long been criticised in academia,[109] but has nevertheless survived several amendments and persists today. Furthermore, reciprocity is required in a very strict sense. First of all, enforcement requires not only substantive reciprocity, but *formal* reciprocity.[110] What makes enforcement in Austria so difficult is that the reciprocity must not only be plain reciprocity, but rather, it must be proven by an administrative or diplomatic act: § 406 EO requires an international treaty or an Austrian ordinance ('*Verordnung*').[111] In Austria, this is generally called 'qualified reciprocity'.

The treaties referred to in § 406 EO are, however, not general treaties on the recognition of foreign judgments, which would as a *lex specialis* derogate § 406 EO and establish their own rules anyway.[112] Rather, this refers to treaties merely guaranteeing reciprocity – yet this has proven entirely impractical: if a treaty is concluded, it generally also regulates the substantive requirements for recognition and enforcement and not just reciprocity.[113] A residual scope of application for this provision is given in the Convention on the Contract for the International Carriage of Goods by Road (CMR)[114] and the Convention concerning International Carriage by Rail (COTIF),[115] as they both require the Member States to reciprocally enforce judgments based on the substantive rules of the respective treaty, without establishing substantive enforcement law themselves.[116] A much more practical way to fulfil the requirement of qualified reciprocity would be ordinances. Ordinances on reciprocity are issued by the minister of justice[117] if the minister concludes that formal reciprocity is given with respect to a particular country. In practice, however, this only happens very rarely.

Due to the normative, law-like effect of both treaties and ordinances, courts cannot refuse enforcement if either of the two exists for a certain country, even if the legal situation might have changed since the enactment of the ordinances and formal reciprocity

[108] Garber (n 78) para 23; Höllwerth (n 78) para 16.

[109] Already H Sperl, 'Die internationale Vollstreckung gerichtlicher Entscheidungen' (1912) *Gerichts-Zeitung* 535, 537; W Kralik, 'Die Gegenseitigkeit bei der Zwangsvollstreckung ausländischer Titel' (1959) *Österreichische Jurist:innenzeitung* 253, 258.

[110] J Höllwerth, '§ 406 EO', para 6.

[111] This is already evident from the wording in § 406 EO, but was made eminently clear by Oberster Gerichtshof, 24 January 1989, 2 Ob 611/88.

[112] Neumayr and Nunner-Krautgasser (n 53) 119; Höllwerth (n 110) para 11.

[113] D Czernich, 'Zu den Voraussetzungen der Anerkennung und Vollstreckung fremder Entscheidungen nach autonomem Recht (§ 79 EO)' (1996) *Juristische Blätter* 495, 498.

[114] 1956.

[115] 1985.

[116] Art 31(3) CMR; Art 18 COTIF; see also Neumayr and Nunner-Krautgasser (n 53) 122.

[117] *cf* § 483a EO; even though the wording used to be different (and confusing with regards to who should issue the ordinance) before, it has always been issued by the minister of justice; see Czernich (n 113) 498.

is no longer given.[118] While this was originally thought as a means to relieve courts of the burden of examining in every single case whether reciprocity actually exists and to provide maximum legal certainty,[119] this aim is not achieved. As any normative source of law must be subject to constitutional review of the Austrian Constitutional Court, this also applies to ordinances. If the ordinance no longer conforms with its statutory requirement, namely that reciprocity is given, it becomes unconstitutional. Any judge who has doubts about an ordinance's constitutionality must submit an application for review to the Constitutional Court.[120] Judges are thus constitutionally required to do at least some cursory review of whether reciprocity actually exists – and the purpose of the rule is defeated.[121]

Even more problematic than the binding effect of treaties and ordinances is the 'binding' effect of their absence. The deciding court has no authority to determine by itself whether formal reciprocity is given.[122] In the absence of a reciprocity ordinance, foreign decisions can thus not be enforced. This has been criticised as overly restrictive and without any actual use since the early days of the rule,[123] yet it has nevertheless survived several reforms and persists until this day.

Another heavily disputed question is the time at which reciprocity must be established. The prevailing opinion in Austrian legal literature seems to support that the date when the original judgment was issued is relevant, generally basing this view on the principle of non-retroactivity of legal norms.[124] A smaller – yet more convincing – part of legal literature on the other hand advocates for the relevance of the date of the *exequatur* decision.[125] This is also in line with a previous Supreme Court decision[126] that declares the factual and legal situation at the time of the decision relevant in *exequatur* proceedings – albeit in a different context. Also from a teleological point of view, this solution is preferrable: after all, even justified trust in the mere non-enforcement of a foreign decision is not worthy of legal protection.[127] While there is no final answer to the question of the temporal frame of qualified reciprocity, assessing it at the time of the decision on the declaration of enforceability is thus the preferred solution.

h) Other Requirements

The requirement of sufficient definiteness might be considered a separate requirement, but at a closer look, it becomes evident that it is just a subcategory of enforceability and is thus treated above under Question 3b).

[118] Höllwerth (n 110) para 8; Czernich (n 113) 498.
[119] *Materialien zu den neuen österreichischen Zivilprozeßgesetzen I* (Manz, 1897) 493.
[120] *cf* Art 89 B-VG BGBl Nr 1/1930 idF BGBl I Nr 222/2022.
[121] Czernich (n 113) 499.
[122] RIS-Justiz RS0002322; Czernich (n 113) 499; Garber (n 60) para 19.
[123] G Walker, *Streitfragen aus dem internationalen Civilprocessrechte* (Manz, 1897) 232.
[124] Höllwerth (n 110) para 9; also stated in the decision of Oberlandesgericht Wien, 30 June 1992, 11 R 115/92.
[125] Garber (n 60) para 20; Slonina (n 22) para 31.
[126] Oberster Gerichtshof, 26 April 2000, 3 Ob 258/99h.
[127] Slonina (n 22) para 31.

Question 4. Documents to be Produced

The central document that needs to be submitted is the application for a declaration of enforceability. It initiates the proceedings and must be submitted in German.[128] The other documents to be produced and attached to this application are the documents that prove the positive requirements in § 407 EO. That is the entire decision that is to be enforced (if there is a minority opinion in a separate document, it does not have to be attached[129]) and a confirmation by the deciding authority that this decision is enforceable.[130] It needs to be submitted as an original and not as an (albeit legalised) copy.[131] In addition to the original, a legalised translation into German is necessary,[132] which needs to cover the entirety of the decision, including the reasoning.[133] Legalisation of the translation has to be effected by a certified court interpreter/translator, eg according to the Austrian Court Expert and Interpreter Act (*Sachverständigen- und Dolmetschergesetz*;[134] SDG). The translation does not necessarily have to be made by someone certified in Austria, as long as they are certified as a court interpreter/translator by another state authority[135] and this certification is also translated (in a legalised manner).[136] If the legalisation is in a foreign language, the legalisation must also be translated (and in turn be legalised).[137] For these reasons, it will be advisable in practice to have the translation made by a court interpreter/translator in Austria. In addition, proof that the document initiating the original proceedings was served to the respondent also needs to be submitted (if not in German also in a translated version) in order to prove the requirement of § 407(2) EO.[138]

Question 5. Securities, Bonds and Deposits

For the declaration of enforceability, there is no requirement to provide securities. The application of the general provisions of the ZPO on whether securities have to be provided (but not which types of securities are permissible)[139] are even explicitly excluded by virtue of § 78(2)1 EO.[140] However, there is one – very limited – exception

[128] Höllwerth (n 32) para 5.
[129] RIS-Justiz RS0121018.
[130] Höllwerth (n 32) para 12; *cf* also Oberster Gerichtshof, 28 January 2004, 3 Ob 104/03w.
[131] Slonina (n 22) para 14.
[132] ibid para 15.
[133] RIS-Justiz RS0110840.
[134] BGBl Nr 137/1975 idF BGBl I Nr 61/2022.
[135] Oberster Gerichthof, 11 June 1969, 3 Ob 62/69; 29 May 1996, 3 Ob 2097/96w; T Garber and C Koller, 'Vor § 79 EO' in Peter Angst and Paul Oberhammer (eds), *Kommentar zur Exekutionsordnung EO*, 3rd edn (Manz, 2015) para 582.
[136] Oberster Gerichtshof, 23 October 1991, 3 Ob 88/91.
[137] Oberster Gerichtshof, 28 November 2002, 3 Ob 196/02y.
[138] See above Question 3 e). On the need to furnish this proof, see Höllwerth (n 32) para 12.
[139] *cf* R Fucik, 'Vor § 56 ZPO' in Hans W Fasching and Andreas Konecny (eds), *Zivilprozessgesetze II/1*, 3rd edn (Manz 2014). Therefore, § 56 ZPO is applicable, whereas the rest of the provisions in §§ 57–62 ZPO are not applicable.
[140] R Fucik, '§ 78 EO' in Astrid Deixler-Hübner (ed), *Exekutionsordnung: Kommentar*, 33rd edn (LexisNexis, 2021) para 52.

to this rule: if an appeal is lodged against the declaration of enforceability in Austria of a foreign judgment that is already enforceable but not yet final in the country of origin, it is at the enforcement court's discretion to order the provision of securities until the judgment becomes final before enforcement may commence.[141] This decision is not subject to a further appeal.[142]

In addition, some particularly expensive enforcement acts are subject to the requirement that the applicant pays for their costs in advance before these acts can be performed. This obligation does not depend on whether it is a domestic or a foreign decision that is being enforced. Such acts include among others: getting a locksmith to open locked doors;[143] appointing an enforcement administrator;[144] putting real estate under forced administration;[145] or putting real estate up for auction.[146]

[141] § 411(5) EO.
[142] Höllwerth (n 110) para 44.
[143] § 26a(2) EO.
[144] § 79(1) EO.
[145] § 99(1) EO.
[146] § 136(2) EO.

Belgium

CEDRIC VANLEENHOVE

Question 1. General Overview

Judgments in civil and commercial matters from third countries are, in the absence of a treaty, recognised and enforced in Belgium in accordance with the provisions of the Belgian Code of Private International Law of 2004 (CPIL). The CPIL forms an attempt to codify the private international rules that prior to the entry into force of the CPIL could be found in various places, such as the Belgian Civil Code and the Belgian Code of Civil Procedure. The provisions of the CPIL are interpreted by the courts. Case law, just like doctrine, however, does not have binding authority as Belgium does not follow precedent. Decisions of the highest courts, in particular the Supreme Court, called the Cour de Cassation (*Hof van Cassatie*), do hold strong persuasive authority. The rules in the CPIL have been heavily influenced by the Brussels regime, specifically the Brussels I Regulation (Regulation 44/2001) which was the instrument in force at the time of the drafting and adoption of the CPIL. Although no empirical research has been undertaken to confirm this, the author believes that the courts readily refer to the provisions of the Brussels instruments when interpreting the CPIL.

The CPIL lays down the conditions for the effect in Belgium of foreign judgments in civil and commercial matters (Article 2 CPIL). The term 'judgment' is defined as any decision rendered by an authority exercising judicial power (Article 22 §3, 1° CPIL). This neutral definition should be given a broad interpretation. It could be a binding decision from an organ of the judiciary or from an administrative authority.[1] Arbitral awards are not considered to be judgments in the sense of Article 22.[2] The absence of a list of exclusions in the CPIL ensures that the instrument's scope encompasses the broadest possible range of civil and commercial matters.

Articles 22–25 of the CPIL deal with the recognition and enforcement of judgments. Recognition gives legal force to the foreign judgment (Article 22 §3, 2° CPIL). The foreign judgment obtains in Belgium the same binding effect as it has in the country of origin. Enforcement should be understood as the declaration of enforceability (ie the granting of *exequatur*) of the foreign judgment as a preliminary step for actual execution in Belgium.

[1] H Storme, 'Artikel 22 WIPR' in I Couwenberg, A Hansebout and L Vanfraechem (eds), *Duiding Internationaal Privaatrecht* (Larcier, 2014) 653.

[2] P Wautelet, 'Le nouveau régime des décisions étrangères dans le Code de droit international privé' (2004) *Tijdschrift voor procesrecht en bewijsrecht / Revue de droit judiciaire et de la preuve* 208, 210.

Article 22 lays down the general principles. A foreign judgment is recognised in Belgium, in whole or in part, without the need for any procedure (Article 22 §1, paragraph 2). A foreign judgment, provided it is enforceable in the state in which it was rendered, is declared enforceable in whole or in part in Belgium in accordance with the procedure set out in Article 23 (Article 22 §1, paragraph 1 CPIL). It follows from Article 22 §1, paragraphs 1–2 CPIL that recognition and enforcement can pertain to part of the judgment. Article 23 describes the jurisdiction and procedure for recognition and enforcement, and Article 24 lists the documents to be submitted by the party seeking recognition and enforcement. The judgment may be recognised or declared enforceable only if it does not violate the conditions laid down in Article 25 (Article 22 §1, paragraph 4). Article 25 contains the grounds for refusal of recognition and enforcement. If one of these refusal grounds is found to exist, the refusal of recognition and enforcement is mandatory (evidenced by the word 'shall' in Article 25 §1 CPIL).

Question 2. Procedure

a) Circumstances of Recognition and Enforcement

In Belgium there are three different methods of recognition: recognition *de plano*; judicial recognition on the basis of a principal claim for recognition; and incidental judicial recognition.

The CPIL provides that recognition of a foreign judgment does not require any procedure (Article 22 §1, paragraph 2 CPIL). This is the so-called *de plano* recognition. Various authorities which are confronted with the foreign judgment, such as the Civil Registry, the Immigration Office, a notary and the Pension Office, have the competence to decide on its recognition. In making their determination they have the obligation to check whether the conditions for recognition are fulfilled. They will have to verify *ex officio* whether the incoming judgment does not violate the conditions of Article 25 (Article 22 §1, paragraph 4 CPIL). In any case, under no circumstances will the foreign judgment be reviewed on the merits (Article 25 §2 CPIL). Their decision does not have *res iudicata* effect and is not binding upon the other authorities. It has an inherent precarious status and different authorities can reach conflicting decisions as to the recognition or non-recognition.

An interested party (and also, in matters regarding the status of natural persons, the Public Prosecutor's Office) can therefore request the judicial (non-)recognition, in whole or in part, of the foreign judgment through a principal claim (Article 22 §2 CPIL). The required interest is the one laid down in Articles 17 and 18 of the Belgian Code of Civil Procedure. The claimant must demonstrate a legitimate, personal and immediate interest in bringing the case before the court. He must show that the action may grant him a certain (material or moral) advantage.[3] In recognition procedures the most important consideration is whether the claimant has a personal interest in obtaining recognition, but it is not necessary that the foreign judgment concerned contains a conviction in

[3] P Taelman and C Van Severen, *Civil Procedure in Belgium* (Kluwer Law International, 2008) 77.

favour of the party requesting recognition. The procedure to follow is the one described in Article 23 CPIL for obtaining the declaration of enforceability (see Question 2b) below). The requested court's decision has *res iudicata* effect and ensures that the recognition (or non-recognition) is settled and can no longer be called into question.[4]

The incidental judicial recognition is in essence of form of recognition *de plano*. Article 22 §1, third paragraph CPIL provides that, if the recognition issue is brought incidentally before a Belgian court, the latter has jurisdiction to hear it. The interested party does not have to file a separate principal claim before the court competent for the procedure under Article 23 CPIL, but the court dealing with the pending matter may rule on the request for recognition or non-recognition of the foreign judgment. The court's decision can obtain *res iudicata* effect.[5]

b) Procedural Steps

For enforcement, a declaration of enforceability needs to be obtained (Article 22 §1, paragraph 1 CPIL). This *exequatur* procedure is described in Article 23 CPIL. An interested party (and also, in matters regarding the status of natural persons, the Public Prosecutor's Office) can therefore request that the judgment be declared enforceable or not enforceable, in whole or in part (Article 22 §2 CPIL). The notion of interest is to be interpreted in the same way as in the case of a procedure for recognition (see Question 2 a) above). This allows creditors of the victorious party to obtain the *exequatur* of the judgment. The requested court examines *ex officio* whether the foreign judgment does not violate the conditions of Article 25 (Article 22 §1, paragraph 4 CPIL). In any case, under no circumstances will the foreign judgment be reviewed on the merits (Article 25 §2 CPIL).

The declaration of enforceability results in the foreign judgment being able to be enforced in the same manner as a Belgian judgment. When granting a partial *exequatur*, the judge must ensure that the partially granted enforceability is practically achievable in light of the partial refusal. The court may not amend or add to the foreign judgment.[6] The enforcement itself is governed by Belgian procedural law.[7]

The action is introduced and treated in accordance with the procedure referred to in Articles 1025–1034 Code of Civil Procedure (Article 23 §3 CPIL). The *exequatur* procedure commences through the introduction of a unilateral petition, accompanied by the documents listed in Article 24 CPIL, which must in principle be filed with the court's registry by an attorney. The procedure is conducted as a written ex parte proceeding, whereby the opposite party remains virtual and is not involved in the proceedings, and not even informed thereof. The court may summon the petitioner in order to hear his arguments or ask for additional information, but this does not happen often in practice.[8] The claimant has to elect domicile within the district of the court and the court decides within a short delay (Article 23 §3 CPIL).

[4] Storme (n 1) 655.
[5] ibid.
[6] A change of the currency would be allowed: Court of appeal Brussels, 29 November 1994, *Pas* 1994, II, 5.
[7] Storme (n 1) 656.
[8] Taelman and Van Severen (n 3) 106.

Article 23 §2 CPIL describes the subject matter and territorial (venue) jurisdiction. The procedure takes place before the court of first instance.[9] The court with territorial jurisdiction is the court of the domicile or habitual residence of the defendant. As the procedure is unilateral and does not feature a defendant, the term 'phantom defendant' has been used.[10] In the absence of such domicile or habitual residence, jurisdiction lies with the court of the place of enforcement. In case of a request for (non-)recognition aimed at a defendant outside Belgium or not aimed at any defendant, the claimant may seize the judge of its own domicile or residence in Belgium. In the absence of such domicile or residence in Belgium, the claimant can seize the court of the district of Brussels.

In Belgium the 'winning' party may recover (part of) his attorney's fees from the 'losing' party. The compensation for attorney's fees and expenses is limited to a fixed lump sum indemnification, awarded by the court to the prevailing party.[11] There are tables which contain the basic figures (depending on the amount of the claim), but also minimum and maximum amounts which allow the court to modulate the award according to inter alia the complexity of the case and the losing party's financial capacity. The CPIL is silent regarding the costs of a recognition or *exequatur* procedure. The prevailing opinion seems to accept that the fixed indemnification as recovery of lawyer's fees and expenses can be granted if an opponent can be identified. The minimum amount of the lump sum is usually awarded.[12]

Against the judgment of the court granting recognition or *exequatur*, third-party opposition can be lodged by the person who was not a party to the proceedings and whose rights are adversely affected by the judgment rendered (Article 1033 Code of Civil Procedure). The third-party opposition is brought before the judge who rendered the contested judgment, ie the territorially competent court of first instance. The third-party opposition has to be brought within one month from the date of service of the judgment on the third party (Article 1034 Code of Civil Procedure). Against the 'second' judgment of the court instance, rendered after adversarial proceedings, all ordinary remedies are available (Article 1131 Code of Civil Procedure).

The judgment of the court refusing recognition or *exequatur* is open to appeal by the petitioner. The appeal is conducted in adversarial proceedings and the court of appeal has to review whether the request complies with the necessary formalities, the required documents pursuant to Article 24 CPIL have been submitted and the refusal grounds of Article 25 CPIL are respected. The decision of the court of appeal is only open to a petition for cassation, which is to be filed before the Court of Cassation.[13]

[9] Except for the recognition and declaration of enforceability of: 1) judgments concerning insolvency matters, for which the commercial court has jurisdiction (Art 121 §4 CPIL); 2) judgments in family matters in the sense of Art 572*bis* Code of Civil Procedure, for which the family court has jurisdiction (Art 23 §1, paragraph 2 CPIL); and 3) measures of protection of adults in the sense of Art 594, 23° Code of Civil Procedure, for which the justice of the peace has jurisdiction (Art 23 §1, paragraph 3 CPIL).

[10] H Boularbah, *Requête unilatérale et inversion du contentieux* (Larcier, 2010) 22.

[11] Taelman and Van Severen (n 3) 57.

[12] I Couwenberg, 'Artikel 24 WIPR' in I Couwenberg, A Hansebout and L Vanfraechem (eds), *Duiding Internationaal Privaatrecht* (Larcier, 2014) 659.

[13] ibid.

Question 3. Requirements

As mentioned, in order to be eligible for enforcement, the foreign judgment needs to be enforceable in the state of origin (Article 22 §1, paragraph 1 CPIL). Next to that, Article 25 CPIL lists in an exhaustive manner the circumstances in which a foreign judgment may not be recognised or declared enforceable (Article 22 §1, paragraph 4 CPIL).[14]

a) Jurisdiction of the Court of Origin

The CPIL provides for a limited review of the jurisdiction of the rendering court. The refusal grounds in Article 25 §1, 7° and 8° CPIL impose a check of the jurisdiction of the court of origin, but the scope of this verification is restricted. Only when the foreign court has ruled in a dispute over which the Belgian courts have exclusive jurisdiction (Article 25 §1, 7° CPIL) or when the jurisdiction was exclusively founded on the presence of the defendant or assets located in the state of the court, but without any direct relation with the dispute (Article 25 §1, 8° CPIL), recognition and enforcement of the third state judgment will be refused.

Under Article 25 §1, 7° CPIL a foreign judgment shall not be recognised or declared enforceable if the Belgian courts had exclusive jurisdiction to hear the claim. This refusal ground is assessed on the basis of the jurisdiction rules of the requested court. Article 24.1 of the Brussels I*bis* Regulation grants exclusive jurisdiction to the Belgian courts for adjudicating matters concerning rights *in rem* in immovable property or tenancies of immovable property situated within Belgium. Consequently, judgments from third countries that pertain to these specific matters will not be recognised or enforced in the Belgian legal order. Likewise, Article 25 of the Brussels I*bis* Regulation confers jurisdiction on the Belgian courts (or a specific Belgian court) when the parties, regardless of their domicile, have validly agreed that the Belgian courts (or a specific Belgian court) are to have jurisdiction to settle any disputes which have arisen or which may arise in connection with a particular legal relationship. Such jurisdiction shall be exclusive, unless the parties have agreed otherwise.[15] Under Article 25 §1, 7° CPIL a foreign judgment rendered in violation of such an exclusive jurisdiction agreement will be declined recognition and enforcement in the territory of Belgium.

Pursuant to Article 25 §1, 8° CPIL recognition and enforcement are refused if the jurisdiction of the foreign court was based exclusively on the presence of the defendant or assets located in the state of the court, but without any direct relation with the dispute. A direct relation of the goods with the dispute exists, for example, when the claim seeks the revindication of the goods.[16] This refusal ground approaches the examination of the jurisdiction of the rendering court from the perspective of the jurisdictional rules of the country of origin. The provision blocks judgments rendered on exorbitant grounds of

[14] Storme (n 1) 661.

[15] Art 6 CPIL also grants exclusive jurisdiction to (a) Belgian court(s) designated in a jurisdiction agreement. The relevance of the provision is limited due to the precedence of Art 25 Brussel I*bis* Regulation.

[16] J Erauw et al, *Internationaal Privaatrecht* (Kluwer, 2009) 284, para 209.

jurisdiction, but limited to the two mentioned: presence of the defendant or assets in the state of origin without a direct link to the dispute.[17] If the jurisdiction of the court of origin was founded on another excessive basis, such as the mere nationality of the claimant, recognition and enforcement will not be denied (unless other refusal grounds are triggered).

b) Finality/Enforceability in the Country of Origin

In order to be eligible for enforcement, the foreign judgment needs to be enforceable in the state of origin (Article 22 §1, paragraph 1 CPIL). According to Article 25 §1, 4° CPIL a foreign judgment shall not be recognised or declared enforceable if, according to the law of the state where the judgment was rendered and without prejudice to Article 23 §4 CPIL, the judgment would still be subject to an ordinary recourse in the state of origin. It is the law of the rendering court that determines whether a remedy has an 'ordinary' character.

The reference to Article 23 §4 CPIL intends to take the provisional enforceability of a foreign judgment into account. This provision states that the foreign judgment subject or open to an ordinary recourse can be enforced provisionally and that the judge may make the enforcement subject to the provision of a guarantee. It is contradictory to refuse the grant of enforceability to a foreign judgment that can still be overturned in the rendering state on the one hand, and allow (provisional) enforcement measures on the basis of that judgment on the other hand. Article 23 §4 CPIL could be interpreted as allowing conservatory measures and not enforcement measures.[18] Alternatively, Article 25 §1, 4° CPIL can be disregarded in favour of Article 23 §4 CPIL, thereby permitting the granting of enforceability and consequently enforcement to judgments open to an ordinary recourse and provisionally enforceable in the state of origin.[19]

c) *Res Iudicata*

Under Article 25 §1, 5° CPIL a foreign judgment shall not be recognised or declared enforceable if the judgment is irreconcilable with a Belgian decision or an earlier foreign decision that is amenable to recognition in Belgium. The provision uses the term 'decision' (*beslissing*) instead of 'judgment' (*rechterlijke beslissing*). The notion 'decision' is broader than 'judgment' (which is defined in Article 22 §3, 1° CPIL) and encompasses arbitral awards.[20]

In order to block the recognition and enforcement of a foreign judgment the Belgian decision must no longer be appealable. The date on which the Belgian decision was rendered is irrelevant: the decision may be younger than the foreign requested judgment. The recognition and enforcement of a foreign judgment can also be refused on

[17] Storme (n 1) 669–70.
[18] Wautelet (n 2) 222–23.
[19] Storme (n 1) 667–68. Erauw, who does not engage with any possible interpretation problems, reaches the same conclusion: Erauw (n 16) 285, para 210.
[20] Storme (n 1) 669.

the basis of another foreign decision, but only if the latter is older and amenable to recognition in Belgium.[21]

d) *Lis Pendens*

Article 25 §1, 6° CPIL requires that recognition and enforcement be refused if the foreign claim was brought after a claim, which is still pending between the same parties and with the same subject matter, was brought in Belgium. The foreign judgment that arises from proceedings initiated after the commencement of pending Belgian proceedings between the same parties and with the same cause of action will not be recognised and enforced in Belgium. Upon the completion of the Belgian proceedings, recognition and enforcement of the requested judgment will be precluded on the basis of Article 25 §1, 5° CPIL.[22]

e) Specific Requirements of Due Process

Article 25 §1, 2° CPIL provides that a foreign judgment shall not be recognised or declared enforceable if the rights of the defence were violated. The assessment is carried out *in concreto*: the court cannot resort to an assessment of abstract rules or of the foreign legal order, but must verify whether the fundamental rights of defence have been respected. The refusal of recognition and enforcement can only be justified if there was a breach of fundamental principles of Belgian law.[23] The rights of the defence are determined according to Belgian procedural law.[24] Belgian judges will be bound by the standards of Article 6, paragraph 1 ECHR when applying this provision.[25]

The impartiality of the court belongs to the category of fundamental principles.[26] Another of the fundamental principles of Belgian law requires that the defendant is able to organise his defence in a timely and effective manner. The defendant has to be summoned in such a way that gives him the opportunity to prepare his defence.[27]

The existence of a separate refusal ground dedicated to the rights of the defence underlines the importance the Belgian legislator attaches to the procedural quality of the foreign judgment. Furthermore, the requested court always needs to review the due process integrity of the incoming judgment, irrespective of the degree of connection to the Belgian forum. In that sense Article 25 §1, 2° CPIL differs from the public policy exception in Article 25 §1, 1° CPIL (see Question 3 f) below) as the latter's operation depends on the extent in which the situation is connected to the Belgian legal order and the seriousness of the consequences of recognition and enforcement.[28]

[21] Storme (n 1) 668–69.
[22] ibid 669.
[23] ibid 664.
[24] Court of Cassation, 5 January 1995, *Arr Cass* 1995, 15, *Pas* 1995, I, 15.
[25] Erauw (n 16) 282, para 208.
[26] Court of Cassation, 5 January 1995, *Arr Cass* 1995, 15, *Pas* 1995, I, 15.
[27] Court of Cassation, 11 December 1995, *Rev dr étr* 1996, 185, note M-C Foblets, *RW* 1995–96.
[28] Storme (n 1) 664.

f) Public Policy

Pursuant to Article 25 §1, 1° CPIL a foreign judgment shall not be recognised or declared enforceable if the result of the recognition or enforceability would be manifestly incompatible with public policy. The provision further lays down that upon determining the incompatibility with public policy special consideration is given to the extent to which the situation is connected to the Belgian legal order and the seriousness of the consequences which will be caused thereby. The mention of these two assessment criteria emphasises that the test of the acceptability of the incoming judgments needs to be performed *in concreto*. It further leaves room for the application of the '*effet attenué*' of the international public policy in enforcement cases.[29]

In cross-border matters public policy is to be understood as international public policy.[30] International public policy is a national concept and a subset of the domestic public policy. It refers to those fundamental rules of domestic or internal public policy which a legal system also wants respected in international cases. In enforcement cases a legal system is required to be more tolerant than it would be in purely domestic affairs.

In Belgium, a law is only part of international public policy if, by the provisions of that law, the legislator intended to enshrine a principle that it considers essential to Belgium's moral, political or economic order.[31] The CPIL allows the requested court to verify whether the effects of granting recognition and enforcement would infringe the essential values of its domestic law. However, the use of the word 'manifestly' sets a high bar and indicates that the use of the public policy exception is constrained to situations in which recognition and enforcement of the foreign judgment would be flagrantly infringing upon the fundamental values of the Belgian legal order contained in its international public policy. The distinction between procedural and substantive public policy is known in Belgium. It could be said that Article 25 §1, 2° CPIL, which protects the rights of the defence, acts as the procedural counterpart for the public policy exception of Article 25 §1, 1° CPIL.[32]

Most of the examples in which the Belgian international public policy is triggered are outside the scope of this report (eg polygamy, child marriage, sham marriage, surrogacy and other family matters). The Belgian position regarding the enforcement of foreign punitive damages is unknown. We were unable to find any case law on the matter. The assessment of this legal institution's compatibility with Belgian international public policy will be subject to the discretion of the Belgian courts, and their determination remains to be observed.[33]

[29] H Boularbah, 'Le nouveau droit international prive belge' (2005) 11 *Journal des tribunaux* 173, 185.

[30] H Van Houtte, 'De openbare orde als beletsel voor de erkenning of tenuitvoerlegging van buitenlandse vonnissen' (1973–74) 14 *Rechtskundig Weekblad* 737, 741.

[31] Court of Cassation, 18 June 2007, *Arr Cass* 2007, 1359, *Pas* 2007, 1237.

[32] Erauw (n 16) 281, para 208.

[33] See for suggested guidelines for European judges on how to deal with incoming judgments awarding punitive damages: C Vanleenhove, *Punitive Damages in Private International Law* (Intersentia, 2016) 210–36 and C Vanleenhove, 'A normative framework for the enforcement of U.S. punitive damages in the European Union: transforming the traditional "¡No Pasarán!"' (2016) 41 *Vermont Law Review* 377–401.

g) Reciprocity

The CPIL does not require any form of reciprocity, whether it be de facto or *de iure*. The recognition and enforcement of a foreign judgment is not dependent on whether Belgian judgments have been or will be enforced in the jurisdiction in which the foreign judgment was rendered.

h) Other Requirements

Under Article 25 §1, 3° CPIL a foreign judgment shall not be recognised or declared enforceable if, in a matter in which parties cannot freely dispose of their rights, the judgment is only obtained to evade the application of the law designated by the CPIL. In the section on the applicable law, the CPIL also addresses evasion of the law. Article 18 CPIL provides that, for the determination of the applicable law in a matter where parties may not freely dispose of their rights, facts and acts committed with the sole purpose to evade the application of the law designated by the CPIL are not taken into account. The court has the possibility to ignore connecting factors that the parties have artificially created with the sole purpose to escape from the applicable law that would normally apply.[34] The connecting factor can be wholly fictitious or can correspond to reality, but solely be created to evade the law designated by the CPIL. When the change of the connecting factor also pursues other objectives or when the party accepts all consequences of the change, Article 18 cannot be applied. The intention of the parties therefore plays a crucial role.[35]

When handling requests for recognition and enforcement, the examination of law evasion does not entail an investigation of the law applied by the foreign court. Therein lies the difference with the recognition and enforcement of foreign authentic instruments: in order to obtain legal effect in Belgium the validity of such instruments needs to be established in accordance with the law applicable by virtue of the CPIL (Article 27 §1, paragraph 1). Article 25 §1, 3° CPIL applies to recognition and enforcement of foreign judgments and disapproves of illicit forum shopping.[36] The refusal ground is only applicable when it can be demonstrated that the parties intended to evade the law designated by the conflict of laws rules of the CPIL and the sole purpose of initiating the case in the foreign court was to circumvent those laws. These subjective criteria reduce the refusal ground's pertinence and consequently will only affect a small number of requested judgments.[37]

The CPIL imposes specific regimes for recognition and enforcement, which are to be applied instead of or in addition to the refusal grounds of Article 25. These are the following (not all are relevant in light of the scope of this report): determination

[34] M Traest, 'Artikel 18 WIPR' in J Erauw et al (eds), *Het Wetboek Internationaal Privaatrecht becommentarieerd – Le Code de Droit International Privé commenté* (Intersentia/Bruylant, 2006) 97.

[35] ibid 99.

[36] Erauw (n 16) 283, para 209.

[37] Storme (n 1) 665–66.

or change of name or surnames (Article 39); foreign divorce based on the will of the husband (Article 57); adoptions established abroad (Article 72); intellectual property rights (Article 95); the validity, the functioning, the dissolution or liquidation of a body with separate legal personality (Article 115); and the opening, the conduct or the closure of insolvency proceedings (Article 121).

Question 4. Documents to be Produced

Article 24 §1 CPIL lists the documents that the party that invokes the recognition of or seeks to declare a foreign judgment enforceable needs to submit.

The following documents are required:

(1) a certified copy of the decision, which according to the law of the country where it was rendered meets the conditions required for the authenticity thereof;
(2) if it concerns a decision by default, the original or a certified copy of the document establishing that the act that introduced the proceeding or the equivalent document was served or brought to the notice of the defaulting party in accordance with the law of the country where the decision was rendered; and
(3) any document on the basis of which it can be established that, according to the law of the country where the decision was rendered, the decision is enforceable and has been served or brought to notice.

In order to be produced in Belgium a foreign judgment has to be legalised in its entirety or as an excerpt, in original or copy. The legalisation confirms only the authenticity of the signature, the capacity in which the signatory acted and, as the case may be, the identity of the seal or stamp on the document (Article 30 §1 CPIL). As Belgium is bound by the 1961 Apostille Convention, the apostille (a simplified form of legalisation) will suffice if the judgment originates from another contracting state of the Convention.

The submission of the original or a certified copy of the document establishing that the act that introduced the proceeding or the equivalent document was served or brought to the notice of the defaulting party required by Article 24, 2° CPIL ensures that the Belgian court can verify whether the defaulting party had to opportunity to defend itself in the foreign proceedings.[38]

The document mentioned in Article 24, 3° CPIL proves that the period for filing an ordinary remedy has lapsed or that the available ordinary remedies have been exhausted. The certificate can also show that the judgment is provisionally enforceable. This can also be evident from the judgment itself. If it is impossible to obtain this document, it can also be proven through the relevant foreign legislation that the decision is indeed enforceable. In addition, the requesting party must also demonstrate that this enforceable judgment has been served or notified to the opposing party. The Belgian legislator considered that the opposing party should be made aware of the contents of the judgment and should at least have had the opportunity to either voluntarily perform

[38] Couwenberg (n 12) 660.

or to appeal. This notification must be carried out in accordance with the legislation of the state where the decision was rendered.[39]

The CPIL does not require a translation of the foreign judgment or the other documents. The requested court nevertheless has the power to demand the translation (by a sworn translator) of the documents submitted by the party seeking recognition and/or enforcement.[40] It is therefore advisable to inquire in advance with the court registry whether a translation will be required. It often happens that the court grants the requesting party an additional period for filing this translation.[41]

In the absence of the production of the documents mentioned, the judge may impose a delay in which they are to be produced or may accept equivalent documents or, if he believes himself to be sufficiently informed, grant an exemption (Article 24 §2 CPIL). Whether a document will be considered to be 'equivalent', or in which circumstances the court will considered itself sufficiently informed without additional documents, cannot be laid down in general rules but depends on a factual and case-by-case assessment.[42]

Question 5. Securities, Bonds and Deposits

In Belgium, Article 851 of the Code of Civil Procedure allows the defendant to force the foreign claimant to provide security for the payment of costs and damages that may be awarded against them (*cautio iudicatum solvi*), except in the case of conventions by which states have stipulated that their nationals are to be exempt from the obligation. The Belgian Constitutional Court has ruled that this provision violates the principle of equality and non-discrimination.[43] It must now be interpreted as meaning that it applies to any claimant, irrespective of nationality, who is domiciled or lives abroad and does not have sufficient assets in Belgium to cover the financial consequences of an unfavourable judgment.[44]

[39] Couwenberg (n 12) 660.

[40] Wautelet (n 2) 219. In our opinion, a translation of a foreign judgment in French and English will usually not be demanded: see Couwenberg (n 12) 660; I Couwenberg, 'Stukken over te leggen met het oog op de erkenning of de uitvoerbaarverklaring' in J Erauw et al (eds), *Het Wetboek Internationaal Privaatrecht becommentarieerd – Le Code de Droit International Privé commenté* (Intersentia/Bruylant, 2006) 132.

[41] Couwenberg (n 12) 660.

[42] ibid.

[43] Constitutional Court, 11 October 2018, n 135/2018.

[44] Court of Cassation, 10 March 2023, n C.22.0126.N.

Bulgaria

ILIA LASSIN AND DAFINA SARBINOVA

Question 1. General Overview

In Bulgaria, the general rules for recognition and enforcement of foreign judgments originating from third countries are provided for in the Private International Law Code of 2005 (*Кодекс на международното частно право*; PILC).[1] They fall under the scope of Article 1(1) PILC which encompasses: 1. the international jurisdiction of the Bulgarian courts and authorities and the general rules for international civil procedures; 2. the law applicable to private law relationships with an international element; and 3. the recognition and enforcement of foreign judgments and authentic instruments in the Republic of Bulgaria. The national-autonomous rules concerning the recognition and enforcement of non-EU judgments in civil and commercial matters are stipulated in Part 4, Chapter 12, Articles 117–124 (inclusive) PILC. For issues, not covered by the provisions of PILC and the international treaties or conventions, the general Bulgarian civil procedural legislation remains applicable, and more specifically the Civil Procedure Code (*Граждански процесуален кодекс*; CPC).[2]

This domestic codification of conflict-of-laws provisions serves as one of the three separate systems for recognition and enforcement of judgments acting in parallel to respectively: (i) the system stipulated in the EU legal instruments; and (ii) the system comprised of international treaties and conventions to which Bulgaria is a signatory.[3] These systems use a hierarchical approach to organise the rules for recognising and enforcing foreign judgments and acts into four main categories: (i) EU legislative acts, which take precedence over Bulgarian laws within their scope; (ii) international treaties, which also have priority over Bulgarian laws if they meet constitutional requirements; (iii) specific acts that deal with the recognition and enforcement of foreign judgments; and (iv) general provisions in the PILC. As a result, the recognition and enforcement of foreign judgments under PILC is carried out in cases where there is no regulation of the recognition and enforcement provided in the EU law, an international treaty, another international instrument, or another law.[4]

[1] Promulgated in State Gazette No 42 of 17 May 2005, last amended in State Gazette No 100 of 21 December 2010.

[2] Promulgated in State Gazette No 59 of July 20 2007, last amended in State Gazette No 66 of 1 August 2023.

[3] B Musseva, 'The interested party during recognition and enforcement of a foreign court judgment' (2011) 5 *Contemporary Law* 58.

[4] Pursuant to Supreme Court of Cassation, 26 October 2012, Judgment No. 248 under civil case No 241/2012, PILC rules for recognition and enforcement are relevant only for these foreign judgments for which no regulation exists in EU law instrument, international treaty, or other domestic law (*lex specialis*).

This understanding for the hierarchical coordination of the different sources of law which contain rules for the recognition and enforcement of judgments is also reflected in court practice (eg Court Statement No 411 of 8.06.2015 under commercial case No 1349/2014 of the Supreme Court of Cassation). Furthermore, Judgment No 101 of 9.02.2010 under civil case No 919/2009 of the Supreme Court of Cassation specifies that the rules of PILC do not affect the regulation of private and procedural law relations with international element established in international treaty in force for Bulgaria and because of this PILC is only subsidiary applied to the issues outside of the scope of the treaty.

The review of the court practice on the recognition and enforcement of non-EU judgments reveals the existence of several bilateral treaties for legal assistance which find frequent application before Bulgarian court. In particular: the Bilateral Treaty for Legal Assistance with the Union of Soviet Socialist Republics (now applicable for judgments issued by the Russian courts)[5] and the Bilateral Treaty for Legal Assistance with the Republic of Yugoslavia (now applicable for judgments issued by the Serbian courts).[6]

Article 117 PILC stipulates that the only two types of foreign acts entitled to recognition and enforcement are respectively foreign 'judicial acts' and 'authentic instruments'. Judicial acts are acts that are issued by a court that is independent and on the basis of impartiality and equality within the framework of competitive dispute proceedings resolves a dispute with the effect of a *res judicata*. Authentic instruments are official acts, issued and certified by an authority that are enforceable in the country in which they are issued. According to Article 123 PILC such authentic instruments can be recognised and enforced under the same conditions as judicial acts if they certify an enforceable claim. For recognition and enforcement to occur on the territory of Bulgaria under PILC, the foreign act, of which the recognition and enforcement is sought, must meet certain criteria.

First of all, in order for a foreign judicial act or authentic instrument to be recognisable and enforceable, it must resemble and fall under the notion of a 'judgment'.[7] Insofar as the assessment carried out by the Bulgarian court analyses the effect of the respective act for which recognition and enforcement is sought, the title of the act granted by the authorities of origin is irrelevant. Instead, what is important is to make sure that such an act constitutes a declaration of will over a dispute in adversarial proceedings that is freely executed by a foreign authority with granted jurisdiction. Such a judgment must be able to produce legal consequences in relation to persons, their property, rights and obligations.[8] PILC equates to judgments also the court settlements, provided that they are considered equivalent to court judgments in the country where they were concluded (Article 122 PILC), as well as foreign official documents that certify a claim as enforceable in the country where the document was issued. Due to this, foreign official documents that do not certify specific claims, similar to the writ of enforcement, cannot

[5] In force as of 18 January 1976.
[6] In force as of 26 January 1957.
[7] Supreme Court of Cassation, Commerce Chamber, 17 March 2008, Judgment No 27, commercial case No 510/2007.
[8] ibid.

be subject to recognition and enforcement in the Republic of Bulgaria.[9] According to Article 124 PILC, foreign writs of enforcement and protection are also excluded from the notion of judgment and therefore cannot be recognised and enforced due to them lacking a *res judicata* effect. Instead, such foreign acts only maintain their evidentiary effect and civil consequences upon their presenting. As such, their consequences may become the subject of judicial review and can be ruled upon, but only in the event of a substantive legal dispute regarding other legal relationships and not in an independent proceeding for the recognition of the writ of enforcement and protection itself.[10]

Second, judgments under the meaning of Article 117 PILC must be recognised as 'foreign'. A 'foreign' judgment would refer to any final act and/or instrument issued by a competent authority of a foreign country that concerns the private relationships of the parties under a procedural due process, in spite of the name, format or procedure adopted by the respective foreign court. It should be specified that while judgments and authentic instruments issued by authorities established by international treaties such as the ECJ or the ECHR would technically fall within the same notion, they are excluded from the scope of the PILC due to the applicability of their own specific regimes of regulation under the respective international treaties.

The final prerequisite is for the judgment to have been issued on matters of private law, and more specifically civil and commercial matters. The notion of civil and commercial is not explicitly defined in the PILC and is interpreted under the approach of the Bulgarian legal doctrine which establishes a clear distinction between public and private. Naturally, in Bulgaria the notion of 'civil and commercial matters' is interpreted to fall within the scope of the 'private law relations' and exists as broader category encompassing various legal relationships regulated by PILC. By systematically analysing the chapters provided for in PILC, it can be reasonably concluded that within the notion of 'civil and commercial matters' fall also the private law relations related to: (i) the legal status of subjects; (ii) legal transactions, agency and extinctive prescription; (iii) rights *in rem*; (iv) intellectual property rights; (v) family and succession relationships; (vii) contractual relationships; and (viii) non-contractual relationships. Judgments relating to administrative, criminal or tax matters do not fall within the notion of 'civil and commercial matters' and therefore are not recognisable and enforceable under PILC.

Question 2. Procedure

a) Circumstances of Recognition and Enforcement

PILC does not provide a legal definition of what is meant by the terms 'recognition' and 'enforcement' of foreign judgments. Nevertheless, the Bulgarian legislation conceptually distinguishes recognition from enforcement due to use of separate terms in the provision of Article 117 PILC.

[9] ibid.

[10] Supreme Court of Cassation, III Civil Chamber, 1 December 2020, Court Statement No 461, private civil case No 2073/2020.

By its legal essence, the recognition of a judgment of a foreign authority represents a declarative statement of the respective national authority to respect the legal consequences of the foreign act.[11] The purpose and meaning of the proceedings for the recognition of a foreign judgment in court proceedings is to grant effect of the decreed recognition against all third parties.[12] According to Bulgarian case law and legal theory, the notion of 'recognition' consists of two defining characteristics, as follows: (i) recognition of the *res judicata* effect; and (ii) recognition of the constitutive effect of the foreign judgment (if any).

By virtue of the constitutive effect of a judgment, a right or a legal relationship is created, terminated or modified. Such constitutive effect occurs in the events where a judgment would respect a so-called constitutive claim that aims to unilaterally cause a desired legal amendment in the legal sphere of another party.[13] Through recognition, the legal consequences following from the constitutive effect can be transferred with the same content and volume it originally has in the state of origin, allowing for the respective legal changes to occur also on the territory of Bulgaria.

The institute of enforcement represents an exercise of sovereign judicial power through which the enforceability of a foreign judgment extends to the territory of another country. In its essence it resembles a procedure of recognition of a foreign judgment with the purpose of creation of an enforcement title for the purposes of substantive enforcement in the country of *exequatur*. Due to this, an enforceable judgment must also inevitably undergo a process of recognition. Subject to enforcement however are only judgments ordering the defendant to perform or refrain from a specific action. Such judgments are distinguished by the presence of a so-called enforceability effect which inevitably results to the extension of the legal consequences of the judgment, and respectively the *res judicata* effect.

In summary, the purpose of the recognition and enforcement of foreign court judgments is to consider the force of a *res judicata* and their constitutive effect in the Republic of Bulgaria for the substantive right recognised by them. Through the recognition and enforcement, the enforceability of the foreign judgment is manifested, and it can serve as an enforcement title. In such events creditors are entitled to a right of request for the issuance of a writ of execution.[14]

b) Procedural Steps

The Bulgarian legal doctrine recognises three parallel systems for recognition of foreign judgments: (i) automatic ('*ipso iure*') recognition; (ii) recognition by declaratory proceedings; and (iii) incidental recognition.

Pursuant to the provisions of Article 118(1) PILC, the recognition of the foreign judgment is carried out by the authority before which it is presented, and which is competent

[11] Supreme Administrative Court, 14 May 2014, Court Statement No 6415, administrative case No 6055/2014.

[12] Supreme Court of Cassation, I Commerce Chamber, 16 September 2021, Judgment No 60044, commercial case No 2775/2019.

[13] T Todorov, *Private International Law. EU and the Republic of Bulgaria*, 3rd edn (Sibi, 2010) 388–421.

[14] Supreme Court of Cassation, Commerce Chamber, 17 March 2008, Judgment No 27, commercial case No 510/2007.

to carry out the verification of the foreign judgment. Foreign judgments are automatically recognised by the authority whereto the said judgment is presented as long as the requirements for recognition and enforcement are satisfied. While the automatic character of the recognition allows the party relying on a foreign judgment to evade undergoing a formal procedure in Bulgaria prior to relying on the foreign judgment, it does not mean, however, that the judgment is awarded an effect towards all third parties. Instead, the effect takes place only between the recognising authority and the person requesting the recognition. Judgments are subjected to examination by the respective authority that assesses the conditions for recognition and enforcement set out in Article 117 PILC (see Question 3). When this authority considers that the conditions of the said provision have been met, it issues an express internal act. If one or more of the grounds of refusal are present, foreign judgments are refused recognition. Even though such acts of refusal may resemble administrative acts under the acting Bulgarian legislation, they are not subject to judicial appeal before administrative courts. Instead, such disputes should be resolved according to the general claim procedure by filing a declaratory action.

According to Article 118(2) PILC an interested party may request recognition of the foreign judgment by submitting a declaratory action before Sofia City Court only if the relevant Bulgarian authority has already assumed that the conditions of recognition and enforcement under Article 117 PILC were not met and therefore refuses the recognition. Since the subject of the claim itself is the recognition of the judgment, the only parties that are considered legitimate to request such recognition are the person whose application for automatic recognition was denied by the national authority and the original persons who participated in the proceedings before the court of origin.[15] Therefore, an interested party would be considered to be lacking legal interest in the filing of a claim for judicial recognition of a foreign judgment once the said party has exercised their subjective right to request automatic ('*ipso iure*') recognition by claiming that all requirements for the said recognition are present and the respective competent authority has ruled positively on their request.[16]

The authority's refusal to recognise the foreign judgment represents a procedural prerequisite for the submission and admissibility of the claim. Its admissibility is conditioned by the existence of a legal interest in its submission, which requires the presence of a *dispute concerning the conditions for recognition of the foreign judgment*. If the interested party has not exercised their potestative right before the competent authority, the proceedings for declaratory recognition will be effectively inadmissible.[17] Therefore, the authority's refusal to recognise the foreign judgment is linked to the legal interest as a prerequisite for the submission of the declaratory action before the Sofia City Court.[18]

[15] Supreme Court of Cassation, III Civil Chamber, 1 December 2020, Court Statement No 461, private civil case No 2073/2020.

[16] Supreme Court of Cassation, IV Civil Chamber, 21 December 2015, Court Statement No 808, private civil case No 5686/2015.

[17] Supreme Court of Cassation, IV Civil Chamber, 20 April 2017, Court Statement No 200, private civil case No 1173/2017.

[18] Supreme Court of Cassation, III Civil Chamber, 23 July 2009, Court Statement No 416, civil case No 149/2009; Supreme Court of Cassation, II Civil Chamber, 13 February 2006, Judgment No 23, civil case No 638/2005.

The proceedings before the Sofia City Court are adversarial and are subject to appeal in three-instance process, respectively before the Sofia Appellate Court and then the Supreme Court of Cassation. As a result, a direct consequence of the recognition by declaratory proceedings is that the foreign judgment is deemed to be effective against all third parties, contrary to the effect of the automatic recognition.

In the vast majority of cases, a foreign judgment will be recognised incidentally in the framework of other proceedings since parties can also invoke the effects of such judgment when it is of relevance to the outcome of the dispute with which the court is originally concerned. In pending proceedings courts are required to take into account the consequences of an entered into force judgment of a foreign court, which is presented by a party to the case, only if the conditions under Article 117 PILC are met and there is no dispute between the parties regarding these prerequisites.[19] In such cases the incidental recognition gives effect to the judgment only between the parties to the respective case.[20]

In order to enforce a foreign judgment a deliberate adversarial proceeding must always be initiated before the Sofia City Court pursuant to Article 119(1) PILC. The proceedings are held in accordance with the general rules under the Civil Procedure Code, thereby summoning the defendant and granting them the opportunity at this stage of the court proceedings to defend themselves against the enforcement of the judgment. During the course of the proceedings the court makes an assessment on the requirements for recognition and enforcement in the same way as when a judgment is being recognised. The admissibility assessment is carried out by taking into consideration the content of the foreign judgment, as well as any evidence presented by the parties regarding the presence or absence of the requirements for recognition and enforcement. The ruling of the Sofia City Court is subject to appeal in three-instance process, respectively before the Sofia Appellate Court and the Supreme Court of Cassation (the latter is subject to procedure for admission to cassation). In both cases, the acts of the first-instance Bulgarian court are subject to preliminary enforcement and the appeal proceedings remain adversarial. In such scenarios the court may also rule on the requested provisional and protective measures when ruling on the enforcement of a foreign judgment.[21]

According to Article 120(1) PILC, when presented with a foreign judgment for the purpose of its recognition and/or enforcement, the addressed court must review and verify the conditions covered under Article 117 of its own motion, *ex officio*. The assessment covers all conditions and is not limited solely to the ones raised by the person requesting the recognition and/or enforcement, nor to the grounds for refusal that a previous authority may have based their refusal for *exequatur*. Nevertheless, the assessment does not cover the procedural prerequisites for the initiation of such proceedings outside of the formal ones under Article 119(2) PILC. The court may be assisted, however, by the parties respectively by collecting evidence from them regarding the presence or absence of the conditions for recognition and enforcement, or by verifying and comparing data and findings with sources that they have provided to the court.[22]

[19] Supreme Court of Cassation, 26 October 2012, Judgment No 248, civil case No 241/2012.

[20] Supreme Court of Cassation, 26 July 2013, Court Statement No 485, private civil case No 3074/2013.

[21] Sofia Appellate Court, 14 January 2013, Court Statement No 99, civil case No 67/2013.

[22] Supreme Court of Cassation, IV Civil Chamber, 14 October 2022, Court Statement No 50734, civil case No 1341/2033.

Pursuant to Article 120(2) PILC, during these proceedings the defendant is prevented from challenging the admissibility of the proceedings by invoking violations in connection to the due process that he could have raised before the court of origin since these circumstances are part of the scope of assessment under and may serve as grounds for the refusal of the recognition and/or enforcement of the foreign judgment. The only admissible objections that can be made during the proceedings must refer to the authenticity and details of the submitted certificate by the court of origin, certifying that the foreign judgment has effectively entered into force, thus disputing the evidentiary value of the certificate and the foreign judgment.[23] In addition, refutation of the evidentiary value of the certificate is also admissible by presenting evidence that proceedings have been initiated in the country of origin to appeal the certificate for entry into force and that it is currently under the revision of a competent court.[24]

Article 121 PILC provides clear and specific limits to the assessment of the Bulgarian courts with respect to the foreign judgment. When assessing foreign judgments courts do not examine the merits of the dispute decided by the foreign court.[25] It should be specified, however, that an assessment on whether or not a claim derives from the circumstances specified by the person requesting the exequatur does not represent an assessment of merits as such a verification does not rule beyond the scope of the judgment, but merely assesses the facts from which the claim originates.[26]

Since the purpose of the proceedings does not pertain the assessment of the merits of the foreign judgment, any objections made by the defendant against the decision on the merits are considered inadmissible. Article 121(2)–(3) provides a sole exception for that in the scenario where an objection can be made for the extinguishment of the obligation as long as it has occurred after the foreign judgment took effect. The moment until such an objection can be raised is the entry into force of the decision of the court addressed admitting the enforcement.

Question 3. Requirements

Foreign judgments are recognised and enforced in Bulgaria as long as the requirements in Article 117 PILC are satisfied. Separate from the merits of the foreign judgment, each requirement is subject to judicial assessment on its merits, the result of which also determines the procedural legitimacy of the parties.[27] Article 117 sets out five exhaustive requirements for recognition: (a) indirect jurisdiction of the foreign court; (b) proper service of process; (c) lack of final judgment rendered by a Bulgarian court; (d) lack of pending proceedings before a Bulgarian court initiated before the foreign judgment was requested; and (e) conformity with public policy in

[23] Supreme Court of Cassation, I Commerce Chamber, 16 September 2021, Judgment No 60044, commercial case No 2775/2019.

[24] ibid.

[25] Supreme Court of Cassation, 14 March 2014, Court Statement No 194, commercial case No 2832/2013.

[26] Supreme Court of Cassation, II Commerce Chamber, 3 April 2020, Court Statement No 197, commercial case No 1544/2019.

[27] Supreme Court of Cassation, III Civil Chamber, 1 December 2020, Court Statement No 461, commercial case No 2073/2020.

Bulgaria. Accordingly, if any of the specified requirement is not present, the respective Bulgarian court or authority shall refuse the recognition or execution of the foreign act.

a) Jurisdiction of the Court of Origin

The first criterion for the recognition and enforcement of foreign judgments is the presence of jurisdiction of the foreign authority that issued the foreign judgment. For that the national authority is obliged to assess the extent to which the foreign jurisdiction is compatible with Bulgarian law. This first prerequisite for recognition and enforcement introduces only a rule of indirect jurisdiction to the extent the jurisdiction of the court of origin: (i) should not interfere with the exclusive jurisdiction of the Bulgarian courts as envisaged in the relevant jurisdictional rules (eg Article 24 of Regulation (EU) No 1215/2012 and Articles 12, 13, 19 PILC); and (ii) should not be grounded solely on the citizenship or the registration of the claimant in the country of the court of origin. Except for the latter, Article 117(1) PILC does not explicitly prohibit any other type of exorbitant jurisdiction of the court of origin. This provision in fact duplicates, but in a negative manner, the exorbitant jurisdiction of the Bulgarian courts envisaged in Article 4(1), specifically prohibiting reliance on this basis for jurisdiction for foreign courts.[28] Therefore, due to the 'mirror-image' approach explained below, if a foreign court has issued a judgment where the jurisdiction is based solely on the exorbitant jurisdiction provided by Article 4(1) PILC, the foreign court or authority would find no grounds to recognise the court as competent.

The Bulgarian legal doctrine adopts the so-called 'mirror-image' approach, according to which Bulgarian courts make an assessment from the perspective of the foreign court as to whether they would be granted jurisdiction under Bulgarian legislation if they were presented with the same facts to the case. When determining such jurisdiction, courts are required to take into consideration not only the domestic rules granting jurisdiction, but also all bilateral or multilateral treaties and international conventions.[29] The subject of this assessment is limited only to the presence of international jurisdiction and not the local and material jurisdiction of the authority.[30] Such international jurisdiction is present only when the foreign court or authority had jurisdiction according to the provisions of Bulgarian law. This is considered to be the case in scenarios where the Bulgarian legislation would grant jurisdiction to foreign courts over the disputed matter while at the same time recognises that the Bulgarian courts are lacking exclusive jurisdiction over the case. As such, the mere presence of jurisdiction of the Bulgarian courts or third-country courts does not lead to the lack of jurisdiction of the court of

[28] The provision of Art 4(1) PILC provides for a general jurisdiction of Bulgarian courts when the claimant is a Bulgarian national or a legal person registered in Bulgaria. For the exorbitant jurisdiction of the Bulgarian court under PILC refer to D Sarbinova in T Lutzi, E Piovesani and D Zgrabljic Rotar (eds), *Jurisdiction Over Non-EU Defendants: Should Brussels Ia Regulation be Extended?* (Hart Publishing, 2023) 60–72.

[29] Sofia Appellate Court, 23 December 2009, Judgment No 1644, civil case No 2294/2009.

[30] Sofia Appellate Court, Civil Chamber, 31 March 2014, Judgment No 613, civil case No 4175/2013.

origin under the meaning of Article 117(1) PILC.[31] Grounds for refusal will be present only in the scenarios where the Bulgarian courts or the courts of a third country under the applicable EU law instruments or international conventions would have exclusive jurisdiction similar to the one provided for disputes *in rem* or when the only grounds for foreign jurisdiction over such disputes *in rem* is based on the party's citizenship or registration at state of origin. Thus, a lack of exclusive jurisdiction of the Bulgarian court or the court of a third country should be established for the foreign jurisdiction to be recognised.[32]

b) Finality/Enforceability in the Country of Origin

The criteria of 'finality/enforceability in the country of origin' is not one of the exhaustive conditions for the recognition and enforcement of foreign judgments provided in Article 117 PILC. Nevertheless, to be recognised in Bulgaria, a foreign judgment must be a final and binding judgment, as well as to have enforceability, in order for the *res judicata* effect to be recognised and enforced as described above (see Question 1). A foreign judgment can be defined as 'final' once it enters into force and gives rise to its legal consequences. A final judgment must no longer be subject to ordinary forms of review during the judicial phase of the dispute since the finality of a judgment should be interpreted to include the non-appealability before the court of origin and should not be understood only as finality vis-à-vis other judicial authorities.[33] The characteristics of non-resolvability, finality of the dispute and binding force in relation to the parties involved in the dispute constitute the objective and subjective limits of the *res judicata* effect of judgments in the Bulgarian legal system. The same characteristics constitute the definition of 'judgment entered into force' and establish the inherent legal consequences of a judicial act, namely *res judicata* effect and enforceability. According to the consistent case law, the court addressed does not have the capacity of a control instance in relation to the foreign judgment and does not act as an instance in substance that can review the legal dispute itself. As such, it cannot assess whether the judgment of the court of origin is correct. Instead, the recognition of an act of a foreign authority constitutes a declaration of will of the respective judicial authority to respect the legal consequences of the foreign judgment.[34] In addition, the enforcing court requests and collects certificates from as evidence for the finality of the judgment in order for the enforceability of the foreign judgment to be admissible on the territory of Bulgaria (see Question 1). Therefore, judgments that are not final and binding cannot be recognised and enforced under Article 117 and Article 120 PILC, respectively.

[31] Supreme Court of Cassation, 12 April 2011, Court Statement No 254, commercial case No 854/2010.

[32] Supreme Court of Cassation, I Commerce Chamber, 16 September 2021, Judgment No 60044, commercial case No 2775/2019.

[33] Supreme Court of Cassation, I Commerce Chamber, 3 February 2017, Court Statement No 59, commercial case No 788/2016.

[34] Sofia City Court, IV Commerce Chamber, 7 November 2022, Judgment No 260665, commercial case No 227/2020.

c) *Res Iudicata*

Another condition for the recognising and enforcement of a foreign judgment is the absence of an effective judgment of a Bulgarian court between the same parties on the same claim and on the same grounds. The moment of seizing of the Bulgarian court with the dispute is irrelevant as long as the respective judgment has entered into force at the moment of request of the recognition and enforcement. A situation where a foreign judgment has confirmed an agreement reached by consent of the parents regarding the granting of parental rights does not represent a violation under Article 117(3) PILC. Furthermore, in such cases the judgment of the Bulgarian court effectively recognises the foreign judgment as having entered into force, and its recognition and enforcement constitutes a reevaluation of the issues resolved by the prior judgment as a change in circumstances.[35]

d) *Lis Pendens*

According to Article 117(4) PILC a judgment cannot be recognised and enforced in Bulgaria if there is a pending trial before a Bulgarian court, which was initiated before the foreign judgment was requested. This provision protects the legal certainty of the judicial process against attempts that try to nullify a domestic case by recognising a foreign judgment faster.

In order for the foreign judgment to be refused, the pending trial must be between the same parties, on the same grounds and on the same claim similar to the provision under Article 117(3) PILC. In order for this to be present there needs to be a complete objective and subjective overlap in identity between the two pending proceedings. Subjective identity is present when, in both cases, the addressees of the *res judicata* effect are the same persons – the parties to the proceedings, their universal legal successors, or private legal successors who acquired rights after filing the claim. Objective identity exists when the claim in both cases is identical and is submitted on the same grounds.[36] Therefore, the circumstances of the dispute must overlap both with respect to both the parties and the subject matter of the case. As such, the existence of a pending proceedings before a court of a non-EU country for a claim that cannot be individualised by the grounds for its submission does not represent an obstacle for the recognition of a foreign judgment due to the impossibility of establishing identity between the two claims and the existing possibility that foreign judgment may be subject to recognition and enforcement.[37]

If such an overlap of the circumstances of the dispute does not exist, no obstacle exists for the recognition and enforcement of the foreign judgment. For example, a pending conciliation proceedings before a Bulgarian court is not an obstacle for the recognition of a foreign divorce judgment between the same parties, since in the phase of the conciliation proceedings the matrimonial proceedings are not considered pending.[38]

[35] Sofia Appellate Court, Civil Chamber, 13 July 2009, Judgment No 925, commercial case No 1494/2009.
[36] Supreme Court of Cassation, 24 July 2013, Court Statement No 357, private civil case No 3981/2013.
[37] Supreme Court of Cassation, 24 July 2013, Court Statement No 357, private civil case No 3981/2013.
[38] Supreme Court of Cassation, 23 June 2014, Court Statement No 841, private civil case No 993/2014.

e) Specific Requirements of Due Process

The requirement for due process is another of the criteria subject to assessment by national courts and other authorities. In order for such an objection to be admissible under Article 120(2) PILC, it needs to address circumstances that were unable to be raised before the court of origin.

In order for it to be applicable, courts need to verify: (i) the proper service of a copy of the statement of action; (ii) the due summoning of the parties; and (iii) the lack of violations of fundamental principles of Bulgarian law, related to the defence of the said parties.

Such fundamental principles under Bulgarian law include the opportunity for the defendant to present their objections against the submitted action, to receive all evidence, or to receive a proper translation of the statement of action and the respective evidence. In order to not constitute a violation, the proceedings before the court of origin need to be of a proper duration as to not restrict the right of defence of the defendant. If the proceedings before the foreign court have been held at an extremely fast pace, resulting in a judgment that has been issued within a relatively short period of time from the deadline for possible service of the notice to the defendant, then a violation of the fundamental principles under Bulgarian law has occurred.[39] A violation also exists where a defendant company was not summoned in the complete absence of procedural representative authority through a person wrongly appointed as a representative of all defendants in a case, and was therefore unable to properly participate in the proceedings due to a lack of a proper legal representative.[40] In the event where a dispute would arise in connection to a violation of the due process of a defendant and their summoning before the court of origin, the national authority is obliged to distribute the burden of proof, as well as indicate to the parties that the assessment of the court would also cover the subject of whether the defendant was able to raise their objections during the proceedings before the foreign court. In the event of an appeal of the first instance court ruling, the appellate court is required to give both parties the opportunity to submit and present their own claims and evidence with respect to the principle of competitive due process.[41]

f) Public Policy

When recognising and enforcing foreign judgments, the Bulgarian courts and other authorities should assess the nature of the legal consequences of the foreign judgment. If they are considered incompatible with the Bulgarian public policy, the foreign judgment cannot be recognised or enforced. There is no definition of the concept of 'public order' in the Bulgarian legislation, but it is traditionally understood as the basic and fundamental principles of Bulgarian law. They are initially provided in the Constitution, but also in the constitutive treaties of EU and binding international conventions. Typical examples of public policy principles include the equality of

[39] Sofia Appellate Court, 2 March 2021, Judgment No 115, commercial case No 2647/2020.

[40] Sofia Appellate Court, Commerce Chamber, 12 June 2018, Judgment No 1452, commercial case No 670/2018.

[41] Supreme Court of Cassation, IV Civil Chamber, 14 October 2022, Court Statement No 50734, civil case No 1341/2022.

citizens, the prohibition of discrimination, equality of children born in marriage with those born out of wedlock and inviolability of private property.[42] In the legal doctrine it is indicated that the public policy of the state of the court includes those principles which constitute the basis of the social and economic organisation of the state.[43] As such, contradiction with the fundamental legal principles constituting public policy would inevitably lead to the refusal of recognition and enforcement of the foreign judgment.[44]

In connection to this, contradiction with the Bulgarian public policy does not necessarily mean every discrepancy with the law in general.[45] Instead, it refers to a violation of such legal principles, which are considered to be the foundations of the legal order in the country where the *exequatur* is requested, or concerning basic principles of the administration of justice, which have a universal meaning.[46] Rather than focusing on contradictions with specific legal provisions, an emphasis should be placed on contradictions that would lead to the violation of the public interest and the personal interest of the individual citizen and inadmissible impact on the basic values of society.[47] For example, the recognition of a foreign arbitral award and its enforcement for the payment of costs awarded in arbitration award that has not entered into force could only infringe certain rights of the aggrieved party, but not endanger public policy.[48]

This leads to a differentiation between the conditions for enforcement and recognition provided in PILC. On one hand, the grounds for refusal mentioned above aim to protect the interest of the defendant by giving them tools for objecting to the requested *exequatur*. On the other hand, however, the main goal behind the classification of public policy as grounds for refusal is to protect the legal order of the state of *exequatur*.[49] Such violation against the public policy that leads to the refusal of recognition and enforcement is present when the *exequatur* of a foreign judgment would result into the recognition of the emergence of two enforceable titles from the same claim without having a rule regulation the competition between such enforceable titles. Recognition of such judgment would clearly result in a breach of the public policy in Bulgaria by allowing unjust enrichment.[50]

[42] Sofia Appellate Court, Civil Chamber, 20 June 2013, Judgment No 1242, civil case No 4550/2011.

[43] V Stancheva-Mincheva, *Commentary on Private International Law Code. Comparison with European Union Acts* (Sibi, 2010) 86–94.

[44] For example, conflicts may arise regarding the method and requirements for certifying the origin of a child by identifying each parent's maternal or paternal role and verifying biological parentage. See Supreme Administrative Court, 8 January 2024, Judgment No 113, administrative case No 6071/2023; Supreme Administrative Court, 11 January 2024, Judgment No 287, administrative case No 6776/2023.

[45] Recognition and enforcement of judgments imposing obligations analogous to those regulated under Bulgarian law, such as monetary settlements in the division of family property, do not contravene Bulgarian public policy. See Supreme Court of Cassation, III Civil Chamber, 15 June 2023, Court Statement No 1665, civil case No 262/2023.

[46] Similarly, the recognition and enforcement of a judgment ordering maintenance in an amount deemed excessive by the parent is not contrary to Bulgarian public policy, as Bulgarian law establishes an unconditional and irrevocable legal obligation for every parent to provide child support for a minor, without any limitation on the maximum amount payable. See Supreme Court of Cassation, IV Civil Chamber, 5 June 2024, Court Statement No 2748, civil case No 5079/2023.

[47] Supreme Administrative Court, 10 October 2012, Judgment No 12546, administrative case No 7792/2012.

[48] Supreme Court of Cassation, II Commerce Chamber, 14 December 2016, Court Statement No 901, private civil case No 3627/2015.

[49] Supreme Court of Cassation, 17 May 2010, Court Statement No 264, commercial case No 1014/2009.

[50] Supreme Court of Cassation, 9 February 2015, Court Statement No 85, commercial case No 387/2014.

The institute of the public policy recognises multiple classification based on either the origin or on the field of law in which this institute is used. At its core, however, the institute is mainly based on the fundamental values that are derived by domestic law, international conventions, or EU law. As such, the principles of child protection and prioritising the interest of children are to be considered as primary public policy when solving issues concerning adoption or other issues affecting children.[51] For example, allowing for a child to be adopted without having the permission by their biological parent is not contrary to the public policy in the Republic of Bulgaria when it is a result of the objective impossibility to locate the parent after all available options for determining their location have been exhausted. Since the child's best interest is of primary importance, the Bulgarian legislation also allows adoption without the consent of a parent under certain conditions such as when the parent permanently does not take care of the child and does not provide maintenance or raises and educates him in a way that is harmful for his development.[52] Parents' obligation to pay maintenance to their children when they do not raise them personally is also of key importance to the interests of the child and therefore constitutes a part of the national public policy in the Republic of Bulgaria.[53]

g) Reciprocity

According to Bulgarian law no requirement of reciprocity is required when the application of foreign law is concerned. Furthermore, Article 47 PILC stipulates a rebuttable presumption of the existence of such reciprocity in the events where a statutory instrument would require such reciprocity. This approach is naturally extended to cover the *exequatur* of foreign acts as well, thus making the recognition and enforcement of foreign judgments independent on both contractual and/or factual reciprocity. As such, as a rule when making their assessment on the recognition and enforcement of a foreign judgment, national courts and authorities do not assess whether Bulgarian judgments are recognised in the respective foreign countries and under what conditions.

The requirement for reciprocity is present in the Commerce Act (as *lex specialis*) with respect to judgments issued in insolvency proceedings outside of the scope of application of the Insolvency Regulation. Pursuant to Article 757, foreign judgments declaring the insolvency of the debtor issued by the competent authority in the country where the seat of the debtor is situated, are subject to recognition in Bulgaria under the terms of reciprocity. This rule represents a reminiscence of the preexisting regulation (before the introduction of PILC in 2005) on recognition and enforcement of foreign judgments in the Civil Procedure Code (repealed) which included the reciprocity requirement.

[51] Sofia Appellate Court, Civil Chamber, 20 June 2013, Judgment No 1242, civil case No 4550/2011.

[52] Sofia Appellate Court, Civil Chamber, 26 February 2016, Judgment No 366, civil case No 5013/2015.

[53] Supreme Court of Cassation, III Civil Chamber, 15 May 2023, Court Statement No 50203, civil case No 3528/2022.

h) Other Requirements

None.

Question 4. Documents to be Produced

Pursuant to the provision of Article 119(2) in connection with Article 118 PILC, the application for recognition and enforcement of judgment must be accompanied by two documents: 1. a copy of the judgment duly certified by the court which issued the judgment; and 2. a certificate issued by this court that the judgment has entered into true force and effect. As a rule, these documents should be certified by the Ministry of Foreign Affairs of the Republic of Bulgaria.

The Bulgarian court practice undertakes a formalistic approach upon the examination of the documents to be produced for the purpose of the *exequatur* procedure. However, the court does not insist on the existence of a separate document – a certificate evidencing that the judgment has entered into force when on the front page on the judgment itself has a clear certification (for example, a stamp) that the judgment has entered into force on a specific date (being the date on which the judgment of the appellate court become effective) and the judgment is eligible for initiation of execution proceedings (in this sense are Court Order No 1234 from 28 November 2014 under civil case No 5441/2014 of the Supreme Court Cassation and Court Order No 597 from of 15 July 2019 under civil case No 535/2019 of the Supreme Court Cassation). These court rulings are rendered in the context of procedures for recognition and enforcement of foreign judgments originating from countries with which Bulgaria has entered bilateral treaties for legal assistance incorporating specific rules for *exequatur* of judgments issued by the courts of the respective contracting state. The Bulgarian court applies these specific rules together with the requirements under Article 119(2) PILC, taking into account that PILC supplements the application of the bilateral treaties if need be.

An analysis of the relevant texts of the most frequently applied bilateral treaties of legal assistance reveals that the rules concerning the documents that need to be produced in the *exequatur* proceedings does not differ significantly from or even replicate those envisaged in Article 119(2) PILC. For example, Article 45(2)(a) of the Bilateral Treaty for Legal Assistance with the Republic of Yugoslavia (now applicable for judgments issued by the Serbian courts) requires the same documents to be attached to the application for recognition and enforcement of judgments as those envisaged in Article 119(2) PILC, in particular a copy of the judgments and a certificate that this judgment has entered into force and is eligible for execution.

By the same token, Article 49 of the Bilateral Treaty of Legal Assistance with the Union of Soviet Socialist Republics (now applicable for judgments issued by the Russian courts) provides potentially for three documents that has to be produced before the Bulgarian court seized with an application for *exequatur* of a Russian judgment, namely: a certified copy of the judgment and a certificate that the judgment has entered into force and is eligible for execution. The latter certificate should be provided only in cases where the certification is not incorporated in the judgment itself. In addition, the provision requires the production of a document which evidences the fact that the defendant (or his/her attorney) who did not take part in the proceedings was duly summoned.

As already noted, PILC requires the documents filed with the application to be certified by the Bulgarian Ministry of Foreign Affairs. This indicates that as a rule these documents are subject to a procedure of legalisation under the terms of the Rules for Legislations, Certifications and Translations of Documents and Other Papers.[54] The Bulgarian Ministry of Foreign Affairs legalises documents and other papers originating from another state only if they have been certified aforehand by the diplomatic or the consulate representation of this state in Bulgaria (Article 8 of the Legalizations and Translations Rules). Furthermore, public documents originating from another state are subject to legalisation by the respective Bulgarian diplomatic or consulate representation abroad.

The Legalizations and Translations Rules also contain provisions for the implementation of the Convention of 5 October 1961, abolishing the Requirement of Legalisation for Foreign Public Documents (the Apostille Convention) which applies when the produced document is executed in the territory of one contracting state under this Convention.[55]

As a rule, the bilateral treaties for legal assistance entered into with a number of other states contain provisions under which the public documents originating from the other contracting state are exempt from any legalisation requirements (including apostille). For example, under Article 12(1) of the Bilateral Treaty of Legal Assistance with the Union of Soviet Socialist Republics all public documents duly issued or certified by a competent authority of a contracting state are subject to free circulation on the territory of the other contracting state without the need of legalisation.

In any case, if the document is written in a foreign language, official translation in Bulgarian is also necessary. Such official translation of a document to be produced in Bulgaria is made by a translator whose signature is subject to notary certification in Bulgaria (Article 21a of the Legalizations and Translations Rules). A list of certified translators is also kept with the respective Bulgarian diplomatic or consulate representation abroad (Article 18(3) of the Legalizations and Translations Rules).

Question 5. Securities, Bonds and Deposits

The applicant is not required to provide any type of security, bond or deposit upon initiation of the procedure for recognition and enforcement of non-EU judgments. The filing of the application is only subject to the payment of standardised court fee of nominal nature. Pursuant to the Tariff of the State Fees Collected by the Courts under the Civil Procedure Code, the court fee for the application for recognition and enforcement of foreign judgments is 50 Bulgarian leva (approximately 25 euros).

[54] Promulgated in State Gazette No 73 of 12 September 1958, last amended in State Gazette No 31 of 7 April 2023.

[55] Bulgaria is a Contracting State to the Apostille Convention since 29 April 2001.

Croatia

TENA HOŠKO AND DORA ZGRABLJIĆ ROTAR

Question 1. General Overview

In the Republic of Croatia, rules on recognition and enforcement of foreign judgments are contained in the Private International Law Act. Private international law has been codified in Croatia since 1982 when the 'Act concerning the resolution of conflicts of laws with the provisions of other countries in certain matters' (Zakon o rješavanju sukoba zakona s propisima drugih zemalja u određenim odnosima)[1] (1982 PILA) came into force. The 1982 PILA not only contained rules on conflict of laws, but also jurisdictional rules and rules on recognition and enforcement of foreign judgments.

The 1982 PILA was originally enacted as a federal statute of the former Socialist Federative Republic of Yugoslavia.[2] The original text of the law was taken over as the law of Croatia in 1991, when the country declared independence.[3] The 1982 PILA had remained intact until 4 October 2017 when the new Private International Law Act was passed by the Parliament and came into force 29 January 2019 (2017 PILA).[4]

Rules on recognition and enforcement are found primarily in the PILA 2017. However, the procedure of recognition and enforcement is a non-contentious one thus regulated by the Non-Contentious Proceedings Act (NCPA)[5] and subsidiarily by the Civil Procedure Act (CPA).[6] Prior to entry into force of the NCPA non-contentious proceedings were regulated by a very old piece of legislation – Judicial Non-Contentious Proceedings Act from 1934.[7]

The recognition and enforcement procedure in Croatia is obligatory in order for the foreign judgment to have effect in Croatia. The decision on recognition is considered

[1] Zakon o rješavanju sukoba zakona s propisima drugih zemalja u određenim odnosima, Narodne novine no 53/91.

[2] Službeni list SFRJ nos 43/82, 72/82.

[3] D Babić, 'Private International Law' in T Josipović (ed), *Introduction to the Law of Croatia* (Wolters Kluwer, 2014) 439. The only major change since 1982 was that the rules on recognition and enforcement of arbitral awards were abolished and replaced by the Arbitration Act of 2001 (Narodne novine no 88/01, Art 50).

[4] Zakon o međunarodnom privatnom pravu, Narodne novine no 101/17, 67/23.

[5] Zakon o izvanparničnom postupku, Narodne novine no 59/23.

[6] Narodne novine nos 53/91, 91/92, 58/93, 112/99, 88/01, 117/03, 88/05, 02/07, 84,123/08, 57/11, 148/11, 25/13, 89/14, 70/19, 80/22, 114/22.

[7] Zakon o sudskom vanparničnom postupku, Službene novine Kraljevine Jugoslavije no. 45/34, Narodne novine no 73/9.1.

to be a declaratory one. This is interpreted in the sense that foreign judgments do have effect *ex lege* in the territory of Croatia, but that effect is suspended until recognition procedure is conducted, ie the effectiveness determined.[8] The decision can be rendered in a self-standing procedure or the issue can be decided incidentally, but that decision will have effect only in the legal procedure it was rendered in. The system of recognition and enforcement is one of limited control, and that has remained unchanged from the outset. The new 2017 PILA did introduce some changes – jurisdictional requirement was changed, reciprocity abolished as well as specific requirements for decisions on status of a person. The changes bring the new PILA closer to the Brussels regime, as will be shown in Question 3 of this report.

In June 2023 the recognition and enforcement of foreign adoption decisions was nuanced. This was caused by a recent intercountry adoption case which comes out of the scope of this report, but is important to mention because it was the first time that recognition of foreign decisions has caught the attention of public eye and led to public debate, both professional and political. Otherwise, recognition and enforcement of non-EU judgments has not produced much writings in legal theory, even though its practical importance cannot be irrelevant given the fact that half of the neighboring countries of the Republic of Croatia are not Member States of the European Union (EU).

Article 65 of the 2017 PILA situated at the beginning of Chapter 4 that contains rules on recognition and enforcement declares priority of listed multilateral international treaties and European regulations. This rule is redundant with the declarative purpose to aid in prioritising the sources that emanate either from EU law or the Croatian Constitution. Bilateral treaties are not mentioned, but that does not influence their priority in application that is provided by the Constitution.[9]

The 2017 PILA expressly states that the foreign judgment can also be a court settlement.[10] The judgment can also be issued by a different authority as long as it is equated with the court judgment or a court settlement in the country of origin.[11] The judgment in any case needs to be foreign, issued by an authority of a foreign state, notwithstanding the territory it was issued on.[12]

Question 2. Procedure

a) Circumstances of Recognition and Enforcement

Under a clear wording of Article 66 paragraph 1 2017 PILA, a foreign court decision is equated with a domestic one and has effect in Croatia only if recognised by a Croatian

[8] M Dika, G Knežević and S Stojanović, *Komentar Zakona o međunarodnom privatnom i procesnom pravu* (Nomos, 1990) 277–78.

[9] Art 134; Narodne novine nos 56/90, 135/97, 08/98, 113/00, 124/00, 28/01, 41/01, 55/01, 76/10, 85/10, 05/14.

[10] Art 66 para 2 2017 PILA.

[11] Art 66 para 3 2017 PILA.

[12] Dika, Knežević and Stojanović (n 8) 283; P Bosnić, *Hrvatsko međunarodno privatno i procesno pravo, Knjiga II* (Pravni fakultet Sveučilišta u Splitu, 2003) 77; Đ Vuković and E Kunštek, *Međunarodno građansko postupovno pravo* (Zgombić i partneri, 2005) 423–24.

court. Article 72 paragraph 3 of the 2017 PILA states that the recognition procedure can be a self-standing one or the decision can be recognised incidentally. Incidental recognition may only take place if recognition has not been finally settled by a court decision, when any court can decide on recognition incidentally, for the purpose of the proceedings for which it was seized. Legal theory accepts the literal interpretation of the rule, only courts, and no other authorities, can deal with the recognition incidentally.[13] Incidental recognition might be especially convenient in enforcement proceedings.[14] What is more, Article 19 of the Enforcement Act[15] provides that the enforcement can be ordered based on a foreign decision that fulfils requirements for recognition what is interpreted in case law as an obligation to check whether incidental recognition is viable in enforcement proceedings, ie has to decide on incidental recognition prior to enforcement.[16] From the same rule, it is seen that a foreign decision can, once recognised and declared enforceable, be enforced in Croatia.

b) Procedural Steps

The procedure for recognition and enforcement is regulated primarily by Articles 72 and 73 of 2017 PILA. Since the procedure is a non-contentious one[17] the NCPA is also applicable, and subsidiarily, when necessary, the CPA. The recognition and enforcement procedures are basically the same, often dealt with in one proceeding. Article 73 2017 PILA expressly provides for application of its rules that regulate recognition procedure to enforcement procedure as well.

Article 72 paragraph 1 of the 2017 PILA prescribes the competent court. The competent court is one of the domicile of the person against whom recognition is sought or the court in whose territory the judgment is to be enforced. In case of lack thereof, any court competent *ratione materiae* is competent *ratione teritorii* as well. Courts competent *ratione materiae* are civil courts of first instance (*općinski sud*) or commercial courts (*trgovački sud*) depending on the subject matter.[18]

It is not expressly regulated by the 2017 PILA who can request recognition and enforcement. It is not doubtful that it can be the creditor (or its successor) in proprietary matters[19] or one of the parties to the proceedings in the country of origin.[20] It is held that if the decision is of declaratory nature anyone with legal interest can seek recognition,

[13] Dika, Knežević and Stojanović (n 8) 341–42; Bosnić (n 12) 95.

[14] See Supreme Court, 14 October 2020, Judgment no Rev 410/2018-3; County Court Varaždin, 15 June 2012, Judgment no 27 Gž-2262/2012-2; Supreme Court, 10 March 2004, Judgment no Gž-28/00-2.

[15] Narodne novine nos 112/12, 25/13, 93/14, 55/16, 73/17, 131/20, 114/22.

[16] County Court Varaždin, 25 May 2021, Judgment no Gž Ovr-271/2021-2.

[17] See Art 1 para 3 NCPA. Dika, Knežević and Stojanović (n 8) 339; Bosnić (n 12) 94 on the non-contentious nature of recognition procedure' and A Maganić, 'Zakon o izvanparničnom postupku' (2023) 6778 *Informator* 1, 2 on applicability of the NCPA *ratione materiae*. This is also confirmed in case law; see eg County Court Varaždinu, 2 September 2021, Judgment no Gž-773/2021-3; County Court Varaždinu, 19 March 2021, Judgment no 25 Gž-1845/2019-6.

[18] Art 17 para 5 and Art 21 para 6 Judiciary Act, Narodne novine nos 28/13, 33/15, 82/15, 82/16, 67/18, 126/19, 130/20, 21/22, 60/22, 16/23. Vuković and Kunštek (n 12) 490; Bosnić (n 12) 93.

[19] Vuković and Kunštek (n 12) 490.

[20] Dika, Knežević and Stojanović (n 8) 339.

whereas in condemnatory or constitutive judgments the authorised applicant would be the party that would be authorised to initiate the proceedings on the subject matter.[21]

Further issue mentioned in legal theory and case law is whether the proceedings need to be adversarial, ie whether the request for recognition is to be delivered to the opposing party or the decision can be made ex parte. Both theory[22] and case law[23] support adversarial nature of the proceedings. This is regulated by the new NCPA which in Article 10 paragraph 2 states that the request is to be delivered to all parties to the proceedings, including the ones court finds should be included as parties in accordance with Article 5.

The court has no obligation to conduct an oral hearing if it can decide without it.[24] It can even render a decision based on lack of response of the opposing party, it that party fails to respond in time or to appear before court. The court may consider that the party has agreed to the proposal of the other party and render a decision based on the factual situation with which the party was aware. The court will, however, warn the party of the legal consequences of such conduct.[25]

The question whether the party needs to invoke reasons to refuse recognition and enforcement or can the court do it on its own motion is only partially expressly regulated by the 2017 PILA. The party seeking recognition and enforcement needs to submit proof of finality and certificate of enforceability,[26] but the failure to do so does not automatically lead to inadmissibility. The court will invite the party to submit it, and if it fails to do so, the court will find the request inadmissible.[27] In any case, lack of these requirements lead to inadmissibility and not refusal of the request.

The 2017 PILA also expressly states that the party (against whom recognition is sought) claiming breach of the right to be heard also needs to invoke it.[28] As for the remaining negative requirements (jurisdiction, *res iudicata* and public policy) the PILA 2017 is silent. Theory suggest that they are to be determined *ex officio* by the court.[29]

In any case, there is no review as to the merits, the court is only allowed to check if positive requirements exist and verify that the negative ones do not.[30]

The appeal is allowed within 15 days from delivery of the decision on recognition.[31] The appellate courts are county courts (*županijski sud*) and high commercial courts

[21] Dika, Knežević and Stojanović (n 8) 339–40. Bosnić (n 12) 94 contends that in all cases all the parties with legal interest cane seek recognition.

[22] Dika, Knežević and Stojanović (n 8) 340–41; Bosnić (n 12) 94. Contrary: Vuković and Kunštek (n 12) 492.

[23] County Court Varaždin, 6 November 2020, Judgment no 35 Gž-270/2020-2; County Court Vukovar, 4 February 2008, Judgment no Gž 166/2008-2.

[24] Art 19 NCPA; S Aras Kramar, 'Novi Zakon o izvanparničnom postupku prijedlog iz 2023. godine' (2023) 15 *Pravo i porezi* 19. See also Dika, Knežević and Stojanović (n 8) 340.

[25] Art 18 NCPA.

[26] Art 67 2017 PILA.

[27] Art 109 CPA. Dika, Knežević and Stojanović (n 8) 286; Vuković and Kunštek (n 12) 491.

[28] Art 68 2017 PILA.

[29] Dika, Knežević and Stojanović (n 8) 292, 297, 304; Bosnić (n 12) 80, 82; H Sikirić, 'Zakon o međunarodnom privatnom pravu (2018) 61 *Tradicionalno XXXIII. savjetovanje – Aktualnosti Hrvatskog zakonodavstva i pravne prakse, Godišnjak 25* 132–33.

[30] Dika, Knežević and Stojanović (n 8) 342; Bosnić (n 12) 94; Vuković and Kunštek (n 12) 491. Also confirmed in case law see eg County Court Varaždin, 19 March 2021, Judgment no 25 Gž-1845/2019-6; County Court Varaždin, 2 September 2021, Judgment no Gž-773/2021-3; County Court Varaždin, 26 February 2019, Judgment no 10 Gž-1078/2017-2.

[31] Art 72 para 2 2017 PILA.

(*Visoki trgovački sud*). Previous 1982 PILA contained an explicit rule that second instance courts are competent; it is thought this was omitted by mistake.[32] Still Judiciary Act is to be applied[33] which regulates that if it is not provided otherwise, these courts serve as appellate courts.[34] However, new NCPA provides that the first instance court can in some cases accept the appeal on its own. Most importantly, if it follows from the state of the file that the decision must be revoked and the request that initiated the procedure, on which the decision is based, must be rejected, or that the decision must be changed in its entirety by accepting the request invoked in the appeal.[35]

Issue whether further legal remedies can be submitted has been discussed in legal theory in the past.[36] Nowadays, after the new NCPA the stance is clear – two further remedies are allowed. The second appeal is allowed in same cases as in contentious proceedings (if permitted by the Supreme Court of the Republic of Croatia[37]).[38] Also, a request to alter or revoke the decision that may be based on same reasons on which renewal of proceedings can be sought in contentious proceedings.[39]

Question 3. Requirements

The requirements for the recognition and enforcement of foreign judgments in the 2017 PILA are to a large extent inspired by the Brussels regime. This is not unexpected given that the 2017 PILA was drafted around the time of the Croatian accession to the EU and that all parts of the 2017 PILA are aligned with the European private international law.

There are seven negative and two positive requirements for the recognition and enforcement of non-EU judgments listed in PILA. The negative requirements are grouped in the following sections: jurisdiction of the court of origin; due process; irreconcilability with other judgments; proceedings pending in Croatia on the same matter; and public policy. The positive requirements are finality and enforceability of the requested judgment in the country of origin. Reciprocity was a requirement under the 1982 PILA, but it was abandoned in the 2017 PILA.

a) Jurisdiction of the Court of Origin

The rules on jurisdiction of the court of origin are set in Article 69 of the 2017 PILA as negative requirements. There are three main rules: under paragraph 1 the court will

[32] Sikirić (n 29) 135.

[33] Vuković and Kunštek (n 12) 490; Bosnić (n 12) 93.

[34] Art 19 para 1 and Art 24 para 1 Judiciary Act.

[35] Art 39 para 1 pt 3 NCPA.

[36] Dika, Knežević and Stojanović (n 8) 341.

[37] More on second appeal by permission of the Supreme Court in M Bratković, 'Revizija po dopuštenju: izazovi i dvojbe' in J Barbić (ed), *Novine u parničnom procesnom pravu* (Hrvatska akademija znanosti i umjetnosti (HAZU, 2020) 179–209.

[38] Art 45 NCPA; Arts 382–400 CPA.

[39] Arts 46–47 NCPA; Arts 420–29 CPA. See Aras Kramar (n 24) 20–21.

refuse the recognition of a foreign judgment if Croatian courts have exclusive jurisdiction over the matter at hand; under paragraph 2 the court will refuse a judgment if it was rendered by a court whose jurisdiction was exorbitant; under paragraph 3 the court will refuse a judgment rendered by a court whose jurisdiction contradicts the Brussels Ia rules on protective jurisdiction.

The courts should take care of all three reasons *ex officio*.[40]

1. The first reason is well known in comparative law, and was known in the 1982 PILA as well. A foreign judgment will not be recognised if Croatian courts have exclusive jurisdiction over the matter. This applies notwithstanding the fact that the court that rendered the judgment had jurisdiction according to its domestic law.[41] The prevailing view is that conflict with the rules on exclusive jurisdiction of the Croatian courts should be assessed at the moment when the foreign judgment was rendered.[42] It is worth mentioning that in Croatian legal systems there are no specific rules on exclusive international jurisdiction in civil and commercial matters except those provided by the Brussels Ia Regulation.

2. Judgment based on exorbitant jurisdictional grounds and a judgment based on jurisdiction not in line with the rules on protective jurisdiction found in the Brussels Ia Regulation as the reasons for refusal of recognition and enforcement of a foreign judgment are a novelty in the Croatian legal system, introduced by the 2017 PILA.

Exorbitant jurisdiction is defined by the 2017 PILA as the one 'exclusively based on the presence of the defendant or the defendant's property in the state of the rendering court, while the presence is not in a direct connection to the subject matter'.[43]

Although some Member States also have within their respective legal systems rules that would fall within the Croatian 2017 PILA understanding of an exorbitant jurisdictional ground and thus judgments rendered by the courts of those states could not be recognised, the rule on non-recognition of judgments will in civil and commercial matters only be applicable to the non-EU foreign judgments because the Brussels I Regulation excludes the application of those rules over EU defendants.

Interestingly, until 2022, the CPA allowed for exorbitant international jurisdiction of Croatian courts in several provisions which directly contradicts the reasoning behind the adoption of this rule in the new 2017 PILA.

Namely, Article 58, paragraph 1 CPA provided for jurisdiction when defendant had property in Croatia or the object requested by the claim was situated in Croatia. The term 'property of the defendant' was understood in a broad way. The property could have been a real estate or a movable property, it could have been a claim that the defendant has towards a third person or any other belonging of the defendant. Most importantly, the property did not have to be related to the claim, nor did it have to be of the same value as the claim.[44]

Article 58, paragraph 2 of the CPA determined territorial jurisdiction in cases when international jurisdiction was based on the fact that the dispute arose out of an obligation that arose while the defendant was in Croatia.

[40] Dika, Knežević and Stojanović (n 8) 292, 297, 304; Bosnić (n 12) 80, 82; Sikirić (n 29) 132–33.

[41] Dika, Knežević and Stojanović (n 8) 292.

[42] ibid 294.

[43] Art 69 para 2 2017 PILA.

[44] Dika, Knežević and Stojanović (n 8) 199; T Varadi et al, *Međunarodno privatno pravo* (Pravnifakultet Univerziteta u Beogradu, 2016) 507.

Article 58, paragraph 3 of the CPA provided that:

> In disputes against a person regarding whom there is no general territorial jurisdiction in the Republic of Croatia, with respect to obligations to be performed in the Republic of Croatia, a complaint may be filed with the court in whose territory these obligations are to be fulfilled.

Therefore, the rule provided for jurisdiction of the court of *loci solutionis*, ie the place of performance of the obligation and the Croatian courts were in no way reluctant to base their international jurisdiction on that provision which is evidenced in case law.[45]

However, the rules are out of force as of 2022, thus they no longer serve as the basis for jurisdiction over non-EU defendants. One of the reasons which lead towards deleting those rules from the CPA was the alignment with the rule on the exorbitant jurisdictional ground as a reason for non-recognition of a foreign judgment.

3. A foreign judgment will not be recognised when the court of origin based its jurisdiction contrary to the Chapter II, Sections 3, 4 or 5 of the Brussels Ia Regulation. Thus, recognition of a foreign judgment will be refused when the court of origin breached the Brussels Ia protective jurisdictional rules applied to matters relating to insurance, consumer contracts and individual employment contracts.

This reason for refusal of recognition is found in Article 45, paragraph 1(e) of the Brussels Ia Regulation as well, and thus the same principle in Croatia applies for both EU judgments as well as non-EU judgments.

It should be noted that the wording of the 2017 PILA differs slightly from the wording of the Brussels Ia Regulation. Namely, the 2017 PILA only refers to the non-compliance of the jurisdiction of the court of origin with the protective jurisdictional grounds of the Brussels Ia Regulation, while as the Brussels I Regulation explicitly provides that the judgment will be refused if it conflicts with the provision on protective jurisdiction where the policyholder, the insured, a beneficiary of the insurance contract, the injured party, the consumer or the employee was the defendant. Notwithstanding the differences in the wording, the aim of both provisions is to protect the weaker party and, thus, if we interpret the 2017 PILA teleologically instead of grammatically, the provision of the 2017 PILA should be applied in the same way as the Brussels Ia Regulation. Namely, the protection of the policyholder, the insured, a beneficiary of the insurance contract, the injured party, the consumer or the employee as the defendant stems from the very reasoning of the special protective rules on jurisdiction. The case law might only show that in some occasions the weaker party should also be protected in the role of the claimant, as well as in the role of the defendant.

b) Finality/Enforceability in the Country of Origin

Both finality of the judgment in the country of origin as well as, in case of a request for enforcement of foreign judgment enforceability of the judgment in the country of

[45] High Commercial Court, 12 December 2006, Judgment no Pž 537/04-3; 23 August 2006, Judgment no Pž 2136/03-3; 6 July 1999, Judgment no Pž 2622/99; 14 January 1997, Judgment no Pž-2698/96; 1 February 1994, Judgment no Pž-2826/93; 6 July 1993, Judgment no Pž-7739/93; 30 March 1993, Judgment no Pž-1028/92.

origin, are required under the 2017 PILA. The decision should be final and enforceable according to the law of the state of origin.

Finality and enforceability of the judgment in the country of origin was also required under the 1982 PILA, but due to the slightly different wording of the provision, some discussions occurred on whether the requirement refers to providing a document on finality or a factual finality is required.[46] The outcome of the latter would be that the document of proof of finality of judgment carries the same evidentiary force as any other authentic document and that the opposing party could prove its invalidity.[47]

The wording of the Article 67 2017 PILA provides more accurately that the judgment should be final and enforceable under the law of the state of origin, and that the document on finality and enforceability is a proof of that, leaving this doubt in the past.

c) *Res Iudicata*

Article 70 paragraph 1 of the 2017 PILA recognises the irreconcilability of the judgment with another judgment as a reason for the refusal of recognition. It was inspired by Article 45, paragraph 1(d) of the Brussels Ia Regulation.[48] However, there is a notable difference in the two provisions. Namely, the 2017 PILA provides that the recognition of the judgment will be refused if the court finds that there is a final judgment by the Croatian court in the same matter between the same parties or that there is a prior final judgment of a foreign court that has been recognised or fulfils the conditions necessary for its recognition in Croatia. On the other hand, the Brussels Ia Regulation provides that the recognition of the judgment will be refused if 'is irreconcilable with an earlier judgment'.

Although it stems from the case law of the CJEU that the irreconcilability of judgments should be interpreted narrowly, it seems that the provision of the 2017 PILA is more limited and more precise.

Whether the judgments concern the same matter between the same parties is an issue that is governed by Croatian law.[49]

d) *Lis Pendens*

According to Article 70, paragraph 2 of the 2017 PILA, 'the court will stay the proceedings of recognition of the foreign judgment if proceedings on the same matter between the same parties have already been initiated in front of a Croatian court, until the final termination of that proceeding'.

The existing *lis pendens* should be determined by the court *ex officio*.[50] It is applicable in cases where the proceedings are self-standing, as well as in cases where the

[46] Dika, Knežević and Stojanović (n 8) 285.
[47] I Grbin, *Priznanje i izvršenje odluka stranih sudova* (Informator, 1980), 137; Dika, Knežević and Stojanović (n 8) 285.
[48] Sikirić (n 29) 134.
[49] Dika, Knežević and Stojanović (n 8) 296.
[50] Dika, Knežević and Stojanović (n 8) 298.

recognition of a decision is decided as an incidental question.[51] *Lis pendens* in and of itself is not a reason to deny recognition, but only a stay of recognition proceedings. A final judgment rendered in main proceedings can become a reason to deny recognition as explained above.

e) Specific Requirements of Due Process

According to Article 68 of the 2017 PILA, Croatian courts will refuse the recognition of a foreign judgment if a party proves that its right to participate in the proceedings in which the judgment was rendered was breached.

This provision relies on Article 45, paragraph 1(b) of the Brussels Ia Regulation according to which,

> where the judgment was given in default of appearance, if the defendant was not served with the document which instituted the proceedings or with an equivalent document in sufficient time and in such a way as to enable him to arrange for his defence, unless the defendant failed to commence proceedings to challenge the judgment when it was possible for him to do so.

In essence, both articles have the aim to protect the right to a fair hearing of the defendant, thus if the defendant did not have a fair chance to present its defence the judgment cannot be recognised. The defendant has to prove that his right was breached.

This reason for the refusal of recognition of foreign judgments is not a novelty, since a similar version existed in the 1982 PILA.[52] Prior to the 1982 PILA, there was a theoretical debate on whether the right to a fair trial in the proceedings should be protected through the provision on public policy.[53] The main reason for inclusion of a special provision on due process is the fact that the breach of the right to be heard has to be invoked and proven by the party that is relying on it, while as the incompatibility with the public policy has to be determined *ex officio* by the court.[54]

The notion of participation in the proceedings should be understood broadly and is not limited to only one stage of the proceedings, ie it should be considered that the party could not participate in the proceedings in cases where the party could not be heard by the court, where it could not appeal or answer to the appeal of the other party, etc.[55]

f) Public Policy

The 2017 PILA introduced a public policy provision that is identical to the one in the Brussels Ia Regulation: The court will refuse the recognition of a foreign judgment if such recognition is manifestly contrary to public policy (*ordre public*) of the Republic of Croatia.

[51] ibid 299.
[52] Art 88 1982 PILA.
[53] Dika, Knežević and Stojanović (n 8) 288; Grbin (n 47) 155.
[54] Dika, Knežević and Stojanović (n 8) 288.
[55] ibid 290.

The provision differs in wording from the public policy provision of the 1982 PILA. The 2017 PILA abandoned the 1982 PILA attempt to define the notion of public policy by providing that 'the court will refuse the recognition of a foreign judgment if such recognition is contrary to *the constitutionally established foundations of the society*'.[56] The idea behind the statutory definition of the term public policy is that it provides guidance for the judiciary interpretation, which should, at least in theory, be formed more precisely with the help of this statutory definition.[57] The prevailing view is that the provision should not be interpreted as restricting the *ordre public* exception to constitutional norms.[58] However, *ordre public* does not include all mandatory law, but encompasses only the most fundamental values of Croatian law that have to be protected.[59]

According to the 2017 PILA, the foreign judgment has to be manifestly contrary to public policy. The aim is, of course, to point out that the public policy provision is an exception which should be interpreted narrowly. That was already established by both scholarly[60] and judicial interpretation[61] notwithstanding the fact that it was not explicitly mentioned in the 1982 PILA.

What is decisive in the court's decision to refuse the recognition based on the public policy exception is not whether the foreign law is contrary to the public policy of Croatia, not even whether the decision itself is contrary to the public policy of Croatia, but whether it would produce such effects in Croatia that would go against its public policy.[62] Thus, the courts should not examine whether the law of a foreign state that governed the judgment is compatible or incompatible with the public policy of Croatia.[63]

According to scholarly opinion based on the 1982 PILA, the court could have refused to recognise a foreign judgment based on the *ordre public* exception if it concluded that the jurisdiction of the court of origin was based on a ground it finds absurd.[64] However, since that would not be allowed according to the Brussels I Regulation, and since the 2017 PILA introduced exorbitant jurisdiction as a reason for refusal of a foreign judgment, this scholarly opinion should not apply to the new 2017 PILA.

There are very few reported decisions on the application of the *ordre public* exception in the context of refusal of recognition and enforcement of judgments,[65] and none

[56] Art 911982 PILA.

[57] Dika, Knežević and Stojanović (n 8) 300.

[58] ibid 16.

[59] T Varadi et al, *Međunarodno privatno parvo*, 15th edn (Univerzitet u Beogradu – Pravni fakultet, 2016) 154; Dika, Knežević and Stojanović (n 8) 15, 47; M Pak, *Međunarodno privatno pravo* (Naučna knjiga, 1986), 607; Grbin (n 47) 117; H Sikirić, *Prisilna pravila, pravila neposredne primjene i mjerodavno materijalno pravo u međunarodnoj arbitraži*, (Pravo u gospodarstvu, 1999) 84.

[60] Dika, Knežević and Stojanović (n 8) 19, 300–05; H Sikirić, 'Javni popredak kao razlog za poništaj pravorijeka' (2009) 59 *Zbornik PFZ* 229.

[61] Supreme Court of the Republic of Croatia, 7 October 2009, Revt 74/2007-2, (the decision emphasises that not all mandatory rules are a part of public policy); High Commercial Court, 10 May 2012, Judgment No P ž -7632/11-3, Supreme Court of the Republic of Croatia, 21 September 2011, Judgment No G ž 29/11-2.

[62] Dika, Knežević and Stojanović (n 8) 301, 302.

[63] K Sajko, *Međunarodno privatno pravo* (Narodne novine, 2009) 259; Dika, Knežević and Stojanović (n 8) 16, 17; Varadi et al (n 59) 194; Pak (n 59) 598.

[64] Dika, Knežević and Stojanović (n 8) 192.

[65] County Court in Split, 23 November 2018, Judgment No Gž-606/2015-5; County Court in Varaždin, 10 November 2016, Judgment No Gž-2484/15-2.

in which the recognition was refused. Case law on the judicial review of arbitral awards is more generous. On several occasions, the courts have held that the public policy exception is a very narrow ground for refusal of enforcement of an arbitral award, and encompasses only the most fundamental principles of the Croatian legal order.[66] The view is, by analogy, applicable to judgments. To date, in the case of court judgments, no arbitral award has been set aside or denied enforcement on public policy grounds.

g) Reciprocity

Reciprocity is not a requirement for the recognition and enforcement of foreign judgments according to 2017 PILA, and thus it will not be a requirement in the recognition and enforcement of non-EU judgments in civil and commercial matters.

Reciprocity was a requirement under the 1982 PILA. It was abandoned in line with the view that reciprocity is a consequence of the relationship between countries and not the parties, so they do not have a possibility to influence it and thus should not bear the negative consequences of the lack of reciprocity.[67] In addition, reciprocity is difficult to prove and might lead to extra costs for the parties.[68]

As explicitly determined in Article 92 of the 1982 PILA, reciprocity was presumed until proven otherwise.[69] Reciprocity could either be legal or factual reciprocity.[70] This was also confirmed by case law. Specifically, in cases where Croatia does not have a contractual reciprocity with the state of origin, the courts have decided that the judgment has to be recognised if there is factual reciprocity, ie if the courts of the state of origin have already recognised judgments rendered by the Croatian courts.[71]

An interesting case on proving reciprocity, albeit in connection to reciprocity as to succession, occurred before the Constitutional Court of the Republic of Croatia.[72] In that case, Croatian courts sought a declaration from the Ministry of Justice on the issue of reciprocity in inheritance between Croatia and Jordan in a very lengthy procedure. The Constitutional Court held that the applicant's right to a fair trial was breached and she was awarded reimbursement.

h) Other Requirements

None.

[66] Supreme Court of the Republic of Croatia, 11 July 2007, Judgment No G ž 17/06-2; High Commercial Court, 17 October 2006, Judgment No P ž -4908/04-3; High Commercial Court, 8 November 2006, Judgment No P ž -5712/03-3; High Commercial Court, 12 December 2006, Judgment No P ž -1574/04-6.

[67] Sikirić (n 29) 127.

[68] ibid.

[69] Also confirmed in a succession matter by the Supreme Court, 23 June 1994, Judgment Rev 3341/1993-2.

[70] Dika, Knežević and Stojanović (n 8) 306; Vuković and Kunštek (n 12) 150 and 476.

[71] High Commercial Court, 22 March 2006, Judgment No Pž-1458/03-3; High Commercial Court, 21 September 2006, Judgment N. Pž-3888/03-3.

[72] Constitutional Court of the Republic of Croatia, 8 December 2004, Judgment U-IIIA/1335/2004. As reported in T Ratković, *Private international law of succession – the Croatian experience* (Anali Pravnog fakulteta Univerziteta u Zenici, 2014).

Question 4. Documents to be Produced

Article 67 of the PILA 2017 regulates which documents need to be produced in order for the judgment to be recognised and enforced. Alongside the request for recognition, the proof of finality under the law of the country of origin is to be submitted. Prior rule of Article 87 of the PILA 1982 sought the certificate of finality which lead to discussion whether the certificate of finality or the finality as such is the positive requirement for recognition.[73] With the new PILA 2017 it should be less doubtful that the finality under the law of the country of origin is the necessary prerequisite. Also, if the judgment is to be enforced the certificate of enforceability under the law of the country of origin has to be submitted.

The judgment whose recognition and enforcement are sought has to be translated to Croatian by a certified translator.[74] This is not specifically prescribed by the PILA but a general requirement for all the documents that are to be submitted to court.[75]

Legislative intervention of 2023 brought some doubts as to requirements of legalisation of foreign judgments whose recognition is sought in Croatia. Legalisation of foreign documents is regulated by an old Legalisation of Foreign Documents in International Legal Transactions Act (*Zakon o legalizaciji isprava u međunarodnom prometu*) ('Legalisation Act') from 1970s that has been transposed to Croatian legal system after it gained independence in 1991.[76] The Legalisation Act does not specifically address foreign judgments, but provides that all foreign documents that are to be used in Croatia need to be legalised (subject to international agreements that provide otherwise, such as the Hague Apostille Convention, which Croatia is a contracting state to).[77] This requirement only exists if Croatian documents need to be legalised to be used in the country of origin, ie if the legalisation requirement is reciprocal.[78] Until recently the issue of legalisation of foreign judgments in recognition procedure did not rise any attention either in legal theory or in general public. In December 2022, however, this issue started gaining much attention, albeit regarding adoption decisions stemming from a non-Hague country. Amendments of the 2017 PILA were thus undertaken in June 2023 that provide for an explicit legalisation obligation for non-Hague adoption decision. It is not completely clear if this is a new obligation for this type of decisions only or applies to all decisions, including those in civil and commercial matters, even without an express provision in the 2017 PILA. Some of the public discussion as well as the parliamentary debate point to the direction that the legalisation requirement exists based on the Legalisation Act as such, ie that the term 'used in the territory of the Republic of Croatia' also encompasses recognition procedure. This has also been asserted in legal theory prior to the amendment[79] as well as after.[80] However, an opposite conclusion could be reached if we

[73] Dika, Knežević and Stojanović (n 8) 285–86.
[74] ibid 286.
[75] Arts 6, 104, 232 CPA. Vuković and Kunštek (n 12) 491.
[76] Službeni list SFRJ no 06/73, Narodne novine no 53/91.
[77] Art 1 and Art 3 para 1 Legalisation Act.
[78] Art 3 para 2 Legalisation Act.
[79] M Dika, *Građansko parnično pravo: Utvrđivanje činjenica* (Narodne novine, 2018) 538.
[80] M Župan, P Poretti and J Golub, 'Strane javne isprave u digitalno doba' in J Barbić, *Međunarodno privatno pravo i globalni trenovi* (HAZU, 2024) 115–18.

consider that only the adoption decisions are explicitly mentioned in the 2017 PILA that regulates requirements for recognition.[81] This is even more so if it is taken into account that in the recognition procedure, the judgment's effects are recognised rather than it being used in the territory of Croatia.

Question 5. Securities, Bonds and Deposits

According to the 2017 PILA, a claimant who is not a citizen of the Republic of Croatia or another Member State of the EU or citizen of the Agreement on the European Economic Area (EEA) country or any other international treaty which provides for exemption of the security for costs of procedure, and who has its domicile or seat outside of the Republic of Croatia or another Member State of the EU or citizen of the Agreement on the EEA country or any other international treaty which provides for exemption of the security for costs of procedure, has to, upon request of the respondent, deposit security for costs, unless the decisions on costs made by Croatian court are recognized in the country of the claimant's domicile or seat.[82]

Thus, there are two groups of reasons for the exemption of the deposition of the security for costs. In the first group, the legislator has included a simple and straightforward reason – cases where the claimant is a citizen or is domiciled in an EU Member State, an EEA country or a state which is a party to an international treaty which provides for exemption of the security for costs of procedure. The second group consists of cases where the claimant has its domicile or its seat in a country where the decisions of Croatian courts on costs are recognised. Thus, the latter group is a group of countries with which there is factual reciprocity on decisions on costs. The Croatian Ministry of Justice should, at the request of the competent court, provide information on whether the country of the claimant's domicile recognises the decisions of Croatian courts on costs.[83]

The group of persons that is obligated to provide security on costs is much narrower in the 2017 PILA then in the 1982 PILA, since all citizens and persons domiciled in the EU and EEA are, in line with the European law, exempted from depositing security on costs.

As in the 1982 PILA, the respondent has to make a request for the deposit on costs at the preliminary hearing, or in the case it was not held, on the first hearing on the merits.[84] Security has to be provided in money, unless the court approves otherwise.[85] In case the security was not deposited in a timely fashion, the court will find that the claim was withdrawn.[86]

[81] *cf* ibid 116. M Guštin and B Reštetar, 'Međudržavno posvojenje u Republici Hrvatskoj kroz prizmu slučaja posvojenja djece iz DR Konga' (2023) 73 *Zbornik PFZG* 901 refers to the amendment as introducing an obligation nad not only an option of legalisation with regard to adoption decisions.

[82] Art 61 2017 PILA.

[83] Art 61 2017 PILA provides that Art 8 2017 PILA should be applied accordingly which leads to the conclusion that the Ministry of Justice is competent for providing the information on the recognition of decisions on costs. This view is supported in Sikirić (n 29) 126.

[84] Art 61 para 3 2017 PILA.

[85] Art 61 para 4 2017 PILA.

[86] Art 63 2017 PILA.

The respondent is not allowed the security on costs in cases when: the claim is based on claimants demands from its employment in the Republic of Croatia; it is a marital dispute or a claim on the maternity or paternity or a maintenance claim; it is a counter-claim; the claimant has the right of asylum in the Republic of Croatia.[87]

The majority of published cases deal with the issues of whether the claimant needs to deposit security on costs in case where the claimant is a citizen of a state with which the Republic of Croatia has concluded a multilateral or a bilateral agreement.[88]

However, there are two recent decisions by two different county courts on the basis of Articles 61 and 8 of the 2017 PILA. In both cases the county courts have found that the claimant, domiciled in the US, is obligated to deposit security on costs since it was not proven that the court in the US would recognise the decision on costs provided by the Croatian courts.[89] In one of the two cases, the court reasoned that it was the US claimant's right to try and prove the opposite, but the claimant failed to do that.[90] This would lead to the conclusion that, as for now, the Croatian courts standpoint is that the decisions of the Croatian courts on costs are not recognized in the US, and that, thus, the US claimants in Croatia are obligated to deposit security on costs.

[87] Art 62 2017 PILA.

[88] County Court Varaždin, 18 November 2019, Judgment No Gž 1878/2018-2. County Court Varaždin, 11 August 2010, Judgment No Gž.732/10-2; County Court Zagreb, 16 November 2010, Judgment No Gž-325/10; County Court Vukovar, 9 October 2020, Judgment No Gž 596/2020-2.

[89] County Court Varaždin, 10 January 2022, Judgment No Gž 1576/2021-2; County Court Zadar, 15 March 2023, Judgment No Gž 91/2023-2.

[90] County Court Zadar, 15 March 2023, Judgment No Gž 91/2023-2.

Cyprus

NICOLAS KYRIAKIDES AND KONSTANTINOS ROKAS

Question 1. General Overview

Cyprus,[1] like several other jurisdictions, lacks a unified system for the enforcement of foreign judgments. Depending on the place of issuance of the judgment, different rules apply, and these rules are often prescribed by international conventions.[2] The recognition and enforcement of EU judgments or judgments issued in European Free Trade Association (EFTA) states in civil and commercial matters in Cyprus through Regulations and the Lugano Convention (eg Regulation 1215/2012, Regulation 805/2004) ensures a degree of certainty, efficiency and ease of enforcement. Cyprus as an EU Member State is also bound by The Hague 2005 Convention on Choice of Court Agreements and The Hague 2019 Convention on the Recognition and Enforcement of Foreign Judgments in Civil or Commercial Matters ('the 2019 Hague Convention'). The country is also a contracting party to The Hague Convention on the Recognition and Enforcement of Foreign Judgments in Civil and Commercial Matters ('the 1971 Convention').

Conversely, the recognition and enforcement of non-European Union (EU) judgments depends largely on the existence of a treaty on recognition and enforcement between Cyprus and the countries in which the judgment is issued or the common law regime.[3] Where there is such a treaty, the enforcement of the foreign judgment thereby depends on the specific conventional provisions and their interpretation.[4] In the absence of an applicable treaty, the common law regime applies. A separate regime applies to judgments from the United Kingdom (UK) and other Commonwealth countries.

The national/autonomous rules applicable to the recognition and enforcement of non-EU judgments are to be found in the domestic legislation and the common law regime. The domestic legislation applicable to the recognition and enforcement of non-EU judgments includes the Foreign Court Judgments (Recognition, Registration and Enforcement) Law (121(I)/2000); and The Foreign Judgments (Reciprocal Enforcement) Law of 1935 ('Cap 10'), as amended by the Reciprocal Execution of Certain Judgments

[1] For general information regarding the Cypriot legal traditions, see eg S Symeonides, 'The Mixed Legal System of the Republic of Cyprus' (2003) 78 *Tulane Law Review* 441; N Hatzimichail, 'Cyprus as a Mixed Legal System' (2013) 3 *Journal of Civil Law Studies* 38.

[2] N Koulouris, *Cyprus Civil Procedure* (Nomiki Vivliothiki, 2017) 320; AC Emilianides, *IEL Civil Procedure* (Kluwer, 2020) 234.

[3] ibid.

[4] Loizides & Economou LLC, 'Recognition & Enforcement of Judgments in Cyprus' (10 October 2022), lelaw.com.cy/commercial-litigation/recognition-enforcement-of-judgments-in-cyprus.

of the Commonwealth Countries Law 130(I) of 2000 or, as it is known, The Certain Judgments of Courts of Commonwealth Countries (Reciprocal Enforcement) Law.[5]

The Foreign Court Judgments (Recognition, Registration and Enforcement) Law (121(I)/2000) governs the recognition and enforcement of any foreign judgments issued by any court or tribunal of a foreign country with which Cyprus entered into a bilateral or multilateral agreement for the mutual recognition and enforcement of judgments. From non-EU countries, Cyprus is currently bound by bilateral treaties for the mutual recognition and enforcement of judgments with Belarus, China, Egypt, Georgia, Russia, Serbia, Syria and Ukraine. Moreover, the Republic of Cyprus has concluded bilateral treaties with three EU Member States: Bulgaria, Greece and Czechia.[6] As previously mentioned, Cyprus is also a party to various multilateral conventions concerning the recognition and enforcement of foreign judgments. Consequently, these international conventions play a role in the recognition and enforcement of judgments from non-EU states.

The Foreign Judgments (Reciprocal Enforcement) Law of 1935, Cap 10, as amended by the Reciprocal Execution of Certain Judgments of the Commonwealth Countries Law, 130(I) of 2000, provides for the recognition of judgments issued in the UK, British dominions, protectorates and mandated territories as well as other foreign countries which accord reciprocal treatment to judgments given in the Republic of Cyprus.[7] Cap 10 was enacted when Cyprus was a British Colony, modelling the UK's own Foreign Judgments (Reciprocal Enforcement) Act 1933.[8] This statute now has increasing significance for the UK post-Brexit as a part of the available enforcement regimes. The application of the provisions of Cap 10 means that the recognition and enforcement in Cyprus of judgments given by the UK courts after December 2020 will remain largely unaffected.

In the absence of a convention, treaty or applicable domestic legislation governing the recognition and enforcement of foreign judgments, particularly where the foreign judgment in question does not fall under any of the aforementioned legal frameworks, a final and conclusive judgment for a specified sum rendered by a court in a foreign jurisdiction can be recognised and enforced in Cyprus through a common law action based on the foreign judgment.[9]

In Cypriot law, as in most legal orders, there is a legal distinction between recognition and enforcement.[10] Generally, across all recognition and enforcement regimes, recognition is a mandatory requirement for a foreign judgment to be valid in Cyprus. After recognition, foreign judgments are considered to have the same status and effect as their Cypriot counterparts,[11] and so the judgment can be enforced thereafter. The

[5] A Emilianides, S Shaelou and A Solomou, *IEL Private International Law* (Kluwer, 2015) 114; Koulouris (n 2) 321.

[6] C Demetriades, 'Litigation: Enforcement of foreign judgements in Cyprus' *Lexology* (6 June 2018), lexology.com/library/detail.aspx?g=8218089b-bdfb-45f8-b606-357287279191; C Clerides, 'Enforcement of Foreign Judgments Laws and Regulations Cyprus 2023' *The International Comparative Legal Guide* (31 March 2023), iclg.com/practice-areas/enforcement-of-foreign-judgments-laws-and-regulions/cyprus.

[7] E Christofi et al, 'Law and Practice' (2019), pavlaw.com/wp-content/uploads/2019/09/190829_cyprus_chapter_final.pdf.

[8] N Pirillides, 'Enforcement of English judgments in Cyprus in the post Brexit era' (2021), www.pirilides.com/en/publications/enforcement-of-english-judgments-in-cyprus-in-the-post-brexit-era/ppp-301/220.

[9] Koulouris (n 2) 322; D Campbell et al, *Introduction to Cyprus Law* (Yorkhill Law Publishing, 2000) 105; C Christoforou, *Enforcement of Foreign Judgments* (Kluwer, 2023) 7.

[10] Demetriades (n 6).

[11] Christofi et al (n 7).

recognition of the foreign judgment in Cyprus is a prerequisite to be enforced.[12] Where a foreign judgment is for declaratory relief, or where the defence of *res iudicata* is raised (ie, to prevent the parties from relitigating the same dispute), recognition alone will suffice, and enforcement will not be required.[13]

However, pursuant to Article 5(2) of Law 121 (I)/2000,[14] a judgment creditor is entitled to apply for both recognition and enforcement of a foreign judgment or recognition only.[15] Once a foreign judgment is recognised, it can be enforced in the same way as Cypriot judgments. It results that in principle the recognition and enforcement of a foreign judgment depend on the same basic requirements. Nonetheless, enforcement will not always be necessary for a foreign judgment to produce its effects.

The 2019 Hague Convention has the potential to provide more certainty and stability currently lacking in Cyprus's recognition and enforcement regime. By unifying the law of recognition and enforcement among state parties, it addresses, at least partially, the current lack of cohesion in Cyprus's regime for non-EU judgments, thus offering more certainty to litigants. Of course, the 2019 Hague Convention does leave some space for the application of the default regime for judgments emanating from countries that have not signed and ratified it.

Question 2. Procedure

The procedural requirements for the recognition and enforcement of a judgment might appear to be trivial. Nonetheless, failure to comply with procedural requirements can be crucial for the efficacy of the enforcement of a foreign judgment. Procedural flaws can lead to delays and eventually to a definite frustration of the enforcement.

a) Circumstances of Recognition and Enforcement

The recognition of a foreign judgment happens both informally and incidentally in the context of another trial and as the result of a formal procedure. Informally, a litigant can invoke the recognition of a foreign judgment in the context of another judicial procedure. In that case, the judge must examine whether the applicable conditions under Cypriot law are met to recognise the *res iudicata* effect of the foreign judgment. Besides that, the recognition of a foreign judgment can be requested before a competent court. This will be required when a party seeks the enforcement of this judgment within the Cypriot legal order.

As it concerns the enforcement of a foreign judgment a procedure is required before the competent court. A decision for the enforcement will be required every time a claimant needs to proceed to acts of enforcement in the Cypriot legal order.

[12] ibid.
[13] Pirillides (n 8).
[14] Art 5(2) Foreign Court Judgments (Recognition, Registration and Enforcement) Law of 2000 (121(I)/2000).
[15] Clerides (n 6).

b) Procedural Steps

The competent court for the recognition and enforcement of foreign judgments is the District Court where the respondent has their residence. The litigant who applies for recognition and enforcement bears the burden of proof vis-à-vis the requirements provided by the applicable rules.

Moreover, in Cypriot law, procedural requirements can vary depending on the regime applicable to the recognition and enforcement. A specific regime applies to judgments rendered in the UK, its territories and dominions. The procedural rules regarding judgments issued by the courts of countries with which Cyprus has executed a specific agreement are to be found primarily in this applicable bilateral treaty and, additionally, in the Foreign Court Judgments (Recognition, Registration and Enforcement) Law (2000). Finally, for all judgments not falling within the scope of these two regimes, procedural rules are to be found in common law.

As already explained, judgments obtained in the UK and its territories and dominions are governed by Cap 10, as amended by the Reciprocal Execution of Certain Judgments of the Commonwealth Countries Law 130(I) of 2000.[16] Similar to the common law provisions for recognition and enforcement, Cap 10 indicates that enforcement follows recognition.[17] The procedural requirements are presented in Art 6 of Cap 10 and are similar to common law:

1. The judgment creditor may file an application to the court on an *ex parte* basis (without notifying the other party) requesting the recognition of the foreign judgment.
2. Upon the satisfaction of the court that the foreign judgment should be recognised in Cyprus, an order is issued to that effect.
3. Following its issuance, the order must be served to the judgment debtor, who has the right to dispute the recognition by applying to the court to set aside the registration.

This article also permits the litigating parties to seek an application setting aside the foreign judgment as soon as the judgment is registered, as during the registration process, it cannot be enforced.

The refusal of enforcement is subject to certain factors of enforceability, as well as a question of jurisdictional right, and an assessment of compatibility with Cypriot public policy.[18] More precisely, the judgment can be set aside under Article 6: (i) if the judgment does not constitute a decision or order issued by a court in civil or criminal proceedings involving the payment of compensation or damages to an injured party, or if it is a judgment entered in violation of relevant domestic (Cypriot) legal provisions; (ii) if the courts of the country of origin lacked jurisdiction under the circumstances of the case; (iii) if the judgment debtor, who served as the respondent in the original proceedings, did not receive timely notice of said proceedings, thereby impeding their ability to present a proper defence and participate in the trial; (iv) if the judgment was procured through fraudulent means; (v) if the registration of the judgment would conflict with public policy.

The Foreign Court Judgments (Recognition, Registration and Enforcement) Law 121(I)/2000 ('the Law of 2000') provides a legal framework for foreign

[16] Clerides (n 6).
[17] ibid.
[18] ibid.

judgments passed in jurisdictions with which Cyprus has a bilateral treaty (according to Article 3). The procedure for the Law of 2000 is set out in Article 5[19]

> The procedure begins with the filing by the judgment creditor of an application by summons accompanied by an affidavit, in accordance with the provisions of the Cyprus Civil Procedure Rules.
>
> a. When registering the application, a hearing date is set at a time not exceeding four weeks from the date of its registration.
> b. After the registration of the application, a copy of the application shall be served on the defendant without delay. The Procedural Regulations on Civil Procedure for substitute service may apply.
> c. The defendant submits, if he so wishes, a written objection accompanied by an affidavit on the facts on which he bases his objection at least two days before the date of the hearing of the application.
> d. The reasons on which the defendant may base his objection are limited to the question of the jurisdiction of the court, the proven satisfaction of the decision, and the existence of the conditions laid down in the treaty concerning its application.
> e. The court shall not extend the time limit for filing an objection unless it is convinced that there are special reasons for granting a reasonable extension.
> f. Evidence of the facts may be made either by affidavit or oral testimony at any stage of the proceedings.
> g. At the end of the hearing, the court shall render its decision.

Pursuant to Article 2 of Law 121(1)/2000,[20] Cypriot courts must consider whether they have jurisdiction to proceed with the requested recognition. According to the same article, either the applicant or the respondent must be a resident of Cyprus regardless of the existence of the bilateral treaty between Cyprus and the country that issued the foreign judgment. However, these provisions have been interpreted in different ways by Cypriot courts; in the case *VTB Bank (Open Joint-Stock Company) v Taruta Sergey Alekseyevich*,[21] the Cypriot courts held obiter that Cypriot courts do not have jurisdiction to recognise and enforce foreign judgments where both the judgment creditor and the judgment debtor are foreign residents. The case was issued on the basis of Article 27 of the bilateral Convention between the former Soviet Republic and Cyprus (Law ratifying the Treaty between the Republic of Cyprus and the Union of Soviet Socialist Republics (USSR) on legal assistance in civil and criminal matters, Law 172(1)/86). The judgment leaves room for argument and it is thus uncertain how the issue of jurisdiction will be interpreted by the district courts.[22]

Finally, the Foreign Court Judgments Law of 2000 does provide for specific procedural requirements of form:[23]

> In form, the foreign judgment must: a) Satisfy the conditions necessary to establish its authenticity which are set out in the applicable legal instrument; b) Contain a finality and enforceability clause, unless this is evident by the judgment itself; c) Be accompanied by a

[19] Art 15 Foreign Court Judgments (Recognition, Registration and Enforcement) Law of 2000 (121(I)/2000).
[20] Art 2 Foreign Court Judgments (Recognition, Registration and Enforcement) Law of 2000 (121(I)/2000).
[21] Supreme Court, 2 June 2021, General Application: 378/14 [2021], ECLI:CY:EDLEF:2014:A295, *VTB Bank (Open Joint-Stock Company) v Taruta Sergey Alekseyevich*.
[22] Clerides (n 6).
[23] ibid.

> document certifying that the party against which the judgment was given and who failed to attend the proceedings was duly summoned and in sufficient time to take part in the proceedings according to the law of the contracting party in the territory of which the judgment was given and, in case of incapacity to plead, such party was properly represented; and d) Be accompanied by a certified translation of the application and the above documents in the language of the requested contracting party or into English.

The common law regime is considered the last resort and applies in instances where the foreign judgment in question is not governed by any of the aforementioned regimes. Thus, when no other course of action is available pursuant to any multilateral or bilateral treaty, EU regulation or domestic statute (such as in the case of a British Virgin Islands judgment), the recognition and enforcement of a foreign judgment may be sought via a common law action. This requires initiating a fresh common law action, in which the foreign judgment itself constitutes the cause of action. The judgment creditor may initiate an action before the Cypriot courts requesting an award for damages in the amount of the foreign judgment on the basis of the foreign judgment debt. Within the framework of this procedure, it is possible to apply for the issue of a summary judgment on the ground that the defendant (ie, the judgment debtor) has no defence. This regime is based on common law precedents and is not codified in a statute. Therefore, its application is not absolute and must be approached on a case-by-case basis. Cypriot courts will assume jurisdiction where the judgment debtor's place of residency is Cyprus or, in limited circumstances, when they retain assets in Cyprus. It has not yet been clarified whether common law actions for recognition of foreign judgments could be adjudicated in cases where the judgment debtor is a non-Cypriot resident who retains assets within the jurisdiction that may be used towards the satisfaction of the judgment debt.

Under common law, both of the following options appear to be possible in Cyprus, ie to file an action based on the foreign judgment, requesting its recognition and enforcement, or to file an action based on the cause of action of the foreign judgment, requesting a judgment for a sum of money. In the former case, it would result in a declaratory judgment, while in the latter case it would be a judgment for a sum of money.

The above is based on this Supreme Court judgment *Constantinou Achilleas and ors v Dimokritos Publications Company Ltd and anor* (1996) 1 CLR 206, which stated:

> As we mentioned earlier, it appears from the various authorities to which we have referred, that when a foreign judgment is not registrable, then under common law the beneficiary of the foreign judgment can file an action based on the foreign judgment as a cause of action. He can still file a lawsuit without relying on the foreign decision, but on the facts that give rise to his right.

The procedure is as follows.[24] The claimant has to fill out a claim form with statements of case relying on the facts which created the cause of action for the foreign judgment. The claimant has the burden of proof. Then it is required to apply for a summary judgment under the Cyprus Civil Procedure Rules, on the ground that the defendant has no reasonable prospect of defending the claim. In case of a successful

[24] ibid.

application, the defendant is prevented from defending the case and the Cypriot court can make a declaration of enforceability, allowing the applicant to use any method of enforcement. These available means of enforcement[25] are mentioned in the Civil Procedure Law (Cap 6), the old Civil Procedure Rules (Rules 40–43) and the new Civil Procedure Rules (Parts 47–53).[26] Cypriot courts are precluded, in the context of a common law action, from reviewing the foreign judgment on the merits. However, they can examine, at least incidentally, issues of substance resolved by the foreign court since the defendants have the right to defend themselves by advancing arguments linked to the case judged before the foreign court. The defendant might allege and prove any of the following to secure that the common law action will be dismissed:

(a) The foreign judgment is not final and conclusive. A final judgment is final in the court in which the judgment was made and may not be re-adjudicated by the same court.
(b) The foreign court did not have jurisdiction over the parties. A foreign judgment is only enforceable if the foreign court has jurisdiction according to domestic principles of private international law. It is not sufficient if the foreign court had jurisdiction according to its own legal rules.
(c) The judgment is contrary to the public policy of the forum state. The judgment itself (and not the underlying transaction on which the judgment is based) must offend domestic public policy.
(d) The foreign judgment offends the principles of natural justice or substantial justice enshrined in the domestic legal system; for example, if the defendant was not given due notice of the original proceedings (with the result that judgment was obtained in default) or was not given a fair opportunity to be heard.
(e) The judgment was fraudulently obtained. This could involve fraud on the part of the party in whose favour the judgment is given or fraud on the part of the court delivering the judgment. Where a defendant relies on fraud on the part of a foreign court, it has to adduce evidence to establish that there was an improper influence (bias) of the foreign court and show that the foreign court's findings were deliberately wrong and not merely incompetent.
(f) Recognition of the foreign judgment would result in the contravention of the European Convention on Human Rights (ECHR).
(g) The dispute in question should be submitted to the determination of the courts of another country.
(h) The judgment imposes a fine or a penalty upon the judgment debtor.
(i) There exists a previous final and conclusive judgment of a competent foreign or domestic court with sufficient jurisdiction that conflicts with the judgment that is being sought to be enforced through the common law action/summary judgment.

[25] See N Kyriakides and A Plevri, 'Enforcement in Cyprus in Urgent Need of Reform: A Review and Critical Appraisal of the Current Enforcement Process' (2021) 8 *South East European Law Journal* 103.

[26] For the old and new Civil Procedure Rules in Cyprus see eg Institute of Public Administration, *Progress Report: Review of the Rules of Civil Procedure of Cyprus* (2018); N Kyriakides, 'Cyprus Civil Justice System Reform: Developing a national identity' (2019) 31 *Cyprus Review* 31; N Kyriakides, A Shrikhande and L Stefanatos, 'The Rocket Docket System: A Model for Active Case Management in Countries Facing Judicial Delays' (2021) 34 *New York International Law Review* 79.

The claimant and the defendant can appeal against the Cypriot decision that grants the summary judgment before the Court of Appeal of Cyprus.[27] The judgment on the claim filed is binding for all Cypriot courts.

Since enforcement follows recognition under common law, a judgment cannot be enforced in Cyprus before it is recognised; once recognition takes place, it can be enforced in the same way that a Cypriot judgment would be enforced.[28]

For judgments falling within the common law regime, Cypriot courts do not have the obligation to establish a degree of connection with the Cypriot legal order.[29] If there is no real connection to the jurisdiction in civil actions, the courts can, in exceptional circumstances, dismiss such an action on the basis of the *forum non conveniens* principle.[30]

In addition to the procedural requirements that have just been explained, one should examine the conditions of the 2019 Hague Convention. This Convention was concluded on 2 July 2019 and has been in force throughout the EU (including Cyprus) since 1 September 2023. It has also been signed by Israel, the Russian Federation, Costa Rica, Montenegro, North Macedonia, Ukraine, the United States, and Uruguay. Beyond the EU Member States, the Convention has also entered into force in Ukraine and Uruguay. However, it is worth mentioning that Cyprus has also signed and ratified the 1971 Convention, signed as well and ratified by Albania, the Netherlands, Portugal and Kuwait.[31] Still, this Convention has not come into force, since the supplementary Agreement required under Article 21 of the 1971 Convention has not been signed by Cyprus and the aforementioned contracting states. Had this agreement been signed, this Convention would still be of limited interest given that the only non-EU Member States bound are Albania and Kuwait. That said, the entry into force of the 2019 Hague Convention leaves practically no margin for the future application of the 1971 Convention.

Question 3. Requirements

As noted, the legal requirements that need to be met for recognition and enforcement of a foreign judgment depend on the recognition and enforcement regime applicable to the country of origin of the judgment. Each regime provides for specific positive and negative requirements for the recognition and enforcement of a foreign judgment.

Regarding the bilateral treaties, there is no holistic approach in Law 121(I)/2000.[32] The requirements are determined by the treaty, which is applicable each time. However, some conditions are common to all the treaties,[33] namely: i. The foreign judgment must be final and binding; ii. The defendant should have been duly summoned in sufficient time to take part in the proceedings according to the law of the contracting party in the territory of which the judgment was given and, in case of incapacity to plead, the

[27] *Trans Middle East Trading Ltd v Abdul Aziz Tlais* (1991) 1 CLR 239.
[28] Clerides (n 6).
[29] ibid.
[30] ibid.
[31] ibid.
[32] ibid.
[33] ibid.

defendant was properly represented; iii. The recognition must not be contrary to Cypriot public policy; iv. The judgment has not been obtained by fraud; v. The actionable right should not be covered by *res iudicata*; and vi. The proceedings should not be frivolous or vexatious or constitute an abuse of the court's process.[34]

The different requirements will be examined in the light of each separate regime.

a) Jurisdiction of the Court of Origin

The jurisdiction of the court of origin is one of the basic requirements for the recognition and enforcement of a foreign judgment in Cyprus.[35] This requirement is common to all applicable regimes. According to the Law of 2000 on judgments from countries with which there is a bilateral or multilateral agreement, the judgment must have been rendered by a court of competent jurisdiction.

Under Cap 10 on Judgments of Commonwealth countries, the courts may examine the issue of personal jurisdiction in an application to set aside the recognition or enforcement of the foreign judgment. According to the same rules, the court that has issued the judgment must have been a superior court and must have had jurisdiction in the circumstances of the case.[36] Otherwise, this judgment cannot be recognised.

In relation to the common law regime, the Cypriot court will consider whether the court that issued the foreign judgment had jurisdiction over the defendant in accordance with the rules applicable in Cyprus. Any recognition and enforcement will be refused if the 'issuing court lacks jurisdiction according to the rules of Cyprus'.

Given that Cypriot courts establish their jurisdiction in international cases very broadly it seems that it will be difficult to oppose the recognition of a foreign judgment in Cyprus on grounds of lack of jurisdiction. This will be possible in cases where foreign courts have based their competence on an exorbitant jurisdictional basis or when the conditions of the *forum non conveniens* theory seem to be met.

b) Finality/Enforceability in the Country of Origin

If the foreign judgment is not final or conclusive, the recognition and enforcement of a foreign judgment can be refused. A final judgment is final in the country in which it was made, and it may not be re-adjudicated by the courts that issued it, even if an appeal is pending before the higher courts of the country in which the judgment was made. The judgment therefore creates *res iudicata* for the parties to the foreign proceedings. Bilateral treaties and the Law of 2000 also require that the foreign judgment is final and binding. The same applies to judgments from the Commonwealth. According to section 3(2)(a) of Cap 10, 'any judgment of a superior Court of a foreign country … shall be a judgment to which this Part of this Law applies, if – (a) it is final and conclusive as

[34] ibid.

[35] K Karatsis and A Argyrou, 'Enforcement of Foreign Judgements: Cyprus' *Lexology* (August 2020), pirilides.com/assets/modules/ppp/publications/219/docs/2021_enforcement_of_foreign_judgments_cyprus.pdf.

[36] Loizides & Economou LLC (n 4).

between the parties thereto'. In addition to that, section 4(1) provides that 'a judgment shall not be registered if at the date of the application – … (b) it could not be enforced by execution in the country of the original Court'. Moreover, where an appeal is pending in the country where the judgment was initially issued or may be filed by the judgment debtor, the Cypriot courts have the discretion to set aside the recognition and enforcement of the judgment. Where this is the case, the court will provide the judgment debtor with a timeframe in which the appeal must be heard.[37] Under common law, the foreign judgment must also be final and conclusive.[38]

c) *Res Judicata*

For recognition and enforcement proceedings governed by common law or domestic legislation, the courts will refuse recognition of a foreign judgment if there is a conflicting Cypriot or foreign judgment of a competent foreign or Cypriot court with sufficient jurisdiction on the same cause of action and between the same parties.[39] Necessary adherence to the principle of *res iudicata*, which is applicable in Cyprus, justifies this requirement; these judgments are final, and so cannot be re-litigated by those bound by the judgment. The irreconcilability with another judgment as a negative condition regarding decisions from countries with which there is a bilateral treaty and governed by the Law of 2000 depends on the specific provisions of the applicable treaty.[40] As a principle, the regime applicable under the law of 2000 requires that the actionable right should not be covered by *res iudicata*. As regards Cap 10, the Cypriot courts may set aside a foreign judgment if a final judgment regarding the same matter has already been issued in another court (section 6(1)(b)).[41]

d) *Lis Pendens*

Neither Cypriot nor pending foreign proceedings between the same parties over the same cause of action will hinder the recognition and enforcement of a non-EU judgment under the common law.[42] Under domestic legislation, pending foreign proceedings in general will also not hinder recognition and enforcement of a non-EU judgment. However, recognition and enforcement proceedings in relation to a foreign judgment may be stayed (either partially or completely) by the courts where the pending foreign proceedings are an appeal of the foreign judgment in the court of origin, or where a finding is made that the time for an appeal has not yet expired.[43]

Cap 10 provides that where an appeal is pending in the country where the judgment was initially issued or may be filed by the judgment debtor, the Cypriot courts have the discretion to set aside the recognition and enforcement of the judgment. Where this

[37] Christofi et al (n 7).
[38] Clerides (n 6).
[39] Clerides (n 6).
[40] ibid.
[41] ibid.
[42] Demetriades (n 6).
[43] ibid.

is the case, the court will provide the judgment debtor with a timeframe in which the appeal must be heard.

e) Specific Requirements of Due Process

Due process is also a basic condition for the recognition and enforcement of foreign judgments. The Cypriot courts must assess whether all parties in the original proceedings had been duly served, whether the defendant was given a fair hearing, and whether the defendant received sufficient notice of proceedings to defend or contest them. The requirement for due process is central to the recognition of a foreign judgment as it serves the purpose of ensuring a fair trial. In particular, for judgments covered by a bilateral and multilateral treaty and the Law of 2000, the defendant should have been duly summoned in sufficient time to take part in the proceedings according to the law of the contracting party in the territory of which the judgment was given and, in case of incapacity to plead, the defendant was properly represented. Also under Cap 10, the judgment debtor must have received notice of the original proceedings in England or the respective Commonwealth country in sufficient time to enable him to defend the proceedings, and thus did not appear.[44] Thus, it will not be possible to have recognised and enforced any foreign judgment rendered in violation of the right of defence of the respondent.

f) Public Policy

Public policy is a requirement universally accepted for the recognition and enforcement of foreign judgments. It is a condition present in all international treaties and there is also an explicit reference to it in Cap 10. The same holds for the recognition and enforcement of decisions that fall within the scope of common law. According to common law, recognition and enforcement will be refused where the foreign judgment is contrary to the requirements of natural justice. Such ground, although difficult to define accurately, will most probably coincide with public policy. Under Article 6(1)(a)(v) of Cap 10[45] and the common law, the courts in Cyprus will not recognise or enforce a foreign judgment contrary to public policy. The notion of 'public policy' remains undefined in Cypriot legislation. However, a possible definition for this may be: 'the totality of fundamental values, perceptions and ideas on which the ethical, financial and political order regulate Cypriot society at a certain time'.[46] An example of foreign judgments that may be contrary to public policy can include those: obtained by fraud; obtained in breach of Article 6 of the ECHR or other fundamental rights of the parties.[47] However, if recognition and enforcement are sought under Law 121(I)/2000, the examination of the

[44] Clerides (n 6).
[45] Art 6 Foreign Judgments (Reciprocal Enforcement) Law of 1935.
[46] M Kyriakides, O Shelyagova and A Daoudi, 'Cyprus' in M Moedritzer and KC Whittaker (eds), *Enforcement of Foreign Judgments 2012* (London Business Research Ltd, 2011).
[47] Christofi et al (n 7).

public policy element will depend on the wording of any applicable bilateral or multilateral treaty.[48]

g) Reciprocity

For recognition and enforcement of non-EU judgment where treaties and conventions are applicable, the principle of reciprocity applies, so a foreign judgment cannot be recognised in Cyprus unless the courts of the foreign country are also willing to recognise an identical judgment that had been issued by Cypriot courts.[49] However, the question of reciprocity will also depend on the applicable treaty and one should bear in mind that in practice it will be difficult for Cypriot courts to examine and verify the reciprocity. The Law of 2000 and Cap 10 do not provide such a requirement explicitly, nor does any specific provision exist as regards reciprocity under common law. It is to be noted that one of the positive requirements for recognition and enforcement of Cap 10 is that the Ministry of Councils has extended the applicability of this law to a foreign country.[50] It is reasonable to assume that such an extension will generally not occur in the absence of reciprocity in the recognition and enforcement of Cypriot judgments within that foreign legal order.

h) Other Requirements

Among other requirements, fraud has often been construed as a separate negative requirement for the recognition and enforcement of a foreign judgment. Under common law and domestic legislation, if the judgment is obtained by fraud, the enforcement of the judgment is likely to be refused on such grounds. However, the party who wishes to successfully challenge the recognition of the judgment on this ground must have strong and concrete evidence of the alleged fraud before the Cypriot court.[51] Under Article 6(1)(a)(iv) of Cap 10,[52] a recognised or enforced judgment may be set aside if the judgment is obtained by fraud. It must be stressed that a judgment obtained as a result of fraudulent behaviour can also be sanctioned separately under the public policy exception.

There are also other additional requirements depending on the applicable regime. Thus, under Cap 10, among the negative requirements for recognition and enforcement for which the recognition of the judgment may be set aside are, that the foreign judgment cannot be enforced by execution in the original jurisdiction; and that the rights under the foreign judgment are not attributable to the person who is seeking its registration and enforcement. The same requirement also exists under common law.[53]

[48] Clerides (n 6).
[49] Christofi et al (n 7).
[50] Loizides & Economou LLC (n 4).
[51] Christofi et al (n 7).
[52] Art 6 Foreign Judgments (Reciprocal Enforcement) Law of 1935.
[53] Clerides (n 6).

Under Cap 10, among the positive requirements for recognition and enforcement, it is required that:

> The Ministry of Councils decided to extent the applicability of this Law to that foreign country; the judgment was issued by a superior court; there is a payable thereunder a sum of money, not being a sum payable in respect of taxes or other charges of a like nature or in respect of a fine or other penalty; and the judgment was given after the coming into operation of the order of the Ministry of Councils.[54]

To sum up, whilst the requirements do vary amongst the enforcement regimes, the general requirements for recognition and enforcement of a foreign judgment under all applicable regimes can thus be summarised as following:

> The judgment was given by a court having jurisdiction to entertain the underlying claim under the legal regime applicable to that claim, provided that the case was not within the exclusive jurisdiction of the Cypriot courts; the courts of Cyprus have jurisdiction over the judgment debtor; the judgment is final and conclusive; the judgment is enforceable in the state of origin by way of execution; the judgment was not obtained by fraud and is not contrary to the public policy of Cyprus; there is no conflicting Cypriot judgment issued in proceedings between the same parties, based on the same subject matter; in the case of a judgment rendered in default, if the judgment creditor can prove that the defaulting party received, under the law of the state of origin, sufficient notice that proceedings had been commenced against them, both in terms of form and time.[55]

Moreover, as a general rule, under both common law and domestic legislation, the Cypriot courts cannot review the merits of a foreign judgment at the recognition and or enforcement stage.[56] However, as already explained, the Cypriot courts can examine in the context of a common law action objections based on the substance of the right adjudicated by the foreign judgment. Finally, despite the existence of these general requirements, amongst the enforcement regimes, there are notable distinctions concerning these requirements, which will be drawn out.

By examining the requirements for recognition and enforcement of non-EU judgments, it is apparent that the rules lack consistency across all enforcement regimes, showing the inherent complexity of Cyprus's enforcement regime.

Question 4. Documents to be Produced

The documentary requirements depend on the enforcement regime applicable to the foreign judgment. In general, regarding the recognition and enforcement of non-EU foreign judgments, the judgment creditor must provide the Cypriot enforcing courts with the following documentation:

(i) a complete, certified copy of the foreign judgment, authenticated by its seal;

[54] Loizides & Economou LLC (n 4).
[55] Demetriades (n 6).
[56] E Christofi and Y Lambrianou, 'Enforcement of Judgments 2022' (Chambers and Partners, 2 August 2022), practiceguides.chambers.com/practice-guides/enforcement-of-judgments-2022/cyprus.

(ii) if the foreign judgment was rendered by default, the originals or true copies of the documents required to establish that the summons was duly served on the judgment debtor;
(iii) a Greek translation of the judgment, or, where expressly provided, an English translation, certified as correct by a diplomatic or consular agent, a sworn translator, or any person so authorised; and
(iv) expert legal advice under the law of the country of issue confirming that the foreign judgment is final and enforceable in the country where the foreign judgment was issued.[57]

Question 5. Securities, Bonds and Deposits

The costs involved in the enforcement of a foreign judgment vary depending on the procedure followed, as well as personal factors, such as the agreement between a client and their counsel.[58] The general rule is that the unsuccessful party in litigation is ordered to pay the costs of the successful party.

The old as well as the new Cyprus Civil Procedure Rules also have a provision for security for costs (Order 60 of the old Rules and Part 26 of the new Rules), which states that a defendant who is ordinarily resident outside of the EU may at any stage be ordered to give security for costs while it creates an exception for foreign workers with a low income.[59] The Court does have the power to exercise its discretion where the claimant is due to give security for costs in actions brought by non-EU residents if the claimant's claim is founded on a judgment, order, or negotiable instrument.[60]

The provision specifies what is to happen in the event of bonds being given as security for costs: unless the Court exercises its discretion, the bonds will be given directly to the relevant party, rather than an officer of the Court.[61] Although there is no such specificity with regard to the payment of securities or deposits, it would be safe to assume that these methods of settling costs do not go directly to the relevant parties.

Under the Hague 2019 Convention, Article 14(1) provides that no securities, bonds or deposits are required because the applicant is a foreign national or is not domiciled in the state in which they are seeking enforcement.[62] This is a significant difference from the current provisions in the Civil Procedure Rules, which do make a distinction as to the origins of the parties.

[57] Demetriades (n 6).
[58] Christofi and Lambrianou (n 56).
[59] ibid pt 26.1(1).
[60] ibid pt 26.1(2).
[61] ibid pt 26.1(6).
[62] Art 14(1) Convention on the Recognition and Enforcement of Foreign Judgments in Civil or Commercial Matters (The Hague, 2 July 2019).

Czech Republic

PATRIK PROVAZNÍK AND RADOVAN MALACHTA

Question 1. General Overview

As of 1 January 2014, rules for the recognition and enforcement of foreign judgments have been codified in Act No 91/2012 Coll, on Private International Law ('Czech PILA'). This Act has become an integral part of the overall recodification of private law in the Czech Republic, although one can observe a clear ideological continuity with the previously effective Act No. 97/1963 Coll, on Private International Law and Procedure. The Czech PILA also reflects recent developments at the regional and international level, but it cannot be said that these sources directly shaped the Czech national approach.

The Czech PILA generally applies in situations that are not covered by an EU regulation or a bilateral or multilateral international treaty[1] – questions of recognition and enforcement of foreign judgments being no exception in this respect.[2] Therefore, since several EU regulations and international treaties largely exhaust the issue of recognition and enforcement of foreign judgments, the general regime provided for under the Czech PILA does not attract much scholarly attention. Nevertheless, practitioners still need to resort to national rules on a daily basis in cases falling outside the scope of other instruments.[3]

The general approach of the Czech legislator as to the requirements for recognition and enforcement of foreign judgments follows from the provisions of Sections 14 and 15 of the Czech PILA. Within this framework, the rules are set out as follows. Section 14 lays down the positive requirements for the effectiveness of foreign judgments in the Czech Republic – namely the finality of the foreign judgment and its recognition in the Czech Republic – and defines what is meant by a foreign judgment for its purposes. Section 15 establishes a general framework of exceptions to the otherwise applicable principle of recognition of foreign judgments in the form of a list of grounds for refusal of recognition, and thus also possible enforcement of foreign judgments in the Czech Republic. The grounds for refusal of recognition can be described as negatively defined requirements for recognition, which are appended to the positively defined requirement for the finality of the foreign judgment.

[1] Section 2 Czech PILA.

[2] It should, however, be noted that the rules stipulated in the Czech PILA apply even where a case falls within the scope of application of an international treaty but the treaty does not comprehensively regulate the issue of recognition of foreign judgments.

[3] P Dobiáš, '§ 14' in P Dobiáš et al (eds), *Zákon o mezinárodním právu soukromém: komentář: podle právního stavu k 1. lednu 2014* (Leges, 2013) 93.

Section 15 of the Czech PILA exhaustively sets out a total of six grounds, or categories of grounds, which build ideologically on Section 64 of the Private International Law and Procedure Act of 1963. However, as these are deemed to be exceptions to the recognition of foreign judgments, it is necessary to interpret them strictly, so as to preserve their nature of exceptions to the general rule.

Section 16 addresses the process of recognition and enforcement itself, distinguishing between recognition of foreign judgments in 'property matters' and so-called 'other matters'. The principal difference being whether or not recognition is subject to a separate recognition procedure resulting in a special decision. Modifications to the general framework can be provided for in the special part of the Czech PILA, especially in the areas of family law and status matters.

As for the documentation that is required by Czech public authorities deciding on recognition (and enforcement), it should be noted that the statutory regulation does not provide any overview or list of such documents. Thus, the requirements will vary depending on the subject matter of the foreign judgment to be recognised.

Regarding the enforcement procedure itself, the Czech legislation provides for a double-track policy, which means that enforcement is governed by two acts, namely the Code of Civil Procedure (Act No 99/1963 Coll) and the Enforcement Code (Act No 120/2001 Coll).[4] It is then up to the judgment creditor to choose whether to opt for 'judicial enforcement' or enforcement by a bailiff.

In the enforcement proceedings, it may also be necessary to lodge a deposit for the costs of enforcement. These issues are also governed by national rules in the Code of Civil Procedure and the Enforcement Code. If the judgment creditor is habitually resident abroad, the Czech PILA provides for the possibility of their exemption from having to lodge the deposit under the condition of reciprocity.

The following table provides a brief overview of the rules.

Recognition of foreign judgments	Section 14 Czech PILA	General provision, definition of a 'foreign judgment', requirements for the effectiveness of foreign judgments in the Czech Republic
	Section 15 Czech PILA	Grounds for refusal of recognition of foreign judgments
	Section 16 Czech PILA	Procedure for recognition of foreign judgments, orders for enforcement of judgments

(continued)

[4] In the Enforcement Code, the following rules are stipulated in Section 37 paragraph 3(c) and paragraph 4(b)(c). The creditor is not entitled to file a motion for enforcement if the enforcement title is a foreign judgment or a foreign arbitral award, unless otherwise stipulated in paragraph 4(b) or 4(c). 'The creditor may file a motion for enforcement if the enforcement is to be carried out based on a (b) foreign judgment: 1. for which a declaration of enforceability has been issued pursuant to a directly applicable regulation of the EU or an international treaty; or 2. that is enforceable under a directly applicable regulation of the European Union EU declaration of enforceability; or (c) a foreign judgment or foreign arbitral award that has been recognized by a decision.'

(Continued)

	Sections 38, 40, 51, 52, 55, 58, 63, 66, 67, 79, 111 Czech PILA	Special rules for recognition of foreign judgments (in particular, family, inheritance, bankruptcy, and personal status matters)
Enforcement of foreign judgments	Code of Civil Procedure	Judicial enforcement
	Enforcement Code	Enforcement carried out by a bailiff

Question 2. Procedure

a) Circumstances of Recognition and Enforcement

Recognition and enforcement of foreign judgments represent two different phases of (international) civil procedure. Regarding the recognition phase under Czech law, this phase differs depending on whether it concerns a judgment in 'property matters' or in the so-called 'other (non-property) matters'.[5] The notion of 'property matters' (and 'other matters') has to be interpreted in accordance with the law of the forum and is interpreted extensively by Czech courts. In general, it can be said that a 'property right' is always involved if the result of the court proceedings may affect or does affect the property of the plaintiff.[6] 'Other matters' include, in particular, status issues and certain family law matters, or more generally, judgments involving non-property matters.[7]

b) Procedural Steps

1. Recognition

Section 16 Czech PILA sets these out as follows.

	Recognition of a foreign judgment in 'property matters'	**Recognition of a foreign judgment in 'other matters'**
	No special recognition proceedings apply	Recognised by a special decision
This does not apply:	If a ground for refusal of recognition is invoked which could not have been taken into account *ex officio*; in this case, special recognition proceedings are required.	If the Czech PILA explicitly provides that foreign judgments are recognised without any further (special) proceedings.

[5] Section 16 Czech PILA.

[6] Resolution of the Supreme Court of the Czech Republic, 10 October 2008, Ref No 21 Cdo 3967/2007.

[7] M Jirmanová, '§ 16 (Uznání cizích rozhodnutí)' in M Pauknerová et al (eds), *Zákon o mezinárodním právu soukromém: Komentář* (Wolters Kluwer, 2013) 117–18; T Břicháček, '§ 16 (Postup uznání a výkonu)' in P Bříza et al (eds), *Zákon o mezinárodním právu soukromém: komentář* (CH Beck, 2014) 110.

There are no special recognition proceedings (no separate decision on recognition) for:

(a) foreign judgments in 'property matters';
(b) foreign judgments in 'other matters' where the Czech PILA explicitly provides so. This is the case in 'other matters' involving only foreigners (in other words, in cases that do not concern Czech citizens), specifically in status and family matters.[8]

In these matters, recognition of a foreign judgment is not pronounced by any special statement or judgment. Foreign judgments are recognised simply by means of the fact that the respective public authority takes them into consideration, as if they were a judgment of a Czech public authority, provided that the requirements for recognition under the Czech PILA are met. Recognition can thus occur automatically within another proceedings, such as in the context of enforcement of a judgment.[9] As there is no separate decision on recognition, there is also no possibility of appeal.

Special recognition proceedings are conducted (and a separate decision issued):

(a) for foreign judgments in 'other matters' (except for the cases listed in footnote 7);
(b) for foreign judgments in 'property matters', if a ground for refusal of recognition, which could not have been taken into account *ex officio*, is invoked by a party to the proceedings (ie, any of the grounds listed in Section 15; Czech PILA explicitly mentions the ground based on the breach of public policy). From a procedural point of view, in such a case, the main proceedings are suspended and a deadline for commencing the proceedings for refusal of recognition is designated. The proceedings then continue either after the expiry of the aforementioned deadline (if the party does not initiate proceedings for refusal of recognition within the deadline), or after the proceedings for refusal of recognition are decided (by becoming final) – in such a case, the decision is binding on the court. If the plaintiff is successful in the proceedings for refusal of recognition, the court shall reject recognition;
(c) for foreign judgments in both property and non-property matters, at a separate request of a party.[10]

In these cases, recognition of a foreign judgment is not automatic. The court[11] decides whether the foreign judgment meets the requirements for recognition. Although

[8] Břicháček (n 7) 110–11; J Valdhans, 'Uznání a výkon cizích soudních rozhodnutí' in N Rozehnalová et al, *Úvod do mezinárodního práva soukromého* (Wolters Kluwer ČR, 2017) 276. Specifically, these include matters of the limitation and deprivation of legal capacity and the guardianship of a foreigner, the declaration of a foreigner as dead or missing, the dissolution of marriage, legal separation, the declaration of a marriage as invalid and the designation of whether or not a marriage exists, as well as in matters of the establishment and denial of parenthood, the upbringing, maintenance and custody of minors, the wardship and guardianship of minors, and in the matters of annulment, invalidity and non-existence of a registered partnership or a similar relationship; foreign judgments in matters of registered partnerships and similar relationships are subject to this 'no special recognition treatment', even in cases involving a Czech citizen.

[9] Valdhans (n 8) 276.

[10] Section 16 Czech PILA; P Dobiáš, '§ 16' in P Dobiáš et al (eds), *Zákon o mezinárodním právu soukromém: komentář: podle právního stavu k 1. lednu 2014* (Leges, 2013) 103; Břicháček (n 7) 113; Jirmanová (n 7) 118.

[11] Section 16 Czech PILA does not apply to courts only, as foreign judgments can also be invoked before other public authorities. It is true, however, that in most cases, foreign judgments will be relied on and invoked within judicial proceedings.

possible, there is no need to hold a hearing for such a decision.[12] The form of the court's decision is a judgment. Since a separate judgment is issued, there is a possibility of appeal.[13] An exception are judgments of the Supreme Court, which in certain cases decides on recognition of a foreign judgment in the first instance (see below) which are not subject to appeal.

It should be emphasised that in matters where there are no separate recognition proceedings, the competent public authority will consider recognition as a preliminary question, and such consideration does not constitute *res iudicata*. In contrast, in cases where separate recognition proceedings are conducted and a special recognition judgment issued, this does constitute *res iudicata*.[14]

1.1. Authorities with Subject Matter and Local Jurisdiction

Where there are no separate proceedings for recognition of a foreign judgment, no special rules of jurisdiction apply. Recognition shall be assessed by the court hearing the case in which the recognition of a foreign judgment is invoked or where the foreign judgment is otherwise relevant for the case.[15]

Where separate proceedings for the recognition of a foreign judgment are conducted, the Czech legislation (Section 16(4) of the Czech PILA) establishes that it is district courts (ie, the lowest level of the judicial system in the Czech Republic) that have subject matter jurisdiction in the first instance. Local jurisdiction is exercised by the general court of the party seeking recognition. In order to determine the general court of the petitioner, the rules laid down in the rules of procedure – the Code of Civil Procedure (99/1963 Coll) or the Act on Special Court Proceedings (292/2013 Coll) – are applicable.[16] The petitioner's court of general jurisdiction is the court in whose district the natural person is domiciled or the legal person has its seat (the Code of Civil Procedure lays down further rules), or the court of general jurisdiction of the person in whose interest the proceedings are brought (under the rule stipulated in the Special

[12] The judgment of the Supreme Court of 14 June 2022 can serve as an example. In this case, the Supreme Court annulled a judgment of an appellate court regarding the recognition of a Russian judgment concerning the settlement of the joint property of spouses. The ground for annulment was the alleged lack of jurisdiction of the Russian court – it was disputed whether the change of residence of one party constituted evasion of the law (rules of private international law). According to the Supreme Court, the lower courts are obliged, among other things, to deal with the mentioned objection and thoroughly examine the temporal sequence between the change of residence of the party and the conduct of foreign judicial proceedings, the intention of the party in the proceedings to permanently reside in the new residence, and their motivation. We present this judgment for two reasons: (a) although the case is a case in property matters, separate recognition proceedings were conducted at a request of a party; (b) in the ongoing proceedings, the parties will be heard and, if necessary, evidence will be presented concerning the relevant facts. This is an example where a hearing, although not required to be held by the Czech PILA, may be ordered (similarly to the judgment of the Supreme Court of 15 September 2021, Case No 20 Cdo 705/2021, to which the commented judgment refers) – *cf* Judgment of the Supreme Court of the Czech Republic, 14 June 2022, Ref No 20 Cdo 1375/2022.

[13] Břicháček (n 7) 113; Jirmanová (n 7) 119.

[14] Břicháček (n 7) 113.

[15] Z Kučera et al, *Mezinárodní právo soukromé,* 9th edn (Vydavatelství a nakladatelství Aleš Čeněk, sro, 2022) 396.

[16] For the sake of completeness, we would like to add that the former applies to so-called contested proceedings (eg, property matters), while the latter applies to so-called non-contested proceedings (eg, the question of a person's legal capacity, matrimonial and partnership matters, etc).

Court Proceedings Act). These regulations, however, also provide further rules on how to determine local jurisdiction of the court.

The Czech PILA also accounts for situations where the petitioner does not have a general court in the territory of the Czech Republic. In such a case, it is the district court in whose district the circumstances for which the recognition is relevant have occurred or may occur that has jurisdiction (Section 16(4) of the Czech PILA). However, as pointed out in the commentary literature,[17] the determination of local jurisdiction under this rule is unlikely due to the existence of the broad rules mentioned above.

An interesting exception to these rules is the special provision for foreign judgments in cases of divorce (or legal separation, declaration of nullity of marriage and determination of whether or not a marriage exists) and in cases of establishment and denial of parenthood, provided that at least one of the parties to the proceedings was a citizen of the Czech Republic. In these cases, it is the Supreme Court of the Czech Republic, as the highest court within the system of general courts in the Czech Republic, that has jurisdiction (Sections 51 and 55 of the Czech PILA).

1.2. The Burden of Proving the Requirements for Recognition

Recognition proceedings are initiated upon filing a separate request. It thus follows from the nature of such proceedings that it is the petitioner who must provide the necessary facts or attach evidence to the request (see Question 4). It is the petitioner who bears the burden of proof and it is their responsibility to submit to the court all the documents or fulfil the requirements imposed on them. The court does not, of its own motion, ascertain the existence or non-existence of any such requirements.

1.3. Review of the Judgment on the Merits

Although the Czech PILA does not regulate this issue explicitly, it is generally accepted that the courts are prohibited from reviewing the foreign judgment as to its merits (*révision au fond*). The review is limited to verifying whether the requirements for recognition and enforcement as prescribed by law are met.[18]

2. *Enforcement*

Under Section 16(5) Czech PILA, a foreign judgment on 'property matters' that meets the requirements for its recognition under this Act may be enforced by a decision of a Czech court, which must be reasoned. Thus, enforcement is only available in 'property matters'.[19] As pointed out in the literature,[20] in 'other (non-property) matters', enforcement is envisaged only in matters of care, maintenance and custody of minors (Section 58 Czech PILA), provided that the foreign judgment imposes a proprietary benefit.

[17] Dobiáš (n 10) 103.
[18] Kučera et al (n 15) 369.
[19] Břicháček (n 7) 114; Kučera et al (n 15) 400.
[20] Břicháček (n 7) 114; Kučera et al (n 15) 397.

In general, there are two methods of enforcement in the Czech Republic, namely by a court and by a bailiff, and it is up to the judgment creditor which method they choose.[21] If judicial enforcement is selected, both recognition and enforcement are conducted before the same authority (a court). This is a procedure that can always be resorted to. The enforcement method through a bailiff, conducted in accordance with the Enforcement Code (Act No 120/2001 Coll), is only applicable if the enforcement is to be conducted with respect to a foreign judgment where recognition has been granted by a court decision (Section 37(4)(c) of the Enforcement Code; different rules apply in cases where an EU regulation or an international treaty applies). Thus, the following methods of enforcement are available for the recognition and enforcement of foreign judgments under the Czech PILA:

- If the foreign judgment has not been recognised in special proceedings, then only judicial enforcement is possible. In such cases, a direct application for enforcement is made. It should be recalled that in this procedure, the court will assess whether the foreign judgment meets the requirements for its recognition and resolve this as a preliminary question. If the conditions are met, the court will order enforcement of the foreign judgment. The law requires that reasons be given for the order of enforcement, so that it is possible for the party concerned to submit arguments as to why the assessment was incorrect. The decision ordering enforcement (or even in the case of rejection of the application) is subject to appeal.[22] Enforcement is then governed by the rules set out in the Code of Civil Procedure (Section 251 et seq) and can be carried out in the ways authorised by national legislation.
- If the foreign judgment has been recognised in special proceedings (where there is a separate judgment of recognition), then the so-called double-track legal regime is activated, allowing the choice between judicial enforcement of the judgment and enforcement under the Enforcement Code through a bailiff.[23] This is because the recognition judgment constitutes a domestic enforcement title (Section 40 Enforcement Code). This was confirmed by the resolution of the Supreme Court of the Czech Republic of 1 July 2017 – 'the enforcement of a foreign judgment, which is subject to the provisions of Sections 14–16 Czech PILA, can only be carried out by judicial enforcement of the judgment, while enforcement by means of the Enforcement Code can in such a case only be carried out on the basis of a foreign judgment that has been recognised by a special judgment of a Czech court pursuant to Section 16(2) Czech PILA, ie, by a judgment that must be reasoned, both in the case of granting the application for recognition of the foreign judgment as well as in the case of its rejection'.[24] This case law has been followed in other judgments up

[21] Valdhans (n 8) 281; J Valdhans and T Kyselovská, 'Recognition and Enforcement of Foreign Judgments According to Czech Law' in V Rijavec, K Drnovsek and CH van Rhee (eds), *Cross-Border Enforcement in Europe: National and International Perspectives* (Intersentia, 2020) 146; M Pfeiffer and M Zavadilová, 'Recognition and Enforcement of Judgments in Commercial Matters Rendered by Courts of Non-EU Countries in the Czech Republic' (2020) 4 *Acta Universitatis Carolinae Iuridica* 168.

[22] Jirmanová (n 7) 119–20; Břicháček (n 7) 114.

[23] Břicháček (n 7) 114; Valdhans (n 8) 282; Resolution of the Supreme Court of the Czech Republic, 1 July 2016, Ref No 20 Cdo 1349/2016. For more details see also Valdhans and Kyselovská (n 21) 146–47.

[24] Point 22 of the resolution of the Supreme Court of the Czech Republic, 1 July 2016, Ref No 20 Cdo 1349/2016; freely translated.

to the present day – the assessment of recognition as a preliminary question is not sufficient for enforcement under the Enforcement Code.[25] Since 2022, however, the situation has been simplified so that a motion for recognition can be filed together with an enforcement motion. Unless provided otherwise, it is the enforcement court that is competent to decide on the motion for recognition (see below; Section 35(6) Enforcement Code). The court shall issue a mandate to the bailiff after it has ruled on the motion for recognition, which may be decided without a hearing; the decision on recognition must be reasoned.[26]

2.1. Authorities with Subject Matter and Local Jurisdiction

Subject matter jurisdiction for ordering and carrying out enforcement lies with the district courts. As for local jurisdiction, this refers to the general court of the judgment debtor. If the debtor does not have a general court, or if this court is not in the Czech Republic, then the court in whose district the debtor has property is competent; other subsidiary rules may be applicable (Section 252 of the Code of Civil Procedure). The above two rules apply similarly when the Enforcement Code is applied – district courts have subject matter jurisdiction, and the court where the natural person has their permanent residence or the legal entity has its seat has local jurisdiction; if this place is not in the Czech Republic, the court in whose district the debtor has property has jurisdiction (Section 45 of the Enforcement Code).

2.2. The Burden of Proving the Requirements for Enforcement

Enforcement proceedings are initiated upon filing a separate petition. It thus follows from the nature of such proceedings that it is the judgment creditor who must provide the necessary facts or attach evidence to the petition (see Question 4). It is the judgment creditor who bears the burden of proof, and it is their responsibility to submit to the court all the documents or fulfil the requirements imposed on them. The court does not, of its own motion, ascertain the existence or non-existence of any such requirements.

2.3. Review of the Judgment on the Merits

The courts are prohibited from reviewing the foreign judgment whose recognition is sought on the merits (*révision au fond*).

Question 3. Requirements

The Czech PILA provides for both positive and negative requirements for the recognition and enforcement of foreign judgments.

[25] For example, point 11 of the resolution of the Supreme Court of the Czech Republic, 18 October 2022, Ref No 20 Cdo 2477/2022.

[26] Section 43a(3) Enforcement Code; L Jícha, '§ 37 (Oprávněný návrh)' in Svoboda et al (eds), *Exekuční řád: komentář* (CH Beck, 2022) 239.

The positive requirements follow from Section 14, pursuant to which judgments of the courts of a foreign country and decisions of the authorities of a foreign country on rights and obligations which, according to their private law nature, would be decided in the Czech Republic by courts, are effective in the Czech Republic if they have become final according to the confirmation of the competent foreign authority and if they have been recognised by Czech public authorities. Effectiveness is to be understood as a state in which a foreign judgment is granted the same legal effects as if it were a judgment of a Czech court.[27] The Czech PILA is thus founded on the so-called 'theory of adjustment', whereby a foreign judgment is likened to a Czech judgment and is adapted to Czech procedural conditions.[28]

The general grounds for refusal of recognition and enforcement are then listed in Section 15(1). The current approach to the treatment of refusal grounds could be described as a mixed approach, consisting of three distinct sub-categories.[29]

First, there are grounds for refusal which must be taken into account *ex officio*, ie, without the need for the party concerned to invoke them. These grounds include the existence of exclusive jurisdiction of Czech courts, the fulfilment of the so-called mirror-image jurisdiction, manifest breach of public policy, and the absence of reciprocity.

The second category consists of the existence of irregularities in the proceedings in which the judgment was given. This ground shall be taken into account only if it is invoked by the party against whom the foreign judgment is to be recognised.

The last category represents the grounds for refusal based on *lis pendens* or *res iudicata* obstacles. In these cases, too, it is primarily the party against whom the foreign judgment is to be recognised that must invoke them. However, if these obstacles are otherwise known to the authority deciding on recognition, then the law presupposes their application *ex officio*.

a) Jurisdiction of the Court of Origin

The jurisdiction of the court of origin is the first ground for refusal, which the Czech PILA stipulates in Section 15(1)(a). It follows from the wording of this provision that the legislator differentiates between two types of situations depending on the nature of international jurisdiction.

On the one hand, these are cases where Czech courts have exclusive jurisdiction. In these cases, the recognition of a foreign judgment will be refused outright. National law provides for the exclusive jurisdiction of Czech courts, for example, for proceedings for declaring a Czech citizen dead or missing (Section 39(1)) or for proceedings

[27] Assessment of the Supreme Court of the Czechoslovak Socialist Republic, 27 September 1987, Ref No Cpjf 27/86; This is also confirmed by the explanatory report to the Czech PILA with respect to Section 14.

[28] J Valdhans and T Kyselovská, *Cross border Enforcement of Monetary Claims – Interplay of Brussels I A Regulation and National Rules. National report: Czech Republic* (University of Maribor Press, 2018) 14 with the reference to V Vaške, *Uznání a výkon cizích rozhodnutí v České republice* (CH Beck, 2007) 491 and Assessment of the Supreme Court of the Czechoslovak Socialist Republic, 27 September 1987, Ref No Cpjf 27/86.

[29] This is a significant conceptual change compared to the previous legislation pursuant to which, as confirmed by the Constitutional Court in its judgment of 12 June 2012, Ref No II. ÚS 2455/09, all grounds for refusal had to be assessed *ex officio*.

concerning rights to immovable property located in the Czech Republic (Section 68). Naturally, however, exclusive jurisdiction may also follow from international treaties or EU law.

On the other hand, there are cases of non-exclusive jurisdiction. In these cases, in order to assess whether the ground for refusal is given, it is necessary to assess whether the proceedings could have been brought before the authority of the foreign country if the provisions on jurisdiction of Czech courts had been applied when establishing jurisdiction of the foreign authority. In other words, it is not examined based on what criterion, under the law of the country of origin, the authority which issued the judgment established its jurisdiction.

The decisive question for the assessment is whether jurisdiction of that authority would have been established had it proceeded to its determination under Czech law. However, it is not necessary that the foreign authority actually established its jurisdiction based on such a criterion. The Czech PILA provides in its Section 6(1) that 'jurisdiction of Czech courts is established if, according to the rules of procedure, a court in the territory of the Czech Republic has territorial jurisdiction over the proceedings, unless otherwise provided by this Act or another legal regulation'. The relevant provisions of international treaties and EU law are therefore also relevant for the assessment of the potential jurisdiction of Czech courts. In the remaining cases, reference may be made, in particular, to the criteria of local jurisdiction laid down in the Code of Civil Procedure and the Act on Special Court Proceedings.

If the foreign authority could not establish its jurisdiction to hear the case based on these rules, then under Czech law there is no sufficient relationship to the subject matter and the decision cannot be recognised.[30]

A novelty in comparison to the previously effective legislation is the fact that this 'mirror-image rule' does not apply if the party against whom the judgment is directed has voluntarily submitted to the jurisdiction of the foreign authority. The Czech PILA, however, does not explicitly state what exactly is meant by 'submission'. The assessment of this requirement will certainly not be problematic if the jurisdiction of the authority of origin is established by an express declaration. In other cases, the commentary literature presents the view that, in order to protect the defendant's rights, the assessment should be made in the light of domestic standards and not in the light of the law of the country of origin.[31]

b) Finality/Enforceability in the Country of Origin

Finality is a defined requirement for the recognition of a foreign judgment in the Czech Republic. Unlike other conditions mentioned in this section, it constitutes a positive requirement. The notion of finality must be viewed from the perspective of Czech law, where it implies that the judgment is binding on the parties to the proceedings and

[30] M Jirmanová, '§ 15 (Odepření uznání cizího rozhodnutí)' in M Pauknerová et al (eds), *Zákon o mezinárodním právu soukromém: Komentář* (Wolters Kluwer, 2013) 110 with the reference to Vaške (n 32) 433.

[31] T Břicháček, '§ 15 (Důvody pro odepření uznání cizího rozhodnutí)' in P Bříza et al (eds), *Zákon o mezinárodním právu soukromém: komentář* (CH Beck, 2014) 104–05.

that the judgment is not subject to change.[32] Ascertaining whether a foreign judgment meets this condition, ie, whether it possesses the aforementioned qualities, is however carried out in accordance with the foreign procedural regulations,[33] while the Czech PILA presupposes that a confirmation of finality will be issued by a competent authority of the state of origin.[34] Should the country of origin not know the institute of finality, it would be decisive whether the judgment possesses the characteristics that are associated with finality under Czech law.[35] And although the Czech PILA is silent in this respect, it follows from the logic of the matter that the possibility of subsequent enforcement of a foreign judgment in the Czech Republic requires that it is also enforceable in the state of origin. This requirement is assessed pursuant to the law of the country of origin.[36]

c) *Res Iudicata*

As with regard to the question of international jurisdiction, also in the case of *res iudicata* obstacle, two types of situations must be distinguished.

On the one hand, these are cases where a final judgment of a Czech court on the same legal matter[37] has already been issued. In these cases, both the moment of commencement of the proceedings (the Czech court could have commenced the proceedings earlier or later than the foreign authority) and the moment of issuance of the judgment (the Czech judgment could have been issued earlier or later than the judgment of the foreign authority) are completely irrelevant.

The decisive fact is only whether there already was a decision of a Czech court that had become final at the time of the request for recognition of the foreign judgment. It is the finality of such a judgment that is a necessary requirement for the fulfilment of the above-mentioned ground for refusal. If the judgment of the Czech court had not yet become final, this ground for refusal would not be given and the foreign decision could not be refused recognition on that ground. On the contrary, the recognition of the foreign judgment would result in the establishment of a *res iudicata* obstacle to the judgment of the Czech court, from which it can be inferred that such a judgment would have to be annulled and the proceedings dismissed for the lack of procedural conditions.[38]

The second type of situations are cases where a final judgment of an authority of a third state has already been recognised in the Czech Republic at the time of the application for recognition of the foreign judgment. Also in these cases, the moment when the proceedings were initiated, or the judgment issued in the third state is irrelevant. For

[32] T Břicháček, '§ 14 (Úvodní ustanovení k uznávání cizích rozhodnutí)' in P Bříza et al (eds), *Zákon o mezinárodním právu soukromém: komentář* (CH Beck, 2014) 98; Section 159a Code of Civil Procedure.

[33] Z Kučera et al, *Mezinárodní právo soukromé*, 8th edn (Aleš Čeněk, 2015) 376; Vaške (n 32) 426.

[34] This confirmation may take the form of either a separate document or a clause indicated on the decision. – Valdhans (n 8) 275.

[35] M Jirmanová, '§ 14 (Obecně k uznání a výkonu cizích rozhodnutí)' in M Pauknerová et al (eds), *Zákon o mezinárodním právu soukromém: Komentář* (Wolters Kluwer, 2013) 106.

[36] Valdhans (n 8) 275.

[37] For the interpretation of this concept, see the definition given below regarding *lis pendens*.

[38] Vaške (n 32) 436.

the purposes of this ground of refusal, the only decisive factor is whether a judgment of the authority of the third country had already been recognised.

d) *Lis Pendens*

A new ground for refusal, which was introduced into the Czech concept of recognition and enforcement of foreign judgments only with the entry into force of the new Czech PILA, is the *lis pendens* obstacle. This ground for refusal lies in the fact that a foreign judgment cannot be recognised if proceedings are still pending before a Czech court in respect of the same legal relationship[39] and those proceedings were initiated prior to the commencement of the foreign proceedings in which the judgment whose recognition is sought was rendered.[40]

The decisive factor for this ground for refusal to be given is the moment when the proceedings were initiated before the Czech court. On the contrary, the time when the court of origin issues its decision is completely irrelevant. Thus, if the proceedings before the Czech court were initiated prior to the foreign proceedings, this ground for refusal is given, even though the foreign authority has already issued its decision and the judgment creditor now seeks its recognition and enforcement in the Czech Republic.

However, it should be noted that this ground presupposes that the proceedings before the Czech authority are ongoing and will result in a judgment on the merits. If the Czech proceedings would end otherwise than with a judgment on the merits, and the *res iudicata* obstacle would not arise, the ground for non-recognition would cease to exist and the foreign judgment could be recognised in the Czech Republic.[41]

e) Specific Requirements of Due Process

Another ground for refusal responds to situations of irregularities in the proceedings, ie, the existence of facts which impede a proper hearing of the case and deprive the parties of an equal opportunity to exercise their rights.[42] In particular, the provision in question provides that a final foreign judgment cannot be recognised if the party against whom the decision is to be recognised has been deprived by the foreign authority of the opportunity to participate properly in the proceedings, in particular if they have not been served with a summons or a motion instituting the proceedings.

[39] The notion of the 'same legal relationship' under Czech domestic law presupposes the identity of the parties to the proceedings and the identity of the subject matter of the proceedings. Identity of the subject matter of the proceedings occurs if the same claim arises from the same factual allegations as those which were raised in the previous proceedings. The same subject matter is also involved where the same act is legally classified differently in the new proceedings from that in the original proceedings. However, the authors are not aware of any case law interpreting this concept specifically for the purposes of the Czech PILA. Therefore, the question remains whether Czech courts will prefer the broader EU approach to the interpretation of 'same legal relationship' in extra-EU relations – Pfeiffer and Zavadilová (n 21) 165.

[40] Section 15(1)(b) Czech PILA.

[41] Jirmanová (n 34) 111.

[42] Assessment of the Supreme Court of the Czechoslovak Socialist Republic, 27 September 1987, Ref No Cpjf 27/86.

It follows, therefore, that the possibility of recognising a foreign judgment is conditional upon ensuring that the standards of due process are met in the original proceedings in which the foreign judgment was rendered. The procedure of the foreign authority in this respect is, in principle, assessed in accordance with Czech constitutional principles of procedure, even if the procedure in question is in accordance with the procedural rules of the country of origin.[43] It is clear from the use of the words 'in particular' that the circumstances explicitly provided for by the Czech PILA constitute only a demonstrative list of cases which cannot be regarded as complying with due process standards. In other cases, the fulfilment of this ground of refusal must be assessed in the light of the particular circumstances of the case. At the same time, the obligation to ensure that the right to a fair trial was observed cannot be met merely by reference to the information (allegations) provided by the court of origin but must be verified materially.[44]

f) Public Policy

The Czech legislator adheres to the generally shared doctrines of private international law and procedure and therefore enshrines the breach of public policy as one of the traditional grounds for refusal of recognition.

The Czech PILA, however, does not provide any definition of the concept of public policy, neither in relation to the recognition and enforcement of foreign judgments, nor insofar as it deals with this institute in the general part of conflict of laws. The Explanatory Report merely states that the public policy exception is to be applied if the effects of the application of the foreign rule (in this case, the effects of the recognition of the foreign judgment) would be contrary to such principles of the Czech legal order that must be upheld without reservation and to good morals. Similarly, the commentary literature states that a breach of public policy is found where the recognition of a foreign judgment would contravene the fundamental principles of constitutional and legal order, the social order and public policy in general, and would constitute a breach of such an important principle which must be insisted upon unequivocally and in every respect.[45]

Generally, the public policy exception will be invoked in cases of violation of the right to a fair trial.[46] However, according to the Supreme Court, it could also cover situations where the jurisdiction of the foreign court has been deliberately established in order to evade domestic law.[47] What is clear, however, is that this ground for refusal of recognition does not justify a review of the judgment on its merits. Czech private international law follows the general principle of the prohibition of *révision au fond*.[48]

Following the adoption of the Czech PILA, which is currently in force, the word 'manifest' was explicitly added, which implies that any conflict with public policy

[43] Jirmanová (n 34) 111–12.
[44] Judgment of the Constitutional Court of the Czech Republic, 12 June 2012, Ref No II ÚS 2455/09.
[45] Jirmanová (n 34) 112.
[46] Judgment of the Constitutional Court of the Czech Republic, 25 April 2006, Ref No I ÚS 709/05; Judgment of the Constitutional Court of the Czech Republic, 21 November 2001, Ref No IV ÚS 189/2010.
[47] Assessment of the Supreme Court of the Czechoslovak Socialist Republic, 27 September 1987, Ref No Cpjf 27/86.
[48] Pfeiffer and Zavadilová (n 21) 164.

must be of a certain intensity. In our view, however, this novelty cannot be regarded as a change in the concept of the public policy reservation. Rather, it is an explicit reference to the fact that the application of the reservation is to be approached restrictively as an exception to the otherwise liberal approach to the recognition of foreign judgments, which is, however, a characteristic feature of all grounds for the refusal of recognition.

g) Reciprocity

Absence of reciprocity presents the last ground for refusal of recognition of a foreign judgment under the Czech PILA. The underlying assumption is the existence of material reciprocity, where a finding that the country of origin recognises or would recognise Czech judgments in a legal matter of the same kind is sufficient to meet this requirement. Thus, no guarantee of reciprocity by means of an international treaty[49] is required, nor is the fact that any Czech judgment has already been recognised by the country of origin. It is sufficient that its legislation or practice implies a presumption of recognition and enforcement of such a judgment if it were requested.[50]

It is in principle for the authority deciding on recognition to assess whether the requirement of reciprocity is met.[51] In practice, however, this task may prove difficult. Therefore, the law provides for the possibility[52] for the court to apply to the Ministry of Justice with a request for a notification of reciprocity and the consequent obligation of the Ministry to provide such a notification.[53] Nevertheless, this procedure does not delegate the responsibility for ascertaining reciprocity to the Ministry. If the Ministry fails to provide the information, it is for the court itself to ascertain whether or not there is material reciprocity in relation to the country concerned.[54]

However, even if such a notification is provided, it is not binding on the court, unlike the so-called 'declaration of reciprocity' that was in place under the previous legislation.[55] The court examines this notification as it would any other evidence.[56] By

[49] Although the possibility of concluding them cannot be ruled out. The literature even suggests that in such cases reciprocity should be deemed guaranteed even if the Czech court has knowledge of a specific practice of the authorities of the contracting state which would contradict the respect of reciprocity. To proceed otherwise would constitute a breach of the Czech Republic's treaty obligations. – M Zavadilová, '§ 13 (Sdělení o vzájemnosti)' in M Pauknerová et al (eds), *Zákon o mezinárodním právu soukromém: Komentář* (Wolters Kluwer, 2013) 98.

[50] Břicháček (n 35) 107.

[51] Z Kučera and L Tichý, *Zákon o mezinárodním právu soukromém a procesním: Komentář* (Panorama, 1989) 284.

[52] The Act leaves the matter to the discretion of the court. The court may therefore automatically proceed with the application to the Ministry without examining reciprocity itself, or it may first attempt to assess reciprocity itself and only subsequently, if no or insufficient conclusions are drawn, file an application for a statement of reciprocity.

[53] Section 13 Czech PILA.

[54] Resolution of the Supreme Court of the Czech Republic, 12 September 2006, Ref No 20 Cdo 1688/2006.

[55] Section 54 Czech PILA; these were legal acts officially issued by the Ministry of Justice in agreement with the Ministry of Foreign Affairs on the basis of reciprocal international negotiations and subsequent assurances of reciprocity by the foreign country – Z Fišerová, '§ 13 (Zjišťování vzájemnosti)' in P Bříza et al (eds), *Zákon o mezinárodním právu soukromém: komentář* (CH Beck, 2014) 93; Zavadilová (n 53) 99.

[56] Zavadilová (n 53) 99.

this departure from the previously adopted approach, the legislator intended to respect and strengthen the independence of judicial decision-making. At the same time, it confirms the conclusion that it is the court that bears the primary responsibility for this ascertainment.

Absence of reciprocity, however, does not constitute an absolute obstacle to the recognition of a foreign judgment. Reciprocity is not required if the judgment is not directed against a Czech national or a Czech legal entity. Similarly, absence of reciprocity does not prevent the recognition of final foreign judgments in matters of divorce, legal separation, declaration of nullity of marriage, determination of whether or not there is a marriage,[57] nor in matters of establishment and denial of parenthood,[58] if at least one of the parties to the proceedings was a national of the Czech Republic.

h) Other Requirements

None.

Question 4. Documents to be Produced

The Czech PILA does not contain any provision that would explicitly and in a general manner lay down a list of documents that must be produced in proceedings for the recognition and enforcement of foreign judgments. This is mainly because the documentary requirements imposed might greatly vary depending on the subject matter of the proceedings.

Generally, however, it will be necessary to submit a request for recognition that must be accompanied by the foreign judgment itself, documents declaring the status of the person (depending on the subject matter of the proceedings), if necessary a transcript (a copy) of the petition filed with the foreign court and the record of the proceedings conducted before the foreign court, and, in the case of representation, a power of attorney.

This general scheme applies, for example, with respect to requests for recognition of foreign divorce judgments, as the Supreme Court lists on its website that a request for the recognition of such judgments must be accompanied by:

(1) a document declaring that at least one of the parties to the proceedings was a Czech citizen at the time of issuance of the divorce judgment;
(2) the foreign divorce judgment whose recognition is sought (either an official transcript, or a certified copy – if necessary, it may need to be accompanied by an apostille or its superlegalisation);
(3) the marriage certificate (a copy is sufficient);

[57] Section 51(1) Czech PILA.
[58] Section 55(1) Czech PILA with reference to Section 51(1).

(4) under certain conditions a transcript (a copy) of the petition filed with the foreign court and/or a copy of the record of proceedings conducted before the foreign court;
(5) a judgment on the arrangement of the affairs of a minor child for the period after the divorce;
(6) a power of attorney in case of representation.

All documents drafted in a foreign language will need to be accompanied by a certified translation into Czech. Public instruments issued by a court, a notary public or a public authority abroad will also have the evidential authority of a public instrument in the Czech Republic, provided they include the prescribed authentication.[59] In case the request does not contain all the necessary details, the Supreme court will ask to complete them.[60]

Question 5. Securities, Bonds and Deposits

In view of the double-track nature of enforcement in the Czech Republic (see Question 2.b)), the requirement to provide a deposit must be assessed depending on the procedure chosen by the judgment creditor.

In cases of enforcement of judgments by way of judicial enforcement under the Code of Civil Procedure, the court may order the judgment creditor, who does not qualify for exemption from court fees, to lodge a deposit for the costs of enforcement. If they fail to do so, the court shall stay the enforcement of the judgment.[61]

The requirement to lodge a deposit may also arise in connection with the enforcement of a judgment by a bailiff under the Enforcement Code. The Enforcement Code provides both for the possibility and, in certain circumstances, the obligation to order the judgment creditor to lodge a deposit for the costs of enforcement.[62]

Pursuant to Section 90(3), first sentence, of the Enforcement Code, the bailiff has a right to order the judgment creditor to lodge a deposit for the costs of the enforcement proceedings, the amount of which and the time limit for payment shall be determined by the bailiff. Deposits pursuant to this sentence are optional and it is up to the bailiff to decide whether to require it from the judgment creditor at the beginning of the enforcement proceedings or during the enforcement proceedings if the measures to be carried out require increased expenses.[63] The second sentence of Section 90(3) obliges the bailiff to order the judgment creditor to lodge a deposit if, under the conditions set out in that provision, they reinitiate an enforcement procedure that has already been once stayed. Failure to lodge the deposit shall result in the

[59] Section 12 Czech PILA.
[60] Supreme Court, Proceedings on Recognition of Foreign Decisions, nsoud.cz.
[61] Section 270(3) Code of Civil Procedure.
[62] Section 90(3) Enforcement Code. The Enforcement Code also provides for a category of deposits for the further conduct of the enforcement proceedings, the purpose of which is primarily to discourage the creditors from unreasonably insisting on the further conduct of the unsuccessful enforcement proceedings. However, their detailed description is beyond the scope of this questionnaire.
[63] M Kasíková, '§ 90 (Odměna exekutora, smlouva o vedení exekuce, záloha na náklady)' in M Kasíková et al (eds), *Exekuční řád: Komentář*, 5th edn (CH Beck, 2022) 776.

discontinuation of the enforcement in accordance with Section 55(6) of the Enforcement Code.

With respect to optional deposits within the meaning of the first sentence of Section 90(3) of the Enforcement Code, such deposits may not be imposed upon a judgment creditor within the meaning of Section 55(9)[64] or upon a judgment creditor who is eligible for exemption from court fees within the meaning of Section 138(1)[65] of the Code of Civil Procedure.

However, for foreigners who are habitually resident abroad and foreign legal entities in proceedings before Czech courts, the Czech PILA provides for the possibility of their exemption from court fees and deposits under the same conditions as applicable to citizens of the Czech Republic and Czech legal entities.[66] The law expressly refers only to court fees and deposits, which implies that notary, bailiff and other administrative fees cannot be covered. However, this exemption is conditional on the assurance of reciprocity,[67] which, as in other cases where the Czech PILA refers to reciprocity, is a case of material reciprocity.[68]

[64] If the enforcement is for the recovery of a claim for maintenance for a minor child, a claim for substitute maintenance, compensation for injury caused to the injured party by an occupational accident, occupational disease, bodily harm or a criminal offence, a claim arising from a tort under the Civil Code, unjust enrichment, a claim of a school or school institution for public service provided under the Education Act.

[65] Exemption from court fees where the circumstances of the party so justify and where the claim or defence is not arbitrary or manifestly unfounded.

[66] T Břicháček and P Horák, '§ 10 (Osvobození od soudních poplatků a ustanovení bezplatného zástupce)' in P Bříza et al (eds), *Zákon o mezinárodním právu soukromém: komentář* (CH Beck, 2014) 80.

[67] The requirement of reciprocity does not apply to nationals of the Member States of the EU and other countries forming the EEA; Section 10, second sentence, Czech PILA.

[68] Kučera and Tichý (n 55) 274.

Finland

ONERVA-AULIKKI SUHONEN

Question 1. General Overview

The legal framework for the recognition and enforcement of foreign judgments in civil and commercial matters in Finland consist of international and bilateral agreements, EU law and Finnish national rules.[1] Since the recognition and enforcement of foreign judgments is based on the co-operation between states, the issue is mainly founded on international treaties in different fields of law. The most important international instruments in the field are the Brussels Ia Regulation[2] and Lugano Conventions[3] that are directly applicable in Finnish law.[4] Between Nordic countries, the Convention between Finland, Iceland, Norway, Sweden and Denmark on the recognition and enforcement of judgments concerning claims under private law (Finnish Treaty Series 56/1977; 'Nordic Convention') and the Act on the Recognition and Enforcement of Nordic Judgments Concerning Claims Under Private Law (588/1977),[5] which is based on the convention, are still formally in force in Finland. However, the Act is rarely applied in the recognition and enforcement of Nordic judgments as the EU law and international treaties are given priority over the Nordic Convention.[6] Accordingly, the Brussels Ia Regulation is applied as regards other

[1] English translations of Finnish national legislation and the international treaties Finland has acceded to are available at Finlex Data Bank. See finlex.fi/en.

[2] Regulation (EU) No 1215/2012 of the European Parliament and of the Council of 12 December 2012 on jurisdiction and the recognition and enforcement of judgment in civil and commercial matters.

[3] Lugano Convention of 2007 on jurisdiction and the recognition and enforcement of judgments in civil and commercial matters and the preceding Lugano Convention of 1988.

[4] In addition, Finland is a party to many Hague Conference on Private International Law (HCCH) conventions, such as the Hague Judgments Convention of 2019 (Convention of 2 July 2019 on the Recognition and Enforcement of Foreign Judgments in Civil or Commercial Matters), the Hague Choice of Court Convention of 2005 (The Convention of 30 June 2005 on Choice of Court Agreements), the Maintenance Obligation Protocol of 2007 (Protocol of 23 November 2007 on the Law Applicable to Maintenance Obligations and the Child Support Convention of 2007 (The Convention of 23 November 2007 on the International Recovery of Child Support and Other Forms of Family Maintenance). Finland has also joined the New York Arbitration Convention of the Recognition and Enforcement of Foreign Arbitral Awards of 10 June 1958.

[5] Laki yksityisoikeudellista vaatimusta koskevien pohjoismaisten tuomioiden tunnustamisesta ja täytäntöönpanosta (588/1977).

[6] However, theoretically, the Act can still become applicable in connection with judgment and documents drawn up before the entry into force of the Lugano Treaty.

Nordic EU Member States Sweden and Denmark, and the Lugano Convention of 2007 in respect for Norway and Iceland.[7]

In Finnish national law, the recognition and enforcement of foreign judgments in civil and commercial matters is not comprehensively established.[8] The main law that governs recognition and enforcement is the Act on International Legal Assistance and Recognition and Enforcement of Judgments in Civil and Commercial Matters (462/2015; 'International Legal Assistance Act'),[9] which regulation is supplemented by the principles of private international law and procedural rules set forth in the Code of Judicial Procedure (4/1734; CJP).[10] In practice, the provisions of Chapter 8 of the CJP do not have much significance in recognition and enforcement matters, because the procedural norms generally come from each specific law. In the recognition and enforcement of civil and commercial matters the normative guidance is nevertheless very modest, because the International Legal Assistance Act concentrates mainly on international legal assistance and includes only one chapter (Chapter 8) and six sections, which directly regulate recognition and enforcement issues. Moreover, as the EU law and international agreements, such as the Lugano Convention of 2007 and the Hague Judgments Convention of 2019,[11] take precedence over national rules, Finnish national legislation has only a secondary and complementary role in the regulation of the recognition and enforcement of foreign judgments.

In its approach to the recognition and enforcement of judgments, Finnish national regulation continues to follow the traditional approach of Nordic legal systems, according to which the recognition and enforcement of a foreign judgment in civil and commercial matters is exceptional and requires an explicit legal provision to support it. According to Section 30, subsection 1 of the Act on International Legal Assistance: 'A judgment or a decision in a civil or commercial matter of a court in a foreign state is recognised and enforced in Finland on the basis of a specific agreement on this or if so provided by law.' Consequently, foreign judgments are recognised and enforceable in Finland only to the extent that is expressly stipulated in the law or agreed on international or bilateral agreement. In practice, this means that most judgments in civil and commercial matters issued in a non-EU country are not recognised or enforced in Finland.[12] As an exception to this, decisions on legal cost based on the 1954 and 1980

[7] Lugano Convention of 2007 is also applicable in respect to Switzerland.

[8] HE 216/2014 vp, 40–41. The role of legal practice has also been rather marginal in Finland as there are hardly any legal cases available on the subject.

[9] Laki kansainvälisestä oikeusavusta sekä tuomioiden tunnustamisesta ja täytäntöönpanosta siviili- ja kauppaoikeuden alalla (462/2015). However, as noted in Hallituksen esitys eduskunnalle laiksi kansainvälisestä oikeusavusta sekä tuomioiden tunnustamisesta ja täytäntöönpanosta siviili- ja kauppaoikeuden alalla sekä eräiksi siihen liittyviksi laeiksi, HE 216/2014 vp., 23, the significance of the provision 30 on recognition and enforcement is mainly informative.

[10] Oikeudenkäymiskaari (4/1734).

[11] The Hague Judgment Convention of 2019 that entered into force on 1 September 2023, currently regulates the recognition and enforcement of foreign judgments issued in Ukraine, Uruguay and the United Kingdom as well as Albania and Montenegro (from March 2026).

[12] HE 216/2014 vp, 40. The interpretation has been confirmed in the case Etelä-Karjalan käräjäoikeus 14 April 2020 nro 20/517, where a Russian party applied for recognition of an order to pay issued by the Moscow City Arbitration Court. Since there is no bilateral agreement between Finland and Russia concerning the recognition and enforcement of a judgment imposing a payment obligation, the application was rejected as clearly unfounded.

Hague Conventions[13] are enforceable under Finnish law.[14] In practice, the scope of this exception is nevertheless quite narrow.

Question 2. Procedure

a) Circumstances of Recognition and Enforcement

When discussing the procedure for the recognition and enforcement of foreign judgments, a distinction must be made between the two. Generally, recognition of a foreign judgment means that the judgment is given legal effects in Finland that indicate the validity and binding nature of the judgment, including the effect of legal force. In other words, the foreign judgment is considered to be in force in Finland in the same way as domestic judgments.[15] The enforceability of a foreign judgment, on the other hand, signifies that the judgment has been recognised and the party concerned has the right to demand enforcement, if necessary, with the assistance of an enforcement authority.[16] According to Koulu, conceptually, a court's decision on the enforceability of a foreign judgment contains both a law-confirming and law-creating element. Firstly, in the exequatur procedure, the court geographically extends the validity of the rights established in the original judgment to the country of enforcement. Secondly, the transfer of a judgment to the legal system of the country of enforcement severs the connection of the foreign judgment with the legal system of the country of origin.[17]

When a foreign judgment is recognised in Finland, it acquires the same legal force (*res iudicata*) as domestic judgments. In other words, a recognised foreign judgment serves as grounds for enforcement and can be invoked directly in courts and other authorities. Recognised foreign judgment has both positive and negative legal force. This means that once the foreign judgment has been recognised, the judgment constitutes a basis for decision in future trials (positive legal force) and the same case cannot be re-examined on the merits in Finnish courts (negative legal force).[18] Conceptually, enforcement of a foreign judgment also requires that the judgment has been first recognised.

[13] Convention of 1 March 1954 on civil procedure and Convention of 25 October 1980 on International Access to Justice.

[14] According to section 33, subsection 1 Act on International Legal Assistance, 'A decision in a civil or commercial matter issued by a court of a state party to the Convention on Civil Procedure (Finnish Treaty Series 2/1957) or the Convention on International Access to Justice (Finnish Treaty Series 47/1988), ordering the plaintiff or the intervening party to pay legal costs, is enforceable in Finland after it has, on application, been declared enforceable.'

[15] R Koulu, *Kansainvälinen prosessioikeus pääpiirteittäin* (Talentum, 2003) 212.

[16] ibid 214.

[17] ibid 216–17.

[18] R Koulu, 'Ulkomaisen tuomion voimassaolo' in M Vuorenpää et al (eds), *Prosessioikeus*, 6th edn (Alma Talent Oy, 2021) 792–93 and J Lappalainen, 'Recognition and Enforcement of Foreign Judgment Outside the Scope of Application of the Brussels and Lugano Conventions: Finland', in G Walter and SP Baumgartner (eds), *Recognition and Enforcement of Foreign Judgment Outside the Scope of Application of the Brussels and Lugano Conventions* (Kluwer Law International, 2000), 177.

Judgments given in other EU Member States are automatically recognised in Finland without any special procedure being required. As a result, EU judgments can be directly applied by the enforcement authorities. Judgments issued by Member Sates of the 2007 Lugano Convention (Iceland, Norway and Switzerland) are also automatically recognised, but the enforcement of the judgments requires that the district court confirms the enforceability of the judgment.

If foreign judgment in civil and commercial matters has been issued in a non-EU and non-Lugano state, a specific legal basis such a bilateral agreement is required for the recognition and enforcement. As a result, recognition and enforcement of non-EU judgments in civil and commercial matters are very exceptional situations in Finland due to a lack of statutory support.[19] Even when a bilateral agreement between Finland and a third country would exist, judgments issued in a non-EU country are not directly recognised, but the party concerned must apply for a judgment's formal recognition and separate enforcement order (*täytäntöönpanomääräys*) from a district court.[20]

Since foreign judgments issued in non-EU countries are generally not recognised and enforced in Finland, the plaintiff must bring their case before a Finnish court to obtain a legally binding and enforceable decision on the matter.[21] This has been confirmed also in the case law of the Finnish Supreme Court.[22]

In case KKO:2011:74, the judgment of the American court could not be enforced in Finland because there was no mutual agreement between Finland and the United States on issues related to international procedural jurisdiction. The Finnish Supreme court held that in order for Company T to be able to enforce its claims in Finland, the Finnish court had to have jurisdiction to hear the case again despite the judgment of the American court.

Consequently, if there is no legal basis for recognition and enforcement between Finland and a non-EU country, the parties can re-submit their case to a Finnish court in order to obtain a legally binding solution that serves as the basis for enforcement.[23] In these situations, when evaluating the evidence, the Finnish courts usually give significant evidential effect to the said foreign judgment given between the same parties in the same matter.[24] In particular, if the foreign court has applied its own law to the legal relationship, which a Finnish court would also have to apply according to the private international law rules, a presumption of legality is often attached to the foreign judgment.[25]

[19] Decisions on legal costs based on the 1954 and 1980 Hague Conventions constitute an exception to this general rule.

[20] S Johansson, *Kansainvälisen siviiliprosessioikeuden käsikirja* (Talentum, 2002), 258.

[21] HE 216/2014, 40.

[22] See Finnish Supreme court cases KKO:2011:74 and KKO 1980 II 54.

[23] HE 216/2014 vp, 40.

[24] ibid.

[25] R Koulu, *Kansainvälisen prosessi- ja insolvenssioikeuden pääpiirteet* (Kauppakaari, 2001) 49 and 212–13. According to Koulu, a foreign judgment is accompanied by a presumption of its correctness, which the other party must somehow overturn to win its case. The presumption of correctness is particularly strong when the foreign court has applied its own law to the legal relationship, which the Finnish court would also have to follow according to the conflict of laws rules, and when the procedure in the foreign court has been

b) Procedural Steps

In order for a non-EU judgment in civil and commercial matters to be enforced in Finland, the validity and enforceability of the judgment under Finnish law must be confirmed in a formal *exequatur* procedure.[26] Since the recognition and enforcement procedure are typically agreed upon in relevant international agreements, Finnish national law mainly complements such international procedural rules.[27] Accordingly, national legislation does not have uniform or standardised rules on the exequatur procedure in civil and commercial matters, but provisions of the International Legal Assistance Act and Chapter 8 of the Code of Judicial Procedure on petitionary matters are applied, as appropriate.

The recognition of foreign judgments in Finnish courts takes place in a summary procedure, in which the court makes a decision based on documents without an oral hearing. The summary procedure aims to ensure the speedy processing of the matter.[28] According to Chapter 8, section 1 of the CJP, the petitionary matter shall become pending when it its presented in the office or in the session of the court. To initiate the recognition and enforcement of foreign judgment, the petitioner should submit the application to declare the decision enforceable and necessary annexes to the district court in whose jurisdiction the defendant has domicile or permanent residence.[29] Since the recognition of a foreign judgment is by nature a petitionary matter, the applicants often initiate the case independently without legal assistance. To facilitate processing recognition and enforcement petition without an assistant, the courts have drawn up different application forms, which require the applicant to provide sufficient information and attach all the necessary attachments at the application stage.[30]

At the next stage of recognition, the court conducts an initial examination of the petition. The applicant who is petitioning the recognition of foreign judgment is responsible for obtaining and submitting to the court all documents and translations required for the enforcement. The court may require that documents that have been written in a foreign language are translated into Finnish or Swedish if it does not understand the language used. When necessary, the court can also request any additional information or documents from the applicant. If the petitioner

appropriate. See also M Norros, 'Siviilituomioiden täytäntöönpano Suomen ja Venäjän välillä keskusviranomaisen näkökulmasta' (2015) 1 *Defensor Legis* 139, 154.

[26] Koulu (n 15) 215–16.

[27] HE 216/2014 vp, 41.

[28] Consideration of petitionary matters, at https://oikeus.fi/tuomioistuimet/en/index/asiat/hakemusasiat/considerationofpetitionarymatters.html#. When the court decides the case without hearing the other party, the decision given is practically equivalent to summons, because the other party has not had a chance to act on the application. HE 216/2014 vp, 41.

[29] See more Ch 10 (135/2009) CJP on Jurisdiction in civil matters. Jurisdiction in exequatur proceedings is decentralised in Finland. Currently, there are 20 district courts in Finland. The district courts deal with criminal cases, civil cases and petitionary matters.

[30] The court's conduct of proceedings can also aim to ensure the equal treatment of the parties in the exequatur procedure. M Mohsen and K Puro, 'Helsingin hovioikeuden eksekvatuurimenettelyn erityiskysymyksiä' in T Mikkola and E Konttinen (eds.), *Lapsen asema kansainvälistyvässä maailmassa*, (Helsinki, Helsingin hovioikeuden julkaisuja 2014) 159.

does not supplement the application as required, the court leaves the application unexamined.[31]

In the exequatur procedure, the district court examines *ex officio* whether the foreign judgment meets the prerequisites set for the execution of such a judgment. The court mainly focuses on examining the grounds for refusal on its own initiative. The court does not review the merits of the case or change the content of the foreign judgment, but only determines whether the procedural requirements for enforcement are met and whether there are no further grounds for refusing the enforcement.[32] The court cannot therefore intervene in the content of the foreign judgment, but only declare it fully or partly enforceable or, if necessary, refuse enforcement.

If a foreign judgment is recognised and deemed enforceable in Finland, the court will issue an enforcement order, which obliges the parties to act in accordance with the recognised judgment. According to section 31, subsection 2 of the International Legal Assistance Act, if a foreign judgment has been declared enforceable in Finland without hearing the opposing party and without notifying him of the decision in accordance with Chapter 8, section 11 of the CJP, the district court shall serve the opposing party with the decision.[33]

Recognition of foreign judgment and related enforcement order bind Finnish authorities. As a result, no other court can contest the outcome of the district court without a party's appeal. At the request of the party, a decision given by a district court on the enforceability of foreign judgment can be nevertheless reviewed by the court of appeal provided that the court grants leave for continued consideration.[34] Decisions issued by the court of appeal can be again appealed to the Supreme Court if the leave to appeal is granted. For the appeal process, the rules of Chapter 25 of the CJP apply. If the requirements set forth in chapter 25a, section 11 of the CJP are present, the court of appeal shall grant the leave for continued consideration.[35] According to Chapter 26, section 1 of the CJP, the proceedings in the court of appeal concern the matter that is the subject of the decision of the district court to the extent raised in the appeal and the possible response. The question is whether the decision of the district court is to be amended and how.

If the parties do not apply for amendment within the given timeframe or the court of appeal does not grant the leave for continued consideration, the decision becomes final. Once the foreign judgment has been declared valid and enforceable in the *exequatur* procedure, it serves as grounds for enforcement like automatically recognised foreign judgments and domestic judgments. In practice, an enforceable foreign

[31] Mohsen and Puro (n 30) 194.

[32] Norros (n 25) 147; and Mohsen and Puro (n 30) 158.

[33] The district court is responsible for the service of the decision in accordance with the provisions of Ch 11 CJP on the service of a summons.

[34] Section 32 International Legal Assistance Act.

[35] According to Ch 25a, s 11 CJP, 'Leave for continued consideration shall be granted if: 1) there is reason to doubt the correctness of the result of the decision of the district court; 2) it is not possible to assess the correctness of the result of the decision of the district court without granting leave for continued consideration; 3) in view of the application of the law in other similar matters, it is important to grant leave for continued consideration in the matter; or if 4) there are other serious grounds for granting the leave.'

judgment therefore gives the party concerned the right to apply for enforcement with the help of enforcement authorities.

Finally, it should be noted that the declaration of non-EU judgment as enforceable does not automatically initiate enforcement proceedings, but the enforcement must be sought with the Finnish executive authorities once the court has issued its decision on the enforceability of the judgment. In Finland, the competent authority that enforces court judgments is the National Enforcement Authority Finland, which works under the Ministry of Justice. The agency carries out its statutory enforcement duties independently, and decides, for example, whether the enforceability of foreign judgment is falling under the statute of limitations.[36]

Question 3. Requirements

The requirements set for recognition and enforcement of foreign judgments are laid down in international treaties Finland has acceded to and in the supplementary national rules. As a result, the prerequisites for the recognition of non-EU judgment depend on the applicable rules and vary in different branches of substantive law. In family law matters, issues of recognition and enforcement are comprehensively regulated in national law, but the International Legal Assistance Act does not address the requirements for the recognition and enforcement of non-EU foreign judgments in civil and commercial matters.[37] Consequently, the International Legal Assistance Act is only meant to complement international agreements and supranational legislation, in which the requirements and procedures followed in the recognition and enforcement of foreign judgments are principally agreed upon.

a) Jurisdiction of the Court of Origin

The jurisdiction of the courts is one of the essential procedural requirements that lay the foundation for a fair trial. Issues related to international jurisdiction of Finnish courts are regulated in the Code of Judicial Procedure, in particular in Chapter 10, sections 25 and 26 thereof.

According to section 25 subsection 1, Finnish courts have jurisdiction to examine a case of an international nature that has a connection with Finland, unless the decision of the Finnish court in the case could clearly not have legal significance for the parties involved.[38] Regarding natural and legal persons, the place of jurisdiction is determined by the defendant's domicile, permanent residence or the legal person's

[36] For more information about National Enforcement Authority Finland, see ulosottolaitos.fi/en/index.html #.

[37] In family law matters, the prerequisites of recognition and enforcement of foreign judgments and decisions are more clearly set down also in national laws, such as in Ch 2 Marriage Act (239/1929), Ch 9 Adoption Act (22/2012) as well as in the Act on the Recognition and Enforcement of a Decision on Maintenance Made Abroad (370/1983).

[38] For criteria for sufficient connection, see KKO 2007:68.

principal place of business (Chapter 10, sections 1 and 2 of the CJP).[39] According to section 26, a Finnish court shall, on its own motion, consider whether, in accordance with section 25, it is competent to consider a matter of an international nature. As an exception to this, if the parties have made a valid choice of court agreement, the court will consider its jurisdiction only if a party enters a plea on the lack of jurisdiction.

Currently there is no general provision on Finnish national legislation that would explicitly state that the recognition and enforcement of foreign judgments in civil and commercial matters is subject to a condition related to the court of origin's jurisdiction. This can be partly explained by the fact that the foreign judgments in civil and commercial matters issued outside Lugano and Brussels Ia frameworks are not recognised and enforced in Finland.

However, section 6 of the Act on the Recognition and Enforcement of Judgments in Nordic Civil Law Claims (588/1977) establishes the jurisdiction of the court of origin as a possible ground for refusing the recognition of the Nordic civil law claim judgment.[40] Accordingly, if the court considers that the exclusive jurisdiction to hear the case lies with a court other than the court of the state in which the judgment was given, the judgment will not be considered valid in Finland. In other areas of law where judgments and decisions from non-EU countries are more frequently recognised and enforced, national provisions provide that the enforceability of a foreign decision depends on the jurisdiction of the court of origin or the competence of the foreign authority. This is the case, for example, with the recognition and enforcement of maintenance agreements issued abroad.[41] This shows that the jurisdiction of the court of origin is recognised as ground for refusal in Finnish legal system, although there is currently no express provision in force for civil and commercial judgments.

b) Finality/Enforceability in the Country of Origin

In principle, the recognition and enforcement of foreign judgment in civil and commercial matters requires that the judgment or decision is final and non-appealable in the country of origin.[42] For example, according to section 36 of the Legal Assistance Act, the enforcement of decision on legal costs requires that a certificate indicating the finality and enforceability of the decision in the state in which it was issued is attached

[39] The regulation of international jurisdiction was renewed 2009. Previously, the international jurisdiction of Finnish courts was quite extensive, which was considered problematic. HE 70/2008 vp, 16.

[40] As mentioned in the introduction, the Act on the Recognition and Enforcement of Judgments in Nordic Civil Law Claims (588/1977) is still formally in force in Finland, although it does not have practical relevance due to applicability of Brussels Ia Regulation and Lugano Convention of 2007 between the Nordic Countries.

[41] Section 5 Act on the Recognition and Enforcement of a Decision on Maintenance Made Abroad (370/1983).

[42] See L Lehtinen, *Suomalainen ja venäläinen siviiliprosessi kansainvälisen täytäntöönpanon näkökulmasta*, Lausuntoja ja selvityksiä 2003:2 (Oikeusministeriö, 2003) 120. However, in family law matters, the situation is different, as non-final decisions and preliminary orders (such as preliminary orders on maintenance) issued by foreign courts or administrative bodies can also be recognised and enforced in Finland in certain situations. See eg Lappalainen (n 14) 173 and M Helin, *Suomen kansainvälinen perhe- ja perintöoikeus* (Alma Talent Oy, 2020) 104.

to the application. The finality of a foreign judgment has been set as a requirement also in section 3 of the Act on the Recognition and Enforcement of Nordic Judgments Concerning Claims Under Private Law (588/1977).

c) *Res Iudicata*

Res iudicata effect means that once a judgment has gained a legal force and become final, the same matter cannot be re-examined in court. On the other hand, a judgment must be taken as the basis of a subsequent judgment if the issue decided therein is raised as a preliminary question in a later legal proceeding.[43] In principle, a court cannot therefore re-examine a matter that has already been heard in court or that has been resolved by a final judgment.

The recognition or enforcement of foreign judgment is to be refused by the Finnish court if the foreign judgment conflicts with a previously given domestic judgment on the same matter, or a previously recognised or enforced foreign judgment given in the same case between the same parties.[44] On the other hand, if the foreign judgment is not recognised and enforced in Finland, as is the case with most non-EU judgments, the parties have a right to resubmit their case to a Finnish court in order to obtain a legally binding and enforceable solution to their dispute.[45]

d) *Lis Pendens*

Giving a *lis pendens* effect to ongoing proceedings is an important tool in avoiding overlapping processes and costs, and conflicting decisions. In Finland, domestic proceedings have a *lis pendens* effect, which means that new proceedings on the same matter between the same parties are prevented.[46] However, there are no general provisions in Finnish national legislation on the *lis pendens* effect of proceedings pending on the same matter in foreign courts.[47]

Generally, whether a pending proceeding abroad prevents a Finnish court from taking the case under investigation depends again on whether the future judgment will be recognised and enforced in Finland. If the judgment issued by a foreign court will not be recognised in Finland due to the lack of sufficient legal basis, linking the *lis pendens* effect to the foreign proceedings would be ill-founded. This is because in the absence of a legally binding decision, the parties have a right to have their case resolved in a court with competent jurisdiction.[48]

[43] Koulu (n 18) 792–93, Lappalainen (n 14) 177; and Helin (n 42) 112.
[44] Mohsen and Puro (n 30) 181 and Koulu (n 15) 220–221.
[45] HE 216/2014 vp, 40.
[46] Koulu (n 15) 207.
[47] Again, s 13 Act on the Recognition and Enforcement of Nordic Judgments Concerning Claims Under Private Law (588/1977) contains a *lis pendens* rule that would apply to Nordic judgments if the Brussels Ia Regulation or the Lugano convention did not apply.
[48] Koulu (n 15) 207–08.

e) Specific Requirements of Due Process

The recognition of a foreign judgment can be refused in a Finnish court when a significant procedural error has occurred in the foreign court proceedings.[49] Section 21, subsection 2 of the Finnish Constitution contains a basic provision on fair trial and good governance, which guarantees the right to the public of proceedings, the right to be heard, the right to receive the grounds for decision, and the right to appeal. Generally, the Finnish court could therefore refuse to enforce a foreign judgment if the principles of due process had been compromised in the foreign court proceedings; for example, if the parties concerned have not been heard or if the summons have not been served on the absent party appropriately and on time.[50]

f) Public Policy

The recognition and enforcement of a foreign judgment can be refused in Finland on grounds of public policy. The public policy exception is stated in the chapter 10, section 25, subsection 3 of the CJP on international jurisdiction, according to which, 'a Finnish court has jurisdiction if the procedure to be followed or the legislation to be applied in the court of a foreign State would be contrary to the basis of the Finnish judicial system'. However, the principle of *ordre public* is considered the last resort to counter foreign norms that would violate the foundations of the legal system.

In general, the application of the public policy exception requires that the applicable law or procedure is clearly and fundamentally in conflict with the prevailing Finnish understanding of human rights or the procedural guarantees of legal protection.[51] As a result, a refusal that is based on public policy is possible only if the recognition or enforcement would be clearly contrary to the fundamental principles of the Finnish legal order.

In the context of recognition and enforcement of foreign judgments, the public policy assessment does not focus on the law of a foreign state per se, but the weight must be given to the outcome to which the recognition or enforcement of a foreign decision would lead in the case under consideration.[52] The situation to which the rejection of enforceability of the foreign judgment in this individual case would lead should also be taken into consideration. The enforcement of a foreign judgment cannot therefore be refused on grounds of public policy solely because the outcome of the foreign

[49] Helin (n 42) 109–10 and Lappalainen (n 14) 175. Parties' right to fair trial is highly valued in the Finnish legal system and the foreign proceeding leading to a judgment must also satisfy the basic criteria. Section 21 Constitution of Finland (731/1999) guarantees everyone the right to have his case heard appropriately and without undue delay by a legally competent court or other judicial body, as well the right to have a decision affecting his right and duties reviewed. Article 6 European Convention on Human Rights also provides for the key guarantees of a fair trial.

[50] Helin (n 42) 110 and Koulu (n 18) 799–800.

[51] HE 80/2008 vp, 53. HT Klami and E Kuisma, *Suomen kansainvälinen yksityisoikeus* (Kauppakaari Oyj, Lakimiesliiton kustannus, 2000a) 80. See also HT Klami and E Kuisma, *Finnish Law as an Option: Private International Law in Finland* (Kauppakaari Oyj, 2000b).

[52] Klami and Kuisma (2000a) (n 51) 81.

judgment differs from what would have been achieved if Finnish national law had been applied.[53] Instead, raising *ordre public* argument requires that there is a clear contradiction between the basic principles of Finnish law and the content of the foreign judgment.

In the precedents of the Supreme Court of Finland, the public policy considerations have been raised in cases concerning, for example, the notification of a unilateral judgment (KKO:2013:80) and service of summons application (KKO:2002:34).[54] Based on these precedents, recognition and enforcement could be prevented, for example, if the key procedural principles have been ignored in foreign court proceedings.[55] Due to the open nature of the doctrine of public policy, its application in practice is nevertheless somewhat challenging.

g) Reciprocity

The current national legislation on recognition and enforcement of foreign judgments in civil and commercial matters does not include a clause that would explicitly state that recognition of foreign judgments is based on reciprocity.[56]

h) Other Requirements

None.

Question 4. Documents to be Produced

According to section 33, subsection 3 of the International Legal Assistance Act, the following documents shall be attached to the enforcement application concerning the decision on legal costs:

(1) a certified copy of those sections of the decision that indicate the nature of the matter, the names of the parties and their status in the proceedings, and their obligation to pay legal costs; and
(2) a certificate indicating that the decision is final and enforceable in the state in which it was issued.

[53] Mohsen and Puro (n 30) 184.

[54] However, as both cases have been decided on grounds of the Lugano Convention and not the national law, they are not discussed here in more detail.

[55] See also M Tuulikki, 'Vieraan valtion oikeuden soveltamisen torjuminen ja ordre public' Edilex (22 June 2016) 2–3; and Koulu (n 18) 798–802.

[56] However, the Act on the co-operation between Finnish and foreign authorities in legal proceedings and on the enforcement in certain cases of a decision issued by a foreign court (171/1921) that was repealed when the current International Legal Assistance Act entered into force, included a provision on reciprocal enforcement of decisions of legal costs. HE 216/2014 vp, 6.

If the decision is in a language other than Finnish or Swedish, the application shall be accompanied by a certified translation into either of these languages, unless the district court grants an exemption.

It should be noted that section 33 of the International Legal Assistance Act serves as an express basis only for the recognition and enforcement of foreign decision on legal costs. However, it could provide some analogous support also in relation to the required documents in other enforcement applications.[57]

Accordingly, if there would be a sufficient basis for recognition and enforcement of other kind of foreign judgment, the application for the enforcement should state the requested measure and, as necessary, the circumstances on which the request measure is based. An application for the enforcement of foreign judgment should also include the written evidence that the applicant intends to present in support of the enforcement request.[58] This essentially refers to a copy of the foreign judgment certified by relevant authority that should be attached to the application. Additionally, a statement that indicates that the foreign judgment is legally binding and enforceable in the issuing country should also accompany the application.[59]

In Finnish courts, Finnish or Swedish are used as the languages of proceedings. The court decision is also issued in one of these two languages as provided in the Language Act (423/2003).[60] Subsequently, the court can require that the supporting documents of the recognition and enforcement application, which have been written in foreign languages, are translated into Finnish or Swedish if the court does not understand the language used.[61] However, in legal practice the translation requirement has not been always followed literally; in commercial disputes especially, documents are customarily submitted to the court also in English, French or German.[62]

As a rule, documents issued by a foreign authority must be legalised to have legal effect in Finland.[63] Legalisation of the document aims to ensure that the document or judgment concerned is valid in the issuing country. This may include ensuring that the person signing the document has the right to issue such a document in the issuing country under the laws of the country and that the document has been issued in the correct manner. In practice, the legalisation of foreign judgment or decision is not always a necessary requirement in the *exequatur* procedure in Finland. The Finnish

[57] Similar requirements for the necessary documents are stated in section 10 Act on the Recognition and Enforcement of Nordic Judgments Concerning Claims Under Private Law.

[58] Ch 8, s 2 CJP.

[59] According to s 35 Act of International Legal Assistance and Recognition and Enforcement of Judgments in Civil and Commercial Matters, 'If a judgment, decision or settlement issued in Finland is to be enforced in a foreign state, the court or authority that issued the judgment or other decision, or confirmed the settlement, shall on request issue a certificate of the enforceability of the decision or settlement in Finland.' Such certificate is authorised by the signature and the stamp of the district court.

[60] Ch 4, s 1 CJP.

[61] Obviously, translation of the foreign judgment supports also effective enforcement. The party who applies for the enforcement of foreign judgment in summary proceedings is responsible for providing to the court all the necessary translations required for the enforcement. Mohsen and Puro (n 30) 169.

[62] See Koulu (n 15) 59–60.

[63] A foreign document is legalised with a so-called Apostille certificate if the country has joined the Convention of 5 October 1961 Abolishing the Requirement of Legalisation for Foreign Public Documents. Regulation (EU) 2016/1191 on promoting the free movement of citizens by simplifying the requirements for presenting certain public documents in the EU applies within the EU.

courts have followed the principle that without the support of an explicit norm, the parties involved cannot usually be required to legalise or apostille documents, unless there is a special reason to doubt the authenticity of the documents.[64] However, if the court has doubts about the authenticity of the document, legalisation can be demanded and the application rejected if the legalised document has not been submitted.

Question 5. Securities, Bonds and Deposits

In accordance with Nordic practice, Finnish law does not recognise the possibility of obliging a party to a lawsuit to provide a security or a bond to cover any legal costs that may be awarded to the other party (*cautio judicatum solvi*). Since foreign parties have the same legal protection as Finnish citizens, a foreign applicant cannot be required to provide security for future legal costs.[65]

[64] Mohsen and Puro (n 30) 168. The principle follows the practice valid during the Brussels I Regulation, according to which legalisation of a copy of a foreign judgment was not required (Art 44).

[65] J Lappalainen and T Hupli, 'Oikeudenkäynnin kustannukset' in M Vuorenpää et al (eds), *Prosessioikeus*, 6th edn (Alma Talent Oy, 2021) 809; and HE 216/2014 vp, 6.

France

CLAUDIA CAVICCHIOLI

Question 1. General Overview

Subject to special regimes set out in bilateral or multilateral international conventions,[1] French rules on recognition and enforcement of non-EU judgments in civil and commercial matters are provided for in the French Codes and largely supplemented by relevant case law. These rules have not been influenced by, and are substantially different from, the Brussels regime (see, for instance, Question 3 below, concerning the conditions for recognition and enforcement).

The provisions contained in the French Codes that are specifically related to recognition and enforcement of foreign judgments are rather scarce and they consist mainly of Article 509 of the French code of Civil Procedure,[2] Article L 111-3 of the French Code of Civil Enforcement Procedures[3] and Article R 212-8 of the French Judicial Organisation Code.[4] Due to this scarcity of texts, most national-autonomous rules on recognition and enforcement of non-EU judgments are the work of jurisprudence.

To be subject to the French regime of recognition and enforcement, a judgment must: (i) be rendered by a foreign state or a foreign sovereignty; and (ii) issued by a judicial authority, or by non-judicial foreign authorities, provided that these authorities exercise discretionary power over an individual situation.[5]

Under French law, the concepts of recognition and enforcement are kept distinct: while recognition aims at introducing the situation which has been established by the

[1] For instance, the Convention on jurisdiction and the recognition and enforcement of judgments in civil and commercial matters (Lugano, 30 October 2007), the Convention of 30 June 2005 on Choice of Court Agreements (The Hague, 30 June 2005), the Convention of 2 July 2019 on the Recognition and Enforcement of Foreign Judgments in Civil or Commercial Matters (The Hague, 2 July 2019).

[2] 'Judgments rendered by foreign courts and acts received by foreign officers are enforceable in the territory of the Republic in the manner and in the case provided by law.'

[3] This provision includes, among other enforceable titles, 'foreign judgments … declared enforceable by a decision'.

[4] 'The high court of justice knows, by a single judge, … 2° Requests for recognition and enforcement of foreign judicial decisions and public acts …'. See, also, Art 370-5 on foreign adoptions.

[5] Recognition and enforcement of foreign arbitral awards do not fall within the scope of application of these rules.

foreign judgment in the French legal system, enforcement allows the creditor to take coercive steps on the French territory against the debtor.

Question 2. Procedure

a) Circumstances of Recognition and Enforcement

Foreign non-EU judgments are provisionally recognised *de plano* in France, without any need to obtain a court judgment, insofar as they relate to matters of status and capacity of persons[6] or in case of constitutive patrimonial judgments.[7]

Declaratory patrimonial judgments, on the contrary, are not recognised *de plano* and need to undergo an exequatur procedure.

The foreign decision cannot be enforced itself and an *exequatur* procedure is always necessary to enforce any foreign judgment. The party seeking enforcement of a foreign non-EU judgment must file a request for *exequatur* by way of writ of summons against the opposing party.

b) Procedural Steps

In terms of jurisdiction, the request must be brought:

- before a civil court of first instance (*tribunal judiciaire*);[8]
- before the court of the place where the enforcement is contemplated, or before the court of the opposing party's domicile. In the absence of a domicile in France, the request must be brought to the court of the residence of the defendant (for natural persons) or to the court of its place of business (for legal entities).[9] If the domicile, residence and/or establishment of the defendant are situated abroad or are unknown, the plaintiff may seize the French court of his choice provided that this choice is in accordance with the requirements of the proper administration of justice.

The ruling will be made by a single judge unless the parties expressly require a three-judge panel. The case will be heard through adversarial proceedings, after the exchange of written submissions. Parties must be represented by a lawyer registered with the local bar association.

First-instance enforcement proceedings can usually take from six to 12 months.

The enforcement decision may be appealed within one month of being notified by one party to the other (or three months for parties domiciled abroad). The appeal proceedings usually last approximately 12 to 18 months.

[6] Cour de cassation, 3 March 1930, *Hainard*.
[7] Cour de cassation, civ 1re, 3 November 1983, n° 82-14.003.
[8] Art R 212-8 of the Code of Judicial Organisation.
[9] Art 43 of the Code of Civil Procedure.

In the context of an action aimed at obtaining the recognition and enforcement of a foreign judgment, the burden to prove that the relevant conditions are met follows the principle *actori incumbit probatio*. It is therefore the party requesting the recognition or enforcement of the judgment that must prove the relevant facts. On the contrary, in the context of an action aiming at obtaining a decision on the ineffectiveness of the foreign judgment (*action en inopposabilité*), the claimant must allege and prove the defects which appear to affect the international validity of the judgment.

As regards French courts' role when reviewing foreign judgments, as a principle, French courts may, on their own motion, ascertain the existence of non-existence of the requirements to obtain recognition and enforcement. In this respect, on several occasions the French Supreme Court has stated that 'French courts must ensure [that the conditions for exequatur] are fulfilled'[10] and that French courts 'must, of their own motion, verify whether the foreign decision fulfils the conditions required to be declared enforceable in France'.[11] This is the case whether the foreign judgment is subject of a review on a principal basis (via an action for exequatur or an action for ineffectiveness (*action en inopposabilité*)), as well as when a party relies on the foreign judgment on an incidental basis in the course of an action with a different subject matter (for instance, by raising a plea of *res iudicata*).

However, by way of exception, French courts may not verify on their own motion whether the requirements to obtain recognition and enforcement are met when: (i) the requirement at stake is of private interest; and (ii) if the rights of the parties are freely disposable (*droits librement disponibles*).[12] In this case, French courts may only examine the requirements which have been challenged by the defendant. The French Supreme Court appears to have enshrined this principle by rejecting an appeal directed against a judgment which, in the absence of any challenge by the defendant, had granted exequatur to a foreign patrimonial judgment.[13]

Concerning the assessment of the relevant facts, these must be proven by the parties and the court is not obliged to seek out the relevant factual elements.[14] However, French courts have the power to order any investigative measure on their motion[15] or to request the parties to provide them with the factual information which is necessary for the review of the judgment.[16]

As indicated below (and see Question 3), French courts are prohibited from reviewing the foreign decision on the merits.[17]

[10] Cour de cassation, civ 1re, 7 January 1964, *Munzer*; Cour de cassation, civ 1re, 20 February 2007, n° 05-14.082, *Cornelissen*.

[11] Cour de cassation, civ 1re, 9 November 1971; Cour de cassation, civ 1re, 29 January 2014, n° 12-28.953.

[12] This will be the case in patrimonial matters.

[13] Cour de cassation, civ 1re, 3 June 1969: 'in the absence of any challenge to the applicable law, to the jurisdiction of the foreign court and to the regularity of the procedure that has been followed, the Court of Appeal rightly confined itself to exercising its power of review without having to raise any fact which was not raised before it'.

[14] Cour de cassation, civ 1re, 19 April 1977, n° 76-11.516.

[15] Art 10 French Code of Civil Procedure.

[16] Art 8 French Code of Civil Procedure.

[17] Cour de cassation, civ 1re, 7 January 1964, *Munzer*.

Question 3. Requirements

The requirements for the recognition and enforcement of a foreign judgment have been set by French case law.

Initially, said requirements were set by the *Munzer* judgment, dated 7 January 1964, which abolished the power of French court to fully review the merits of the case (*pouvoir de revision au fond*) that previously existed. In the *Munzer* case, the French Supreme Court held that

> in order to grant exequatur, French courts must ensure that five conditions are met, namely the jurisdiction of the foreign court that rendered the decision, the regularity of the proceedings before that court, the application of the competent law according to the French rules of conflict, conformity with international public policy and the absence of fraud against the law; … this verification, which is sufficient to ensure the protection of the French legal order and interests, the very purpose of the institution of exequatur, constitutes in all matters both the expression and the limit of the supervisory power of the court responsible for rendering a foreign decision enforceable in France, without that court having to review the merits of the decision.[18]

Further to the *Munzer* case, the requirements to obtain recognition and enforcement of a foreign judgments have become even more liberal, as two of the five conditions set out by the French Supreme Court have been abandoned by French case law.

Firstly, the French Supreme Court decided in the case *Bachir*, dated 4 October 1967, that it was not necessary to verify the regularity of the proceedings before the court of origin other than by resorting to the notion of public policy. The Court held in this respect that 'although the exequatur judge must check whether the proceedings before the foreign court were conducted in accordance with the law, this condition of regularity must be assessed solely in relation to French international public policy and respect for the rights of the defence'.[19]

Secondly, French case law abandoned the condition relating to the application of the competent law according to the French rules of conflict. In a decision *Cornelissen* rendered in 2007, the French Supreme Court held that 'the exequatur judge does not … have to verify that the law applied by the foreign judge is the one that is designated by the French conflict-of-laws rule'. As such, the Court stated that

> in order to grant exequatur outside the scope of any international convention, French courts must ensure that three conditions are met, namely the indirect jurisdiction of the foreign court, compliance with international public policy in terms of substance and procedure and the absence of fraud against the law.[20]

In light of the above, further to the *Cornelissen* decision of the French Supreme Court, in order to be recognised and enforced in France, the following requirements must be met:

- the country of origin has an indirect jurisdiction, ie the dispute is clearly connected with the country of origin, French courts do not have exclusive jurisdiction to hear the matter, and the choice of foreign court is not fraudulent;

[18] Cour de cassation, civ 1re, 7 January 1964, *Munzer*.
[19] Cour de cassation, civ 1re, 4 October 1967.
[20] Cour de cassation, civ 1re, 20 February 2007, n° 05-14.082, *Cornelissen*.

- the judgment is not contrary to French international public policy (*ordre public international*), both pertaining to the merits and to the procedure of the case;
- the judgment is not tainted with fraud;
- the judgment does not conflict with a judgment rendered by a French court or a foreign judgment which that has become effective in France. Although this requirement is not expressly mentioned by the *Cornelissen* case, French legal authors consider that it was considered by the French Supreme Court as being part of the review of the compliance by public policy, and is constantly verified by French courts.

In addition, and as a matter of admissibility, in the context of an action aiming at obtaining the *exequatur* of the foreign judgment, French courts must verify that the foreign judgment is enforceable in the country of origin.

a) Jurisdiction of the Court of Origin

Since the thesis of the legal author Bartin, the jurisdiction of the foreign court which handed down the relevant judgment has been described as *indirect* jurisdiction,[21] as opposed to the *direct* jurisdiction of a French court hearing the merits of a case.

Drawing on the thesis of Dominique Holleaux,[22] who had shown that direct and indirect jurisdiction must be considered two distinct notions, the French Supreme Court established a rule specifically designated to the review of the international validity of foreign judgments.[23] In this respect, French courts must verify that: (i) the dispute is clearly connected with the country of origin; (ii) French courts do not have exclusive jurisdiction to hear the matter; and (iii) the choice of foreign court is not fraudulent.

As regards the first requirement (the dispute is clearly connected with the country of origin), if one of the grounds of jurisdiction enshrined in a French rule of direct jurisdiction has arisen in the country of origin, this condition will be met. Thus, for instance, since Article 42 of the Code of Civil Procedure gives jurisdiction to the court of the defendant's domicile, the dispute will be deemed as being clearly connected with a country if the defendant is domiciled in such country. If no grounds for direct jurisdiction points to the country of origin, the existence of a clear connection with said country is assessed on a case-by-case. For instance, French courts held that this criterion was met in a case where English courts were seized of an application for divorce, as the wife had a British nationality and domicile, and the spouses had married in England where they had established their first domicile and where the

[21] E Bartin, *Principes de droit international privé* (Domat-Montchrestien, 1930) 127, 205 and 206.

[22] D Holleaux, *Compétence du juge étranger et reconnaissance des jugements* (Dalloz, 1970) 407.

[23] Cour de cassation, civ 1re, 6 February 1985, n° 83-11.241, Simitch: 'whenever French rules on conflict of jurisdictions do not confer exclusive jurisdiction on the French courts, the foreign court must be deemed to have jurisdiction if the dispute is clearly connected with the country at stage and if the choice of court has not been fraudulent'.

husband owned certain assets.[24] On the contrary, French courts have held that temporary residence in a foreign state is insufficient to constitute a clear connection for the purposes of establishing indirect jurisdiction.[25] In another case, French courts have held that the identity between applicable law and country of origin is insufficient to establish indirect jurisdiction.[26]

As regards the second requirement (French courts do not have exclusive jurisdiction to hear the matter), this is notably the case: (i) in matters which involve the French state (for instance, in case of injunctions against state agents, or matters relating to the granting of French nationality); or (ii) in case of actions for a seizure in France;[27] or (iii) in case of actions *in rem* concerning immovable property located in France.[28] The French Supreme Court has also held that the requirement relating to indirect jurisdiction is not complied with in a case where the dispute had been submitted to a foreign court in breach of a jurisdiction clause in favour of French courts.[29] On the contrary, French case law has notably established that French courts do not have exclusive jurisdiction over the matter on the sole ground that the claimant[30] or the defendant[31] is French.

As regards the third requirement (the choice of foreign court is not fraudulent), French courts must assess that there was no fraud on the part of the claimant to create an artificial ground on which to base the jurisdiction of the country of origin. This criterion is said to partially overlap the general criterion of fraud (see below, Question 3 e)).

b) Finality/Enforceability in the Country of Origin

As a matter of admissibility of the claim, foreign non-EU judgments can be enforced in France if they are enforceable in the country of origin, according to the law of that jurisdiction. They do not need to be final.

c) *Res Iudicata*

Recognition or enforcement may be denied in cases of irreconcilability with a prior conflicting judgment.

In the event of irreconcilability between a foreign judgment (which has not yet been recognised or enforced in France) and a French judgment, French courts consider that the French judgment prevails,[32] even if the French judgment is subsequent.[33]

[24] Cour de cassation, civ 1re, 6 February 1985, n° 83-11.241, *Simitch*.
[25] Cour de cassation, civ 1re, 5 May 1998, n° 95-22.020.
[26] Cour de cassation, civ 1re, 24 November 1993, n° 91-21.368.
[27] Cour de cassation, civ 1re, 6 November 1979; Cour de cassation, civ 1re, 18 November 1986.
[28] Cour de cassation, civ 1re, 14 November 1961.
[29] Cour de cassation, civ 1re, 15 May 2018, n° 17-17.546.
[30] Cour de cassation, civ 1re22 May 2007, n° 04-14.716, *Fercométal*.
[31] Cour de cassation, civ 1re, 23 May 2006, n° 04-12.777, *Prieur*.
[32] Cour de cassation, civ 1re, 15 May 1963, *Patino*.
[33] Cour de cassation, civ 1re, 24 September. 2002, n° 01-11.237; Cour de cassation, civ 1re, 27 April 2004, n° 02-13.490.

In the event of irreconcilability between two foreign judgments, French courts will apply the criteria *prior tempore potior jure*. Therefore, the first judgment to be recognised or granted *exequatur* will prevent the other judgment from being recognised or granted exequatur in France, regardless of the date on which the case was referred to court or the date on which the judgments were issued.

d) *Lis Pendens*

If recognition or enforcement proceedings are brought in France while other proceedings are still pending before a French court, the latter will not be taken into account.

Enforcement proceedings in France may also be stayed if there are proceedings pending before the French courts at the time the enforcement of the foreign judgment is sought, which have the same or similar subject matter as the foreign judgment.[34] However, if the application for *exequatur* was lodged before the proceedings on the merits, French Supreme Court held that it may be examined first.[35]

e) Specific Requirements of Due Process

French courts will assess whether due process has been followed and whether the right of the defence have been complied with. Under French law, these principles are considered part of the broader category of public policy pertaining to the procedure of the case.

As such, French courts will verify whether the fundamental principles of the procedure have been complied with,[36] such as proper service on the defendant,[37] sufficient time to prepare the defence,[38] independence and impartiality of the foreign court,[39] due process[40] and provision of reasoning in the judgment where no documents are produced that could serve as an equivalent to the insufficient reasoning.[41]

These requirements will always be considered as a 'full' public policy and do not produce any attenuated effect[42] (see section f) below).

[34] Cour d'appel Paris, 27 juin 1964, *Rougeron*: 'Where two sets of proceedings are pending in France, one seeking a decision on the merits of a dispute and the other seeking enforcement of a foreign decision that has ruled on the merits between the same parties in the same dispute, the court before which enforcement is sought may not, on pain of a possible conflict of decisions prejudicial to public policy, either rule on the questions referred to the judges hearing the case on the merits, or grant enforcement as it stands, as long as the judges hearing the case on the merits have not given a ruling.'

[35] Cour de cassation, civ 1re, 13 April 1976, n° 74-14.163.

[36] Cour de cassation, civ 1re, 19 September 2007, n° 06-17.096.

[37] Cour de cassation, civ 1re, 1 June 1994, n° 92-13.523; Cour de cassation, civ 1re, 20 December 2000, n° 99-12.777.

[38] Cour de cassation, civ 1re, 29 November 1994, n° 92-19.648.

[39] Cour de cassation, civ 1re, 3 December 1996, n° 94-20.986.

[40] Cour de cassation, civ 1re, 21 October 1997, n° 95-17.577.

[41] Cour de cassation, civ 1re, 17 May 1978, n° 76-14.843.

[42] Cour de cassation, civ 1re, 6 June 1990, n° 99-17.877.

f) Public Policy

French courts must verify that the foreign judgment does not contravene other principles of French international public policy rules, both pertaining to the merits and the procedure of the case.[43]

Public policy is generally applied as a basis for refusing to enforce foreign judgments in a restrictive way. The French Supreme Court held that 'a foreign decision can only be considered as contrary to French public policy if it is shown that the interests of a party have been objectively compromised by a violation of the fundamental principles of procedure'.[44]

Concerning public policy pertaining to the merits, this notion consists of the 'essential principles of French law'.[45] French courts will not assess the conformity of the foreign applicable law to French public policy, but whether the substantial solution adopted by the foreign judgment complies with these essential principles. For instance, the French Supreme Court held that a foreign judgment issuing punitive damages that are disproportionate to the harm sustained and the contractual breach is contrary to public policy.[46]

French substantive public policy will apply with varying degrees of intensity depending on the case.[47] Unless there are special links with France (for instance, where one of the parties is a French national or has his or her domicile or residence in France),[48] a foreign judgment will in principle be accepted in France on liberal terms, since 'the French concept of international public policy only comes into play in this case with attenuated effect'.[49] In certain situations, however, the foreign judgment will be considered unacceptable on the basis of a 'full' public policy exception, irrespective of the links with France. This is the case, for instance, when a foreign divorce judgment was based on the concept of marital power.[50]

Public policy pertaining to the procedure of the case has been discussed above, under section e).

g) Reciprocity

Not applicable.

[43] Cour de cassation, civ 1re, 20 February 2007, n° 05-14.082, *Cornelissen*.

[44] Cour de cassation, civ 1re, 19 September 2007, n° 06-17.096.

[45] Cour de cassation, civ 1re, 8 July 2010, n° 08-21.740.

[46] Cour de cassation, civ 1re, 1 December 2010, n° 09-13.303: 'although the principle of an award of punitive damages is not, in itself, contrary to public policy, that is not the case when the amount awarded is disproportionate in relation to the harm suffered and the debtor's breaches of contractual obligations'.

[47] Cour de cassation, civ 1re, 17 April 1953, *Rivière*; Cour de cassation, civ 1re, 7 January 1964, *Munzer*.

[48] Cour de cassation, civ 1re, 17 February 2004, n° 02-10.755, 02-17.479, 01-11.549, 02-11.618, 02-15.766.

[49] Cour de cassation, civ 1re, 28 February 1984, n° 83-10.041, *Klopp*.

[50] Poitiers Court of Appeal, 24 July 1980, Jurisdata n° 1980-601180.

h) Other Requirements

French courts also verify the absence of fraud.[51] There is a debate among legal authors as to how this requirement should be construed.

Strictly speaking, the requirement of fraud refers to a fraudulent application of the law (*fraude à la loi*), ie a manoeuvre consisting of modifying a connecting factor (nationality, domicile, residence) with a view to ousting the law of a state that would have been applicable and artificially benefiting from the law of another state. In this respect, French courts have in the past refused to enforce in France a foreign judgment that had applied the law that had been made applicable fraudulently.[52]

However, following the *Cornelissen* case referred to above,[53] which held that the *exequatur* judge must not check that the law applied by the foreign court is the one that would have been designated pursuant to the French conflict-of-laws rule, some legal authors state that French courts cannot review whether a fraudulent application of the law (*fraude à la loi*) exists.[54] Other legal authors indicate that this requirement should be maintained, by interpreting it as 'the absence of fraud to all the rules of private international law of the forum', in order to use this criterion when 'the judgment was sought abroad for the sole purpose of evading [the rules of private international law of the forum'.[55]

Broadly speaking, this criterion may be understood as referring to a fraud on the judgment (*fraude au jugement*), ie 'going to litigate abroad with the main (if not sole) aim of invoking the judgment in (another country) which would have refused to pronounce it if its judges had been seized directly; fraud consists in seeking to obtain indirectly what one would not have been able to obtain directly'.[56] For instance, *exequatur* of a foreign judgment was denied based on fraud in a case where a husband obtained a divorce judgment abroad, even though he was domicile in France with his wife and a French court had previously ordered him to contribute to the costs of the marriage.[57] Similarly, *exequatur* was denied in a case where the plaintiff seized United States courts after having travelled on several occasions to United States with the

> sole purpose, by misrepresenting the existing situation in such a way as to give credence to the fact that the family's residence was established on American soil … to obtain, by deliberately misleading the foreign judge, that the children's residence be established in the United States.[58]

[51] Cour de cassation, civ 1re, 30 January 2013, n° 11-10.588.

[52] Cour de cassation, civ 1re, 9 May 1900, *de Wrède*.

[53] Cour de cassation, civ 1re, 20 February 2007, n° 05-14.082, *Cornelissen*.

[54] P Mayer, V Heuzé and B Remy, *Droit international privé* (LGDJ 2019) 391.

[55] M-L Niboyet, 'L'abandon du contrôle de compétence législative indirecte' *Gazette du Palais*, 3 May 2007, 2.

[56] Mayer, Heuzé and Remy (n 54) 408.

[57] Cour de cassation, civ 1re, 20 June 2012, n° 11-30.120; Cour de cassation, civ 1re, 28 March 2006, n° 03-18.934; Cour de cassation, civ 1re, 6 June 1990, n° 88-15.008, *Akla*.

[58] Cour de cassation, civ 1re, 17 December 2014, n° 13-21.365.

Question 4. Documents to be Produced

The party seeking to recognise or enforce a foreign non-EU judgment must provide the court with:

- Proof of the foreign judgment, by producing an authenticated copy of the decision.[59] The copy must be authenticated by the French consul in the country of origin of the judgment, the consul's signature itself being authenticated by the Ministry of Foreign Affairs. The signature of the foreign document must be legalised. Legalisation is not required on pain of nullity, and the *exequatur* judge may declare that the document is authentic on the basis of other evidence.[60]
- A translation if the judgment is not issued in French. French courts will generally require that foreign judgments be accompanied by a translation issued by a sworn translator.
- Proof that the judgment has been served on the opposing party.

Question 5. Securities, Bonds and Deposits

The claimant to an action aiming at obtaining the recognition or enforcement of a foreign non-EU judgment is not required to provide securities, bonds or deposits.

[59] In this respect, a simple extract of the foreign judgment is not sufficient: Cour de cassation, civ 1re, 18 April 1967; Cour de cassation, civ 1re, 26 June 1990, n° 88-18.721.

[60] In addition, international conventions may provide for different requirements. See, for instance, the Convention on international access to justice (The Hague, 25 October 1980), which state that no legalisation or analogous formality may be required (Art 17).

Germany

KARIN ARNOLD AND LEON THEIMER

Question 1. Overview

The framework for the recognition and enforcement of foreign judgments in civil and commercial matters in Germany is set forth in the Code of Civil Procedure (*Zivilprozessordnung*; ZPO). Conceptually, German law draws a strict distinction between recognition and enforcement: § 328 ZPO governs recognition, whereas §§ 722, 723 ZPO are concerned with enforcement. Pursuant to § 723(2) cl 2 ZPO, the recognition of a foreign judgment is a prerequisite for its enforcement. Following the structure of § 328(1) ZPO, there are six statutory requirements for recognition, all of which are phrased negatively, as grounds for refusal. In addition, two uncodified requirements must be met. Finally, § 723(2) cl 1 ZPO requires finality for the purpose of enforcement, but it is disputed whether this also extends to recognition. Put positively, the requirements for recognition and enforcement are as follows:

(1) Jurisdiction of the Court of Origin
(2) Finality/Enforceability in the Country of Origin
(3) Compatibility with a German judgment or with an earlier foreign judgment
(4) Compatibility with proceedings that have become pending earlier in Germany
(5) Due Process
(6) Compatibility with public policy
(7) Reciprocity
(8) Validity of the judgment (uncodified)
(9) Jurisdiction of the Court of Origin under public international law (uncodified).

Requirements (3) and (5) are modelled after Article 27 no 2, 3 and 5 Brussels Convention. They are thus interpreted in accordance with these provisions and, in so far as they still coincide, with the corresponding provisions in the Brussels I and Brussels Ia Regulations. Importantly, this includes taking into account the relevant case law of the Court of Justice of the European Union (CJEU).[1] The other requirements, however, can be found – in varying forms and combinations – in both academic discussions and legislation since at least the end of the eighteenth century.

[1] See R Geimer, '§ 328' in R Zöller (ed), *Zivilprozessordnung*, 35th edn (Dr Otto Schmidt, 2024) paras 155 ff., 199. See below, Question 3 c), e).

In particular, requirements (1) and (7) were already widespread and the subject of intense debate in the nineteenth century.[2] Although requirement (5) in its current form is based on EU law, the German Code of Civil Procedure of 1877 already contained a similar provision which, however, only applied in favour of German debtors.[3] Today, European (EU) law even plays a role in the interpretation of the 'old' requirements, such as requirement (6).[4]

Against the background of the Brussels framework, the practical relevance of German autonomous law has declined. Furthermore, international treaties on recognition and enforcement with non-EU and non-European Free Trade Association (EFTA) states exist, ie with the United Kingdom (UK), Tunisia and Israel.[5] In particular, the 1960 Treaty with the UK has recently come back into the limelight as its legal revival after Brexit is being discussed among scholars.[6]

Question 2. Procedure

a) Circumstances of Recognition and Enforcement

1. *Recognition: Informal vs Formal Recognition*

Recognition of a foreign judgment under the ZPO is informal.[7] The requirements for recognition are examined when the effects of the foreign judgment become relevant in Germany, eg as a preliminary question in civil or administrative proceedings.

Decisions in marital matters, however, have to be recognised in a formal procedure: § 107 Act on Proceedings in Family Matters and in Matters of Non-contentious

[2] See, eg, legislation in Prussia: General Court Order of 1791, Title 24, Section 1, § 30, and Explanatory Report, 244 f., and Draft Code of Civil Procedure of 1864, § 972; in Bavaria: Ordinance of 2 June 1811, Draft Codes of Civil Procedure of 1825, §§ 1059 ff, and of 1861, Art 770(1) no 2, and Code of Civil Procedure of 1869, §§ 823 f; in Württemberg: Enforcement Act of 1825, Art 7, Draft Enforcement Act of 1840, Art 13, and Code of Civil Procedure of 1868, Arts 10(1), 11(2), (4), (5); in Hanover: Lower Court Order of 1828, § 161(1), General Code of Civil Procedure of 1848, § 84, and Hanoverian Code of Civil Procedure of 1850, § 29; in Baden: Code of Civil Procedure of 1830, §§ 952 f; German Code of Civil Procedure of 1877, § 661; KS Zachariae, 'Ueber die Rechtskraft eines in einer Civil-Sache von einem auswärtigen Gericht gesprochenen Urtheils, nach den Grundsätzen des Staatsrechts der rheinischen Bundes-Staaten' (1809) 2 *Germanien, Eine Zeitschrift für Staats-Recht, Politik und Statistik von Deutschland*, 229, 235, 247; KA von Kamptz, 'Ueber die Rechtskraft eines, in einer Civil-Sache von einem auswärtigen Gerichte gesprochenen Urtheils nach den Grundsätzen des Staatsrechts der rheinischen Bundesstaaten' (1809) 3 *Germanien, Eine Zeitschrift für Staats-Recht, Politik und Statistik von Deutschland*, 231, 233 ff; PJA Feuerbach, *Themis oder Beiträge zur Gesetzgebung* (Krüll, 1812) 75 ff; L von Bar, *Theorie und Praxis des Internationalen Privatrechts, Zweiter Band*, 2nd edn (Hahn, 1889) 506513.

[3] § 661(2) no 4 of the German Code of Civil Procedure of 1877. Similarly, Art 11(5) of the Württemberg Code of Civil Procedure of 1868.

[4] See Geimer (n 1) paras 208 ff.

[5] For more details on these treaties, see R Schütze, '§ 328' in B Wieczorek, R Schütze and M Gebauer (eds), *Zivilprozessordnung und Nebengesetze – Großkommentar*, 5th edn (de Gruyter, 2023) paras 204 ff.

[6] See R Wagner, 'Justizielle Zusammenarbeit in Zivilsachen nach dem Brexit' (2021) *Praxis des Internationalen Privat- und Verfahrensrechts* 2, 7; G Rühl, 'Die Wahl englischen Rechts und englischer Gerichte nach dem Brexit' (2017) *Juristenzeitung* 72, 80 f.

[7] In family matters, this is expressly stated in § 108(1) FamFG, whereas the ZPO lacks an explicit provision.

Jurisdiction (*Gesetz über das Verfahren in Familiensachen und in den Angelegenheiten der freiwilligen Gerichtsbarkeit*, FamFG).[8] Here, the requirement of formal recognition is justified by the fact that the existence or non-existence of a marriage directly affects a large number of other family matters and has repercussions in the context of inheritance law, aliens law and tax law.[9] Conflicting decisions must therefore be prevented.[10] For non-marital matters, formal recognition is optional under § 108(2) FamFG.

2. *Enforcement: Requirement of a Domestic Judgment*

Under the ZPO, enforcement always requires a formal procedure: a declaration of enforceability must be pronounced by a court in a so-called 'enforcement judgment' (*Vollstreckungsurteil*), issued in response to a formal action (*Vollstreckungsklage*): §§ 722, 723 ZPO. The subject matter of this action is not the original claim (see also, the prohibition of the *révision au fond*[11]), but the admissibility of enforcement of the foreign judgment in Germany.[12] The enforcement judgment – and not the foreign judgment – then forms the basis for enforcement in Germany.[13]

The ZPO does not provide for a special type of procedure for an enforcement action. It is therefore an ordinary action to which the general provisions of the ZPO apply.[14] In particular, the plaintiff must file a formal claim, which is usually heard orally,[15] and the proceedings are adversarial. This is criticised by scholars as inefficient since it is costly, time-consuming, and makes rapid enforcement impossible.[16]

In contrast, in certain family matters,[17] a declaration of enforceability is neither admissible nor necessary;[18] see §§ 110(2), 95(1) FamFG.

[8] This does not apply to decisions made in the country of which both spouses were nationals at the time of the decision; these decisions are recognised informally, §107(1) cl 2 FamFG.

[9] R Hüßtege, '§ 107 FamFG' in H Thomas and H Putzo (eds), *Zivilprozessordnung*, 46th edn (CH Beck, 2025) para 2.

[10] U Spellenberg, '§ 107' in J von Staudinger (ed), *J. von Staudingers Kommentar zum Bürgerlichen Gesetzgebuch mit Einführungsgesetz und Nebengesetzen – Einführungsgesetz zum Bürgerlichen Gesetzbuche/IPR – Internationales Verfahrensrecht in Ehesachen 2* (Sellier-de Gruyter, 2016) paras 1 f.

[11] See below, Question 2 b) 4.

[12] CF Nordmeier, '§ 723 ZPO' in H Thomas and H Putzo (eds), *Zivilprozessordnung*, 46th edn (CH Beck, 2025) para 9; R Schütze, '§ 722' in B Wieczorek, R Schütze and M Gebauer (eds), *Zivilprozessordnung und Nebengesetze – Großkommentar*, 5th edn (de Gruyter, 2023) para 30.

[13] Prevailing opinion, see R Geimer, '§ 722' in R Zöller (ed), *Zivilprozessordnung*, 35th edn (Dr Otto Schmidt, 2024) para 93; for a contrary opinion, see Schütze (n 12) para 45, who considers as the basis for enforcement the German enforcement judgment together with the foreign judgment.

[14] Geimer (n 13) para 36; P Gottwald, '§ 722' in T Rauscher and W Krüger (eds), *Münchener Kommentar zur Zivilprozessordnung*, 7th edn (CH Beck, 2025) para 45; Nordmeier (n 12) paras 7, 13; Schütze (n 13) paras 26, 37.

[15] Nordmeier (n 12) para 13.

[16] Geimer (n 13) para 36.

[17] Decisions concerning the surrender of children and contact arrangements.

[18] J Dimmler, '§ 110' in W Sternal (ed), *FamFG Kommentar*, 21th edn (CH Beck, 2023) para 71; U Spellenberg, '§ 110' in J von Staudinger (ed), *J. von Staudingers Kommentar zum Bürgerlichen Gesetzgebuch mit Einführungsgesetz und Nebengesetzen – Einführungsgesetz zum Bürgerlichen Gesetzbuche/IPR – Internationales Verfahrensrecht in Ehesachen 2* (Sellier-de Gruyter, 2016) para 15.

b) Procedural Steps

1. Recognition

As foreign decisions are generally recognised informally in the context of other proceedings, all authorities and courts involved in such proceedings are competent for recognition.

2. Enforcement

Enforcement jurisdiction is governed by § 722(2) ZPO, which partly refers to the general provisions of the ZPO. In particular, the regional courts (*Landgerichte*) at the defendant's domicile (§ 12 ZPO) or registered office (§ 17 ZPO) have jurisdiction. If the defendant is not domiciled in Germany or has no registered office in Germany, the *Landgerichte* in whose districts the defendant's assets are located possess subsidiary jurisdiction (§ 23 ZPO). In this case, no further connection to Germany is necessary. In addition, the assets need not be sufficient for enforcement.[19] No provision exists as to which court should have jurisdiction if the location of the defendant's assets is unknown. Scholars suggest that the courts at the seat of the federal government should have jurisdiction,[20] but there is no case law in this regard.

Moreover, the federal states (*Länder*) have recently been authorised under § 722(4) ZPO to concentrate jurisdiction for the enforcement of foreign judgments in one or more *Landgerichte*. Multiple *Länder* may even agree on the joint jurisdiction of one or more *Landgerichte*.

For a comprehensive overview of the different heads of jurisdiction under German law, the reader is kindly referred to the third project of the EAPIL Young Research Network.[21]

3. Burden of Proof

A distinction must be drawn between the examination of the requirements for recognition and enforcement on the one hand and the burden of proof for the facts relating to the existence of the requirements on the other.

3.1. Examination of Requirements

According to the prevailing view, the requirements for recognition and enforcement are examined *ex officio*.[22] Therefore, the defendant need not apply to the authority or

[19] Bundesgerichtshof, 28 October 1996, X ARZ 1071/96, sub II.2–3.

[20] Geimer (n 13) para 46; Schütze (n 13) para 13. This solution is similar to § 107(2) cl 3 FamFG.

[21] T Lutzi and FM Wilke, 'Germany' in T Lutzi, E Piovesani and D Zgrabljić Rotar (eds), *Jurisdiction Over Non-EU Defendants*, Studies in Private International Law 36 (Hart, 2023) 111.

[22] Bundesgerichtshof, 30 March 2011, XII ZB 300/10, sub II.3.b) for § 109 FamFG; P Gottwald, '§ 328' in T Rauscher and W Krüger (eds), *Münchener Kommentar zur Zivilprozessordnung*, 7th edn (CH Beck, 2025) para 10; U Spellenberg, '§ 109' in J von Staudinger (ed), *J. von Staudingers Kommentar zum Bürgerlichen Gesetzbuch mit Einführungsgesetz und Nebengesetzen – Einführungsgesetz zum Bürgerlichen Gesetzbuche/ IPR – Internationales Verfahrensrecht in Ehesachen 2* (Sellier-de Gruyter, 2016) para 12; S Huber in R Dierck, T Morvilius and G Vollkommer (eds), *Handbuch des Zwangsvollstreckungsrechts* (CH Beck, 2009) para 304.

the court for their examination. However, there is an exception for the requirement of due process: this ground for refusal must be invoked by the defendant in order to be assessed,[23] as it is seen as only serving to protect the defendant, rather than the interests of the state.[24] The defendant should therefore have the possibility to accept the foreign judgment despite not having been duly served in sufficient time.[25]

Some scholars wish to generalise this idea: the requirements which serve the defendant's protection should be examined only if she invokes them, while the requirements which (also) serve the state's interests should be examined *ex officio*.[26] According to this scholarly opinion, a violation of procedural public policy as well as the finality of the judgment and the jurisdiction of the court of origin should be examined only if the defendant invokes them.[27] With regard to the jurisdiction of the court of origin, one court of second instance has endorsed this opinion.[28] However, in family matters, the Federal Court of Justice (Bundesgerichtshof) has ruled that all requirements except for the requirement of due process have to be examined *ex officio*.[29]

3.2. Facts Relevant for the Requirements of Recognition and Enforcement

At the same time, examination *ex officio* does not mean that the authority or the court itself determines the facts relevant for the existence of the requirements for recognition and enforcement.[30] In contrast, the plaintiff bears the burden of proof – in principle.[31] In detail, the different requirements must be considered separately. Problems arise where the assessment of the requirements depends not only on facts, but on legal provisions as well. An example for this is the requirement of due service.[32] According to the case law, the plaintiff bears the burden of proof for the jurisdiction of the court of origin,[33] for due service[34] in sufficient time,[35] and for reciprocity.[36] On the other hand, the defendant bears the burden of proof for an alleged violation of public policy.[37]

[23] Bundesgerichtshof, 30 March 2011, XII ZB 300/10, sub II.3.b) for § 109 FamFG; Schütze (n 5) para 92.

[24] I Bach, '§ 328' in V Vorwerk and C Wolf (eds), *Beck'scher Online-Kommentar ZPO*, 57th edn (CH Beck, 2025) para 49.

[25] Spellenberg (n 22) para 43.

[26] Bach (n 24) para 49.

[27] Schütze (n 5) para 93; with regard to the jurisdiction of the court of origin: Geimer (n 1) para 142. For a contrary view with regard to public policy and § 109 FamFG, see R Hausmann, *Internationales und Europäisches Familienrecht*, 3rd edn (CH Beck, 2024) Part 2, K, para 389.

[28] Oberlandesgericht Schleswig, 5 May 2008, 12 Va 5/07, para 7. For a different view in marital matters, see Bayerisches Oberstes Landesgericht 19 September 1991, BReg 3 Z 113/91 sub II.2.c) (rationale: choice of court agreements in marital matters are prohibited).

[29] Bundesgerichtshof, 30 March 2011, XII ZB 300/10, sub II.3.b) for § 109 FamFG.

[30] Gottwald (n 22) para 10; *cf* Schütze (n 5) para 92; Huber (n 22) para 304.

[31] Schütze (n 5) para 94; for a contrary opinion, see B Völzmann-Stickelbrock, '§ 328' in H Prütting and M Gehrlein (eds), *Zivilprozessordnung Kommentar*, 16th edn (Wolters Kluwer, 2024) para 1, who places the burden of proof on the plaintiff only with regard to the jurisdiction of the court of origin and to reciprocity.

[32] See below, Question 3 e) 2.

[33] Oberlandesgericht Koblenz, 16 October 2003, 7 U 87/00, above sub A; Geimer (n 1) para 144.

[34] Oberlandesgericht Karlsruhe, 22 January 1996, 13 W 220/92.

[35] Oberlandesgericht Stuttgart, 18 May 2017, 17 VA 1/16, sub II.3.d) for § 109(1) no 2 FamFG.

[36] Bundesgerichtshof, 29 April 1999, IX ZR 263/97, sub IV.4.d); Oberlandesgericht Koblenz, 16 October 2003 – 7 U 87/00, above sub A; Geimer (n 1) para 264.

[37] Bundesgerichtshof, 14 November 1996, IX ZR 339/95, sub III.2.f); Oberlandesgericht Koblenz, 16 October 2003, 7 U 87/00, above sub A; Geimer (n 1) paras 269, 271.

The case law on the reciprocity requirement has not found universal approval among scholars. Rather, it is noted that under German law the plaintiff can only be required to prove facts. However, foreign law is not treated as fact in German law, but as law. It follows that, according to this scholarly opinion, the plaintiff cannot bear the burden of proof for the requirement since reciprocity depends on the content of foreign law. It is therefore suggested that a distinction be made: facts should be proved by the plaintiff, while the authority or the court should be responsible for assessing the requirements depending on the content of foreign law.[38] This can be understood as an expression of the principle *iura novit curia*.[39] Crucially, the argument is not limited to reciprocity but extends to the requirements of validity and finality of the foreign judgment as well as due service of the document initiating the proceedings.[40]

In the context of reciprocity, the determination of foreign law may prove difficult. There are various lists of countries to be found in legal literature indicating whether or not reciprocity is guaranteed. However, these lists often contain outdated information. In addition, there is the possibility of obtaining expert opinions from universities or the Max Planck Institute for Comparative and International Private Law in Hamburg; however, this increases the cost of the enforcement proceedings.[41]

The situation is different in those family matters which require a formal recognition procedure:[42] in these cases, the relevant facts are also determined *ex officio*.[43] However, if the facts cannot be established, the rules on the distribution of the burden of proof apply.[44]

4. *Prohibition of* Révision au Fond

Neither in the context of recognition nor in the context of enforcement may the foreign judgment be reviewed on the merits. This principle is expressly laid down in § 723(1) only for enforcement, but it also applies to recognition.[45]

5. *Appeals*

Appeals against a decision granting or refusing recognition are possible and depend on the context in which the foreign judgment is either recognised or refused recognition. Enforcement judgments can also be appealed. Since the general provisions of the ZPO apply,[46] the enforcement judgment can be challenged like any other judgment under the ZPO.[47]

[38] Bach (n 24) para 51.

[39] See with regard to the examination of reciprocity by the court, D Martiny, 'Recognition and Enforcement of Foreign Money Judgments in the Federal Republic of Germany' (1987) 35 *American Journal of Comparative Law* 721, 751.

[40] Bach (n 24) para 51.

[41] Martiny (n 39) 751 f.

[42] §§ 107, 108(2) FamFG.

[43] § 26 FamFG; Hüßtege (n 9) para 23; Hausmann (n 27) Part 2, K, para 328; Spellenberg (n 10) para 180.

[44] Spellenberg (n 10) para 31.

[45] Geimer (n 1) para 208. In family matters, the *révision au fond* is expressly prohibited by § 109(5) FamFG.

[46] See above, Question 2 a) 2.

[47] Geimer (n 13) para 92.

6. *Binding Effect*

In cases of informal recognition, the decision of the respective authority or court has no binding effect on other authorities and courts, thus creating a risk of conflicting decisions.[48]

As an ordinary judgment, the enforcement judgment is endowed with binding effect. However, it is important to note that the binding effect relates to the enforceability of the foreign judgment in Germany, not to the original claim, since the latter is not the subject matter of the dispute (see Question 2 a) 2.

Question 3. Requirements

a) Jurisdiction of the Court of Origin

1. *Recognition Jurisdiction and the 'Mirror Image Principle'*

Pursuant to § 328(1) no 1 ZPO, recognition of a foreign judgment shall be denied if 'The courts of the state to which the foreign court belongs do not have jurisdiction according to German law'.[49] Crucially, jurisdiction is to be understood in an international sense: whether the particular foreign court was locally competent is irrelevant as long as it had international jurisdiction.[50] This recognition jurisdiction (*Anerkennungszuständigkeit*) is assessed on the basis of the so-called 'mirror image principle' by which the German rules of jurisdiction are hypothetically applied to the foreign court.[51] Put differently, the foreign court must have exercised jurisdiction in circumstances in which a German court would also have exercised jurisdiction.

The rationale behind the 'mirror image principle' is to use the concept of jurisdictional justice embodied in the German rules of jurisdiction as a standard against which to measure whether foreign judgments should be given effect in Germany. In the absence of an internationally uniform understanding of jurisdictional justice, it is considered fair to treat the judgments of foreign courts no less favourably than those of German courts.[52] In particular, the 'mirror image principle' ensures that the country of origin's *lex fori processualis* conforms, as a minimum, with internationally accepted principles.[53] Moreover, it protects the defendant[54] from having to defend herself before

[48] Geimer (n 1) para 85. See, in contrast, § 107(9) FamFG and Spellenberg (n 10) paras 1 f.

[49] Official translation by the German Federal Ministry of Justice, available at gesetze-im-internet.de/englisch_zpo. The same applies to family matters, § 109 FamFG.

[50] Bundesgerichtshof (Federal Court of Justice) 29 April 1999, IX ZR 263-97, BGHZ 141, 286, sub III.1; Martiny (n 39) 734; Gottwald (n 22) para 90; H Schack, *Internationales Zivilverfahrensrecht*, 9th edn (CH Beck, 2025) para 986.

[51] See, eg, Bundesgerichtshof, 16 May 2019, V ZB 101/18, NJW 2019, 3575, sub III.3.a) ('mirror image principle'); Bundesgerichtshof, 3 December 1992, IX ZR 229/91, BGHZ 120, 334, sub II.1 ('mirroring application' of the German rules on jurisdiction).

[52] Martiny (n 39) 734; Schack (n 50) para 982; Gottwald (n 22) para 85.

[53] Bundesgerichtshof, 29 April 1999, IX ZR 263-97, BGHZ 141, 286, sub III.2.b); Gottwald (n 22) para 85.

[54] Terminology of the FamFG: respondent, see § 113(5) no 3 FamFG.

foreign courts lacking a sufficiently close connection to the subject matter as seen from the domestic perspective.[55]

While figuratively appealing, the term 'mirror image principle' is misleading in so far as it suggests that the foreign court must have based its jurisdiction on a provision which corresponds to an equivalent – 'mirror image' – provision under German law. However, it is irrelevant on which provision the foreign court based its jurisdiction.[56] In fact, the question of whether jurisdiction existed under the applicable foreign law bears no relevance at all.[57] It is thus equally beside the point to enquire whether the foreign court based its jurisdiction on a provision considered exorbitant or alien to German law. Recognition is only refused where jurisdiction could not have been established under any of the German rules.[58]

2. *The Rules on Recognition Jurisdiction*

Generally speaking, however, German law contains no statutory rules on international jurisdiction. Instead, courts extend the applicability of the rules governing local jurisdiction (venue) to international cases under the principle of double functionality (*Doppelfunktionalität*); codified only for family courts in § 105 FamFG.[59] Simply put, whenever a German court is locally competent, it is also internationally competent. The 'mirror image principle' further extends the applicability of these provisions to the recognition of foreign judgments. In this sense, the German rules on local jurisdiction can be said to feature triple functionality (*Dreifachfunktionalität*). Furthermore, some scholars have suggested that the 'mirror image principle' also projects onto the foreign court the jurisdictional rules of the Brussels I(a) Regulation.[60] While the issue has not been settled by authority, it bears little practical relevance. Given the numerous and relatively broad bases of jurisdiction under German law, the requirement is already often inconsequential under the law as it currently stands.[61] Indeed, the recognition of foreign judgments only rarely fails for lack of recognition jurisdiction.[62]

Moreover, the 'mirror image principle' allows for concurrent jurisdiction. This means that even where jurisdiction is established in Germany (eg the defendant

[55] Bundesgerichtshof, 29 April 1999, IX ZR 263-97, BGHZ 141, 286, sub III.2.b); Bundesgerichtshof, 3 December 1992, IX ZR 229/91, BGHZ 120, 334, sub II.1.c).

[56] Schack (n 50) para 986; H Roth, '§ 328' in R Bork and H Roth (eds), *Kommentar zur Zivilprozessordnung (Stein/Jonas)* 23rd edn (Mohr Siebeck, 2015) para 76.

[57] Martiny (n 39) 734; Roth (n 56) para 76.

[58] Gottwald (n 22) para 86; Roth (n 56) para 76.

[59] Bundesgerichtshof (Grand Panel for Civil Matters) 14 June 1965, GSZ 1/65, BGHZ 44, 46, sub 2; see also, Bundesgerichtshof, 3 December 1992, IX ZR 229/91, BGHZ 120, 334, sub II.1; Bundesgerichtshof, 2 July 1991, XI ZR 206/90, BGHZ 115, 90, sub B.I. For a comprehensive overview of the rules on jurisdiction, see Lutzi and Wilke (n 21) 111.

[60] In favour, C Kern, 'Anerkennungsrechtliches Spiegelbildprinzip und europäische Zuständigkeit' (2007) 120 *Zeitschrift für Zivilprozess* 31; A Stadler, '§ 328' in HJ Musielak and W Voit (eds), *Zivilprozessordnung*, 22nd edn (Vahlen, 2025) para 10; against, C Schärtl, '"Spiegelbildprinzip" des § 328 I Nr. 1 ZPO und Zuständigkeitsvorschriften der EuGVO' (2006) *Praxis des Internationalen Privat- und Verfahrensrechts* 438; Gottwald (n 22) para 93.

[61] Gottwald (n 22) para 87.

[62] Martiny (n 39) 736; Gottwald (n 22) para 93.

is domiciled in Germany), a foreign judgment is recognised if the foreign court is competent under a concurrent head of jurisdiction (eg the place of the performance). In contrast, an important limit to recognition jurisdiction under the 'mirror image principle' is set by the rules on exclusive jurisdiction. Where German courts have exclusive jurisdiction, foreign courts necessarily lack jurisdiction and recognition of their judgments is thus barred.[63] For example, a foreign judgment dealing with proprietary claims to immovable property situated in Germany would not be recognised.[64]

Two heads of jurisdiction deserve particular attention with regard to their application under the 'mirror image principle'. First, § 23 ZPO applies to claims in economic matters against persons without domicile in Germany and provides for the jurisdiction of the courts of the place where the defendant's assets are located. In an effort to limit this jurisdiction – widely considered exorbitant[65] – the Bundesgerichtshof has imposed the additional requirement of a sufficiently close connection to Germany.[66] Given that § 23 ZPO applies to foreign courts under the 'mirror image principle', the question arises whether this requirement also applies to the recognition jurisdiction under § 328(1) no 1 ZPO.[67] Second, § 39 ZPO establishes jurisdiction on the basis of the defendant's submission. However, the Bundesgerichtshof has limited this provision's application under the 'mirror image principle' to cases in which the foreign court would have lacked jurisdiction but for the defendant's submission. Crucially, § 39 ZPO cannot establish recognition jurisdiction where the foreign court was otherwise competent under its *lex fori processualis*, thus rendering futile any contestation of jurisdiction by the defendant.[68]

3. *Details of the Enquiry*

The details of the application of the 'mirror image principle' to foreign judgments from states comprised of territorial units with separate legal systems has not been fully settled. This concerns judgments from federal states such as the United States (US) and Canada, but also from unitary states such as the UK or Spain. At least where judgments from a federal judiciary are concerned, the recognition jurisdiction of the federal state – rather than the territorial unit in which the federal court is located – is

[63] Oberlandesgericht Hamm, 14 April 1976, 15 W 253/75, NJW 1976, 2079, 2080; Schack (n 50) para 985; Gottwald (n 22) para 92.

[64] See § 24 ZPO.

[65] See, eg, the 'black lists' of exorbitant heads of jurisdiction under Art 5(2), Art 76(4) of the Brussels Ia Regulation and Art 3(2), Annex I of the Lugano Convention which both contain § 23 ZPO.

[66] Bundesgerichtshof, 2 July 1991, XI ZR 206/90, BGHZ 115, 90, sub II.1.b). For criticism of this requirement, see Schack (n 50) paras 389–99, 404; A Junker, *Internationales Zivilprozessrecht*, 6th edn (CH Beck, 2023) § 18, para 36.

[67] Explicitly left open in Bundesgerichtshof, 29 April 1999, IX ZR 263-97, BGHZ 141, 286, sub III.1. In favour, HP Mansel, 'Vermögensgerichtsstand und Inlandsbezug bei der Entscheidungs- und Anerkennungszuständigkeit am Beispiel der Anerkennung US-amerikanischer Urteile in Deutschland' in HP Mansel, T Pfeiffer, H Kronke, C Kohler and R Hausmann (eds), *Festschrift für Erik Jayme. Band 1* (Sellier, 2004) 561, 570–73; against, U Haas, 'Zur Anerkennung US-amerikanischer Urteile in der Bundesrepublik Deutschland' (2001) *Praxis des Internationalen Privat- und Verfahrensrechts* 195, 197.

[68] Bundesgerichtshof, 3 December 1992, IX ZR 229/91, BGHZ 120, 334, sub II.1.c). For criticism, see Schack (n 50) para 987.

decisive.[69] Having been left open by the Bundesgerichtshof,[70] the question of whether judgments rendered by state courts require the recognition jurisdiction of the respective territorial unit remains a matter of controversy.[71]

Importantly, German courts are not bound by findings of law or fact when applying the 'mirror image principle'.[72] The question of whether the foreign court had recognition jurisdiction must be established independently and afresh, even where it is based on facts which also underpin the substantive claim and which must otherwise only be conclusively asserted (*doppelrelevante Tatsachen*).[73] Both parties may make new submissions, including where the recognition of a default judgment is concerned.[74]

In principle, the relevant point in time at which recognition jurisdiction must exist is the last oral hearing before the foreign court.[75] Thus, it suffices that the facts establishing jurisdiction arose only after the action was initiated (eg acquisition of assets in the country of origin).[76] At the same time, if the circumstances giving rise to jurisdiction cease to exist before the last oral hearing, the foreign court nevertheless retains jurisdiction under the 'mirror image principle' where a *perpetuatio fori* can be affirmed pursuant to § 261(3) no 2 ZPO.[77]

b) Finality/Enforceability in the Country of Origin

Pursuant to § 723(2) cl 1 ZPO, 'The judgment for enforcement is to be delivered only once the judgment handed down by the foreign court has attained legal validity pursuant to the laws applicable to that court.'[78] Legal validity in this sense means finality (*formelle Rechtskraft*) and exists when the judgment is no longer subject to ordinary forms of appeal or review in the rendering state.[79] Neither the possibility of reopening the case in separate later proceedings (eg an action for annulment or an action for retrial) nor that of a constitutional challenge prevent enforcement.[80]

[69] Bundesgerichtshof, 29 April 1999, IX ZR 263-97, BGHZ 141, 286, sub III.2; calling for a more nuanced approach based on the type of jurisdiction, R Stürner and J Bormann, 'Internationale Anerkennungszuständigkeit US-amerikanischer Bundesgerichte und Zustellungsfragen im deutsch-amerikanischen Verhältnis' (2000) 55 *Juristenzeitung* 81, 83–85.

[70] Bundesgerichtshof, 29 April 1999, IX ZR 263-97, BGHZ 141, 286, sub III.2.

[71] In favour, Landgericht München I, 28 June 1988, 28 0 15047/85, RIW 1988, 738; Stürner and Bormann (n 69) 83; Schack (n 50) para 1065; against, Landgericht Heilbronn, 6 February 1991, 1b O 2122/89 III, RIW 1991, 343; B von Hoffmann and W Hau, 'Zur internationalen Anerkennungszuständigkeit US-amerikanischer Zivilgerichte' (1998) *Recht der Internationalen Wirtschaft*, 344, 351–52; Gottwald (n 22) para 91.

[72] Bundesgerichtshof, 25 November 1993, IX ZR 32/93, BGHZ 124, 237, sub A.III.4.b); Bundesgerichtshof, 26 March 1969, VIII ZR 194/68, BGHZ 52, 30, paras 35–39; see also L Theimer, 'Protection against the breach of choice of court agreements: A comparative analysis of remedies in English and German courts' (2023) 19 *Journal of Private International Law* 208, 223.

[73] Bundesgerichtshof, 25 November 1993, IX ZR 32/93, BGHZ 124, 237, sub A.III.3.

[74] Bundesgerichtshof, 25 November 1993, IX ZR 32/93, BGHZ 124, 237, sub A.III.4.b); Bundesgerichtshof, 26 March 1969, VIII ZR 194/68, BGHZ 52, 30, sub 3.e).

[75] Bundesgerichtshof, 29 April 1999, IX ZR 263-97, BGHZ 141, 286, sub III.1.

[76] ibid.

[77] ibid; see also, Bundesgerichtshof, 5 March 2009, IX ZR 150/05, NJW-RR 2009, 1652, para 8.

[78] See § 110(3) FamFG for family matters.

[79] Bundesgerichtshof, 29 April 1999, IX ZR 263-97, BGHZ 141, 286, sub IV.1; Martiny (n 39) 732.

[80] Gottwald (n 22) para 71; Roth (n 56) para 66.

Whether the finality requirement also applies to the recognition of foreign judgments is subject to debate and has recently been left open by the Bundesgerichtshof.[81] The dominant view supports the extension of the requirement to recognition.[82] Others, however, argue for the recognition of the legal effects which the rendering foreign state attributes to the judgment even before it becomes final.[83]

c) *Res Iudicata*

A foreign judgment can only be recognised if it is not incompatible with another judgment. Once considered a question of public policy, the problem of conflicting judgments now constitutes a separate ground for refusal of recognition in § 328(1) no 3 ZPO.[84] In so far as the provision is concerned with other judgments, it distinguishes between two scenarios: the incompatibility with a German judgment (var 1); and the incompatibility with an *earlier* foreign judgment (var 2).

Crucially, this means that a conflicting domestic decision takes precedence over a foreign judgment, irrespective of whether it was rendered earlier or later than the latter. While this 'egoistic principle' may be justified with the protection of the domestic decision's legal effects,[85] it has also attracted considerable criticism in the literature.[86] In any case, it has been firmly embedded in § 328(1) no 3 var 1 ZPO.[87] In contrast, where incompatibility with a *foreign* judgment is concerned, only an earlier decision may constitute a bar to recognition under § 328(1) no 3 var 2 ZPO. This must be assessed by reference to the point in time when the conflicting judgment became final and conclusive, rather than the initiation of the action.[88] Importantly, the earlier foreign judgment must be recognised or at least be capable of recognition in Germany.

§ 328(1) no 3 ZPO does not contain any guidance as to when judgments are incompatible.[89] Since the provision is modelled after what is now Article 45(1) lit c, d Brussels Ia Regulation, it must be interpreted according to the relevant jurisprudence of the CJEU.[90] On this basis, judgments are incompatible where 'they entail legal

[81] Bundesgerichtshof, 16 May 2019, V ZB 101/18, BGH NJW 2019, 3575, sub III.4.b).

[82] Schack (n 50) para 970; Roth (n 56) para 65; Stadler (n 60) para 5.

[83] H Dörner, '§ 328' in I Saenger (ed), *Zivilprozessordnung*, 10th edn (Nomos, 2023) para 18; Geimer (n 1) para 69.

[84] Martiny (n 39) 743; see, eg, Bayerisches Oberstes Landesgericht, 28 January 1983, BReg 1 Z 48/82, BayObLGZ 1983, 21; see § 109(1) no 3 FamFG for family matters.

[85] Schack (n 50) para 1004; Roth (n 56) para 94.

[86] Gottwald (n 22) para 119; M Sonnentag, 'Anerkennungs- und Vollstreckbarkeitshindernisse im autonomen deutschen Recht' (2014) 113 *Zeitschrift für Vergleichende Rechtswissenschaft* 83, 92; FK Juenger, 'The Recognition of Money Judgments in Civil and Commercial Matters' (1988) 36 *American Journal of Comparative Law* 1, 26.

[87] See § 109(1) no 3 FamFG for family matters.

[88] Gottwald (n 22) para 118; Roth (n 56) para 97.

[89] Nor does § 109(1) no 3 FamFG for family matters.

[90] Oberlandesgericht Hamm, 30 October 2000, 1 U 1/00, FamRZ 2001, 1015, para 23; Gottwald (n 22) para 121; T Rauscher, '§ 109' in T Rauscher (ed), Münchener Kommentar zum FamFG, 4th edn (CH Beck, 2025) para 35; advocating for a narrower interpretation: Roth (n 56) para 96.

consequences that are mutually exclusive'.[91] Importantly, the cause of action underlying the judgments need not be formally identical.[92] Rather, the relevant test is whether the two actions concern the same 'core issue'.[93] For example, a judgment declaring the rescission or discharge of a sales contract would be incompatible with a judgment enforcing the same contract, both having at their heart the 'core issue' of whether the contract is binding.[94]

d) *Lis Pendens*

According to § 328(1) no 3 var 3 ZPO,[95] recognition of a foreign judgment is also denied if it is 'incompatible with proceedings that have become pending earlier in Germany'. This concerns the situation where foreign proceedings have resulted in a judgment without taking account of earlier German proceedings. Whether the foreign court had knowledge of these German proceedings[96] or was obliged to take them into account[97] is irrelevant. The point in time at which the foreign proceedings became pending is assessed according to the foreign procedural law.[98] Incompatibility is determined in the same way as under § 328(1) no 3 var 1, 2, ie by reference to the relevant CJEU jurisprudence.[99]

e) Specific Requirements of Due Process

Pursuant to § 328(1) no 2 ZPO, a foreign judgment is not recognised if 'the defendant, who has not entered an appearance in the proceedings and who takes recourse to this fact, has not duly been served the document by which the proceedings were initiated, or not in such time to allow him to defend himself'.[100]

§ 328(1) no 2 ZPO sets out two conditions for the recognition and enforcement of default judgments which must be met cumulatively:[101] *due service* of the document

[91] Case 145/86 *Hoffman v Krieg*, para 22.
[92] Case 144/86 *Gubisch Maschinenfabrik KG v Giulio Palumbo*, para 17.
[93] ibid, para 16 (from the German version: 'Kernpunkt'). For more detail, see R Fentiman, 'Article 29', in U Magnus and P Mankowski (eds), *Brussels Ibis Regulation, European Commentaries on Private International Law, Volume I* (Otto Schmidt, 2023) paras 6–22.
[94] Case 144/86 *Gubisch Maschinenfabrik KG v Giulio Palumbo*, paras 16, 19.
[95] See § 109(1) no 3 var 3 FamFG for family matters.
[96] Oberlandesgericht Stuttgart, 2 May 2002, 20 U 13/01, NJOZ 2002, 2539, sub III.6.; Gottwald (n 22) para 120.
[97] Bayerisches Oberstes Landesgericht, 28 January 1983, BReg. 1 Z 48/82, BayObLGZ 1983, 21, sub II.3.c) bb)(2) (considered, then, as a matter of public policy).
[98] Oberlandesgericht Stuttgart, 2 May 2002, 20 U 13/01, NJOZ 2002, 2539, sub III.2; Bayerisches Oberstes Landesgericht, 28 January 1983, BReg. 1 Z 48/82, BayObLGZ 1983, 21, sub II.3.c)bb)(2) (considered, then, as a matter of public policy).
[99] See above, Question 3 c).
[100] The same requirement applies in family matters pursuant to § 109(1) no 2 FamFG, see Hüßtege, '§ 109 FamFG' in H Thomas and H Putzo (eds), *Zivilprozessordnung*, 46th edn (CH Beck, 2025) para 2.
[101] Bundesgerichtshof, 2 December 1992, XII ZB 64/91, sub III.1.d); Oberlandesgericht Stuttgart, 18 May 2017, 17 VA 1/16, sub II.3.b) for § 109(1) no 2 FamFG; for a contrary view, see Geimer (n 1) paras 158–160, who wishes to waive the requirement of proper service.

initiating the proceedings; and service *in sufficient time*. The provision is similar to Article 45(1) lit b) Brussels Ia Regulation as well as to Article 34 no 2 Brussels I Regulation and is therefore interpreted in the same way, in so far as the provisions coincide.[102] This is the case with the requirement of service *in sufficient time*. However, § 328(1) no 2 ZPO corresponds even more closely to Article 27 no 2 Brussels Convention since it requires not only that the document initiating the proceedings was served on the defendant in sufficient time, but also that it was *duly* served. Furthermore, neither § 328(1) no 2 ZPO nor Article 27 no 2 Brussels Convention require that the defendant has challenged the foreign judgment in the country of origin. Therefore, the case law on Article 27 no 2 Brussels Convention can also be applied to § 328(1) no 2 ZPO.[103] It is interesting to note that the German legislator has maintained the requirement of due service even against the background of the contrary provisions in the Brussels I and Brussels Ia Regulations.[104]

1. *Document Initiating the Proceedings*

The document initiating the proceedings is the document by which the defendant is to be officially informed of the proceedings.[105] The information contained in the document must be such as to enable her to decide whether or not to enter an appearance.[106] The document must therefore indicate what the plaintiff is claiming and on what grounds.[107] However, it does not have to contain a formal request.[108]

2. *Due Service*

The law of the country of origin determines whether the defendant has been *duly* served. Due service is to be assessed strictly according to the relevant legal provisions which include the EU Service Regulation and applicable international treaties, such as the Hague Service Convention.[109] In its examination, the German court is not bound by the assessment of the foreign court.[110] When applying international treaties, it is important to take into account the objections against certain provisions declared by Germany.[111]

[102] CF Nordmeier, '§ 328 ZPO' in H Thomas and H Putzo (eds), *Zivilprozessordnung*, 46th edn (CH Beck, 2025) para 9.
[103] Bundesgerichtshof, 2 December 1992 XII ZB 64/91 sub III.1.d).
[104] In 2009, it even introduced the requirement of due service in family matters, § 109(1) no 2 FamFG, see Bundesgerichtshof, 3 April 2019, XII ZB 311/17, sub II.2.b)aa)(3).
[105] Geimer (n 1) para 168.
[106] Bundesgerichtshof, 29 April 1999, IX ZR 263/97, sub IV.2.a).
[107] ibid; for Art 34 no 2 Brussels I Regulation: Bundesgerichtshof, 3 August 2011, XII ZB 187/10, sub II.2.a) aa); Bundesgerichtshof, 10 March 2022, IX ZB 36/20, para 17, with reference to the case law of the CJEU.
[108] Bundesgerichtshof, 29 April 1999, IX ZR 263/97, sub IV.2.a).
[109] Bundesgerichtshof, 2 December 1992, XII ZB 64/91, sub III.2. (with regard to the possibility to remedy service); Bundesgerichtshof, 29 April 1999, IX ZR 263/97, sub V.1.a), b) (with regard to the necessity of a translation and the possibility to remedy service).
[110] Bundesgerichtshof, 2 December 1992, XII ZB 64/91, sub III.1.c); Bundesgerichtshof, 28 November 2007, XII ZB 217/05, sub III.2. for Art. 27 no 2 Lugano Convention.
[111] See Bundesgerichtshof, 2 December 1992, XII ZB 64/91, sub II.1.c).

3. *Service in Sufficient Time*

The question whether the document was served on the defendant in sufficient time must be assessed on a case-by-case basis in order to balance the interests of the plaintiff and the defendant. The decisive factor is the period of time the defendant had at her disposal to prevent the issuance of a judgment.[112] Fictitious service is therefore generally not considered timely, but does not constitute a general obstacle to recognition and enforcement: for example, it must be taken into account whether the defendant herself has caused the necessity of fictitious service.[113]

4. *No Necessity to Challenge the Foreign Judgment*

In contrast to Article 45(1)(b) Brussels Ia Regulation, recognition cannot be refused on the ground that the defendant could have challenged the foreign judgment but failed to do so. This is justified by the fact that § 328(1) no 2 ZPO refers to the document initiating the proceedings. Hence, the provision is linked to the time of the opening of proceedings and not to later procedural stages. Furthermore, a defence against the issued judgment is not equivalent to a defence before the judgment is issued: if the mere possibility to challenge the judgment were sufficient to bar recognition, the defendant could be deprived of a judicial instance.[114] Some scholars suggest that the requirement to challenge the foreign judgment under Article 45(1)(b) Brussels Ia Regulation is a general principle of cross-border recognition and enforcement and should therefore be read into § 328(1) no 2 ZPO.[115] The Bundesgerichtshof, however, has rejected this suggestion.[116]

f) Public Policy

Public policy or, more precisely, its violation, constitutes a bar to recognition under German law. Pursuant to § 328(1) no 4 ZPO, the recognition of a foreign judgment shall be denied if it 'would lead to a result that is obviously incompatible with essential principles of German law, and in particular if the recognition is not compatible with fundamental rights'.[117] As is clear from the wording of these provisions, it is

[112] Bundesgerichtshof, 6 October 2005, IX ZB 360/02, sub II.2.a)bb) for Art 27 no 2 Brussels Convention.

[113] Bundesgerichtshof, 28 November 2007, XII ZB 217/05, sub IV.1.a), b) for Art 27 no 2 Lugano Convention with reference to CJEU Case 49/84 *Debaecker v Bouwman*, para 32.

[114] Bundesgerichtshof, 2 December 1992, XII ZB 64/91, sub III.3, following the case law of the CJEU with regard to Art 27 no 2 Brussels Convention (Case C-123/91 *Minalmet v Brandeis*); Bundesgerichtshof, 3 April 2019, XII ZR 311/17, sub II.2.c) for § 109(1) no 2 FamFG; for a contrary view, see Geimer (n 1) para 163.

[115] R Geimer, *Internationales Zivilprozessrecht*, 9th edn (Dr Otto Schmidt, 2024) para 2921.

[116] With regard to Art 27 no 2 Brussels Convention Bundesgerichtshof, 22 July 2004, IX ZB 2/03, sub II.3.a); 20 January 2005, IX ZB 154/01, sub II.2.b)aa), bb); with regard to § 328(1) no 2 ZPO Bundesgerichtshof, 2 December 1992, XII ZB 64/91, sub III.3.; with regard to § 109(1) no 2 FamFG Bundesgerichtshof, 3 April 2019, XII ZB 311/17, sub II.2.c).

[117] In some of the cases cited in this segment, not § 328(1) no 4 ZPO, but rather the respective public policy provisions contained in other instruments were applicable, eg those of the Brussels–Lugano Regime or bilateral conventions on the recognition and enforcement of judgments. Since all of these provisions refer to

the *result* of the recognition of the foreign decision that must be incompatible with German public policy. The reason for this incompatibility may be found either in the foreign law itself or in its incorrect application.[118] In contrast, the potential incompatibility of individual aspects in the judgment's reasoning is irrelevant.[119] Finally, partial recognition and enforcement of a foreign judgment is possible if it awards several legally independent claims of which only some are compatible with public policy.[120]

Against the background of the prohibition of *révision au fond*,[121] the refusal of recognition on grounds of public policy is restricted to exceptional cases of 'obvious' incompatibility. In line with this, German courts have adopted a relatively liberal approach to public policy over the last decades.[122] Though not sketched out by § 328(1) no 4 ZPO, a distinction is drawn between a substantive and a procedural dimension. In contrast, the application of the foreign court's private international law is no longer considered to be in the realm of public policy.[123] The recognition of foreign judgments does not depend on the application of the law which the rules of German private international law would have selected.[124] The relevant point in time for the application of the public policy exception is the time of the recognition decision of the receiving court, rather than the time of the decision of the court of origin.[125]

Finally, it must be emphasised that public policy in the context of the recognition and enforcement of foreign judgments is not identical with public policy in the application of foreign law.[126] Also called *ordre public international* or *ordre public attenué*, the former is considerably weaker than the latter.[127] The distinction pertains to both substantive and procedural public policy: the fact that a German judge would have reached a different decision on the basis of domestic mandatory substantive or procedural law is not sufficient to bar recognition of a foreign judgment.[128] This is due to the fact that the primary

German public policy, the cases are also relevant for German autonomous law. See § 109(1) no 4 FamFG for family matters.

[118] Gottwald (n 22) para 125.

[119] Bundesgerichtshof, 19 July 2018, IX ZB 10/18, GRUR 2018, 1074, sub II.2.b)aa); Gottwald (n 22) para 125; Stadler (n 60) para 24; Roth (n 56) para 101.

[120] Bundesgerichtshof, 4 July 1992, IX ZR 149/91, BGHZ 118, 312, sub A.VI.

[121] See above, Question 2 b) 4.

[122] Gottwald (n 22) para 123; Stadler (n 60) para 23; Martiny (n 39) 745 (already for the time before the German private international law reform in 1986).

[123] Formerly, § 328(1) no 3 ZPO (old version) contained reservations in favour of a number of German rules of private international law in the fields of family law and the law of persons. The provision was abolished in 1986. For the time prior, see, eg, Bundesgerichtshof, 7 March 1979, IV ZR 30/78, BGHZ 73, 378.

[124] Bundesgerichtshof, 4 July 1992, IX ZR 149/91, BGHZ 118, 312, sub A.IV.3.a); Gottwald (n 22) para 126; Martiny (n 39) 745–46.

[125] Bundesgerichtshof, 21 April 1998, XI ZR 377–97, BGHZ 138, 331, sub II.2.b); Bundesgerichtshof, 11 April 1979, IV ZR 93/78, NJW 1980, 529, sub III.2.b)bb).

[126] Bundesgerichtshof, 18 October 1967, VIII ZR 145/66, BGHZ 48, 327, sub 3.; Bundesgerichtshof, 15 May 1986, III ZR 192/84, BGHZ 98, 70, sub II.3.

[127] Bundesgerichtshof, 17 June 2015, XII ZB 730/12, BGHZ 206, 86, sub IV.2.b)bb)(2); Bundesgerichtshof, 21 April 1998, XI ZR 377–97, BGHZ 138, 331, sub II.2.b).

[128] Bundesgerichtshof, 18 October 1967, VIII ZR 145/66, BGHZ 48, 327, sub 3 (procedural); Bundesgerichtshof, 16 September 1993, IX ZB 82/90, BGHZ 123, 268, sub I.5 (substantive).

objective of the law on recognition and enforcement is the preservation of international harmony of decisions.[129]

1. *Substantive Public Policy*

Consequently, substantive public policy is only violated where 'the result of the application of the foreign law stands in contradiction to the fundamental notions of German law and the concepts of justice contained therein to such an extent that it appears intolerable according to domestic conceptions'.[130] In this assessment, the extent and significance of the connection between the facts underlying the foreign judgment and Germany (*Inlandsbezug*) is a decisive factor.[131] The substantive public policy is thus subject to a 'graduated standard of review':[132] the weaker the foreign judgment's connection to Germany, the larger the deviations from fundamental notions of German law needed to constitute a violation of public policy. There exists a plethora of German decisions dealing with various aspects of foreign judgments in the context of public policy, only some of which can be highlighted here.

Certain idiosyncrasies of US law have proven to be especially contentious in the context of substantive public policy. The Bundesgerichtshof has held that a US judgment for 'exemplary and punitive damages', which were awarded as a lump sum and in addition to material and immaterial damages suffered, is 'obviously' incompatible with fundamental notions of German law.[133] More specifically, the court considered that such damages are ordinarily characterised by the purposes of punishment and deterrence, and thus incompatible with the principle of proportionality and the notion of compensation underlying the German law of damages.[134] The same reasoning extends to treble damages, such as under the US Racketeer Influenced and Corrupt Organizations (RICO) Act, though treble damages were not subject of the decision.[135]

Interestingly, the Bundesgerichtshof has relied directly on fundamental rights of the Basic Law (*Grundgesetz*; GG) in a more recent decision, holding a Polish judgment to be incompatible with public policy. The judgment had ordered a German public broadcaster to publish a statement on its website, regretting a falsification of history and apologising for a violation of personality rights. This was held to constitute a violation of the broadcaster's right to negative freedom of expression, which also protects against having to disseminate someone else's opinion as one's own.[136]

[129] Bundesgerichtshof, 17 June 2015, XII ZB 730/12, BGHZ 206, 86, sub IV.2.b)bb)(2).

[130] Bundesgerichtshof, 19 July 2018, IX ZB 10/18, GRUR 2018, 1074, sub II.2.b)aa); Bundesgerichtshof, 21 April 1998, XI ZR 377–97, BGHZ 138, 331, sub II.2.b); Bundesgerichtshof, 16 September 1993, IX ZB 82/90, BGHZ 123, 268, sub I.5; Bundesgerichtshof, 4 July 1992, IX ZR 149/91, BGHZ 118, 312, sub A.IV.3.b).

[131] Bundesgerichtshof, 4 July 1992, IX ZR 149/91, BGHZ 118, 312, sub B.I.1.

[132] Bundesgerichtshof, 4 July 1992, IX ZR 149/91, BGHZ 118, 312, sub B.I.1.

[133] Bundesgerichtshof, 4 July 1992, IX ZR 149/91, BGHZ 118, 312, sub A.V.3.

[134] Bundesgerichtshof, 4 July 1992, IX ZR 149/91, BGHZ 118, 312, sub A.V.3. Whether this is still tenable in light of recent increasing number of 'penal elements' in German private law is questioned by Stadler (n 60) para 25.

[135] R Stürner, 'Die Vereinbarkeit von »treble damages« mit dem deutschen ordre public' in B Bachmannet al (eds), *Grenzüberschreitungen, Beiträge zum Internationalen Verfahrensrecht und zur Schiedsgerichtsbarkeit, Festschrift für Peter Schlosser zum 70. Geburtstag* (Mohr Siebeck, 2005) 967, 979–83; Gottwald (n 22) para 129.

[136] Bundesgerichtshof, 19 July 2018, IX ZB 10/18, GRUR 2018, 1074, sub II.2.b)bb).

2. *Procedural Public Policy*

Public policy's second, procedural dimension is violated where

> the decision is based on proceedings which deviate from fundamental principles of German procedural law to an extent that it cannot be regarded as having been rendered in an orderly manner in accordance with the rule of law by the German legal order.[137]

It bears repeating that it is irrelevant whether a German judge would have violated fundamental principles of German procedural law in the same situation. In order to further concretise this standard, German courts rely on the principles protected by the right to be heard under Article 103(1) GG.[138] For one, the principle of the rule of law generally prohibits rendering a decision without giving the person concerned the opportunity to express their views.[139] Moreover, the respect for human dignity requires that a party must be able to actively influence the course of the proceedings.[140]

However, the right to be heard only protects the *opportunity* to participate in the proceedings. In principle, it is the parties' responsibility to defend themselves and ensure their proper legal representation.[141] Thus, there is no violation of the right to be heard if the defendant has deprived herself of this opportunity. In this regard, the Bundesgerichtshof has recognised and enforced a judgment against a maintenance debtor who had been excluded from the English proceedings on the basis of contempt of court.[142] It was later clarified, however, that any exclusion from the proceedings must be proportionate in light of the circumstances of the individual case, denying recognition of a judgment rendered against a defendant in contempt of court.[143] Furthermore, the right to be heard does not entitle a party to a specific procedure, but only to be heard in the manner prescribed or admissible by law.[144]

Other cases of incompatibility with procedural public policy concern a foreign judgment which contained neither the grounds for the decision nor the underlying facts[145]

[137] Bundesgerichtshof, 10 September 2015, IX ZB 39/13, NJW 2016, 160, sub III.2.a)bb); Bundesgerichtshof, 4 July 1992, IX ZR 149/91, BGHZ 118, 312, sub A.III.3.b); Bundesgerichtshof, 18 October 1967, VIII ZR 145/66, BGHZ 48, 327, sub 3. For due process as a specific but (now) separate category of procedural public policy, see above, Question 3 e).

[138] Bundesgerichtshof, 10 September 2015, IX ZB 39/13, BGH NJW 2016, 160, sub III.2.a)bb); Bundesgerichtshof, 29 April 1999, IX ZR 263-97, BGHZ 141, 286, sub IV.3.a); Bundesgerichtshof, 4 July 1992, IX ZR 149/91, BGHZ 118, 312, sub A.III.3.b.

[139] Bundesgerichtshof, 29 April 1999, IX ZR 263-97, BGHZ 141, 286, sub IV.3.a); Bundesgerichtshof, 4 July 1992, IX ZR 149/91, BGHZ 118, 312, sub A.III.3.b); Bundesgerichtshof, 19 September 1977, VIII ZR 120/75, NJW 1978, 1114, sub II.2.

[140] Bundesgerichtshof, 29 April 1999, IX ZR 263-97, BGHZ 141, 286, sub IV.3.a); Bundesgerichtshof, 4 July 1992, IX ZR 149/91, BGHZ 118, 312, sub A.III.3.b); Bundesgerichtshof, 19 September 1977, VIII ZR 120/75, NJW 1978, 1114, sub II.2.

[141] Bundesgerichtshof, 29 April 1999, IX ZR 263-97, BGHZ 141, 286, sub IV.3.a); Bundesgerichtshof, 4 July 1992, IX ZR 149/91, BGHZ 118, 312, sub A.III.3.b); Bundesgerichtshof, 19 September 1977, VIII ZR 120/75, NJW 1978, 1114, sub II.2.a).

[142] Bundesgerichtshof, 18 October 1967, VIII ZR 145/66, BGHZ 48, 327, sub 4.b)c).

[143] Bundesgerichtshof, 2 September 2009, XII ZB 50/06, BGHZ 182, 204, sub 5.

[144] Bundesgerichtshof, 4 July 1992, IX ZR 149/91, BGHZ 118, 312, sub A.III.3.b); Bundesgerichtshof, 25 March 1970, VIII ZR 202/69, BGHZ 53, 357, sub II.4.d).

[145] Bundesgerichtshof, 10 September 2015, IX ZB 39/13, BGH NJW 2016, 160, sub III.2.b). However, the fact that a foreign judgment was rendered without written reasons does not *per se* constitute a violation of public policy, see Bundesgerichtshof, 26 August 2009, XII ZB 169/07, BGHZ 182, 188, sub II.3.b).

and anti-suit injunctions which are considered an 'infringement of the judicial sovereignty of Germany'.[146] More extremely, the Bundesgerichtshof has held that a judgment obtained by intentional deception of the foreign court violates public policy, though this allegation was not borne out by the facts of the case.[147] Lastly, neither the fact that a foreign judgment was preceded by a pre-trial discovery nor the fact that it does not provide for the reimbursement of costs in favour of the prevailing party (American rule of costs) renders it incompatible with German procedural public policy.[148]

g) Reciprocity

In principle, the recognition and enforcement of a foreign judgment in Germany requires reciprocity. Pursuant to § 328(1) no 5 ZPO, recognition shall be denied if 'Reciprocity has not been granted'. However, the requirement is waived according to § 328(2) ZPO 'if the judgment concerns a non-pecuniary claim and if, according to the laws of Germany, no place of jurisdiction was established in Germany'.[149] This means that, generally, foreign judgments are only recognised if the country of origin, conversely, recognises German judgments. Simply put, the reciprocity requirement is intended to function as a bargaining chip.[150] By pre-emptively sanctioning the non-recognition of German judgments, its purpose is to incentivise foreign countries to adopt recognition-friendly practices in relation to Germany.[151]

§ 328(1) no 5 ZPO contains no definition of reciprocity, but there exists a significant amount of jurisprudence on the requirement. Perhaps most importantly, a formal 'granting' of reciprocity by a German or foreign authority or in a bilateral agreement is not necessary – *substantive* reciprocity suffices.[152] The Bundesgerichtshof has adopted a wide interpretation of the concept and, in fact, has expressed its opposition to a 'formal and petty standard' on several occasions.[153] Crucially, the domestic and foreign law on the recognition and enforcement of foreign judgments need not be identical. Instead, it must be examined whether 'essentially equivalent conditions' exist when assessed as a whole.[154] This means that, in practice, the legislation and jurisprudence on the recognition of foreign judgments of the country of origin must be compared with the requirements contained in § 328(1)(4) ZPO, as interpreted by the German courts. Restrictions in one respect may be compensated for by facilitation in other respects.[155]

[146] Oberlandesgericht Düsseldorf, 10 January 1996, 3 VA 11/95, ZIP 1996, 294, para 26–31.

[147] Bundesgerichtshof, 29 April 1999, IX ZR 263-97, BGHZ 141, 286, sub V.2.

[148] Bundesgerichtshof, 4 July 1992, IX ZR 149/91, BGHZ 118, 312, sub A.III.4.

[149] Reciprocity is also not required in most family matters, see § 109(1), (4) FamFG.

[150] More crudely, HJ Puttfarken, 'Zur Anerkennung und Vollstreckung ausländischer Urteile deutscher Kläger – verfassungswidrige Gegenseitigkeit' (1976) *Recht der Internationalen Wirtschaft* 149, 150 ('thumbscrew for legal policy').

[151] Martiny (n 39) 749; Gottwald (n 22) para 135.

[152] Bundesgerichtshof, 24 October 2000, XI ZR 300/99, NJW 2001, 524, sub II.2.a); Gottwald (n 22) para 137.

[153] Bundesgerichtshof, 8 May 1968, VIII ZR 43/65, BHGZ 50, 100, sub II.; Bundesgerichtshof, 30 September 1964, VIII ZR 195/61, BGHZ 42, 194, sub III.

[154] Bundesgerichtshof, 29 April 1999, IX ZR 263-97, BGHZ 141, 286, sub IV.4; Bundesgerichtshof, 8 May 1968, VIII ZR 43/65, BHGZ 50, 100, sub II; Bundesgerichtshof, 30 September 1964, VIII ZR 195/61, BGHZ 42, 194, sub III.

[155] Bundesgerichtshof, 30 September 1964, VIII ZR 195/61, BGHZ 42, 194, sub III.

In other words, the recognition and enforcement of a German judgment in the foreign country must not encounter 'significantly greater difficulties' than a foreign judgment would in Germany.[156] This is, for example, the case where the foreign country subjects German judgments to a *révision au fond*.[157] Reciprocity with France could therefore only be established after the Cour de cassation ceased to review foreign judgments on their merits in 1963/1964.[158]

The application of the reciprocity requirement is further softened by its divisibility. Not all German judgments need to be recognised or enforced in the foreign country. Instead, *partial* reciprocity suffices and extends to a number of different respects. First, the reciprocity requirement may be satisfied with regard to specific classes of judgments, such as money judgments or default judgments.[159] Secondly, partial reciprocity for specific heads of jurisdiction is possible. More concretely, in assessing whether 'essentially equivalent conditions' exist, German courts only examine the specific head of jurisdiction relied on by the foreign court rather than the jurisdictional regime as a whole.[160] Thus, the Bundesgerichtshof has held that reciprocity existed for French judgments based on a choice of court agreement and on submission, even though French law generally contained 'jurisdictional privileges' providing that nationals could both sue and only be sued before French courts.[161] However, recognition of another French judgment based on the nationality of the French plaintiff was refused for lack of reciprocity since the 'jurisdictional privilege' would have prevented recognition of an equivalent German judgment.[162] Thirdly, partial reciprocity may exist even in relation to foreign countries which do not extend certain types of jurisdiction to foreign courts for the purpose of recognition if recognition of a German judgment would be possible on the basis of an alternative head of jurisdiction.[163] Lastly, in federal states comprised of territorial units with separate legal systems, reciprocity is required only in relation to the respective territorial unit where the judgment was rendered.[164]

The relevant point in time at which reciprocity must be established is the time of recognition and enforcement of the judgment in question.[165] If reciprocity is established only after the foreign judgment has been rendered, no legitimate expectation of non-recognition exists.[166] Conversely, if the foreign judgment has been recognised or

[156] Bundesgerichtshof, 24 October 2000, XI ZR 300/99, NJW 2001, 524, sub II.1; Bundesgerichtshof, 5 July 1972, VIII ZR 118/71, BGHZ 59, 116, sub 4.a); Bundesgerichtshof, 8 May 1968, VIII ZR 43/65, BHGZ 50, 100, sub II; Bundesgerichtshof, 30 September 1964, VIII ZR 195/61, BGHZ 42, 194, sub III.

[157] Gottwald (n 22) para 137; Martiny (n 39) 750.

[158] Bundesgerichtshof, 8 May 1968, VIII ZR 43/65, BHGZ 50, 100, sub I, citing Cour de cassation, 8 January 1963, Hohenzollern, Rev crit 52, 109 and Cour de cassation, 7 January 1964, Munzer, Rev crit 53, 344. See also National Report on France, Question 3.

[159] Bundesgerichtshof, 8 May 1968, VIII ZR 43/65, BHGZ 50, 100, sub II; Bundesgerichtshof, 30 September 1964, VIII ZR 195/61, BGHZ 42, 194, sub III; Gottwald (n 22) para 138.

[160] Bundesgerichtshof, 30 September 1964, VIII ZR 195/61, BGHZ 42, 194, sub IV.1.

[161] Bundesgerichtshof, 8 May1968, VIII ZR 43/65, BHGZ 50, 100, sub III.1.a); Bundesgerichtshof, 5 July 1972, VIII ZR 118/71, BGHZ 59, 116, sub 4.

[162] Bundesgerichtshof, 16 March 1970, VII ZR 125/68, BGHZ 53, 332, sub I.2.c).

[163] Bundesgerichtshof, 29 April 1999, IX ZR 263-97, BGHZ 141, 286, sub IV.4.

[164] ibid; Gottwald (n 22) para 136; Roth (n 56) para 120.

[165] Gottwald (n 22) para 136; Dörner (n 83) para 63.

[166] Gottwald (n 22) para 136; Roth (n 56) paras 35, 126.

enforced, it remains effective in the receiving country, even if reciprocity subsequently ceases.[167]

The reciprocity requirement has long been criticised.[168] In contrast to the other conditions under § 328 ZPO, reciprocity says nothing about the intrinsic quality of the foreign judgment.[169] In fact, its purpose to induce foreign countries to adopt recognition-friendly practices is entirely political. It is questionable to what extent this purpose has been achieved in the past[170] and, indeed, whether it can even be achieved by the reciprocity requirement in its current form.[171] The immediate negative consequences of a lack of reciprocity are suffered not by the non-cooperative state but by the private parties unable to obtain recognition and enforcement of their judgments. Notably, this includes German plaintiffs seeking to enforce their foreign judgments in Germany. For this reason, it has been suggested that the reciprocity requirement is unconstitutional.[172] Moreover, it is equally unjust to refuse recognition and enforcement of a judgment in favour of a foreign plaintiff on the basis that the country of origin does not recognise German judgments. Thus, the requirement places a considerable burden on private parties and constitutes an obstacle to international cooperation.[173] Despite this wealth of criticism, the German legislator has retained the requirement in the 1986 reform of private international law, considering its abolishment 'premature'.[174] The overwhelming majority of scholars continue to support the striking of § 328(1) no 5 ZPO from the statute books,[175] but whether the legislator will answer their calls remains to be seen.

h) Other Requirements

1. *Validity*

Though not codified, a basic condition for recognition and enforcement is the validity of the foreign judgment under the law of the rendering state.[176] If the foreign legal order considers a judgment void or invalid, it generates no effects which could be recognised

[167] Gottwald (n 22) para 136; Roth (n 56) para 126.
[168] See already, von Bar (n 2) 506–13.
[169] ibid 506–07; Martiny (n 39) 749.
[170] Gottwald (n 22) para 135; for an example to the contrary, see J Coyle, 'Rethinking Judgements Reciprocity' (2014) 92 *North Carolina Law Review* 1109, 1131–34.
[171] T Pfeiffer, 'Kooperative Reziprozität: § 328 I Nr. 5 ZPO neu besichtigt' (1991) 55 *Rabel Journal of Comparative and International Private Law* 734 (suggesting instead an alternative interpretation on the basis of 'cooperative reciprocity' which would arguably enhance international cooperation).
[172] Puttfarken (n 150) 150. This is, however, a minority view. For arguments in favour of constitutionality, see D Martiny, *Handbuch des internationalen Zivilverfahrensrechts Band III/1* (Mohr Siebeck, 1984) paras 1222–28; see also, Gottwald (n 22) para 135; Roth (n 56) para 116.
[173] Gottwald (n 22) para 135; Martiny (n 39) 749.
[174] BT-Drs 10/504, 88.
[175] Shortly after the reform, Martiny (n 39) 749; more recently, Schack (n 50) para 1031; Gottwald (n 22) para 135; Roth (n 56) para 116.
[176] This requirement is distinct from the 'legal validity' pursuant to § 723(2) cl 1 ZPO, see above, Question 3 b).

and enforced in Germany.[177] If, on the other hand, the judgment is merely voidable, recognition and enforcement are possible as long as the judgment has not been set aside. This includes the possibility of reopening the case in novel proceedings (eg, through an action for annulment or an action for retrial) and the possibility of a constitutional challenge.[178]

2. *Jurisdiction under Public International Law*

For a foreign judgment to be recognised and enforced, the rendering state must have had jurisdiction over the defendant and the subject matter under public international law (*Gerichtsbarkeit* or *facultas iurisdictionis*).[179] Not mentioned in § 328 ZPO, the Bundesgerichtshof considers this to follow indirectly from the requirements of recognition jurisdiction under § 328(1) no 1 ZPO and of public policy under § 328(1) no 4 ZPO.[180] The requirement is, however, also justified on another level: the recognition and enforcement of a foreign judgment rendered in violation of public international law would be equally contrary to public international law.[181] Thus, the prohibition of recognising and enforcing such foreign judgments constitutes a general rule of public international law and is transformed into German law under Article 25 cl 1 GG.[182] As a consequence, foreign judgments rendered against a subject benefitting from immunity – such as the Federal Republic of Germany, a foreign state or state organ, an international organisation, or a consul – cannot be recognised and enforced.[183] In contrast, state-owned enterprises are not usually considered to be able to claim immunity.[184]

Question 4. Documents to be Produced

German law does not specify which documents have to be produced. As case law and statements by scholars are rare and differ from one another, much remains unclear. One court of second instance has ruled that a certified copy of the foreign title must be submitted.[185] While some scholars do not consider a translation to be required,[186]

[177] Bundesgerichtshof, 4 July 1992, IX ZR 149/91, BGHZ 118, 312, sub III.2.a); Gottwald (n 22) para 83.
[178] ibid; Stadler (n 60) para 7.
[179] Bundesgerichtshof, 30 March 2011, XII ZB 300/10, BGHZ 189, 87, sub II.3.a); Bundesgerichtshof, 26 June 2003, III ZR 245/98, BGHZ 155, 279, sub B.I.2; Oberlandesgericht Frankfurt, 21 October 1980, 5 W 24/80, para 18; Gottwald (n 22) para 84.
[180] Bundesgerichtshof, 26 June 2003, III ZR 245/98, BGHZ 155, 279, sub B.I.2. See § 109(1) no 1, 4 FamFG for family matters.
[181] Oberlandesgericht Frankfurt, 21 October 1980, 5 W 24/80, para 19; Gottwald (n 22) para 84 Geimer (n 1) para 99.
[182] Oberlandesgericht Frankfurt, 21 October 1980, 5 W 24/80, para 19.
[183] See, eg, § 18–20 GVG.
[184] Oberlandesgericht Frankfurt, 21 October 1980, 5 W 24/80, para 20; Gottwald (n 22) para 84.
[185] Oberlandesgericht Hamm, 4 June 1997, 1 U 2/96, IPRax 1998, 474, 476, sub II.1.
[186] See Nordmeier (n 12) para 12a.

others argue that a translation[187] or even an official translation of the title[188] is necessary. According to the latter view, the court may, if a translation is missing, either order the plaintiff to produce one or obtain it *ex officio*.[189] *Ex officio* obtainment is considered in particular if the plaintiff is impecunious.[190] According to one scholar, it should be left to the discretion of the competent authority or court whether to require a translation.[191] In order to prove the finality of the judgment, some scholars suggest the presentation of a certificate of finality while others propose that all means of evidence be admitted on the other.[192] With reference to the FamFG, scholars have commented on the requirement of 'legalisation'. According to one author, documents (without specifying which) may (but do not have to) be legalised.[193] Another scholar suggests, again, that the requirement of legalisation should be left to the discretion of the competent authority or court.[194]

With regard to a declaration of enforceability under the German–Israeli Convention on Recognition and Enforcement, the Bundesgerichtshof has ruled that no documents need to be submitted at all, provided that the German court was able to convince itself by other means that the requirements for recognition and enforcement were met.[195]

Question 5. Securities, Bonds and Deposits

Plaintiffs may, under certain circumstances, be required to provide security. Since the ZPO does not provide for a special procedure for the enforcement judgment, the general provisions of the ZPO apply.[196] The obligation to provide security is governed by §§ 110–113 ZPO. Pursuant to § 110(1) ZPO, the plaintiff – on the application of the defendant – must provide security for the costs of the proceedings if she is habitually resident outside the EU and the European Economic Area (EEA). For legal persons, the administrative seat is decisive.[197] The defendant bears the burden of proof for the fact that the plaintiff is habitually resident outside the EU and the EEA,[198] without imposing excessive requirements on the presentation of evidence.[199]

[187] Spellenberg (n 10) para 181.
[188] Gottwald (n 14) para 48.
[189] ibid; Spellenberg (n 10) para 181.
[190] Spellenberg (n 10) para 181.
[191] Hausmann (n 27) Part 2, K, para 328.
[192] Dimmler (n 18) para 75 (with regard to § 110 FamFG); C Heinze, '§ 723', in R Bork and H Roth (eds), *Kommentar zur Zivilprozessordnung (Stein/Jonas)*, 23rd edn (Mohr Siebeck, 2024) para 3; Nordmeier (n 12) para 14a; similarly, Geimer (n 13) para 64.
[193] Spellenberg (n 10) para 181.
[194] Hausmann (n 27) Part 2, K para 328.
[195] Bundesgerichtshof, 12 October 2017, IX ZB 64/14, sub II.2.c)bb)(1).
[196] See Geimer (n 13) para 74; Gottwald (n 14) para 45.
[197] Bundesgerichtshof, 23 August 2017, IV ZR 93/17, sub II.2.b).
[198] Bundesgerichtshof, 23 August 2017, IV ZR 93/17, sub II.3.b).
[199] Oberlandesgericht Düsseldorf, 16 March 2017, I-15 U 67/16, 15 U 67/16, sub II.2.b)aa); K Herget, '§ 110' in R Zöller (ed), *Zivilprozessordnung*, 35th edn (Dr Otto Schmidt, 2024) para 7.

Pursuant to § 110(2) nos 1–3 ZPO, there is no obligation to provide security:

- Where, due to international treaties, no such security may be demanded;
- Where the decision as to the defendant's reimbursement of the costs it has incurred in the proceedings would be enforced based on international treaties;
- Where the plaintiff possesses real estate assets, or claims secured in rem, in Germany that suffice to cover the costs of the proceedings.

The court has a discretion in determining the amount of security (§ 112(1) ZPO). The exercise of discretion is based on the costs that the defendant has already incurred and is likely to further incur, including possible appeals (§ 112(1) cl 1 ZPO).[200] The court sets a time limit for the plaintiff to provide security (§ 113 cl 1 ZPO). If the plaintiff fails to comply with this, the enforcement action is declared withdrawn on the application of the defendant (§ 113 cl 2 ZPO).

[200] Bundesgerichtshof, 1 April 1982, VIII ZR 159/80, sub III.1.b).

Greece

EVA LITINA

Question 1. General Overview

The national rules governing recognition and enforcement of foreign judgments in Greece can be found in the Greek Code of Civil Procedure (Κώδικας Πολιτικής Δικονομίας in Greek; CCP). The requirements and procedure are provided by Articles 323 (recognition of *res iudicata* of contentious proceedings), 780 (recognition of legal effect of judgments of non-contentious proceedings) and 905 (declaration of enforceability) of the CCP.

There is a clear distinction between recognition and enforcement under Greek law. Recognition refers to the binding effect of a foreign judgment and differs from enforcement in that it happens without any special procedure if the requirements are fulfilled (Article 323). In cases of dispute over the fulfilment of such requirements, the interested party may seek a declaratory judgment from Greek courts. For enforcement, in the absence of a special legal framework, and especially of an applicable European Union (EU) regulation on direct enforcement of a foreign judgment, a declaration of enforceability is necessary in accordance with Article 905.

Under the CCP, only judgments ordering the defendant to perform as obliged (payment of money or specific performance – καταψηφιστική, *katapsifistiki* in Greek) can be enforced.[1] A declaratory (αναγνωριστική, *anagnoristiki* in Greek) or constitutive (ordering judicial modification of a legal relationship – διαπλαστική, *diaplastiki* in Greek) judgment can only be enforced to the extent it awards judicial costs.[2] It should further be noted that in contrast to the definition of the 2019 Hague Conference on Private International Law (HCCH) Convention on the Recognition and Enforcement of Foreign Judgments in Civil or Commercial Matters (HCCH 2019 Judgments Convention), which excludes interim measures of protection from the definition of judgment (Article 3 paragraph 1(b)), interim measures may be enforced under the CCP.[3] However, it is not

[1] P Mazis, 'Art 905' in K Kerameus, D Kondylis and N Nikas (eds), *Interpretation of Code of Civil Procedure* (Sakoulas, 2021) para 6.

[2] ibid. See K Kerameus, 'Chapter 16: Judicial Organization and Civil Procedure' in K Kerameus and P Kozyris (eds), *Introduction to Greek Law* (3rd ed, Kluwer Law International, Sakoulas, 2008) 350-351 on the types of actions under Greek law.

[3] ibid.

possible to enforce interim measures related to real property located outside Greece, since Greek courts would not have jurisdiction to order such measures for real property situated abroad.[4] It is also not possible to enforce interim measures issued by a foreign court for real property located in Greece.[5]

Greek courts consider the definition of judgment on the basis of the law of the state to which the body that issued it belongs. From the combination of Articles 905 paragraphs 1–4 and 323 of the CCP, a foreign judgment is defined as decision of an organ of a foreign state, which, according to its law and having the relevant jurisdiction, is charged with the resolution of private disputes according to a prescribed, even summary, procedure, while the type or characterisation by the law of the foreign state as a judgment, decree, act, decision, etc is irrelevant.[6] The validity of the judgment is considered in accordance with the foreign law, which applies in the state where the decision is issued and it is irrelevant whether the judgment bears the form determined by the local procedural rules, even if the latter are mandatory rules and form part of domestic public policy.[7] For example, the Supreme Court held that a decision of the competent District Court of the United States (US) that confirms an arbitral award and registers a decision ordering the defendant to pay the amount in dispute plus interest and costs, while it is also subject to appeal, is a judgment in accordance with Article 905 paragraph 3 of the CCP.[8]

The type of the dispute, ie whether it is a private dispute, will be considered in accordance with Greek law and therefore it is irrelevant whether it was issued by a civil, criminal or administrative court.[9] The judgments of the European Court of Human Rights can also be enforced in accordance with Articles 323 and 905 of the CCP.[10]

Recognition and enforcement of foreign judgments is governed by the CCP in the absence of a special regime, originating from EU legislation, or international and bilateral treaties. In accordance with Article 28, paragraph 1 of the Greek Constitution, international treaties signed by Greece form an integral part of Greek law and prevail over any contrary provision. Apart from treaties in force in all EU Member States (such as the Lugano Convention) or special regimes (such as the Convention on the Contract for the International Carriage of Goods by Road (CMR), ratified by Law 559/1977, or the Berne Convention Concerning International Carriage by Rail 1980 (COTIF), ratified by Law 1593/1986), there are also bilateral treaties between Greece and non-EU states, such as Albania,[11] Armenia,[12] China,[13]

[4] Single-member First Instance Court (SFIC) Piraeus 3127/1981 (1981) *Peiraiki Nomologia (PeirN)* 366.
[5] SFIC Piraeus 854/1989 ISOKRATIS.
[6] Areios Pagos (Supreme Court; SC) 496/1994 (1995) *Nomiko Vima (NOV)* 552.
[7] ibid.
[8] SC 340/1998 NOMOS.
[9] Mazis (n 1) para 6.
[10] ibid para 37.
[11] Greece–Albania Treaty of 17 May 1993, ratified by Law 2311/1995, on civil and criminal matters.
[12] Greece–Armenia Treaty of 21 November 2000, ratified by Law 3007/2002, on civil, family, and criminal matters.
[13] Greece–China Treaty of 17 October 1994, ratified by Law 2358/1995, on civil and criminal matters.

Georgia,[14] Great Britain and Australia,[15] Lebanon,[16] (former) Socialist Federal Republic of Yugoslavia,[17] Switzerland,[18] Syria,[19] Tunisia,[20] Ukraine,[21] and (former) Union of Soviet Socialist Republics (USSR).[22] With a few exceptions, those bilateral treaties contain recognition and enforcement provisions.[23] These are important as, in accordance with the express provision of Article 323, they supersede domestic law.[24] The procedure under those bilateral treaties is broadly the same as that provided by the CCP, and involves a petition to the Greek Court either directly or in certain cases through diplomatic channels (eg Article 6 paragraph 1 of the Greece–(former) Socialist Federal Republic of Yugoslavia Treaty of 18 June 1959, ratified by Law 4007/1959).

The provisions of the CCP are aligned with both EU legislation and multilateral treaties. Both Article 323 and Article 905 provide their residual application, while Article 905 has been amended by Article 18 of Law 4055/2012 to provide that it applies without prejudice to EU Regulations. The residual application of those rules perhaps explains, to a certain extent, the fact that they have received less scholarly attention compared to EU Regulations.

Question 2. Procedure

a) Circumstances of Recognition and Enforcement

In accordance with Article 323 of the CCP, if the requirements are fulfilled, recognition takes place automatically (*ipso jure*). Greek courts are divided on whether recognition can

[14] Greece–Georgia Treaty of 10 May 1999, ratified by Law 2813/2000, on civil and criminal matters.

[15] Greece–Great Britain Treaty of 27 February 1936, ratified by Law 730/1937, on judicial cooperation in civil and commercial matters. Australia acceded to the Treaty, in accordance with Arts 15 and 16, on 14 December 1938, with effect from the same day (Government Gazette A 445/1938). SC 974/2023 NOMOS concerns the application of the Treaty to Australia.

[16] Greece–Lebanon Treaty of 5 April 1975, ratified by Law 1099/1980, on civil, commercial, and criminal matters.

[17] Greece–(former) Socialist Federal Republic of Yugoslavia (and now Bosnia – Herzegovina, Croatia, Montenegro, North Macedonia, Serbia, and Slovenia) Treaty of 18 June 1959, ratified by Law 4007/1959, on civil, commercial, and criminal matters. Greek courts applied the CCP for the recognition and enforcement of a judgment from North Macedonia, as the Intermediate Treaty between Greece and FYROM of 13 September 1995 which provided for the application of Greece–(former) Socialist Federal Republic of Yugoslavia Treaty of 18 June 1959 had not been ratified by law, see SFIC Thessaloniki 17483/2018 (2018) *Armenopoulos* 1705.

[18] Greece–Switzerland Treaty of 30 March 1934, ratified by Law 729/1937, on judicial cooperation in civil and commercial matters. SC 22/2009 NOMOS; SC 23/2009 NOMOS; Court of Appeal (CA) Piraeus 336/2020 NOMOS.

[19] Greece–Syria Treaty of 2 June 1981, ratified by Law 1450/1984.

[20] Greece–Tunisia Treaty of 12 April 1993, ratified by Law 2228/1994, on civil and commercial matters.

[21] Greece–Ukraine Treaty of 2 July 2002, ratified by Law 3281/2004, on civil matters.

[22] Greece–(former) USSR Treaty of 21 May 1981, ratified by Law 1242/1982, on civil and criminal matters.

[23] For example, Greece–Great Britain Treaty and Greece–Switzerland Treaty do not refer to recognition and enforcement of judgments.

[24] CA Piraeus 830/1987 NOMOS.

be affirmed by a Greek court even incidentally, for example during other proceedings.[25] The interested party may present the foreign judgment to Greek public authorities, which should not oblige the party to seek a domestic court judgment for recognition.[26] In case of dispute, the issue of recognition may be resolved by an action for declaratory judgment if the interested party has a legitimate interest.[27] This remedy does not seem to work in practice, as the process would be lengthy.[28]

In the absence of an EU regulation or an international or bilateral treaty, Article 905 of the CCP applies for the enforcement of a foreign judgment. The interested party must seek a declaration of enforceability of the foreign judgment by a Greek court judgment.

The petition for the declaration of enforceability of a foreign judgment is heard according to the rules applicable to non-contentious proceedings (Article 905 paragraph 1). In addition to the general requirements provided by Article 905 paragraph 2 (enforceability in accordance with the law of the country of origin, and not being contrary to good morals or public policy), specifically with respect to foreign judgments, the court declares enforceability if the judgment also meets the requirements of Article 323 paragraphs 2–5.[29] This procedure is mandatory and exclusive, as there is no other remedy or procedure for the enforcement of a foreign judgment.[30]

The court examines the requirements of its own motion. The court does not adjudicate the case and the Greek judgment does not replace the foreign judgment – it merely provides to the judgment executory power so that it can be enforced in the Greek legal order.[31]

Once the foreign judgment is declared enforceable by the Greek court, the foreign judgment is an executory title on the basis of which enforcement can be attempted against assets owned by the debtor.[32] The procedure to be followed and the methods of enforcement available thereafter are the same as those provided by Greek law for the enforcement of domestic court judgments. An executory mark (απόγραφο, *apografo* in Greek) must be affixed to the foreign judgment, which will then be a writ of execution (Article 918 of the CCP).

b) Procedural Steps

From the combination of the provisions of Articles 323 and 905 paragraphs 1, 2 and 3 of the CCP, for a foreign judgment to be enforced in Greece, there must be an application before the competent Single-member First Instance Court (SFIC) seeking a declaration of enforceability of the judgment. In accordance with Article 905 paragraph 1 of CCP, the competent authority to enforce a foreign judgment is the

[25] In favour: CA Thessaloniki 2367/1998 (1998) Arm 1233; CA Athens 7359/2005 (2006) *Dikaiosini (D/ni)* 856. Against: CA Athens 1330/1996 (1997) *D/ni* 1873; CA Dodekanisa 140/2005 NOMOS.

[26] A Anthimos, 'Art 323' in H Apalagaki and S Stamatopoulos (eds), *The New Code of Civil Procedure* (Nomiki Vivliothiki, 2022) para 3.

[27] Art 70 CCP.

[28] Anthimos (n 26) para 3.

[29] Art 905 paras 2 and 3 CCP.

[30] Mazis (n 1) para 2.

[31] ibid para 17.

[32] SC 767/2019 NOMOS.

SFIC of the place of domicile of the debtor or, if there is no such place of domicile in Greece, the SFIC of Athens. The SFIC decides in accordance with the procedure of Articles 740–781, which means that the petition is heard according to the rules applicable to non-contentious proceedings.

The petition is filed by the person who under the foreign law has the right to enforce the judgment, in accordance with the judgment and its legal successor (eg assignor or successor in right).[33] The CCP does not provide a limitation period to recognise and enforce a foreign judgment.[34] The petition need not be addressed to the debtor. However, the debtor may be summoned to appear by the court of its own motion in accordance with Article 748 paragraph 3 of the CCP. In this case, the judge orders that the debtor is summoned to the hearing within a specific deadline. The debtor cannot file an appeal unless it becomes a party to the proceeding, either by intervention (Article 752 CCP) or impleader (Article 753 CCP).[35] At the date of the hearing, which is fixed by the court, the parties must submit pleadings and all supporting evidence.

The petition needs to plead the requirements of Articles 905 paragraphs 2 and 3 and 323 paragraphs 2–5 in general, while the facts may arise from the judgment itself.[36] In contrast to EU Regulations, Article 323 does not distinguish between requirements for recognition and enforcement, and grounds for refusal of recognition. Thus, the burden of proving the requirements for recognition and enforcement is upon the party seeking recognition and enforcement.[37] Greek courts examine the requirements of their own motion during both first instance proceedings and appeal.[38]

Greek courts do not have the power to examine the merits of a judgment to be enforced, but only to verify whether the conditions for recognition and enforcement are met. This means that the court does not adjudicate the case and its judgment, which is constitutive, merely provides to the foreign judgment enforceability in the Greek legal order.[39] Greek courts have no power to change the content, interpret or correct the foreign judgment.

In accordance with Article 778 of the CCP, for the cases adjudicated in accordance with the rules applicable to non-contentious proceedings, if an application is accepted or rejected, with a final decision, a new application of the parties on the same subject matter is inadmissible. From the combination of this provision with Article 758, which provides that if new facts arise or the circumstances change, the court may order that the revoking or reforming decision has retroactive force, it follows that the decisions issued during the special procedure of non-contentious proceedings do not constitute *res iudicata* (in the sense of Articles 321 et seq of the CCP).[40] However, a new petition of the parties on the same facts is inadmissible and has similar effects to the negative

[33] Art 919 CCP.

[34] P Rentoulis, 'Art 905' in H Apalagaki and S Stamatopoulos (eds), *The New Code of Civil Procedure* (Nomiki Vivliothiki, 2022) para 13.

[35] If the debtor has not become a party to the proceedings, the following remedies are available: an application initiating third-party proceedings (τριτανακοπή, *tritanakopi* in Greek); and opposition to enforcement (challenging the validity of the executory title) (Art 933). See Mazis (n 1) para 14.

[36] ibid para 15.

[37] Anthimos (n 26) para 6.

[38] CA Athens 14501/1988 (1993) *D/ni* 1358.

[39] Mazis (n 1) para 17.

[40] SC 281/1997 NOMOS.

function of *res iudicata*.[41] In case the petition is rejected, a new one can be filed on the basis of different facts.[42]

Question 3. Requirements

Article 323 of the CCP sets out five cumulative requirements for the recognition of *res iudicata* of foreign judgments. In contrast to EU Regulations and the HCCH 2019 Judgments Convention, the CCP does not distinguish between requirements for recognition and enforcement, and grounds for refusal of recognition. Some bilateral treaties between Greece and third states provide for grounds for refusal.[43]

In accordance with Article 323, a foreign judgment is valid and *res iudicata* in Greece without any special procedure if:

(1) it is *res iudicata* under the law of the state it was issued;
(2) the judgment was delivered by a competent court in accordance with Greek law;
(3) the losing party was not deprived of its right to defend itself and in general to participate in the proceedings, unless deprivation is according to a provision that also applies to the nationals of the state of the court that issued the foreign judgment;
(4) the judgment is not contrary to a Greek court judgment issued in the same case and constituting *res iudicata* for the parties for which the foreign court judgment was issued;
(5) it is not contrary to good morals or public policy.

A foreign judgment resolving a private dispute can be enforced in Greece in accordance with the procedure and requirements set out in Article 905 of the CCP. The requirements set out in Article 905 paragraph 3 overlap with the requirements of Article 323, except for the requirement that the judgment is *res iudicata* under the law of the state in which it was issued. From the combination of the provisions of Articles 323 and 905 (paragraphs 2 and 3) of the CCP, for a foreign judgment to be enforced in Greece the following requirements must be met:

(1) the judgment is enforceable in accordance with the law of the country of origin;
(2) the judgment has been delivered by a competent court in accordance with Greek law;
(3) the losing party was not deprived of its right to defend itself and in general to participate in the proceedings;
(4) the judgment is not contrary to a Greek court judgment issued in the same case that constitutes *res iudicata* for the parties for which the foreign court judgment was issued;

[41] ibid.
[42] ibid.
[43] For example, see Greece–China Treaty of 17 October 1994, ratified by Law 2358/1995, on civil and criminal matters, Art 23.

(5) it is not contrary to good morals or public policy.

There are also special provisions regarding enforcement of the judgments of Mufti (Law 4964/2022, Article 146 paragraphs 8–11), which refer to family relationships of Muslims in the region of Thrace.

The requirements mirror the classic grounds for the refusal of recognition and enforcement of foreign judgments, accepted in all European legal orders and provided by the Brussels Ia Regulation and the HCCH 2019 Judgments Convention. Indeed, Article 323 paragraph 3 refers to the protection of due process, Article 323 paragraph 4 refers to irreconcilability with a judgment between the same parties on the same subject matter, and Article 323 paragraph 5 refers to public policy.

a) Jurisdiction of the Court of Origin

In accordance with Articles 323 paragraph 2 and 905 paragraph 3, for a judgment to be enforced in Greece, the court that issued the foreign judgment must have jurisdiction to hear the case under Greek law.[44]

Greek courts examine whether the foreign court had jurisdiction over the defendant on the basis of the internal rules governing jurisdiction of Greek courts (mirror-image principle).[45] This means that courts make an assessment from the perspective of the foreign court as to whether they would have jurisdiction under Greek law if they were presented with the same facts of the case.[46]

Specifically, Greeks and foreigners are submitted to the jurisdiction of Greek civil courts, provided that said courts have territorial competence (Article 3 paragraph 1 of the CCP). Article 22 of the CCP establishes the general jurisdiction of the defendant's domicile. The CCP also includes special jurisdictional rules – such as those for company disputes,[47] disputes concerning real property located in Greece,[48] disputes concerning succession,[49] contractual disputes,[50] disputes arising out of torts[51] – while it also provides that litigant parties may submit to the jurisdiction of the court by virtue of an explicit or implicit agreement.[52] The foreign judgment is not enforceable, if Greek courts have exclusive jurisdiction to hear the case in accordance with Greek law. For example, Greek courts have exclusive jurisdiction in proceedings which have as their object rights *in rem* in immovable property situated in Greece.[53]

[44] For a more detailed analysis of Greek (domestic) jurisdictional rules, see V Marazopoulou, 'Greece' in T Lutzi, E Piovesani and D Zgrabljić Rotar (eds), *Jurisdiction Over Non-EU Defendants: Should the Brussels Ia Regulation be Extended?* (Hart Publishing, 2023) 127.

[45] SC 1053/2003 NOMOS; CA Thessaloniki 3836/1996 NOMOS.

[46] ibid.

[47] Art 27 CCP.

[48] Art 29 CCP.

[49] Art 30 CCP.

[50] Art 33 CCP.

[51] Art 35 CCP.

[52] Art 42 CCP.

[53] SC 12/1986 NOMOS.

b) Finality/Enforceability in the Country of Origin

In accordance with Article 905 paragraph 2, the judgment must be enforceable in accordance with the law of the country of origin. It is not necessary that the judgment is final or unappealable in accordance with the law of the country of origin, nor it is necessary that it is *res iudicata*.[54] The enforceability of the foreign judgment and any related issues are considered in accordance with the law of the country of origin.[55] If the judgment was declared enforceable in Greece but was later suspended in the country of origin, the enforcement of the foreign judgment cannot continue in Greece since the foreign judgment is the executory title on the basis of which enforcement is attempted.[56]

c) *Res Iudicata*

A final judgment of a Greek court not subject to application to set aside a default judgment or appeal is characterised (in Greek) as τελεσίδικη, *telesidiki* (final judgment not subject to appeal) and has *res iudicata* effect.[57] Such judgment has *res iudicata* effect on the same parties with the same capacity to the dispute only for the claim that was adjudicated, as long as the subject matter, facts and legal basis are the same.[58]

In accordance with Articles 323 paragraph 4 and 905 paragraph 3, such Greek court judgment is a reason for the court to refuse enforcement of the foreign judgment. It is irrelevant if the Greek court judgment was issued before or after the foreign judgment.[59] On the contrary, a final judgment subject to appeal, an interim judgment, or proceedings pending on the same matters do not block enforcement.[60]

In practice, the judgment debtor bears the burden to prove this requirement by presenting certificates from the secretary of any competent SFIC in Greece, which clearly leads to legal uncertainty.[61]

d) *Lis Pendens*

Under the CCP, proceedings pending on the same matters do not block enforcement.[62] However, special frameworks regulate this issue differently, such as the Greece–(former) USSR Treaty of 21 May 1981, ratified by Law 1242/1982 (Article 24 paragraph 3). The Greece–China Treaty of 17 October 1994, ratified by Law 2358/1995 provides that the court may refuse enforcement of the foreign

[54] SC 1660/1983 ISOKRATIS; SC 340/1998 (n 8).
[55] SC 767/2019 (n 32).
[56] ibid.
[57] Art 321 CCP.
[58] Arts 322 and 324 CCP.
[59] S Kousoulis, 'Art 323' in K Kerameus, D Kondylis and N Nikas (eds), *Interpretation of Code of Civil Procedure* (Sakoulas, 2000) para 8.
[60] SC 108/2001 NOMOS on a family law dispute.
[61] Anthimos (n 26) para 10.
[62] SC 108/2001 (n 60); CA Athens 11244/1980 NOMOS.

judgment if proceedings are pending before the courts of the state to which the application is filed involving the same cause of action and between the same parties, provided that such court was the court first seized (Article 23 paragraph e). The Greece–Tunisia Treaty of 12 April 1993, ratified by Law 2228/1994, provides that if proceedings are pending involving the same cause of action and between the same parties before the courts of either state, the courts of the other state may, upon petition of a party, reject the application or stay the proceedings (Article 30 paragraph 1).

e) Specific Requirements of Due Process

The rule of law ensures the right to a fair trial. Article 10 of the Universal Declaration of Human Rights and important international legal texts assert that access to a fair hearing by an impartial tribunal is a fundamental human right. At the national level, it is also found in constitutions and national legislation. Greece is bound by Article 14 paragraph 1 of the International Covenant on Civil and Political Rights, Article 6 of the European Convention for the Protection of Human Rights and Fundamental Freedoms (ECHR), and Article 47 of the Charter of Fundamental Rights of the EU.

In accordance with Articles 323 paragraph 3 and 905 paragraph 3, for a judgment to be enforced in Greece, the court will examine whether the losing party was deprived of its right to defend itself and in general to participate in the proceedings, unless deprivation is according to a provision that also applies to the nationals of the state of the court that issued the foreign judgment.

This requirement refers to cases in which the document which instituted the proceedings or an equivalent document, including a statement of the essential elements of the claim was not served on the defendant[63] or was not duly served in accordance with the legal provisions.[64] For example, it may be considered that the defendant was deprived of the right to defend when the document was not served on the defendant in sufficient time.[65]

The Supreme Court found that the claim was not notified when the lawsuit never reached the defendant via the Iranian Embassy.[66] The publication of announcement in Albanian newspapers was not considered sufficient, when it was proved that the claimant knew the domicile of the defendant.[67] Similarly, service of documents to non-authorised persons does not suffice.[68] The mere fact that the defendant could not participate in the proceedings (and hire a lawyer) due to financial constraints is not considered as deprivation.[69] The judgment as to whether the circumstances and the procedure at the foreign court constitute the legal concept of depriving the losing party of its right to defend itself is subject to appeal (cassation – αναίρεση, *anairesi* in Greek) to the Supreme Court, while the judgment of whether the losing party was deprived of

[63] SC 687/2003 NOMOS.
[64] CA Athens 14501/1988. Anthimos (n 26) para 9.
[65] SC 1383/1987 NOMOS; CA Athens 10601/1995 NOMOS.
[66] SC 687/2003 (n 63).
[67] SC 2264/2014 NOMOS.
[68] SC 1522/2007 NOMOS; See SC 2293/2009 NOMOS for valid service.
[69] SFIC Thessaloniki 4728/1999 NOMOS.

its right to defend itself or not refers to a question of fact and therefore is not subject to appeal to the Supreme Court.[70]

Finally, in contrast to the Brussels Ia Regulation, which does not include provisional measures ordered by a court or tribunal without the defendant being summoned to appear (Article 2 paragraph a), English court orders have been enforced under the CCP.[71]

f) Public Policy

Articles 323 paragraph 5 and 905 paragraph 3 require that the foreign judgment is not contrary to good morals or public policy. The term 'good morals' is considered to be narrower than public policy and forms part of it.[72] However, it is mentioned expressly for the avoidance of doubt to exclude the recognition and enforcement of judgments which are contrary to good morals.[73] During enforcement proceedings, Greek courts review only compatibility with international public policy in accordance with Article 33 of the Civil Code and do not review errors of fact or law.[74] The review of the merits of the judgment (*révision au fond*) is prohibited.[75] Public policy also appears in bilateral treaties, except for the Greece–China Treaty of 17 October 1994 (Article 23) and the Greece–(former) USSR Treaty of 21 May 1981 (Article 24), which do not include public policy as a ground for refusal of recognition and enforcement. Typically, public policy will be invoked by the defendant who is resisting enforcement.

The Supreme Court has interpreted international public policy as follows:

> International public policy in the context of Article 33 of the Civil Code consists of fundamental rules and principles, which prevail at a given time in a country and which reflect the social, economic, civil, political, religious, moral, and other perceptions that govern its standard of living and constitute a barrier to the application of foreign rules within the domestic territory when this application may disrupt the aforementioned prevailing standard of living in this country.[76]

It should be noted from the outset that Greek courts have exercised their powers regarding public policy sparingly. The notion of international public policy has been construed in line with the Brussels regime and international best practices: Greek courts describe it as a flexible, vague principle that can only be used in exceptional cases.[77] The judge has to make a careful fact-based determination of public policy on a case-by-case basis.[78]

[70] SC 2293/2009 (n 68); SC 2264/2014 (n 67).

[71] CA Athens 10647/1987 (1990) D/ni 1514. See also Mazis (n 1) para 6.

[72] A Kaisis, *Public Policy Aspects in Recognition and Enforcement of Foreign Court Judgments and Foreign Arbitral Awards* (Sakoulas Athens-Thessaloniki, 2003) 69.

[73] ibid.

[74] SC 579/2019 NOMOS. See also Kaisis (n 72) 67.

[75] ibid.

[76] ibid. For a more detailed analysis of public policy in the context of recognition and enforcement of foreign judgments, see Kaisis (n 72) 67–141; I Delicostopoulos, 'Public Policy as a Ground to Refuse Enforcement of a Foreign Judgment' in *In Memoriam St. Kousouli* (Sakoulas, 2012) 103–115.

[77] CA Athens 2382/2011 (2012) *Dikaio Epiheiriseon & Etairion (DEE)* 63; CA Piraeus 548/2020 NOMOS.

[78] ibid.

Over time, public policy is subject to changes, usually reflected in the amendments of the legal provisions.[79]

The mere fact that Greek law is unaware of a particular foreign legal provision or that the issue is regulated differently in Greek law does not mean that the judgment is contrary to public policy.[80] The crucial time for the court to ascertain the violation of public policy is the time of recognition of the foreign judgment.[81] The correct interpretation and application of public policy as a legal concept is subject to appeal to the Supreme Court.[82]

1. *Procedural Public Policy*

Procedural public policy includes fundamental procedural principles which express the rule of law:[83] judicial independence and impartiality; the right to be heard; equal treatment of the parties; and due process.[84] The lack of reasoning in a foreign judgment does not violate international public policy,[85] unless such lack of reasoning aims at a disguised breach of the right to fair trial or leads to a resolution of the dispute that violates public policy.[86] The mere fact that the foreign court denied examination of two more witnesses does not constitute a violation of public policy nor due process.[87]

Greek courts found excessive judicial costs to be: a) contrary to the principle of proportionality; and b) indirect restrictions of a party's access to justice.[88] However, there is a shift in this approach in the recent Greek jurisprudence.[89] The Supreme Court in a recent judgment ruled that the mere imposition of high judicial costs does not amount to a violation of public policy.[90] Provided that judicial costs are actual and they do not constitute a disguised punitive damages award, they should not be reviewed for excessiveness, as this would amount to a prohibited review of the merits.[91]

Greek case law has also faced the controversial issue of anti-suit injunctions. Parallel proceedings can lead to increased costs and conflicting judgments, which complicate enforcement proceedings. A court or tribunal order, known as an anti-suit injunction, restrains a party from starting or continuing legal action in a jurisdiction or forum other

[79] ibid.
[80] SC 17/1999 NOMOS.
[81] Kaisis (n 72) 70.
[82] SC 17/1999 (n 80); SC 579/2019 (n 74).
[83] SC 496/1994 (n 6); SC 579/2019 (n 74).
[84] CA Piraeus 548/2020 (n 77). See Kaisis (n 72) 71–72.
[85] SC 1518/1979 NOMOS; SC 950/1991 NOMOS.
[86] SC 1134/1975 (1976) *NOV* 418.
[87] SC 580/1982 NOMOS.
[88] SC 1829/2006 NOMOS; CA Athens 6115/2005 NOMOS. CA Piraeus 1273/1981 (1981) *PeirN* 434 had not found excessive judicial costs. For a more detailed analysis, see P Giannopoulos, 'Violation of Greek Public Policy by Foreign Judgment Due to the Imposition of Excessive Judicial Costs' (2006) *Armenopoulos* 1832; H Meidanis, 'The Imposition of Excessive Judicial Costs by a Foreign Judgment. Enforcement Issues in Light of the Principle of Proportionality and Access to Justice' (2007) *Chronika Idiotikou Dikaiou* 833.
[89] CA Piraeus 548/2020 (n 77).
[90] SC 579/2019 (n 74) which applied Regulation 44/2001.
[91] ibid.

than the one that has been contractually agreed upon. Anti-suit injunctions can be used as a remedy to prevent foreign proceedings started in breach of an exclusive jurisdiction or arbitration agreement. This practice, which has been employed predominantly by common law state courts, as well as by arbitrators,[92] has created a field of conflict between the civil and common law legal systems.

Especially with regard to anti-suit injunctions issued by English courts, this has also been an area where the European notion of mutual trust has been tested.[93] Following the United Kingdom (UK)'s departure from the EU, anti-suit injunctions are now available in a wider range of cases than previously.

The maritime bench of the Court of Piraeus faced the issue of anti-suit injunctions from English courts.[94] Citing Article 8 paragraph 1, Article 20 paragraph 1 of the Greek Constitution, and Article 6 paragraph 1 of the ECHR regarding the right of fair trial, the Court held that the enforcement of such an injunction is against public policy.[95] In general, a court or tribunal order which directly restricts a party's access to justice in the form of an anti-suit injunction will be considered contrary to Greek public policy.[96]

The criticism against this approach has been that the prohibition of a suit before Greek courts does not necessarily violate the party's access to justice since it could still pursue its claim before the court or tribunal that issued the anti-suit injunction.[97] Especially in light of the Brussels I and Brussels Ia Regulations and the underlying principles of mutual trust and equality among the courts of the EU Member States, it is questionable whether such concern is valid. Instead, Greek courts could invoke the principle of mutual trust, which has public policy status under EU law, as a more convincing ground to refuse enforcement of anti-suit injunctions.[98]

[92] L Levy, 'Anti-suit Injunctions Issued by Arbitrators' in E Gaillard (ed), *Anti-suit Injunctions in International Arbitration* (JurisNet, 2005) 115–29. The power of the arbitral tribunals to issue anti-suit injunctions depends on whether the arbitration agreement will be seen as a contract or as a procedural agreement; see P Ortolani, 'Anti-suit Injunctions in Support of Arbitration under the Recast Brussels I Regulation' (2015) *MPILux Working Paper* 6, 11–12, mpi.lu/fileadmin/mpi/medien/research/Pietro_Orotolani_WPS_2015-1.pdf.

[93] In the context of the EU, anti-suit injunctions had been considered contrary to the Council Regulation (EC) No 44/2001 of 22 December 2000 on jurisdiction and the recognition and enforcement of judgments in civil and commercial matters [2001] OJ L 12/1 (Brussels I Regulation) by the European Court of Justice (ECJ) C-185/07 *Allianz SpA and Generali Assicurazioni Generali SpA v West Tankers Inc* ECLI:EU:C:2009:69. The debate revived after the Regulation (EU) No 1215/2012 of the European Parliament and of the Council of 12 December 2012 on jurisdiction and the recognition and enforcement of judgments in civil and commercial matters [2012] OJ L 351/1 (Brussels Recast Regulation) and the judgment of the ECJ C-536/13 *Gazprom OAO v Lietuvos Respublika* ECLI:EU:C:2015:316 on anti-suit injunctions issued by arbitral tribunals.

[94] CA Piraeus 110/2004 NOMOS; CA Piraeus 31/2012 NOMOS; CA Piraeus 548/2020 (n 77).

[95] CA Piraeus 31/2012 (ibid) further found that anti-suit injunctions violate the sovereignty of the Greek state, by limiting the jurisdiction of Greek courts. See also H Meidanis, 'Notes on CA Piraeus 110/2004' (2005) *Dike International* 835, 839–40 and Kaisis (n 72) 91–92 embracing this reasoning and citing German authorities on this issue.

[96] See SFIC Trikala 709/2000 ISOKRATIS denying the enforcement of an anti-suit injunction issued by a US court. See also S Stamatopoulos and P Giannopoulos, 'Enforcement Issues of English Judgment Imposing Damages in Case of Pursuing Proceedings before Greek Courts' (2015) *Epitheorisi Politikis Dikonomias* 145, 163.

[97] CA Piraeus 548/2020 (n 77) mentions this argument. See also H Meidanis, 'Notes on CA Piraeus 110/2004' (n 95) 840; H Meidanis, 'Anti-suit Injunction in England and the Regulation 44/2001: Conflict (and Comparison) of Two Legal Traditions' (2005) *DEE* 152, 155.

[98] For further arguments in favour of invoking mutual trust to deny enforcement of anti-suit injunctions in the form of arbitral awards, see Ortolani (n 92) 15–16.

It remains to be seen how the political and legal developments on this issue will affect the stance of Greek courts following Brexit. As injunctions travel and reach the courts of civil law countries, the concept of public policy comes into play and it will be the judge who will have the final say in this legal battle.

2. *Substantive Public Policy*

Earlier case law addressed the legality of over-insurance and blocked the enforcement of a London maritime arbitration award that allowed for coverage exceeding the actual cash value of the vessel.[99] Greek courts have also addressed the issue of interest. The Supreme Court found that a foreign arbitral award does not violate public policy by providing daily interest of 0.4 per cent even if it exceeds the maximum interest rate allowed in Greece.[100]

The remedy of punitive damages is one of the most representative areas of conflict among the European and Anglo-Saxon legal systems. Greek courts have held that awards of punitive damages are not in principle violations of international public policy, provided that they are not excessive or disproportionate.[101]

The Supreme Court (in full plenary 17/1999), after having acknowledged that Greek law provides for remedies comparable to punitive damages,[102] held that foreign judgments or arbitral awards ordering punitive damages must pass the proportionality test and any potential violation of public policy is considered on a case-by-case basis.[103] Partial recognition and enforcement of a foreign judgment is possible in cases of excessive punitive damages.[104]

This approach is pragmatic and quite progressive, as it does not ignore the legal reality that in an era of globalisation the interaction between different legal systems and cultures is inevitable. The conflicts and challenges during enforcement proceedings of punitive damages are also clearly reflected in the dissenting opinions of the Supreme Court.[105] The Court correctly identified the underlying legal principles and appropriately balanced the apparent commonalities, as well as the divergences arising

[99] SC 1469/1988 NOMOS; SC 6/1990 and 9/1990 NOMOS; CA Athens 2135/1987 NOMOS. For an analysis of this issue see I Rokas, 'Note: Prohibition of Enrichment and Evaluation of the Insured Property' (1987) *NOV* 1411.

[100] SC 1710/1997 NOMOS. In SFIC Piraeus 494/1998 unpublished, the court provides specific criteria for assessing whether contractual interest violates public policy; see H Meidanis, *Public Policy in European Private International Law* (Sakoulas, 2004) 96.

[101] SC 17/1999 (n 80). This was the first judgment that addressed the issue of punitive damages in the context of a US court judgment. In 1260/2002 NOMOS, the SC established the same principles for the enforcement of foreign arbitral awards imposing punitive damages. See also Kaisis (n 72) 101, 198.

[102] For example, Arts 404–09 of the Greek Civil Code allow parties to insert penalty clauses in their contract.

[103] SC 17/1999 (n 80) and SC 1260/2002, ibid, refer to the criteria on which judgment on excessiveness will be based: type and seriousness of the debtor's wrongful behavior; the degree of culpability; the interests of the creditor; moral and financial condition of the parties and any other special conditions. SFIC Piraeus 722/2019 NOMOS enforces a US judgment awarding punitive damages.

[104] SC 17/1999 (n 80).

[105] Apart from the prevailing view, two dissenting opinions were formed. The first was the complete rejection of punitive damages, as they violate Greek public policy. The second was the opposite, ie that the principle of full compensation cannot be considered as part of the international public policy and thus punitive damages are not contrary to public policy.

out of the different legal systems. However, there is an inherent contradiction in this rationale: if punitive damages are not incompatible with international public policy, why does the court have to further check excessiveness?[106] As can be expected, such a compromise approach does not resolve all the issues.

From a policy perspective, it is understandable that the Supreme Court wishes to maintain some control over the amount of punitive damages, given their uncertain and controversial character even in the Anglo-Saxon legal traditions.[107] However, to apply the proportionality test, the enforcing authority will have to enter the restricted area of the merits.[108]

Furthermore, the criteria on how to determine the excessiveness of punitive damages lack specificity. This leaves the lower courts without guidance on what constitutes disproportionality.[109] Therefore, the stance of the Supreme Court in this respect does not lead to clear-cut and predictable outcomes. However, in such controversial areas, where vague principles such as public policy come into play, judicial discretion is at the end inevitable and potentially even desirable.

In accordance with Article 10 of the HCCH 2019 Judgments Convention, recognition or enforcement of a judgment may be refused if, and to the extent that, the judgment awards damages, including exemplary or punitive damages, that do not compensate a party for actual loss or harm suffered. Therefore, the possibility of partial enforcement, as ordered by Greek courts, is expressly provided in the Convention and may facilitate enforcement among contracting states. This provision is expected to become more relevant, if states that impose exemplary or punitive damages ratify the Convention. The UK has already done so, while the US have only signed the Convention.

g) Reciprocity

Unlike other jurisdictions, Greece does not impose any reciprocity requirements for the recognition and enforcement of foreign judgments.[110]

h) Other Requirements

None.

[106] I Karakostas, 'Note I' (2000) *DEE* 183.

[107] E Vasilakakis, 'Enforcement of Foreign Arbitral Awards of Punitive Damages' (2006) *DEE* 459.

[108] Karakostas (n 106) 183; see also C Vanleenhove, *Punitive Damages in Private International Law: Lessons for the European Union* (Intersentia, 2016) 210 on the prohibition of *révision au fond* in the enforcement of US punitive damages judgments.

[109] For an analysis of the same issues arising from this approach also adopted by the French Supreme Court, see Vanleenhove (n 108) 133.

[110] Kousoulis (n 59) para 10.

Question 4. Documents to be Produced

The CCP does not provide for any formal requirements, but in practice the claimant must submit to the court:

(a) the foreign judgment or a certified copy thereof along with evidence of its authenticity (apostille) and their certified translation into Greek and
(b) a certificate or similar document issued by the state of origin proving that the judgment is enforceable according to the laws of the state of origin and its certified translation into Greek.[111]

Since the claimant has the burden to prove that all conditions for the declaration of the enforceability of the foreign judgment are met in accordance with the applicable law (Greek law, bilateral treaty or international convention), it will be typically required to provide additional documents. For example, in case of a foreign default judgment, the claimant will be required to submit a certificate of service or similar document to prove that the absent party was served in due time.[112]

Question 5. Securities, Bonds and Deposits

There are no specific provisions regulating securities, bonds or deposits for the recognition and enforcement of foreign judgments. In accordance with Article 932 of the CCP, the costs of enforcement are prepaid by the claimant and shall be recovered by the person against whom enforcement is sought.

[111] Mazis (n 1) para 15. For example, see SC 767/2019 (n 32).
[112] For example, this is expressly required in Art 6 para 2 of the Greece–(former) Socialist Federal Republic of Yugoslavia Treaty of 18 June 1959, ratified by Law 4007/1959.

Hungary

FERENC SZILÁGYI

Question 1. General Overview

§ 2 of the Private International Law Code of 2017 (PIL Code)[1] specifies that, within their material, personal, temporal and territorial scope, European Union (EU) regulations and international conventions (treaties) take precedence over the provisions of domestic law outlined in the PIL Code. Additionally, only *some* of the bilateral legal assistance treaties[2] concluded by Hungary provide rules for the recognition and enforcement of any civil judgments, and such recognition is not limited to judgments rendered in specific matters.[3]

The domestic rules can be found in Chapter XI on 'Recognition and Enforcement of Foreign Judgments' of the PIL Code *and* in Chapter XII on 'Enforcement of a Foreign Judgment' of the Judicial Enforcement Act of 1994 ('Judicial Enforcement Act').[4] The domestic rules, i.e. the provisions of the PIL Code on the recognition and enforcement of foreign judgments in civil and commercial matters, apply *when* the judgment is from

[1] 2017. évi XXVIII. törvény a nemzetközi magánjogról/Act XXVIII of 2017 on Private International Law; ELI: njt.hu/eli/v01/TV/2017/28. An unofficial English translation of this act as in force on 2 January 2018 provided by the Ministry of Justice is available at njt.hu/translations/-:-:2017:28/1/10.

[2] Three examples for bilateral legal assistance treaties, which also contain provisions on the mutual recognition of judgments and enforcement that regard cases that fall under the category of 'civil and commercial' matters are 1984. évi 4. törvényerejű rendelet a Magyar Népköztársaság és a Kubai Köztársaság között a polgári, családjogi és bűnügyi jogsegély tárgyában Havannában, az 1982. évi november hó 27. napján aláírt szerződés kihirdetéséről/Decree-Law No 4 of 1984 on the proclamation of the Treaty between the People's Republic of Hungary and the Republic of Cuba on legal assistance in civil, family and criminal matters, signed in Havana on 27 November 1982 (see Art 43); ELI: https://njt.hu/eli/TVR/1984/4. 1997. évi LXII. törvény a Magyar Köztársaság és a Kínai Népköztársaság között a polgári és kereskedelmi ügyekben történő kölcsönös jogsegélyről szóló, Pekingben, 1995. év október hónap 9. napján aláírt szerződés kihirdetéséről/Act LXII of 1997 on the proclamation of the Treaty between the Republic of Hungary and the People's Republic of China on Mutual Legal Assistance in Civil and Commercial Matters, signed in Beijing on the 9th day of October 1995 (see Art 16(1)(a); ELI: https://njt.hu/eli/TV/1997/62. 2018. évi LXXXVII. törvény a Magyarország és a Vietnami Szocialista Köztársaság között a polgári ügyekben nyújtandó kölcsönös jogsegélyről szóló megállapodás kihirdetéséről/Act LXXXVII of 2018 on the promulgation of the Agreement between Hungary and the Socialist Republic of Vietnam on mutual legal assistance in civil matters (see Art 21(2)); ELI: njt.hu/eli/TV/2018/87.

[3] S Boreczki, 'XI. fejezet: Külföldi határozatok elismerése és végrehajtása' in L Vékás, Z Nemessányi and A Osztovits (eds), *A nemzetközi magánjogról szóló törvény kommentárja* (HVG-Orac, 2020) 480, 481.

[4] 1994. évi LIII. törvény a bírósági végrehajtásról/Act LIII of 1994 on Judicial Enforcement; ELI: njt.hu/eli/TV/1994/53.

a non-EU country. The domestic rules follow a 'two-stage scheme'. In the first stage, as a matter of substantive law, the question of the recognition of a judgment in civil and commercial matters falling within the scope of the PIL Code is decided on basis of §§ 109–115 PIL Code. The second stage consists of the procedural rules for the recognition of the judgment (§ 122 PIL Code) and for the enforcement of the judgment (§ 123 PIL Code and §§ 205–210 Judicial Enforcement Act).

The PIL Code first sets out the general rules on the conditions for the recognition and enforcement of foreign judgments (Title 38, §§ 109–112 PIL Code), and then sets out the derogations from the general rules for decisions rendered in proprietary matters (Title 39, §§ 113–115 PIL Code)[5] and decisions rendered in matters of family law and status of persons (Title 40, §§ 116–121 PIL Code).[6] These derogations from the general rules include the modification of the general conditions, the addition of further conditions or the deletion of certain conditions.[7] Pursuant to § 110 PIL Code the recognition and enforcement of settlements made in proceedings before a foreign court, or another authority is possible according to the conditions set out for judgments.

The recognition of judgments in civil and commercial matters falls under the category 'decisions rendered in proprietary matters', in Hungarian *Vagyonjogi ügyben hozott határozatok* (§§ 113–115 PIL Code), and more precisely under § 113 PIL Code as § 114 PIL Code deals with decisions in insolvency proceedings and § 115 PIL Code defines the meaning of the requirement of 'well-founded jurisdiction' of the foreign court proceeding in succession matters. The term 'property/proprietary matters' (in German: 'Verm ögenssachen'/'Vermögensstreitigkeiten') is broader than the term 'civil and commercial matters' as under Brussels Ia Regulation. In his article on the new Hungarian PIL Code of 2017, Tamás Szabados refers to this category of cases as 'matters involving economic interest'.[8] This might provide a better description or explanation of the nature of the cases included in the category of *vagyonjogi ügyek*.[9] Finally, procedural rules are provided in § 122 PIL Code on the recognition and in § 123 PIL Code on the enforcement of foreign judgments (Title 41),[10] while § 123 PIL Code is also supplemented by §§ 205–210 Judicial Enforcement Act. The aforementioned provisions of the Judicial Enforcement Act channel the judgment of the foreign court recognised in Hungary into the system of Hungarian judicial enforcement law, ie the Judicial Enforcement Act. From the point of view of the enforceability of the foreign judgment, the decision on the costs of the proceedings is also considered a decision rendered in proprietary matters.[11]

According to the Supreme Court, a provision of an international treaty which provides that nationals of a contracting state are free to bring proceedings to the courts of the other contracting state cannot, even with a broad interpretation of that provision,

[5] '39. Vagyonjogi ügyben hozott határozatok'.

[6] '40. Családjogi és személyállapoti ügyekben hozott határozatok'.

[7] Boreczki (n 3) 481.

[8] T Szabados, 'The New Hungarian Private International Law Act: New Rules, New Questions' (2018) 82 *Rabels Zeitschrift für ausländisches und internationales Privatrecht* 972, 1001.

[9] F Szilágyi, 'Hungary' in T Lutzi, E Piovesani and D Zgrabljić Rotar (eds), *Jurisdiction Over Non-EU Defendants: Should the Brussels Ia Regulation be Extended?* (Hart Publishing, 2023) 137, 137.

[10] '41. Eljárási rendelkezések'.

[11] Fővárosi Bíróság (Budapest Municipal Court), 47. Pkfv 24 872/1998/3, no BDT2000.196 in the commercial legal sources database Jogtár, uj.jogtar.hu.

be interpreted as implying recognition of the enforceability of a judgment issued in that other state. Similarly, even if two contracting states mutually recognise the evidentiary (probative) force of authentic instruments issued by the courts, notaries or administrative authorities of the other state, this does not automatically mean that the documents are enforceable in both jurisdictions. The recognition of enforceability is a separate matter.[12]

Question 2. Procedure

a) Circumstances of Recognition and Enforcement

1. General

A person seeking enforcement of a foreign judgment has *two* options. One option is to request the court in a separate optional preliminary procedure pursuant to § 122 (2)–(6) PIL Code to assess the preconditions of recognisability of the foreign judgment in Hungary on basis of §§ 109–113 PIL Code for judgments rendered in 'property/ proprietary' matter. The other option is, as it follows from § 122(1) PIL Code, that the applicant directly requests the issuance of the *enforcement certificate*, meaning the initiation of the *exequatur procedure* pursuant to §§ 205–210 Judicial Enforcement Act, in the course of which the court will also examine the existence of the preconditions for recognition (concerning judgments rendered in 'property/proprietary' matters as set out in §§ 109–113 PIL Code). The general rules underlying both procedures are set out in the Act on the Rules Applicable to Non-Contentious Civil Proceedings in the Courts ('Non-Contentious Civil Procedure Act').[13] According to § 1(1) of this Act, in civil non-contentious proceedings before the courts, the rules of the Civil Procedure Code[14] (CPC) apply with modifications resulting from the specific nature of civil non-contentious proceedings. In this proceeding, the court will issue a formal decision (*végzés*)[15] on the merits of the case (ie request to establish the recognisability), which is subject to appeal.[16]

If an optional preliminary procedure pursuant to 122(2)–(6) PIL Code has been initiated, *exequatur* proceedings may be initiated if the court has established in a final decision that the foreign judgment is recognisable in Hungary. Since the optional preliminary procedure is a non-contentious procedure replacing the

[12] Legfelsőbb Bíróság (Supreme Court), 24 September 1999, Pfv VIII 23.958/1997, no BH2000.212 in the commercial legal sources database Jogtár, uj.jogtar.hu. According to the judgment, it was not possible to issue an enforcement certificate under Hungarian law for a bill payment order of the Austrian Commercial Court.

[13] 2017. évi CXVIII. törvény a bírósági polgári nemperes eljárásokban alkalmazandó szabályokról, valamint egyes bírósági nemperes eljárásokról/Act CXVIII of 2017 on the Rules Applicable to Judicial Civil Non-Contentious Proceedings and on Certain Judicial Non-Contentious Proceedings; ELI: njt.hu/eli/TV/2017/118.

[14] 2016. évi CXXX. törvény a polgári perrendtartásról/Act CXXX of 2016 on the Code of Civil Procedure, ELI: njt.hu/eli/v01/TV/2016/130. An unofficial English translation provided by the Ministry of Justice is available at njt.hu/translations/-:-:2016:130/1/10.

[15] This type of decision is standard in judicial civil non-contentious proceedings.

[16] § 1(5) of Act CXVIII of 2017.

contentious procedure which is ending with a decision on the merits of the case (§ 1(1) Non-Contentious Civil Procedure Act), to the decision is attached full substantive force within the meaning of § 360(1) CPC. Thus, the substantive force of a final decision precludes to have another action brought by the same parties against one another for the same right under the same factual grounds, and it constitutes an absolute bar for such parties to dispute a decision with substantive force already rendered in the case (*res iudicata*).

If an optional preliminary procedure under § 122(2)–(6) PIL Code has been initiated, it is not possible to initiate the *exequatur* procedure under §§ 205–210 Judicial Enforcement Act in parallel, but must await the final decision of the optional procedure on the issue of enforceability. This follows from the CPC provisions on *lis pendens*: the court will reject the request since the legal effects of bringing a procedure have already arisen in another procedure between the same parties for the same right under the same factual grounds (§ 176(1)(d) CPC), respectively the court may terminate the procedure at any time during the procedure of its own motion if the request should already have been rejected for *lis pendens* (§ 240(1)(a) CPC). This will also be true vice versa, ie it will no longer be possible to initiate an optional preliminary procedure on the issue of recognisability once the *exequatur* procedure has been initiated.

The issue of *recognizability* of a foreign judgment may also arise in a civil procedure before a Hungarian court when considering foreign *lis pendens* and foreign *res iudicata* under § 69(1) PIL Code, which corresponds to § 176(1)(d) CPC. *Lis pendens* involves two elements: the requirement of identical or related proceedings; and priority in time. It is not necessary for the Hungarian and foreign proceedings to be identical in subject matter and parties; it is sufficient if the ongoing foreign proceeding is related to the action subsequently filed with the Hungarian court (related action).[17] Regarding the requirement of a related action, the explanatory note to § 69 of the PIL Code essentially follows the definition provided in Article 30(3) Brussels Ia Regulation. However, as pointed out by Tibor Szőcs, the EU legal definition does not align well with the system of the PIL Code, as the former places too much emphasis on the convenience of consolidating and jointly deciding cases. The PIL Code, however, does not permit the termination of domestic proceedings for reasons of convenience, in order to allow two related claims to be adjudicated in a consolidated proceeding by a foreign court.[18] Regarding the concept of priority in time, the autonomous definition provided in § 69(5) PIL Code applies.[19] The procedural prerequisite for taking into account foreign *lis pendens* is that the potential recognition of the judgment expected to be rendered by the foreign court in Hungary is not precluded. Since the foreign court has not yet rendered a judgment, the examination cannot, of course, extend to all conditions for recognition; it must only consider those that allow sufficient certainty at this stage of the proceedings to conclude that the judgment to be rendered by the foreign court will not be recognized

[17] T Szőcs, 'IV. fejezet: 'A polgári perjog nemzetközi vonatkozásainak belső jogi szabályozása a nemzetközi magánjogról szóló 2017. évi XXVIII. törvényben (Nmjtv.)' in I Varga (ed), *A polgári perrendtartás és a kapcsolódó jogszabályok kommentárja III/III.* (HVG-Orac, 2018) 2319 (para 6271), 2326 (para 6284).
[18] ibid 2326 (para 6285).
[19] ibid 2326 (para 6286).

in Hungary.[20] It is possible that the conditions for recognition are governed not by the PIL Code, but by the terms set out in a bilateral legal assistance treaty, if such a treaty exists.[21] With regard to considering *res iudicata* arising from a judgment rendered by a foreign court, the court examines all conditions for the recognition of the foreign judgment that must be assessed *ex officio* under § 122(5) PIL Code. The Hungarian court does not need to issue a separate formal decision on the matter of recognition; it is sufficient for the court to indicate in its decision terminating the ongoing proceedings that, in its view, the foreign court's judgment is recognisable in Hungary.[22] According to § 69(4) PIL Code, termination of the proceedings is possible if the foreign court's judgment has become final or has 'the same legal effect'.[23] This is also reflected in the second sentence of § 176(1)(d) and § 240(1)(a) CPC concerning proceedings before the Hungarian court.[24]

2. *Optional Preliminary Procedure to Establish the Recognisability of a Foreign Judgment under the PIL Code*

The court decides on such a request in a *non-contentious* proceeding. It is important to highlight that this procedure *is not the exequatur procedure itself*, but an optional separate preliminary procedure governed by § 122(2)–(6) PIL Code. The court which is exclusively competent (material jurisdiction and exclusive territorial jurisdiction; see Question 2 b) 1. below) according to § 122(3) PIL Code is qualified to decide on the existence of the preconditions for recognition. In this procedure, the court examines the grounds for refusal (listed in § 109(4) PIL Code) of its own motion or on request.[25]

The provisions of the Judicial Enforcement Act on the issuance of the *enforcement certificate* shall apply *mutatis mutandis* to the optional preliminary recognition proceeding, including the means of appeal available against a decision rendered in such proceedings (§ 122(4) PIL Code). It follows from the appropriate application of the rules on the issue of the enforcement certificate that the court will normally decide on the request within 15 days of receipt of the request. If the request needs to be completed, the 15 days will be counted from the date of completion (§ 12(4) Judicial Enforcement Act).

The court, at the request of the party concerned (creditor seeking recognition of the foreign judgment and enforcement thereof, 'judgment creditor'), may order a security measure pursuant to §§ 185–201/B Judicial Enforcement Act in advance. Such an order for security measure *will not prevent* the enforcement certificate to be issued (§ 122(6) PIL Code).

It is important to note that the decision on the existence of the preconditions for the domestic recognition of the foreign judgment as outcome the optional preliminary

[20] ibid 2327 (para 6288).
[21] ibid 2327 (para 6289).
[22] ibid 2329 (para 6296).
[23] ibid 2329 (para 6297).
[24] ibid 2329 (para 6298).
[25] K Gombos, 'Joghatóság, külföldi határozatok elismerése és végrehajtása az új nemzetközi magánjogi törvényben' (2019) 74 *Jogtudományi Közlöny* 141, 149.

procedure under § 122(2)–(6) PIL Code *does not replace* the *exequatur* procedure pursuant to §§ 205–210 Judicial Enforcement Act. In order for a foreign judgment to be enforceable domestically, an *exequatur procedure* is necessary (§ 123 PIL Code).

3. *Exequatur Procedure (végrehajthatóvá nyilvánítási eljárás)*

In the absence of a separate optionafl preliminary recognition procedure for the assessment and establishment of recognisability of the foreign judgment (see Question 2 a) 2. above), the court will examine the existence of the preconditions for recognition (as set out in §§ 109–113 PIL Code) within the framework of the *exequatur procedure* (*végrehajthatóvá nyilvánítási eljárás*, governed by §§ 205–210 Judicial Enforcement Act).[26]

As stipulated in § 123 PIL Code, the judgment declared *enforceable* in accordance with the provisions of the Judicial Enforcement Act (ie as a result of the *exequatur procedure*) can be enforced in Hungary according to the provisions of the relevant legislation. According to § 205 Judicial Enforcement Act, a judgment of a foreign court may be enforced based on statutory provision, international convention, or reciprocity. Pursuant to § 206 Judicial Enforcement Act, the judgment of a foreign court may be enforced if the judgment, by its nature, complies with the provisions of § 15 Judicial Enforcement Act. Prerequisite of the *enforcement order* is the *enforcement sheet* (*végrehajtási lap*) which is issued by the first instance court on the basis of a civil judgment rendered by the court containing an obligation, ie a ruling against the judgment debtor (§ 15(1)(a) Judicial Enforcement Act), on the basis of the clause of a ruling in a criminal case concerning civil law claim, and on awarding the costs of criminal proceedings for a person participating in the criminal proceedings (§ 15(1)(b) Judicial Enforcement Act) or on basis of a judicial (court-approved) settlement (§ 15(1)(c) Judicial Enforcement Act).

In the context of the *exequatur* procedure, the conditions for the *enforcement order* (*végrehajtás elrendelése*, commencing with the issuance of the enforcement sheet) laid down in § 13 Judicial Enforcement Act *do not need to be fully* examined. Among these conditions, however, it is necessary to examine whether the foreign judgment imposes an obligation on the judgment debtor (usually the defendant). This depends on the nature of the claimant's request for action. A request is directed to impose an obligation if it requires the defendant to do, refrain from doing or tolerate something. The judgment must specify exactly what the judgment debtor's obligation is. A declaratory judgment (in the sense of *Feststellungsurteil*) cannot be enforced.[27] The same applies here as for the recognition of judgments: the nature of the judgment is not decisive.

A foreign judgment, or any decision having the effect of a judgment – such as a judgment that can be likened to a default judgment (in Hungarian: *bírósági meghagyás*, corresponding to the *Versäumnisurteil* under German law) under Hungarian procedural law – or a settlement approved by a court or notary public, or, eventually, any other court decision

[26] D Gelencsér and R Muzsalyi, 'XII. fejezet: Külföldi határozat végrehajtása' in D Gelencsér and S Udvary (eds), *A bírósági végrehajtásról szóló törvény és a kapcsolódó jogszabályok kommentárja* (HVG-Orac, 2021) 678, 683 (para 1960).

[27] ibid 685 (para 1969).

imposing an obligation on the defendant, can be enforceable.[28] From the point of view of the enforceability of the foreign judgment, the decision on the costs of the proceedings is also considered a decision rendered in proprietary matters.[29] The request filed according to § 207 Judicial Enforcement Act initiating the *exequatur* procedure amounts formally to a *request for enforcement*, and thus must comply with the requirements of the Judicial Enforcement Act and other requirements of the underlying applicable legislation.[30] The request initiating the *exequatur* procedure must be submitted *together* with the *request for the enforcement order*, amounting in the issuance of the enforcement sheet, so the *two requests are merged*. The existence of the conditions is examined separately by the court for each of the two requests.[31] In doing so, the conditions for enforceability are assessed first, and the conditions related to ordering enforcement are only examined if enforceability is established.

The court shall decide on the *enforcement requests* within 15 days of receipt of the request, or, if the request needs to be completed, the 15 days shall be counted from the date on which the deficiencies are completed (§ 12(4) Judicial Enforcement Act).

If the judgment is enforceable according to § 205 Judicial Enforcement Act, the court competent for the *exequatur* procedure (§ 208 in conjunction with § 16(c) Judicial Enforcement Act) will by its formal decision (*végzés*) issue an *enforcement certificate* for the foreign judgment, certifying that the judgment is enforceable under Hungarian law in the same manner as a judgment of a Hungarian court (§ 208 Judicial Enforcement Act).

In the *exequatur* proceedings under §§ 207–208 Judicial Enforcement Act, ie proceedings for the issuance of the *enforcement certificate*, the court will examine compliance with the requirements of § 205–206 and § 15 Judicial Enforcement Act.[32] The enforcement certificate serves solely to enable the subsequent ordering of enforcement through the issuance of an *enforcement sheet* or other *enforceable instrument* equivalent to an enforcement sheet. Before issuing the enforcement certificate, the court examines, among other factors, the type of decision to be enforced and whether there is any legal possibility for its enforcement.[33] Of the requirements set out in § 15, in the case of a judgment in a civil or commercial case, compliance with § 15(1)(a) is the relevant requirement, and § 15(1)(c) Judicial Enforcement Act is the relevant legal basis if not a judgment, but a court-approved settlement is the subject of the *exequatur* proceedings.[34]

If the court comes to the conclusion that the foreign judgment is not enforceable, it refuses the request. If the request of the applicant for enforcement represented by a lawyer is incomplete, the court rejects the request in accordance with section 12(2) of the Judicial Enforcement Act.[35]

[28] ibid 685 (para 1971).
[29] Fővárosi Bíróság (Budapest Municipal Court), 47 Pkfv 24 872/1998/3 (no BDT2000.196).
[30] Gelencsér and Muzsalyi (n 26) 686 (para 1972).
[31] Kúria (Highest judicial body as from 2012), 23 June 2021, Pfv.I.21.094/2020/5, para 18, Case ID K-PJ-2021-245 in the case law database 'Bírósági Határozatok Gyűjteménye (BHGY)', eakta.birosag.hu/anonimizalt-hatarozatok.
[32] ibid para 17.
[33] ibid para 16.
[34] Gelencsér and Muzsalyi (n 26) 687 (para 1978).
[35] ibid 688 (paras 1984–85).

As stipulated in § 210 Judicial Enforcement Act, when enforcing a foreign judgment, the provisions stipulated in a specific legislation and in international conventions must also be applied, and case law based on reciprocity must also be taken into consideration. This means that even an administrative decision rendered by a foreign authority can be declared enforceable under the provisions of the PIL Code.[36]

The issuance of the *enforcement certificate* amounts to the *declaration of enforceability*. Once the decision made has become final, the court, on basis of the foreign judgment complemented by the *enforcement certificate*, will issue an *enforcement sheet* (*végrehajtási lap*) or other *enforceable instrument* (*végrehajtható okirat*) equivalent to an enforcement sheet (§ 209 2nd sentence Judicial Enforcement Act). The declaration of enforceability, as the outcome of the successful *exequatur* procedure and amounting to the issuance of the *enforcement certificate*, is distinct from the *enforcement order* amounting to the issuance of the enforcement sheet or other enforceable instrument by which the actual enforcement proceeding is commenced.[37] Another *enforceable instrument* may be the formal decision (*végzés*) ordering enforcement through wage garnishment (§ 24 Judicial Enforcement Act).

Thus, issuing the enforcement sheet or other enforceable instrument constitutes an additional act of the court (enforcement order) in addition to its formal decision (*végzés*) on the declaration of enforceability, whereby the latter means that the foreign judgment is provided with an enforcement certificate. If enforcement is ordered by the issuance of an enforcement sheet (intended for enforcement against the debtor's assets), no formal decision is issued by the court in this regard, and therefore no basis exists for an appeal against it. However, if enforcement through garnishment of the debtor's wages (§ 24 Judicial Enforcement Act) is ordered, a formal decision is issued by the court, against which an appeal may be lodged by the parties (most likely the debtor) (§ 213(1) Judicial Enforcement Act).

4. *Ordering the Enforcement*

As stated above, on basis of the foreign judgment supplemented by the *enforcement certificate* the court will issue an *enforcement sheet* (§ 209 2nd sentence Judicial Enforcement Act). Thus, the successful completion of the *exequatur* procedure, ie issuance of the enforcement certificate, is a *prerequisite* for the opening of the actual enforcement proceedings,[38] ie for ordering the enforcement (*végrehajtás elrendelése*) which commences with the issuance of the enforcement sheet. As a general rule, the enforcement ordered by the court is carried out (*végrehajtás foganatosítása*) by a court bailiff (*cf* § 5(4) and § 225(1) Judicial Enforcement Act).

The court examines and decides separately on the conditions for the issuance of the enforcement sheet, but this will generally not require a new application for enforcement, as the request for a declaration of enforceability (*exequatur procedure*) and

[36] Boreczki (n 3) 541.
[37] Kúria, 23 June 2021, Pfv.I.21.094/2020/5, para 18 (Case ID K-PJ-2021-245).
[38] Boreczki (n 3) 541.

for an enforcement order must be submitted together.[39] By issuing the certificate of enforcement, the foreign judgment has the same legal effect as an enforceable domestic judgment/decision.[40]

The court issues the enforcement sheet or other enforceable instrument once the decision on issuing the enforcement certificate has become final – that is, when the parties have not exercised their right of appeal under § 209 1st sentence Judicial Enforcement Act, or when the court of second instance has upheld the court of first instance's decision.

For the requested ordering of enforcement, the additional conditions stipulated in § 13 Judicial Enforcement Act must be met – conditions that are not, or not fully, examined during the exequatur procedure.[41] One of the conditions also to be examined in the context of ordering the enforcement is whether the time limit for performance has already expired, ie whether the claim is due, the lack of which may constitute an obstacle to the enforcement measure,[42] or the judgment may be enforceable in advance.[43] In line with this, the Supreme Court has ruled, for example, that a reduction in the amount of the claim due to enforcement abroad should only be considered when the enforcement sheet is issued.[44]

On submission of the request for ordering the enforcement amounting to the issuance of the enforcement sheet, the judgment creditor as requesting party must indicate the judgment debtor's name and any data necessary for their identification (§ 11(2)(a) Judicial Enforcement Act), furthermore, depending on the circumstances of the case, at least one item from the following information must be provided: the judgment debtor's domicile; workplace or registered address; place of business; and the venue where the judgment debtor's enforceable assets are located (§ 11(2)(b) Judicial Enforcement Act). In case of a request for enforcement in an immovable property, the immovable registry data of that immovable property must be provided (§ 11(3) Judicial Enforcement Act). If the hypothec securing the claim is subject to a so-called 'subordinated hypothec' registered in the immovable registry, the information necessary to identify the creditor secured by the subordinated hypothec and the immovable property subject to the hypothec must be provided, together with the certified 'proof of ownership sheet' of the immovable property, not older than 15 days (§ 11(2)(c)–(e) Judicial Enforcement Act).

Instead of issuing an enforcement sheet, the court directly issues a garnishment decision if the claim is to be collected solely from the debtor's wages (§ 24(1) Judicial Enforcement Act). Claims should generally be enforced through direct garnishment in two key scenarios. First, if the judgment creditor specifically requests it, or if the claim involves alimony or other amounts payable in instalments, and the portion of

[39] Gelencsér and Muzsalyi (n 26) 690 (para 1991).
[40] ibid 688 (para 1983).
[41] Kúria, 23 June 2021, Pfv.I.21.094/2020/5, para 17 (Case ID K-PJ-2021-245).
[42] Boreczki (n 3) 541.
[43] Gelencsér and Muzsalyi (n 26) 688 (para 1983).
[44] Legfelsőbb Bíróság (Supreme Court), 6 March 2007, Pfv XI 22.270/2006, no BH2007.130 in the commercial legal sources database Új Jogtár, uj.jogtar.hu.

the wages available for garnishment is sufficient to cover the amount due (§ 26 Judicial Enforcement Act). Second, pursuant to § 27 Judicial Enforcement Act, wage garnishment is preferred if the principal claim is HUF 60,000 or less, or if the court considers it appropriate according to § 7(1) Judicial Enforcement Act.

b) Procedural Steps

1. *Competent Authorities*

1.1. Optional Preliminary Procedure to Establish the Recognisability of a Foreign Judgment (§ 122(2)–(6) PIL Code)

§ 122(3) PIL Code regulates which court is exclusively competent (material jurisdiction and exclusive territorial jurisdiction) to conduct the non-contentious proceeding for the establishment of the recognisability of the foreign judgment: a) the first instance court of the domicile (seat) or, in the absence of such, the habitual residence of the opposing party (in Budapest the Central District Court of Buda) *or, failing that*; b) the first instance court of the domicile (seat) or, in the absence of such, the habitual residence of the requesting party (in Budapest the Central District Court of Buda); or c) the Central District Court of Buda or, if the requesting party has no domicile (seat) or habitual residence in Hungary.

1.2. Exequatur Procedure (*végrehajthatóvá nyilvánítási eljárás*) and Ordering the Enforcement (*végrehajtás elrendelése*)

The request for the declaration of enforceability (*exequatur* procedure) and the request for ordering the enforcement (request for issuance of the enforcement sheet) are merged, which also implies that the rules on competence will be the same, ie § 16 l(c) Judicial Enforcement Act designating the court competent to issue the enforcement sheet in case of foreign judgment.

Thus, according to § 208 Judicial Enforcement Act in conjunction with § 16(c) Judicial Enforcement Act, the competent authority for the *exequatur* procedure is the court competent to issue the so-called enforcement sheet, which is the first instance court of the debtor's domicile, the place of the debtor's registered office or, in the absence of such place, the place of the debtor's enforceable assets, the place of the branch or, in the case of a direct commercial representation of a foreign company, the place of the branch or representation.

2. *The Burden of Proving the Requirements for Recognition and Enforcement*

Pursuant to § 122(5) 2nd sentence PIL Code, the requirement of well-founded jurisdiction (§ 109(1)(a) PIL Code), of the final character of the judgment (§ 109(1)(b) PIL Code), of the existence of reciprocity (§ 113(1) PIL Code) and of non-conflicting with Hungarian public policy (§ 109(4)(a) PIL Code) is assessed by the court *ex officio*, while the absence of all other remaining grounds of refusal (§ 109(1)(b)–(e) PIL Code) is presumed until proven otherwise.

3. *The Extent to which the Requested Court may Review the Merits*

Among the procedural provisions on the recognition, § 122(5) PIL Code provides that there shall be no review on the merits (*révision au fond*) of a foreign judgment.[45] Allowing this would mean a reopening of the foreign proceedings, ie the Hungarian court could check whether the foreign court had correctly decided the case on the facts and law. This would mean, as Boreczki points out, that the court acting on recognition would have to establish the facts underlying the foreign proceedings and draw the legal conclusions, which would in turn call into question the very nature of the recognition itself.[46] As a result, the Hungarian court cannot review the foreign judgment from a substantive point of view and thereby decide that the foreign court incorrectly established the facts due to a possible violation of its procedural rules, unless this violation amounts to a breach of the fundamental principles of Hungarian procedural law.[47] A judgment that cannot be recognised in Hungary cannot have direct legal effect in Hungary, but may be considered in other ways, for example as evidence.[48]

4. *Appeal against the Decision Granting or Refusing Recognition and/or Enforcement*

4.1. Appeal in the Optional Preliminary Procedure on Enforceability and in the Exequatur Procedure

§ 122(4) PIL Code stipulates that the provisions of the Judicial Enforcement Act on the issuance of a certificate of enforcement apply *mutatis mutandis* to the optional preliminary procedure to establish the recognisability of a foreign judgment/decision under § 122(2)–(6) PIL Code, including the available ways of appeal. From this it follows that the same means of appeal are available in this procedure as in the *exequatur* procedure.

Against a decision issuing the enforcement certificate *an appeal may be lodged*, as well as against a decision refusing or rejecting the request for enforcement (§ 209 1st sentence Judicial Enforcement Act). Pursuant to § 9 Judicial Enforcement Act, the rules of Chapter XXVII of the CPC shall apply *mutatis mutandis* to the appeal. The appeal must be lodged with the court of first instance within 15 days of the date of notification of the decision. The appeal has suspensory effect on the enforcement of the decision: no enforcement sheet or other enforceable instrument may be issued until the appeal has been decided.

[45] *cf* F Mádl and L Vékás, *Nemzetközi magánjog és nemzetközi gazdasági kapcsolatok joga* (ELTE Eötvös Publishing, 2012) 565 (para 812).

[46] Boreczki (n 3) 540.

[47] Kúria, 10 July 2013, Pfv.I.20.368/2013 in the commercial legal sources database Jogkódex, jogkodex.hu/doc/5362000.

[48] Legfelsőbb Bíróság (Supreme Court) Pkf IV 23.066/1997, 4 March 1998, no BH1999.169 in the commercial legal sources database Új Jogtár, uj.jogtar.hu. Tenor of the judgment: the judgment of the foreign court is not binding for the court in a proceeding for cancellation of a Hungarian trade mark.

If the appeal is against a decision rejecting or refusing a request for an enforcement certificate, the court of first instance may overrule it, as it is not bound by its own decision to reject or refuse (§ 390(1) CPC). In contrast, an appeal against the decision issuing the enforcement certificate is lodged by the court of second instance (§ 390(1) CPC). Before forwarding the documents to the court of second instance, the appeal shall be served by the court of first instance on the opposing party of the appellant and on those concerned, with the warning that they may submit their observations to the court of first instance within eight days after receiving the appeal (§ 390(2) CPC). A cross-appeal shall not be admitted (§ 390(3) CPC). The court of second instance decides on the appeal outside the hearing; however, it shall hear the parties if deemed appropriate (§ 391(1) CPC). The court of second instance may uphold or modify the decision of the court of first instance or set it aside and order the court of first instance to conduct a new proceeding (§§ 379–387 CPC).[49]

In the event that the decision on issuing the enforcement certificate has become final at the first or second instance, and the court has ordered enforcement by wage garnishment (§ 24 Judicial Enforcement Act) – which constitutes ordering enforcement by rendering a formal decision (*végzés)* – this decision may (also) be appealed by the parties pursuant to § 213(1) Judicial Enforcement Act. Furthermore, under § 213(2) Judicial Enforcement Act, the party requesting enforcement may appeal the court's decision denying the issuance of the enforceable instrument (eg, the enforcement sheet). Ordering enforcement by issuing the enforcement sheet (the most common method) does not qualify as enforcement rendered by a formal decision (*végzés*) that can be appealed.

If the court orders enforcement by issuing an enforcement sheet (ie, not by rendering a decision), the debtor cannot appeal this. In such a case, the debtor may claim that the enforcement sheet was issued by the court in violation of the law and may request its withdrawal. The court that ordered enforcement will render a decision on this request (§§ 211(1) and 212(1) Judicial Enforcement Act). The parties may lodge an appeal against that decision (§ 212(2) Judicial Enforcement Act).

Additionally, pursuant to § 214 of the Judicial Enforcement Act, a supervisory/review procedure (in German: *Revisionsantrag*) may be initiated against the final second-instance decision by which the court decided to issue (or not to issue) an enforcement certificate for a foreign judgment or ordered (or did not order) the actual enforcement.[50] The CPC's Chapter XXIX on review shall apply *mutatis mutandis* to the admission and adjudication of the request for review. In order for a request for review to be admissible, the party must have exhausted the ordinary remedies, so there is no right of review against the decision which has become final at first instance (§ 407(1)(a) CPC).[51] In the review procedure, the Kúria (Hungary's highest judicial body as from 2012) may render the following decisions (CPC § 424): if the request for review is well founded, it sets aside the final decision and either upholds the first-instance court's decision or, by modifying it, rejects the judgment

[49] Gelencsér and Muzsalyi (n 26) 689 (para 1988).

[50] D Gelencsér et al, 'XV. fejezet: A végrehajtás elrendelésével kapcsolatos jogorvoslatok' in D Gelencsér and S Udvary (eds), *A bírósági végrehajtásról szóló törvény és a kapcsolódó jogszabályok kommentárja* (HVG-Orac, 2021) 755, 764 (para 2307).

[51] ibid 764 (paras 2306–07).

creditor's request for enforcement. If the request for review is unfounded, the final decision is upheld. Although it is quite rare in practice, in principle the Kúria may also terminate the enforcement procedure or instruct the court of second instance to conduct a new proceeding.[52]

4.2. Remedies During Actual Enforcement

The issuing court shall terminate or limit the enforcement order if it can be established from a public deed that the decision (judgment) on which the enforcement is based has been modified or deemed ineffective (§ 56(1)(a) Judicial Enforcement Act). Another possibility is an action brought by the debtor under the CPC for the termination and limitation of the enforcement ordered by the issuance of the enforcement sheet, if the fact to be disclosed in the action occurred when it could not have been disclosed in the proceedings prior to the decision (judgment) on which basis the enforcement sheet was issued, or occurred after the conclusion of the judicial settlement serving as the ground for issuing the enforcement sheet (§ 528(1) CPC).

Under § 217(1) Judicial Enforcement Act, a party or any other interested person may lodge a so-called 'objection to enforcement' (*végrehajtási kifogás*), with the court supervising the enforcement (ie the court which ordered enforcement by issuance of the enforcement sheet), against a measure of the executor (bailiff), or the failure to take a measure, which substantially infringes the rules of the enforcement procedure and the right or legitimate interest of the person lodging the objection. A substantial infringement of the rules of the enforcement procedure is a breach of law which had a decisive impact on the implementation of the enforcement procedure.

5. *Binding Nature of the Decision for Other Courts*

The question of binding force arises in the relationship between the optional preliminary procedure (§ 122(2)–(6) PIL Code) and the *exequatur* procedure (§§ 205–210 Judicial Enforcement Act). The obvious question is whether a final decision in the optional preliminary proceedings on the question of recognisability is binding on the court if *exequatur* procedure is sought. The binding force in such a case derives from the substantive *res iudicata* effect under § 360(1) CPC attached to the decision on recognisability.

Question 3. Requirements

The PIL Code rules on the recognition and enforcement of foreign judgments are stricter than the equivalent EU rules. The PIL Code's approach on recognition of foreign judgments differs strikingly from the EU regulations in two respects. On the one hand, it requires, as a general rule, reciprocity if the judgment has been rendered in proprietary

[52] Gelencsér and Muzsalyi (n 26) 689 (para 1990).

matters (§ 113(1) PIL Code).[53] On the other hand, a significant difference compared to EU regulations lies in the requirement of the jurisdiction of the foreign court (where the case has been decided) to be well founded in conformity with the rules on jurisdiction of PIL Code, cf § 109(2) PIL Code.[54]

§ 111 PIL Code allows for the recognition of a judgment under the rules of the PIL Code even if the judgment does not comply with the terms of an international agreement (bilateral treaty) concluded by Hungary that is applicable to the recognition of the judgment. In such a case, as also provided by § 111 PIL Code, the reciprocity with that country must be considered as existing (*fictio iuris*). This is an exception to § 2 PIL Code, which provides that the provisions of the PIL Code apply if the issue is not regulated by an EU regulation or an international treaty. However, this subsidiary application of the PIL Code is out of the question if the recognition of the foreign judgment falls within the scope of an EU regulation or an international treaty concluded by the EU, binding Hungary.[55] In such cases, Hungarian national rules cannot be applied.

§ 109(1) of the PIL Code imposes *three general conjunctive requirements* for the recognition and enforcement of a foreign judgment. Two of them are positive requirements: the jurisdiction of the foreign court must be well founded in accordance with the PIL Code, and the judgment has become final. The negative requirement is that there shall not be grounds for refusal as under § 109(4) PIL Code. Regarding judgments rendered in civil and commercial matters one additional positive requirement follows from § 113(1) PIL Code which sets out the existence of reciprocity between Hungary and the state of the court rendering the judgment.

§ 109(4) PIL Code sets out the following grounds for refusal: a) its recognition would violate Hungarian public policy; b) the person against whom the decision was rendered did not attend the procedure either in person or by way of an authorised representative because the summons, statement of claim, or other document instituting the procedure was not served at the domicile or habitual residence in a time and manner allowing for adequate preparation of defence; c) the *lis pendens* (initiated and pending proceeding[case]) has already been established in Hungary before the foreign proceedings were instituted; or (d)–(e) a final judgment has been made in Hungary or a foreign judgment which must be recognised in Hungary, ie it is an internal or external *res iudicata*.[56] It follows from § 122(5) of the PIL Code that the court shall examine the infringement of Hungarian public policy of its own motion, and the absence of other grounds for refusal shall be presumed until proven otherwise.[57]

a) Jurisdiction of the Court of Origin

Jurisdiction of the court of origin is assessed on the basis of the so-called 'mirror principle'. This means that the rules of jurisdiction laid down in the PIL Code are mirrored

[53] § 113(1) PIL Code: 'Reciprocity between Hungary and the state of the court rendering the judgment shall be another requirement of the recognition of decisions rendered in proprietary matters.'

[54] Mádl and Vékás (n 45) 564–565 (para 812).

[55] Boreczki (n 3) 494.

[56] Mádl and Vékás (n 45) 565–66 (para 813); Boreczki (n 3) 488–93.

[57] Mádl and Vékás (n 45) 566 (para 813).

and indirectly applied to the foreign court that issued the judgment.[58] As pointed out by Boreczki, it is important to note that when assessing whether jurisdiction is well founded, not only the direct jurisdictional rules in Chapter X and the indirect jurisdictional rules in Chapter XI PIL Code must be taken into account, but also the immunity standards set out in §§ 83–84 and 86 PIL Code.[59] These provisions are jurisdictional rules in the sense of public international law, and compliance with them is also a condition for the recognition of a foreign judgment. In addition, private international jurisdiction must be well founded.[60] As Boreczki explains by way of an example, if a civil law contract concluded by an organ of the Hungarian state is the subject of a lawsuit, the Hungarian state will not be exempt from the jurisdiction of the foreign court under § 84(2)(a) PIL Code. If, however, the place of performance of the obligation in dispute was not in the forum (*cf* § 93(d) PIL Code) and the defendant Hungarian State organ did not have assets there (*cf* § 97 PIL Code), the requirement of established jurisdiction is not met.[61] Therefore, when examining whether the jurisdiction of the foreign court is well founded, the Hungarian court must also take into account the rules on jurisdiction under public international law in addition to the rules on jurisdiction under private international law.

Besides the general provisions on exclusive (§ 88 PIL Code) and excluded (§ 89 PIL Code) jurisdiction, in cases in proprietary matters ('matters involving economic interest'[62]), the following grounds of jurisdiction (connecting factors) are of particular importance:

- the domicile, respectively, the seat of the defendant in Hungary (§ 92 PIL Code);
- the place of performance situated in Hungary in contract disputes (§ 93 PIL Code), the legal fact giving rise to non-contractual liability for damages, or the effect of such legal fact occurred or could occur in Hungary (§ 94 PIL Code), the legal dispute is related to the operations in Hungary of a branch or a representation of a business having its seat abroad, respectively the contract on behalf of the business having its seat abroad was concluded in Hungary (§ 96 PIL Code);
- assets located in Hungary which may be subjected to enforcement if the defendant is not domiciled, respectively has not its seat in Hungary (§ 97 PIL Code);
- the parties' choice-of-court agreement (§ 99 PIL Code);
- the domicile, respectively seat or central place of administration of one of the defendants is in Hungary, if suing more than one defendant simultaneously, provided that there is a close relationship between the actions so that it is practical to assess and decide on them jointly in order to avoid contradictory decisions rendered in separate procedures (§ 90(1) PIL Code);
- the domicile or seat of the primary obligor is in Hungary, if the primary and secondary obligors are sued simultaneously (§ 90(2) PIL Code);

[58] O Brávácz and T Szőcs, *Jogviták határok nélkül. Joghatóság, külföldi határozatok elismerése és végrehajtása polgári ügyekben* (HVG-ORAC, 2003) 195.
[59] Boreczki (n 3) 487.
[60] ibid.
[61] ibid.
[62] Term used by Tamás Szabados. See Szabados (n 8) 998.

- Hungarian jurisdiction to decide on a claim, it shall also have jurisdiction in respect of the counter-claim (§ 90(3) PIL Code).

b) Finality/Enforceability in the Country of Origin

A prerequisite for the recognition of the effects of a foreign judgment is that the judgment must have legal force (in the meaning of the term *jogerő* in Hungarian, and *Rechtskraft* in German, respectively) or equivalent legal effect under the law of the forum (§ 109(1)(b) PIL Code). In assessing compliance with this requirement, the so-called formal legal force (in the meaning of the term *alaki jogerő* in Hungarian, and *formelle Rechtskraft* in German, respectively) is decisive. This means that, according to the law of the forum, there is no right of appeal against the foreign judgment which is the subject of the recognition, no ordinary appeal is possible and the judgment is final.[63] It is therefore possible to recognise an interim measure which has become final, but not a decision which is enforceable in advance but can be challenged by ordinary appeal.[64]

c) *Res Iudicata*

With regard to the *res iudicata* effect attached to a final judgment of a Hungarian court, it should be noted that a foreign judgment can only be recognised in Hungary if the foreign proceedings were initiated before the proceedings in Hungary in the same case and the foreign court or authority delivered its judgment/decision earlier than the Hungarian court (§ 109(4)(d) PIL Code).[65]

In relation to the *res iudicata* effect of a foreign court's judgment as a ground for refusal, it should be pointed out that § 109(4)(e) PIL Code also took into account the possibility of several 'competing' foreign judgments from different countries in the same case and therefore provides that a foreign judgment previously given and meeting the conditions for recognition is a ground for refusal in relation to a foreign judgment given later in the same case.[66] Recognition of an earlier foreign judgment may be based not only on relevant provisions of the PIL Code, but also on an EU regulation or an international treaty.[67] An earlier judgment which takes priority under § 109(4)(e) PIL Code is also sufficient to have the equivalent effect of a final judgment (formal legal force), depending on the law of the forum that gave the judgment.[68] Recognition may not require formal legal force, for example if the recognition is based on EU regulations or the Lugano Convention. In such cases, the time from which the law of the forum

[63] Boreczki (n 3) 488.
[64] ibid.
[65] See, eg, Fővárosi Törvényszék (Budapest-Capital Regional Court), 16 March 2023, G.40848/2021/60, para 40, Case ID 1-GJ-2023-36 in the case law database Bírósági Határozatok Gyűjteménye (BHGY), eakta.birosag.hu/anonimizalt-hatarozatok.
[66] Boreczki (n 3) 492.
[67] ibid.
[68] ibid.

attaches legal effects to the earlier judgment should be taken into account when deciding about 'priority'.[69]

d) *Lis Pendens*

As regards the *lis pendens* before a Hungarian court, the requirement of 'same right arising from the same factual basis between the same parties' shall be interpreted in accordance with § 69(1) PIL Code.[70] The date of commencement of proceedings shall be determined in accordance with § 69(5) PIL Code.[71] This ground for refusal also applies if the Hungarian proceedings terminate later without a judgment on the merits.[72]

Although this is not explicitly stated in the wording of § 109(4)(c) PIL Code, the proceedings instituted before the Hungarian court means the concept of *lis pendens* (in the meaning of *perfüggőség* in Hungarian, and *Rechtshängigkeit* in German). Besides this, the interpretative provision of § 3(a) PIL Code is also applicable in this case, stating that the 'term court shall also accordingly cover other authorities acting in civil matters'.

e) Specific Requirements of Due Process

Pursuant to § 109(4)(b):

> A foreign decision shall not be recognised if … b) against whom the decision was rendered did not attend the procedure either in person or by way of an authorised representative because the summons, statement of claim, or other document instituting the procedure was not served at his domicile or habitual residence in a time and manner allowing for adequate preparation of defence, …'

The PIL Code aims to strike a balance between the defendant and the plaintiff. In line with this objective, the lack of formally correct delivery is not in itself a bar to recognition if the addressee has otherwise actually received the document instituting the proceedings, thus effectively putting him in a position to prepare their defence.[73] It is important to note that the delivery of the document instituting the proceedings is relevant, ie the service of the statement of claim or any other document (eg order

[69] ibid 493.
[70] § 69(1) PIL Code: 'If, at the time of the commencement of the procedure, a procedure launched previously is in progress before a foreign court, concerning the same right arising from the same factual basis, the Hungarian court may, either ex officio or upon request, suspend the procedure, provided that the recognition of the foreign court's decision is not excluded in Hungary.'
[71] § 69(5) PIL Code: 'For the purposes of this Act, the procedure shall be deemed to commence a) at the time when the document instituting the procedure is submitted to the court, provided that the plaintiff does not fail afterwards to carry out the actions set forth in order to facilitate the service of documents to the defendant, or b) if the document shall be served prior to its submission to the court, at the time when it is received by the authority having the competence to serve the document, provided that the plaintiff does not fail afterwards to perform the action set forth to facilitate the submission of the document to the court.'
[72] Boreczki (n 3) 491. For a contrary opinion with reference to the corresponding provision of the old PIL Code [1979], see O Brávácz andT Szőcs, *Jogviták határok nélkül. Joghatóság, külföldi határozatok elismerése és végrehajtása polgári ügyekben* (HVG-ORAC, 2003) 224.
[73] Boreczki (n 3) 490; [Unofficial] Explanatory Statement to § 109 PIL Code.

for payment[74]) which informs the defendant or the debtor, in accordance with the law of the forum, that proceedings have been instituted against them and provides information on the subject matter of those proceedings.[75] The mere fact that the foreign judgment has not been delivered to the party whom it concerns does not exclude the recognition of the judgment.[76]

In order for the ground of refusal to apply, it is not sufficient that the recipient, due to a defect in delivery, was unable to prepare their defence. It is also necessary that due to this defect they were unable to participate in person or through an authorised representative.[77] So the focus lies on the failure to be able to participate in the merits of the case.[78] The existence of such a ground for refusal must be examined in each individual case. As pointed out by Boreczki, a ground for refusal may exist, for example, if the domestic time limit applies to a defendant living abroad who does not know the language of the proceedings. For example, the requirement of actual knowledge means that the method of delivery by announcement, ie fictitious delivery, constitutes usually a ground for refusal of recognition.[79]

f) Public Policy

The reference point is provided by the public policy clause in § 12(1) PIL Code. Accordingly, the foreign law applicable violates Hungarian public policy if the results of its application in the given case clearly and seriously breach the fundamental values and constitutional principles of the Hungarian legal system. The object of the examination is whether the concrete result of the recognition of the foreign judgment would manifestly and seriously violate these values and principles.[80] In the context of the examination of the enforceability of a foreign arbitral decision under Hungarian law, the Supreme Court of Hungary explained that the possibility of establishing the existence of a public policy violation presupposes the existence of a real and sufficiently serious threat to a fundamental interest of society. According to the court, the fact that the debtor is placed in a difficult financial situation by the payment of the high amount awarded by the arbitral tribunal affects the debtor's individual economic situation, but does not affect the public interest of society.[81] With regard to the violation of public policy in its judgment of 2014, the Kúria (Hungary's highest judicial body as from 2012) ruled that

> a violation of public policy can only be established if the consequences of the breach of fundamental rights or social values, which go beyond the legal relationship of the parties and cause a breach of public policy, can be established. Public policy is prejudiced if the judgment

[74] In the meaning of *fizetési meghagyás* in Hungarian. The competent authority for issuing payment orders in Hungary is the public notary. The corresponding term in German would be *gerichtliche Mahnung/gerichtlicher Mahnbescheid*. Here, the authority for issuing payment orders is a specific court, the so-called Mahngericht.
[75] Boreczki (n 3) 490–91.
[76] ibid 491.
[77] ibid.
[78] ibid.
[79] ibid.
[80] Boreczki (n 3) 488.
[81] Legfelsőbb Bíróság (Supreme Court), 6 March 2007, Pfv XI 22.270/2006 (no BH2007.130).

> directly affects the foundations of the socio-economic order. It is not a breach of the fundamental principles of judicial procedure to rely on personal circumstances which may have prevented the party relying on them from exercising their procedural rights or from exercising them fully.[82]

The public policy clause can be used to exclude the application of foreign substantive and procedural rules in a specific case. The application of the public policy clause always requires a case-by-case assessment.[83] Hungarian law does not distinguish between substantive and procedural public policy. However, the distinction between substantive and procedural public policy can indeed be encountered in legal scholarship.[84]

g) Reciprocity

With regard to judgments rendered in proprietary matters § 113(1) PIL Code requires the existence of reciprocity between Hungary and the state of the court rendering the judgment. In connection with this requirement, placed among the final provisions of the PIL Code, § 124 PIL Code empowers the Minister of Justice to determine in a decree the existence of reciprocity relating to the recognition and enforcement of foreign judgments. Thus, under Hungarian law, the administrative model of establishing reciprocity prevails, presumably inspired by Austrian legislation.[85] The Minister may also establish reciprocity in part, for a defined range of civil cases only.[86] Still, all the conditions set out by law (§ 109(1)–(2), (4) § 113 PIL Code) must be met for a judgment to be recognised, and reciprocity alone is not sufficient.

However, § 113(2) PIL Code[87] provides for two exceptions to the requirement of reciprocity in relation to the recognition of judgments. First, if the jurisdiction of Hungarian courts was excluded, and second, if the jurisdiction of the foreign court is based on an agreement of the parties which is in compliance with the provisions of Hungarian law, ie with § 99 PIL Code. Regarding the first exception (§ 113(2)(a) PIL Code), Boreczki explains that in the case of a civil law relationship falling within the scope of excluded Hungarian jurisdiction (§ 89 PIL Code), the need for legal protection may also arise in a domestic context. In connection with this, it must necessarily be possible for the foreign judgment to have legal effects in Hungary, irrespective of the

[82] Kúria, 13 July 2013, Pfv.I.20.368/2013 in the commercial legal sources database Jogkódex, jogkodex.hu/doc/5362000.

[83] Mádl and Vékás (n 45) 176 (para 183).

[84] *cf* K Raffai, 'Az exequatur (tervezett) teljes felszámolása és annak közrendi összefüggései' (2012) 59 *Magyar Jog* 546, 546–53.

[85] Boreczki (n 3) 506.

[86] Establishing reciprocity with regard to judgments rendered in 'proprietary matters' (a category including 'civil and commercial matters') in relation to Italy (judgments which have become final on or after 1 April 2003) and Germany (judgments which have become final after 26 February 1992): 36/2017. (XII. 29.) IM rendelet a nemzetközi jogsegélyre és a külföldi határozatok elismerésére és végrehajtására vonatkozó viszonosság megállapításáról/ 36/2017 (of December 29) Minister of Justice establishing reciprocity in international legal assistance and the recognition and enforcement of foreign judgments; ELI: njt.hu/eli/R/2017/IM/36.

[87] § 113(2) PIL Code: 'A decision may be recognised without reciprocity if a) the jurisdiction of Hungarian courts was excluded in the case, or b) the jurisdiction of the proceeding foreign court is based on an agreement between the parties which is in compliance with the provisions of Hungarian law.'

existence of reciprocity. The first exception therefore essentially serves the realisation of the right to free access to justice as a fundamental right. Regarding the second exception (§ 113(2)(b) PIL Code), as also pointed out by Boreczki, it is important to note that if the jurisdiction of the foreign court is based on the parties' stipulation, this must comply with § 99 PIL Code even if reciprocity exists, otherwise the requirement of well-founded jurisdiction as a first condition for recognition of the foreign judgment would not be fulfilled (§ 109(1)(a) PIL Code). According to case law, the agreement on the jurisdiction of a foreign court must correspond to the form of the contract established in the business relationship between the parties.[88]

h) Other Requirements

None.

Question 4. Documents to be Produced

Since the provisions of the Judicial Enforcement Act applicable to the *exequatur* procedure (§§ 205–210 Judicial Enforcement Act) also apply *mutatis mutandis* to the optional preliminary procedure to establish the recognisability of a foreign judgment under § 122(2)–(6) PIL Code there will be no difference about the documents to be produced between the optional preliminary procedure and the *exequatur* procedure. The only difference may be that, as the applicant submits the request for enforcement order together with the request for declaration of enforceability (*exequatur* procedure), the former necessarily includes the completed form 'enforcement sheet'.

The request for enforcement may only be submitted using the official form designated for this purpose. The request for enforcement must comply with § 114 (1)[89] CPC, § 11–12 of the Judicial Enforcement Act as regards the mandatory content and § 18 of the Judicial Enforcement Act as regards the number of copies.[90] The person requesting enforcement shall attach to the request for enforcement the foreign judgment to be enforced and, if necessary, at the request of the court, a Hungarian translation thereof (§ 207 Judicial Enforcement Act). § 207 regulates the formal requirements for the declaration of enforceability. The foreign judgment is considered foreign public deed which, according to § 593 CPC, has to be legalised by the competent Hungarian diplomatic mission of the place of issue, unless another requirement is specified in an international treaty entered into with the country in which it was issued. Whether a Hungarian

[88] Legfelsőbb Bíróság (Supreme Court), 23 February 2009, Gpkfv XI 30.470/2008, no BH2010.45 in the commercial legal sources database Új Jogtár, uj.jogtar.hu.

[89] § 114 [Form-related requirements for submissions] (1) CPC 'On the submission, the proceeding court to which the submission is addressed, the full name, domicile or seat, and any known electronic mail address of each party and their representatives, as well as the subject matter of the action and the case number in pending cases, shall be indicated. If a party or his representative has a place of residence that is different from his domicile, or any other address that is suitable for summoning, it shall also be indicated on the submission.'

[90] Gelencsér and Muzsalyi (n 26) 686 (para 1972).

translation is necessary is at the discretion of the court, and a partial translation, for example limited to the dispositional part (the ruling itself), may be sufficient.[91]

Question 5. Securities, Bonds and Deposits

The question of the provision of security can be interpreted in the context of the ordering of the enforcement, ie actual enforcement proceedings (see above Question 2 a) 4.), so there are no special rules for the enforcement of a foreign judgment, since the issuance of an enforcement certificate means that the foreign judgment is enforceable in the same way as a judgment of a Hungarian court. The enforcement procedure itself involves the advance of costs incurred in the enforcement process, which is regulated in § 34 Judicial Enforcement Act. The costs to be advanced are the costs incurring in connection with the ordering of the enforcement, which are part of the claim to be included in the enforceable instrument, ie they constitute the claim to be enforced. This also applies to the enforcement fee, the service charge for ordering of the enforcement, the fees of the lawyer representing the applicant for enforcement, and other costs related to the enforcement.[92] The latter may include the costs of transport and storage in the event of the transfer of the seized property, the costs of opening and re-closing the sealed premises, the costs of a witness present at the enforcement proceedings, the postal charges incurred, the costs of making photocopies to be sent to the court or the bailiff *ex officio*,[93] the fees of a custodian or a guardian *ad litem*, if any.[94] As an advance on costs in enforcement proceedings for the recovery of pecuniary claims, 50 per cent of the bailiff's fees and 50 per cent of the costs established on lump sum basis shall be paid, but the total amount shall not be less than HUF 9,000, which, together with the HUF 8,000 administration and document management fee chargeable at the beginning of the proceedings, shall not exceed HUF 85,000.[95] These costs are advanced by the creditor seeking enforcement and borne by the debtor.[96]

If an appeal is successfully lodged against the enforcement order, resulting in the revocation of the enforcement sheet or the enforceable instrument, the enforcement costs incurred will be borne by the creditor seeking enforcement.[97]

[91] Boreczki (n 3) 541.

[92] N Kiss et al, 'Vht. 34. §' in A Osztovits (ed), *A bírósági végrehajtásról szóló 1994. évi LIII. törvény nagykommentárja* (Opten, 2015), 156; B Martonovics and S Udvary, 'III. fejezet: A végrehajtás foganatosításának közös szabályai' in D Gelencsér and S Udvary (eds), *A bírósági végrehajtásról szóló törvény és a kapcsolódó jogszabályok kommentárja* (HVG-Orac, 2021) 312, 322 (paras 735–36).

[93] 8/2021. (X. 29.) SZTFH rendelet a bírósági végrehajtói díjszabásról/Regulation of the Authority for the Supervision of Regulated Activities 8/2021 (X. 29.) on the fees of bailiffs, see § 11(1); ELI: njt.hu/eli/R/2021/SZTFH/8.

[94] Martonovics and Udvary (n 92).

[95] § 18(1)(a) Regulation of the Authority for the Supervision of Regulated Activities 8/2021 (X. 29).

[96] Martonovics and Udvary (n 92) 326 (para 748).

[97] Kiss et al (n 92) 156.

Ireland

YAĞMUR HORTOĞLU GRANT

Question 1. General Overview

The Republic of Ireland has not entered into any bilateral treaties regarding reciprocal recognition and enforcement of foreign judgments. However, there are a number of multilateral treaties that are relevant to the recognition and enforcement of non-EU judgments and in effect in the Republic of Ireland, such as the Lugano Convention,[1] the Hague Convention on Choice of Court Agreement[2] and more recently the Hague Judgments Convention.[3] Irish common law applies to the decisions rendered in civil and commercial matters, and originated from states other than the ones to which the latter sources apply. More precisely, Irish common law applies solely to monetary foreign judgments.[4]

For historical reasons, the Republic of Ireland shares a common law tradition with other English-speaking countries, and particularly with England.[5] Irish common law enforcement principles are also very heavily influenced by English common law rules[6] and the English case law is of persuasive value for Irish courts in the interpretation or the establishment of the rules on enforcement of foreign judgments.

Irish common law rules on recognition and enforcement of foreign judgments regime is not codified in a statute/legislation and is based on case law. The limited case law in the field[7] sets up a more or less restrictive procedure, especially when compared to the recognition and enforcement of judgments obtained in European Union (EU) Member States and the European Free Trade Association (EFTA) countries. Considering the field is regulated by precedents, hence on a case-by-case basis, it is ironic to note the outdated nature of this regime. Indeed, we would have expected a position more aligned

[1] Convention on jurisdiction and the recognition and enforcement of judgments in civil and commercial matters (Lugano Convention; SR 0.275.12).

[2] Choice of Court (Hague Convention) Act 2015.

[3] Convention of 2 July 2019 on the Recognition and Enforcement of Foreign Judgments in Civil or Commercial Matters.

[4] For more information, see below Question 3 h).

[5] Prior to the expansion of English common law to Ireland in the 17th century (also described as the 'first adventure of the common law'), Ireland had its own indigenous system of law, originated from its Celtic period, called Brehon Law.

[6] See High Court of Ireland, 31 May 2011, [2011] IEHC 220, *Bussoleno v Kelly*.

[7] However, English common law is considered as a persuasive source in Ireland as it is not significantly different from Irish common law. See High Court of Ireland, 31 May 2011, [2011] IEHC 220, *Bussoleno v Kelly*.

with globalisation. The lack of cases often maintains the reign of English case law from the Victorian period.[8]

Although in some other common law countries[9] this field has been reformed or modernised, Irish courts have recently refused to adopt such modern common law rules on recognition and enforcement of foreign judgments. Indeed, in *Flightlease (Ireland) Limited (In Voluntary Liquidation) & Cos Act*,[10] even though O'Donnell J noted the archaic character of the current Irish common law rules on recognition and enforcement of foreign judgments, he also unexpectedly indicated that it is the legislator's responsibility, and not that of the courts, to make a change in the field.[11] This approach has been criticised in the doctrine[12] and does not seem to be in line with the spirit of common law.

In any event, it is possible to observe that because of the significant role occupied by other regimes and the narrow scope of enforcement rules, the application of common law rules is relatively less usual in the field.

Question 2. Procedure

a) Circumstances of Recognition and Enforcement

Regarding the circumstances in which a judgment can be recognised and enforced, it is first necessary to draw a distinction between enforcement and recognition of a foreign judgment. Under Irish common law, enforcement of a foreign judgment requires its recognition. Conversely, a foreign judgment can be recognised without being enforced.

Recognition and enforcement of foreign judgments under Irish common law is permissible only in respect of money judgments, meaning that the damages or costs awarded must have been assessed and quantified, or at least be susceptible to a simple arithmetical process.[13] The decision must also be final and conclusive,[14] which means that it must be final and unalterable (ie, cannot be reviewed/revisited) by the court which pronounced it.

[8] See Supreme Court of Ireland, 23 February 2012, [2012] IESC 12, *Flightlease (Ireland) Limited (In Voluntary Liquidation) & Cos Act.*

[9] See Supreme Court of Canada, 18 December 2003, [2003] SCC 72, (2003) 3 SCR 416, *Beals v Saldanha.* For a doctrinal overview on the issue, see eg A Briggs, 'Crossing the River by Feeling the Stones: Rethinking the Law on Foreign Judgments' (2004) 8 *Singapore Yearbook of International Law* 1.

[10] *Flightlease* (n 9).

[11] See *Flightlease* (n 9). In this matter, O'Donnell J noted that a modernisation of the law on the recognition and enforcement of foreign judgments in Ireland, similarly to the reform conducted by the Supreme Court in Canada over the past few decades would exceed the judicial functions of the Supreme Court in Ireland to 're-state the common law in such a way'. O'Donnell J concluded that until the legislator intervenes, Dicey's Rules should be applied. See also, High Court of Ireland, 27 February 2008, [2008] IEHC 90, *Goshawk Dedicated v Life Receivables Ireland*, 4.15.

[12] See D Kenny, 'Re Flightlease: The "Real and Substantial Connection" Test for Recognition and Enforcement of Foreign Judgments Fails to Take Flight in Ireland' (2014) *The International and Comparative Law Quarterly* 197.

[13] For more detail, see below Question 3 h).

[14] The fact that the foreign court made a mistake or misinterpreted its own law does not prevent the foreign judgment from being conclusive. See Court of Queen's Bench, 1 January 1862, [1892] 2 B & S 11, *Scott v Pilkington*; Court of Common Pleas, 19 November 1863, [1863] 15 CBNS, *Vanquelin v Bouard* 341.

Even if an appeal is pending against the foreign judgment, the judgment may still be considered final and conclusive unless the appeal stays the judgment. In this hypothesis, Irish courts can use their discretion to place a stay on the enforcement proceedings before the appeal decision is determined. If the application lodging an appeal in the foreign jurisdiction stay the proceedings, enforcement in the Republic of Ireland will not be permissible during the stay period. Even if no stay is decided, the Irish courts may require security to be given as a condition for being allowed to proceed with the enforcement.

Under Irish common law, recognition of foreign judgments is not automatic, and an application must be made to court.[15] The claimant should prove that the defendant either submitted to the foreign court or was present at in the foreign jurisdiction during proceedings.

It is only where enforcement is not required that recognition alone might be sought (eg, declaratory relief, or where it is relied upon as *res iudicata* to prevent the parties relitigating the same dispute). Since only foreign money judgments can be recognised and enforced at common law in the Republic of Ireland, it is rare for recognition to be sought on its own in respect of such foreign judgments, as enforcement (execution) is typically the objective in pursuing the proceedings.

It is in the Irish courts' discretion whether to recognise a foreign judgment. However, as a general principle, and on the basis of respect and comity between international courts, the approach of the Irish court to proceedings seeking recognition and enforcement is generally positive, provided the requirements are fulfilled.[16] However, there are grounds on which recognition and enforcement of such judgments may be refused, as referred to in Question 3.

As mentioned earlier, under Irish common law, recognition of a foreign judgment is a requirement for its enforcement. It could be in the applicant's interest to introduce a case directly against the defendant or against their assets within the jurisdiction where the application for enforcement has been initiated in multiple different jurisdictions where assets are available. Once the foreign judgment has been recognised or declared enforceable, it is akin to an Irish judgment, and can be enforced like one. In Irish law, there are several enforcement methods at the disposal of the plaintiffs that would also be applicable in this hypothesis.

b) Procedural Steps

In the Republic of Ireland, an application for recognition or enforcement of a foreign judgment should be submitted to the Master of the High Court, usually on an ex parte basis grounded upon an affidavit (by way of commencing fresh proceedings through originating High Court summons). It consists of a summary judgment procedure where a summary summons (the originating court document that presents the details of the claim) issued against the defendant and served is followed by a motion seeking an order for judgment introduced by the applicant before the courts.

[15] For the procedure of recognition, see below Question 2 b).
[16] For an overview of these requirements, see below Question 3.

Unlike an application prepared pursuant to the Lugano Convention or the Hague Convention, an application for recognition and enforcement of a foreign judgment under Irish common law is made on notice to the defendant. In other words, the defendant can challenge the application by filing a replying affidavit pursuant to Order 11 of the Rules of the Superior Courts,[17] which could result in a decision that is subject to appeal. If the defendant is domiciled in the Republic of Ireland, an appearance at the application to challenge should be entered within eight days of service of the summons. If the defendant is domiciled outside the Republic of Ireland, the jurisdiction of the defendant's domicile will be determining the time limit for appearance.

There are also a number of defences available for the defendant to contest the recognition and enforcement of a judgment. The defendant can claim that the judgment does not fulfil the conditions referred to in Question 3. A claim that the foreign judgment has been procured by fraud constitutes another ground the defendant can rely on in order to resist enforcement of the foreign judgment. Allegations of fraud can be raised for the first time before Irish courts and eventually succeed.[18] The defendant can also finally claim that the judgment conflicts other judgment on the same facts involving the same parties.[19]

In accordance with the maxims *interest rei publicae ut sit finis litium* and *nemo debet bis vexari pro eadem causa*, Irish courts refuse to review the foreign judgments on the merits. However, the judgment given by the High Court regarding the recognition and enforcement of a foreign judgment can be appealed to the Court of Appeal. In this case, the usual Court of Appeal Rules apply to the action.

If an enforcement order has been obtained by the plaintiff, this foreign decision will have the same legal effect as a High Court judgment and will be enforced as such.

Question 3. Requirements

a) Jurisdiction of the Court of Origin

Irish courts can refuse to recognise or enforce a foreign judgment if the defendant proves that the ruling has been given by a court that lacks jurisdiction.

The question of competence of jurisdiction is one of the requirements for recognition and enforcement of foreign judgments under Irish common law. In this regard, it is necessary to prove that the foreign court had jurisdiction in relation to the defendant, and to deliver the final and conclusive judgment in respect of which recognition and enforcement is sought, in accordance with the Irish conflict of laws rules. Indeed, providing for the jurisdiction of the foreign court according to its domestic or conflict of laws rules would not be sufficient according to Irish common law. In this regard, Irish courts will verify if the original court had *personal* jurisdiction according to the Irish conflicts of law rules, which imply submission to the jurisdiction of the foreign court

[17] The Rules of the Irish Superior Courts do not indicate any period during which such a challenge should be made, but the Irish court can prescribe a timeframe for the filing of the affidavit and enforce it.

[18] It is, nonetheless, important to note that Irish courts hold discretion to give more or less importance to this request.

[19] For further detail, see Question 3 c) below.

by the defendant, or whether there are sufficient connections between the plaintiff and the foreign state.

Other possible connections such as reciprocity,[20] domicile[21] and nationality of the defendant,[22] applicable law,[23] the possession of property by the defendant in the foreign country[24] or the sole fact that the dispute arose in the foreign country[25] do not constitute sufficient basis of jurisdiction of foreign courts.

Under the Irish common law, for a foreign court to be considered to have personal jurisdiction over the defendant for the purposes of the enforcement of foreign judgments, there are several possible grounds: the defendant must have consented to the jurisdiction in a contractual clause;[26] be present, as a resident or not, in the foreign country at the time of commencement of the action;[27] or have simply submitted to the foreign proceedings whether by filing a voluntary appearance as a plaintiff[28] or by making a counterclaim in the matter.[29] In this regard, the defendant's appearance only to contest jurisdiction cannot constitute submission if the challenge to jurisdiction is made prior to submission. Companies will be considered as being within the jurisdiction of a foreign court where they have business.[30]

Under Irish common law, the question of jurisdiction of the court of origin for the purposes of recognition and enforcement of foreign judgments finds its origins in *Conflict of Laws Rules* written by AV Dicey.[31] In this regard, Dicey's Rule 36 provides that a foreign court has jurisdiction if the defendant submitted to the jurisdiction

[20] See High Court of Ireland, 31 July 1961, [1962] IR 95, *Russell Rainford et al v Frederick Norman Newell-ZRoberts*. In this matter, the Irish courts held that the similarity between English and Irish legislations would not justify the use of principle of reciprocity in the recognition and enforcement of English judgments.

[21] Under Art 1 of Order 11 of the Rules of the Superior Courts, Irish courts can still have jurisdiction on the basis of the domicile of the defendant, which is a concept that has been avoided in various international instruments in the favour of the habitual residence.

[22] See *Russell Rainford* (n 21). This case deals with an English judgment rendered on the basis of service out of the jurisdiction against the defendant, a British subject resident in Ireland, for payment of an amount found due on an account of dealings of a medical partnership in England of which the defendant had been a member. Here, the Irish High Court held that this English judgment could not be enforced in Ireland on the sole basis of the defendant's British nationality. It has been judges that the fact that English rules of jurisdiction supported the granting of a judgment was irrelevant. This position has been approved by the doctrine multiple times. See eg A Briggs, 'Foreign Judgments: The Common Law Flexes its Muscles' (2011) *17 Trusts & Trustees* 328, 331–32; E Young Exshaw, 'The Enforcement of a Foreign Judgment *in Personam*' (1964) *30 Irish Jurist* 1. Court of Appeal, Civil Division, 27 July 1989, [1990] Ch 433 (CA) 518, *Contra Adams v Cape Industries plc*.

[23] See Court of Appeal, 12 February 1909, [1910] 2 IR 416, *Limerick Corporation v Crompton & Co*. See also for an example from Australia, Supreme Court of New South Wales, *Ltd.* 70 SR NSW 219, [1968] 2 Lloyd's Rep 394, *Dunbee Ltd v Gilma, & Co (Australia) Pty*[**AQ?**], according to which an agreement to submit to the exclusive jurisdiction of a foreign court must be expressly stated and cannot be deduct from the applicable law.

[24] See eg Court of Appeal, 14 November 1907, [1908] IKB 302, *Emmanuel v Symon*.

[25] See Privy Council (India), 28 July 1894, [1894] AC 670, *Sirdar Gurdyal Singh v Rajah of Faridkot*.

[26] See *Russell Rainford* (n 21); High Court, 22 October 1965, [1965] IR 264, *International Alltex Corporation v Lawler Creations Ltd*. See also, High Court, Eire, 72 IR LTR 142, *Edelstyn v Coleman*, in which the High Court of Ireland held that international jurisdiction of a foreign court cannot be based on the fact that the dispute arose from a breach of contract within the foreign state.

[27] See *Russell Rainford* (n 21).

[28] See *Russell Rainford* (n 21); *International Alltex Corporation* (n 27).

[29] See *Russell Rainford* (n 21); *International Alltex Corporation* (n 27). See also, King's Bench Division, 29 April 1914, [1914] 3 KB 145, *Guiard v De Clarmont*, in which a defendant was held to have voluntarily submitted to a jurisdiction where he had set aside default judgment restored by an appeal court.

[30] See Court of Appeal, 27 February 1901, [1901] 2 IR 337, *Dennis v Leinster Paper Co*.

[31] AV Dicey's *Conflict of Laws Rules* consists of a *Digest of the English Conflict of Laws* written by Professor Albert Venn Dicey. Today, with its updated version and new title, *Dicey, Morris & Collins on The Conflict of Laws*, this source is considered as a renowned authority on Irish private international law.

or was present in the foreign jurisdiction when proceedings started.[32] This position has been adopted by the Irish High Court.[33]

Even if it is possible to criticise jurisdiction on the basis of the mere presence of the defendant in the foreign country, Irish courts accept jurisdiction on the same ground. Additionally, it would also be possible for Irish courts to refuse recognition or enforcement of the decision at hand on the basis of fraud, and more specifically abuse of process if the defendant came to the foreign state solely to induce the jurisdiction of the foreign courts.

As for the jurisdiction of Irish courts to enforce foreign judgments under common law, courts have a discretionary power pursuant to Order 11 of the Rules of the Superior Courts. Under Order 11, Irish courts hold a discretionary power to decide for the recognition or enforcement of a foreign judgment under common law and the grounds to refuse to recognise and enforce the foreign judgment are not exhaustive and should be reviewed on a case-by-case basis. However, it is possible to note that as long as the requirements are met,[34] the courts tend to have a positive attitude towards these requests.

The above-mentioned discretionary power has implications that are illustrated in *Albaniabeg Ambient Shpk v Enel SpA and Enelpower SpA*.[35] In this case, it has been upheld that High Court's decision to judge in the favour of an application for leave to issue and serve proceedings seeking to enforce a foreign judgment depends on the fulfilment of three criteria: a good arguable case;[36] the probability of obtaining a practical benefit, that could be at the very least be prospective or indirect from the proceedings in the Republic of Ireland;[37] and satisfaction of comparative cost and convenience pursuant to Order 11, Rule 2.[38]

In *Albaniabeg Ambient Shpk v Enel SpA and Enelpower SpA*, the Court of Appeal also indicated that under Irish common law, there is not any *ex ante* rule that requires that the defendant of the case possesses assets in order to receive leave to commence

[32] See more recently, *Adams* (n 23).

[33] See *Russell Rainford* (n 21); *Flightlease* (n 9).

[34] For more detail, see above Question 2.

[35] High Court of Ireland, 8 March 2016, *Albaniabeg Ambient Shpk v Enel SpA* [2016] IEHC 139. See also previously, in the context of international commercial arbitration, High Court of Ireland, 13 March 2014, [2014] IEHC 115, *Yukos Capital SARL v OAO Tomskneft VNK*. Yukos Capital had received a favourable award in an International Criminal Court arbitration dated back in 2007 and was seeking enforcement in Ireland, just prior the expiry of the legal limitation period of six years. The Irish High Court refused to accept jurisdiction on the basis that the case lacked connections with Ireland, and the parties to arbitration did not have or were likely to have in the future any assets on the Irish territory. The Court also added that it was the fourth time the claimant was requesting the enforcement of the award (having already received the enforcement of the award in the Netherlands and Russia, and having initiated the proceedings for an enforcement in Singapore), which would create a significant financial burden on the defendant. All of these points showed that the claimant was not able to show that a 'solid practical benefit' was to be gained from an enforcement in Ireland, a judgment from a 'respectable' court having already been obtained elsewhere.

[36] In this matter, according to Hogan J, it was sufficient for the appellant to demonstrate that the foreign judgment is for a definite sum of money in order to establish a good arguable cause pursuant to Order 11 of the Rules of the Superior Courts.

[37] In other words, the plaintiff is expected to demonstrate that the application for recognition or enforcement of the judgment is not futile.

[38] In this regard, in *Albaniabeg Ambient Shpk* (n 36), Hogan J highlighted the unfairness of requiring the defendants to go through a second set of enforcement proceedings, especially considering the possible supplementary costs and the lack of any prospective success for the claimant (the proceedings being futile).

proceedings seeking to enforce a foreign judgment under Order 11 of the Rules of the Superior Courts.[39] The Court finally affirmed that the motivation of the claimant to obtain a decision from a neutral and a respected jurisdiction could constitute a legitimate and sufficient benefit to apply for an enforcement in the Republic of Ireland unless enforcement proceedings have already been determined or are pending in other jurisdictions. Nonetheless, the Court of Appeal has also highlighted that courts should still be reluctant to allow enforcement on the sole basis of this claim.[40]

b) Finality/Enforceability in the Country of Origin

The judgment subject to a recognition and enforcement in the Republic of Ireland is required to be final and conclusive,[41] binding in its own jurisdiction and hence unalterable by the latter, and given on the merits. A judgment that can be challenged by one of the parties in the same court will not be enforceable in the Republic of Ireland as it will not be considered final and conclusive.

The question then arises whether the possibility of an appeal could prevent foreign judgments from being recognised or enforced in the Republic of Ireland. The fact that the foreign judgment is subject to appeal or that an appeal is pending against it does not make that judgment unenforceable in the Republic of Ireland.[42] In this hypothesis, it is nonetheless likely that Irish courts exercise their discretion to grant a stay of execution, pending the outcome of the appeal.

c) *Res Iudicata*

Under Irish common law, there is no specific rule which indicates the approach of the courts to recognition and enforcement of foreign judgments where there is a conflicting judgment involving the same parties. However, in practice and according to English common law rules, which are, as previously mentioned, considered as persuasive in Irish law, if the plaintiff claims that the submitted foreign judgment is inconsistent with an existing Irish judgment based on the same cause of action between the same parties, Irish courts can refuse recognition and enforcement depending on which judgment has priority. In line with the 'first in time' approach, a conflicting Irish judgment may be effective, hence prevent the recognition and enforcement of a foreign judgment where the former was first rendered.

[39] See also in this sense, Court of Appeal, Civil Division, 26 July 2007, [2007] EWCA Civ 799, *Tasarruf Mevduati Sigorta Fonu v Demirel and another*.

[40] In this regard, see also, *Yukos Capital SARL* (n 36). The same test has recently been applied in the context of international commercial arbitration: High Court of Ireland, 11 November 2016, [2016] IEHC 636, *Avobone NV v Aurelian Oil & Gas Limited*.

[41] See Chancery Division, 18 July 1880, [1880] 8 LR Ir 298, *Nunn v Nunn*; Court of Appeal, 14 February 1924, [1924] 1 KB 807, *Beatty v Beatty*; King's Bench Division, 1 January 1921, [1921] 2 IR 148, *M'Donnell v M'Donnell*; High Court of Ireland, 9 October 1984, [1984] IR 368, *G v G*.

[42] See *Scott* (n 15); Court of Appeal, 7 June 1966, [1966] 1 WLR 1287, *Colt Industries Inc v Sarlie (No 2)*; House of Lords, 22 November 1889, [1889] 15 App Cas 1 HL (Eng), *Nouvion v Freeman*.

d) *Lis Pendens*

Under Irish common law, there is not any specific rule that states the position that the courts should take regarding the recognition and enforcement of a foreign judgment in case of parallel proceedings. However, it is possible to state that, in accordance with what has been explained in the Question 3 c) above, the existence of parallel proceedings should have no effect on the recognition and enforcement of a foreign judgment, which has priority on the basis of the 'first in time' approach.

e) Specific Requirements of Due Process

The respect of due process by the proceedings taken place in the foreign country is not a requirement under Irish common law. Instead, Irish courts have previously searched for 'equivalence' in terms of the approach and procedure adopted by the foreign court.[43] However, the contrariety of the foreign judgment to principles of natural justice[44] can serve as a ground to contest its enforcement by the defendant.

f) Public Policy

A judgment which is contrary to the principles of Irish public policy can be refused recognition and enforcement by an Irish court.[45] Irish common law does not provide any standard applicable to the public policy exception in respect of recognition and enforcement.

It is possible to refer to the manner in which Irish public policy has been defined by Irish courts within the framework of international commercial arbitration law.

In this regard, it is important to note the case *Brostrum Tankers AB v Factorias Vukano SA*,[46] in which the Irish High Court addressed the public policy exception to the enforcement of arbitral awards under the New York Convention.[47] In this ruling, Irish courts stated that the public policy exception to Irish common law can only be invoked where there is 'some element of illegality' or that the enforcement of the judgment 'would be clearly injurious to the public good' or 'offensive to the ordinary responsible and fully informed member of the public'. The interpretation of public policy exception by Irish courts is then strict and narrow in scope.

[43] This approach has been used as a basis for the recognition of foreign bankruptcy procedures and liquidations. See in this sense, High Court of Ireland, 5 March 2012, [2012] IEHC 97, *Mount Capital Fund Limited (In Liquidation) & Ors v Companies Act*.

[44] In this sense, a foreign judgment that has not been adequately served on the judgment debtor, might risk to be unenforceable. Indeed, such procedure would violate the right to be given due notice of the proceedings and the right to be heard by an impartial tribunal. See also, Question 3 f).

[45] See Court of Appeal, 1897, 31, ILTR 141, *Denman v O'Callaghan* (on contrariety to 'natural justice'); *Maubourquet v Wyse*, 1867, IR 1 CL 471 (more precisely, on contrariety to maxim *audi alteram aldem*). See also, Court of Appeal, 27 February 1901, [1901] 2 IR 337, *Dennis v Leinster Paper Co.*

[46] High Court of Ireland, 19 May 2004, [2004] 2 IR 19, *Brostrum Tankers AB v Factorias Vukano SA*.

[47] United Nations Convention on the Recognition and Enforcement of Foreign Arbitral Awards (New York, 10 June 1958).

g) Reciprocity

The principle of reciprocity (or *comity of courts*) is no more a requirement for the enforcement of foreign judgments under Irish common law. As the Republic of Ireland has not entered into any bilateral treaty arrangements regarding the reciprocal recognition and enforcement of foreign judgments, this principle is not itself sufficient for Irish courts to accept the jurisdiction of foreign courts.

On the contrary to Brussels Regulations or Hague Conventions, under Irish common law there is no prescription as to what to take into consideration while deciding on the recognition or enforcement of judgments. Irish courts have the discretion to take into consideration reciprocity as a factor in their decisions. However, in practice, the courts tend to reject the principle of reciprocity in favour of the doctrine of obligation.[48]

h) Other Requirements

Irish courts do not enforce orders for delivery of goods, specific performance or injunctions. For recognition and enforcement of foreign judgments in the Republic of Ireland, the foreign judgment submitted by the applicant seeking the enforcement must be for a definite sum of money, in other words, only money judgments can be enforced.[49] Further, Irish courts do not enforce tax or penalty judgments nor revenue law related orders and judgments.

It is also necessary that the application for enforcement has been brought to Irish courts within the limitation period, which is six years from the date on which the foreign judgment was given or made as under Irish common law, the foreign judgment being considered as similar to a contractual debt.[50] In the same line, in accordance with Order 86A of the Superior Courts Rules, parties can appeal the decision of the High Court within 28 days of perfection of the order.

Question 4. Documents to be Produced

An application for recognition and enforcement of a foreign judgment pursuant to Irish common law is made on an ex parte basis before the Master of the Irish High Court. The applicant should bring an originating summons, more specifically a summary summons, as well as a verified, certified and sealed copy of the judgment. Once the summons has been filed, a notice setting out the relief sought and a grounding affidavit should be brought by the plaintiff in order to receive a motion. A separate affidavit proving the service of the proceedings and the motion papers on the defendant should also

[48] See *Russell Rainford* (n 21) at 104, in which the idea was to inquire if the defendant was 'under any duty or obligation to comply with the judgment upon which th[e] action [was] brought'.

[49] See High Court of Ireland, 1 January 1807, [1808] 170 ER 948, *Sadler v Robins; M'Donnell* (n 42). For an example from New Zealand, see Supreme Court, 1932, [1932] NZLR 286, *Taylor v Begg*. See also, Question 2 a), above.

[50] For this reason, the rules applicable to such a claim apply. For more information, see below Question 4.

be presented. A prior ex parte application to the High Court may be required seeking to serve the defendant located outside of the jurisdiction.

If the foreign judgment is not in an official language of the Irish State (ie, Irish or English), a translation into either of these languages will be necessary. It is preferable that this translation is certified by a notary public, but a translation by a qualified person in the foreign jurisdiction can also be received if it is authenticated by affidavit.

Question 5. Securities, Bonds and Deposits

Security for costs is not a requirement in an application for recognition and enforcement of a foreign judgment before Irish courts unless an application for such an order by the respondent has been successful. Indeed, if there are concerns about a plaintiff's financial state, the respondent can apply for an order for security for costs. If the application is successful, the plaintiff will have to lodge a sum of money into the court to meet the costs of the defendant in the proceedings if the respondent is successful.

Bonds and deposits do not constitute requirements in an application for recognition and enforcement of a foreign judgment before Irish courts.

Italy

MARCO PASQUA

Question 1. General Overview

National-autonomous rules on the recognition and enforcement of non-EU judgments in civil and commercial matters are contained, mainly, in Law 31 May 1995 no 218, the Reform of the Italian system of private international law ('Law 218/1995').[1] However, Article 2 Law 218/1995 provides that the provisions of Law 218/1995 do not prejudice the application of the international conventions in force for Italy.[2]

Title IV Law 218/1995, which deals with the effectiveness of foreign judgments, begins with Article 64.[3] This article introduces the principle of automatic recognition of foreign judgments, establishing that they are recognised without the need to resort to any proceedings when they satisfy specific requirements. These requirements are summarised as follows: a) jurisdiction of the court issuing the judgment according to Italian jurisdiction principles; b) proper service of the document initiating proceedings and no violation of essential rights of defence; c) compliance with parties' appearance requirements, or declaration of default of appearance, according to the law where the proceeding took place; d) finality of the judgment according to the law of the issuing place; e) absence of conflict with another final judgment issued by an Italian court; f)

[1] Legge of 31 May 1995 no 218, Riforma del Sistema italiano di diritto internazionale privato, Gazzetta Ufficiale no 128 of 3 June 1995 – Supplemento Ordinario no 68. For English translation of Law 218/1995, see A Montanari and VA Narcisi, 'Italy' in J Basedow et al (eds), *Encyclopedia of Private International Law*, Vol IV (Edward Elgar, 2017) 3329.

[2] The reference encompasses both multilateral international conventions (eg, the 2007 Lugano Convention on jurisdiction and the recognition and enforcement of judgments in civil and commercial matters) and bilateral international conventions. For a comprehensive list of the international conventions in force for Italy, consult the archive held by the Italian Ministry of Foreign Affairs at itra.esteri.it.

[3] *cf* S Bariatti, 'Articoli 64-68' in F Pocar et al (eds), *Commentario del nuovo diritto internazionale privato* (Cedam, 1996) 318 ff; R Luzzatto, 'Il riconoscimento di sentenze e provvedimenti stranieri nella riforma del diritto internazionale privato italiano' in F Salerno (ed), *Convenzioni internazionali e legge di riforma del diritto internazionale privato* (Cedam, 1997); M Maresca, 'Artt. 64-66' in S Bariatti (ed), *Legge 31 maggio 1995 n. 218, Riforma del Sistema Italiano di Diritto Internazionale Privato*, in *Le Nuove Leggi Civili Commentate*, 1460 ff; M Torsello, 'Articoli 64-71' in M Torsello (ed), *Commento alla legge 31 maggio 1995, n. 218 di riforma del sistema italiano di diritto internazionale privato*, e-book connected to M Franzoni et al (eds), *Codice civile commentato con dottrina e giurisprudenza* (Giappichelli, 2018) 136 ff; N Boschiero, *Appunti sulla riforma del sistema italiano di diritto internazionale privato* (Giappichelli, 1996) 149 ff; E D'Alessandro, *Il riconoscimento delle sentenze straniere* (Giappichelli, 2007) 14 ff; G Carella, 'Sentenze civili e atti stranieri' in *Enciclopedie del diritto* (Annali, vol IX) (Giuffrè, 2016), 843 ff; F Salerno, 'Riconoscimento delle sentenze straniere in materia civile e commerciale [dir. proc. civ. int.]' in *Treccani* (Diritto online, 2014); MA Lupoi, 'Italy' in G Walter and S Baumgartner (eds), *Recognition and enforcement of foreign judgments outside the scope of the Brussels and Lugano Conventions* (Kluwer Law International, 2000) 347 ff.

absence of a pending proceeding in Italy involving the same parties and cause of action that began before the foreign proceeding; and g) provisions of the judgment do not produce effects contrary to public policy.

Article 67 addresses the enforcement of foreign judgments, outlining which procedure shall or can be instituted when a foreign judgment, assumed to be effective in Italy, is not complied with and it becomes necessary to enforce it, or when its recognisability is contested. It stipulates that anyone with an interest can request the court to verify the existence of the recognition requirements. The Court of Appeal of the place where the enforcement of the judgment is sought has jurisdiction for such proceeding. Pursuant to Article 30 Legislative Decree 1 September 2011 no 150,[4] as amended by Legislative Decree 10 October 2022 no 149,[5] the (new) simplified cognition proceeding is the one to be followed. The foreign judgment, along with the Italian judgment establishing the existence of the recognition requirements, serves as enforcement title. Finally, the case of incidental verification of recognisability conditions: if the existence of these conditions is contested during a proceeding, it is up to the court seized to assess them; however, the judgment issued for this purpose holds limited effectiveness solely within the proceeding concerned.

A clarification is necessary regarding an implicit requirement under Title IV Law 218/1995: the presence of a foreign act that qualifies as a 'judgment'.[6] Arts 64 and 67 Law 218/1995 do not provide for the notion of 'judgment', and it is the accompanying Ministerial Report ('Report') that provides guidance based on legal scholars' interpretations and case law under previous legislation. An act qualifies as a 'judgment' if it concludes a legal proceeding, which, by its content, would result in a judgment if conducted in Italy. Moreover, the Report states that a foreign decision which has the effect of ascertaining, establishing, modifying or extinguishing a subjective right, a capacity or a situation, along with any consequent condemnation, should be regarded as a judgment, even if it does not align precisely with its Italian counterpart. Regarding the authority issuing the foreign judgment, the Report employs the criterion of equivalence, suggesting that administrative decisions or decisions made by public authorities, not analogous to judicial authorities but pertaining to matters handled and decided by the judiciary in Italy, should also be subject to the rules governing recognition and enforcement of foreign judgments in Italy.

The Italian system on recognition and enforcement of foreign judgments differs from the Brussels Ia Regulation[7] regime in several aspects. Firstly, the different formulation: the Italian system positively establishes the necessary requirements for recognition,

[4] Decreto Legislativo of 1 September 2011 no 150, Disposizioni complementari al codice di procedura civile in materia di riduzione e semplificazione dei procedimenti civili di cognizione, ai sensi dell'articolo 54 della legge 18 giugno 2009, n. 69, Gazzetta Ufficiale no 220 of 21 September 2011.

[5] Decreto Legislativo of 10 October 2022 no 149, Attuazione della legge 26 novembre 2021, n 206, recante delega al Governo per l'efficienza del processo civile e per la revisione della disciplina degli strumenti di risoluzione alternativa delle controversie e misure urgenti di razionalizzazione dei procedimenti in materia di diritti delle persone e delle famiglie nonche' in materia di esecuzione forzata, Gazzetta Ufficiale no 243 of 17 October 2022, Supplemento Ordinario no 38.

[6] G Conetti, S Tonolo and F Vismara, *Commento alla riforma* (Giappichelli, 2009), 312; C Consolo, 'Evoluzioni nel riconoscimento delle sentenze straniere' in F Salerno (ed), *Convenzioni internazionali e legge di riforma del diritto internazionale privato* (Cedam, 1997) 272 ff; A Migliazza, 'Nazionalismo e internazionalismo nel sistema italiano di diritto processuale civile internazionale' (1996) *Rivista di diritto processuale* 686.

[7] Regulation (EU) No 1215/2012 of the European Parliament and of the Council of 12 December 2012 on jurisdiction and the recognition and enforcement of judgments in civil and commercial matters (recast), OJ L 351/1, 20 December 2012.

whereas the Brussels Ia regime provides negatively for obstacles which preclude recognition. Secondly, the Italian system, unlike Brussels Ia, does not contain a definition of what is meant by 'judgment'. Additionally, in the Italian system a judgment must be final in order to be recognised, while this element is not required in the Brussels Ia regime. Finally, the procedure: for the Brussels Ia regime, the specific reference is to Article 30-*bis* Legislative Decree 1 September 2011 no 150 which, however, as amended by Legislative Decree 10 October 2022 no 149 paragraph 4, similarly provides for the simplified cognition proceeding as the one to be followed.

Question 2. Procedure[8]

a) Circumstances of Recognition and Enforcement

Recognition of foreign judgments is automatic, without the need to resort to any proceedings, when they satisfy the aforementioned requirements. If the existence of these recognition requirements is contested during a proceeding, the court seized with the matter undertakes an incidental verification and assess them; any judgment issued for this purpose has limited effectiveness to the proceeding concerned.

In the event of non-compliance with or objection to the recognition of the foreign judgment, or when it is necessary to proceed with its enforcement, a request may be brought to the ordinary judicial authority to verify the requirements for recognition according to the procedure outlined below. The foreign judgment, along with the Italian judgment confirming the existence of the recognition requirements, serves as enforcement title.

b) Procedural Steps

Pursuant to Article 67, paragraph 1-*bis* Law 218/1995, the proceeding in the event of non-compliance with or objection to the recognition of the foreign judgment, or when it is necessary to proceed with its enforcement, is disciplined by Article 30 Legislative Decree 1 September 2011 no 150,[9] as amended by Legislative Decree 10 October 2022

[8] This author emphasises that the procedure in question raises many issues, including more general ones of civil procedural law. This author has focused more on the issues of private international law that emerge, while still addressing the relevant procedural aspects. Given the aim to provide a concise, yet clear and comprehensive report, this explains why the analysis and the footnotes are reduced to the essential and do not extensively deal, as they should, with references to the general theory of Italian civil procedural law.

[9] *cf* S Turatto, 'Commento all'art. 30' in C Consolo (ed), *La semplificazione dei riti e le altre riforme processuali 2010-2011* (IPSOA, 2012), 379 ff; M Abbamonte, 'Commento all'art. 30' in R Martino and A Panzarola (eds), *Commentario alle riforme del processo civile dalla semplificazione dei riti al decreto sviluppo* (Giappichelli, 2013) 376 ff; MA Lupoi, 'Commento all'art. 30, d. legisl. 150 del 2011' in F Carpi and M Taruffo (eds), *Commentario breve al codice di procedure civile*, (CEDAM, 2012) 3228–29; M Farina, 'Sub art. 30' in B Sassani and R Tiscini (eds), *La semplificazione dei riti civili* (Dike Giuridica, 2011) 266; R De Nictolis, *Riti speciali di cognizione – commentario al d.lgs 1° settembre 2011, n. 150* (Zanichelli, 2012) 606 ff; MG Civinini, *Il riconoscimento delle sentenze straniere* (Giuffrè, 2001), 89 ff; G Gaja, 'Le convenzioni internazionali e le nuove norme sulla giurisdizione e sul riconoscimento delle sentenze straniere' (1997) *Rivista trimestrale di diritto e procedura civile* 837 ff.

no 149, which provides the (new) *simplified cognition proceeding* (in Italian, *procedimento semplificato di cognizione*) as the one to be followed.[10] Disciplined under the Code of Civil Procedure (CPC),[11] this procedure, alternative to the ordinary one, is governed by Article 281-*decies* ff CPC.[12] It is characterised – without prejudice to the fullness of cognition – by a summary preliminary activity and by a procedure inspired by speed and non-formalisation.[13] Briefly, the chronological structure of this procedure includes: filing of the recourse and appearance of the claimant before court; scheduling of the first hearing; notification of the recourse and the decree fixing the hearing date; appearance of the defendant before court; first hearing; potential submission of supplementary briefs and replies; hearing for the assumption of evidence; submission of the clarifications of the conclusions; submission of final notes; oral discussion hearing; issuance of the judgment.

The Italian courts have always jurisdiction over such proceedings in Italy. Despite the absence of an explicit criterion of jurisdiction in this regard, the proceeding pursuant to Article 67 Law 218/1995 aims to ascertain the effectiveness or lack thereof of foreign judgment in Italy, thereby establishing a sufficient connection with the Italian state. This holds true regardless of other circumstances that may render recognition and enforcement relevant within the Italian legal system. Affirming this, the Court of Cassation has clarified that the potential absence of assets subject to enforcement in Italy does not constitute a reason for denying Italian jurisdiction.[14] The *Court of Appeal* is the competent authority for such proceeding under Article 67 Law 218/1995 and renders decisions in a single instance.

Regarding *venue jurisdiction*, as outlined in Article 30 Legislative Decree 1 September 2011 no 150, the competent court is the *Court of Appeal of the place where execution is to take place*. The place of execution is determined by the location where the effects of the foreign judgment, which are particularly relevant, are intended to occur. For instance, in the case of a proceeding for enforcement purposes, the Court of Appeal of the place where the assets, on which enforcement action is intended, are located would be competent. Similarly, for proceedings related to transcription, registration or annotation in

[10] Art 35 para 1 Legislative Decree 10 October 2022 no 149 has provided that 'The provisions of this decree, unless otherwise provided, apply from 30 June 2023 and apply to proceedings initiated after that date. The provisions previously in force apply to proceedings pending as of 30 June 2023.' Legislative Decree 10 October 2022 no 149, as amended by Art 35 para, 1 Legge 29 December 2022 no 197, Gazzetta Ufficiale no 12 of 16 January 2023, Supplemento Ordinario no 3, has provided that 'The provisions of this decree, unless otherwise provided, apply from 28 February 2023 and apply to proceedings initiated after that date. To the proceedings pending as of 28 February 2023 provisions previously in force shall apply.' *cf* MA Lupoi, 'Art. 30 d. legisl. 1° settembre 2011, n.150' in F Carpi and M Taruffo (eds), *Commentario breve al codice di procedure civile* (CEDAM, 2023), Appendix – VIII, 499–500; F Pesce, 'Luci ed ombre delle norme di rilievo internazional(privat)istico nella recente riforma del processo civile' (2023) *Jus – Rivista di Scienze Giuridiche* 293; A Carratta, 'La riforma del processo civile nella prospettiva del diritto processuale civile internazionale' (2023) *Rivista di diritto internazionale* 929.

[11] Regio Decreto of 28 October 1940 no 1443, Codice di procedura civile, Gazzetta Ufficiale no 253 of 28 October 1940.

[12] *cf* B Gambineri, 'Il procedimento semplificato di cognizione (o meglio il "nuovo" processo di cognizione di primo grado)' (2023) *Questione giustizia*; R Masoni, 'Il procedimento semplificato di cognizione' (2023) *Giustizia civile* 291 ff; A Giussani, 'Le nuove norme sul rito semplificato di cognizione' (2023) *Rivista di diritto processuale* 632 ff; G Balena, 'Il (seminuovo) procedimento semplificato di cognizione' (2023) *Il giusto processo civile* 1 ff; M Abbamonte, 'Il nuovo procedimento semplificato di cognizione: osservazioni a prima lettura' (2023) *Studium iuris* 166 ff.

[13] Corte di Cassazione, Ufficio del Massimario, Relazione no 110 of 1 December 2022, 76.

[14] Corte di Cassazione, Sezioni Unite, 23 October 2006, no° 22663, (2007) *Riv dir int priv proc* 1064.

the public registers, the Court of Appeal of the place where these registers on which the aforementioned operations shall be carried out would be competent. In scenarios where the judgment can be enforced in more than one place – for example, because the debtor's assets are located in different places – multiple courts may concurrently have venue jurisdiction. The same principle applies to multi-parts judgments capable of being implemented in different places, unless there is a main or pre-eminent ruling to which the exclusive jurisdiction of the Court of Appeal, within whose district enforcement is sought, is attached.[15]

However, applying this criterion becomes challenging in cases where judgments are not suitable to any form of execution – such as when the place of execution cannot be identified due to the absence of assets subject to enforcement in Italy – or when a party claims only for the purposes of ascertaining the effectiveness of the *res iudicata*. In such instances, the Court of Cassation has ruled that if a *forum* cannot be determined using the criterion of execution, the ordinary venue jurisdiction rules apply. These rules typically rely on the defendant's *forum* as a primary criterion, along with other alternatives. However, utilising venue jurisdiction criteria alternative to the defendant's *forum* seems questionable in this context: these criteria are designed to be applied based on the subject matter of the proceeding at hand. In order to apply them to such proceeding under Article 67 Law 218/1995 it would be necessary to go back to the relationship addressed in the foreign judgment. Yet, in these proceedings, the underlying relationship is not pertinent; rather, only the existence of the requirements for the foreign judgment's effectiveness in Italy matters. Therefore, it appears preferable to use the general criterion of the defendant's *forum* as the subsidiary criterion to that of the place of execution. This criterion remains applicable unless the defendant neither resides nor is domiciled in Italy. In such cases, the additional residual criterion of the place where the plaintiff resides applies. Moreover, if the plaintiff also lacks residence in Italy, any Court of Appeal would be competent.[16]

Lastly, a question arises whether the criterion of venue jurisdiction referred to by Article 67 Law 218/1995 can be derogated. The issue is uncertain because, compared to the previous CPC recognition and enforcement system of foreign judgments, Article 67 Law 218/1995 no longer expressly provides for the mandatory participation of the public prosecutor. Consequently, by applying the CPC rules, venue jurisdiction shall be considered derogable, as indirectly affirmed by the Court of Cassation.[17]

In the Italian civil trial, there are conditions for the legal action. These include the legal standing and the interest to act. Legal standing involves demonstrating to be the holder of the legal position by the party initiating the action (standing to act), as well as by the party against whom the action is directed (standing to be sued). Its basis is established *a contrario* by Article 81 CPC, which states that, except in cases explicitly

[15] Corte d'Appello di Roma, 12 April 2000, (2001) *Riv dir int priv proc* 126; Corte d'Appello di Bari, 11 May 2000, (2001) *Riv dir int priv proc* 135. *cf* O Lopes Pegna, *I procedimenti relativi all'efficacia delle decisioni straniere in materia civile* (Cedam, 2009), 155; S Turatto, 'Problemi interpretativi sul riconoscimento delle sentenze straniere' (2005) *Rivista trimestrale di diritto e procedura civile* 677.

[16] Lopes Pegna (n 15) 157. The Italian report chapter draws extensively on insights and passages from Lopes Pegna's book, particularly in sections discussing the procedural steps. While the book is written in Italian, its contents have been adapted and referenced throughout this Italian report chapter, with citations provided in the footnotes where relevant.

[17] Corte di Cassazione, Sezione Civile I, 29 May 2003, no° 8588, (2005) *Riv dir int priv proc* 1414.

provided for by law, no one can claim for the rights of others in their own name during proceedings. On the other hand, the interest to act is outlined in Article 100 CPC, which stipulates that one must have an interest in either proposing a claim or contesting it. This interest exists when tangible legal benefits can be derived from the proceeding, and its manifestation varies depending on the type of legal action proposed. These conditions, as delineated in the proceedings specified in Article 67 Law 218/1995, are further elaborated below.

In line with Article 67 Law 218/1995, the *legal standing to act* is conferred upon anyone who has an interest. Thus, third persons not parties in (and unrelated to) the foreign proceeding also have legal standing, provided they can demonstrate an interest.[18] This aligns with the introduction of automatic recognition of foreign judgments, where the judgment arising from the recognition proceeding serves merely to establish whether recognition has occurred or whether the recognition requirements are absent. The decision to adopt such a form of standing is rooted in the non-availability of the legal relationship and/or the involvement of public interests. Proceedings under Article 67 seek to verify a situation already existing as resulting from legal provisions, thus removing recognition from the parties' control. Furthermore, the parties' interest is accompanied by a public interest in ensuring legal certainty, which also legitimises third parties to request the recognition assessment. The question arises regarding who the legitimate third persons are in requesting verification of the requirements for recognition of foreign judgments. It is reasonable to argue that all persons with legal situations impacted by the foreign judgment have the right to request the verification. Thus, under Article 67, those entitled to act include not only those claiming to hold a right, but also those claiming to hold a related legal situation. Based on this assumption, third persons who possess legal situations dependent on the relationship addressed in the foreign judgment may act, provided they are affected by its effectiveness in the legal system.[19] However, the Court of Cassation has adopted a more restrictive approach, limiting legal standing (both to act and to be sued) to the parties (or their heirs or assignees) involved in the foreign trial.[20]

Regarding the *interest to act*,[21] the legislator, in regulating the procedure under Article 67, acknowledges the existence, in principle, of certain situations that give rise to the interest to act, and has established this procedure as a measure. In addition to cases where one seeks to confer executive effects on the judgment, necessitating recourse to

[18] Bariatti, 'Articolo 67' (n 3) 342; Lopes Pegna (n 15) 163; Torsello, 'Articolo 67' (n 3) 143; A Attardi, *La nuova disciplina in tema di giurisdizione italiana e di riconoscimento delle sentenze straniere* (CEDAM, 1995) 781; A Carlevaris, 'Il nuovo procedimento per accertare l'efficacia delle sentenze straniere e le prime difficoltà applicative' (1999) *Rivista di diritto internazionale* 1013 ff; A D'Amato, *L'efficacia degli atti giurisdizionali stranieri in giudizio pendente* (Cacucci, 2000) 132 ff.

[19] Lopes Pegna (n 15) 163 ff.

[20] Corte di Cassazione, Sezione Civile I, 12 March 2018, no° 5895, (2019) *Riv dir int priv proc* 403; Corte di Cassazione, Sezioni Unite, 23 October 2006, no° 22663, (2007) *Riv dir int priv proc* 1064; Corte di Cassazione, Sezione Civile I, 16 February 1999, no° 1301, (2000) *Riv dir int priv proc* 787. And even under the previous legislation on the matter, see Corte di Cassazione, Sezione Civile I, 10 November 1994, no 9383, (1995) *Riv dir int priv proc* 729; Corte di Cassazione, 14 March 1985, no 1977, (1986) *Riv dir int priv proc* 617; Corte di Cassazione, 4 March 1980, no 1436, (1981) 489. On the same interpretation, see De Nictolis (n 9) 607, on Corte di Cassazione, Sezioni Unite, 18 November 2008, no° 27338, (2009) *Riv dir int priv proc* 670.

[21] Lopes Pegna (n 15) 167 ff.

the procedure, non-compliance with and objection to are the circumstances that may create uncertainty, thereby prompting interest in verifying the recognition requirements. In such instances, it can be inferred that the interest to act exists inherently, without the need for additional checks not mandated by law;[22] nevertheless, the counterparty retains the opportunity to demonstrate that, in the specific case, such interest does not exist, rendering the action non-actionable. Hence, it is crucial to delineate the meanings of 'non-compliance with' or 'objection to'. The failure to fulfil an obligation stemming from the foreign judgment, whether to do or not to do, undoubtedly falls under the category of non-compliance with. On the other hand, the scenario of an objection arises whenever there is a disagreement regarding the effectiveness of the judgment in Italy. This may occur when the existence (or non-existence) of the requirements for recognition is questioned, or more broadly, to contest the existence of the right or legal relationship that constituted the subject of the foreign judgment. The fact that Article 67 has provided for typical situations (non-compliance with and objection to) which denote an interest to act, however, raises the question of whether there may be an interest to act even in the presence of different situations not explicitly mentioned, and if so, whether the action outlined in Article 67 remains viable in such cases. Uncertainty regarding a legal situation may not necessarily stem from a non-compliance or objection; it can also arise from a state of fact or law. Simply because a judgment is recognised in the Italian system only if it meets specific requirements, one may find oneself in a state of uncertainty due to the impossibility (or extreme difficulty) of definitively ascertaining whether or not the judgment meets these requirements. This observation is not intended to critique or undermine the scope of automatic recognition. Thus, it cannot be discounted that situations may arise wherein this uncertainty prejudices the holder of the legal situation involved, and such prejudice can only be rectified through a definitive ruling by the court.

The scenario may arise where the claimant is interested in requesting verification of the existence of the requirements solely concerning *one or more independent parts of the judgment*. This possibility is considered permissible under the framework of Article 67. When the non-compliance with or objection to pertains only to specific parts of the judgment, or when only certain parts are subject to enforcement in Italy, it would be reasonable to allow a party to limit their request for assessment to these particular parts.[23]

The considerations outlined above regarding the standing to act inevitably also impact the question of the *standing to be sued*.[24] Thus, determining the holder of the standing to be sued depends on the circumstances that necessitate resorting to the assessment in each specific case. In instances of non-compliance with or objection to, the plaintiff seeks a definitive assessment regarding the recognition that has occurred, which can be enforced against the party failing to comply or objecting. When the counterparty of the foreign trial is the one contesting, there are no issues: this procedure will involve the original parties of the foreign trial. The same applies when one party requests a negative assessment against the other. Similarly, when the recognition is sought for the enforcement procedure, the party failing to comply with the obligation arising from the

[22] Corte di Cassazione, Sezione Civile I, 1 August 2007 no 16991, (2008) *Riv dir int priv proc* 755.
[23] Lopes Pegna (n 15) 179 ff.
[24] ibid 181 ff.

foreign judgment will be the holder of the standing to be sued. However, as previously noted, the person contesting does not necessarily coincide with the counterparty; it may also be a third person affected by the effectiveness of the foreign judgment, as they are the holder of a related legal situation. In this scenario, the holder of the standing to be sued can only be the third person, as the plaintiff seeks a definitive assessment enforceable against them.

The scenario where this assessment proceeding involves a party from the foreign trial and a third person who did not participate in that trial raises the question of whether the other party or parties from the foreign trial must always participate in the assessment proceeding in Italy, ie if they are compulsory joinder of parties (in Italian, *litisconsorti necessari*). It cannot be discounted that there may be instances of joinder of parties even when not explicitly stipulated by the legislator. The principles regarding joinder of parties, when applied to proceedings under Article 67, suggest that the parties from the foreign trial are indispensable parties in the trial disputing the effectiveness of the judgment in Italy, particularly when it concerns legal rights they hold. This holds true whether the action is initiated by any interested party, such as a third person, or when one of the parties initiates action against a third person. Otherwise, the judgment rendered may not fully achieve its intended effects, specifically the certainty regarding the judgment's effectiveness concerning that relationship in the Italian legal system. Such certainty could only be attained through the involvement of parties from the foreign trial in the assessment proceeding. Nevertheless, the issue persists regarding the necessity of having all parties from the foreign trial present. This inquiry becomes particularly pertinent when there is a non-compliance with or objection to over the recognition of a judgment that has condemned multiple persons jointly and severally.

Regarding *intervention in the proceeding of third persons*, there is no justification for departing from the general rules of the CPC. However, it is necessary to identify specifically which types of intervention are compatible with the proceeding under Article 67 at stake. The standing to intervene in this proceeding will be determined by to be holder of legal situations that are directly or indirectly affected by the effectiveness of the foreign judgment in Italy. The standing for voluntary intervention (Article 105 CPC) extends to both parties from the foreign trial who are not compulsory joinder of parties (or their heirs or assignees), and to third persons who, as holders of dependent relationships, are subject to the indirect effectiveness of the foreign judgment. These parties and/or persons may also be called upon to intervene at the request of a party (Article 106 CPC) or by order of the court (Article 107 CPC).

With reference to the burden of proving the requirements for recognition, it is necessary to preliminarily observe that *the court has an autonomous duty, of its own motion, to ascertain the existence or non-existence of all such requirements.*[25] This obligation stems from the fact that these requirements pose safeguards deemed essential by the Italian legal system for foreign judgments to have effect within its territory. Consequently, these requirements are not solely for the exclusive interest of one party. This also means that, in carrying out the verification of the existence of these requirements, the court

[25] Corte di Cassazione, Sezione Civile I, 22 July 2004, no 13662, (2005) *Foro it* 1458.

has an own independent power of assessment, not being bound by what is declared in the foreign judgment. And the exercise of such assessment power is all the more important today as the necessary presence of the public prosecutor is no longer generally required. It follows that the assessment should also include those requirements which have not been contested. Indeed, the principle according to which facts not contested by the party appeared before court are to be considered established does not apply in matters such as this under analysis which are not characterised by the dispositive principle (ie the principle according to which, as a general rule, only parties are entitled to indicate the evidence to support the facts alleged in court). There is no prescribed order for assessing the requirements, and it is clear that the possible assessment of the absence of a requirement renders the assessment of the other requirements irrelevant.[26]

In the absence of a specific rule, *the burden of proving these requirements* is disciplined by Article 2697 Civil Code (CC),[27] which establishes the common rule in civil proceedings regarding the allocation of the burden of proof. In proceedings characterised by the existence of *ex officio* powers on the part of court, this rule functions as a procedural guideline to determine the party who bears the risk of failure to prove a fact. Obviously, the issue of the burden of proof only pertains to requirements that presuppose the establishment of 'facts'. As per Article 2697 CC, whoever wants to assert a right in court shall prove the facts that constitute its foundation, and whoever objects to the ineffectiveness of such facts or objects that the right has been modified or extinguished shall prove the facts on which the objection is founded. This rule has been defined as a blank rule: the distinction between constitutive facts on the one hand, and impeding, modifying or extinguishing facts on the other, relevant for the allocation of the burden of proof, derives from the interpretation of the substantive rule that governs the case in question. Therefore, even in such proceeding under Article 67 Law 218/1995, establishing who bears the burden of proof is a question of interpretation of the relevant substantive rule. It follows that the burden of proving the existence of all the requirements for recognition rests on the claimant,[28] with the exception of the 'negative' ones posed by Article 64 paragraph 1(e) Law 218/1995 and Article 64 paragraph 1(f) Law 218/1995. The non-existence of an Italian judgment irreconcilable with the one at stake in the proceeding and the absence of a pending proceeding in Italy on the same matter are to be considered impeding facts, with the consequence that their burden of proof is upon the defendant who contests the recognition. Otherwise, the claimant would find himself in obvious difficulty if he had to prove them. Hence, the same *ratio* should also operate with reference to the condition that the essential rights of defence have not been violated, a requirement set by Article 64 paragraph 1(b), second part, Law 218/1995. Only the defendant can introduce specific de facto circumstances pertaining to the foreign trial that substantiate violations of the right to defence and, thus, are susceptible to prevent recognition. In essence, the risk of failure to prove the requirements under Article 64 paragraph 1(b), second part, Article 64 paragraph 1(e) and Article 64 paragraph 1(f)

[26] Lopes Pegna (n 15) 225 ff.

[27] Regio Decreto of 16 March 1942 no 262, Codice Civile, Gazzetta Ufficiale no 79 of 4 April 1942.

[28] More precisely, it rests on who claims for recognition on a substantive level; it does not matter whether he is the defendant in the proceedings. *cf* P Biavati, 'Riconoscimento ed esecuzione dei provvedimenti stranieri, con particolare riferimento alla materia familiare' (2017) *Judicium* 22.

Law 218/1995 is upon the defendant. However, the burden of proof differs in cases where there is a claim for assessing the non-existence of the recognition requirements. Always respecting the court's *ex officio* powers, the general principles suggests that it is the claimant who bears the risk of failure to prove the existence of an impeding fact or the non-existence of a constitutive fact.

Next, there is the issue of *the extent to which the requested decision may be reviewed on the merits.* While in the previous Italian system on this matter the review of the merits was expressly consented, in the presence of certain circumstances indicated under Article 798 CPC, with its repeal by the reform carried out with Law 218/1995, such review of the merits is now not permitted.

The fact that the procedure for verifying the requirements involves an adversarial process with the party against whom the judgment is to be enforced means that this party is informed of the enforcement intention. This can lead to a risk that, during the time required for the proceedings, actions may be taken that make executing the judgment impossible or more difficult. To mitigate this risk, those seeking to enforce a foreign judgment can utilise generally *conservative measures* available under the Italian legal system to secure the effectiveness of future enforcement actions. Specifically, to ensure the future enforcement of a judgment ordering the payment of a sum of money, the plaintiff can resort to precautionary seizure (Article 671 CPC), which is a measure designed to preserve the guarantee of credits. For ensuring the effectiveness of future enforcement by delivery or release, the appropriate measure is judicial sequestration (Article 670 CPC). Additionally, interim protection under Article 700 CPC can be sought as a precautionary measure of a residual nature with atypical content. It is also worth considering whether some form of precautionary protection is permissible for requests to verify the existence of requirements for the effectiveness of foreign judgments that are not for enforcement purposes and, therefore, not subject to enforcement. The question of whether precautionary measures can be used to anticipate the effects of judgments that are purely declaratory, without additional enforcement measures, is debated. The primary concern is the compatibility between the 'legal certainty' aimed at by the request for verification of a right and the provisional nature of precautionary measures.[29] Regarding the competence issue, a request for precautionary measures can be made either before initiating the proceedings to assess the requirements outlined in Article 67 Law 218/1995 or during such proceedings. In both scenarios, pursuant to Articles 669-*ter* and 669-*quate*r CPC, the competent court is the Court of Appeal of the place where the foreign judgment is to be enforced, as it is the court with jurisdiction over the merits of the case.

When all the legal requirements for the valid initiation and conduct of the trial are met, the procedure outlined in Article 67 Law 218/1995 typically results in a decision on the merits of the claim, determining whether the requirements for recognition are satisfied. Regarding the form of this decision, which the law vaguely describes as a 'measure accepting the request' (Article 67 paragraph 2), it must take the form of a *judgment.* This is because it is a conclusive decision in a cognition proceeding, aimed at resolving any uncertainty about whether a foreign judgment meets the recognition requirements. As with any judicial measure, the final judgment in this procedure must be motivated

[29] Lopes Pegna (n 15) 235.

(Article 111 paragraph 6 of the Italian Constitution[30]). The acceptance (or rejection) of the application can also be partial. This situation may arise when the foreign judgment, for which verification of requirements is requested, contains multiple parts. In such cases, the Court of Appeal may determine that the requirements for recognition are met for some parts but not for others.[31]

Once the judgment accepting the application pursuant to Article 67 Law 218/1995 has been issued, the foreign judgment can be *enforced immediately* without waiting for the judgment confirming the recognition requirements to become final. This is evident from the wording of Article 67 paragraph 2, which states that the foreign judgment, along with the measure accepting the verification request referred to under Article 67 paragraph 1, serves as a title for the enforcement procedure. This approach, which facilitates immediate enforceability, aligns with the reform's goal of promoting the circulation of judgments.[32] However, foreign judgments that merely establish or verify a relationship or legal situation and are not subject to any form of execution, even in a broad sense, are excluded from immediate enforceability.

The procedure for verifying the requirements under Article 67 Law 218/1995, like any other cognition proceeding, can be *terminated* by withdrawal of the judicial documents (Article 306 CPC) or by inactivity of the parties (Article 307 CPC).

The judgment ruling on the existence of the requirements for recognition (by either accepting the application for positive recognition or rejecting the application for negative recognition), once it becomes final, is conclusive for all purposes between the parties, their heirs, or successors (Article 2909 CC). The determination of the existence of the recognition requirements and, thus, recognition already occurred of the foreign judgment within the Italian legal system becomes incontestable and *binds the other courts* in any subsequent proceedings where the issue is relevant.[33]

Finally, *the decision ruling on the existence or not of the recognition requirements can be challenged* via the ordinary means of appeal provided for in the Italian legal order: given that it is a judgment rendered in a single instance, these means include recourse to the Court of Cassation, revocation and third-party opposition.[34]

1. *Recourse to the Court of Cassation*

Regarding the recourse to the Court of Cassation, the general principles that regulate this proceeding apply. Judgments can be challenged before the Court of Cassation relying upon grounds comprising both *errores in procedendo* and *errores in iudicando* (Article 360 CPC). These include:

(a) grounds relating to jurisdiction;
(b) violation of the rules on venue jurisdiction, when the 'regulation of venue jurisdiction' proceeding is not prescribed;

[30] Costituzione della Repubblica Italiana, Gazzetta Ufficiale no 298 of 27 December 1947.
[31] Corte d'Appello di Trento, Sez. distaccata di Bolzano, 16 August 2008, (2009) *Riv dir int priv proc* 448.
[32] Lopes Pegna (n 15) 269.
[33] ibid 289.
[34] ibid 273.

(c) violation or false application of legal rules and national collective labour contracts and agreements;
(d) nullity of the judgment or of the proceeding; and
(e) failure to examine a fact decisive for the judgment which was the subject of discussion between the parties.

Given that the powers of the Court of Cassation are limited to a review of legitimacy, a re-examination of the existence of the requirements of the foreign judgment which involves an assessment of fact is prevented. Consequently, the Court of Cassation cannot re-examine the documents and facts already evaluated by the Court of Appeal, but shall limit itself to verifying that the rules governing the assessment of the requirements have not been violated. Nevertheless, the Court of Cassation retains the ability to adjudicate on the substance of the case if no further factual assessments are required (Article 384 CPC); with reference to the proceeding under analysis, this may occur, for example, in the presence of legal reasons that exclude the recognition. Notably, the recourse to the Court of Cassation does not suspend the enforceability of the challenged judgment (Article 373 CPC); hence, with reference to the proceeding at stake, the enforceability of the executive title constituted by the foreign judgment and the contested Italian judgment persists. Nonetheless, when serious and irreparable damage could result from the execution, the court which issued the contested judgment may be claimed to suspend the execution or provide adequate security (Article 373 CPC).[35]

2. *Revocation*

The decision ruling on the existence or not of the recognition requirements can also be challenged through revocation, provided that the circumstances outlined in Article 395 CPC are met. These circumstances include:

(a) if the decision is the effect of fraud by one of the parties to the detriment of the other;
(b) if the judgment was based on evidence recognised or declared false after the judgment or which the losing party was unaware had been recognised or declared false before the judgment;
(c) if after the judgment one or more decisive documents were found that the party had not been able to produce in court due to *force majeure* or actions of the other party;
(d) if the judgment is the effect of a factual error resulting from the acts or documents of the case – this error exists when the decision is based on the supposition of a fact whose truth is incontrovertibly excluded, or when the non-existence of a fact is supposed whose truth is positively established, and in both cases if the fact did not constitute a controversial point on which the judgment had to be pronounced;
(e) if the judgment is contrary to another precedent having the authority of *res iudicata* between the parties, provided that it has not ruled on the relevant exception;
(f) if the judgment is the result of the fraud of the court, ascertained by a final judgment.

[35] ibid 273 ff.

The application for revocation is submitted before the same Court of Appeal that issued the judgment (Article 397 CPC). The object of this appeal can only be the judgment that concludes the proceeding to ascertain the requirements (ie the decision of the Italian court); thus, the mentioned grounds shall necessarily directly concern this judgment. Only this judgment can potentially be revoked and substituted with a new ruling sharing the same objective: verifying the requirements. Any defects relating to the foreign judgment may exclusively be the subject of challenge in the legal order of origin, with then, in the event of annulment or revocation of the foreign judgment, automatic effects in the Italian legal order. However, even if these defects do not allow a challenge in the legal order of origin, it is to be assumed that they can be asserted during the assessment of the requirements to the extent that they translate into a defect in the assessment of requirements.[36]

3. *Third-party Opposition*

Lastly, the means of challenging the decision ruling on the existence or not of the recognition requirements may be proposed not only by the parties, but also by third persons who did not assume the role of party in the proceeding via the third party opposition. This opposition can take two forms: a third party can challenge the final or executable judgment issued between other people when it prejudices his rights ('ordinary third party opposition', Article 404 paragraph 1 CPC); the assignees and creditors of one of the parties can challenge the judgment when it is the effect of fraud or collusion to their detriment ('revocatory third party opposition', Article 404 paragraph 2 CPC). The opposition is filed before the same court that issued the judgment (Article 405 CPC). This means of challenging is also to be considered admissible against the judgment assessing on the recognition requirements. Although recognition operates automatically under Law 218/1995, it cannot be excluded that there could be third parties whose legal positions may be undermined by the ascertaining of the existence of the recognition requirements of a foreign judgment. However, even in this scenario, this means of challenge can only be exercised with reference to the subject of the Italian judgment and cannot in any way delve into the merits of the foreign judgment. However, a distinction needs to be drawn concerning the two modes of this means of challenging, the ordinary and the revocatory one. In relation to the proceeding ruling on the existence or not of the recognition requirements, the ordinary opposition of the third party who claims to be the holder of a right or a relationship irreconcilable with that which is the subject of the judgment seems to be excluded: if the object of the judgment in question is solely to ascertain the existence of the requirements (without any examination of the merits of the dispute decided abroad), a right or relationship that is irreconcilable with that which was the subject of the foreign ruling cannot be asserted. While there may certainly be third parties who would suffer prejudice from the verification of recognition requirements, the direct source of the prejudice is not the Italian judgment, rather the foreign one: therefore, the protection must be sought abroad with any means of challenging provided for by the country of origin of the judgment. These third parties, ultimately, will be able to assert their irreconcilable rights in Italy through different means such as ordinary cognition proceeding or by opposing the forced execution procedure.

[36] ibid 274 ff.

Remaining in this first typology under Article 404 paragraph 1 CPC, the ordinary third party opposition by the party, in the case of compulsory joinder of party, who did not participate in the proceeding to ascertain the recognition requirements can be considered admissible: in this scenario, the proceeding remains unchanged and the judgment is defected because it was issued in the absence of the necessary litigant, thus it must be eliminated and the assessment must be renewed, affording the latter the opportunity to assert his reasons. Unlike the first typology, there are no impediments to the admissibility of the revocatory third-party opposition (Article 404 paragraph 2 CPC) against the judgment verifying on the requirements. The right or relationship of which the third party claims to be the holder does not become part of the object of the proceeding, constituting only the basis for the prejudice. If the opposition is ruled founded, it results in the elimination of the judgment issued *inter alios* and the renewal of the proceeding verifying on the requirements.

This means of challenging, expressly provided only for creditors and assignees of one of the parties, is generally also extended to holders of relationships linked by a prejudicial-dependence relationship as they are subject to the 'reflected effect' of the judgment, but only when it is the effect of fraud or collusion to their detriment. Since fraud or collusion must concern the Italian judgment, it occurs only when the fraud or collusion between the parties take place during the proceeding to ascertain the requirements and concern the existence or absence of such requirements. Otherwise, fraud or collusion perpetrated in the foreign proceeding can be asserted by the third party only in the legal order of origin of the judgment through the means provided for by it, and its revocation, if any, will also have effect in Italy.[37]

Question 3. Requirements

As previously noted, in order for a judgment to be recognised in Italy, without the need to resort to any proceedings, Article 64 provides for the requirements it has to meet.[38]

a) Jurisdiction of the Court of Origin

Article 64 paragraph 1(a) Law 218/1995 requires that the court which issued the judgment could hear the case according to the principles of jurisdiction of the Italian legal order. The interpretation of this provision requires clarification. It is not expected that the court of origin will have relied upon jurisdiction criteria (even similar) in force in Italy in order to assess its jurisdiction. Rather, it means to let the recognition of foreign judgments subject to the condition that they originate from the country with which the dispute presents the kind of connections the Italian legal order requires its courts to use

[37] ibid 276 ff.

[38] *cf* P Franzina, *Introduzione al diritto internazionale privato* (Giappichelli, 2021) 285; F Mosconi and C Campiglio, *Diritto internazionale privato e processuale, Volume I, Parte generale e obbligazioni*, 10th edn (UTET, 2022) 395; G Conetti at al, *Manuale di diritto internazionale privato* (Giappichelli, 2020) 85; Conetti, Tonolo and Vismara (n 6) 313 ff.

in order to determine their jurisdiction when claims similar to the one decided abroad are brought before them. In essence, it is necessary for the foreign court to have what is commonly referred to as 'international jurisdiction' concerning the specific case, serving as a filter for recognisability.[39]

Challenges concerning the requirement of 'international jurisdiction' arise due to the evolving criteria that determine the jurisdiction of Italian courts. Since the adoption of Law 218/1995, these criteria have undergone significant changes, influenced by the substantial uniform international discipline and the European Union's growing competence in this field. These shifts have led to persistent interpretative difficulties in judicial practice, resulting in inconsistent rulings that contribute to significant legal uncertainty.[40]

The reference to the 'principles of international jurisdiction' within the Italian legal order raises complex issues regarding the identification of the sources from which these principles are derived. Following the enactment of Law 218/1995, it was clear that this reference pertained specifically to the jurisdictional criteria outlined within the provisions of Law 218/1995 itself. Hence, it is appropriate to refer to the connections Law 218/1995 identifies as relevant for the Italian jurisdiction to exist in civil and commercial matters.[41] The 'general' rule on jurisdiction is contained in Article 3 Law 218/1995, which provides for three separate rules:

(a) the Italian jurisdiction exists when the defendant is domiciled, resident or has a representative authorised to stand in trial in accordance with Article 77 CPC in Italy, and in other cases when it is provided by law;
(b) the Italian jurisdiction may additionally exist based on the criteria set forth in Sections 2, 3 and 4 of Title II of the 1968 Brussels Convention[42] and following amendments in force for Italy, even if the defendant is not domiciled in the territory of a contracting state, insofar as one of the matters falling within the scope of said Conventions is concerned;
(c) with respect to other matters, the jurisdiction also exists based on national rules on venue jurisdiction.

The other jurisdictional rules contained in Law 218/1995 are those on prorogation and derogation of jurisdiction (Article 4); actions concerning rights in rem in immovable

[39] See Corte di Cassazione, Sezione Civile I, 28 November 2022, no 34969, onelegale.wolterskluwer.it; Corte di Cassazione, Sezione Civile I, 10 December 2021, no 39391, (2022) *Riv dir int priv proc* 650; Corte di Cassazione, Sezioni Unite, 28 October 2015, no 21946, (2017) *Riv dir int priv proc* 382; Corte di Cassazione, Sezioni Unite, 28 May 2004, no 10378, (2005) *Riv dir int priv proc* 129; Corte di Cassazione, Sezioni Unite, 6 November 1996, no 9655, (1997) *Riv dir int priv proc* 948; Corte di Cassazione, Sezione Civile I, 21 April 1997, no 3411, (1997) *Riv dir int priv proc* 971; Corte d'Appello di Milano, 16 May 1997, (1997) *Riv dir int priv proc* 1087; Corte di Cassazione, Sezione Civile I, 14 January 2003, no 365, (2003) *Riv dir int priv proc* 201; Corte di Cassazione, Sezioni Unite, 23 September 2013, no 21672, (2014) *Riv dir int priv proc* 654.

[40] O Lopes Pegna, 'L'accertamento della «competenza internazionale» del giudice straniero ai sensi della legge n 218/1995' (2024) *Rivista di diritto internazionale* 77.

[41] For the complete legal framework, see E Piovesani and S Dominelli, 'Italy' in T Lutzi, E Piovesani and D Zgrabljić Rotar (eds), *Jurisdiction Over Non-EU Defendants: Should the Brussels Ia Regulation Be Extended?* (Hart Publishing 2023) 147 ff.

[42] 1968 Brussels Convention on jurisdiction and the enforcement of judgments in civil and commercial matters, Brussels, 27 September 1968, executed in Italy with Legge 21 June 1971 no 804, Gazzetta Ufficiale no 254 of 8 October 1971.

properties located in Italy (Article 5); preliminary questions (Article 6); protective measures (Article 10). Finally, some national rules on venue jurisdiction, relevant pursuant to Article 3 Law 218/1995, are found in the CPC and in the Code of Navigation.[43]

In the case of international conventions establishing jurisdictional criteria that are unilaterally 'rendered' applicable *erga omnes* by the Italian legislator,[44] the provisions referenced effectively undergo a 'transformation' into domestic rules. This occurs, for instance, through the aforementioned Article 3 paragraph 2 Law 218/1995, which references certain criteria set forth in the 1968 Brussels Convention. In such scenarios, it becomes possible to also consider the criteria established in these international instruments for purposes related to Article 64 paragraph 1(a) Law 218/1995, to the extent that they have been 'nationalised' into the domestic legal framework.

In the case of EU regulations establishing jurisdictional rules – Brussels Ia Regulation in civil and commercial matters – a deepened reasoning is required.

The applicability of (some and even) the criteria contained therein can be regarded as resolved, given that in the Italian legal order the 'expansion' provided by Article 3 paragraph 2 Law 218/1995 allows special jurisdictional grounds to apply even to defendants domiciled in non-EU states. However, the issue becomes more complex when identifying the jurisdictional criteria referenced by this provision. Since the 1968 Brussels Convention was first replaced by Brussels I Regulation[45] and subsequently by Brussels Ia Regulation, the Italian legislator has left Article 3 paragraph 2 Law 218/1995 unchanged. In the meantime, several jurisdictional provisions originally set forth in the Convention have been significantly revised. This has led to a critical question: should Article 3 paragraph 2 Law 218/1995 still be interpreted as referring to the jurisdictional grounds as they appeared in the 1968 Brussels Convention, or should it instead be applied in light of the subsequent revisions introduced by the Brussels I and Ia Regulations? For over 15 years, the Italian Supreme Court oscillated between these two interpretations, at times adhering to the original wording of the 'Convention' and at other times embracing its revised forms. In a recent ruling[46] aimed at resolving this ongoing uncertainty, the Court clarified that the reference in Article 3 paragraph 2 Law 218/1995 must be understood as extending to the jurisdictional rules as modified by the subsequent EU Brussels I and Ia Regulations.[47]

Regarding specific provisions of the Brussels Ia Regulation, such as those establishing exclusive jurisdiction (Article 24 Brussels Ia) – regardless of the defendant's domicile – referring to national criteria in areas covered by such criteria would be inconsistent with the underlying rationale of the framework at hand.

Another source of interpretative uncertainty lies in the rules governing acceptance and derogation of the jurisdiction of Italian courts. The question is whether, and to

[43] Regio Decreto of 30 March 1942 no 327, Codice della Navigazione, Gazzetta Ufficiale no 93 of 18 April 1942.

[44] F Marongiu Buonaiuti, 'Il rinvio della legge italiana di riforma del diritto internazionale privato alle convenzioni internazionali, tra adeguamento al mutato contesto normativo e strumentalità alla tutela dei valori ispiratori' (2021) *Riv dir int priv proc* 266.

[45] Council Regulation (EC) No 44/2001 of 22 December 2000 on jurisdiction and the recognition and enforcement of judgments in civil and commercial matters, OJ L 12/1, 16 January 2001.

[46] Corte di Cassazione, Sezioni Unite, 28 February 2024, no 5303, (2024) *Riv dir int* 921.

[47] P Franzina, 'Il rinvio ai criteri di giurisdizione della convenzione di Bruxelles: le Sezioni Unite pongono fine a una lunga stagione di incertezza' (2024) *Il diritto processuale civile italiano e comparato* 778.

what extent, these rules can be considered 'principles of international jurisdiction' for the purposes of Article 64 paragraph 1(a) Law 218/1995. A preferable approach is to include these principles through an 'indirect' application, similar to other jurisdictional criteria, as they also help define the scope of Italian judicial jurisdiction. Article 4 paragraph 1 Law 218/1995 provides that, when jurisdiction cannot be established under Article 3, it may still exist if the parties have contractually agreed to it and such agreement is proven in writing, or if the defendant appears in court without raising an objection to the lack of jurisdiction in their first defence. Furthermore, Article 4 paragraph 2 Law 218/1995 states that Italian jurisdiction may be contractually derogated in favour of a foreign court or foreign arbitration if the derogation is proven in writing and the case concerns disposable rights. The relevance of these provisions in assessing the 'international jurisdiction' is a source of uncertainty. The Italian Supreme Court has ruled in favour of recognising the significance of both express and tacit acceptance for the purposes of 'international jurisdiction' under Article 4 Law 218/1995.[48] In this context, it is also necessary to consider the impact of supranational rules that establish uniform discipline for the prorogation of jurisdiction. It appears reasonable to account for those rules that replace national ones, such as Article 25 Brussels Ia Regulation, which applies regardless of the parties' domicile.

Determining the extent to which the failure to challenge jurisdiction in the original proceedings impacts the assessment of 'international jurisdiction' presents significant complexities. Italian case law does not provide a uniform resolution to this issue. In some cases, rather than addressing the matter under the 'principles of international jurisdiction' pursuant to Article 64 paragraph 1(a) Law 218/1995, Italian courts have focused on whether such conduct creates an eventual 'preclusion', effectively preventing a party from contesting the lack of jurisdiction of the original court during proceedings to assess recognition requirements in Italy. The Italian Supreme Court recently reaffirmed this approach,[49] referencing an earlier ruling[50] that held the lack of jurisdiction under Article 64 paragraph 1(a) Law 218/1995 cannot be raised for the first time before an Italian court if such objections, when raised in a timely manner before the foreign court, could have invalidated its proceedings. The issue, however, is more nuanced as it involves two distinct objections: the foreign court's 'direct' jurisdiction (assessed in the original proceedings) and its 'indirect' or 'international' jurisdiction, which must be evaluated based on the principles of jurisdiction of the Italian legal order. For the purposes of determining the conditions for recognition, only the failure to raise an objection related to the latter (second) condition by the party opposing recognition in the recognition proceedings themselves should be considered relevant. Given that procedural rules governing these two (distinct) objections depend on the *lex fori* of their respective jurisdictions, the failure to contest jurisdiction in the original proceedings becomes a matter of verifying the existence of the foreign court's 'international jurisdiction' under the Italian jurisdiction principles. Specifically, the absence of an objection to the foreign court's jurisdiction may influence the evaluation of its 'international jurisdiction' if such conduct constitutes 'implicit' acceptance according to the relevant

[48] Corte di Cassazione, Sezione Civile I, 22 July 2004, no 13662, (2005) *Riv dir int* 516.

[49] Corte di Cassazione, Sezione Civile I, 28 November 2022, no 34969, onelegale.wolterskluwer.it. Later, see Corte di Cassazione, Sezioni Unite, 26 June 2023, no 18199, (2024) *Riv dir int priv proc* 236.

[50] Corte di Cassazione, Sezioni Unite, 28 October 2015, no 21946, (2017) *Riv dir int priv proc* 382.

parameters (ie according to Article 4 paragraph 1 Law 218/1995 or, if considered applicable, Article 26 Brussels Ia Regulation).[51]

b) Finality/Enforceability in the Country of Origin

Article 64 paragraph 1(d) Law 218/1995 requires that the judgment has become final according to the law of the place in which it was issued. Non-final judgments, even if enforceable in the country of origin, are radically unsuitable for recognition.[52]

c) *Res Iudicata*

Article 64 paragraph 1(e) Law 218/1995 requires the foreign judgment not to be contrary to another judgment issued by an Italian court which has become final. This condition is aimed at avoiding the risk that the recognition of a foreign judgment could lead to a conflict of judgments.[53]

d) *Lis Pendens*

Article 64 paragraph 1(f) Law 218/1995 requires that a proceeding is not pending before an Italian court involving the same cause of action and between the same parties, which began before the foreign proceeding. This requirement, akin to the preceding one, aims to avoid conflicts of judgments. The rules on *lis pendens*, whether provided for by uniform rules or domestic rules, should generally prevent the occurrence of such scenarios. Failure to adhere to these provisions renders the foreign judgment non-recognisable in Italy.[54]

e) Specific Requirements of Due Process

Article 64 paragraph 1(b) and Article 64 paragraph 1(c) Law 218/1995 concern the respect of the safeguards of due process in the foreign proceeding. Article 64 paragraph 1(b) Law 218/1995 requires that the defendant was served the document

[51] Lopes Pegna (n 40) 98.

[52] Corte d'Appello di Milano, 27 February 1998, (1999) *Riv dir int priv proc* 563; Corte di Cassazione, Sezione Civile I, 9 January 2004, no 115, (2004) *Riv dir int priv proc* 1377. *cf* F Carpi, 'Dal riconoscimento delle decisioni all'esecuzione automatica' (2005) *Rivista di diritto processuale* 1134.

[53] Corte di Cassazione, Sezione Civile I, 29 August 2018, no 21367, (2018) *Riv dir int priv proc* 1065; Corte di Cassazione, Sezioni Unite, 29 May 2008, no 14199, (2009) *Riv dir int priv proc* 425.

[54] Corte d'Appello di Milano, 28 December 1999, (2000) *Riv dir int priv proc* 1081; Corte di Cassazione, Sezione Civile III, 21 August 2018, no 20841, (2019) *Riv dir int priv proc* 176; Corte di Cassazione, Sezioni Unite, 28 November 2012, no 21108, (2013) *Riv dir int priv proc* 762; Corte di Cassazione, Sezione Civile I, 1 December 2016, no 24542, (2017) *Riv dir int priv proc* 1026; Corte di Cassazione, Sezione Civile I, 8 March 1995, no 2718, (1996) *Riv dir int priv proc* 124; Corte di Cassazione, Sezione Civile I, 21 October 1996, no 9153, (1997) *Riv dir int priv proc* 713.

which instituted the proceedings in accordance with the provisions of the law of the place where the proceeding took place and that the essential rights of defence were not violated. In addition, Article 64 paragraph 1(c) Law 218/1995 requires that the parties have appeared before the court according to the law of the place where the proceeding took place, or the default of appearance was declared in compliance with this law.

The condition of respect for the essential rights of defence cannot be considered satisfied if the rights of a fair trial have been disregarded in the foreign proceeding. In order to establish whether a violation of the essential rights of defence has occurred, it is necessary to proceed with a global evaluation of the foreign proceeding. Thus, even a significant violation of the safeguards to a fair trial does not affect the recognisability of the judgment if, during the foreign proceeding, it was possible to remedy the violation. Specifically, the rights of defence referred to under Article 64 (1)(b) are those recognised by Italian law. However, this does not mean that, to affirm the recurrence of a such violation, the evaluation parameter is represented by the Italian procedural rules: by referring to the 'essential' rights of defence, the legislator envisaged an evaluation based on the respect for the principles underlying procedural rules, rather than their specific declinations in domestic procedural law.[55]

f) Public Policy

Article 64 paragraph 1(g) Law 218/1995 requires that foreign judgment provisions do not produce effects contrary to public policy.[56] This term refers to a set of principles which, in a given historical moment, the Italian legal order regards as fundamental, to the extent that adherence to them takes precedence over embracing foreign legal principles incorporated in a judgment.[57] When this concept comes into play in relation to the effectiveness of a judgment, it involves a substantial and a procedural dimension.

To grasp its significance regarding the substantial dimension, let us consider the evolution in the Italian case law regarding the recognition of foreign decisions

[55] Corte di Cassazione, Sezione Civile II, 12 July 2023, no 19900, (2024) *Riv dir int priv proc* 959; Corte di Cassazione, Sezione Civile I, 29 September 2011, no 19932, (2013) *Riv dir int priv proc* 121; Corte di Cassazione, Sezione Civile I, 25 July 2006, no 16978, (2007) *Riv dir int priv proc* 432; Corte d'Appello di Roma, 12 April 2000, (2001) *Riv dir int priv proc* 126; Corte di Cassazione, Sezione Civile I, 11 July 2006, no 15730, onelegale.wolterskluwer.it; Corte di Cassazione, Sezione Civile I, 22 July 2004, no 13662, (2005) *Riv dir int priv proc* 152; Corte di Cassazione, Sezione Civile I, 17 February 2011, no 3919, (2011) *Riv dir int priv proc* 779; Corte di Cassazione, Sezione Civile I, 4 May 2009, no 10207, onelegale.wolterskluwer.it; Corte di Cassazione, Sezione Civile I, 18 July 2019, no 19453, (2020) *Riv dir int priv proc* 891; Corte di Cassazione, Sezione Civile I, 3 September 2015, no 17519, (2016) *Riv dir int priv proc* 785. *cf* A Carlevaris, 'Violazione dei diritti essenziali della difesa nel giudizio estero e rispetto del contraddittorio nel procedimento di riconoscimento delle sentenze straniere' (2005) *Riv dir int priv proc* 1017.

[56] Corte di Cassazione, Sezione Civile I, 24 March 2023, no 8462, (2024) *Riv dir int priv proc* 226.

[57] Corte di Cassazione, Sezione Civile I, 27 September 2012, no 16511, (2013) *Riv dir int priv proc* 447; Corte di Cassazione, Sezione Civile I, 12 January 2017, no 597, onelegale.wolterskluwer.it; Corte di Cassazione, Sezione Civile I, 3 September 2015, no 17519, (2016) *Riv dir int priv proc* 785; Corte di Cassazione, Sezione Civile III, 19 January 2007, no 1183, (2007) *Riv dir int priv proc* 777; Corte di Cassazione, Sezione Civile I, 15 April 2019, no 10540, (2019) *Riv dir int priv proc* 926; Corte di Cassazione, Sezione Civile VI, 15 June 2016, no 12364, (2017) *Riv dir int priv proc* 408; Corte di Cassazione, Sezione Civile I, 17 January 2013, no 1163, (2013) *Riv dir int priv proc* 465; Corte di Cassazione, Sezione Civile I, 7 August 2020, no 16804, (2021) *Riv dir int priv proc* 107; Corte di Cassazione, Sezione Civile I, 6 December 2002, no 17349 (2002) *Giur comm mass* 2133.

on the issue of punitive damages. These rulings afford to the responsibility of the perpetrator of an offence deemed particularly reprehensible a compensation obligation that exceeds, in amount, the repair of the damage suffered, for reasons, precisely, punitive or deterrence in nature. The contrary position traditionally held by Italian courts was reconsidered by the Court of Cassation in 2017.[58] The Court noted that even in the Italian legal order, as a result of various sectoral reforms, there are rules that allow ultra-compensation, and concluded the recognition of a foreign judgment for the payment of punitive damages does not conflict with public policy, provided it adheres to imperatives of Article 25 Italian Constitution given the punitive nature of the measure.

Conversely, to better understand the procedural dimension of public policy, let us consider the recognisability of a foreign judgment within the context of proceedings where a freezing injunction was granted. The Court of Cassation ruled that there is no violation of essential defence rights and guarantees under the Italian procedural public policy, which would justify the denial of recognition of a foreign judgment, merely because the judgment was rendered following proceedings during which the judgment debtor was subject to an *in personam* interim measure, granted *inaudita altera parte*, according to the English model of a freezing injunction. Recognition of a foreign judgment preceded by an interim measure can only be denied if the issuance of such a measure resulted in a violation of fundamental procedural guarantees, such that it significantly affected the right to defence throughout the entire trial.[59]

The limit of public policy – considered in both its substantive and procedural declinations – requires a prudent approach, consistent with its exceptional nature. Italian case law has shown considerable caution in this regard. Although the public policy exception is frequently invoked before Italian courts, it is actually applied in a relatively small number of cases.

g) Reciprocity

Law 218/1995 does not require any form of reciprocity. The recognition and enforcement of a foreign judgment is not dependent upon whether Italian judgments have been or will be enforced in the jurisdiction in which the foreign judgment was issued.

h) Other Requirements

No additional requirements are requested beyond those previously described.

[58] Corte di Cassazione, Sezioni Unite, 5 July 2017, no 16601, (2017) *Riv dir int priv proc* 1049; P Franzina, 'The purpose and operation of the public policy defence as applied to punitive damages' in S Bariatti, L Fumagalli and Z Crespi Reghizzi (eds), *Punitive Damages and Private International Law: State of the Art and Future Developments* (Wolters Kluver, 2019) 43.

[59] Corte di Cassazione, Sezione Civile I, 16 September 2021, no 25064, (2022) *Riv dir int priv proc* 355; P Franzina, 'La concessione di una freezing injunction non preclude la riconoscibilità in Italia della successiva sentenza di merito resa nel medesimo giudizio' (2022) *Trust e Attività fiduciarie*, 356.

Question 4. Documents to be Produced[60]

Law 218/1995 *does not explicitly indicate the list of documents that shall be produced.*

It is crucial, however, to produce the *foreign judgment* being the subject of the assessment request pursuant to Article 67 Law 218/1995. Since Law 218/1995 does not expressly require the legalisation of the judgment, it could be deduced that the production of a certified copy is sufficient. Nevertheless, the Court of Cassation ruled on this point giving a more rigid solution, establishing that, in the silence of the law, the problem of conformity with the original or authenticity of the document produced shall be resolved by the Court of Appeal with the correct application of the international standards implemented and presupposed by Law 218/1995.[61] Therefore, according to the Court of Cassation, in application of the Convention of 5 October 1961 Abolishing the Requirement of Legalisation for Foreign Public Documents ('HCCH 1961 Apostille Convention'),[62] the exemption from the legalisation of a foreign judgment is conditional on the release by the designated authority of 'Apostille'. HCCH 1961 Apostille Convention limits itself to exempting documents from the authorities of the state parties from the requirement of legalisation, replacing it with the formality of the 'Apostille'.

However, it does not appear that HCCH 1961 Apostille Convention can be interpreted in the sense of always requiring the 'Apostille' on foreign public documents, regardless of whether domestic legislation provides for such a requirement. HCCH 1961 Apostille Convention in Article 3 paragraph 2 establishes:

> However, the formality mentioned in the preceding paragraph cannot be required when either the laws, regulations, or practice in force in the State where the document is produced or an agreement between two or more Contracting States have abolished or simplified it, or exempt the document itself from legalisation.

And the Explanatory Report makes it clear that 'The requirement of the certificate is optional. The State in whose territory the document is to be produced is thus free not to require it for documents of one category or another'.

To conclude, the issue at hand is to determine whether the Italian legal order requires the formality of legalisation of signatures on foreign judgments. Legislative Decree 28 December 2000 no 443[63] in Article 33 paragraph 2 establishes that signatures on acts and documents drafted abroad by foreign authorities and to be valid in the Italian state are legalised by Italian diplomatic or consular representations abroad. In the absence of specific guidance in Article 67 Law 218/1995, it is from this aforementioned provision which, if necessary, can result a general legalisation obligation, without prejudice to any special conventions (multilateral or biliteral) on the matter.

[60] Lopes Pegna (n 15) 145.

[61] Corte di Cassazione, Sezione Civile I, 28 March 2003, no 4742, (2004) *Riv dir int priv proc* 1070.

[62] Convention of 5 October 1961 Abolishing the Requirement of Legalisation for Foreign Public Documents, executed in Italy with Legge 20 December 1966 no 1253, Gazzetta Ufficiale no 26 of 30 January 1967.

[63] Decreto Legislativo of 28 December 2000 no 443, Gazzetta Ufficiale no 42 of 20 February 2001, Supplemento Ordinario no 30.

The other relevant aspect (and document) to deal with is the *translation of the judgment.* As a general principle, documents drafted in foreign languages can also be produced in the original language, without translation. From Articles 122 paragraph 1 and 123 CPC, it can be deduced that the use of the Italian language is required only for procedural documents in the strict sense, and not also for the documents produced by the parties. If the court is proficient in the foreign language, a translation may be unnecessary; the court will request translation only if it deems it essential. This principle is also applicable in matters of recognition of foreign judgments. However, in coherence with the aforementioned stricter jurisprudential interpretation regarding the applicability of the obligation of legalisation (or the need of 'Apostille' on judgments originating from states parties to the HCCH 1961 Apostille Convention), Article 33 paragraph 3 Legislative Decree 28 December 2000 no 443 should also be applied. It establishes that the acts and documents referred to in paragraph 2 drafted in a foreign language shall be accompanied by a translation into Italian certified as compliant with the foreign text by the competent diplomatic or consular representation or by an official translator. This burden of allegation has not generally been considered applicable in matters of recognition of foreign judgments by the case law.

Question 5. Securities, Bonds and Deposits

The applicant, in the specific proceeding for recognition of foreign judgments under Law 218/1995, is not required to provide securities, bonds or deposits.

Generally, CPC addresses bail in a singular rule – Article 119 CPC – according to which the court, in the order by which it imposes a security, must outline the object of the security, the method of providing it, and the timeframe within which it must be provided.

Latvia

ALEKSANDRS FILLERS AND IVAN ALLEGRANTI*

Question 1. General Overview

The recognition and enforcement of non-EU judgments is governed by the Latvian Civil Procedure Law (*Civilprocesa likums*)[1] (CPL),[2] to the degree that it is not governed by international conventions. Hence, the legal requirements are concentrated in one legal act. Currently, Latvia also has seven bilateral treaties on judicial assistance. These are with the following non-EU states: Ukraine, Belarus, Kirgizstan, Moldova and Uzbekistan.[3] A similar treaty with the Russian Federation was denounced by Latvia in 2024. There is also a bilateral treaty with Poland and a tripartite treaty with Estonia and Lithuania. These treaties have their own rules on recognition/enforcement of judgments that take precedence over national legislation. For Estonia, Lithuania and Poland, of course, this is relevant only so far as judgments in question fall outside the scope of application of the EU regime of recognition and enforcement of judgments. The authors are unaware of any cases when courts would have applied the HCCH 2005 Choice of Court Agreement Convention and the HCCH 2019 Judgments Convention.

It is important to note that, in principle, Latvia has a single procedure for recognition and enforcement of foreign judgments. Grounds for refusal are also identical. However, the CPL provides special provision aimed exclusively at enforcement. For example, Section 643 provides that a judge can grant interim measures to secure enforcement of a foreign judgment (or to be more precise of *exequatur*), Section 644[1] deals with postponement, division into time periods, and other adaptions of a foreign judgment.

Moreover, the CPL expressly describes only a procedure for a self-standing recognition/enforcement of a foreign decision. Scholars, however, acknowledge that

* Aleksandrs Fillers worked on questions 1, 3 and 4. Ivan Allegranti worked on questions 2, 5 and 6.

[1] Civil Procedure Law of the Republic of Latvia, adopted 14 October 1998, in force on 1 March 1999, published in Latvijas Vēstnesis [Herald of Latvia] No 326/330, 03 November 1998, likumi.lv/ta/en/en/id/50500-civil-procedure-law#_ftn1&pd=1.

[2] B Rudevska, 'Latvia' in J Basedow et al (eds), *Encyclopedia of Private International Law* (Edward Elgar Publishing Limited, 2017) 2252.

[3] The list of treaties is available at www.tm.gov.lv/lv/starptautiskais-regulejums-tiesiskas-palidzibas-ligumi-ar-krievijas-federaciju-ukrainu-baltkrievi?utm_source=https%3A%2F%2Fwww.google.com%2F. However, it is not updated and fails to mention that on 18 January 2024, the Latvian parliament decided to denounce a similar treaty with the Russian Federation. See: saeima.lv/en/news/saeima-news/33051-saeima-denounces-treaty-with-russia-on-legal-assistance.

recognition of a foreign decision could also take place within the scope of existing litigation of another dispute,[4] such as when the issue decided in a foreign judgment serves as a preliminary issue in an ongoing Latvian procedure. Scholars consider that in such an event, the Latvian court in question is competent to receive the application for the recognition of a foreign judgment and decide whether to recognise the judgment,[5] even though the CPL does not regulate this situation. Similarly, the CPL provides only a positive procedure: a person can apply for recognition and enforcement of a foreign judgment. However, there is no negative procedure: a person cannot apply to ask the court to declare that the foreign judgment is not recognisable in Latvia.[6]

Before we move to specific questions, it is necessary to observe that in Latvia, judgments in civil cases decided in open (public) proceedings are published online.[7] However, in Latvian terminology, a judgment is only a decision that resolves the substance of the dispute. Other types of rulings are decisions. Decisions do not resolve the merits of the case. For instance, procedural decisions are not judgments. For the purposes of this study, it is important to note that applications for recognition/enforcement of foreign judgments are likewise decided in the form of decisions since the dispute is already decided by the court of origin. Courts have no obligation to publish such decisions. Hence, most of them remain unknown. As a result, the authors of this report cannot base their conclusions on the case law with just a few examples from practice available to the broader public.

The scarcity of published case law is accompanied by an extreme scarcity of literature dealing with the recognition and enforcement of foreign judgments outside the EU or international treaty regimes. The most relevant source is the commentary on the CPL. In fact, it is almost the only source that actually explains the application of the relevant CPL provisions; there are hardly any other publications.

Question 2. Procedure

a) Circumstances of Recognition and Enforcement

The procedure for recognition and enforcement of judgments is set out in the CPL. Section 638 describes the steps that the applicant must take. Normally, the applicant must submit an application for recognition and enforcement, meaning that it requires

[4] K Torgāns, *Civilprocesa likuma komentāri. III daļa (61.-86.nodaļa)* (Tiesu namu aģentūra, 2014) 635; B Rudevska, *Ārvalstu tiesu nolēmumu atzīšanas un izpildes attīstības tendences civillietās un komerclietās Eiropas Savienībā un Hāgas Starptautisko privāttiesību konferencē* (PhD thesis, 2012) 96.

[5] Torgāns (n 4) 635; Rudevska (n 4) 96.

[6] Torgāns (n 4) 641–42.

[7] Section $28^2(5)$ of the Law 'On Judicial Power', adopted 15 December 1992, in force 1 January 1993, published in Latvijas Republikas Augstākās Padomes un Valdības Ziņotājs [Reporter of the Republic of Latvia Supreme Soviet and Government], No 1/2, 14 January 1933, likumi.lv/ta/en/en/id/62847-on-judicial-power. It is important to underline that while the law 'On Judicial Power' was adopted in 1992, Section $28^2(5)$ was adopted in 2013. According to Section 11(3) CPL, a court may declare that the case will be heard in a closed hearing in order to protect several interests, eg, trade secrets or interests of a minor.

a formal procedure. The CPL does not expressly discuss the possibility of recognition within another procedure. However, as mentioned above, scholars suggest that when the recognition is a preliminary issue in a separate litigation, the court hearing the dispute must be able to decide the question of recognition. Nonetheless, this is currently a doctrinal construct that is not directly represented in the CPL.

With regard to enforcement, Section 644(1) CPL states that 'A ruling of a foreign court, which is to be enforced in the state wherein it was given, after its recognition shall be enforced in accordance with the procedures laid down in this Law.' This may create an erroneous impression that the foreign judgment is enforced directly in Latvia. However, scholars have underlined that it is never a foreign judgment (unless provided by an EU or international source) that is enforced, but rather a local decision (*exequatur*) that permits the enforcement of the foreign judgment.[8] Hence, a local decision is *a conditio sine qua non* for enforcement of foreign judgments.[9]

b) Procedural Steps

A judgment creditor who wants to have a foreign judgment recognised or enforced in Latvia must submit an application to the district court of the place where the judgment is to be enforced or at the place where the defendant – a natural person – has a declared address or, in case of its absence, domicile or where the defendant – a legal person – has a legal address. Hence, the applicant can choose between these domestic courts.

It is at this stage that it is possible to identify a difference between recognition/enforcement and pure recognition procedures. The place of enforcement as a venue is relevant only if the applicant requests the local court to enforce the decision. The remaining grounds for venue might likewise work for judgments that the applicant does not want to (or cannot) enforce. However, in case the applicant exclusively requests recognition, and the defendant has no declared address/domicile or legal address, the only solution proposed by scholars is to rely on the applicant by analogy to Section 31[1] CPL[10] and to submit the application to any district court in Latvia.[11]

Pursuant to Section 640 CPL, the decision on recognition and enforcement of a foreign judgment is taken by a single judge on the basis of the application submitted by the applicant and documents attached to that application. Neither the applicant nor the judgment debtor is invited to participate in this procedure. In other words, the decision is taken by a single judge ex parte on the basis of the application and the documents submitted by the applicant without the involvement of the defendant.[12]

[8] Torgāns (n 4) 703–04.

[9] *cf* ibid 704.

[10] Section 31[1] CPL states: 'If in accordance with the international agreements binding upon the Republic of Latvia and legal norms of the European Union a case is within the jurisdiction of a Latvian court, however, the provisions of this Law regarding jurisdiction do not provide for the court before which an action should be brought, a plaintiff may bring an action before any Latvian court of his or her choice in conformity with the provisions of Sections 23 and 24 of this Law.'

[11] Torgāns (n 4) 634–35.

[12] ibid 656–58.

Moreover, the decision must be rendered during the period of 10 days (Section 640 CPL).

Concerning the burden of proof, as stated before, the application for recognition/enforcement is subject to ex parte proceedings. The judge makes a decision on the basis of the submitted documents. Hence, in principle, all the grounds for non-recognition/non-enforcement can be invoked by a judge *sua sponte* (*ex officio*).[13]

Concerning the potential review of the decision on recognition/enforcement, Section 641(1) CPL provides that:

> In respect of a decision of a court of first instance in the case regarding recognition of a ruling of a foreign court, an ancillary complaint may be submitted to the regional court, and a decision by the regional court on an ancillary complaint may be appealed to the Supreme Court by submitting an ancillary complaint.

This means that either of the parties can appeal the decision of the district court to the Regional Court. The decision of the Regional Court can be further appealed to the Supreme Court of the Republic of Latvia.

Complaints can be submitted both about a positive and a negative decision.[14] It is at the stage of review where the defendant can submit their arguments and evidence supporting the refusal of recognition/enforcement. In fact, the CPL goes even further. Section 642(2) CPL provides that 'The [regional] court may request explanations from the parties or additional information from the foreign court that had made the ruling.' This is understood to mean that during the first ancillary complaint[15] procedure, the regional court has a right to request necessary information (be it documents, explanations, or other proof) *sua sponte*.[16] Such information may be necessary for the regional court to decide that the foreign judgment cannot be recognised/enforced in Latvia, in particular, when it is contrary to the Latvian public policy.

Regarding the scope of review of the foreign judgment, it is provided in Section 637(4) that in deciding an issue on whether, in conformity with Section 637(2), a court ruling is to be recognised, the judge or court shall be guided by the circumstances, which are established by the ruling of the foreign court. It follows that the court cannot review the facts of the case. Thus, the Supreme Court has ruled that the Latvian court at the stage of recognition and enforcement, must take into account that the foreign court, in the judgment, established that the parties have been informed about the original court proceedings.[17] Based on Section 637(4) and the absence of any ground in Section 673(2) that allows the court to review the merits of the foreign decision, scholars consider that the Latvian court is prohibited from reviewing the merits of the foreign decision.[18]

[13] ibid 657.
[14] ibid 667.
[15] The term 'ancillary complaint' is used for the same reason that the decision in question is not called a judgment. Since the decision does not resolve the substantive issue, then it cannot be appealed pursuant to the CPL terminology. Instead, it can be reviewed following an 'ancillary complaint'.
[16] Torgāns (n 4) 684.
[17] Supreme Court of the Republic of Latvia (Latvijas Republikas Augstākā tiesa), 16 December 2021, Decision n° C33530920 (SKC-1232/2021).
[18] Torgāns (n 4) 617.

Question 3. Requirements

Section 636(1) CPL states that a decision by a foreign court within the meaning of the CPL are: 1) judgments made by foreign courts in which the issue of dispute between the parties has been tried on the merits; and 2) out-of-court settlements from a foreign country court.[19] This provides an important requirement for recognition/enforcement: a foreign decision of a procedural nature (eg, decisions on interim measures) cannot be recognised/enforced in Latvia.[20] Thus, the Supreme Court refused to recognise and enforce a decision rendered in Switzerland concerning attorney fees following an unsuccessful attempt to set aside an arbitration award in Switzerland. The Supreme Court considered that the decision concerned arbitration and thus was not subject to the Lugano Convention. However, it was likewise not enforceable in Latvia on the basis of the CPL as it dealt with a procedural issue of attorney fees and did not resolve any actual dispute on merits.[21]

Other requirements are formulated in a negative manner in Section 637(2) which contains a list of the grounds that serve as obstacles to the recognition/enforcement of a foreign judgment in Latvia.[22] It is enough if the foreign judgment fails to meet one of the criteria listed for recognition/enforcement to be refused.

a) Jurisdiction of the Court of Origin

Section 637(2)(1) states that the recognition/enforcement is to be refused if a foreign court that issued the ruling did not have the necessary jurisdiction according to Latvian law to examine the dispute, or such dispute falls under the exclusive jurisdiction of the Latvian courts. Scholars insist that this assessment is done based on Latvian jurisdictional rules.[23]

[19] Section 636(2) also equates to foreign judgments 'rulings from foreign competent authorities, being enforceable in their native land and subject to recognition in alignment with the European Union's direct legal standards or treaties binding the Republic of Latvia.'

[20] Torgāns (n 4) 580.

[21] Supreme Court of the Republic of Latvia (Latvijas Republikas Augstākā tiesa), 29 June 2018, Decision n° C30499317 (SKC-781/2018).

[22] Torgāns (n 4) 602.

[23] ibid 605. The commentary underlines that only Latvian rules of jurisdiction are to be taken into account, although in a previous page it generally observes that jurisdictional rules can be unified at international or EU level. However, recently it was suggested in academic literature that Latvian *lex fori* jurisdictional rules should include EU jurisdictional rules. See: I Kačevska and A Fillers, 'Ārvalstu spriedumu atzīšana un izpilde Latvijas nacionālajās tiesībās: Atsevišķi problēmjautājumi' in *Likumdošana un tās rezultāts Latvijā: pagātnes mācības, mūsdienu tendences, problēmas un risinājumi. Latvijas Universitātes 82. staarptautiskās zinātniskās konferences tiesību zinātnes rakstu krājums* (LU Akadēmiskais apgāds, 2024) 14–17. The opinion can be illustrated by the following example: the CPL does not establish exclusive jurisdiction for the tenancy claims over immovable property. The Brussels Ibis Regulation does (Art 21(1)). In Latvia, a case involving cross-border tenancy of immovable property could be decided only based on Art 21(1) of the Brussels Ibis Regulation. It might seem illogical to ignore the Brussels Ibis Regulation when assessing compliance with the Latvian jurisdictional rules at the stage of recognition/enforcement of a foreign judgment. However, currently, this is just a very tentative suggestion made by scholars. There are no indications in the case law, known to the authors of this report, suggesting the application of the EU jurisdictional rules. Hence, for practical purposes, currently, the CPL is subject to jurisdictional control of foreign judgment to the Latvian domestic rules on jurisdiction. Domestic both because they emanate from domestic legislation and because their primary focus is to determine local jurisdiction.

Hence, the CPL clearly prioritises the allocation of jurisdiction as understood by Latvian law. Thus, if according to the Latvian law, jurisdiction was vested into the Latvian court or a court of the state other than the one that issued the ruling, that is a ground for refusal of recognition/enforcement. In fact, one could even question if the separate reference to the exclusive jurisdiction in this context is not redundant; clearly, when the Latvian court has exclusive jurisdiction under the Latvian law all other courts lack jurisdiction from the perspective of the said law.

Concerning the specific connecting factors for jurisdiction, it should be observed that Section 29(1) CPL mentions that

> an action for the ownership rights or any other property rights to immovable property or accessories thereof, or an action for registration of such rights in the land register or extinguishment of such rights and exclusion of property from the inventory statement shall be brought based on the location of the property.[24]

However, specific laws could provide for other cases of exclusive jurisdiction.[25]

It is necessary to mention that the CPL does not contain special rules for international jurisdiction: the international jurisdiction of Latvian courts is determined using the exact same rules that determine territorial jurisdiction in domestic cases.[26] This means that rules that are primarily aimed at domestic situations are likewise determining international jurisdiction. Latvian jurisdictional rules then must be bilateralised to determine which foreign court is competent to hear the case from the Latvia's perspective.[27] There is hardly any court practice known to the authors of actually performing this bilateralisation. And it could be a rather ambiguous exercise. For instance, Section 26(1) CPL provides that 'Actions against natural persons shall be brought before a court based on their declared place of residenc,' while Section 27(1) CPL states that 'An action against a defendant who does not have a declared place of residence shall be brought based on their place of residence.' Section 27(2) adds:

> An action against a defendant whose place of residence is unknown or who has no permanent place of residence in Latvia shall be brought before a court based on the location of their immovable property or their last known place of residence.

When the Latvian court has to determine local jurisdiction, it would most likely regard these rules as a part of a cascade: if one rule does not establish jurisdiction, then the next is employed. But if so, then the next rule in line is relevant only if the first one does not apply. Hence, let us imagine that a person has a declared address in Latvia, but its

[24] Section 29(2) concerns succession and states that 'Where the confirmed heirs to an inheritance or the heirs who have accepted an inheritance are unknown, jurisdiction with respect to actions of creditors regarding the whole estate lies in the court based on the declared place of residence or place of residence of the estate-leaver, but, if the declared place of residence or place of residence of the estate-leaver is not in Latvia or is unknown – in the court based on the location of the property of the estate or a part thereof.'

[25] Section 29(3).

[26] I Allegranti and A Fillers, 'Latvia' in T Lutzi, E Piovesani and D Zgrabljić Rotar (eds), *Jurisdiction Over Non-EU Defendants: Should the Brussels Ia Regulation be Extended?* (Hart Publishing, 2023) 159; B Rudevska, 'Latvia' in J Basedow et al (eds), *Encyclopedia of Private International Law* (Edward Elgar Publishing Limited, 2017) 2253. See also: Torgāns, *Civilprocesa likuma komentāri. I daļa (1.-28.nodaļa)* (Tiesu namu aģentūra, 2016) 102.

[27] Torgāns (n 4) 606.

actual place of residence is in Japan, while it also owns immovable property in China. Could the court conclude that only the Latvian court was competent to hear the case? Or would Japanese and Chinese courts likewise be competent? There seems to be no established answer to this question in scholarship or court practice.

b) Finality/Enforceability in the Country of Origin

Section 637(2)(2) provides that the court must refuse recognition/enforcement if the ruling of a foreign court has not entered into lawful effect. The assessment should be done from the point of view of the law of the court that rendered the decision.[28] This provision has been applied by Latvian courts whose practice is available to the broader public. Thus, one regional court heard an ancillary complaint about the decision of the district court concerning the recognition/enforcement of a judgment from Russia.[29] The judgment in question was a court decision from Moscow confirmed by the Russian Appellate Court. However, the regional court observed that the same Russian Appellate Court had annulled its previous ruling based on newly discovered facts. The regional court considered that to mean that the original ruling by the Moscow court lost its legal force. Hence, there was no ruling that had entered into lawful effect to be recognized/enforced in Latvia. In another case – though it was a family law dispute – the Supreme Court noted that the Israeli ruling had been annulled in Israel due to significant procedural violations.[30] As a result, the Supreme Court decided that it was not subject to recognition/enforcement.

c) *Res Iudicata*

Similarly to the Brussels Regime, the CPL has two provisions dealing with the irreconcilability of decisions. Firstly, the CPL deals with irreconcilability between foreign decisions. Section 637(2)(5) states that recognition/enforcement is to be refused if the ruling of the foreign court is not compatible with such ruling of another foreign court, which has already been given earlier and has entered into lawful effect, in the same dispute between the same parties, which may be recognised or is already recognised in Latvia. However, the problem with the requirement is that the decision on recognition/enforcement is made ex parte during 10 days, hence a judge might be unaware of incompatible decisions already recognised in Latvia and much more so of those that satisfy the requirements for recognition/enforcement. Hence, this ground could be more apt for assessment once the decision of the District Court is reviewed by the Regional Court and the party opposing recognition/enforcement can provide information to the relevant court.[31]

[28] Torgāns (n 4) 606.

[29] Riga Regional Court Chamber of Civil Cases (Rīgas apgabaltiesas Civillietu tiesas kolēģija), 22 February 2016, Decision n° C33501114.

[30] Supreme Court of the Republic of Latvia (Latvijas Republikas Augstākā tiesa), 3 November 2022, Decision n° C33530920 (SKC-904/2022).

[31] Torgāns (n 4) 615.

Secondly, the CPL deals with irreconcilability between a foreign decision and a Latvian decision. Section 637(2)(4) provides that recognition/enforcement is to be refused if the ruling of the foreign court is not compatible with a court ruling already given earlier and entered into lawful effect in Latvia in the same dispute between the same parties or with already earlier commenced court proceedings between the same parties in a Latvian court. In the first scenario, it is important that the Latvian court has already rendered a decision before the foreign decision was rendered, but the Latvian decision must have entered into force by the moment when the Latvian court has to decide upon recognition/enforcement of a foreign decision.[32] The same section also deals with the *lis pendens* issues that will be described in the next sub-section.

d) *Lis Pendens*

The CPL has no provision that would extend the prohibition of recognising/enforcing a judgment when the identical dispute is pending before any foreign court. However, it does cover a *lis pendens* situation between a dispute decided in a foreign decision and pending proceedings in Latvia. As mentioned above, Section 637(2)(4) also provides that recognition/enforcement is to be refused if the ruling of the foreign court is not compatible with court proceedings already commenced between the same parties in a Latvian court. The provision does not explain what it means by 'earlier commenced court proceedings'. Scholars argue that the litigation abroad must have been initiated before the litigation in Latvia in order for the foreign decision to be recognisable and enforceable.[33] If the litigation was first initiated abroad, but parallel litigation in Latvia was initiated before an application for recognition and enforcement was submitted to a Latvian court, this should not be an obstacle to recognition/enforcement of that foreign decision. However, there is a risk that courts might understand the *lis pendens* extensively and refuse a recognition and enforcement of a foreign decision simply because proceedings in Latvia were initiated before the application for recognition and enforcement was submitted in Latvia.

e) Specific Requirements of Due Process

The decision of a foreign court, according to Section 637(2)(3) cannot be recognised in Latvia if the defendant was not granted the opportunity to defend his or her rights, particularly when the defendant, who did not engage in the examination of the case, was not appropriately informed in good time about the court appearance, unless the defendant did not contest such ruling despite having the opportunity to do so. It is clear that this provision is an almost verbatim copy of Article 34(2) of the Brussels I Regulation[34] and has rather similar content. Nonetheless, the provision is broader as it extends to situations when the defendant had participated in the proceedings, but was

[32] ibid 613.
[33] ibid 614.
[34] ibid 607.

prevented from defending itself, eg, submitting evidence or expressing its views during the hearing.[35]

Moreover, the duty of notification in this provision is not tied to the 'document which instituted the proceedings' as in Article 34(2) of the Brussels I Regulation. Rather, the defendant must simply be informed in a timely manner about the time and place of the proceedings.[36] If such information is provided then it had to be provided timely so that the defendant had an opportunity to actually prepare for defence.[37] If there was no notification whatsoever, then the ruling clearly violated the provision in question,[38] unless the defendant was informed about the ruling and its content in a timely manner that allowed it to appeal to it.

f) Public Policy

The CPL also contains a public policy exemption. Section 637(2)(6) states that the recognition/enforcement should be refused if 'the ruling of the foreign court is in conflict with the public structure of Latvia'. The rather clunky language of the translation of this provision actually means that foreign judgments in conflict with Latvian public policy must not be recognised or enforced. In principle, that is a rather standard provision. Scholars underline that neither Section 637(2)(6) nor any other allows a Latvian court to review a foreign ruling on merits.[39] The public policy violation can concern both the substantive and procedural effects of the foreign judgment.[40] Regarding procedural public policy, Section 637(2)(6) is a *lex generalis* in relation to Section 637(2)(3); hence the judge must first assess whether the judgment complies with Section 637(2)(3) and only if it does comply, assess its compliance with the procedural aspect of public policy.[41]

g) Reciprocity

Not applicable.

h) Other Requirements

Finally, Section 637(2)(7) contains the most archaic obstacle to recognition/enforcement.[42] It provides that recognition/enforcement must be refused if 'in giving

[35] ibid 607.
[36] ibid 608.
[37] ibid 607–08.
[38] ibid 609.
[39] ibid 617.
[40] ibid 617–18.
[41] ibid 618–19.
[42] For a more extensive critique of this provision, see I Kačevska and A Fillers, 'Ārvalstu spriedumu atzīšana un izpilde Latvijas nacionālajās tiesībās: Atsevišķi problēmjautājumi' in *Likumdošana un tās rezultāts Latvijā: pagātnes mācības, mūsdienu tendences, problēmas un risinājumi. Latvijas Universitātes 82. starptautiskās zinātniskās konferences tiesību zinātnes rakstu krājums* (LU Akadēmiskais apgāds, 2024) 17–23.

the ruling of the foreign court, the law of such state was not applied as should have been applied in conformity with the rules on conflict of laws of the Latvian international private law'. The concept of 'conflict of laws of the Latvian international private law' is not limited to national conflict-of-laws rules but extends to those arising from EU law or international conventions.[43] If the national conflict-of-laws rules are applied, then it also includes the *renvoi*.[44]

If applied literally, then any foreign judgment applying different substantive law than required by Latvian conflict-of-laws or EU conflict-of-laws rules does not qualify for recognition/enforcement. Scholars have argued that the provision should find no application if the difference in applicable law does not result in a difference in outcomes.[45] This, however, means that the Latvian court must de facto re-decide the dispute to come to a conclusion about how the case would have been solved under the law applicable pursuant to conflict-of-laws rules binding on the Latvian court and how it was actually decided in the foreign judgment. And this exercise should be done ex parte during the 10-day period. Moreover, this exercise would not be necessary if the foreign court decided the case in accordance with the law that – possibly by accident – would also apply had the case been heard in Latvia.

Overall, the ratio of Section 637(2)(7) seems hard to explain. It can serve only as a rather random mechanism of restricting recognition/enforcement of foreign judgments. It is questionable why a foreign judgment that does not contradict Latvian public policy should be rejected simply on the basis of the law applicable being different from that applied by Latvian courts. At the same time, there is no data showing how often Section 637(2)(7) is used by courts –and, if and when it is used, how strictly it is applied. Therefore, it is not clear to what degree it serves as an actual obstacle to the recognition/enforcement of foreign judgments.

Question 4. Documents to be Produced

Pursuant to Section 638 CPL, a number of documents need to be attached to the application of recognition/enforcement. In fact, Section 638(6) explicitly mentions that the application must list all the attached documents. Section 638(3) specifies that the application must have attached following documents:

1) a ruling of a foreign court with a statement certifying that the ruling has entered into lawful effect;
2) a document issued by a foreign court which certifies that the defendant, who has not participated in the examination of the case, was notified of the time and place of examination of the case in a timely and proper manner;

[43] Torgāns (n 4) 622.
[44] ibid 627; Rudevska (n 4) 198.
[45] Torgāns (n 4) 627. Interestingly, Section 637(2)(6) does not mention that the conflict with the public policy must be 'manifest'. Scholars seem to make no specific conclusion from the absence of this term. In practice, however, its absence could be potentially used to argue that a conflict of lesser magnitude should be sufficient to deny recognition/enforcement.

3) a document issued by a foreign court or a competent authority regarding the enforcement of the ruling if the ruling of the foreign court is already partially enforced;
4) a document issued by a foreign court, which certifies that a ruling of the foreign court is to be enforced in the state wherein it was given if the applicant requests the recognition and enforcement of the ruling of the foreign court;
5) a translation into the official language of the application and the documents certified according to specific procedures referred to in Clauses 1-3 of this Paragraph;
6) a document, which certifies the payment of the State fee according to the procedures and in the amount laid down in law.

In addition, Section 638(4) states that the application must be signed by the applicant or its representative. In the latter case, an authorisation or another document certifying the authorisation of the representative to apply to the court with an application must be attached to the application.

Section 638(3) deserves a few remarks. Firstly, the statement certifying that the ruling has entered into lawful effect can be a separate document or a statement at the end of the foreign judgment indicating that it has entered into force.[46] Secondly, in a similar manner, a document certifying a timely notice to the defendant might be missing if this information is indicated in the judgment in question.[47] Thirdly, obviously some of these documents do not need to be attached in all cases: Section 638(3)(3) only applies if the judgment was already partially enforced in the state of origin; Section 638(3)(4) only applies if the applicant wants to enforce the judgment (and not only to recognise it).[48]

Section 638(3)(5) makes it clear that the application itself, a foreign judgment and statement of entry into force; document certifying notification of the defendant, and certificate of enforceability must be submitted both in their original language and their translation in Latvian.[49] Moreover, the translation of foreign judgment and the statement of entry into force, statement of notice, and certificate of enforceability must be certified.[50] The certification of the translation can be performed by a Latvian notary or a Latvian translator who has translated the text.[51]

Concerning some of the documents, Section 638(3)(5) is ambiguous. The application for recognition/enforcement is, in principle, expected to be in Latvian.[52] However, even if it is submitted in a foreign language with the translation in Latvian, it is surprising that Section 638(3)(5) does not require the translation to be certified. Bearing in mind that Section 13(2) contains the most general rule that 'The participants in the case shall submit foreign language documents by attaching a translation thereof into the official language certified in accordance with the specified procedures.' Similarly, it

[46] Torgāns (n 4) 644.
[47] ibid 644.
[48] ibid 645.
[49] The application itself must also be in Latvian.
[50] Section 638(3)(5).
[51] Section 10(3) of the Official Language Law, adopted 9 December 1999, in force on 1 September 2000, published in Latvijas Vēstnesis [Herald of Latvia] No 428/433, 21 December 1999, likumi.lv/ta/en/en/id/14740-official-language-law, and Art 6 of the Republic of Latvia Cabinet Regulation No 291 'Procedures for the Certification of Document Translations in the Official Language', adopted 22 August 2000, in force on 1 September 2000, published in Latvijas Vēstnesis [Herald of Latvia] No 302, 29 August 2000, likumi.lv/ta/en/en/id/10127-procedures-for-the-certification-of-document-translations-in-the-official-language.
[52] It seems to indirectly follow from Section 13(2) CPL.

is unclear why Section 638(3)(5) does not specify that the certificate of enforceability must be accompanied by a certified translation. Based on Section 13(2) we would still submit that this has to be done.

The CPL does not state that all foreign public documents themselves need to be legalised. Yet, in accordance with Section 10(1) of the Document Legalisation Law, 'For a public document issued in a foreign state to have legal force in Latvia, it shall be legalised.'[53] Hence, it is submitted that all foreign public documents must be legalised. Other scholars also agree with this opinion – legalisation is required unless the EU or international instrument expressly omits the requirement.[54]

Question 5. Securities, Bonds and Deposits

Pursuant to Point 2(9) of Annex 3 to CPL, when submitting an application for the recognition and enforcement of a ruling of a foreign court and adaptation of the rights and obligations laid down in the ruling of a foreign court for the implementation thereof in Latvia, a State fee shall be paid – EUR 80. Pursuant to Section 43^1(1) CPL,

> The security deposit shall be paid in the following amount: for an ancillary complaint, except for an ancillary complaint regarding a decision by which the release from the payment of the security deposit or court expenses in the State income is refused – EUR 80.

Finally, pursuant to Section 641(1) CPL:

> In respect of a decision of a court of first instance in the case regarding recognition of a ruling of a foreign court, an ancillary complaint may be submitted to the regional court, and a decision by the regional court on an ancillary complaint may be appealed to the Supreme Court by submitting an ancillary complaint.

Thus, the CPL does not require the applicant to submit any securities, bonds or deposits when submitting the original application for recognition/enforcement of a foreign judgment. However, the applicant must pay EUR 80 for the application requesting recognition/enforcement. The decision can be twice appealed via the ancillary complaint. Each complaint will require the applicant to pay a security in the amount of EUR 80.

[53] Document Legalisation Law, adopted 22 March 2007, in force on 18 April 2007, published in Latvijas Vēstnesis [Herald of Latvia] No 56, 4 April 2007, likumi.lv/ta/en/en/id/155411-document-legalisation-law.

[54] Torgāns (n 4) 646.

Lithuania

KATARZYNA BOGDZIEWICZ AND GIEDRIUS OŽIŪNAS

Question 1. General Overview

The recognition and enforcement of non-EU judgments in Lithuania are governed by the Code of Civil Procedure[1] (*Lietuvos Respublikos civilinio proceso kodeksas*); COCP) and bilateral agreements entered into by Lithuania. Lithuania is currrently party to 10 bilateral agreements with non-EU countries, which provide rules on recognition and enforcement of judgments. These are the bilateral agreements with: Armenia, Azerbaijan, Belarus, Kazakhstan, China, Moldova, Russian Federation, Turkey, Ukraine and Uzbekistan.[2] The aforementioned international treaties govern the process by which judgments rendered by the courts of the contracting states are recognised, as well as the available defences to recognition. According to case law, if an international treaty has been concluded between the Republic of Lithuania and a foreign state, the grounds for non-recognition provided in the COCP will not be considered when deciding whether to recognise a foreign judgment in Lithuania.[3]

According to Article 810(1) COCP, foreign judgments will be recognised based on the aforementioned international treaties. In the absence of an international agreement, the recognition of a judgment will be regulated by the provisions of the COCP. The recognition of such a judgment may be denied if any of the grounds for refusal of recognition stated in Article 810 of the COCP are present. When the recognition of a foreign judgment is only governed by the rules of the COCP, the Lithuanian Court of Appeal conducts a limited judicial assessment of the foreign judgment, based on a comprehensive list of grounds specified in the COCP. The process of recognising and enforcing a foreign judgment is a formal procedure that focuses solely on determining the existence of a potential ground for not recognising a foreign judgment. It establishes the necessary legal conditions for enforcing the specific foreign judgment within the territory of the Lithuanian Republic.[4]

Recognising a foreign judgment in Lithuania entails giving it the legal effect of a national court judgment. A judgment attains enforceability in the state of recognition when it is recognised and permitted to be enforced; consequently, it is subject to the

[1] The Code of Civil Procedure of the Republic of Lithuania of 4 April 2002, No IX-743.
[2] Further participation in bilateral agreements with Russia and Belarus is, however, under consideration.
[3] Court of Appeal of Lithuania, 27 September 2018, no e2T-62-370/2018.
[4] Court of Appeal of Lithuania, 14 May 2018, no e2T-40-823/2018.

same requirements for enforcement as a judgment rendered in the state of enforcement.[5] The Senate of the Supreme Court of Lithuania has adopted a review which defines the recognition of a foreign judgment as follows: 1) it attains preliminary effect in the recognising state; 2) it acquires *res judicata* effect in the recognising state; 3) the state that recognises the foreign judgment also affirms that the principles of fair procedure were adhered to during the case hearing in the foreign state; and 4) it becomes enforceable in the state that has recognised the judgment.[6] In other words, the legal effects of a foreign judgment are recognised and extended throughout the territory of the Republic of Lithuania. Until the foreign judgment is recognised in accordance with the procedure outlined in the COCP, it has no *res judicata* or preliminary consequences.[7] It is important to note that judgments without legal effect cannot be recognised.[8] Furthermore, a judgment that recognises another judgment cannot be eligible for recognition itself.[9]

Finally, it is worth noting that recognition can be sought not only for a traditionally understood 'judgment', but also for decisions of other foreign competent authorities. According to bilateral agreements, not only court judgments from foreign countries can be recognised, but also decisions from other institutions of foreign countries that have the authority to decide on matters within the jurisdiction of the court system of the Republic of Lithuania. This includes decisions from administrative authorities of foreign states in areas such as adoption, guardianship, custody of a child and dissolution of a marriage.[10] For instance, according to Article 42 of the Treaty between the Republic of Lithuania and the Republic of Ukraine on legal assistance and legal relations in civil, family and criminal matters decisions regarding guardianship, custody, civil registry and other matters in civil and family affairs that do not need to be enforced will be recognised in the territories of the contracting parties without the need for specific procedure. Similarly, Article 809(4) provides that the provisions laid out in the COCP regarding the recognition of decisions rendered by foreign courts shall also be extended to judgments (acts) issued by other foreign authorities that, as per the legislation of the originating state, possess the jurisdiction to render decisions on subjects falling within the authority of the court in Lithuania. According to the case law, the following documents can be recognised in the same way as court judgments: notarial deed;[11] Israeli Registrar's of Inheritances decision on a will;[12] and Norwegian NAV Family Benefits and Pensions – Child Support decision.[13]

[5] Supreme Court of Lithuania, 3 March 2016, no 3K-3-95-695/2016.

[6] Resolution of the Senate of the Supreme Court of Lithuania no 28 of 21 December 2001 on the Review of the Summary of Judicial Practice in the Republic of Lithuania regarding the Application of Private International Law.

[7] Supreme Court of Lithuania, 26 November 2015, no 3K-3-544-684/2015.

[8] Court of Appeal of Lithuania, 17 September 2015, no 2T-90-370/2015.

[9] Supreme Court of Lithuania, 15 June 2017, no 3K-3-267- 611/2017.

[10] Court of Appeal of Lithuania, 10 February 2017, no 2T-12-381/2017.

[11] Supreme Court of Lithuania, 21 November 2019, no 3K-3-345-916/2019.

[12] Court of Appeal of Lithuania, 25 August 2022, no e2T-73-407/2022.

[13] Court of Appeal of Lithuania, 25 February 2021, no e2T-22-381/2021.

Question 2. Procedure

a) Circumstances of Recognition and Enforcement

Foreign court (arbitrations) judgments may only be enforced in the Republic of Lithuania if they have been recognised by the Lithuanian Court of Appeals. Lithuanian law does not give the power to recognise a foreign decision informally, for instance, within the context of other proceedings. In other words, an enforceable foreign judgment from a third country will have no effect in Lithuania until it is formally recognised. In such a case, Lithuanian institutions are not required to consider the foreign judgment.[14]

Foreign court judgments that have become final in non-property disputes between non-Lithuanian citizens do not require recognition, unless the judgment is the basis for the celebration of a marriage, the registration of any other civil status act, or the registration of other rights in a public registry.

Without a particular procedure for the recognition of foreign judgments, final judgments of foreign courts on divorce, legal separation or annulment of marriage are recognised, and civil status records in Lithuanian registers are altered and updated in accordance with such judgments. Interested persons may apply to the Court of Appeal of Lithuania for a declaration that the record based on the foreign judgment is invalid within one year of becoming aware of such amendment or renewal of civil status records, in accordance with the procedure and grounds set out in Articles 810, 811 and 812 of the COCP (Article 809(3) COCP).

A foreign decision to be enforced requires both recognition and authorisation to be enforced. The Supreme Court in its case law has explained that recognising a judgment and authorising its enforcement are different legal actions, and once a judgment has been recognised, it cannot be enforced – it also needs authorisation for enforcement.[15]

Finally, it is worth noting that despite that the exequatur procedure is required for the foreign judgment to be recognised and enforced, it is still the foreign judgment that is enforced. In other words, the enforcement doesn't require a domestic judgment.

b) Procedural Steps

The Lithuanian Court of Appeal hears applications for recognition and/or permission to enforce in the Republic of Lithuania decisions of foreign courts (and arbitral tribunals) in civil cases, as well as applications for refusal to recognise decisions of foreign courts (and arbitral tribunals).

An application for recognition (or refusal of recognition) and/or enforcement of a foreign court decision (or arbitral award) in the Republic of Lithuania must be submitted to the Lithuanian Court of Appeal. Articles 111–114 and 811 of the COCP set out

[14] Supreme Court of Lithuania, 10 March 2016, no 3K-3-125-313/2016.
[15] Supreme Court of Lithuania, 27 May 2020, no e3K-3-173-469/2020.

what must be included in the request for recognition (or refusal of recognition) and/or enforcement of a foreign court (arbitral) award in the Republic of Lithuania.

Article 805 of the COCP regulates that if the foreign party has not appointed a representative in the case, it is obliged to appoint an authorised person residing in the Republic of Lithuania to be served with procedural documents relating to the case (paragraph 1). If the party residing abroad does not appoint an authorised person, all procedural documents addressed to the party residing abroad remain in the case and are deemed to be served. This effect must be made clear to the party at the time of first service. The party must also be made aware of the obligation to lodge a statement of defence and the consequences of failing to do so, as well as of who may be the authorised person (paragraph 2).

Article 812–1 of the COCP provides that if the applicant resides outside the Republic of Lithuania and has not appointed a representative or an authorised person residing in the Republic of Lithuania or having a place of business in the Republic of Lithuania to receive procedural documents, instead of the applicant's address in the Republic of Lithuania, an email address, a fax number, the addresses of other electronic means of communication available for the purpose of service of procedural documents, as well as a telephone number may be indicated.

The authenticity of foreign judgments and other official documents of foreign authorities must be authenticated by consular legalisation stamps, except where recognition is sought of a judgment rendered by a foreign state which is a party to the 1961 Hague Convention on the Abolition of Legalisation of Foreign Instruments.[16] The authenticity of such foreign judgments and official documents of foreign authorities must be certified by a certificate of legalisation and authentication (Apostille).

The application and its annexes may be delivered to the Court of Appeal of Lithuania in person, sent by post[17] or submitted through the Electronic Services Portal (EPP) system.

An application for recognition and/or enforcement of a foreign court (arbitration) award in the Republic of Lithuania is exempt from stamp duty.[18]

The examination of applications for recognition and (or) enforcement of an arbitral award in the Republic of Lithuania is regulated by Article 811–1 of the COCP, while the procedure for examination of applications for recognition and (or) enforcement of a foreign judgment is regulated by Article 812 of the COCP.

Article 812 of the COCP provides that:

- Applications for recognition (refusal of recognition) of foreign judgments shall be heard by a single judge of the Court of Appeal of Lithuania, however, the President of the Court of Appeal of Lithuania or the President of the Civil Division, taking into account the complexity of the case, shall have the right to set up a three-judge panel to hear the application. The single judge of the Court of Appeal of Lithuania who is hearing the application shall also have the power to refer the application to a three-judge panel by order. Applications

[16] Art 807 of the COCP; Art 3 of the 1961 Hague Convention on the Abolition of Legalisation of Foreign Instruments.

[17] Court of Appeal of Lithuania, Gedimino pr 40, LT-01503 Vilnius, Lithuania.

[18] Art 811(4) of the COCP.

shall be heard by written procedure unless the court decides, having regard to the circumstances of the case, to hear the application by oral procedure. The court's order on recognition of a foreign judgment shall enter into force on the day of its adoption. The court's order may be appealed against in cassation in accordance with the Rules of Procedure of the Court of Cassation. The proceedings may also be reopened.[19]

- The court hearing the application for recognition of a foreign judgment may recognise only part of the foreign judgment.[20]
- The applicant has the right to apply for recognition of part of the foreign judgment and also to refuse recognition of part of the judgment.[21]
- The court hearing an application for recognition of a foreign judgment has the right to stay the proceedings if the judgment is subject to an appeal against the judgment by the ordinary forms of review of judgments of the courts of the state concerned or if the time-limit for lodging such an appeal has not yet expired.[22]
- If the court finds that the application for recognition of a foreign judgment has not been filed in accordance with the procedure laid down in the COCP or international treaties, it may declare the application to be out of order and return it to the applicant, or, if the application has already been accepted, leave it pending. The court may impose a time limit for remedying defects in the form or content of the application[23] if the applicant is domiciled in the Republic of Lithuania, has indicated an address in the Republic of Lithuania at which procedural documents may be served on the applicant or has appointed a representative or an authorised person to receive the procedural documents, who is domiciled in the Republic of Lithuania (having a place of business).[24] If the defects are not remedied within the time limit set by the court, the application shall be deemed to be out of order and shall be returned to the applicant or, where the application has already been admitted, shall be left pending;[25]
- An application for recognition of a foreign judgment may be accompanied by an application for authorisation to enforce that judgment.[26]

Question 3. Requirements

As stated by the Supreme Court of Lithuania, the process of recognising a foreign judgment entails confirming that there are no valid reasons for non-recognition. During this verification, the facts of the case and the legality and foundation of the foreign state court's judgment cannot be re-established.[27]

Lithuanian law provides for an exhaustive list of grounds for non-recognition of a foreign judgment. Article 810(1) of the COCP states that foreign judgments are

[19] Art 812(1) of the COCP.
[20] Art 812(2) of the COCP.
[21] Art 812(3) of the COCP.
[22] Art 812(4) of the COCP.
[23] Art 115 of the COCP.
[24] Art 805 of the COCP.
[25] Art 812(5) of the COCP.
[26] Art 812(6) of the COCP.
[27] Supreme Court of Lithuania, 5 October 2009, no 3K-3-375/2009; Supreme Court of Lithuania, 8 May 2012, no 3K-3-278/2012.

recognised on the basis of international treaties. In the absence of an international treaty, recognition of foreign judgments shall be refused if:

(1) The judgment has not become final under the law of the State in which it was given.
(2) Under the law of the Republic of Lithuania or the provisions of an international treaty, the case falls exclusively into the competence of the courts of the Republic of Lithuania or of a third State.
(3) The party who did not participate in the proceedings was not duly notified of the institution of the civil proceedings and, in the course of the proceedings, was not given the opportunity to present his defence, or, in cases where the party lacked capacity in a certain area or had his capacity limited in a certain area, was not given the possibility of proper representation.
(4) The foreign judgment whose recognition is sought is not compatible with a judgment of a court of the Republic of Lithuania rendered in a case between the same parties.
(5) The judgment is contrary to the public policy enshrined in the Constitution of the Republic of Lithuania.
(6) The foreign court, in rendering the judgment, has resolved issues concerning the capacity of a citizen of the Republic of Lithuania, legal capacity or legal capacity of a citizen of the Republic of Lithuania, legal representation under the law, or legal relations concerning family property or succession, and it is in conflict with the private international law of the Republic of Lithuania, unless Lithuanian courts would have rendered the same judgment.

Article 813(1) of the COCP provides that foreign judgments may be enforced if:

(1) the judgment is enforceable in the State whose courts rendered it;
(2) it has been recognised in accordance with the procedure laid down in the fourth section of Chapter LIX of Part VII of this Code.

a) Jurisdiction of the Court of Origin

Jurisdiction of the court of origin is relevant in a twofold assessment. First assessing the grounds stated in Article 810(1)(2) of COCP. Pursuant to Article 810(1)(2) of the COCP, recognition of foreign judgments shall be refused if, according to the law of the Republic of Lithuania or the provisions of an international treaty, the case falls within the exclusive competence of the courts of the Republic of Lithuania or of the third state. This provision establishes the so-called indirect jurisdiction, where the competence of the court which heard the case and issued the judgment is examined by a court of another state, which decides on the question of recognition of the foreign judgment in its own state. According to Article 810(1)(2) of the COCP, the test is whether there has been an infringement of the exclusive jurisdiction of the courts of the Republic of Lithuania or of the courts of a third State. Pursuant to Article 810(1)(2) of the COCP, a court of the Republic of Lithuania, when deciding on the issue of recognition/non-recognition of a foreign judgment, shall decide on a possible breach of the exclusive jurisdiction of its own courts or of the courts of a third state in the light of the law of the Republic of Lithuania and the provisions of the international agreements.

In this context, the national rules of international civil procedure law of the Republic of Lithuania must be interpreted as including the conflict of laws rules of procedure laid down in Part VII of the COCP, which determine the rules of jurisdiction in cases with a foreign (international) element. Meanwhile, international treaties, as a source of law to be assessed when deciding whether there has been a breach of the exclusive jurisdiction of the courts of the Republic of Lithuania or of the courts of a third state, must be interpreted as encompassing all the international treaties to which the Republic of Lithuania and the state which has delivered the foreign judgment sought to be recognised are parties. Once an international treaty has been ratified and entered into force, it becomes an integral part of the Lithuanian legal system and its procedural rules, including those governing the jurisdiction of courts, become an integral part of the rules governing international civil proceedings in the Republic of Lithuania. Therefore, a court of the Republic of Lithuania decides on the exclusive competence of its own courts or of the courts of a third state in accordance with all the rules of international civil procedure law in force in Lithuania, whether laid down in the COCP, international treaties to which Lithuania is a party, or any other applicable rules.[28]

Article 781 of the COCP establishes the priority of national jurisdiction where the courts of the Republic of Lithuania have jurisdiction at the time the action is brought (Article 781(1) of the COCP), but this provision does not specify whether the action must be brought before the courts of the Republic of Lithuania. Analysing Article 781 of the COCP in its entirety, it can be concluded that the courts of the Republic of Lithuania retain priority in cases where the action is brought before the courts of the Republic of Lithuania, notwithstanding the fact that the circumstances have changed subsequently or the case is pending before another court of a foreign state, ie the priority of the national jurisdiction is linked to the moment when the case was brought before the courts of the Republic of Lithuania.[29]

Second, jurisdiction is also assessed in light of exclusive jurisdiction, that is whether the court of the foreign state has, in the course of its decision, resolved issues concerning the legal capacity of a citizen of the Republic of Lithuania, legal representation under the law, family property or inheritance legal relations, and the decision is contrary to private international law of the Republic of Lithuania, unless the Lithuanian courts in the case would have rendered the same decision.[30]

There are four main areas of exclusive jurisdiction:

- family proceedings if both spouses have their habitual residence in the Republic of Lithuania, the courts of the Republic of Lithuania have exclusive jurisdiction over their family proceedings (Article 784(2) of the COCP);
- cases of legal relations between parents and children, legal relations of adoption, if at least one of the parties is a citizen of the Republic of Lithuania or a stateless person and that party's permanent place of residence is in the Republic of Lithuania, or if both parties have their habitual residence in the Republic of Lithuania (Article 785 of the COCP);

[28] Court of Appeal of Lithuania, 2 November 2016, no e2T-70-381/2016.
[29] Art 137 of the COCP; the ruling of the Supreme Court of Lithuania, 29 May 2015, no 3K-3-360-378/2015.
[30] Supreme Court of Lithuania, 25 April 2023, no e3K-3-127-916/2023.

- cases concerning legal relations in rem relating to immovable property in the Republic of Lithuania (Article 786 of the COCP);
- cases on declaring a natural person to be incapacitated in a certain field or to have limited capacity in a certain field, pronouncing him dead or declaring him to be a person of unknown whereabouts, if he is a citizen of the Republic of Lithuania or a person without citizenship, but has his habitual place of residence in the Republic of Lithuania (Article 789(1) of the COCP).

b) Finality/Enforceability in the Country of Origin

Finality and/or enforceability of the requested judgment in the country of origin is one of the criteria in assessing possible refusal grounds (Article 810(1)(1) of the COCP). The COCP does not set out a list of criteria for the court to ascertain whether or not the judgment sought to be recognised and enforced. Moreover, Article 811(2) of the COCP does not specify which documents evidencing the entry into force of the judgment must be submitted to the court. This is done by assessing both the content of the foreign procedural law and other evidence, such as the judgment itself, recognition in other countries, affidavits from lawyers acting in the foreign country.[31]

c) *Res Iudicata*

Under Article 810(1)(4) of the COCP, recognition of foreign judgments is refused if the foreign judgment whose recognition is sought is not compatible with a judgment of a court of the Republic of Lithuania in a case between the same parties.

There is almost no case law regarding this even though this COCP entered into force in 2003. This in turn, compared to case law on other grounds suggest that it exists as a theoretical possibility, but one that does not occur in practice. It could be explained by the fact that this would be the very last stage in a conflict between the parties: for it to happen, the parties must be duly notified of the process, there must be uncontested grounds for the process to continue, no issues on *lis pendens* raised.

d) *Lis Pendens*

Proceedings pending on the same matters is a highly problematic issue in the COCP.

Article 781 of COCP states that if the courts of the Republic of Lithuania have jurisdiction at the time the action is brought, that jurisdiction shall continue notwithstanding any subsequent change in conditions.[32] If the courts of the Republic of Lithuania are competent to hear civil proceedings in accordance with the rules of jurisdiction laid

[31] See Court of Appeal of Lithuania, 10 September 2019, no e2T-62-370/2019; Court of Appeal of Lithuania, 3 February 2016, no 2T-11-370/2016.

[32] Art 781(1) of the COCP.

down in this Code, that jurisdiction shall not lapse when the same proceedings are pending before a court of a foreign state.[33]

Thus, the words 'jurisdiction shall not lapse' used in Article 781(2) of COCP means that there will not be *lis pendens* legal consequences unless an international treaty, to which the Republic of Lithuania is a party, governs the relevant relationships differently.[34]

For example, the Supreme Court of Lithuania in its ruling of 26 April 2011 in the civil case No 3K-3-191/2011 clarified that in the absence of a treaty between the Republic of Lithuania and the Republic of Georgia on the legal relations in civil matters, there is no legal instrument which would allow avoiding parallel court proceedings in different countries, where overlapping or partially overlapping issues would be examined. Pursuant to the provisions of Article 781(2) of COCP, if the courts of the Republic of Lithuania are competent to hear civil proceedings in accordance with the rules of jurisdiction laid down in COCP, this competence does not lapse when the same (similar) case is pending before a court of a foreign state. Judgments of a foreign court (except in the cases provided for in Article 809(2) of COCP) have legal effects in Lithuania and may be enforced only if they are recognised in accordance with the procedure established by the COCP (Article 809(1) of the COCP). As long as a foreign judgment (in the case at hand, the judgment of the Court of the Republic of Georgia of 26 March 2010) has not been recognised, it has neither *res iudicata* nor preliminary effect in the Republic of Lithuania, and there are therefore no legal obstacles for the courts of the Republic of Lithuania to analyse and assess even the same circumstances that were analysed in the foreign proceedings, or even to adopt different decisions than those adopted by the court of the foreign state. On the other hand, if legal proceeding in Lithuania is pending, a foreign judgment on the same matter between the same parties can be recognised and enforced in Lithuania.

e) Specific Requirements of Due Process

Article 810(1)(3) of the COCP provides that recognition of foreign judgments shall be refused if the party who was absent from the proceedings has not been duly notified of the institution of the civil proceedings and has been denied the possibility of a procedural defence in the course of the proceedings. Furthermore, it shall be refused where he or she has been declared to be mentally incompetent or to have had his or her faculties impaired, in respect of a particular subject matter, of being properly represented.

Case law regarding this ground for refusal heavily relies on European Convention on Human Rights (ECHR). For example, the Supreme Court of Lithuania relies on the case law of the European Court of Human Rights (ECtHR) that in disputes, the outcome of which is decisive for civil rights, Article 6(1) of the ECHR is applicable to the enforcement of foreign final judgments.[35] Thus, a decision to allow the enforcement of a foreign judgment cannot be considered compatible with the requirements of Article 6(1) of the ECHR if it was taken without giving the losing party any effective opportunity to

[33] Art 781(2) of the COCP.
[34] Art 780 of the COCP.
[35] Supreme Court of Lithuania, 18 May 2022, no e3K-3-150-916/2022.

complain about the unfairness of the proceedings in the state of origin of the judgment or in the state addressed.[36]

In other cases the Court of Appeal, following the case law of the ECtHR, clarified that in cases where civil proceedings are heard in the absence of one of the parties, the following circumstances must be assessed: first, whether the court was sufficiently diligent in informing the parties of the proceedings and whether the parties can be considered to have waived their right to stand trial and defend themselves; and second, whether national law allows persons who have learned of a judgment against them to request a new trial that complies with the principle of adversarial proceedings. In deciding whether a person can be regarded as having waived his right to stand trial, a precondition is that he must have been duly informed of that right and of the pendency of the proceedings.[37]

If the court is uncertain about whether the defendant has been properly informed about the commencing of legal proceedings in a foreign court, the applicant may be asked to provide evidence that would allow the court seeking recognition and enforcement to determine how and to which address the court in question sent notices to the defendant. This evidence should also include information about how the defendant was informed about the initiation of the civil proceedings, the date, time and location of the proceedings, the specific measures taken by the court to inform the defendant about decision concerning them, and any evidence indicating that the defendant has waived their right to be heard and defend themselves. Additionally, it should be determined whether the national law of the foreign state provides the defendant with adequate means to secure a new trial in accordance with the principle of fair and adversarial proceedings.[38]

f) Public Policy

Article 810(1)(5) of the COCP aims to safeguard public order within the Republic of Lithuania. The Constitution and other legislation do not provide a specific definition for the concept of public order. However, certain criteria have been established by case law to guide the implementation of public policy. In situations where the recognition or enforcement of a foreign judgment in the Republic of Lithuania would be contrary to its legal system and compromise fundamental principles, the public policy provision may be invoked. The threat should result from a clear violation of a fundamental rule of law or a fundamental right in the legal system of the state where the recognition of the foreign judgment is in question. Therefore, the requirement of conformity with public policy may be invoked as an exceptional circumstance to prevent the recognition or enforcement of a judgment, provided that the repercussions of doing so unequivocally contradict the public policy of Lithuania, specifically its foundational principles, or the constitutional rights and liberties of an individual.[39] In accordance

[36] Grand Chamber's judgment, 23 May 2016, n 17502/07, para 98, *Avotinš v Latvia*.
[37] Court of Appeal of Lithuania, 22 November 2022, no e2T-63-467/2022.
[38] ibid.
[39] Court of Appeal of Lithuania, 9 July 2013, no 2T-49/2013.

with the jurisprudence of Lithuanian courts, the recognition of judgments would be considered incompatible with the *ordre public* if it would interfere with the protection of private property as guaranteed by the Lithuanian Constitution. The Constitution of the Republic of Lithuania enshrines the principles of property protection and equality of persons (including creditors being in the same legal position). This means that during the transfer of property, consideration must be given to the interests of creditors whose claims have been secured by the debtor's property pursuant to final court judgments.[40]

Moreover, in several cases the courts considered whether the amount of the damages awarded can constitute a breach of public policy.[41] The Court of Appeal concluded that the mere fact that the parties to a dispute have contractually agreed on a disproportionate amount of liquidated damages does not constitute a ground for disregarding the entirety of a foreign court's judgment in the matter of liquidated damages.[42]

Finally, as part of the public order test, since 2022, the courts have considered whether recognition of a foreign judgment or arbitral award will not violate European Union (EU) sanctions, as their purpose reflects the fundamental principles of EU and Republic of Lithuania law.[43]

The Supreme Court of Lithuania has ruled in this regard that the universally recognised principles of international law, as well as the legal acts of the EU, which Lithuania undertook to comply with upon its accession to the EU, are an integral part of the legal system of the Republic of Lithuania, and the fundamental principles enshrined therein are elements of the content of public policy. In the view of the court, payments prohibited by EU sanctions can be made possible simply because they have been the subject of a foreign court decision. In such a case, the binding and directly applicable rules of EU law, which form, inter alia, part of the public policy of the Republic of Lithuania, would become ineffective.[44]

g) Reciprocity

Reciprocity is neither recognised as a defence to recognition, nor as a basis for it. This ground is only relevant in cases of specific bilateral treaties. For example, Article 52 of the Treaty of 20 October 1992 between the Republic of Lithuania and the Republic of Belarus on Legal Assistance and Legal Relations in Civil, Family and Criminal Matters establishes the principle of mutual recognition of judgments rendered by the judicial authorities of the contracting parties. According to Article 52 of the Bilateral Treaty, the contracting parties shall mutually recognise and enforce final judgments of judicial authorities in civil and family matters, as well as judgments on compensation for damages caused by crime.

[40] Court of Appeal of Lithuania, 17 January 2023, no e2T-7-330/2023.
[41] Court of Appeal of Lithuania, 24 September 2007, no 2T-144/2007; Court of Appeal of Lithuania, 10 December 2013, no 2T-75/2013; Court of Appeal of Lithuania, 13 November 2019, no e2T-92-943/2019.
[42] Court of Appeal of Lithuania, 10 December 2013, no 2T-75/2013.
[43] eg, Court of Appeal of Lithuania, 20 December 2022, no e2T-91-881/2022.
[44] Supreme Court of Lithuania, 9 November 2022, no 3K-3-255-611/2022.

In several cases, the Court of Appeal has applied the reciprocity principle to recognise a foreign judgment without a legal basis found in a bilateral agreement.[45] In one case the Court argued:

> [T]he Republic of Lithuania and the United States have not signed any international treaties on family law relations, nor have these two States joined any common international treaties in the field of family law relations; therefore, the panel of judges recognises the US judgment on the basis of *bona fides* and reciprocity in accordance with the national legislation (*lex fori*), namely the Civil Procedure Code of the Republic of Lithuania.[46]

h) Other Requirements

Article 811(1) of the COCP provides that any person who has a legal interest in the case has the right to apply for recognition of a foreign judgment. Applications for recognition of a foreign judgment (refusal of recognition) must comply with the general requirements for procedural documents.

Article 810(1)(6) of the COCP, which regulates the conditions for the recognition of foreign judgments, provides that, in the absence of an international treaty, the recognition of foreign judgments shall be refused if the foreign court's decision has resolved issues relating to the legal capacity of a citizen of the Republic of Lithuania, the representation under the law, or the family property or succession relations, and it is in conflict with the international private law of the Republic of Lithuania, except for the cases in which the courts of the Republic of Lithuania in the case would have rendered an identical decision.

Article 789(1) of the COCP stipulates that only the courts of the Republic of Lithuania may exclusively hear cases on declaring a natural person to be incapacitated in a certain sphere or to have limited legal capacity in a certain sphere, on declaring him or her dead or on declaring them to be a person of unknown whereabouts, if they are a citizen of the Republic of Lithuania or a stateless person, but their habitual place of residence is in the Republic of Lithuania.

The areas listed in Article 810(1)(6) of the COCP (questions of the legal capacity of a citizen, legal representation, family property or succession law) are particularly socially sensitive, involving the protection of the rights and legitimate interests of persons in need of additional protection. Thus, it is presumed that the purpose of this legal norm is to protect weaker persons, in certain cases without forcing them to litigate a second time, even if the jurisdiction of the Lithuanian courts is violated in a foreign court.[47]

The COCP provides for a number of cases in which a breach of exclusive jurisdiction is not regarded as an absolute ground for refusing recognition and enforcement of a foreign judgment. For example, Article 789(1) of the COCP provides that only the courts of the Republic of Lithuania may exclusively hear cases concerning the recognition of a natural person as incapacitated in a certain field or as having limited capacity in

[45] eg, Court of Appeal of Lithuania, 17 December 2010, no 2T-301/2010; Court of Appeal of Lithuania, 28 September 2009, no 2T-189/2009.

[46] Court of Appeal of Lithuania, 17 December 2010, no 2T-301/2010.

[47] Supreme Court of Lithuania, 25 April 2023, no e3K-3-127-916/2023.

a certain field, if that person is a citizen of the Republic of Lithuania or a stateless person, but his habitual place of residence is in the Republic of Lithuania. Meanwhile, pursuant to Article 810(1)(6) of the COCP, in the absence of an international treaty, the recognition of foreign judgments shall be refused if the foreign court's judgment resolved issues concerning the capacity of a citizen of the Republic of Lithuania, representation under the law, family property or inheritance legal relations and it is contrary to the international private law of the Republic of Lithuania, unless the Lithuanian courts in the case would have made the same decision. Having assessed this legal regulation, the Court of Cassation has concluded that both the inclusion of the issue of limitation of the legal capacity of a Lithuanian citizen in the area of exclusive jurisdiction and the reference to it in Article 810(1)(6) of the COCP indicate the legislator's decision not to give absolute significance to the violation of the exclusive jurisdiction in certain cases.[48]

Question 4. Documents to be Produced

Applications for recognition (or refusal of recognition) of a foreign judgment must comply with the general requirements for procedural documents. Pursuant to Article 811(2), together with the application for recognition of a foreign judgment, a person must submit the foreign judgment sought to be recognised and a translation of that judgment into Lithuanian certified in accordance with the procedure established by law, a confirmation that the judgment has become final, as well as evidence that the party who was absent during the proceedings has been duly notified of the time and place of the hearing of the civil case.[49]

According to Article 813(3), the creditor must attach to the application for enforcement of a foreign judgment the documents referred to in Article 811(2) of this Code and a statement that the judgment is enforceable in the state of the court that issued it. Article 813(4) of the COCP provides that recognised foreign arbitral awards are enforceable documents and shall be enforced in accordance with the rules of Part VI of this Code.

Question 5. Securities, Bonds and Deposits

There are no requirements to provide securities, bonds or deposits in the COCP.

[48] Supreme Court of Lithuania, 1 June 2022, no e3K-3-145-969/2022.
[49] Art 810(1)(3) of the COCP.

Malta

IOANNIS REVOLIDIS

Question 1. General Overview

Under Maltese law, there are two primary methods for recognising and enforcing foreign judgments. The first is indirect enforcement, where the plaintiff initiates a local legal action before the Maltese courts based on the foreign judgment itself, aiming to enforce it within the local jurisdiction. The second method is direct enforcement. This involves registering the foreign judgment in the relevant local registry. Direct enforcement tends to be more straightforward and swift, since both the requirements and the procedure for recognition and enforcement are usually much more relaxed by comparison to the more rigid regime that usually regulates indirect enforcement.

Articles 825A–828 of the Code of Organisation and Civil Procedure[1] (COCP) regulate the indirect enforcement of foreign judicial decisions within the Maltese legal order. In terms of direct enforcement, one has to refer to the British Judgments (Reciprocal Enforcement) Act,[2] which sets up a specific regime for the recognition and enforcement of British judicial decisions.

The basic requirements for the indirect recognition and enforcement of foreign judicial decisions in Malta are outlined in Articles 826 and 827 of the COCP. While these criteria largely align with the typical requirements found in other legal systems and international conventions, there are also strong national particularities that are unique to the Maltese legal order.

The positive requirements for the recognition and enforcement of foreign judicial decisions can be deduced from Article 826 COCP. According to this provision, it is evident that for a foreign judicial decision to be recognised and enforced in Malta, the following positive requirements must be met: a) there must be a judicial decision (not a decree); b) the judicial decision must have been delivered by a competent court outside of Malta; c) the judicial decision must constitute *res iudicata*; and d) there must be an application before the competent court in Malta containing a demand that the enforcement of such judgment be ordered.

The negative requirements for the enforcement of foreign judicial decisions in Malta are established in Article 827(1) COCP.

[1] Ch 12 of the Laws of Malta.
[2] Ch 52 of the Laws of Malta.

The negative requirements listed in Article 827(1)(b) and (c) represent classic grounds for the refusal of recognition and enforcement of foreign judicial decisions. Indeed, Article 827(1)(b) refers to the protection of due process, while Article 827(1)(c) refers to the classic refusal ground of public policy. In contrast, the reference made by Article 827(1)(a) to Article 811 constitutes an important deviation from traditional national and international standards, since the provision of Article 811 regulates the extraordinary appeal method of retrial within the domestic Maltese legal order. While Article 811 serves an important role within the internal legal order of Maltese civil procedural law, the 12 grounds of retrial listed in Article 811 might put the recognition and enforcement of foreign decisions under strong limitations. They might also not be easily transferable to cross-border situations, as many of the modalities and institutions regulated in Article 811 are specific to the Maltese legal order. It needs to be stressed that while in domestic situations the application of Article 811 will result in a retrial, in cross-border situations it will result in a refusal of recognition and/or enforcement of a foreign judicial decision. In that sense, Article 811 displays a double functionality: for domestic situations it behaves as a method of appeal; while for cross-border situations it regulates grounds of refusal of recognition and/or enforcement of foreign judicial decisions.

The requirements for direct enforcement established in the British Judgments Act are less cumbersome. Instead of seeking a separate local judicial decision that will declare the recognition and enforcement of the foreign decision, British judgments are submitted to the Court of Appeal for direct registration with the Public Registry Office. No further steps are required for their recognition and enforcement in Malta. While the Court of Appeal enjoys latitude on whether it will allow the registration of a British judgment or not, Article 3(2) of the British Judgments Act stipulates considerably fewer requirements for this to happen. Most importantly, Article 3(2) of the British judgments Act does not impose on British judgments the extra scrutiny of Article 811 COCP that applies to all other foreign judicial decisions.

Question 2. Procedure

a) Circumstances of Recognition and Enforcement

Recognition and enforcement of foreign judicial decisions in Malta requires a formal procedure. Maltese law does not distinguish between recognition and enforcement. Therefore, they are both subject to the same procedure.

Judgments that fall under the indirect recognition and enforcement path[3] cannot be recognised and/or enforced on their own; there must always be a domestic Maltese judgment that orders the recognition and/or enforcement of the foreign judgment in Malta. This Maltese decision can only be obtained via contentious proceedings.[4]

[3] See Arts 825A–28 COCP.
[4] Art 826 COCP.

On the contrary, foreign judgments that fall under the direct recognition and enforcement path[5] are recognised and/or enforced per se and without the necessity for an accompanying Maltese decision. In this case, the only requirement is the registration of the foreign judgment in one of the superior courts of Malta. Such registration is ordered by the Court of Appeal on the basis of an application submitted there by the judgment creditor.[6]

b) Procedural Steps

According to Article 826 COCP the party that seeks (indirect) recognition and/or enforcement of a foreign judgment in Malta must bring an application containing a demand that the enforcement of such judgment be ordered. The party seeking recognition and/or enforcement should submit the application before the First Hall of the Civil Court via a normal application (hence not sworn).[7] After the application is submitted, the defendant has 20 days at their disposal to challenge the recognition and enforcement of the foreign judgment on the basis of any of the grounds provided in Article 811 and 827 of the COCP.[8] While Maltese courts will not review the merits of the foreign judicial decision, several grounds of refusal listed in Article 811 of the COCP allow for a rather extensive interference with the foreign judicial decision.

The burden of proof as regards the positive requirements for recognition and/or enforcement lies with the party seeking recognition and/or enforcement, while the burden of proof of the grounds of refusal lies with the defendant that contests the recognition and/or enforcement on the basis of Articles 811 and 827 of the COCP. The defendant cannot request injunctive relief while the application for enforcement is pending, but can apply for any of the precautionary warrants listed in Article 830 in order to cover potential damages in case the enforcement is deemed unlawful at a later stage.

The decision on the recognition and enforcement of a foreign judgment can be appealed. According to Article 143 of the COCP, the application for an appeal shall contain a reference to the claim and the judgment appealed together with detailed reasons on which the appeal is entered and a request that the claim be allowed or dismissed. The appeal must be submitted within 30 days from the delivery of the judgment at first instance. The decision on recognition and enforcement of a foreign judgment is binding for all other Maltese courts. The foreign judgment is to be given the same effect as a local judgment and will be enforced as judgments delivered in Malta, as soon as its recognition and enforcement is ordered by the competent Maltese court.

For direct recognition and/or enforcement the procedure is rather simplified. The judgment creditor must simply apply before the Court of Appeal asking for the foreign judgment to be registered in the superior courts of Malta. The application must be

[5] See the British Judgments (Reciprocal Enforcement) Act, Ch 52 of the laws of Malta.
[6] See ibid Art 3(1).
[7] First Hall Civil Court, 22 May 2023, *Avukat Dottor Louis Pulliċino ,bħala mandatarju speċjali għannom u in rapprezenza ta' Keith Jefferey Algie u Mark John Wilson v Michael James Halligan.*
[8] See Question 3 for the details.

submitted within 12 months from date of publication of the foreign judgment, unless the Court of Appeal grants a longer application period.[9] The substantially limited (in comparison to indirect enforcement) refusal grounds will be examined during the registration process by the Court of Appeal.[10] The judgment shall, as from the date of registration, be of the same force and effect, and enforcement proceedings may be taken thereon, as if it had been a judgment originally obtained or entered up before the courts of Malta.[11]

Question 3. Requirements

a) Jurisdiction of the Court of Origin

One of the most universally[12] accepted prerequisites for the recognition and enforcement of foreign judicial decisions is the jurisdiction of the court that rendered the foreign judgment in the original venue of adjudication. Malta adheres to this convention as is evident by Article 826 which explicitly prescribes the jurisdiction of the foreign court as a requirement for the recognition and/or enforcement of a judicial decision in Malta.

Maltese courts have traditionally followed the international trend, which dictates that the courts of the country where recognition and/or enforcement are being sought should refer to their own rules of international jurisdiction when assessing the jurisdiction of the court that delivered the foreign judicial decision. For example, in the case of *Salvatore Camilleri v Spiridione Mizzi*,[13] the commercial court referenced Article 742 of the COCP to ascertain the jurisdiction of the foreign court involved. Similarly, in *Dr Victor Caruana v G Demarco*,[14] a judgment was deemed unenforceable because the foreign court that issued it lacked jurisdiction under Maltese law. These judgments suggest that Maltese courts apply the principles of Maltese private international law to determine the jurisdiction of foreign courts.[15]

It must be stressed that the Maltese bases of jurisdiction are rather exorbitant and, therefore, it will usually not be difficult for Maltese courts to accept that the foreign court had jurisdiction to adjudicate over the case, as the generous Maltese regime will

[9] See Art 3(1) of the British judgments (Reciprocal Enforcement) Act, Ch 52 of the laws of Malta.

[10] See ibid Art 3(2).

[11] See ibid Art 3(3).

[12] For the universal acceptance of international jurisdiction as a prerequisite for the cross-border circulation of judicial decisions in civil and commercial matters, see M Pagenstecher, 'Gerichtsbarkeit und internationale Zuständigkeit als selbständige Prozeßvoraussetzungen' (1937) 11 *RabelsZ*, esp 360 where he notes: 'Ein von den meisten Kulturstaaten anerkannter Grundsatz des internationalen Prozerßrechts ist: Ausländische Urteile werden nur anerkannt, wenn die internationale Zuständigkeit des Urteilstaates besteht', as well as AT von Mehren and DT Trautman, 'Recognition of Foreign Adjudication. A survey and a suggested approach' (1968) 81 *Harvard Law Review* 1601, esp 1610 where they call international jurisdiction a 'universal requirement' for the recognition and enforcement of foreign judicial decisions.

[13] Commercial Court, 25 November 1952, *Salvatore Camilleri v Spiridione Mizzi.*

[14] Commercial Court, 30 June 1948, *Dr Victor Caruana v G Demarco.*

[15] For a detailed overview of the Maltese jurisdictional system see I Revolidis, 'Country Report – Malta' in T Lutzi, E Piovesani and D Zgrablic Rotar (eds), *Jurisdiction over Non-EU Defendants – Should the Brussels Ia be Extended?* (Hart Publishing, 2023) 181–94.

lower the requirements for the establishment of the jurisdiction of the court issuing the foreign judgment. It must be added, though, that the combination of Article 827(1)(a) and (2) with Article 811(d) of the COCP creates an additional layer of jurisdictional interference. In particular, the combined interpretation of the aforementioned provisions introduces a distinction that Maltese courts must observe when examining the jurisdiction of the foreign court.

When, according to Article 811(d) of the COCP, the defendant has raised no jurisdictional plea before the foreign court where the original proceedings took place, Maltese courts are entitled to apply Article 742 of the COCP and refer to all the jurisdictional venues provided by the Maltese legislator in order to assess whether the foreign court could claim jurisdiction over the case.

On the contrary, when the defendant raised a jurisdictional plea before the foreign court and the foreign court rejected the plea (confirming its own jurisdiction over the case), Article 827(2) of the COCP allows the defendant to submit a new jurisdictional plea before the Maltese courts on the basis that the foreign country where the judicial decision originates from is not their domicile or residence. If the defendant can prove that they were not domiciled or resident in the country where the original proceedings took place, the decision will not be recognised and/or enforced in Malta. It is widely accepted[16] that when examining whether the defendant was domiciled or resident in the country where the foreign judgment originates, Maltese courts will apply the Maltese interpretation of the notions of domicile and/or residence.[17] In this sense, the jurisdictional venues of domicile and residence obtain elevated status by comparison to the other jurisdictional bases established in Article 742 of the COCP. The opportunity to raise a new jurisdictional plea according to Article 827(2) of the COCP might create certain inconsistencies. The foreign court, for example, might consider that the defendant was domiciled within its territory under its national law, while the Maltese courts might come to a different conclusion by applying their own national standards with regards to the notion of domicile.

b) Finality/Enforceability in the Country of Origin

According to Article 826 COCP only a foreign decision that constitutes *res iudicata* or is deemed 'final and conclusive' by the court that issued it can be recognised and/or enforced in Malta. This means that the judgment should have resolved all disputes between the parties. If the judgment can be modified in subsequent proceedings involving the same parties in the same court, then it cannot be enforced. The appropriate law to consult in determining this is the foreign law under which the judgment was issued. This principle was affirmed by Maltese case law in *Avv Gaetano Vassallo nom. v Antonio Licata*.[18] In this case, concerning child custody and care, the Court of Appeal ruled that the execution of judgments issued by foreign judicial authorities can only be

[16] First Hall Civil Court, 16 March 1949, *Camilleri v Avv Dr G Degiorgio*.

[17] On the Maltese understanding of 'domicile' and 'residence' in terms of private international law see Revolidis (n 15) 185–87.

[18] Court of Appeal, 18 July 1906, *Avv Gaetano Vassallo nom v Antonio Licata*.

ordered in Malta if the judgment is final and conclusive. To ascertain whether a judgment is final and conclusive, reference must be made to the law of the country where the foreign judgment was issued.[19]

This perspective is rooted in the understanding that even if a judgment does not meet the Maltese definition of *res iudicata*, there is no justification to deny its enforcement if it is considered final and binding in its country of origin, ensuring that no opposing judgment from the same country can be procured.

c) *Res Iudicata*

Under Maltese law, the pendency of a case before a foreign court does not lead to an obligation of Maltese courts to decline jurisdiction. In that sense, the possibility that irreconcilable judgments might occur is not negligible. It is exactly in situations like this where Article 811(h) of the COCP becomes of paramount importance. Article 811(h) of the COCP prescribes that the recognition and/or enforcement of a foreign judgment should be denied where the judgment is conflicting with a previous judgment given in a suit on the same subject matter and between the same parties, and constituting a *res iudicata*, provided no plea of *res iudicata* had been raised and determined.

The assessment as to whether a foreign decision is delivered on the same subject matter and between the same parties will be done under Maltese law. On the contrary, the assessment as to whether the foreign decision constitutes *res iudicata* will be performed under the law of the country from where the decision originates.

d) *Lis Pendens*

The problem of pending parallel proceedings is addressed under Article 742(2) of the COCP, which stipulates that the jurisdiction of the courts of civil jurisdiction is not excluded by the fact that a foreign court is seized with the same cause or with a cause connected with it. Where a foreign court has concurrent jurisdiction, the Maltese courts may, at their discretion, declare the defendant non-suited or stay proceedings on the ground that, if the action were to continue in Malta, it would be vexatious, oppressive, or unjust to the defendant.

This provision seems to be amalgamating two different institutions, namely that of *lis alibi pendens* and that of *forum conveniens/forum non conveniens*. Indeed, unlike Article 29 of the Brussels Ia Regulation, where earlier pendency before a foreign court leads to automatic suspension of domestic proceedings, Article 742(2) of the COCP does not impose any such obligation upon Maltese courts. While the earlier pendency of the case before a foreign court is taken into account, it is not by itself sufficient to oblige a Maltese court to decline its jurisdiction in favour of that of the foreign court. On the contrary, when a Maltese court identifies that a case with the same cause of action

[19] The original passage in Italian reads as follows: 'perche' ai termini dell'articolo 843 delle dette Leggi, possa esser ordinata in Malta la esecusione di sentenze pronunziate da autorita' giudiziarie straniere; se si abbia, cioe', oppur no, una sentenza passata in giudicato; Che per l'esame della questione se una sentenza sia passata in giudcato e' uopo attendere le Legge del paese in cui essa ju pronunziata'.

and between the same parties is pending before a foreign court, it retains the latitude to decide whether to decline jurisdiction in favour of the foreign court or not. In doing so, Article 742(2) of the COCP invites the Maltese court to assess whether continuing the proceedings in Malta will be vexatious, oppressive or unjust to the defendant. If this is the case, the Maltese court should decline its jurisdiction and allow the case to carry on abroad. If, on the other hand, the Maltese court does not consider that the Maltese proceedings are vexatious, oppressive or unjust to the defendant, then it will adjudicate over the case despite the pending proceedings abroad. The assessment of whether the continuation of the proceedings in Malta will be vexatious, oppressive or unjust to the defendant follows the criteria established in the traditional *forum conveniens/forum non conveniens* doctrine.[20]

e) Specific Requirements of Due Process

Due process concerns constitute an important impediment in the area of the recognition and/or enforcement of foreign judicial decisions. Maltese law takes a very proactive approach in this regard. One can identify two separate refusal grounds that express due process concerns: i) fraud;[21] and ii) problems related to the service of the documents instituting the original proceedings before the foreign court.[22]

1. *Fraud*

According to Article 811(a), which via the reference of Article 827(1)(a) COCP is also applicable with regards to the recognition and enforcement of foreign judicial decisions, a foreign judgment will not be recognised and/or enforced in Malta where the judgment was obtained by fraud on the part of any of the parties to the prejudice of the other party.

This refusal ground is mostly unknown to civil law jurisdictions, but appears relatively often in common law jurisdictions. Article 811(a) of the COCP does not define the notion of fraud, which is, therefore, dynamic, flexible and open-ended. Maltese case law is a crucial tool in the effort to demystify the exact content of the notion of fraud under Article 811(a) COCP. It must be noted, however, that Maltese courts have predominantly applied the provision of Article 811(a) in purely domestic situations and that, therefore, their findings might not always perfectly align with the nature of cross-border recognition and enforcement. Nevertheless, this case law still sheds some light to what the Maltese legal order understands as fraud from a procedural point of view and provides some insights into the types of procedural behaviours that would endanger the recognition and/or enforcement of a foreign judicial decision within Malta.

At the outset, it must be highlighted that Maltese courts apply a strict interpretation to the notion of fraud. They usually underline that not any kind of fraud would justify a retrial

[20] For an excellent comparative analysis of the doctrine of *forum conveniens/forum non conveniens* between different common law jurisdictions see DJ Svantesson, *Private International Law and the Internet*, 4th edn (Wolters Kluwer, 2021) 212–35.

[21] Art 827(1)(a) in combination with Art 811(a) COCP.

[22] Art 827(a) in combination with Arts 811(b) and 827(1)(b) COCP.

under Maltese law (or refusal of recognition and enforcement of a foreign judicial decision for the scope of this report). For this to happen, it must be established that one of the litigating parties has undertaken culpable machinations of such intensity that they result in the other party losing the case on the basis of such culpable machinations.[23] It is also important to observe that the notion of fraud that justifies the refusal of recognition and enforcement of foreign judgments must be understood in procedural terms, namely fraud should not refer to the merits of the case, but must take the form of procedural machinations that deprive the other party of the opportunity to properly exercise their procedural rights.[24] Finally, Maltese courts have consistently held that it is only the fraudulent behaviour displayed by the litigating parties that triggers the application of Article 811(a) COCP, while the fraudulent behaviour of third parties or other actors participating in the proceedings (eg witnesses) will not trigger this provision.[25] The fraudulent behaviour of third parties, other actors in the proceedings or the court (in the rare cases where something like that would happen) can lead to the deployment of public policy as a ground for refusal of recognition and enforcement of a foreign judicial decision.[26]

Additional guidance as regards the exact content of the notion of fraud could be sought in international legal scholarship in the area of private international law. Such scholarship has identified four types of possible fraud that justifies the refusal of the recognition and/or enforcement of a foreign judicial decision:[27] a) fraud as to the jurisdiction of the court that delivered the foreign judicial decision, in the sense that one of the parties has manipulated the connecting jurisdictional factors in order to bring the case before the courts most favourable to their interests to the detriment of the interests of the other party and those of justice; b) fraud as to the determination of the law applicable, in the sense that one of the parties manipulated the connecting factors in order to achieve the application of the law most favourable to their interests to the detriment of the interests of the other party and those of justice; c) fraud concerning service to the defendant in the foreign proceedings; and d) fraud as regards the evidence submitted before the foreign court. While of Article 826, 827 and 811 of the Maltese COCP already recognise such behaviours as standalone grounds for refusal of recognition and/or enforcement, the more abstract and open-ended nature of fraud could allow Maltese courts to safeguard the integrity of the recognition and/or enforcement process by adapting their assessment to the particularities of the manipulative behaviour displayed in each particular case.

2. Service of the Documents Instituting the Original Proceedings before the Foreign Court

Maltese law regulates two distinct situations where problems, as regards the service of the documents instituting the original proceedings, might appear: a) where the party

[23] Commercial Court, 31 March 1894, *Giorgio Zonda v Artiside Parthenis*.
[24] AL Ellul, 'The Institute of Retrial' (Master's dissertation, University of Malta, 2003) 99.
[25] Commercial Court, 16 November 1933, *Charles Portelli v Giovanni Micallef*.
[26] Art 827(1)(c) COCP.
[27] C Kessedjian, 'Synthesis Of The Work Of The Special Commission Of March 1998 On International Jurisdiction And The Effects Of Foreign Judgments In Civil And Commercial Matters' (1998), assets.hcch.net/docs/3385edb5-6f63-4624-934c-4d4245fdcef6.pdf.

contesting the recognition and/or enforcement of the foreign judicial decision has not been served at all with the documents instituting the proceedings before the foreign court; and b) where the foreign court has delivered a decision by default and the affected parties were not contumacious according to the civil procedural rules of the country where the decision was delivered.

As regards the first situation, namely the case where there has been no service of the documents instituting the original proceedings before the foreign court, it must be highlighted that the mere lack of service does not lead to a refusal of recognition and enforcement. Article 811(b) of the COCP is clear, as it lists a further requirement for a refusal to be ordered: that of not entering an appearance before the foreign court that delivered the decision. If the party that has not been served with the documents instituting the proceedings enters an appearance before the foreign court (and contests the merits of the case), it is considered that they have had enough time to prepare their defence. The lack of service per se should not impede the recognition and/or enforcement of the foreign decision in Malta. It remains ambiguous under which law one should determine whether the party was either served with the initiating documents of the original proceedings or made an appearance before the foreign court. Should Maltese courts refer to their own provisions on the service of documents[28] in order to decide whether the party has been served with the documents instituting the proceedings, or should they apply the service of documents provisions of the country from where the foreign decision originates? The same question arises as regards the second requirement under Article 811(b) of the COCP: which law should define whether a party has entered an appearance before the foreign court that delivered the original decision?

The answer to these questions bears a lot of significance, since the requirements of service or the requirements under which a party is considered to have entered an appearance before a court vary significantly between different legal orders. Traditionally and prior to the 1995 amendments to the COCP, Maltese courts favoured a mixed approach established in the case of *Dott Gius Degiorgio v Zammit*.[29] According to this case law, Maltese courts would apply foreign law when service was supposed to be effected outside of Malta. On the contrary, in cases where service was initiated outside of Malta but was supposed to be effected within Malta, both the law of the country where service was initiated and the provisions of Maltese law would be taken into account. It seems, though, that the Maltese legislator was not satisfied with this interpretation and was of the opinion that the issue of service and appearance before a foreign court should be

[28] Especially Art 187(3) COCP, which regulates, among others, the service of judicial documents for persons domiciled outside of Malta. As per this provision, if the certificate from the officer responsible for serving a written pleading or any judicial act indicates that the person to be served is abroad, the court may direct that service be effected by posting a copy of the written pleading or act at a designated location in the town or district where official notices are typically posted. Additionally, the court may require a summary of the written pleading or act to be published in the *Gazette* and one or more daily newspapers as directed. Where possible, if any residence of the addressee is known in Malta, a copy of the pleading should also be posted on the door of the residence. The court may also implement any other measures it deems appropriate to ensure the pleading or act comes to the attention of the person to be served. In such cases, service shall be considered complete on the third working day after the date of the last publication or posting, whichever is later. In cases where urgent service has been ordered, service shall be considered complete at the time specified by the court, which is to be stated in the publication or posting.

[29] Commercial Court, 18 November 1926, *Dott Gius Degiorgio v Zammit*.

decided by the law of the country where the original proceedings took place. A strong indication for this is Article 827(1)(c) of the COCP which, after the 1995 amendments, provides that the provisions of the last preceding article shall not have effect: (b) in the case of a judgment by default, if the parties were not contumacious according to foreign law.[30]

Although Article 827(1)(c) does not regulate the issue of lack of service and of entering appearance before the foreign court despite the lack of such service, it refers to the inextricably linked problem of the contumacy of the litigating parties. It specifically stipulates that the issue of party contumacy should be decided under foreign law, namely the law of the country where the original proceedings took place. If the issue of contumacy is to be decided under foreign law, the same should also apply to the issue of whether service was effected in the first place as well as to the issue of whether a party, despite the lack of service, entered an appearance before the foreign court. After all, these are all problems related to the service of the documents instituting the proceedings before the foreign court. It would be contrary to intuition to apply foreign law to some of them and Maltese law to others.

Apart from assisting with the interpretation of Article 811(b) of the COCP, Article 827(1)(b) regulates, as mentioned just above, an important due process requirement. It applies in situations where a party in the original proceedings has been lawfully served with the documents instituting the proceedings, but has failed to enter an appearance before the foreign court within the time limits prescribed by the applicable foreign procedural law. In this case, Article 827(1)(b) dictates that Maltese courts should not allow the recognition and/or enforcement of a foreign judicial decision unless it is established that the party that failed to enter an appearance despite being properly served was contumacious according to the provisions of the procedural law of the country where the original proceedings took place.

f) Public Policy

Article 827(1)(c) of the COCP stipulates that a foreign judicial decision will not be recognised and/or enforced in Malta if the judgment contains any disposition contrary to public policy or to the internal public law of Malta.

When interpreting the notion of public policy, Maltese courts draw heavily from English law, which is considered a general source of Maltese private international law.[31] In that sense, Maltese courts will, for example, refuse the recognition and/or enforcement of a foreign judicial decision when: a) it is discriminatory on the grounds of sex, race or religion; b) it enforces transactions against the public interest of Malta (eg trading with hostile jurisdictions); c) it is contrary to established principles of international law (eg infringing human rights); or d) it tries to enforce institutions that are unknown to the legal order of Malta.[32] In general, any disposition of a foreign judicial decision that is contrary to the basic moral, social, economic

[30] Emphasis added.

[31] See First Hall Civil Court, 4 February 1936, *Smith v Muscat Azzopardi*.

[32] For an overview of typical instances where the public policy refusal ground is triggered under English law, see P Rogerson, *Collier's Conflict of Laws* (Cambridge University Press, 2013) 253–54.

and regulatory foundations of the Maltese legal order will trigger the application of public policy.

It is generally accepted that the refusal ground of public policy should only be applied when there is a manifest contradiction between the foreign judicial decision and the local legal order. For example, in *Joseph Attard v Av Dr Rene' A Cremona*,[33] the Commercial Court held that the refusal ground of public policy is not triggered merely because the civil procedural rules of the foreign jurisdiction are different from those of Malta. In the same vein, in *Dr Renato Cefai v Valletta Freight Services Ltd*,[34] the First Hall of the Civil Court rejected the plea that the Maltese legal order was breached because the applicable foreign contract law imposed an interest rate in excess of eight per cent. Mere deviations of the foreign law (procedural or law of substance) from local Maltese laws are not, therefore, enough to support a plea of refusal on the basis of public policy.

g) Reciprocity

Unlike other jurisdictions,[35] Malta does not impose any reciprocity requirements for the recognition and/or enforcement of foreign judicial decisions.

h) Other Requirements

Further negative requirements for the recognition and enforcement of foreign judicial decisions in Malta are established in Article 811 of the COCP. These include:

1. *Incapacity of One of the Parties to be Part of Judicial Proceedings*

According to Article 811(c) of the COCP the recognition and/or enforcement of a foreign judgment can be refused where any of the parties to the suit was under legal disability to sue or be sued, provided no plea thereanent had been raised and determined.

According to relevant case law,[36] the capacity of the parties to participate in judicial proceedings must be determined by reference to Maltese law and, more precisely, Articles 780 and 781 of the COCP.[37]

[33] Commercial Court, 26 March 1965, *Joseph Attard v Av Dr Rene Cremona*.

[34] First Hall Civil Court, 20 March 2000, *Dr Renato Cefai v Valletta Freight Services Ltd*.

[35] For example Germany under § 328(1)(5) ZPO.

[36] See Court of Appeal, 24 January 1997, n° 288/90, *Carmelo Busuttil v Mary armla minn Joseph Gauci*.

[37] These provisions read as follows: '780. The plea as to the capacity of the plaintiff or the defendant may be raised, if the one or the other is under any legal disability to sue or be sued or if he sues or is sued in the name and on behalf of others without being lawfully authorized for the purpose. 781. The following persons may not sue or be sued: (a) a minor, except in the person of the parent exercising paternal authority, or, in the absence of such parent, of a tutor or a curator; (b) an insane person, a person with a mental disorder or other condition, which renders him incapable of managing his own affairs, and any other person who is not vested with the free exercise or administration of the rights to which the action refers, except in the person of the party to whom such administration is lawfully entrusted, or of a curator ad litem.'

2. *Wrong Application of the Law*

Under Article 811(e), a wrong application of the law is one of the 12 grounds that can permit a retrial and, for the purposes of this report, lead to refusal of recognition and/or enforcement of foreign judicial decisions. In a way, this ground allows Maltese courts to re-examine the application of the law of substance during the original proceedings, something that substantially expands their level of interference with the adjudicatory power of the foreign court. Since Article 811(e) does not make a distinction, the ground can be evoked not only when the foreign court applied Maltese law to the merits of the case, but also when it applied a foreign law to the merits of the case. While the involvement of the Maltese courts in the interpretation of Maltese law by a foreign court might present certain advantages in view of the enhanced expertise of Maltese courts, it might also create complications, especially if the foreign court applied either its native or any other foreign law to the merits of the case.

What constitutes a wrong application of the law under Article 811(e) of the COCP is not straightforward, and successful pleas on this basis are rare. This is because the ground is narrowly defined and Maltese courts have displayed a lot of restraint when interpreting the provision.

For instance, in the case of *Com Francesco Azzopardi v Francesco Galea*,[38] the Court of Appeal noted that a wrong application arises when there's a blatant breach of a clear law that isn't open to interpretation. Similarly, the Constitutional Court in *Edward Ferro v Housing Secretary*[39] highlighted that a wrong application of the law occurs when the decision does not align with the law's wording. The Court of Appeal has also consistently held that when the plea of Article 811(e) is being raised, the court should not re-examine the facts of the case, but should only verify if the wrong application of the law resulted from the facts established in the contested judgment. From the above, it becomes clear that Article 811(e) does not apply when there is a mere misinterpretation of the applicable law, but mostly when the court did not apply the right provisions on the facts established in the contested dispute.

Article 816 of the COCP mandates that when alleging a wrong application of the law, the plaintiff must reference the law that should have been applied. Failure to do so invalidates the request. The party claiming a wrong application of a foreign law will have, therefore, to not only make a plea that the legal provisions applied were not right, but also indicate which provisions should have been applied in the contested case.

3. *When the Court Decides on Matters not Present in the Initial Demand or in Excess of the Demand*

According to Article 811(f) and (g) a court should not decide on matters not present in the initial demand, nor should it decide in excess on the demand made by the plaintiff. In determining the scope of the plaintiff's original claim and assessing the extent to which the foreign court adjudicated matters beyond or outside the ambit of the initial claim, Maltese law should be the governing authority.

[38] Court of Appeal, 17 February 1876, *Com Francesco Azzopardi v Francesco Galea*.
[39] Constitutional Court, 19 June 1973, *Ferro Edward v Housing Secretary*.

4. *Contrary Dispositions*

According to Article 811(i) of the COCP, a foreign judgment should be refused recognition and/or enforcement in Malta when it contains contrary dispositions. Maltese courts have been stringent in interpreting what qualifies as contradictory dispositions in a judgment, leading to several limitations on applying this ground.

In *Edward Ferro v Housing Secretary*, the Constitutional Court emphasised that contradictory dispositions should be found in the *dispositivo* (operative part) of the judgment and not in the *motivi* (reasons), while in *Carmelo Busuttil v Mary armla minn Joseph Gauci*,[40] the Court of Appeal stated that the *motivazioni* (explanations) of a judgment might sometimes help identify contradictions. It was further clarified that the conflicting dispositions should nullify each other to the extent that none can be executed. If dispositions conflict but are not irreconcilable, a refusal of recognition and/or enforcement of the foreign judgment isn't warranted.

5. *The Foreign Decision was Based on False Evidence*

According to Article 811(j) COCP the recognition and/or enforcement of a foreign judgment can be denied where the judgment was based on evidence that, in a subsequent judgment, was declared to be false or which was so declared in a previous judgment but the party cast was not aware of such fact.

For this ground of refusal to be triggered the following requirements must be met: the challenged judgment should be based on false evidence. The evidence's falsity should be determined in a separate judgment, not in the judgment referring to the recognition and/or enforcement of the foreign judgment. The judgment determining the evidence's falsity can either come before or after the challenged judgment. If the separate judgment determining falsity comes before the challenged judgment, the party demanding the retrial shouldn't have known about it.

In several cases, there were debates about the validity of proceedings aimed at obtaining a declaration that certain evidence is false. For instance, in *Joseph Zammit v Carmelo Dingli*,[41] the Civil Court clarified that before demanding a retrial, the plaintiff must first seek a judgment declaring the contested evidence as false. The court defined false evidence as anything that maliciously presents itself as true (eg false testimony). Simple errors by witnesses or experts and inaccuracies in documents do not qualify as false evidence under Article 811(j) COCP.

6. *Discovery of a Conclusive Document*

Article 811(k) COCP outlines conditions for refusal of the recognition and/or enforcement of a foreign judgment on the discovery of a conclusive document. For a retrial to be granted, the party presenting the document must prove that they had no prior knowledge of the document before the original judgment was given and that they could

[40] Court of Appeal, 24 January 1997, *Carmelo Busuttil v Mary armla minn Joseph Gauci*.
[41] Court of Appeal, 25 May 2001, *Joseph Zammit v Carmelo Dingli*.

not legally present the document before the original judgment. It is not enough to just discover and present a previously unknown document. The party must demonstrate they made significant efforts to obtain the document, akin to the diligence of a *bonus pater familias*. The application of Article 811(k) should be reserved for extraordinary cases and should not be granted merely based on the discovery of a new document without considering the circumstances of its discovery.

7. *Error of Fact*

According to Article 811(l) a foreign judgment may be denied recognition and/or enforcement in Malta where the judgment was the effect of an error resulting from the proceedings or documents of the cause.

The ground of error of fact is applicable in limited situations. It is invoked when a judgment is based on a clearly false assumption of a fact or when it assumes a fact is false despite its proven truth, provided the fact was not a contested point in the judgment. The error must arise from the case's proceedings or documents and must be evident in the judgment itself. The error should be a significant factual mistake, not one of interpretation. It is also crucial that this error significantly influenced the judge's decision. In *Carmelo Busuttil v Mary armla minn Joseph Gauci*,[42] the Court of Appeal emphasised that if a judgment contains a clear factual error but is also supported by other valid reasons, there is no basis for a retrial or, in the case of this report, for a refusal of a recognition and/or enforcement of a foreign judgment.

Question 4. Documents to be Produced

The documents to be produced with the application for the recognition and/or enforcement of a foreign judgment include a certified copy of the original judgment, a certified translation of the original judgment in English or Maltese, and a certificate of no appeal.

Question 5. Securities, Bonds and Deposits

There are no specific provisions regulating securities, bonds or deposits as regards the procedure of recognition and/or enforcement of foreign judicial decisions. If the party requesting the recognition and enforcement of the foreign judgment avail themselves of the precautionary warrants available under the COCP,[43] security shall be given according to Articles 830(2) and 836. If there is an appeal against the decision on the recognition and/or enforcement of the foreign judicial decision, the party lodging the appeal must make a security deposit according to Article 249 COCP.

[42] Court of Appeal, 24 January 1997, *Carmelo Busuttil v Mary armla minn Joseph Gauci*.
[43] Arts 829–38 COCP.

Netherlands

TESS BENS AND BIRGIT VAN HOUTERT

Question 1. General Overview

The Dutch Code of Civil Procedure (*Wetboek van Burgerlijke Rechtsvordering*) does not contain a systematic and comprehensive national-autonomous regime that governs the recognition and enforcement of foreign judgments in civil and commercial matters in the Netherlands.[1] In fact, Article 431(1) of the Dutch Code of Civil Procedure (DCCP) prohibits the enforcement of foreign judgments and authentic acts in the Netherlands, unless they are recognised pursuant to an international convention and a Dutch court granted leave for their enforcement, ie an *exequatur*, in a procedure in accordance with Articles 985–994 DCCP.[2] Absent an international convention, an enforceable title in the Netherlands can only be obtained by a new decision on the merits of the foreign case by a Dutch court in proceedings pursuant to Article 431(2) DCCP. The prohibition of enforcement, however, did not preclude the Supreme Court (*Hoge Raad*) from developing national-autonomous rules that govern the recognition of foreign judgments,[3]

[1] The Kingdom of the Netherlands comprises four constituent countries: Aruba; Curacao; the Netherlands; and Sint Maarten. The BES islands (Bonaire, Sint Eustatius and Saba) enjoy the status of special municipalities of the Netherlands. In this national report, we only discuss the national-autonomous rules on the recognition and enforcement of non-EU judgments in civil and commercial matters in the Netherlands, excluding the BES islands. The term 'non-EU judgments' excludes judgments originating from the 'Caribbean' part of the Kingdom of the Netherlands. The interregional recognition and enforcement of judgments within the Kingdom of the Netherlands is subject to Art 40 of the Charter for the Kingdom of the Netherlands (*Statuut voor het Koninkrijk der Nederlanden*). See generally GCC Lewin, *Interregionaal Privaatrecht* (Maklu, 2014) 109–18. Unless indicated otherwise, the term 'foreign judgments' refers to non-EU judgments for the purpose of this report.

[2] According to Art 985 DCCP, an *exequatur* could also be obtained if a foreign judgment or authentic act is recognised pursuant to a Dutch statutory provision. However, such a provision did not exist at the time of its introduction in 1964 (see Kamerstukken II, 1962/63, no 7179, 3, 3), nor has one been introduced since. Pursuant to Art 992 DCCP, the national *exequatur* procedure is not applicable where an international convention establishes specific or uniform procedural arrangements to obtain an *exequatur*.

[3] The term 'foreign judgment' is generally understood in the Netherlands as referring to any decision given by a foreign court, irrespective of its name. See L Strikwerda and SJ Schaafsma, *Inleiding tot het Nederlandse Internationaal Privaatrecht*, 12th edn (Wolters Kluwer, 2019) 375. Settlements formally approved by a foreign court are treated as judgments. See Rechtbank Amsterdam, 9 November 2022, ECLI:NL:RBAMS:2022:6444, 5.9. See B van Houtert, 'Het 2019 Haags Vonnissenverdrag: een *game changer* in Nederland? Een rechtsvergelijkende analyse tussen het verdrag en het Nederlandse commune IPR' (2023) *Nederlands Internationaal Privaatrecht* 573, 576–77. See Kamerstukken II, 1962/63, no 7179, 3, 4.

including in civil and commercial matters,[4] in its case law on the interpretation of Article 431 DCCP.[5]

Article 431 DCCP was never amended in substance since its introduction 1838.[6] While it was initially interpreted by the Supreme Court as precluding both the recognition and the enforcement of foreign judgments in the Netherlands,[7] this interpretation was abandoned in the early twentieth century.[8] In 1924, the Supreme Court established in its seminal *Fur Coat* ruling that a Dutch court has discretion to determine whether – and to what extent – it recognises a foreign judgment, subject to certain minimum requirements.[9] These minimum requirements were further refined over the course of the twentieth century and became the norm for the recognition of all foreign judgments in the absence of an international convention.[10] In 2014, the Supreme Court formulated four exhaustive national-autonomous requirements for recognition in its ruling in *Gazprombank*.[11] A foreign judgment is in principle recognised in the Netherlands if:

(1) the jurisdiction of the court of origin is based on an internationally generally accepted ground of jurisdiction;
(2) the judgment was given in proceedings that meet due process-standards;
(3) the recognition of the judgment is not contrary to Dutch public policy; and
(4) the judgment is not irreconcilable with a judgment given by a Dutch court between the same parties, or with an earlier foreign judgment given in proceedings that

[4] The national-autonomous requirements for recognition developed in the case law of the Supreme Court are not restricted to foreign judgments in civil and commercial matters. These rules may also apply in matters of insolvency, as well as certain family matters in the absence of a codified national-autonomous rule on recognition. Notwithstanding the limitation of the scope of this report to civil and commercial matters, judgments in family matters and matters of insolvency are considered if they concern the interpretation of requirements for recognition.

[5] See JB van de Velden, *Finality in Litigation: The Law and Practice of Preclusion – Res Judicata (Merger and Estoppel), Abuse of Process and Recognition of Foreign Judgments* (Wolters Kluwer International, 2017) 298; P Vlas, 'On the Development of Private International Law in The Netherlands: From Asser's Days to the Codification of Dutch Private International Law (1910–2010)' (2010) 57 *Netherlands International Law Review* 167, 178.

[6] The national *exequatur* procedure formerly envisaged in Arts 431(3) and (4) DCCP (old) was revised in 1964 and moved to Arts 985–994 DCCP. This revision concerned the procedure and formalities to obtain an *exequatur* and did not involve other amendments to Art 431 DCCP. See Kamerstukken II, 1962/63, no 7179, 3, 3.

[7] Hoge Raad, 31 January 1902, *Weekblad van het recht* 7717.

[8] According to Verschuur, the opinion that Art 431 DCCP only prevents the enforcement of foreign judgments – and not their recognition – already prevailed in the case law of the Dutch (lower) courts during the 19th century. See RCh Verschuur, 'Recognition and Enforcement of Foreign Judgments in the Netherlands' in G Walter and SP Baumgardner (eds), *Recognition and Enforcement of Foreign Judgments Outside the Scope of the Brussels and Lugano Conventions* (Kluwer Law International, 2000) 403, 405.

[9] Hoge Raad, 14 November 1924, *Nederlandse Jurisprudentie* 1925/91. The *Fur Coat* ruling was considered to apply to all types of judgments, except constitutive judgments in matters of personal status. The recognition of the latter type of foreign judgments had already been addressed in Hoge Raad, 24 November 1916, *Nederlandse Jurisprudentie* 1917/5, in which it was held that Art 431(1) DCCP did not preclude a Dutch court from recognising a legal status established by such a judgment.

[10] Hoge Raad, 26 January 1996, *Nederlandse Jurisprudentie* 1997/258. See M Freudenthal, 'Dutch national rules on the recognition and enforcement of foreign judgments, Article 431 CCP' (2014) *Nederlands Internationaal Privaatrecht* 563, 566–68 for an elaborate historical account of the developments in Dutch case law and doctrine prior to 2014.

[11] Hoge Raad, 26 September 2014, ECLI:NL:HR:2014:2838, 3.6.4. The Supreme Court confirmed these requirements in Hoge Raad, 18 January 2019, ECLI:NL:HR:2019:54, *Yukos Oil*, 4.3.4 and Hoge Raad, 16 July 2021, ECLI:NL:HR:2021:1170, *ABA/ENEL*, 3.2.2.

involve the same parties and the same cause of action, provided that the earlier foreign judgment is susceptible to recognition.

A foreign judgment that meets the requirements for recognition set out in the *Gazprombank* ruling still cannot automatically be enforced in the Netherlands due to the prohibition in Article 431(1) DCCP.[12] An enforceable title in the Netherlands can instead be obtained in proceedings pursuant to Article 431(2) DCCP. According to the Supreme Court, two claims can be submitted in this procedure.[13] The first claim is to rule in accordance with the foreign judgment. If the requirements for recognition of the *Gazprombank* ruling are met, a Dutch court will accept the binding effect of the decisions of the foreign court and decide the claim in favour of the claimant, unless the judgment is not (yet) or no longer enforceable in the state of origin.[14] The second claim is for a new decision on the merits of the foreign dispute, in which case the foreign judgment has evidentiary value. This claim can be submitted as a principal claim, or as an alternative claim if a principal claim to rule in accordance with the foreign judgment is dismissed. Either way, a successful claim results in new Dutch judgment that can be enforced in the Netherlands.[15]

In 2017, the WODC published a study on the application of Article 431 DCCP in the Netherlands that was conducted by researchers from the University of Groningen.[16] The study highlighted the peculiar nature of the system for the recognition and enforcement of foreign judgments that was developed by the Supreme Court from a comparative perspective, which is also at odds with the outdated text of the provision. While the system is 'workable' in practice, it also leaves many gaps and uncertainties that could be addressed through a revision of Article 431 DCCP.[17] The Dutch State Committee on Private International Law reached a more firm conclusion in an advice published in February 2023, which insists on revision of this unclear and complex provision.[18] No reform attempt has (yet) been made by the Dutch legislator.

[12] The prohibition of enforcement naturally pertains to foreign judgments that could be subject to execution, ie condemnatory judgments (usually money judgments). The prohibition of enforcement is irrelevant if there is nothing to enforce. *cf* Strikwerda and Schaafsma (n 3) 376, 404.

[13] Hoge Raad, 26 September 2014, ECLI:NL:HR:2014:2838, 3.6.5–3.6.11.

[14] See the answer to Question 3 b).

[15] The result of a successful claim on the basis of Art 431(2) DCCP is very similar to the result of an action upon a foreign judgment under the English common law. Both systems essentially substitute a foreign judgment with a domestic judgment for the purpose of enforcement. See TAG Bens, 'Brussel na de Brexit: nieuwe regels in burgerlijke en handelszaken?' (2021) *Nederlands Internationaal Privaatrecht* 471, 488–89. After the ruling of the CJEU in C-568/20 *H Limited*, questions have arisen amongst Dutch academics and practitioners concerning the extent to which a judgment given in proceedings pursuant to Art 431(2) DCCP is recognised and can be enforced in all EU Member States under the Brussels Ia Regulation. See, inter alia, KJ Krzeminski, 'Actio iudicati onder de Brussel I-bis Vo: een open deur of een geopend "achterdeurtje"?' (2022) *Nederlands Internationaal Privaatrecht* 650. However, there are no reported cases from other EU Member States.

[16] The WODC (Research and Documentation Centre) is the knowledge centre of the Dutch Ministry of Justice and Security, which carries out or commissions scientific research for policy and implementation purposes. See MH Ten Wolde, JG Knot and KC Henckel, *Tenuitvoerlegging van buitenlandse civielrechtelijke vonnissen in Nederland buiten verdrag en verordening (art. 431 Rv)* (WODC, 2017) ('WODC Study').

[17] ibid 135–36.

[18] Staatscommissie voor Internationaal Privaatrecht, *Advies herziening van artikel 431 Rv inzake de erkenning en tenuitvoerlegging van buitenlandse civielrechtelijke vonnissen buiten verdrag en verordening* (21 February 2023).

Question 2. Procedure

a) Circumstances of Recognition and Enforcement

There is no special national procedure in which a party can apply for the formal (refusal of) recognition of a foreign judgment.[19] Questions concerning the 'mere' recognition of a foreign judgment can arise in any procedure, regardless of the type of judgment that is invoked.[20] A foreign judgment in which the same claim between the same parties was decided may for example be invoked as a defence. In such a case, a Dutch court should determine whether that judgment must be recognised and establish its effects for the proceedings at hand.[21] Recognition is therefore not automatic, but rather established on a case-by-case basis in the light of the requirements formulated in *Gazprombank*.[22]

Given that a foreign judgment in itself cannot be declared enforceable or enforced in the Netherlands absent an international convention or EU regulation, a Dutch judgment must be obtained in proceedings pursuant to Article 431(2) DCCP for the purpose of enforcement.[23] Apart from the extent of a review on the merits of the foreign judgment and the burden of proving the requirements for recognition, all procedural aspects discussed below only concern the latter procedure. Differences with the *exequatur* procedure pursuant to Article 985 DCCP are discussed where appropriate to illustrate the peculiar nature of proceedings pursuant to Article 431(2) DCCP.

From a formal point of view, a procedure pursuant to Article 431(2) DCCP is a new procedure on the merits of the foreign case.[24] The procedure is governed by the general rules of civil procedure, as the Dutch legislator did not make any special procedural arrangements. In practice, a Dutch court can dispense with a claim to rule in accordance with a foreign judgment if that judgment meets the requirements for recognition formulated in the *Gazprombank* ruling.[25] If one neglects the formal differences with the *exequatur* procedure pursuant to Article 985 DCCP, both procedures in substance result in an enforceable title in the Netherlands on the basis of a foreign judgment, without a review on the merits.[26] However, this parallel only applies insofar a successful claim to rule in accordance with the foreign judgment is submitted. The claimant retains the option to submit a claim for a new decision on the merits, either as a principal claim or as an alternative claim.[27] The formal starting point in this respect remains that a claim

[19] See Verschuur (n 8) 416.

[20] See Strikwerda and Schaafsma (n 3) 376.

[21] See Rechtbank Amsterdam, 2 November 2016, ECLI:NL:RBAMS:2016:7287, 5.1–5.10 (US defamation judgment invoked as defence against defamation claim in Dutch proceedings). See also Rechtbank Rotterdam, 13 March 2019, ECLI:NL:RBROT:2019:1954, 4.5–4.12 (findings on the non-existence of a contractual relationship between the parties in Russian negative judgment on jurisdiction invoked as a defence against contractual claim).

[22] See F Fernhout, 'Enforcing Foreign Titles Regarding Monetary Claims in the Netherlands' in V Rijavec, K Drnovšek and CH van Rhee (eds), *Cross-Border Enforcement in Europe: National and International Perspectives* (Intersentia, 2020) 153, 164.

[23] See the answer to Question 1.

[24] Hoge Raad, 26 September 2014, ECLI:NL:HR:2014:2838, *Gazprombank*, 3.6.2.

[25] See the answer to Question 1.

[26] See Strikwerda and Schaafsma (n 3) 412–13.

[27] See the answer to Question 1.

on the basis of Article 431(2) DCCP amounts to a new procedure on the merits of the foreign case, notwithstanding the substantive result of this procedure.

A procedure pursuant to Article 431(2) DCCP is initiated by a writ of summons (*dagvaarding*).[28] The general order of such proceedings is that the claimant arranges service of the writ of summons on the defendant, including a statement of claim, and registers the case with the competent court. Absent any procedural complications, the defendant can submit a statement of defence, after which the case is argued orally in court and/or further written statements can be submitted. The proceedings are concluded with a judgment. A default judgment can be given if the defendant did not appear, provided that the defendant was properly summoned.[29]

The *exequatur* procedure pursuant to Article 985 DCCP is instead initiated by means of a petition (*verzoekschrift*).[30] In general, a petition must be filed at the competent court, which schedules an oral hearing and invites the respondent and/or interested third parties to submit a statement of response. A court decision takes the form of an order (*beschikking*) instead of a judgment.[31] However, it should be noted that Articles 985–990 DCCP establish several specific rules that supplement or derogate the general rules of civil procedure applicable to petition proceedings.[32] Petition proceedings that were erroneously initiated on the basis of Article 985 DCCP, eg because there is no international convention that governs the recognition of an English judgment post-Brexit, can be converted into summons proceedings pursuant to Article 431(2) DCCP.[33]

b) Procedural Steps

1. Competent Authorities

Nearly all first instance civil cases in the Netherlands start at the District Court (*rechtbank*).[34] Several (sub-)sections must be distinguished. The cantonal judge (*kantonrechter*) has

[28] The general rules that govern summons proceedings can be found in Arts 78–259 DCCP. The default rule is that a procedure must be initiated by a writ of summons, unless a specific procedure is prescribed (Art 78(1) DCCP).

[29] See on summons proceedings, M van Hooijdonk and P Eijsvoogel, *Litigation in the Netherlands* (Wolters Kluwer, 2012) 37–53; HJ Snijders et al (eds), *Nederlands Burgerlijk Procesrecht*, 7th edn (Wolters Kluwer, 2022) 176–216.

[30] The general rules that govern petition proceedings can be found in Arts 261–302 DCCP. These rules apply only if the DCCP specifically prescribes petition proceedings (Art 261(1) DCCP), such as in Art 986(1) DCCP.

[31] See on petition proceedings Van Hooijdonk and Eijsvoogel (n 29) 70–73; Snijders et al (n 29) 403–17.

[32] The petitioner must for example submit an authentic, and potentially legalised and/or translated, copy of the foreign judgment (Art 986(2)–(4) DCCP), while the party against whom enforcement is sought must be properly summoned by the petitioner, rather than invited by the court, to appear in the oral hearing (Art 987(1)–(4) DCCP).

[33] Art 69 DCCP allows repair if a procedure was initiated by the wrong document, as well as transfer to a different judge. See Rechtbank Amsterdam, 15 November 2022, ECLI:NL:RBAMS:2022:7521, 4.14. There has been discussion in the Netherlands whether the 1967 bilateral treaty on recognition and enforcement between the UK and the Netherlands 'revived' after Brexit. However, it appears to be accepted now that it this treaty only remains in force in relations between the UK and the Caribbean part of the Kingdom of the Netherlands, as well as relations between the Netherlands and Guernsey, Jersey and the Isle of Man. See, inter alia, Bens (n 15) 482–83.

[34] Art 42 Act on the Organisation of the Judiciary (*Wet op de Rechterlijke Organisatie*).

exclusive competence for monetary claims up to EUR 25.000, as well as specific types of contracts irrespective of the monetary value of the claim.[35] The provisional relief judge (*voorzieningenrechter*) has exclusive competence in preliminary relief proceedings (*kort geding*).[36] Other cases are either decided by a single judge (*enkelvoudige kamer*) or a chamber of three judges (*meervoudige kamer*), depending on the complexity of the case.[37]

Claims pursuant to Article 431(2) DCCP can be decided by a cantonal judge,[38] although the total value of the claim(s) will in practice often exceed EUR 25.000. A claim on the basis of Article 431(2) DCCP is therefore usually decided by one or three judges of the district court. In provisional relief proceedings, the provisional relief judge cannot decide a claim on the basis of Article 431(2) DCCP.[39] However, the extent to which a foreign judgment is susceptible to recognition can be provisionally assessed to determine whether interim measures can be granted or lifted.[40]

2. *International and Venue Jurisdiction*

Determining which district court has venue jurisdiction to decide a claim on the basis of Article 431(2) DCCP is theoretically complicated on the account of three reasons. First, the claimant may submit a claim to rule in accordance with the foreign judgment and/or a claim for a new decision on the merits. In addition, the claimant can submit a claim that was not dealt with in the foreign case.[41] In principle, international jurisdiction ought to be established for each individual claim.[42] Second, all claims could, for the purpose of establishing international jurisdiction, either fall within the material scope of the Brussels Ia Regulation, or be excluded from that scope and governed by the domestic rules in Articles 1–14 DCCP. Third, neither Article 431 DCCP itself, nor the domestic general rules on venue jurisdiction in summons proceedings (Articles 99–109 DCCP), provide an indication as to the territorially competent district court.[43] The rules on venue jurisdiction for the *exequatur* procedure in Article 985 DCCP do not apply.[44]

[35] Art 93 DCCP. The type of contracts includes employment, tenancy, agency, consumer credit and consumer sales contrast. In cases before a cantonal judge, legal representation is not mandatory. See Art 89 DCCP.

[36] Art 254(1) DCCP.

[37] Art 15 DCCP.

[38] The Dutch case that led to one of the first CJEU rulings on the interpretation of the 1968 Brussels Convention was based on a case decided by a cantonal judge pursuant to Art 431(2) DCCP. See Case 42/76 *De Wolf*.

[39] Only provisional remedies can be granted. See Van Hooijdonk and Eijsvoogel (n 29) 110–12.

[40] See Rechtbank Amsterdam, 12 December 2018, ECLI:NL:RBAMS:2018:9144 (prospect of recognition of judgment in proceedings pending before English High Court precludes lifting attachment levied in the Netherlands); Rechtbank Noord-Holland, 15 July 2022, ECLI:NL:RBNHO:2022:6208, 4.5–4.11 (jurisdiction of the US court presumed to be based on an internationally accepted ground of jurisdiction, but final decision reserved for main proceedings pursuant to Art 43 (2) DCCP. Prospect of recognition of US judgment did not allow attachment levied in the Netherlands on the basis of that judgment to be lifted).

[41] See Rechtbank Amsterdam, 12 April 2023, ECLI:NL:RBAMS:2023:2524, 4.7 (jurisdiction established separately for claims that exceed the amount awarded in Serbian judgments).

[42] See in this sense WODC Study (n 16) 28–31.

[43] See N Peters, 'Bevoegdheid van de Nederlandse rechter bij een exequaturprocedure en een *actio iudicati*' (2010) *Nederlands Internationaal Privaatrecht* 220.

[44] WODC Study (n 16) 28. *cf* Hof Arnhem-Leeuwarden, 27 October 2015, ECLI:NL:GHARL:2015:8059, 4.2 (Art 985 DCCP apparently applied by analogy to justify venue jurisdiction based on presence of assets); Rechtbank Amsterdam, 2 October 2024, ECLI:NL:RBAMS:2024:6245, 4.3 (Art 985 DCCP applied to determine venue jurisdiction).

The question whether a claim on the basis of Article 431(2) DCCP against a defendant that is domiciled in the Netherlands or in another EU Member State falls within the material scope of the Brussels Ia Regulation is pertinent, but underappreciated. Due to the Court of Justice of the European Union (CJEU)'s ruling in *Owens Bank*,[45] it is commonly assumed that a claim to rule in accordance with a foreign judgment falls outside the scope of the Brussels Ia Regulation, but not a claim for a new decision on the merits.[46] The *Owens Bank* ruling, however, rather excludes the *exequatur* procedure pursuant to Article 985 DCCP.[47] Moreover, while the CJEU ruling in *De Wolf* makes clear that proceedings pursuant to Article 431(2) DCCP cannot be used to obtain a Dutch judgment against an EU defendant on the basis of an EU judgment,[48] it says nothing on non-EU judgments. Consequently, it cannot be excluded, nor taken for granted that a claim pursuant to Article 431(2) DCCP is excluded from the material scope of the Brussels Ia Regulation.

Either way, the potential (in)applicability of the Brussels Ia Regulation makes little difference if the defendant is domiciled in the Netherlands. The application of Article 4 Brussels Ia Regulation and Article 2 DCCP both lead to venue jurisdiction of the district court of the defendant's domicile.[49] In practice, most claims on the basis of Article 431(2) DCCP are initiated against defendants that are domiciled in the Netherlands. In this context, it does not matter if Article 431(2) DCCP itself is considered instead of – or in conjunction with – Article 4 Brussels Ia Regulation as a basis for jurisdiction.[50]

However, the matter becomes more salient if the defendant is domiciled in another EU Member State. If both claims fall within the material scope of the Brussels Ia Regulation, the Dutch courts would not have international jurisdiction vis-à-vis defendants domiciled in EU Member States in proceedings pursuant to Article 431(2) DCCP.[51] If both claims fall outside the material scope of the Brussels Ia Regulation, the Dutch courts could have international jurisdiction on the basis of an attachment levied in the Netherlands pursuant to Articles 10 and 767 DCCP.[52] The presence of assets in the Netherlands has been sufficient for some district courts to base their international jurisdiction on Article 431(2) DCCP itself,[53] including against EU defendants.[54]

[45] Case C-192/92 *Owens Bank*.

[46] WODC Study (n 16) 28–31. *cf* Peters (n 43) 220, who argues that both claims are excluded from the scope of the Brussels Ia Regulation.

[47] See Peters (n 43) 220.

[48] *De Wolf* (n 38).

[49] Neither Art 4 Brussels Ia Regulation nor Art 2 DCCP govern venue jurisdiction. In either case, the district court of the defendant's domicile has venue jurisdiction pursuant to Art 99 DCCP.

[50] See Hof Arnhem-Leeuwarden, 8 June 2021, ECLI:NL:GHARL:2021:5620, 5.3; Rechtbank Amsterdam, 4 April 2023, ECLI:NL:RBAMS:2023:2040, 5.1; Hof Arnhem-Leeuwarden, 15 November 2024, ECLI:NL:GHARL:2024:6373, 4.2.

[51] See also Peters (n 43) 220.

[52] See WODC Study (n 16) 29. A court cannot base its jurisdiction on Arts 10 and 767 DCCP in case of an exclusive choice of forum for a foreign court. See Hoge Raad, 17 December 1993, ECLI:NL:HR:1993:ZC1183; Hoge Raad, 16 June 1995, ECLI:NL:HR:1995:ZC1761, 5.53. Arts 10 and 767 DCCP operate as a residual basis for establishing jurisdiction on a basis not mentioned in Arts 1–14 DCCP. See TAG Bens, 'Netherlands' in T Lutzi, E Piovesani and D Zgrabljic Rotar (eds), *Jurisdiction over Non-EU Defendants: Should the Brussels Ia Regulation Be Extended?* (Hart Publishing, 2023) 195, 195–96.

[53] Rechtbank Amsterdam, 9 November 2022, ECLI:NL:RBAMS:2022:6444, 5.2 (international and venue jurisdiction for claim against South African defendant on the basis of attachments levied in the Netherlands).

[54] Hof Amsterdam, 3 December 2019 ECLI:NL:GHAMS:2019:4260, 2.10 (claim to rule in accordance with Albanian judgment against defendants domiciled in Italy).

The treatment of EU defendants would in this case not be any different from non-EU defendants.

3. *Burden of Proof*

The main rule concerning evidence in civil proceedings in the Netherlands is that the party who asserts the legal consequences of facts or rights also bears the burden of proof, unless provided otherwise.[55] Consequently, the party that invokes a foreign judgment is in principle required to demonstrate its existence,[56] as well as assert and prove that the requirements for recognition are met.[57] In practice, however, it will often be up to the party that invokes the non-recognition of the foreign judgment to assert and prove that these requirements were not met.[58] If necessary, a court can examine the requirements for recognition of a foreign judgment *ex officio*.[59]

Whether the mere recognition of a foreign judgment is sought or a judgment is sought in proceedings pursuant to Article 431(2) DCCP for the purpose of enforcement does not affect the allocation of the burden of proof with respect to the requirements for recognition. However, if a Dutch judgment is sought in proceedings pursuant to Article 431(2) DCCP, the defendant bears the burden of proof to assert and establish that the foreign judgment is not (yet) or no longer enforceable in the country of origin.[60]

4. *Permissibility and Extent of a Review on the Merits*

The examination whether a foreign judgment meets the requirements for recognition formulated in the *Gazprombank* ruling can take place if the mere recognition of a foreign judgment is sought, or if a Dutch judgment is sought in proceedings pursuant to Article 431(2) DCCP for the purpose of enforcement.[61] In general, the merits of a foreign judgment cannot be reviewed in examining whether the judgment meets requirements for recognition.[62] A foreign judgment that meets those requirements is in principle recognised, without a review on the merits.[63]

Nonetheless, a review on the merits of the foreign judgment is permissible in proceedings pursuant to Article 431(2) DCCP, provided that a claim for a new decision on the merits of the foreign case has been submitted.[64] In principle, such a claim amounts to a full

[55] Art 150 DCCP.

[56] See the answer to Question 4.

[57] WODC Study (n 16) 36. If the jurisdiction of the foreign court was based on a choice of forum, submitting the choice of forum as evidence is sufficient to demonstrate the existence of a an internationally accepted ground for jurisdiction. See Hoge Raad, 17 December 1993, ECLI:NL:HR:1993:ZC1183, *Esmil/Enka*, 3.3.6.

[58] WODC Study (n 16) 37.

[59] See eg Rechtbank Rotterdam, 15 July 2015, ECLI:NL:RBROT:2015:6172, 4.3–4.9; Rechtbank Rotterdam, 13 March 2019, ECLI:NL:RBROT:2019:1954, 4.9; Rechtbank Noord-Holland, 1 April 2020, ECLI:NL:RBNHO:2020:2425, 4.13.

[60] Hoge Raad, 26 September 2014, ECLI:NL:HR:2014:2838, 3.6.9–3.6.10.

[61] See the answer to Question 1.

[62] *Yukos Oil* (n 11) 4.1.4.

[63] See eg Rechtbank Noord-Holland 16 September 2015, ECLI:NL:RBNHO:2015:7778, 2.9.

[64] If a claimant submits a claim to rule in accordance with a foreign judgment, but does not submit an alternative claim for a new decision on the merits, the court is not obliged to examine the merits of the case if it dismisses the claim to rule in accordance with a foreign judgment. See Rechtbank Zeeland-West-Brabant, 16 August 2017, ECLI:NL:RBZWB:2017:5251, 3.6.

examination of the merits of the foreign case, although the foreign judgment is admissible as evidence. A Dutch court must therefore establish the 'evidentiary value' of foreign judgment.[65] In other words, a court is not bound to any findings of law or fact in the foreign judgment and has significant freedom in establishing whether and to what extent it adopts the findings of the foreign court.[66]

5. *Appeal*

A judgment in proceedings pursuant to Article 431(2) DCCP can be subject to ordinary remedies, including appeal (*hoger beroep*),[67] cassation (*cassatie*)[68] and opposition (*verzet*),[69] as well as extraordinary remedies, such as third-party opposition (*derdenverzet*),[70] revocation (*herroeping*)[71] and cassation in the interest of law (*cassatie in het belang der wet*).[72] The differences between ordinary and extraordinary remedies are, inter alia, that the ordinary remedies suspend the enforceability of the judgment,[73] while the extraordinary remedies can also be requested after the expiry of the time limits for ordinary remedies.[74] Only the ordinary remedies will be discussed below.[75]

Almost all final judgments given by a District Court in first instance proceedings can be appealed.[76] The competent court is the Court of Appeal (*Gerechtshof* or *Hof*) in the area where the District Court is located.[77] An appeal must be lodged within three months after the date on which the first instance judgment was given.[78] The Court of Appeal conducts a full review of the merits of the first instance case on issues of both law and fact. Appellate proceedings are in formal terms very similar to first instance proceedings, although the appellant and respondent must in appeal concentrate all their claims in their statements of claim and defence.[79]

[65] *ABA/ENEL* (n 11) 3.4.2; Hoge Raad, 26 September 2014, ECLI:NL:HR:2014:2838, 3.6.11.
[66] See eg Rechtbank, Amsterdam 12 April 2023, ECLI:NL:RBAMS:2023:2524, 4.19–4.20 (new decision on the merits of a Serbian case, as the Serbian default judgment is not susceptible to recognition. The judgment was not considered to have evidentiary value as a default judgment).
[67] Arts 332–56 DCCP.
[68] Arts 396–429 DCCP.
[69] Arts 143–48 DCCP.
[70] Arts 367–80 DCCP.
[71] Arts 386–429 DCCP.
[72] Art 78 Act on the Organisation of the Judiciary. The Supreme Court case that led to the referral in *De Wolf* (n 38) was brought by the Advocate-General as an appeal in cassation in the interest of law against a judgment given by a cantonal judge.
[73] Arts 145, 330 and 404 DCCP. Pursuant to Art 233 DCCP, a party can request the court declare a judgment provisionally enforceable (*uitvoerbaar bij voorraad*) in summons proceedings, in which case an ordinary remedy will not suspend enforcement. As a rule, such a request will be granted. However, if the judgment is enforced and later overturned, the party that took enforcement measures is strictly liable for damages. See Van Hooijdonk and Eijsvoogel (n 29) 50–51.
[74] See Snijders et al (n 29) 329–32.
[75] See on extraordinary remedies generally Snijders et al (n 29) 396–401.
[76] Art 332 DCCP. Appeal is excluded if the value of the claim does not exceed EUR 1.750, as well as other cases expressly provided for by law.
[77] Art 60 Act on the Organisation of the Judiciary.
[78] Art 339(1) DCCP.
[79] Van Hooijdonk and Eijsvoogel (n 29) 66–68.

Judgments given by a Court of Appeal can be appealed in cassation before the Supreme Court.[80] The time limit for lodging an appeal in cassation is three months after the date on which the appellate judgment was given.[81] The Supreme Court does not re-examine the facts of the case and only considers whether a decision must be quashed on a point of (procedural) law.[82] An Advocate-General will in this context deliver a non-binding opinion to the Supreme Court.[83] If a decision is quashed, the Supreme Court either gives a decision itself, or refers it back to the Court of Appeal.[84] However, a case may also be disposed of without a review if the appeal in cassation is manifestly unfounded or does not raise any new legal questions.[85]

Default judgments in first instance proceedings pursuant to Article 431(2) DCCP are uncommon, but can be given due to the applicability of the general regime for summons proceedings.[86] A default judgment in first instance proceedings can be opposed before the same district court within four weeks after the judgment was served on the defendant or any act of enforcement was commenced, or eight weeks if the defendant is domiciled outside the Netherlands.[87] Opposition in essence entails that a procedure is re-opened to hear the defendant that did not appear in first instance proceedings.[88] There are several examples of such opposition cases against default judgments given in first instance proceedings pursuant to Article 431(2) DCCP.[89]

In contrast, the ordinary remedies against *exequatur* judgments pursuant to Articles 985 DCCP are more restricted. Opposition against *exequatur* judgments is explicitly ruled out.[90] The time limits for appeal and cassation are both limited to one month after the judgment was given.[91] Moreover, appeal and cassation do not suspend the enforceability of the *exequatur* judgment.[92] All other aspects are governed by the regime for appeal and cassation in petition proceedings.[93]

[80] Art 398 DCCP. Appeal in cassation against a first instance judgment is also possible if appeal to a Court of Appeals is excluded, or in case of an appeal in cassation in the interest of law.

[81] Art 402(1) DCCP.

[82] Art 79 Act on the Organisation of the Judiciary.

[83] See for example the Conclusions of Advocate-General Vlas in ECLI:NL:PHR:2014:530, *Gazprombank* and ECLI:NL:PHR:2018:1017, *Yukos Oil*, and the Conclusion of Advocate-General De Bock in *ABA/ENEL* (n 11).

[84] Arts 419–23 DCCP. The case may also be referred to another Court of Appeal.

[85] Art 81 Act on the Organisation of the Judiciary.

[86] Arts 139–42 DCCP.

[87] Art 143 DCCP. Opposition is also possible against default judgments given in appellate proceedings (Art 353(1) DCCP), although there are no known examples of such default judgments in proceedings pursuant to Art 431(2) DCCP. Opposition against judgments given in cassation proceedings is excluded (Art 425 DCC).

[88] Snijders et al (n 29) 345.

[89] See Rechtbank Amsterdam, 15 July 2015, ECLI:NL:RBAMS:2015:4465 (opposition against default judgment in which the district court rules in accordance with an Israeli judgment); Rechtbank Amsterdam, 23 May 2018, ECLI:NL:RBAMS:2018:4278 (opposition against default judgment in which the District Court ruled in accordance with US default judgments).

[90] Art 989(1) DCCP.

[91] Arts 989(2), 990 DCCP.

[92] Art 988(2) DCCP.

[93] Arts 358–62 (appeal); Arts 426–29 (cassation).

Question 3. Requirements

a) Jurisdiction of the Court of Origin

The first requirement for recognition is that the jurisdiction of the court of origin must be based on an internationally generally accepted ground of jurisdiction.[94] These grounds are not equal to the direct grounds of international jurisdiction according to rules laid down in Articles 1–10 DCCP. Nonetheless, they have to be interpreted in accordance with Dutch standards[95] and seem to correspond to some of the Dutch direct grounds of jurisdiction, in particular the ones that do not deviate substantially from the Brussels Ia Regulation. To determine whether a ground of jurisdiction is considered internationally acceptable, EU Regulations and Conventions that rely on a broad international consensus, such as the HCCH 2019 Judgments Convention,[96] can provide an indication.[97] The Dutch court should assess the first requirement for recognition on the basis of the facts of the case.[98] The actual ground on which the court of origin based its jurisdiction is irrelevant.[99] The following grounds are considered as internationally generally acceptable grounds of jurisdiction in Dutch case law and literature.

The place where the claimant filed its claim has since the *Fur coat* case been regarded as an internationally generally accepted ground of jurisdiction to establish jurisdiction of the court of origin, provided that the claimant voluntarily submitted itself to the jurisdiction of this court.[100] Jurisdiction based on voluntary appearance also serves as a ground in the case that a judgment has been delivered against the claimant in counterclaim proceedings.[101] The court before which the defendant has appeared in the foreign proceedings and defended itself on the merits without contesting jurisdiction has also been regarded to establish jurisdiction on an internationally accepted jurisdiction ground based on voluntary submission.[102]

[94] Hoge Raad, 26 September 2014, ECLI:NL:HR:2014:2838.

[95] See RC Verschuur, *Vrij Verkeer van Vonnissen* (Deventer, 1995) 51; WODC Study (n 16) 39. See also Hof Arnhem-Leeuwarden, 27 October 2015 ECLI:NL:GHARL:2015:8059, 4.4.

[96] According to Vanleenhove, the indirect jurisdiction grounds in Arts 5 and 6 of the HCCH 2019 Judgments Convention are 'globally acceptable minimum standards'. C Vanleenhove, 'Het Haags Vonnissenverdrag: op weg naar mondiale wederzijdse erkenning en tenuitvoerlegging van beslissingen in burgerlijke en handelszaken' (2023) 19 *Tijdschrift voor Belgisch Handelsrecht* 29. The Court of Appeal of Amsterdam pointed out that 'as an indication of the international support for the relevant standards', it can be considered how many states are parties to the Convention, see Hof Amsterdam, 1 September 2015, ECLI:NL:GHAMS:2015:3596, *Nederlands Internationaal privaatrecht* 2016/4, 4.4.

[97] Hoge Raad, 23 September 2016 ECLI:NL:HR:2016:2184, 4.4. The WODC Study (n 16) points out that caution has to be exercised with respect to the application by analogy of treaties and EU Regulations.

[98] WODC Study (n 16) 13, 39.

[99] See, inter alia, Hof Arnhem-Leeuwarden, 27 October 2015 ECLI:NL:GHARL:2015:8059, 4.4.

[100] Hoge Raad, 14 November 1924, *Nederlandse Jurisprudentie* 1925, 91 (*Fur coat*). See also N Rosner, *Cross-border Recognition and Enforcement of Foreign Money Judgments in Civil and Commercial Matters* (Ulrik Huber Institute for Private International Law, 2004) 32, 36. See also JP Verheul, *Erkenning en tenuitvoerlegging van vreemde vonnissen* (TMC Asser Institute, 1989) 33.

[101] See Dutch case law referred to by Rosner (ibid), 36. See also Verheul (n 100) 33.

[102] See also Rosner (n 100) 36; Verheul (n 100) 33. See, inter alia, Rechtbank Midden-Nederland, 11 September 2019, ECLI:NL:RBMNE:2019:4310, 4.10; Rechtbank Rotterdam, 13 May 2020, ECLI:NL:RBROT:2020:4402, 2.6; Hof Arnhem-Leeuwarden, 6 June 2021 ECLI:NL:GHARL:2021:5620, 5.7.

The jurisdiction of the court of origin is based on an internationally generally accepted ground of jurisdiction if this court has been chosen by the parties (*forum prorogatorum*).[103] Academics have generally argued that the validity of the choice of forum agreement should be assessed by the law referred to by Dutch rules of private international law, instead of the rules of private international law of the chosen forum.[104] It has been stated that if a valid exclusive choice of forum has been ignored by the court of the state of origin, the judgment cannot be recognised.[105] Considering the broad international consensus underlying Article 7(1)(d) of the HCCH 2019 Judgments Convention, it can nonetheless be argued that the Dutch court has a discretionary power to refuse recognition of a judgment if an exclusive choice of forum was ignored.[106] Moreover, in case this jurisdiction clause has not been expressly invoked there may still be a ground of jurisdiction on the basis of the voluntary acceptance of jurisdiction.[107]

Furthermore, academics have considered jurisdiction of the court of origin over counterclaims or third-party proceedings as an internationally generally accepted ground of jurisdiction, provided that there no choice of forum or an exclusive ground of jurisdiction was infringed.[108]

The jurisdiction of the court of origin is based on an internationally generally accepted ground of jurisdiction if the defendant is domiciled or habitually resident in the state of origin (*forum rei*).[109] A Dutch court is not bound to any determinations made by the court of origin regarding the defendant's domicile or habitual residence, which should be verified independently.[110] Whether and to what extent the domestic notions of domicile and habitual residence, which are used in establishing direct jurisdiction under Article 2 DCCP,[111] can be used for this purpose is unclear.[112] With respect to the habitual residence, the autonomous interpretation of this concept in Conventions concluded under the auspices of the Hague Conference on Private International Law, and EU Regulations has been followed.[113]

The presence of a branch or agency of the defendant in the state of origin has been considered an internationally generally accepted ground of jurisdiction provided that the dispute on which the judgment is based arose out of the activities of that branch

[103] Hoge Raad, 17 December 1993 ECLI:NL:HR:1993:ZC1183, *Esmil/Enka*, 3.3.6. Rosner (n 100) 36; WODC Study (n 16) 44.

[104] See WODC Study (n 16) 45. See also Verheul (n 100) 32.

[105] Hof Amsterdam, 16 November 2010, ECLI:NL:GHAMS:2010:BO4077, *Nederlands Internationaal privaatrecht* 2011/52, 3.11–3.13. See also Verheul (n 100) 37, 39; WODC Study (n 16) 46.

[106] van Houtert (n 3) 592–93.

[107] Verheul (n 100) 37. Hof Amsterdam, 16 November 2010, ECLI:NL:GHAMS:2010:BO4077, *Nederlands Internationaal privaatrecht* 2011/52, 3.10.

[108] See Rosner (n 100) 36–37; Verheul (n 100) 33–34.

[109] See, inter alia, Rechtbank Amsterdam, 2 November 2016, ECLI:NL:RBAMS:2016:7287, 5.3. See Verheul (n 100) 31; Rosner (n 100) 34; WODC Study (n 16) 41–42.

[110] WODC Study (n 16) 42.

[111] Art 2 DCCP confers jurisdiction to Dutch courts if the defendant is domiciled or habitually resident in the Netherlands. On the notions of domicile and habitual residence, see Bens (n 52) 195, 199–200.

[112] WODC Study (n 16) 42.

[113] See, for instance, Hoge Raad, 23 September 2016, ECLI:NL:2016:2184, 3.4.3. See also Verheul (n 100) 31. 'The concept of habitual residence is regularly used as a ground of indirect jurisdiction regarding judgments on family law matters.' Verheul (n 100) 35.

or agency.[114] Academics have justified this indirect ground of jurisdiction by referring to Article 7(5) Brussels Ia Regulation, as well as (the precursor of) the HCCH 2019 Judgments Convention,[115] although – from a domestic point of view – branch and agency jurisdiction could be considered as a subset of domicile.[116]

In case of judgments concerning claims against multiple defendants that are based on the same factual and legal situation, the domicile of one of these defendants in the state of origin has been considered sufficient to constitute an internationally accepted ground of jurisdiction.[117] The rationale of this indirect ground of jurisdiction has been linked to Article 8(1) Brussels Ia Regulation.[118]

With respect to judgments involving a claim based on tort,[119] or unjust enrichment,[120] Dutch courts have considered jurisdiction based on the place where the harmful event occurred in the state of origin (*forum delicti*) as an internationally accepted jurisdiction ground.[121] This ground covers both the place of the harmful event given rise to the damage and the place where the damage occurred.[122] The Arnhem-Leeuwarden Court of Appeal has recognised the place of performance of the obligation in the state of origin (*forum solutionis*) as an internationally generally accepted ground of jurisdiction by referring to Article 6 DCCP and Article 7(1) Brussels Ia Regulation.[123] This Court of Appeal also considered that 'the assessment as to the place of performance of the obligation in question should be made in accordance with the law applicable to the contract'.[124] The WODC study argues that in case parties do not agree on the applicable law, this law should be determined on the basis of Dutch private international law.[125]

In the context of the recognition of a foreign judgment relating to proceedings concerning a dispute on the ownership of immovable property, the Hof

[114] Rechtbank Amsterdam, 29 June 2016, ECLI:NL:RBAMS:2016:5691, 4.12. See WODC 42. Academics have justified this indirect ground of jurisdiction by referring to Art 7(5) Brussels Ia Regulation and Conventions. See Rosner (n 100) 35; Verheul (n 100) 31.

[115] Rosner refers to former Art 5(5) Brussels I Regulation and Art 9 of the 1999 draft of the HCCH Judgments Convention (currently Art 5(1)(d) of the HCCH 2019 Judgments Convention). See Rosner (n 100) 35. According to Verheul this forum appears in many international conventions, see Verheul (n 100) 31.

[116] See Bens (n 52) 200. Pursuant to Art 1:14 of the Dutch Civil Code, legal persons that are incorporated outside of the Netherlands, but keep an office or branch in the Netherlands are considered to be domiciled there for matters relating to that office of branch.

[117] See Rechtbank Middelburg, 5 April 2006, *Nederlands Internationaal privaatrecht* 2007, 52, 2.3.1; Rechtbank Amsterdam, 29 June 2016, ECLI:NL:RBAMS:2016:5691, 4.12. See WODC Study (n 16) 44. See also Dutch case law mentioned by Rosner (n 100) 35.

[118] See Rechtbank Amsterdam, 29 June 2016, ECLI:NL:RBAMS:2016:5691, 4.12.

[119] See also Verheul (n 100) 34; WODC Study (n 16) 44. See, inter alia, Hof Den Bosch, 31 August 2021, ECLI:GHSHE:2021:2699, 3.5.3.

[120] Rechtbank Amsterdam, 6 March 2019, ECLI:NL:RBAMS:2019:1802, 4.12–4.13.

[121] ibid.

[122] ibid; Hof Den Bosch, 31 August 2021, ECLI:GHSHE:2021:2699, 3.5.3 (Hof s-Hertogenbosch ruled that the *forum delicti* even includes the centrum of interests of the victim). See also the referral by the WODC Study (n 16) 44, fn 90, to Rechtbank Amsterdam, 2 November 2016, ECLI:NL:RBAMS:2016:7287, 5.3.

[123] Hof Arnhem-Leeuwarden, 27 October 2015, ECLI:NL:GHARL:2015:8059, 4.6. Rotterdam District Court considered the fact that 'the agreed place of delivery' of the good had been located in the state of origin as one of the factors contributing to the establishment of jurisdiction on a ground that is acceptable by international standards. Rechtbank Rotterdam, 2 July 2014, ECLI:NL:RBROT:2014:5600, 4.9. The WODC Study (n 16) indicates that Dutch academics are divided on the recognition of *forum solutionis* as an internationally generally accepted ground of jurisdiction. See WODC Study (n 16) 42.

[124] Hof Arnhem-Leeuwarden, 27 October 2015, ECLI:NL:GHARL:2015:8059, 4.6.

[125] WODC Study (n 16) 43.

Arnhem-Leeuwarden pointed out that exclusive jurisdiction based on the place of the immovable property is an internationally generally accepted ground of jurisdiction.[126] With respect to the recognition of a judgment regarding a claim on rights *in rem* in immovable property and tenancies in immovable property, scholars have argued that the place where the property is situated (*forum rei sitae*) is an internationally generally accepted ground of jurisdiction.[127]

The place of domicile of the claimant in the state of origin is generally not regarded as an internationally accepted jurisdiction ground.[128] With reference to Articles 10–23 Brussels Ia Regulation, it has nonetheless been argued that the forum of the claimant (*forum actoris*) being an economically weaker party – namely employee, consumer, insurance policy-holder – could be considered an internationally accepted ground of jurisdiction.[129] As regards the recognition and enforcement of a judgment concerning these (economically) weaker parties, there is no Dutch case law (yet). Dutch legal doctrine is ambiguous as to the consequences if the court of origin did not take account of the special jurisdiction provisions protecting these parties.[130]

According to scholars, jurisdiction based on the place where an attachment was levied (*forum arresti*) cannot be regarded as an internationally accepted jurisdiction ground except in case 'the dispute is related to the cargo or freight of a ship which has been arrested in order to secure that payment'.[131] Unlike common law-based states,[132] jurisdiction based on the 'transient presence' of the defendant in the state of origin at the time of the institution of the claim ('tag' jurisdiction)[133] will not be regarded as an internationally accepted ground of jurisdiction according to Dutch standards.

b) Finality/Enforceability in the Country of Origin

The Supreme Court has in principle not required that the foreign judgment must to be final in order to be recognised.[134] Although academics and district courts adhered to the view that the finality of the foreign judgment is a requirement for its recognition prior to

[126] Hof Arnhem-Leeuwarden 15 October 2024, ECLI:N:GHARL:2024:6373, 4.15.

[127] Rosner (n 100) 37 f; Verheul (n 100) 34.

[128] Verschuur (n 95) 51. The place of domicile or habitual residence of the defendant has nevertheless been regarded as an internationally accepted jurisdiction ground in case of judgments involving family law related matters. See Verheul (n 100) 10, 35.

[129] See Rosner (n 100) 38.

[130] Verheul (n 100) 32; WODC Study (n 16) 46.

[131] See Rosner (n 100) 38; Verheul (n 100) 35 f.

[132] See Bens (n 52), 488.

[133] See C Ryngaert, 'The Restatement and the Law of Jurisdiction: A Commentary' (2022) 4 *The European Journal of International Law* 1455, 1464.

[134] See Hoge Raad, 14 November 1924, *Nederlandse Jurisprudentie* 1925, *Fur coat*, 91; Hoge Raad, 26 September 2014, ECLI:NL:HR:2014:2838; *Yukos Oil* (n 11) 4.3.3–4.3.4; Hoge Raad, 16 July 2021, ECLI:NL:HR:2021:1170, *ENEL*, 3.3.2; Hoge Raad, 29 September 2023, ECLI:NL:HR:2023:1265, 3.6.2. van Houtert (n 3) 578. With respect to Hoge Raad, 26 September 2014, ECLI:NL:HR:2014:2838, Van Hoek has stated that the Dutch Supreme Court did not require that the foreign judgment should be final in order to be recognised. See AAH van Hoek, 'Over een vonnis dat vastzat in de Russische pijplijn' (2015) *Ars Aequi* 502, 508.

the *Gazprombank* ruling,[135] Dutch courts nowadays generally do not employ this requirement.[136] The Supreme Court has nonetheless ruled that recognition may be postponed or refused if the judgment is the subject of review in the state of origin or if the time limit for seeking ordinary review has not yet expired.[137] A refusal on the latter ground does, however, not prevent a renewed application for recognition of the decision.[138] Furthermore, a Dutch court is allowed, on application or of its own motion, to require that the party seeking recognition of a foreign judgment which is not final provides security for damages of which this party could be ordered to pay according to the final judgment.[139]

A claim to rule in accordance with a foreign judgment on the basis of Article 431(2) DCCP may be dismissed on the ground that the foreign judgment subject to recognition is not, not yet or no longer enforceable under the law of the country of origin.[140] In this context it is important on which ground the unenforceability of the foreign judgment is based.[141] In light of the CJEU's interpretation of enforceability in the former Article 38(1) of the Brussels I Regulation,[142] the Supreme Court ruled that the ground relates only to the formal enforceability of the foreign judgment, and not to the conditions under which that judgment can be enforced in the state of origin.[143] An obstacle to the formal enforceability of a foreign judgment exists, inter alia, if an appeal with suspensive effect has been lodged against the (not provisionally enforceable) judgment in the country of origin; or if the judgment has been set aside by a higher court of the country of origin; or a certain period of time in which the judgment can be enforced has been stipulated in the judgment, or arises from the judgment, and this period has not yet started or has already expired.[144] However, an obstacle to the formal enforceability does not include the limitation or the lapse of the power to enforce the judgment under the law of its country of origin, since this in itself does not affect the authority of the judgment.[145]

[135] As regards case law before the *Gazprombank* judgment, the research of Verschuur (concluded in July 1994) shows that Dutch courts did impose the condition that a foreign judgment must be final in the state of origin. See Verschuur (n 95) 50. While academics have argued that the judgment must be final in the state of origin in order to be recognised, this is not regarded as a condition regarding the enforcement of a foreign judgment. See van Hoek (n 134) 502, 508; Freudenthal (n 10) 569.

[136] See Rechtbank Rotterdam, 1 February 2017, ECLI:NL:RBROT:2017:882, 3.14. While the district court of Rotterdam recognised the foreign judgment on the refusal of an adoption, the court nonetheless declared its decision on the basis of Art 431(2) DCCP not enforceable until the foreign judgment has become final.

[137] Hoge Raad, 29 September 2023, ECLI:NL:HR:2023:1265, 3.6.2. The Supreme Court has referred in this context to Art 4(4) HCCH 2019 Judgments Convention and F Garcimartin and G Saumier, *Explanatory Report on the Recognition and Enforcement of Foreign Judgments in Civil or Commercial Matters* (The Hague Conference on Private International Law, 2020) paras 127-32.

[138] Hoge Raad, 29 September 2023, ECLI:NL:HR:2023:1265, 3.6.2.

[139] ibid.

[140] ibid, 3.6.6.

[141] ibid.

[142] Case C-267/97 *Coursier v Fortis Bank*.

[143] Hoge Raad, 26 September 2014, ECLI:NL:HR:2014:2838, 3.6.7–3.6.8.

[144] Hoge Raad, 26 September 2014, ECLI:NL:HR:2014:2838, 3.6.8. With respect to the lack of enforceability of a foreign default judgment that has been set aside, see Hof Arnhem-Leeuwarden 15 October 2024, ECLI:N:GHARL:2024:6373, 4.20.

[145] Hoge Raad, 26 September 2014, ECLI:NL:HR:2014:2838, 3.6.8. As pointed out in van Houtert (n 3) 579, the State Commission on Private International Law nonetheless argues that the limitation of the power of execution under the law of the country of origin does constitute an obstacle to the enforceability of the foreign judgment in the Netherlands. See Staatscommissie voor Internationaal Privaatrecht (n 18) 13.

The defendant in proceedings pursuant to Article 431(2) DCCP may also argue that the sum of money or other remedy awarded in the foreign judgment is not or no longer due, in whole or in part, provided that this defence could not have been raised in the proceedings that led to the foreign judgment, or that this defence arose afterwards.[146] For instance, the defence can be raised that the sum of money awarded by the judgment has been paid, or a settlement took place after the judgment has been issued.[147]

c) *Res Iudicata*

One of the four requirements for recognition concerns that the foreign judgment should not be incompatible with a judgment of a Dutch court given between the same parties, or with an earlier judgment of a foreign court given between the same parties in a dispute concerning the same subject matter and based on the same cause of action, provided that such earlier judgment is susceptible of recognition in the Netherlands.[148] This requirement was only explicitly introduced with the *Gazprombank* ruling. In previous Dutch case law, a foreign judgment was often not recognised for being contrary to public policy in case the judgment was incompatible with a previous judgment rendered by a Dutch court between the same parties and cause of action.[149]

The Arnhem District Court ruled that the court should assess *ex nunc* whether recognition of the foreign judgment would result in two incompatible judgments.[150] Furthermore, the judgments should be enforceable; the fact that a judgment is not final or an appeal has been lodged against an enforceable decision is therefore irrelevant.[151] However, the Dutch court's decision in a preliminary relief proceeding has no *res judicata* effect because of its temporary character; this decision can therefore not entail 'incompatibility of judgments' in the context of the requirement for recognition of the foreign judgment.[152]

d) *Lis Pendens*

The absence of parallel proceedings between the same parties on the same subject matter inside or outside of the Netherlands is not a condition for recognition of a foreign judgment by the Dutch court. However, while the finality of a foreign judgment is generally not regarded as requirement for recognition,[153] several Dutch courts have ruled in the case of parallel proceedings between the same parties that proceedings had to be stayed

[146] Hoge Raad, 26 September 2014, ECLI:NL:HR:2014:2838, 3.6.10.
[147] ibid.
[148] ibid 3.6.4. The condition that the foreign judgment should be susceptible to recognition and enforceable in the Netherlands could be interpreted in a same manner as the similar condition in Art 12 DCCP (see the answer to Question 3 d)).
[149] See Van Hoek (n 134) 508.
[150] Rechtbank Arnhem, 21 June 2010, ECLI:NL:RBARN:2010:BM8462, 3 sub c and 4.
[151] Rechtbank Arnhem, 21 June 2010, ECLI:NL:RBARN:2010:BM8462, 3 sub c.
[152] Hof Amsterdam 24 September 2024, ECLI:NL:GHAMS:2024:2678, 4.17.
[153] See the answer to Question 3 b).

until a final judgment had been rendered by the court of the foreign state after which the latter judgment could possibly be recognised in proceedings pursuant to Article 431(2) DCCP.[154] Despite the fact that the requirements of the *lis pendens*-provision of Article 12 DCCP had not be fulfilled,[155] the Amsterdam District Court stayed the proceedings by reasoning that this stay 'serves the requirements of due process, because it serves the interests of efficient administration of justice and the prevention of the danger of conflicting judgments'; in this particular case these important interests outweighed the interest served by immediate continuation of the proceedings, particularly as the proceedings in the foreign state were in their final stage and it has neither been argued nor proved that the defendant had a reasonable interest in continuing the proceedings without waiting for the foreign judgment to be rendered.[156]

In case of parallel proceedings between the same parties on the same subject matter first brought before the court of origin and subsequently the Dutch court, Article 12 DCCP compels the Dutch court to decline jurisdiction in case the foreign judgment has been final,[157] and is prone to recognition and enforcement in the Netherlands. If the foreign court's decision is not yet final, the Dutch court may not decline jurisdiction to prevent that the situation that both the Dutch and foreign court decline jurisdiction, which would mean that the dispute cannot be settled anywhere in court.[158] Article 12 DCCP is only applicable in case the foreign judgment can be recognised, and in case of a condemnatory judgment enforced, on the basis of an international convention,[159] or recognised pursuant to the four requirements in *Gazprombank*.[160]

e) Specific Requirements of Due Process

One of the four conditions for recognition is that the foreign decision must be obtained in judicial proceedings that meet the requirements of due process.[161] The assessment of the due process-requirements has to be based on legal principles of due process

[154] van Houtert (n 3) 593 refers to Hoge Raad, 16 April 1999, ECLI:NL:HR:1999:ZC2888, *Nederlandse Jurisprudentie* 2001/1, 3.3.3; Rechtbank's-Hertogenbosch, 13 June 2007, ECLI:NL:RBSHE:2007:BA7236, 3.1; Hof Amsterdam, 26 October 2021, ECLI:NL:GHAMS:2021:3248, 4.8.

[155] As part of the Dutch rules on international jurisdiction, Art 12 DCCP stipulates, inter alia, that in case proceedings between the same parties on the same subject matter that are pending before a foreign court and subsequently a Dutch court, the Dutch court may stay proceedings until this foreign court has rendered a final judgment, provided that the latter judgment is susceptible to recognition and enforceable in the Netherlands. The Supreme Court pointed out that a Dutch court may, for instance, decide not to stay proceedings where it is expected that the foreign court will take a long time to render the final judgment. See Hoge Raad, 29 September 2023, ECLI:NL:HR:2023:1265, 3.3.5.

[156] Hof Amsterdam, 26 October 2021, ECLI:NL:GHAMS:2021:3248, 4.8.

[157] See Hoge Raad, 29 September 2023, ECLI:NL:HR:2023:1265, 3.3.6. With respect to the definition of the finality of a foreign judgment, the Supreme Court refers to Art 4(4) HCCH 2019 Judgments Convention; Garcimartin and Saumier (n 137) paras 127–32.

[158] See Hoge Raad, 29 September 2023, ECLI:NL:HR:2023:1265, 3.3.6.

[159] Kamerstukken II, 1999/00, no 26 855, 3, 45 f.

[160] See Hoge Raad, 29 September 2023, ECLI:NL:HR:2023:1266, 3.2.3.

[161] Hoge Raad, 26 September 2014, ECLI:NL:HR:2014:2838, 3.6.4.

according to Dutch procedural law with Article 6 European Convention on Human Rights (ECHR) being the minimum standard.[162] These requirements include:

- 'a proper and timely service of process';[163]
- 'the defendant should have been given the opportunity and sufficient time to adequately defend itself';[164]
- the right to be heard;[165]
- the possibility to appeal;[166]
- parties must have had the opportunity to pose and challenge statements, present their views and provide means of evidence;[167]
- hearing of the case by an independent and impartial tribunal.[168]

The lack of proper reasoning of the judgment may constitute a ground for non-recognition due to failing to meet due process requirements.[169] Furthermore, an 'arbitrary and manifestly unreasonable' judgment has been considered to violate the principles of due process.[170]

With respect to a claim that the requirements of due process have not been met, the Supreme Court held that, depending on the circumstances of the case, it may be relevant if all available effective remedies that could actually lead to a reconsideration have been exhausted in the country of origin.[171] A default judgment may therefore be recognised if the defendant was summoned too late[172] or the summons was not properly served,[173] but received the notification of this judgment in time to oppose or appeal it and did not make use of this opportunity.[174]

[162] WODC Study (n 16) 47.

[163] Rosner (n 100) 43; WODC 47. The Dutch court does not need to examine whether the defendant was properly summoned if that party appeared timely in the proceedings. See Rechtbank Rotterdam, 15 July 2015, ECLI:NL:RBROT:2015:6172, 4.5. See also the Conclusion of Advocate-General L Strikwerda at the case of Hoge Raad, 25 September 1992, *Nederlands Internationaal privaatrecht* 1992, 310.

[164] WODC Study (n 16) 48. See, for instance, Rechtbank Utrecht, 9 June 2010, *Nederlands Internationaal privaatrecht* 2010, 496.

[165] Rosner (n 100) 43; Verheul (n 100) 52. See Rechtbank Midden-Nederland, 11 September 2019, ECLI:NL:RBMNE:2019:4310, 4.18; Rechtbank Amsterdam 14 December 2022, ECLI:NL:RBAMS:2022:8257, 5.26.

[166] Rosner (n 100) 43. See Rechtbank Zeeland West-Brabant, 16 August 2017, ECLI:NL:RBZWB:2017:5251, 3.7.

[167] Verheul (n 100) 50; WODC Study (n 16) 48. See, inter alia, Rechtbank Amsterdam, 2 September 2016, ECLI:NL:RBAMS:2016:7287, 5.4.

[168] WODC Study (n 16) 48. See, for instance, Hof Den Haag, 9 February 2016, ECLI:NL:GHDHA:2016:280, 10.5; Rechtbank Amsterdam, 6 March 2019, ECLI:NL:RBAMS:2019:1802, 4.19. Hof Den Haag, 9 February 2016, ECLI:NL:GHDHA:2016:280, 10.5.

[169] Rosner (n 100) 45; WODC Study (n 16) 49. See, for instance, Rechtbank Zwolle, 16 August 1995, *Nederlands Internationaal privaatrecht* 1996, 143. The lack of proper reasoning of the judgment may also be contrary to the Dutch public policy (see the answer to Question 3 f)). See Verheul (n 100) 49.

[170] Hof Amsterdam, 17 July 2018, ECLI:NL:GHAMS:2018:3008, 3.33. The Amsterdam Court of Appeal held that the obligation to comply with an 'arbitrary and manifestly unreasonable' judgment is also contrary to Dutch public policy.

[171] *Yukos Oil* (n 11) 4.3.3, 4.3.4; Hoge Raad, 16 July 2021, ECLI:NL:HR:2021:1170, *ENEL*, 3.3.2. 'Effective' remedies are means of appeal that may actually lead to a reconsideration.

[172] See Verheul (n 100) 51 f; Rosner (n 100) 48 refers to Hof Amsterdam, 21 March 1996, *Nederlands Internationaal privaatrecht* 1997, 362, 4.4.

[173] Hof Arnhem-Leeuwarden 15 October 2024, ECLI:N:GHARL:2024:6373, 4.6–4.14, 4.16.

[174] See Verheul (n 100) 51 f; Rosner (n 100) 48 refers to Hof Amsterdam, 21 March 1996, *Nederlands Internationaal privaatrecht* 1997, 362, 4.4.

f) Public Policy

One of the four requirements for recognition is that the recognition of a foreign judgment should not be contrary to the Dutch public policy.[175] The Dutch public policy ground used to concern principles of both substantive law and procedural law.[176] However, it has been argued that the 'public policy'-requirement nowadays does not concern the procedure.[177] Dutch courts have stated that the 'due process'[178] and 'public policy' requirements cover the procedural and substantive side of the public policy assessment; these courts have explained this distinction as follows. The 'due process' requirement in particular concerns the procedure in which the foreign decision was reached; the assessment of this requirement is based on the criteria as referred to in Article 6 ECHR.[179] The 'public policy' requirement concerns the consequences of the recognition for the Dutch public policy that means the recognition of the foreign decision may not lead to consequences which are detrimental to fundamental values and principles of the Dutch legal order.[180]

According to Dutch legal doctrine and case law, a two-pronged test can be applied with respect to the public policy ground.[181] First, according to the 'external border' criterion (*buitengrenscriterium*), the content of the foreign judgment should not violate fundamental legal principles and values derived from national, international and EU law that have an absolute nature according to Dutch standards.[182] Contrary to the Dutch public policy are, inter alia, judgments rendered on the basis of fraud,[183] as well as judgments that have awarded extraordinary high damages, known as punitive damages.[184] Second, the 'internal border' criterion related to public policy (*binnengrenscriterium*) focuses on whether recognising the foreign judgment in the concrete case would lead to consequences that should not be tolerated in the Dutch legal order.[185] With respect to the latter criterion, it has been argued that the greater the

[175] Hoge Raad, 26 September 2014, ECLI:NL:HR:2014:2838, 3.6.4.

[176] See, inter alia, Rosner (n 100) 41.

[177] Van Hoek (n 134) 502, 507.

[178] See the answer to Question 3 e).

[179] See Rechtbank Midden-Nederland, 11 September 2019, ECLI:NL:RBMNE:2019:4310, 4.14; Hof Amsterdam, 17 July 2018, ECLI:NL:GHAMS:2018:3008, 3.23. See also the answer to Question 3 e).

[180] See Rechtbank Midden-Nederland, 11 September 2019, ECLI:NL:RBMNE:2019:4310, 4.14; Hof Amsterdam, 17 July 2018, ECLI:NL:GHAMS:2018:3008, 3.23.

[181] Rosner (n 100) 41–42; WODC Study (n 16) 52. See, inter alia, Rechtbank Amsterdam, 29 June 2016, ECLI:NL:RBAMS:2016:5691, 4.17; Rechtbank Amsterdam, 9 November 2022, ECLI:NL:RBAMS:2022:6444, 5.14. This two-pronged test has also been used with respect to the public policy exception regarding foreign applicable law. See APMJ Vonken et al, *Mr. C. Assers Handleiding tot de beoefening van het Nederlands Burgerlijk Recht. 10. Internationaal privaatrecht. Deel I. Algemeen deel IPR* (Wolters Kluwer, 2018) 494.

[182] See *Yukos Oil* (n 11) 4.1.3; Hof Amsterdam, 17 July 2018, ECLI:NL:GHAMS:2018:3008, 3.33. With respect to the interpretation of the Dutch public policy, see Rosner (n 100) 41; WODC Study (n 16) 52; Vonken, et al (n 181) 419, 485, 505ff.

[183] Verheul (n 100) 48; Verschuur (n 95) 56; WODC Study (n 16) 53.

[184] WODC Study (n 16) 53. Dutch case law indicates that a judgment involving *punitive* damages will only be partially recognised and enforced with respect to the award of compensatory damages. See van Houtert (n 3) 592, referring to Rechtbank Midden-Nederland, 11 September 2019, ECLI:NL:RBMNE:2019:4310, 4.28–4.30; Hof's-Hertogenbosch, 31 Augustus 2021, ECLI:GHSHE:2021:2699, 3.7.3–3.7.5, 3.9.

[185] Rosner (n 100) 42; WODC Study (n 16) 52. See, inter alia, Hof Amsterdam, 17 July 2018, ECLI:NL:GHAMS:2018:3008, 3.23; Rechtbank Midden-Nederland, 11 September 2019, ECLI:NL:RBMNE:2019:4310, 4.14; Rechtbank Noord-Holland, 9 June 2021, ECLI:NL:RBNHO:2021:4954, 4.9.

involvement of the Netherlands in the case, the more likely there will be a breach of public policy.[186]

For a successful invocation of the public order exception, the Supreme Court held that, depending on the circumstances of the case, it may be relevant whether all available effective remedies have been exhausted in the country of origin.[187] Unlike Article 45(1)(a) of the Brussels Ia Regulation, the Dutch Supreme Court has not reiterated the 'manifestly contrary' requirement with respect to the public policy exception.[188] Because of the lack of this requirement, it has been argued that the public policy exception is more likely to be met in Dutch proceedings.[189] However, case law of lower courts shows that a foreign judgment will only be contrary to public policy in exceptional cases.[190]

g) Reciprocity

Reciprocity is not a requirement for recognition and enforcement.[191]

h) Other Requirements

None.

Question 4. Documents to be Produced

Except in the context of the exequatur procedure pursuant to Article 985 DCCP,[192] there are no specific rules regarding the documents that should be produced in Dutch proceedings in which the recognition of a foreign judgment is requested. The main rule of evidence provides that a party invoking legal consequences of facts or rights asserted by it shall, in principle, bear the burden of proving them.[193] The party that requests the recognition of a foreign judgment must therefore bring this judgment into the proceedings as any other document, which may have to be legalised and/or translated.

In general, legalisation of the foreign judgment is advisable to establish the authenticity of the foreign judgment.[194] If a foreign judgment is not in English, German or

[186] See, inter alia, the annotation of ThM de Boer on the *Yukos* case, 'HR 18-01-2019, ECLI:NL:HR:2019:54, m. nt. Th.M. de Boer,' (2019) 364 *Nederlandse Jurisprudentie* 5. See also Rosner (n 100) 41–42; Conclusion P Vlas at *Yukos Oil* (n 11) 3.48.

[187] *Yukos Oil* (n 11) 4.3.3–4.3.4; *ABA/ENEL* (n 11) 3.3.2.

[188] See Hoge Raad, 26 September 2014, ECLI:NL:HR:2014:2838; *Yukos Oil* (n 11); *ABA/ENEL* (n 11).

[189] WODC Study (n 16) 51.

[190] See van Houtert (n 3) 591 referring, inter alia, to Rechtbank Amsterdam, 29 June 2016, ECLI:NL:RBAMS:2016:5691, 4.17; Rechtbank Amsterdam, 25 August 2021, ECLI:NL:RBAMS:2021:4730, 4.9.

[191] See, inter alia, Verschuur (n 95) 56.

[192] Art 986 (2)–(4) DCCP.

[193] Art 150 DCCP.

[194] See Rechtbank Rotterdam, 15 July 2015, ECLI:NL:RBROT:2015:6172, 4.7; Rechtbank Rotterdam, 13 May 2015, ECLI:NL:RBROT:2020:4402, 2.3. The claimants in both proceedings provided legalised copies of the Turkish judgments that were invoked, albeit during the proceedings and not beforehand. Legalisation was in this context mainly relevant to anticipate defences based on the formal (in)validity of the foreign judgments under the law of the country of origin.

French, a translation must in principle be submitted, although a Dutch court may in any case require a translation if considered necessary or desirable for the assessment of the case considering the interests of the other parties involved.[195] The court may determine that this translation is prepared and signed by a sworn translator.[196] A party that disagrees with a translation of the foreign judgment provided by the other party should submit its own translation.[197]

Question 5. Securities, Bonds and Deposits

A claimant that is not domiciled or habitually resident in the Netherlands may be required to provide security for the costs of the proceedings (*cautio iudicatium solvi*) at the request of the defendant pursuant to Article 224(1) DCCP. Such a request must be lodged before submitting a statement of defence.[198] However, such a request cannot be submitted if, inter alia, an international convention or EU regulation prohibits the requirement to provide security for costs,[199] or if a Dutch cost order is enforceable in the state where the claimant is domiciled on the basis of an international convention or EU regulation.[200] Peculiarly, the requirement to provide security for costs is not generally excluded with respect to claimants domiciled in the EU and European Economic Area (EEA).[201]

In general, orders to provide security for the costs of proceedings in the Netherlands are rare.[202] However, De Rooij highlighted in 2018 that the number of requests seems to have increased, including requests against claimants domiciled in the EU and EEA.[203] According to De Rooij, granting such requests may, in the absence of an international convention or EU Regulation, nonetheless violate fundamental rights concerning non-discrimination and the right of access to a court in the EU Charter of Fundamental Rights and/or the ECHR.[204]

[195] Art 2.16 of the National rules of procedure for civil summons cases at district courts (July 2025) (*Landelijk procesregelement voor civiele dagvaardingszaken bij de rechtbanken handel en kanton*).

[196] ibid.

[197] See Rechtbank Amsterdam, 6 March 2019, ECLI:NL:RBAMS:2019:1802, 4.25.

[198] Art 224(3) DCCP.

[199] Art 224(2)(a) DCCP. See eg Arts 17–19 of the 1954 HCCH Convention on Civil Procedure and Arts 14–17 of the 1980 HCCH Convention on International Access to Justice.

[200] Art 224(2)(b) DCCP.

[201] See M de Rooij, 'De cautio en de fundamentele rechten van de buitenlandse eiser onder VWEU en EVRM – verschil in benadering tussen Duitsland, Nederland en het Verenigd Koninkrijk' (2018) *Nederlands Internationaal Privaatrecht* 294, 305. According to Van Rooij, such an explicit exclusion for claimant's domiciled in the EU or EEA for example exists in Germany.

[202] In the context of proceedings pursuant to Art 431(2) DCCP, see only Rechtbank Noord-Holland, 1 April 2020, ECLI:NL:RBNHO:2020:2425, 1.1 (request for security for costs pursuant to Art 224 DCCP against Monegasque claimant was apparently dismissed in an earlier decision).

[203] de Rooij (n 201) 294–96.

[204] ibid 308–09.

Poland

ANNA WYSOCKA-BAR*

Question 1. General Overview

In Poland, provisions on international civil procedure, including rules on recognition and enforcement of foreign judgments, are contained in the Code of Civil Procedure ('the Code').[1] The Code entered into force on 1 January 1965. Provisions on international civil procedure were subject to substantive, sometimes also referred to as 'revolutionary' amendments,[2] which entered into force as of 1 July 2009 (Amendment 2009).[3] As underlined in the Explanatory Note[4] to Amendment 2009, the main aim of the amendment was to adapt the provisions of the Code to the laws of the European Union (EU),[5] in particular the Brussels I Regulation.[6] The rules contained in the Code as amended by the Amendment 2009 (which are presented in this national report) apply to recognition and enforcement of foreign judgments, rulings or settlements if handed down, concluded or approved after the date of entry into force of the Amendment 2009, namely after 1 July 2009. Hence, foreign judgments, rulings or settlements handed down, concluded or approved until 1 July 2009 (including on that day) are subject to recognition and enforcement in accordance with rules in place before 1 July 2009.

The Code is divided into parts. Part Four, 'Provisions on International Civil Procedure', is further divided into five books, where Book Four, 'Recognition and

* The national report was prepared within a research supported by a grant under the Strategic Programme Excellence Initiative at Jagiellonian University.

[1] Ustawa z 17 listopada 1964 r Kodeks postępowania cywilnego [Act of 17 November 1964 – Code of Civil Procedure] Dz U z 2021 r, poz 1805. All Polish legislation might be located in the official journal (Dziennik Ustaw, in short Dz U) by year, number (nr) and position (poz), or – starting from 2012 – year and position (poz) only. Dziennik Ustaw is available online at isap.sejm.gov.pl.

[2] W Graliński, 'Wpływ rozporządzenia nr 44/2001 na dokonaną w 2008 r nowelizację polskiego Kodeksu postępowania cywilnego w zakresie uznawania orzeczeń zagranicznych' in T Demendecki (ed), *Mechanizm uznania lub odmowy uznania orzeczenia sądu państwa obcego w sprawach cywilnych przez sąd polski – analiza de lege lata i wniosku de lege ferenda* (Instytut Wymiaru Sprawiedliwości, 2019) 8.

[3] Ustawa z 5 grudnia 2008 r o zmianie ustawy – Kodeks postępowania cywilnego oraz niektórych innych ustaw [Act of 5 December 2008 on the amendment to the act – Code of civil procedure and some other acts] Dz U z 2008 r, nr 234, poz 1571.

[4] Explanatory Note to the Amendment 2009 is available at orka.sejm.gov.pl/Druki6ka.nsf/wgdruku/949.

[5] Graliński (n 2) 8.

[6] Council Regulation (EC) No 44/2001 of 22 December 2000 on jurisdiction and the recognition and enforcement of judgments in civil and commercial matters [2001] OJ L 12/1.

Enforcement of Certain Decisions of Courts of European Union Member States and Settlements, Authentic Instruments and Agreements originating from these States', applies to decisions subject to recognition and enforcement in accordance with EU Regulations (for example, Brussels I bis Regulation[7]). Book Three, 'Recognition and Enforcement', applies to all remaining decisions, including in civil and commercial matters handed down in non-EU states. Please note that these rules might also apply to judgments given in EU Member States if there is no EU regulation or international agreement which could serve as a basis for recognition and enforcement.[8]

Book Three, 'Recognition and Enforcement' (Articles 1145–1152), is in turn divided into two titles: Title I – 'Recognition of decisions of foreign courts or decision of other authorities of foreign states' (Articles 1145–1149[1]); and Title II, 'Enforcement of decisions of foreign courts or decision of other authorities of foreign states and settlements concluded in front of or confirmed by such courts or authorities' (Article 1150–1152). The difference between procedure governing recognition and procedure governing enforcement is explained below (see Question 2 b)).

The provisions on recognition and enforcement contained in Book Tree of Part Four of the Code are of the 'last resort'. They apply only if no EU regulation or international agreement is applicable to recognition/enforcement of a given judgment. EU regulations (for example, the Brussels I bis Regulation, the Maintenance Regulation,[9] the Succession Regulation[10]), multilateral agreements (for example, the 2005 HCCH Choice of Court Convention[11] or the 2019 HCCH Judgment Convention[12]) and bilateral agreements, in general, take precedence before provisions of Part Four of the Code.

Here it should be mentioned that Poland is party to numerous bilateral agreements, some of which do contain rules on international civil procedure (for example, with respect to security deposits) and/or recognition and enforcement of judgments in civil and commercial matters. These agreements were concluded with both EU Member States and non-EU states. These bilateral agreements might regulate recognition and enforcement, including when it comes to grounds of refusal, documents to be provided or/and security deposits differently than the Code. In accordance with constitutional rules on sources of law in Poland, such bilateral agreements take precedence before rules contained in the

[7] Regulation (EU) No 1215/2012 of the European Parliament and of the Council of 12 December 2012 on jurisdiction and the recognition and enforcement of judgments in civil and commercial matters (recast) (2012) OJ L 351/1.

[8] For example, a judgment concerning division of property between ex-spouses will be recognised/enforced in accordance with rules contained in the Code (provided that no bilateral agreement is in place) as Poland is a non-participating Member State with respect to Council Regulation (EU) 2016/1103 of 24 June 2016 implementing enhanced cooperation in the area of jurisdiction, applicable law and the recognition and enforcement of decisions in matters of matrimonial property regimes [2016] OJ L 183/1 (8 July).

[9] Council Regulation (EC) No 4/2009 of 18 December 2008 on jurisdiction, applicable law, recognition and enforcement of decisions and cooperation in matters relating to maintenance obligations (2009) OJ L7/1.

[10] Regulation (EU) No 650/2012 of the European Parliament and of the Council of 4 July 2012 on jurisdiction, applicable law, recognition and enforcement of decisions and acceptance and enforcement of authentic instruments in matters of succession and on the creation of a European Certificate of Succession (2012) OJ L201/107.

[11] Council Decision of 26 February 2009 on the signing on behalf of the European Community of the Convention on Choice of Court Agreements (2009) OJ L 133/1.

[12] Convention on the Recognition and Enforcement of Foreign Judgments in Civil or Commercial Matters (2022) OJ L187/4.

Code. Such agreements, which contains rules on recognition and enforcement are in place with (in alphabetical order): Austria (1963),[13] Algeria (1976),[14] Belarus (1994),[15] Bulgaria (1961),[16] Cuba (1982),[17] China (1987),[18] Cyprus (1996),[19] Egypt (1992),[20] Estonia (1998),[21] Greece (1979),[22] Hungary (1959),[23] Italy (1989),[24] Iraq (1988),[25] Latvia (1994),[26] Lithuania (1993),[27] Mongolia (1998),[28] North Korea (1986),[29] Romania (1999),[30] Russia (1996),[31]

[13] Umowa między Polska Rzecząpospolitą Ludowa a Republika Austrii o wzajemnych stosunkach w sprawach z zakresu prawa cywilnego oraz o dokumentach, podpisana w Wiedniu dnia 11 grudnia 1963 r, Dz U z 1974 r nr 6 poz 33.

[14] Umowa między Polską Rzecząpospolitą Ludową a Algierską Republiką Ludowo-Demokratyczną dotycząca obrotu prawnego w sprawach cywilnych i karnych, podpisana w Algierze dnia 9 listopada 1976 r, Dz U 1982.10.73.

[15] Umowa między Rzecząpospolitą Polska a Republika Białorusi o pomocy prawnej i stosunkach prawnych w sprawach cywilnych, rodzinnych, pracowniczych i karnych, sporządzona w Mińsku dnia 26 października 1994 r, Dz U 1995 r nr 128 poz 619.

[16] Umowa między Polska Rzecząpospolitą Ludową a Ludową Republiką Bułgarii o pomocy prawnej i stosunkach prawnych w sprawach cywilnych, rodzinnych i karnych, podpisana w Warszawie dnia 4 grudnia 1961 r, Dz U 1963 r nr 17 poz 88.

[17] Umowa między Polska Rzecząpospolitą Ludowa a Republika Kuby o pomocy prawnej w sprawach cywilnych, rodzinnych i karnych podpisana w Hawanie dnia 18 listopada 1982 r, Dz U 1984 r nr 47 poz 247.

[18] Umowa między Polska Rzecząpospolitą Ludowa a Chińską Republika Ludowa o pomocy prawnej w sprawach cywilnych i karnych, podpisana w Warszawie dnia 5 czerwca 1987 r, Dz U 1988 r nr 9 poz 65.

[19] Umowa między Rzecząpospolitą Polską a Republiką Cypru o współpracy prawnej w sprawach cywilnych i karnych, sporządzona w Nikozji dnia 14 listopada 1996 r, DzU1999.39.383.

[20] Umowa między Rzecząpospolitą Polska a Arabska Republika Egiptu o pomocy prawnej w sprawach cywilnych i handlowych, sporządzona w Kairze dnia 17 maja 1992 r, Dz U 1994 r nr 34 poz 126.

[21] Umowa między Rzecząpospolitą Polska a Republika Estońską o pomocy prawnej i stosunkach prawnych w sprawach cywilnych, pracowniczych i karnych, sporządzona w Tallinie dnia 27 listopada 1998 r Dz U 2000 r nr 5 poz 49.

[22] Umowa Polska Rzecząpospolitą Ludową a Republiką Grecką o pomocy prawnej w sprawach cywilnych i karnych, podpisana w Atenach dnia 24 października 1979 r, Dz U 1982 r nr 4 poz 24.

[23] Umowa między Polska Rzecząpospolitą Ludowa a Węgierską Republiką Ludową o obrocie prawnym w sprawach cywilnych, rodzinnych i karnych, podpisana w Budapeszcie dnia 6 marca 1959 r, Dz U 1960 r nr 8 poz 54.

[24] Umowa między Polska Rzecząpospolitą Ludową a Republiką Włoską o pomocy sadowej oraz o uznawaniu i wykonywaniu wyrok w sprawach cywilnych, podpisana w Warszawie dnia 28 kwietnia 1989 r, Dz U 1992 r nr 23 poz 97.

[25] Umowa między Polską Rzecząpospolitą Ludową a Republiką Iraku o pomocy prawnej i sądowej w sprawach cywilnych i karnych sporządzona w Bagdadzie dnia 29 października 1988 r, DzU z 1989 r, nr 70, poz 418.

[26] Umowa między Rzecząpospolitą Polską a Republiką Łotewską o pomocy prawnej i stosunkach prawnych w sprawach cywilnych, rodzinnych, pracowniczych i karnych, sporządzona w Rydze dnia 23 lutego 1994 r, Dz U 1995 r nr 110 poz 534.

[27] Umowa między Rzecząpospolitą Polską a Republiką Litewską o pomocy prawnej i stosunkach prawnych w sprawach cywilnych, rodzinnych, pracowniczych i karnych, sporządzono w Warszawie dnia 26 stycznia 1993 r, Dz U 1994 r nr 35 poz 130.

[28] Umowa między Rzecząpospolitą Polską a Mongolią o pomocy prawnej i stosunkach prawnych w sprawach cywilnych, rodzinnych, pracowniczych i karnych, sporządzoną w Warszawie dnia 19 października 1998 r, Dz U 2003 r nr 43 poz 370.

[29] Umowa między Polską Rzecząpospolitą Ludową a Koreańską Republiką Ludowo-Demokratyczna o pomocy prawnej w sprawach cywilnych, rodzinnych i karnych, podpisana w Phenianie dnia 28 września 1986 r, Dz U 1987 r nr 24 poz 135.

[30] Umowa między Rzecząpospolitą Polską a Rumunią o pomocy prawnej i stosunkach prawnych w sprawach cywilnych, sporządzoną w Bukareszcie dnia 15 maja 1999 r, Dz U 2002 r nr 83 poz 752.

[31] Umowa między Rzecząpospolitą Polska a Federacją Rosyjską o pomocy prawnej i stosunkach prawnych w sprawach cywilnych i karnych, sporządzona w Warszawie dnia 16 września 1996 r, Dz U z 2002 r, nr 83, poz 750.

Syria (1985),[32] Turkey (1998),[33] Ukraine (1993)[34] and Vietnam (1993).[35] The agreement concluded with Czechoslovakia (1987)[36] applies now in relations with the Czech Republic and Slovakia. The agreement concluded with Yugoslavia (1960)[37] applies nowadays in relations with Bosnia and Herzegovina, Croatia, North Macedonia, Serbia and Slovenia. Some of the above bilateral agreements bind Poland with other EU Member States. In case such bilateral agreements with other EU Member State contains rules on jurisdiction, as well as recognition and enforcement of judgments in civil and commercial matters within the meaning of Brussels I bis Regulation, the latter regulation takes precedence before the bilateral agreement.[38] Given the amount of bilateral agreements in place, one should not overlook their existence, as they are (or at least some of them are) applied in practice.[39]

At the same time, there are non-EU states, for example the United States (US), with which Poland does not have a bilateral agreement in place and which are not (yet) party to global multilateral conventions (for example, the HCCH 2019 Judgments Convention), while there are instances where recognition/enforcement of judgments originating from such states is sought in Poland.[40] In these cases the provisions on recognition/enforcement included in the Code become of practical importance.

[32] Umowa między Polska Rzecząpospolitą Ludowa i Arabską Republiką Syryjską o pomocy prawnej w sprawach cywilnych i karnych, podpisana w Damaszku dnia 16 lutego 1985 r, Dz U 1986 r nr 37 poz 181.

[33] Umowa między Polska Rzecząpospolitą Ludową a Republiką Turecką o pomocy prawnej w sprawach cywilnych i handlowych, podpisana w Warszawie dnia 12 kwietnia 1988 r, Dz U 1992 r nr 3 poz 13.

[34] Umowa między Rzecząpospolitą Polska a Ukraina o pomocy prawnej i stosunkach prawnych w sprawach cywilnych i karnych sporządzona w Kijowie dnia 24 maja 1993 r, Dz U z 1994 r, nr 96, poz 465.

[35] Umowa między Rzecząpospolitą Polska a Socjalistyczna Republika Wietnamu o pomocy prawnej i stosunkach prawnych w sprawach cywilnych, rodzinnych i karnych, sporządzona w Warszawie dnia 22 marca 1993 r, Dz U z 1995 r, nr 55, poz 289.

[36] Umowa między Polska Rzecząpospolitą Ludową a Czechosłowacką Republiką Socjalistyczną o pomocy prawnej i stosunkach prawnych w sprawach cywilnych, rodzinnych, pracowniczych i karnych, podpisana w Warszawie dnia 21 grudnia 1987 r, Dz U 1989 r nr 39 poz 210.

[37] Umowa między Polską Rzecząpospolitą Ludowa a Federacyjną Ludową Republiką Jugosławii o obrocie prawnym w sprawach cywilnych i karnych, podpisana w Warszawie dnia 6 lutego 1960 r, Dz U 1963 r nr 27 poz 162.

[38] Pursuant to Art 69 Brussels I bis Regulation, as between the EU Member States, Brussels I bis Regulation supersedes the conventions that cover the same matters as those to which the regulation applies. At the same time, these bilateral agreements might still be applicable with respect to matters not covered by Brussels I bis Regulation, for instance matrimonial property matters. Rules on such matters are included, for example in the bilateral agreement with Croatia, and should be applied in relations between Poland and Croatia, as Poland is a non-participating Member State with respect to EU regulations on property matters (Council Regulation (EU) 2016/1103 of 24 June 2016 implementing enhanced cooperation in the area of jurisdiction, applicable law and the recognition and enforcement of decisions in matters of matrimonial property regimes [2016] OJ L183/1 and Council Regulation (EU) 2016/1104 of 24 June 2016 implementing enhanced cooperation in the area of jurisdiction, applicable law and the recognition and enforcement of decisions in matters of the property consequences of registered partnerships [2016] OJ L183/30).

[39] See for example: postanowienie Sądu Okręgowego w Warszawie (District Court of Warsaw), 16 October 2015, z 16 X 2015 r, sygnatura akt: XX GCo 316/14 (concerning enforcement of a judgment handed down in Belarus); postanowienie Sądu Najwyższego (Supreme Court), 14 April 2016, z 14 IV 2016 r, sygnatura akt: IV CSK 507/15 (concerning enforcement of a judgment handed down in Russia); postanowienie Sądu Apelacyjnego w Łodzi (Court of Appeal Lodzi), 25 June 2013, z 25 VI 2013 r, sygnatura akt: I ACz 955/13 (concerning enforcement of a judgment handed down in Russia); postanowienie Sądu Apelacyjnego w Poznaniu (Court of Appeal Poznan City, 9 December 2014, z 9 XII 2014 r, sygnatura akt: I ACz 2073/14 (concerning enforcement of a judgment handed down in Ukraine). Judgments handed down by common courts in Poland might be found by the name of the court, date and signature in paid databases (for example LEX or Legalis) or on the governmental website, orzeczenia.ms.gov.pl.

[40] See for example postanowienie Sądu Najwyższego (Supreme Court), 8 December 2016, z 8 XII 2016 r, sygnatura akt: III CSK 21/16; postanowienie Sądu Najwyższego (Supreme Court), 9 January, z 11 X 2013 r; sygnatura akt: I CSK 697/12.

Additionally, bilateral agreements concluded by Poland became of age (for example, the bilateral agreement with Ukraine, which is one of the newest, has already been in place for 30 years). Consequently, the rules included in such bilateral agreements are often more conservative (for example, when it comes to requirements) than these included in the Code. As a result, there are voices in the legal literature suggesting that the provisions of the Code should apply to judgments which do fall under the bilateral agreement if application of the rules of the Code would be more favourable to recognition/enforcement of the foreign judgment than these included in the bilateral agreement.[41] If this standpoint becomes more popular and applied in practice,[42] the importance of the rules of the Code would be further enhanced.

When it comes to legal literature, quite naturally, scholars are more interested in developments with respect to recognition and enforcement in EU instruments on judicial cooperation in civil and commercial matters, as well as in the jurisprudence of the Court of Justice of the European Union in that respect,[43] than in 'domestic' rules contained in the Code and jurisprudence of 'domestic' courts in that respect. This, however, does not mean that the rules of the Code are not subject to any scholarly work. These rules are contemplated mainly, but not only,[44] in comprehensive commentaries to the Code.[45]

Question 2. Procedure

a) Circumstances of Recognition and Enforcement

Articles 1145–1149[1] of the Code govern recognition, whereas Articles 1150–1152 of the Code regulate enforcement. As indicated in the Explanatory Note to the Amendment 2009, 'recognition' refers to any judgment irrespective of whether it is enforceable by way of execution or not, whereas 'enforcement' is dedicated solely to judgments which are enforceable by way of execution (which includes the possibility of reporting to the use of coercive measures).[46]

[41] P Czubik, 'Uznanie z mocy prawa, uznanie sądowe, odmowa uznania orzeczenia sądów państw obcych w świetle praktyki notarialnej i wieczystoksięgowej' in T Demendecki (ed), *Mechanizm uznania lub odmowy uznania orzeczenia sądu państwa obcego w sprawach cywilnych przez sąd polski – analiza de lege lata i wniosku de lege ferenda* (Instytut Wymiaru Sprawiedliwości, 2019) 81–82.

[42] The courts seem to adhere to the view that a bilateral agreement must be applied even if the rules of the Code would be more favourable to recognition of a judgment. See: wyrok Wojewódzkiego Sądu Administracyjnego w Krakowie (Provincial Administrative Court Krakow), 14 May 2019, z 14 V 2019 r, sygnatura akt: III SA/Kr 1228/18; wyrok Naczelnego Sądu Administracyjnego (Supreme Administrative Court), 22 June 2022, z 22 IX 2022, sygnatura akt: II OSK 1352/21 (these judgments were handed down by administrative courts in cases concerning recognition of divorces pronounced by Ukrainian administrative authorities, but the arguments presented in these judgments may be equally applied to recognition or enforcement of judgments in civil and commercial matters, as well as to other bilateral agreements).

[43] See for example A Frąckowiak-Adamska, *Uznawanie i wykonywanie orzeczeń w sprawach cywilnych w Unii Europejskiej: ujęcie systemowe* (CH Beck, 2018).

[44] See for example T Demendecki, *Mechanizm uznania lub odmowy uznania orzeczenia sądu państwa obcego w sprawach cywilnych przez sąd polski – analiza de lege lata i wniosku de lege ferenda* (Instytut Wymiaru Sprawiedliwości, 2019).

[45] See for example T Ereciński, *Kodeks postępowania cywilnego. Komentarz. Tom VI. Międzynarodowe postępowanie cywilne. Sąd polubowny (arbitrażowy)* (Wolters Kluwer, 2017).

[46] Sejm Rzeczpospolitej Polskiej VI kadencji, druk nr 949.

In accordance with Article 1145 of the Code, judgments of courts of foreign states handed down in civil matters are recognised by operation of law (*ex lege*, *ipso iuris*, *de plano*), unless there are obstacles specified in Article 1146 (for these 'obstacles' see Question 3 below). Hence, it is not necessary for an interested party to apply to the court for the recognition of a judgment of a foreign court in a separate proceeding. Such judgment may be subject to an ad hoc recognition by courts or other authorities in the course of other proceedings (for example, a foreign judgment is recognised within a proceeding aimed at updating data entered into a land register). Such ad hoc recognition does not bind other courts or authorities in other proceedings. Hence, the Code provides for a preventive procedure, which allows anyone with a legal interest to apply to the court that it determines, in a separate facultative proceeding, that a given foreign judgment is or is not recognised (Article 1148 § 1 of the Code). Such a decision on recognition or non-recognition will then bind other courts and authorities in all other proceedings.

Pursuant to Article 1150 § 1 of the Code, foreign judgments, which can be enforced, become execution titles after their enforceability is declared by a court. Declaration of enforceability (*exequatur*) is granted if the judgment is enforceable in the country of origin and there are no obstacles specified in Article 1146 (for these 'obstacles' see Question 3 below). Declaration of enforceability (*exequatur*) is granted at the application of the creditor by way of attaching an enforceability clause to the foreign judgment (Article 1151 § 1 of the Code). Once a foreign judgment is declared enforceable in Poland it constitutes in Poland an execution title (just like a final domestic judgment with enforceability clause attached). Based on such execution title the creditor may initiate the execution proceeding in accordance with *lex fori processualis* (namely in accordance with the provision contained in Part III 'Execution Proceeding' of the Code).

b) Procedural Steps

The procedure in which application with respect to recognition or enforcement is dealt with may not be classified either as contentious or non-contentious proceeding. It is considered a special, separate type of proceeding regulated in Part Four of the Code.[47]

An application with respect to recognition (or non-recognition) is filed with the regional court[48] that would have territorial competence to hear the case (decided by the foreign judgment) or in the region of which the territorially competent district court is located, or in the absence of such, the Regional Court in Warsaw (Article 1148[1] § 1 of the Code). The application to have an enforceability clause granted is filed with the regional court of the place of residence or seat of the debtor, or, in the absence of such a court, by the regional court in whose region enforcement is to be carried out (Article 1151[1] § 1).

[47] Ereciński (n 40) 713–14; M Muzyka, 'Koszty postępowania w sprawach o uznanie orzeczenia sądu zagranicznego oraz w sprawach o ustalenie, że orzeczenie sądu państwa obcego podlega lub nie podlega uznaniu' in T Demendecki (ed), *Mechanizm uznania lub odmowy uznania orzeczenia sądu państwa obcego w sprawach cywilnych przez sąd polski – analiza de lege lata i wniosku de lege ferenda* (Instytut Wymiaru Sprawiedliwości, 2019) 61.

[48] The common courts in Poland are district courts (*sądy rejonowe*), regional courts (*sądy okregowe*) and courts of appeal (*sądy apelacyjne*). They are competent to hear civil law cases, family and custody law cases, labour law cases and social insurance cases and criminal law cases. The Supreme Court (*Sąd Najwyższy*) is the highest central judicial organ in the Republic of Poland, and thus the highest court of appeal.

In the case of both and application concerning recognition, and application concerning enforcement being filed, the copy of the application is served respectively on the other party or the debtor. The other party or the debtor may present their position on the case within two weeks counting from the service of a copy of the application (Article 1148^1 § 2 first sentence of the Code for recognition; Article 1151^1 § 2 first sentence for enforcement). The Code states that with respect to recognition the court may hear the case at a closed session (Article 1148^1 § 2 second sentence), whereas with respect to enforcement the court decides the case in closed session (without 'may' – Article 1151^1 § 2 second sentence).

Furthermore, the decision of the regional court may be appealed against, and the decision of the Court of Appeal may be appealed in cassation (Article 1148^1 § 3 first sentence for recognition; Article 1151^1 § 3 for enforcement). Additionally, other recourse mechanisms are available (namely, resumption of proceedings which ended with a final decision may also be requested, as well as a declaration that a final decision issued in that regard is unlawful (Article 1148^1 § 3 second sentence for recognition; Article 1151^1 § 3 in fine for enforcement).

During the proceedings instituted by an application concerning recognition or application concerning enforcement, as well as within another proceeding when *ex lege* recognition is contemplated, the court is to examine whether the conditions for recognition and enforcement are met. Hence, the court verifies whether any of the 'obstacles' referred to in Article 1146 exist and additionally with respect to enforcement whether the judgment is enforceable in the state of origin (see Question 3 below for details). As rightly explained in the literature, the court has to review circumstances which concern: (1) the decision itself (for example, whether its recognition would be contrary to *ordre public*); (2) the proceedings in which the decision was made (for example, whether the party was not deprived of the right to defend); and (3) certain external circumstances (for example, whether the case falls within the exclusive jurisdiction of Polish courts or whether the case has been already decided or commenced before a Polish court).[49]

It was underlined in one of the decisions of the Supreme Court that the examination by the court of the circumstances ('obstacles') listed in Article 1146 of the Code is not dependent on a plea by the parties to the proceedings, but instead is a duty of the court, the exercise of which is incumbent upon it *ex officio*.[50] Any arguments raised by the parties do not determine the examination made by the court, but may serve as a sign that a particular issue requires special consideration.[51] According to the general rule on burden of proof, it falls on the applicant, regardless of the nature of the request (recognition or non-recognition). However, as rightly pointed in the literature, in practice some circumstances listed in Article 1146 are impossible for the applicant to prove; for example, non-contradiction with *ordre public*. Another example is the impossibility for the applicant to prove that that the case is not pending before a Polish court. This should rather be left for the other party/the debtor to bring to the attention of the court.[52]

Analysing the conditions ('obstacles') of recognition and enforcement requires, to a certain extent, an examination of the content of the judgment. This necessity exists, for

[49] Ereciński (n 40) 724–25.
[50] Postanowienie Sądu Najwyższego (Supreme Court), 31 January 2018, z 23 VIII 1990 r, sygnatura akt: I CR 415/90.
[51] Ereciński (n 40) 724–25.
[52] Ereciński (n 40) 724–25.

example, when the court contemplates the consistency of the recognition/enforcement with the *ordre public*. However, it must be underlined that this examination is limited to a review of the circumstances determining the lack of an 'obstacle' and cannot constitute a substantive review of the judgment, namely a review of its fairness and correctness.[53] The Supreme Court has underlined on many occasions that the foreign judgment is not subject to substantive review.[54]

Referring to enforcement only now, after the decision on the granting of an enforceability clause has become final, an enforcement on the basis of a foreign judgment may be initiated (Article 1151^2 § 1 first sentence of the Code). Until the time limit for lodging an appeal has expired, or, if an appeal has been lodged, before it has been examined by the Court of Appeal, the decision constitutes a security title. The security measure to be taken is indicated by the creditor in the application for granting security. For judgments on pecuniary claims, only certain types of measures, listed in Article 747, are permissible (for example, seizure of a movable property, seizure of a remuneration for work, seizure of a bank account or encumbering of an immovable property with a mortgage). If necessary, the type of security may also be specified by the court in the order granting the enforcement clause if requested by the creditor. The execution of the measure may be made conditional by the regional court on the creditor giving a security deposit (Article 1151^2 § 2). If the appeal against the decision granting an enforceability clause is dismissed or the decision granting an enforceability clause is issued, the appellate court may make the enforcement conditional on the creditor providing a security deposit. The court may, if irreparable damage could result to the debtor as a result of the enforcement of the foreign judgment, suspend the enforcement until the time limit for filing a cassation appeal has expired and, if filed, until it has been examined by the Supreme Court (Article 1151^2 § 2).

Question 3. Requirements

Requirements (drafted in a negative manner and therefore referred to as 'obstacles' in Article 1145 on recognition and Article 1151 § 1 on enforcement) are listed in Article 1146 of the Code. These requirements/grounds for refusal are explained in detail below.

a) Jurisdiction of the Court of Origin

Pursuant to Article 1146 § 1 point 2 of the Code, a foreign judgment will not be recognised/enforced if it was handed down in a case falling within the exclusive jurisdiction

[53] ibid 725.

[54] Postanowienie Sądu Najwyższego (Supreme Court), 10 October 1975, z 21 X 1975 r, sygnatura akt: I CR 672/75, PiP 1976; postanowienie Sądu Najwyższego (Supreme Court), 5 November 1975, z 5 XI 1975 r, sygnatura akt: I CR 625/75; postanowienie Sądu Najwyższego (Supreme Court), z 7 V 1980 r, sygnatura akt: IV CR 116/80.

of Polish courts. Hence, the jurisdiction of the court of origin in general is not assessed as a requirement of recognition/enforcement. The only exception is the existence of exclusive jurisdiction of Polish courts, which is assessed from the perspective of Polish rules on jurisdiction.[55]

The examples of exclusive jurisdiction of Polish courts include cases involving immovable property rights and possession of immovable property located in Poland, as well as cases arising from a lease or rental relationship or other relationship involving the use of such immovable property, except cases involving rent and other charges related to using or benefiting from such immovable property (Article 1103^8 § 1 of the Code). Also, cases other than those listed above fall under exclusive jurisdiction insofar as their adjudication concerns property rights or possession or use of immovable property located in Poland (Article 1103^8 § 2).[56] It is unclear whether nowadays, since Succession Regulation started to be applied, these rules apply when it comes to recognition or enforcement of a judgment given in succession matters. The above rules would not be used to establish jurisdiction of a Polish court in a succession matter of a person who died starting from 17 August 2015. Hence, the question remains whether they still could be used as jurisdictional filters with respect to a judgment given in a non-EU state.

Pursuant to Article 1109^1 § 1 of the Code exclusive jurisdiction encompasses also matters of registration proceedings concerning a register held in Poland. Similarly, exclusive jurisdiction exists with respect to cases concerning dissolution of a legal entity or an organisational unit without legal personality, if this legal entity or unit have their seat in Poland (Article 1109 § 2).

Exclusive jurisdiction exists also in family matters in case interested parties are habitually resident and domiciled in Poland and additionally have Polish nationality (for example, with respect to matrimonial matters, including matrimonial property matters[57] – Article 1103^1 § 2).

b) Finality/Enforceability in the Country of Origin

Pursuant to Article 1146 § 1 point 1 of the Code, a foreign judgment will not be recognised/enforced if is not final (pl: *prawomocne*) in the country where it was given. Additionally, Article 1150 provides that a foreign judgment may be declared enforceable in Poland only if it is enforceable and could in fact be enforced in the country of origin.

The Supreme Court explained, in one of its decisions, that a foreign judgment is 'final' once the parties are not entitled to an appeal or other remedy. Hence, whether a judgment is final is determined in accordance with procedural rules of the law of the state where the judgment was handed down.[58] As noted below (see Question 4), it is for the interested party to provide a document stating that the foreign judgment is final. It

[55] A Wysocka-Bar 'Poland' in T Lutzi, E Piovesani and D Zgrabljić Rotar (eds), *Jurisdiction over Non-EU Defendants* (Hart, 2023) 209-220.

[56] Similar rules are contained in Arts 1107^1 and 1110^2 of the Code which concern cases handled in non-contentious proceedings.

[57] Poland is a non-participating Member State with respect to Twin Property Regulations.

[58] Postanowienie Sądu Najwyższego (Supreme Court), 6 Febraury 1975, z 6 II 1975 r, sygnatura akt: II CR 849/74.

happens, however, that parties claim that foreign courts, in particular in the US, are not willing to produce such documents.[59] It is suggested in the legal literature that more liberal approach is needed and therefore other kinds of documents should be allowed in such cases, for example confirmation produced by a Polish consulate in the country where the judgment was given or by a respective foreign consulate in Poland, as well as explanation on foreign law provided for by Polish Ministry of Justice.[60]

c) *Res Iudicata*

Pursuant to Article 1146 § 1 point 6 of the Code, a foreign judgment will not be recognised/enforced if it is inconsistent with a previously handed down final judgment of a Polish court or a previously handed down final judgment of a court of a foreign state, which fulfills the requirements for its recognition in Poland, given in a case involving the same claim between the same parties.[61] Article 1146 § 2 adds that this 'obstacle' also applies *mutatis mutandis* when there is a decision made by a Polish authority or a foreign authority other than a court.

d) *Lis Pendens*

Pursuant to Article 1146 § 1 point 5 of the Code, a foreign judgment will not be recognised/enforced if a case concerning the same claim between the same parties was pending in Poland earlier than before the foreign court.[62] Article 1146 § 2 of the Code adds that this 'obstacle' also applies *mutatis mutandis* when a case was pending before a Polish or a foreign authority other than a court.

The assessment on whether a case was pending in Poland is made in accordance with Polish civil procedure, namely Article 192 of the Code,[63] which provides that the case is pending starting from the moment when the document initiating proceeding was served on the other party. The assessment on whether a case was pending in a foreign court is done in accordance with foreign law (*lex fori processualis*).[64]

[59] W Graliński, 'Prawomocność orzeczenia zagranicznego jako przesłanka jego uznania w Polsce' in T Demendecki (ed), *Mechanizm uznania lub odmowy uznania orzeczenia sądu państwa obcego w sprawach cywilnych przez sąd polski – analiza de lege lata i wniosku de lege ferenda* (Instytut Wymiaru Sprawiedliwości, 2019) 34.

[60] ibid 34.

[61] Pursuant to Art 1146 § 3 of the Code, this 'obstacle' does not apply when a foreign judgment establishes, in accordance with its own provisions on jurisdiction, the acquisition by way of succession by a person residing or having a seat in Poland of a property located on the territory of the foreign state.

[62] Pursuant to Art 1146 § 3 of the Code, this 'obstacle' does not apply when a foreign judgment establishes, in accordance with its own provisions on jurisdiction, the acquisition by way of succession by a person residing or having a seat in Poland of a property located on the territory of the foreign state.

[63] W Graliński, 'Zawisłość sporu oraz sprzeczność z wcześniej wydanym orzeczeniem w sprawie o to samo roszczenie między tymi samymi stronami' in T Demendecki (ed), *Mechanizm uznania lub odmowy uznania orzeczenia sądu państwa obcego w sprawach cywilnych przez sąd polski – analiza de lege lata i wniosku de lege ferenda* (Instytut Wymiaru Sprawiedliwości, 2019) 50.

[64] ibid 50.

e) Specific Requirements of Due Process

Pursuant to Article 1146 § 1 point 3 of the Code, a foreign judgment will not be recognised/enforced if the defendant, who did not enter into a dispute as to the merits of the case, was not served properly and in time to defend himself with the letter initiating the proceedings. Also, in accordance with Article 1146 § 1 point 4 Code, a foreign judgment will not be recognised/enforced if the party was deprived of the opportunity to defend during the proceedings.

The most important element of the opportunity to defend is the possibility to familiarise oneself with the arguments on which the claim is based. Hence, the court must serve a defendant with the copy of the claim/application. As a result, the mere notification of the defendant by anyone, including the plaintiff, that a proceeding has been initiated, or even the notification of the defendant of the date of the hearing in such a case, especially if it is before a foreign court, cannot be considered sufficient.[65]

While assessing the existence of the obstacle listed in Article 1146 § 1 point 3 of the Code, the court must first determine whether and how service of the document initiating the proceedings was made, then whether the service was proper and, later, whether, considering the circumstances of the case, it was made in time to enable the defence. While examining these issues the court is not constrained by the view of the court of origin.[66]

In the jurisprudence, it was submitted on many occasions that the examination of whether a party was deprived of the possibility to defend before the court of the state of origin should be based on the procedural law of the state of origin, in accordance with *lex fori processualis* rule. However, the assessment of whether this deprivation occurred is not limited to the verification of the correctness of the application of foreign procedural law. This assessment is made by the Polish court, which is not bound in this regard by the findings of the court of origin.[67] While assessing this obstacle to recognition/enforcement, attention should be paid not so much to compliance with specific provisions of foreign law, but rather the actual opportunity to participate in the proceedings and undertake a defence.[68]

It was reported in the legal literature that it happens that judgments given in the US (in particular in family matters, namely divorce) are not recognised in Poland based on the above-mentioned obstacles, due to lack of proper service, which in the case of defendants domiciled in Poland should be done in accordance with the Hague Service Convention and is not (or in the case of defendants domiciled in the US is) done only through public notice in a newspaper published in a given state.[69]

[65] Postanowienie Sądu Najwyższego (Supreme Court), 25 March 1998, z 25 XI 1998, sygnatura akt: II CKN 70/98.

[66] Postanowienie Sądu Najwyższego (Supreme Court), 2 June 2017, z 2 VI 2017, sygnatura akt: II CSK 704/16.

[67] ibid.

[68] Postanowienie Sądu Najwyzszego (Supreme Court), 6 July 2000, z 6 VII 2000, sygnatura akt: V CKN 1350/00.

[69] M Derdak, 'Zachowanie prawa do obrony – uwagi na tle art. 1146 §1 pkt 3 i 4 k.p.c.' in T Demendecki (ed), *Mechanizm uznania lub odmowy uznania orzeczenia sądu państwa obcego w sprawach cywilnych przez sąd polski – analiza de lege lata i wniosku de lege ferenda* (Instytut Wymiaru Sprawiedliwości, 2019) 44–46.

f) Public Policy

Pursuant to Article 1146 § 1 point 7 of the Code, a foreign judgment will not be recognised/enforced if recognition/enforcement would be contrary to the fundamental principles of the legal order of the Republic of Poland (public policy clause).

It is underlined in the literature that the wording of the public policy clause requires that it is the recognition/enforcement which must be contrary to the fundamental principles and not the judgment itself for the clause to come into play. Hence, the object of the assessment are the potential effects/consequences of the recognition/enforcement.[70] The fundamental principles of the legal order of the Republic of Poland are not only constitutional principles, but also most important principles governing different branches of law, for example civil law, and also procedural law.[71] When it comes to procedural law the principles which should be perceived as fundamental are that of adversarial process and equal rights of the parties.[72]

In one of its important decisions the Supreme Court explained the nature and operation of the public policy clause.[73] The case concerned enforcement of a US judgment awarding both actual damages (250,000 USD and 750,000 USD respectively towards both claimants) and punitive damages (4,000,000 USD for both claimants) as a result of an allegedly defamatory article, which appeared in a newspaper published in Poland in paper and online, and also distributed in the US.

First, the Supreme Court elaborated in general about the system of recognition/enforcement of foreign judgments, stating that:

> It is a principle of international law, underpinned by the sovereignty of states, that a court decision as an act emanating from an organ of a state has its own effect only in the territory of the state of origin. Respect for any of its effects, including its enforcement, in the territory of another state – justified by the needs of international trade – is therefore possible only insofar as the law of that state permits it. The prerequisites for this may be determined by the norms of the internal law of that state or international agreements concluded by it, and, in the case of European Union members, also by the norms of regulations of Union institutions.

In this case, as none of the EU regulations and international agreements apply, these prerequisites are those listed in the Code.

In this case, the Supreme Court contemplated in detail one of the prerequisites listed in Article 1146 of the Code, namely that the enforcement is not incompatible with public policy. The Court explained that

> the mere dissimilarity of a foreign law, even a very far-reaching or even blatant one …, is not sufficient to refuse to apply it or to refuse to recognize or declare enforceability of a judgment based on it by invoking the public policy clause. What is necessary for this is a contradiction, i.e. an obvious, blatant incompatibility of the effects of … the recognition or declaration of enforceability of a foreign judgment with the fundamental principles of the legal order of the state … of recognition or enforcement.

[70]Ereciński (n 40) 699.
[71] ibid 699.
[72] ibid 700.
[73] Postanowienie Sądu Najwyższego (Supreme court), 11 October 2013, z 11 X 2013 r, sygnatura akt: I CSK 697/12.

After analysing the system of actual and punitive damages in the US, and comparing it with delict law in Poland, the Court arrived at the following conclusion:

> The consequence of declaring the submitted judgment enforceable insofar as it covers the entirety of the punitive damages would be to allow in the territory of Poland the legal effect of the possibility of enforcing a monetary benefit, awarded in a civil case for violation of honor, in a very large amount, detached from the extent of the damage. Such a result would undoubtedly be unacceptable from the point of view of the principle, interpreted in accordance with the constitutional requirement of proportionality, that compensation serves to compensate for damage and cannot exceed the extent of the damage. It would remain in obvious incompatibility with it and would destabilize the system of liability for damages adopted in Polish law, allowing foreign creditors, able to take advantage of the broad jurisdiction of U.S. courts, to satisfy themselves in Poland on the basis of titles awarding such amounts to an extent unavailable to Polish creditors …

The Court did not exclude the possibility of enforcing the judgment in part related to actual damage.

g) Reciprocity

There is no reciprocity requirement for recognition and enforcement. Such requirement existed previously, but was abolished by the 2009 Amendment to the Code.

h) Other Requirements

No other requirements exist in Poland for the recognition and enforcement under the Code. Other requirements existed previously (namely, application of Polish law in cases it was the applicable law), but they were abolished by the 2009 Amendment to the Code.

Question 4. Documents to be Produced

As explained above, a foreign judgment (and also other decision of a foreign authority) is recognised in Poland by virtue of law (*ex lege, de plano*), unless there exists one of the 'obstacles' specified in Article 1146 of the Code. Pursuant to Article 1147 § 1, a person relying on the recognition is obliged to present certain documents: an official copy of the judgment; a document stating that the judgment is final, unless the finality of the judgment follows from the content of the judgment; and a certified translation into Polish of the above documents.

Article 1147 § 1 of the Code provides that if the judgment was issued in proceedings in which the defendant did not enter into a dispute as to the merits of the case, a document confirming that the document initiating the proceedings was served must be presented, together with its certified translation.

In case an application to the court is made to have confirmed that a judgment is recognised, the same documents as listed in Article 1147 § 1 of the Code must be provided.

However, if the application concerns non-recognition it is enough to provide an official copy of the judgment and its certified translation (Article 1148 § 2).

In case of application for declaration of enforceability, the documents listed in Article 1147 § 1 of the Code must be provided (ie, an official copy of the judgment, a document stating that the judgment is final, unless the finality of the judgment follows from the content of the judgment and a certified translation into Polish of the above documents), as well as a document stating that the judgment is enforceable in the state of origin, unless its enforceability follows from the content of the judgment or the law of that state (Article 1151 § 2).

Foreign judgment for its recognition or enforcement in general does not need to be legalised or have apostille attached to it as, in accordance with Article 1138 of the Code, foreign official documents have the same evidentiary force as Polish official documents.[74] The provision further states that only a document concerning the transfer of ownership of real property located in Poland or a document whose authenticity has been denied by a party should be authenticated by a Polish diplomatic representation or consular office.

Question 5. Securities, Bonds and Deposits

The application for determining whether a foreign judgment is subject to recognition and an application to declare a foreign judgment (or a decision of another foreign authority or a settlement concluded or confirmed by such court or authority) is enforceable is subject to a court fee in the amount of PLN 300 (approximately EUR 65). Other obvious expenses are costs of translations and costs of professional representative during the proceeding.

Additionally, in accordance with Article 1119 of the Code, a plaintiff who does not have domicile or habitual residence, or a seat in Poland or in another EU Member State is obliged to give a security deposit for the costs of the trial. This obligation might be put on the plaintiff only if the defendant so requests. Article 1120 lists circumstances in which the plaintiff is not under the obligation to give a security deposit. These circumstances include having in Poland assets sufficient to pay the costs; being entitled to or having obtained exemption from court costs, or where a judgment of a Polish court awarding the reimbursement of costs from the plaintiff to the defendant would be enforceable in the state where the plaintiff has domicile or habitual residence or seat. In certain cases the security deposit is not applicable, for example in non-pecuniary matrimonial cases, in counterclaims and in injunction, writ of payment and summary proceedings or in cases which the parties have unanimously submitted to the jurisdiction of the Polish courts. Pursuant to Article 1121 § 1 the defendant may make a request for security for costs before entering into a dispute on the merits.

There is no clear provision in the Code indicating that provisions on security deposit also apply in proceedings concerning recognition or enforcement. However, in

[74] Postanowienie Sądu Najwyższego (Supreme Court), z 28 I 2018 r, sygnatura akt: II CSK 174/17.

the literature, authors support the view that the security deposit might be required in proceedings concerning recognition or enforcement.[75]

Where a security deposit is requested, the court determines the amount of the security deposit having in mind the probable amount of costs to be borne by the defendant (Article 1123 § 1 of the Code). The amount is deposited on the account of the Ministry of Finance unless the court determines another way of depositing it. The court sets a time limit for the plaintiff to make the deposit (Article 1124 § 2). Upon the ineffective expiry of the time limit, the court will reject the application (Article 1124 § 3). Once the proceeding is over, the court, at the request of the defendant, orders that the costs awarded to the defendant be satisfied from the deposit (Article 1126 § 1). Such a request must be made within one month from the (requested) decision becoming final. If the application has not been made, the court, upon the expiry of that period, orders that the security deposit be released to the plaintiff (Article 1126 § 1). If the defendant has not been awarded costs, the court orders that the deposit be given back to the plaintiff immediately after the (requested) decision becomes final (Article 1126 § 1).

[75] J Ciszewski in T Ereciński (ed) *Kodeks postępowania cywilnego. Komentarz. Tom VI. Międzynarodowe postępowanie cywilne. Sąd polubowny (arbitrażowy)* (Wolters Kluwer, 2017) 415.

Romania

RAMONA CIRLIG AND DANIEL-FLORIN PETRACHE

Question 1. General Overview

As a background to the analysis that will follow, it is important to note that the Romanian law system combines features from both the adversarial and inquisitorial systems. Nevertheless, the inquisitorial side is more pregnant in litigation. Therefore, the judge plays an active role in finding the truth, subject to the principle that the judge can only rule within the limits of the claim. The judge can assess the evidence based on their own conviction, taking into account each piece of evidence and all the evidence as a whole.

The national autonomous rules on the recognition and enforcement of non-EU judgments in civil and commercial matters are set forth in the Romanian Code of Civil Procedure (RCCP), Book VII (International Civil Proceedings), Title III (The Effectiveness of Foreign Judgments), Chapter I (Recognition of Foreign Judgments) and Chapter II (Enforcement of Foreign Judgments).[1]

Article 1094 RCCP defines the notion of foreign judgments in a very broad manner as including contentious and non-contentious jurisdictional acts, notarial acts, and acts belonging to any competent authority of a non-member state of the European Union (EU).

Article 1065 RCCP establishes the scope of application of the RCCP rules. These rules are applicable in private law proceedings with a foreign element only where EU law, international treaties or special laws are not applicable.

The RCCP has been influenced by the Brussels regime, which was one of the sources of inspiration for the drafters of the regulation. However, the RCCP is also inspired by the national views of the Private international law act of 1992 (Law no 105/1992) and thus, the national rules on the recognition and enforcement of non-EU judgments in civil and commercial matters present some particularities that we will emphasise in the following pages.

We mention that Romania is a party to several bilateral treaties on cooperation in civil matters that apply in relation to Algeria, Bosnia, Serbia, Montenegro, Cuba, Egypt, Macedonia, Morocco, Moldova, Tunisia, Turkey, Albania, China, North Korea, Mongolia, Russia and Ukraine. All these treaties include provisions on the recognition and enforcement of judgments.

[1] The Romanian Code of Civil Procedure (Law 134/2010) was published in the *Official Gazette* (Part I, 545) on 3 August 2012, and entered into force on 15 February 2013 (replacing the Code of Civil Procedure 1865).

Question 2. Procedure

a) Circumstances of Recognition and Enforcement

The request for recognition can be formulated as a main claim or can be settled incidentally by the court seized with a matter having a different object, in which one party invokes the *res iudicata* effect or a preliminary matter based on the foreign judgment.[2]

When the request for recognition of the foreign judgment was submitted through the statement of claim, the recognition will be decided by a final ruling. When the recognition was invoked in an incidental manner, the matter will be decided by an interlocutory minute.

In both cases, the decision will be rendered after summoning all parties so that they can express their views. By exception, the request for recognition can be settled without summoning the parties if it results from the foreign judgment that the defendant agreed to the admission of the claim.

The request for approval of the enforcement, on the other hand, is settled by a final ruling, after summoning the parties. There is no scenario where the decision can be rendered without summoning the parties. Enforcement always requires a domestic judgment confirming that the requirements for recognition and enforcement are fulfilled.

b) Procedural Steps

1. *The Procedure for Recognition*

When the request for recognition is formulated as a main claim, Article 1099 RCCP sets forth that the court competent to handle the recognition procedure is the tribunal where the party refusing the recognition is domiciled or headquartered. If such tribunal cannot be established, the Bucharest Tribunal will settle the matter. When the request for recognition is incidental, the court competent to handle the recognition procedure is the court seized with the main matter.

The foreign judgment benefits from probative force in Romanian proceedings with regard to its findings, if it satisfies the requirements necessary for its authenticity according to the law of the state of origin. The proof against the facts ascertained by the foreign court can be done by any means. Findings made by a foreign court do not benefit from probative force if they are manifestly incompatible with Romanian public policy.

Article 1101 RCCP provides that the statute of limitation term for enforcement of the foreign ruling will be interrupted upon the request for recognition. This means that a new statute of limitation term of the same length as the initial one will start lapsing. In order to secure enforcement of a foreign judgment in Romania, it is not required to provide proof that the decision has not become time-barred and this issue cannot be raised by the judge of its own motion.

[2] D Lupașcu and D Ungureanu, *Drept international privat* (Universul Juridic, 2012) 311.

Given its wording, Article 1101 RCCP indirectly sets forth that a foreign ruling is qualified as enforceable in Romania as of the date when it is deemed enforceable according to the law of the state where it was rendered.[3]

2. *The Procedure for Enforcement*

Article 1103(1) RCCP provides that foreign judgments that are not complied with voluntarily can be enforced on the Romanian territory based on the approval granted by the tribunal where the enforcement will take place. When the claimant demands simultaneously the recognition and the approval of enforcement, the request may be submitted either to the tribunal where the debtor of the ruling has the domicile/headquarters, either to the tribunal where the enforcement will take place.

Article 1103(2) RCCP expressly provides that foreign judgments ordering conservatory measures as well as interim decisions cannot be enforced on the territory of Romania.[4]

The request for approval of the enforcement is settled by a final ruling, after summoning the parties.

If the foreign judgment contains decisions on several claims which are dissociable, approval can be granted separately.

The decision approving the enforcement of a pecuniary award in a foreign currency will also impose the conversion into national currency at the exchange rate of the day when the judgment became enforceable in the state of origin. Until the date of conversion, the interest is governed by the law of the state of origin and for the subsequent period, the interest will be calculated by reference to the Romanian laws.

On the basis of the final decision approving the enforcement, an enforceable deed is issued in accordance with the conditions of Romanian law. This title will also mention the decision to approve the enforcement.

Following this exequatur procedure, the judgment creditor will need to go through additional court formalities applicable to any enforceable deed, including national courts' rulings. Thus, the judgment creditor submits a request to the enforcement officer and the latter addresses to the court in order to obtain approval of enforcement. This approval and the enforcement of the ruling in its entirety may be subsequently contested to the local courts (a lower grade than the tribunals) in accordance with the rules on the challenge of enforcement of the RCCP (Book 5).

Suspension of enforcement proceedings is possible as set out in Article 719 RCCP until the challenge to the enforcement or any other request regarding the enforcement proceedings is resolved, at the request of the interested party and only for reasonable grounds. The suspension may be requested alongside the challenge to the enforcement or by means of a separate request.

A party seeking to suspend enforcement proceedings is required to provide a bond, the amount of which must be determined based on the value of the amount challenged, according to the thresholds set out under Article 719(2) RCCP.

[3] ŞA Stănescu in VM Ciobanu and M Nicolae (eds), *Noul Cod de Procedură Civilă. Comentarii pe articole*, Vol II – Art 527–1134 (Universul Juridic, 2016) 1733.

[4] See also High Court of Cassation and Justice, Civil Section, 25 June 2004, no 4813.

Pursuant to Article 719(6) RCCP, the court must rule on the suspension request by means of enforceable minutes, which may be challenged by means of appeal. The parties must be summoned for the hearings.

In urgent cases and provided that the bond has been properly constituted, upon the request of the interested party, a court may order provisional suspension of the enforcement proceedings until the request for suspension is resolved. To obtain provisional suspension, in addition to the requirement of 'reasonable grounds', the interested party must prove the 'urgency' of the situation.

A particularity of the provisional suspension of the enforcement proceedings is that in respect of such proceedings, the court will rule without summoning the parties. Minutes rendered by a court in respect of a request for provisional suspension are not subject to appeal and are enforceable. However, the ruling of a court in respect of a request for provisional suspension will produce effects only until the main suspension request is resolved.

As regards foreign court settlements, Romanian law provides that they will be granted the effects deriving from the law under which they were concluded. Article 1103(1) RCCP and Articles 1104–1108 RCCP will apply accordingly.

3. The Burden of Proving the Requirements for Recognition and Enforcement

The burden of proving the requirements for recognition and enforcement (including whether the competent authority may, of its own motion, ascertain the existence or non-existence of any such requirements) is not clearly regulated by the RCCP.

The existence of an article – 1096 RCCP with the marginal title 'Conditions of recognition' – and of another article – 1097 RCCP named 'Grounds for refusal of recognition' – suggests that the Romanian judge has the obligation to check *ex officio* the requirements of Article 1096 RCCP, and not those from Article 1097 RCCP.

In other words, the drafting of two different articles regarding the requirements for the recognition of a foreign decision could be based on a distinction between the aspects that must be verified *ex officio* and those that will be analysed by the judge exclusively when they are invoked by the party opposing to the recognition or enforcement.[5]

The obligation to verify the conditions regulated by Article 1096(1) RCCP is indicated by Article 1096(3) RCCP. Thus, the non-definitive character of the foreign judgment, arising from the omission to serve a subpoena to the person who did not participate in the trial before the foreign court, can only be invoked by that person. Via a *per a contrario* interpretation, it results that other requirements laid down in Article 1096 RCCP must be verified by the own motion of the court.

Likewise, Article 1104 RCCP provides that the approval of the enforcement is carried out in compliance with the conditions provided for in Article 1096 RCCP, to which the requirement of enforceability of the foreign judgment, according to the law of the state of origin court, is added. Grounds for refusal of Article 1097 RCCP are also applied in enforcement cases, but they are not treated as preconditions for approval.

[5] D Petrache, *Ordinea publică de drept internațional privat* (Universul Juridic, 2019) 215–17.

At the same time, the documents attached to a request for recognition or enforcement suggest that the grounds for refusal of Article 1097 RCCP are not necessarily analysed in all cases.

For instance, if one of the parties does not specifically invoke non-compliance with fundamental procedural principles, the simple reading of the court decision, which does not necessarily contain a section on how the trial was conducted, does not allow the judge to notice a breach of a fundamental rule of procedure.

Therefore, based on the current regulation of the RCCP, it seems that the grounds for refusal of recognition should not be invoked *ex officio* by the court.

However, there are inflections to this statement. The delimitation between conditions for recognition and grounds for refusal of recognition shows that the judge is not obliged to examine, each time, the non-existence of grounds for refusal. But, by virtue of his active role, he should be able to invoke one of the grounds for refusal, where he ascertains or is aware of its existence.

Thus, it is likely that the court ascertains that the foreign ruling manifestly infringes the fundamental values of the Romanian state, even though none of the parties invoked the breach of public policy.[6]

Also, the breach of the exclusive jurisdiction rules can be noticed by the judge without having to be invoked by one of the parties.

In such cases, the judge should be able to invoke, by his own motion, the grounds for refusal invoked by Article 1097 RCCP.

As a conclusion on this matter, the conditions for recognition provided by Article 1096 RCCP must be assessed *ex officio* by the court in all cases (with the exception set forth in Article 1096(3) RCCP, where only the harmed party may invoke that the decision was not final). In what concerns the grounds of refusal provided by Article 1097 RCCP, the court can exercise its active role by raising a certain ground in a specific case, but the judge does not have an obligation to always analyse them.

4. The Extent to which the Requested Decision may be Reviewed on the Merits

Concerning the extent to which the requested decision may be reviewed on the merits, Article 1098 RCCP provides that: 'Except for the verification of the conditions provided for in Art. 1.096 and 1.097, the Romanian court cannot proceed with the substantive examination of the foreign judgment nor to its amendment.'[7]

Even though the wording may be confusing, the intention of the lawmaker was to emphasise that the substantive examination of a foreign ruling may only concern the fulfilment of the conditions laid down in Articles 1096 and 1097 RCCP. In those cases where the judge ascertained a breach of one of the conditions provided by Articles 1096 and 1097 RCCP, the court cannot intervene on the merits of the foreign ruling and will resume to rejecting the request for recognition and/or enforcement.[8]

[6] For a relevant case confirming our interpretation, please see Bucharest Court of Appeal, Sixth Civil Section, 13 February 2023, no 193.

[7] On this matter, please also see High Court of Cassation and Justice, Civil Section, 29 January 2003, no 293.

[8] Stănescu (n 3) Art 527–1134, 1730.

As such, the Romanian court has the prerogative to analyse the conduct of the proceedings, the evidence administered, the rules of procedure, the rules applied on the merits, factual elements arising after the dispute has been settled abroad to assess the grounds for refusing recognition. What the Romanian court cannot do is to question the merits of the case, to administer evidence in order to establish what the outcome should have been.

In practice, the Romanian courts usually deal appropriately with the prohibition to review the merits of the case.

However, we have identified a criticisable solution, in which we consider that the High Court of Cassation and Justice (HCCJ) has mistaken the examination of a public policy breach with the review of the merits.[9] In the case at issue, the applicant HH, residing in Syria, requested against the defendant AAM, a German-Syrian citizen residing in Târgu Jiu (Romania), that the court recognises on Romanian territory the judgment No 316/2003, delivered by the Sharia II Court of Aleppo, Syria, and enforce the judgment in order to return the minor daughter SAM to the defendant AAM in Syria.

Craiova Court of Appeal took into account the child's physical, emotional and psychological needs, the child's views[10] and the war situation in Syria at that time. In view of these aspects, it held that the recognition and enforcement of the judgment violated the best interests of the child and rejected the applicant's request.[11]

On the final appeal, HCCJ held that the assessment of the best interests of the child by the Craiova Court of Appeal amounted to an examination of the merits of the case:

> The appellate court assessed the admissibility of the plaintiff's application having regard also to the physical, emotional and psychological needs of the child, including the child's need for stability, the age and developmental stage of the minor, the child's views and preferences as ascertained by the first court, the nature, strength and stability of the relationship between the child and his father, the child's care history who suffers from certain medical conditions requiring specialized treatment, and the climate of war in the country where the plaintiff resides, that entrusting the minor to her mother would be contrary to the child's best interests, concluding that all these factors taken together prevent the Syrian judgment from being recognized and enforced, matters which concern the examination of the merits of the case.[12]

In our opinion, Craiova Court of Appeal did not examine the merits of the case, but took into account the circumstances that arose after the foreign judgment was rendered, in order to see to what extent the judgment is compatible with a public policy value, namely the best interests of the child. The child had been living in Romania for years with her father, had integrated into the community and was enjoying a nurturing environment. In Aleppo in November 2013, at the time of the judgment, the city was destroyed because of the civil war in Syria. These elements show that the execution of the judgment is manifestly contrary to the best interests of the child.[13]

[9] Petrache (n 5) 220.

[10] The child declared that she has been in Romania for more than five years in her father's care, enjoys the affection of her family and, although she has daily phone conversations with her mother, whom she has not seen since 2004, she does not want to return to Syria.

[11] Craiova Court of Appeal, First Civil Section, 19 October 2012, no 80.

[12] High Court of Cassation and Justice, Second Civil Section, 21 November 2013, no 4099.

[13] Petrache (n 5) 221.

The decision is open to criticism and stems from misunderstanding the powers of the court of recognition. It is open to the court of recognition to examine any relevant matters of fact or of law in order to determine compatibility with public policy or with any other ground of refusal.[14]

5. Challenging the Decision Granting or Refusing Recognition and/or Enforcement

If recognition and/or enforcement has been sought in separate proceedings, the decision to grant or to refuse recognition/enforcement is subject to appeal before the Court of Appeal and this decision may be subsequently challenged by an appeal on points of law before the HCCJ. This means that every *exequatur* procedure governed by the RCCP could reach the HCCJ, which could add a significant amount of time to the length of the trial. However, the award of the Court of Appeal is enforceable and therefore enforcement could be sought before the ruling of the Supreme Court is rendered.

If the recognition has been requested by an incidental manner, the means of challenging the decision are determined by the rules applicable to the statement of claim.

An important difference between recognition of a foreign judgment and that of a foreign arbitral award in Romania is that the latter is subject to only one instance of appeal.

Question 3. Requirements

Before describing the requirements, we must mention that foreign judgments on citizens' personal status will be automatically recognised in Romania if they refer to the personal status of the citizens of the state where they were rendered or, if rendered in a different state, they were recognised first in the citizenship state of each party. If there is no such recognition, the foreign judgments must have been rendered under the applicable law established in accordance with the Romanian private international law, should not be contrary to the Romanian public policy and the right of defence should have been observed. This is all set forth in Article 1095 RCCP.

For the judgments that do not fall under Article 1095 RCCP, the requirements are regulated by two different Articles, mentioned above: on one hand, Article 1096 RCCP provides for the cumulative conditions required for recognition; on the other hand, Article 1097 RCCP provides for the grounds on which recognition can be denied.

Furthermore, legal doctrine explains that, should the requirements be complied with, the recognition of the foreign judgment should not be hindered by the fact that Romania does not recognise the country of origin of the judgment as a matter of

[14] 'A court is obviously entitled to conduct so much of a review as is necessary to determine whether any of the substantive defences to recognition is made out, even where this involves an examination of the procedure before the foreign court, and even where the merits of that procedure are assessed.': A Briggs and P Rees, *Civil jurisdiction and judgments*, 5th edn (Informa, 2009) 686.

public international law.[15] For instance, a ruling from Kosovo that complies with the requirements of the RCCP will be recognised, even though Romania does not recognize the existence of the state of Kosovo.

a) Jurisdiction of the Court of Origin

The judgment will be recognised only if the court of origin had jurisdiction in accordance with the law of the country where the court of origin is located. Nevertheless, the jurisdiction cannot be based exclusively on the defendant's presence or on assets being located in the country of the court of origin, without a direct connection with the dispute. This is provided for in Article 1096(1)(b) RCCP, and it is a cumulative condition that must be met for recognition.

The jurisdiction of the court of origin is determined by observing the rules of law applicable in the state where the judgment is issued. The proof of the content of the foreign law is subject to Article 2562 of the Romanian Civil Code, the European Convention on Information on Foreign Law concluded in London on 7 June 1968 and its Additional Protocol (to which Romania adhered on 26 March 1991 by way of Government Decision Number 153/1991), as well as Law Number 189/2003 on international judicial assistance in civil and commercial matters.

Regarding proof of the law of the country of origin of the foreign judgment, the HCCJ[16] has held that Romanian law provides for the collaboration between the courts and the parties to the dispute. The courts, in accordance with the principle of the judge's active role in the proceedings, must implement, *ex officio*, measures required to establish the content of the foreign law and administer the proof deemed necessary. At the same time, the court has the option (not the obligation) to request the aid of the parties to determine the content of the foreign law.

Furthermore, the HCCJ held that if the interested party invokes the foreign law provisions, that party may be requested to prove its content. However, imposing such an obligation must be justified, meaning that the court must show why it did not use other institutional methods in order to determine the content of the foreign law.

The fact that, in our system of law, the court is required to establish the foreign law, with the assistance of the parties to the dispute, means that the parties must, on the one hand, provide evidence of the foreign law on which they rely, but at the same time the court, which has an active role in ascertaining the truth of the case and has appropriate methods of proving the foreign law, must also take steps to identify the content of the applicable foreign law.

As a rule, the parties have recourse to certificates issued by public authorities of the foreign state or even to a specialist, remunerated by the parties, to provide advice on foreign law.

In return, the court may not order specialised expertise, as it has institutional solutions at its disposal to obtain proof of foreign law. The main instruments used in the area of judicial cooperation in civil and commercial matters are the European Convention

[15] I Deleanu, V Mitea and S Deleanu, *Noul Cod de Procedură Civilă. Comentarii pe articole*, Vol II (Universul Juridic, 2013) 556.

[16] High Court of Cassation and Justice, First Civil Section, 18 April 2019, no 819.

on Information on Foreign Law and the European Judicial Network. Both give the court both the possibility to obtain information on the content of foreign law and on how foreign legal rules are interpreted in the home state.

b) Finality/Enforceability in the Country of Origin

The foreign judgment must be final according to the law of the country of origin, pursuant to Article 1096(1)(a) RCCP. Nevertheless, the lack of finality of the foreign judgment, deriving from the omission to summon the party that did not take part in the proceedings before the court of origin, can be invoked only by that party, pursuant to Article 1096(3) RCCP.

Usually, the proof of finality is made by means of the judgment itself if it contains such a mention. Should there be no such mention, the proof can be made by means of the relevant legal provisions from the state of origin.[17]

As a ground to deny recognition, Article 1097(1)(g) RCCP provides for the situation when the foreign judgment can be appealed in the country where it was rendered. This provision excludes from recognition foreign judgments that are enforceable in the country of origin but can still be appealed.[18]

c) *Res Iudicata*

This requirement is split under two different articles under Romanian law. Article 1097(1)(c) RCCP deals with a prior Romanian judgment between the same parties, which is final, while Article 1097(1)(d) RCCP deals with a prior foreign judgment, which has the vocation to be recognised in Romania.

First, Article 1097(1)(c) RCCP provides for the hypothesis when there is a prior Romanian judgment between the same parties and this judgment is final.

Second, Article 1097(1)(d) RCCP provides for the situation when the foreign judgment cannot be reconciled with a prior judgment rendered abroad, which has the vocation to be recognised in Romania. Therefore, under this ground for denying recognition the irreconcilable judgments are both foreign judgments. On the one hand, there is a foreign judgment submitted for recognition before Romanian courts. On the other hand, there is a prior foreign judgment that is susceptible of being recognised in Romania. There is no condition as to the existence of a prior request for recognition for the prior foreign judgment. The court faced with this problem will have to analyse which foreign judgment was the first, and whether they both fulfil the legal requirements for recognition.[19]

Both grounds, under Article 1097(1)(c) (prior Romanian judgment) and Article 1097 (1)(d) RCCP (prior foreign judgment), must be invoked by the party opposing the recognition as there is no obligation for the Romanian court to check the existence of a prior conflicting judgment.

[17] Deleanu, Mitea and Deleanu (n 15) 560.
[18] FG Păncescu, *Drept procesual civil internațional* (Editura Hamangiu, 2014) 208.
[19] ibid 218.

d) *Lis Pendens*

Article 1097(1)(c) RCCP provides for the situation when the dispute between the same parties was resolved by a judgment of the Romanian courts, which is not final or the dispute was pending before Romanian courts at the date when the foreign court was seized. Under this ground for denying recognition, there are two hypotheses: (1) there is a prior Romanian judgment between the same parties and the judgment is not final; (2) there was a case already pending before Romanian courts between the same parties at the date when the foreign court was seized.

Scholars analysing these two hypotheses deem that they are more questionable as regards a proper legal explanation, since the foreign judgment is final before the Romanian judgment. An explanation is offered by relying on the principle of the pre-eminence of the national judgment. Nevertheless, such situations rarely occur, since they are usually avoided by *lis pendens* mechanisms.[20]

In one case, the HCCJ ruled that the admission of the request for recognition in Romania of a foreign judgment under the pre-existence of a judgment given by a Romanian court does not constitute a case of unlawfulness, because the recognition of the foreign judgment is an independent power of the Romanian court,[21] which has a margin of discretion. This decision was criticised by the scholars, who consider that courts are bound to refuse recognition when there is a prior award from Romania which conflicts with the foreign ruling.[22]

e) Specific Requirements of Due Process

In case the judgment was rendered without the losing party being present, the judgment must ascertain that such party was issued with a timely subpoena for the final hearing, that it received the statement of claim and had the possibility to defend itself and to file an appeal against the judgment. This requirement is set forth in Article 1096(2) RCCP, and it is a cumulative condition that must be met for recognition.

Distinctively, Article 1097(1)(f) RCCP provides for a ground to deny recognition in case due process was breached. Even though the notion of due process is included in the notion of public policy, the lawmaker decided to regulate the breach of due process as a standalone ground for refusal.

f) Public Policy

Public policy is enshrined as a potential ground for denying recognition of a foreign judgment. In this respect, Article 1097(1)(a) RCCP provides as a ground to deny recognition the hypothesis when the foreign judgment is manifestly against the Romanian

[20] ibid 218.
[21] High Court of Cassation and Justice, Civil Section, 22 February 2007, no 1645.
[22] Stănescu (n 3) Arts 527–1134, 1728; S Popovici, *Drept internațional privat* (CH Beck, 2019) 124.

private international law public policy. It also mentions that this incompatibility will be assessed especially by taking into account the proximity of the case with the Romanian legal system and the seriousness of its effect.

Guidance as to the content of the Romanian private international law public policy can be found in Article 2564 of the Civil Code dealing with the grounds to remove the application of a foreign law. Thus, this article provides that there may be a breach of the Romanian private international law public policy when the result is incompatible with fundamental principles of Romanian law or EU law, or with the fundamental human rights.

The distinction between procedural and substantive public policy is not enshrined in the legal provisions, but only used by scholars to better explain the content of public policy.

Substantive public policy is often invoked by the debtor of the judgment as an attempt to obtain a reassessment of the merits of the case and, as a consequence, Romanian courts rarely admit such a ground for denying recognition.[23]

For example, HCCJ ruled that the mere fact that

> the foreign court has ruled on the manner of payment of social security benefits to the underaged child, as well as on the payment of maintenance, does not violate the Romanian public policy. On the contrary, the solution serves to respect a fundamental value, namely the best interests of the child.[24]

However, we can mention a recent judgment of Bucharest Court of Appeal,[25] where public policy was applied to refuse the effects of a foreign ruling.

The case concerned the recognition of a foreign judgment rendered in Belarus where the creditor of the judgment was a company included in Annex 1 to the Regulation (EC) no 765/2006 concerning restrictive measures in view of the situation in Belarus and the involvement of Belarus in the Russian aggression against Ukraine.

According to Article 2(2) of Regulation no 765/2006, no funds or economic resources shall be made available, directly or indirectly, to or for the benefit of the natural or legal persons, entities or bodies listed in Annex I.

In explaining the prohibition stipulated in Article 2(2), Article 8 d(1)(a) provides that no claims in connection with any contract or transaction the performance of which has been affected, directly or indirectly, in whole or in part, by the measures imposed under the Regulation no 765/2006, if they are made by legal persons listed in Annex I.

According to Article 1 point 15 (v) of Regulation (EC) no 765/2006, the notion of 'claim' includes a request for the recognition or enforcement, including by the procedure of *exequatur*, of a judgment, an arbitration award or an equivalent decision, wherever made or given.

The Bucharest Court of Appeal considered that the above-mentioned texts are included in the public policy concept and, therefore, invoked *ex officio* the breach of

[23] DA Sitaru, *Drept international privat* (CH Beck, 2013) 102.
[24] High Court of Cassation and Justice, First Civil Section, 13 April 2011, no 3423.
[25] Bucharest Court of Appeal, Sixth Civil Section, 13 February 2023, no 193.

public policy in order to block the enforcement of a ruling favourable to a company of Belarus mentioned by the Annex I of the Regulation (EC) no 765/2006.

The HCCJ fully confirmed this decision rendered by the Bucharest Court of Appeal.[26]

An issue that arose not only in theory, but also in practice, was whether the Romanian court can refuse to recognise a foreign ruling on the ground that it violates public policy, although the law applicable on the merits was Romanian. HCCJ has been clear on this point,[27] stating that

> such ground for refusing to recognize and enforce a foreign judgment (i.e. public policy) can only be based on the premise that the … tribunal applied a foreign law, the provisions of which are irreconcilable with the legal system of the country where recognition is sought.[28]

However, the answer must be nuanced.[29] Indeed, if Romanian law is the *lex causae*, there is no question of this law leading to a judgment contrary to a fundamental value of the Romanian legal order. But the law applicable to the proceedings is the law of the forum, ie a foreign law. It is not excluded that the application of the procedural rules of the foreign law may result in the infringement of a fundamental procedural right, in which case, even if the *lex causae* was Romanian law, the Romanian court may refuse to recognise the foreign judgment on the ground of breaching (procedural) public policy.

g) Reciprocity

As a positive condition that must be met for recognition, Article 1096(1)(c) RCCP requires reciprocity of effects regarding foreign judgments between Romania and the state of origin.

It is generally admitted that a factual reciprocity should be sufficient, without having to check whether the requirements are similar.[30] Moreover, reciprocity should be presumed until proven otherwise, as per Article 2561 of the Romanian Civil Code. More precisely, this provision sets forth that if the condition of factual reciprocity is required, its fulfilment is presumed until the contrary is proven.

h) Other Requirements

There are two grounds for denying recognition which do not fit the above categories.

The first one, provided for by Article 1097(1)(b) RCCP, refers to fraud, defined as the situation when the judgment was rendered in an area of law where the parties cannot freely dispose of their rights and it was obtained in order to avoid the applicable law in accordance with the Romanian private international law rules.

[26] High Court of Cassation and Justice, Second Civil Section, 10 October 2023, no 2017.

[27] In order to be accurate, we must mention the dispute concerned the recognition of an arbitral award, but the reasoning is the same in the case of a court decision.

[28] High Court of Cassation and Justice, Commercial Section, 2 December 2009, no 3181.

[29] Petrache (n 5) 352–53.

[30] Păncescu (n 18) 212.

The second one, provided for by Article 1097(1)(e) RCCP, concerns the hypothesis when the Romanian courts had exclusive jurisdiction.

The law also sets forth what a Romanian court cannot do when requested to recognise a foreign judgment.

In this respect, Article 1097(2) RCCP specifically mentions that recognition cannot be denied only because the court rendering the judgment applied a different law than the applicable law under the Romanian private international law.

There is one exception to the previously mentioned rule, namely when the subject matter of the proceedings concerned the civil status and capacity of a Romanian citizen, and the solution rendered by the court of origin was different than the one under Romanian law.

Therefore, in matters concerning the civil state and capacity of a Romanian natural person, if the solution differs from that under Romanian law, the judgment will not be recognised. The purpose of the rule is to protect the Romanian individual against violations of the essential values included in the notion of public policy. The lawmaker establishes that whenever the solution differs from the Romanian law, the decision infringes the fundamental values of the Romanian forum. This inflexibility in protecting the public policy values is an unwise choice of legislative policy. The rule goes far beyond the purpose for which it was instituted: not every regulatory variation leads to the prejudice of the Romanian citizen.[31]

To illustrate our statement, we can offer an example from the practice of Romanian national courts.[32] The petitioner KA applied for the recognition of an adoption judgment rendered in Switzerland, by the effect of which the petitioner – a Romanian citizen, born on 15 December 1980, was adopted by MH, born on 7 October 1955. MH was the husband of the adoptee's mother, KA, and had been married to her since 1998. The three lived together in Switzerland. The best interests of the child and the protection of fundamental rights with regard to marriage, the establishment of a family and the private life of the individual were invoked in favour of recognition. HCCJ refused to allow the final appeal and to recognise the adoption on the basis that the solution under Romanian law would have been different. More specifically, Romanian law required that the petitioner must have grown up during his minority with the adopter. In this case, the child had lived with the adopter since the age of 18.

We thus see how the legal text prevents an *in concreto* assessment of the infringement of fundamental values and leads to solutions that can be qualified as inequitable.[33]

Distinctively from the requirements for recognition of a foreign judgment, Article 1104 RCCP sets forth the conditions for granting the enforcement of the foreign judgment.

First, all the positive conditions set for the recognition of the judgment must be fulfilled.

Second, it is specifically mentioned that the judgment must be enforceable in accordance with the law of the state where it was rendered.

[31] Petrache (n 5) 279.
[32] High Court of Cassation and Justice, First Civil Section, 15 November 2007, no 7738.
[33] Petrache (n 5) 279.

Third, the grounds for denying enforcement are the same as the grounds for denying recognition. Reference is made to Article 1097 RCCP.

Fourth, reference is made to Article 1098 RCCP, forbidding the Romanian court to review or modify foreign judgments as to their substance in a request for granting the enforcement of a foreign ruling.

Question 4. Documents to be Produced

The request for recognition of a foreign judgment must comply with the general requirements provided by the RCCP for any request addressed to the court. Therefore, the request should include at a minimum: the parties' names and other identifying elements; the claims; the factual and legal reasons behind the claims; the supporting evidence; and the submitting party's signature.

Besides registering it at the court registry, the request can also be sent via email or fax. A document sent by email or fax is deemed as filed with the court from the date and time of receipt as evidenced by the court's receiving computer or fax. Moreover, it has recently become possible to submit requests via an online portal specially created for this purpose.[34]

Before sending a copy of the complaint to the defendant, the court can request the claimant to modify or complete the claim, as well as to provide the court with the original proof of payment of judicial stamp duty. The court serves a copy of the complaint to the defendant and informs the defendant of its obligation to submit a statement of defence within 25 days from reception of the complaint. The penalty for non-compliance is the loss of the right to submit evidence and to raise grounds for summary judgment, except grounds of public order. The statement of defence is sent to the claimant, who can answer to the statement of defence within 10 days from the day of reception. Submission of an answer to the statement of defence is not compulsory.

Pursuant to Article 1100(1) RCCP, the documents that must be attached to the request for recognition are: a copy of the foreign judgment; proof that the judgment is final; proof of service in case the debtor was not present; and any other document proving compliance with the requirements provided for in Article 1096 RCCP.

For the court to be able to review the service of process, the claimant must attach to the request proof that the summons and a copy of the claim were delivered to the missing party in the foreign court, or another official document stating that the summons and the claim were known in due time by the party against whom the ruling was pronounced. As per the HCCJ, with regard to the regularity of service of the judgment, the rule *locus regit formam actus* applies, according to which the issue of the summons is subject to the law of the state from which it originates, and its receipt must be performed in accordance with the law of the domicile of the party concerned.[35]

Pursuant to Article 1100(2) RCCP, the documents must be accompanied by authorised translations and must be legalised, in accordance with the conditions set forth in

[34] registratura.rejust.ro.

[35] High Court of Cassation and Justice, Civil Section, 17 October 2003, no 4119.

Article 1093 RCCP. Legalisation is not required when the parties agree with the submission of copies of the documents that are certified for conformity.

Article 1093(1) RCCP provides that public documents drawn up or legalised by a foreign authority or a foreign public agent can be produced before the Romanian courts only if they are legalised, through a hierarchical administrative process in the state of origin and then by the diplomatic mission or the Romanian consular office, to certify the authenticity of the signatures and the seal applied to them. Furthermore, Article 1093(2) RCCP details that legalisation by administrative means is subject to the procedure established by the state of origin of the act, followed by the legalisation carried out either by the Romanian diplomatic mission or the Romanian consular office in this state, or by the diplomatic mission or consular office in Romania of the state of origin and, afterwards, in either of the two situations, by the Ministry of Foreign Affairs.

Article 1093(3) RCCP explains that the exemption from legalisation is allowed when provided by the law, by an international treaty to which Romania is a party or on the basis of reciprocity. Since the Convention of 5 October 1961 Abolishing the Requirement of Legalisation for Foreign Public Documents (HCCH 1961 Apostille Convention) has over 125 Contracting Parties, the legalisation requirements are rather the exception and not the norm.

Pursuant to Article 1100(3) RCCP, in case some of the documents required in accordance with Article 1100(1) RCCP are not produced, the court may set a deadline for the production of the documents or it can accept equivalent documents or, if the court deems everything sufficiently clear it may dispense the party with the production of the said documents.

As regards the request for enforcement, in addition to the documents necessary for recognition, Article 1105 RCCP requires the production of a proof of enforceability of the foreign judgment, to be issued by the court of origin.

Question 5. Securities, Bonds and Deposits

According to Article 1085 RCCP, subject to the condition of reciprocity, the claimant, a foreign citizen or legal entity of foreign nationality, cannot be required to submit a bail or to provide any other guarantee because he is a foreigner or does not have his domicile or headquarters in Romania.

Therefore, as a general rule, there are no securities, bonds or deposits asked from a foreign party. By 'foreigner' we understand a natural not having Romanian citizenship, while the nationality of a legal entity is indicated by its statutory seat (registered office), as per Article 2571 of the Romanian Civil Code (RCC).

Nevertheless, the interpretation *a contrario* of the above-mentioned text reveals a scenario where, if the claimant is a foreigner, he could be bound to submit a guarantee. Thus, the only cases where the claimant may be asked for a guarantee are those where reciprocity does not exist, ie the national state of the claimant also imposes securities for Romanian claimants.

However, reciprocity is presumed, according to Article 2561(2) RCC. Thus, RCC provides that fulfilment of the factual reciprocity requirement is presumed until the contrary is established by the Ministry of Justice, in consultation with the Ministry of Foreign Affairs.

In general, legal actions filed before the courts are subject to various judicial stamp duties, depending on whether their object is financially determinable. Claims that are not financially determinable are stamped with a fixed stamp duty specified by law, according to the nature of the petition. There is also a specific procedure for requesting judicial aid, either as a waiver/reduction of the stamp duty or as payment by instalments. A request for recognition or for the approval of enforcing a foreign judgment is subject to a fixed stamp fee of RON 20 (approximately four euros).

Spain

BLAS PIÑAR GUZMÁN AND ANNA MARÍA RUIZ MARTÍN

Question 1. General Overview

The Spanish recognition and enforcement regime has its own domestic rules enacted in a specific body of law separated from the domestic jurisdictional and from the conflict of law rules.[1] This body of law is the Spanish Act 29/2015 of 30 July on International Legal Cooperation in Civil Matters (hereinafter, Spanish Act 29/2015).[2] It entered into force in 2015, having been discussed for many years by the Spanish Parliament to comply with the Twentieth Final Provision of the Spanish Civil Procedure Act of 2000 (SCPA).[3] The SCPA and the Spanish Organic Law on the Judiciary (OLJ)[4] complement the provisions of the Spanish Act 29/2015 as the Spanish procedural *lex fori*.

Previous to the enactment of this Law, these rules could be found in Articles 951–958 of the former Spanish Civil Procedure Act of 1881.[5] However, seminal case law of the Spanish Supreme Court widely differed from what was established in these articles. This case law is important, as it shed light on the complexity of the old Spanish recognition and enforcement system, and added some different requirements from those established in the aforementioned Articles. As a matter of fact, it was an inspiration to draft the Spanish Act 29/2015 including some of the requirements and favourable conditions of recognition. Finally, with the enactment of this Law, the Spanish system was simplified and modernised, in line with what was established in the European Union (EU) private international law (PIL)

[1] AM Ruiz Martin and MA Cebrián Salvat, 'Spain' in T Lutzi, E Piovesani and D Zgrabljić Rotar (eds), *Jurisdiction Over Non-EU Defendants. Studies in Private International Law* (Hart Publishing, 2023) 221–37; F Gascón Inchausti, 'Reconocimiento y ejecución de resoluciones judiciales extranjeras en la Ley de Cooperación jurídica internacional en materia civil' (2015) 7 *Cuadernos de Derecho Transnacional* 15; AL Calvo Caravaca and J Carrascosa González, *Tratado de Derecho internacional privado I* (Tirant lo Blanc, 2021) 889, 910–12.

[2] Ley 29/2015, de 30 de julio, de cooperación jurídica internacional en materia civil, *Official State Gazette* 182 [BOE], available in Spanish at boe.es/buscar/act.php?id=BOE-A-2015-8564.

[3] Spanish Act 1/2000 on Civil Procedure, *Official State Gazette* 90–180 [BOE], official translation available at mjusticia.gob.es/es/AreaTematica/DocumentacionPublicaciones/Documents/Law%2012000%20of%207%20January.pdf; M Virgos Soriano et al, 'Una propuesta de Ley de Cooperación jurídica internacional en materia civil (o cómo colmar una laguna legislativa difícil de entender y fácilmente remediable)' (2012) 2143 *Boletín Oficial del Ministerio de Justicia*, 3, 3; A Rodríguez Benot, 'La Ley de cooperación jurídica internacional en materia civil' (2016) 8 *Cuadernos de Derecho Transnacional*, 234, 250–51.

[4] Spanish Organic Law, 6/1985, of 1 July on the Judiciary, *Official State Gazette* 157 [BOE].

[5] Royal Decree of 3 February 1881 (*Gazette of Madrid* 36, 5 February 1881, 326–29) (historic).

regulations and recognition conventions.[6] Thus, it can be said that Spanish recognition and enforcement system has been influenced and inspired by the EU PIL rules on the subject, as will be explained in this report.

Besides, the provisions of the Spanish Act 29/2015 and the EU regime, Spain has signed several bilateral agreements on recognition, enforcement and mutual assistance in civil and commercial matters with third countries, which are still in force. They are of relevance and application when the resolution that comes from the courts of these countries fits in its material scope. Some of these bilateral treaties are as follows: (i) Treaty on the enforcement of civil resolutions (judgements) signed between Spain and Colombia, of 30 May 1908;[7] (ii) Treaty on mutual assistance signed between Spain and the Oriental Republic of Uruguay, of 4 November 1897, which contains rules on recognition and enforcement of civil and commercial resolutions and arbitral awards;[8] (iii) Treaty on mutual assistance in civil matters signed between Spain and Brazil, of 13 April of 1989, which contains rules on recognition and enforcement of civil and commercial resolutions and arbitral awards;[9] (iv) Treaty on the recognition and enforcement of judgments and arbitral awards signed between Spain and Mexico, of 17 April 1989;[10] (v) Treaty on mutual assistance in civil matters between Spain and the former URSS, of 26 October 1990;[11] (vi) Treaty on mutual assistance in civil and commercial matters between Spain and the Popular Republic of China, of 2 May 1992;[12] (vii) Treaty on cross border cooperation in civil and commercial matters signed between Spain and the Kingdom of Morocco, of 30 May 1997;[13] (viii) Treaty on jurisdiction and the recognition and enforcement of civil and commercial resolutions signed between Spain and the Republic of El Salvador, of 7 November 2000;[14] (ix) Treaty on the mutual assistance and the recognition and enforcement of civil and commercial resolutions signed between Spain

[6] Gascón Inchausti (n 1) 159.

[7] Convenio de ejecución de sentencias civiles entre España y Colombia, hecho en Madrid, el 30 de mayo de 1908 (historic), migrarconderechos.es/legislationMastertable/legislacion/Convenio_30_05_1908.

[8] Convenio de Cooperación jurídica entre el Reino de España y la República Oriental del Uruguay, hecho en Montevideo, el 4 de noviembre de 1987, *Official State Gazette* 103 [BOE].

[9] Instrumento de ratificación del Convenio de Cooperación jurídica en materia civil, entre el Reino de España y el gobierno de la República Federal de Brasil, firmado en Madrid el 13 de abril de 1989, *Official State Gazette* 164 [BOE].

[10] Convenio sobre reconocimiento y ejecución de sentencias judiciales y laudos arbitrales, en materia civil y mercantil entre España y México, hecho en Madrid, el 17 abril de 1989, *Official State Gazette* 85 [BOE].

[11] Convention affected by a succession of states. Since 2004, it is no longer in force for Estonia, Latvia and Lithuania as they became Member States of the EU; Convenio entre el Reino de España y la Unión de Repúblicas Socialistas Soviéticas, sobre asistencia judicial en materia civil, hecho en Madrid, el 26 de octubre de 1990, *Official State Gazette* 51 [BOE].

[12] Tratado entre el Reino de España y la República Popular China sobre asistencia judicial en materia civil y mercantil, hecho en Pekín el 2 de mayo de 1992, *Official State Gazette* 26 [BOE].

[13] Convenio de Cooperación judicial en materia civil, mercantil y administrativa entre el Reino de España y el Reino de Marruecos, hecho en Madrid el 30 de mayo de 1997, *Official State Gazette* 151 [BOE].

[14] Instrumento de Ratificación del Tratado entre el Reino de España y la República de El Salvador sobre competencia judicial, reconocimiento y ejecución de decisiones en materia civil y mercantil, *Official State Gazette* 256 [BOE]; see further, PA de Miguel Asensio, 'Tratado Bilateral entre España y El Salvador sobre competencia judicial international, reconocimiento y ejecución de decisiones en materia civil y mercantil de 7 de noviembre 2000', (2003) VIII *Anuario Español de Derecho Internacinal Privado* 587.

and the Republic of Tunisia, of 24 September 2001;[15] (x) Treaty on mutual assistance on civil and commercial matters signed between Spain and the Republic of Algeria, of 24 February 2005;[16] and (xi) Treaty on mutual assistance on civil and commercial matters signed between Spain and the Islamic Republic of Mauritania, of 12 September 2006.[17]

In addition, the Spanish Act 29/2015 contains not only rules on recognition and enforcement, but also rules on cooperation such as rules on the taking of evidence abroad, as well as on cross-border procedural phenomena such as *lis pendens* or related actions. Rules on recognition and enforcement are located in Title V (Articles 41–61), which is divided into: Chapter I. General provisions: definitions (Articles 41–43); Chapter II. Recognition: requirements and proceedings (Articles 44–49); Chapter III. aEnforcement (Articles 50–51); Chapter IV. *Exequatur* proceeding (Articles 52–55); and Chapter V. Efficacy of resolutions and judicial settlements-authentic documents (Articles 56–61).

Its main features with regard to the recognition and enforcement are as follows:

(i) It is based in a 'positive' recognition system rather than a negative one, according to its Article 3 which shields the cooperation principle ('*principio general favorable de cooperación*').[18] Unlike the former Spanish system, the current recognition and enforcement regime no longer rely upon the treatment given by the courts of origin or authorities to the Spanish resolutions, but on objective criteria.[19]

(ii) Its material scope is devoted to civil and commercial matters (all civil and commercial matters are included) as well as resolutions of non-contested jurisdiction ('*jurisdicción voluntaria*').[20] The term 'civil and commercial matters' is interpreted as in all EU PIL Regulations, namely Article 1(1) of Brussels Ia Regulation. Nonetheless, in contrast with the Article 1(2) of said Regulation, the Spanish Act 29/2015 does not exclude the same subject matters in its scope (namely family law matters, insolvency and others).

(iii) It clearly distinguishes between the proceeding of recognition without formalities, from the proceeding of enforcement and the *exequatur*, as will be further detailed under Question 2. The enforcement, in opposition to a mere declaration of recognition, will always need a declaration of enforceability or *exequatur*.[21]

[15] Convenio entre el Reino de España y la República de Túnez sobre asistencia judicial en materia civil y mercantil y reconocimiento y ejecución de resoluciones judiciales, hecho en Túnez el 24 de septiembre de 2001, *Official State Gazette* 52 [BOE].

[16] Convenio relativo a la asistencia judicial en el ámbito civil y mercantil entre la República Argelina Democrática y Popular y el Reino de España, hecho en Madrid el 24 de febrero de 2005, *Official State Gazette* 103 [BOE].

[17] Convenio relativo a la asistencia judicial en el ámbito civil y mercantil entre el Reino de España y la República Islámica de Mauritania, hecho en Madrid el 12 de septiembre de 2006, *Official State Gazette* 267 [BOE].

[18] Calvo Caravaca and Carrascosa González (n 1) 920–21; former bilateral recognition system was based in negative and positive reciprocity that is abolished when the Spanish Act 29/2015 is enacted.

[19] See also Section 3g.

[20] Gascón Inchausti (n 1) 161.

[21] ibid 160.

(iv) It is also allowed to request a partial recognition and enforcement, as well as a recognition of incidental questions of certain resolutions.[22]

(v) In accordance with its Preamble, Article 2 and First Additional Provision, the implementation and application of the Spanish Act 29/2015 is subsidiary.[23] Article 2 enshrines two principles of public international law: primacy (Article 2(a)) and specialty (Article 2(b)). On the one hand, according to the principle of primacy, international and EU law have primacy over domestic law, according to what is set out in Article 96 of the Spanish Constitution.[24] On the other hand, following the principle of specialty ('*principio de especialidad*'), the Spanish Act 29/2015 will only be applicable when the EU rules on recognition and enforcement, other bilateral and multilateral treaties and specific domestic rules on recognition cannot be applied to the specific case.[25]

A general and broad definition of *judgment* is provided by Article 43(a) of the Spanish Act 29/2015 as follows:

> [A]ny judgment given by a court or tribunal, whatever the judgment may be called, including a decree, order, decision, or writ of execution, as well as a decision on the determination of costs or expenses by an officer of a court.[26]

This definition is quite similar to the one provided by the EU PIL Regulations, explicitly, the Brussels Ia Regulation.[27] Under this definition, a court or an authority with analogous judicial functions in the state of origin is a body bestowed with state power to enforce the law and its resolutions might be recognised by the Spanish courts when comply with all the positive requirements established by the Spanish Act 29/2015.

In addition, subsequent paragraphs of Article 43 provide for definitions on authentic instruments, judicial settlements ('*transacciones judiciales*')[28] and the court of origin. Some Spanish scholars, such as Calvo Caravaca and Carrascosa González, inter alia, consider that these definitions have been wisely included in the Spanish Act 29/2015, as those are proper PIL definitions, in accordance with the former case law of the Spanish Supreme Court and the current EU PIL trends.[29]

[22] See Question 2 a) 2.

[23] On this feature, there is Spanish case law that shows the interplay between the implementation of the Spanish Act 29/2015 and the treaties signed between Spain and third countries. Sometimes, these treaties cannot be applied to the case in its whole as its material scope does not cover certain aspects, and the provisions of the Spanish Act 29/2015 must be applied to complement these loopholes; see for instance, Judgment of the Provincial Court of Barcelona, 17 October 2017, no 12949/2017, Secc 18 (ECLI:ES:APB:2017:12949); further details, JC Fernandez Rozas, 'No se aplica el Tratado entre España y Colombia de 1908 al reconocimiento de una sentencia colombiana por referirse éste exclusivamnete a la "ejecución"' (2018), fernandezrozas.com/2018/02/15/no-se-aplica-el-tratado-entre-espana-y-colombia-de-1908-al-reconocimiento-de-una-sentencia-colombiana-por-referirse-este-exclusivamente-a-la-ejecucion.

[24] Constitución española, *Official State Gazette* 311 [BOE].

[25] As the Preamble says: 'Dentro de un complejo marco de relaciones internacionales con numerosos tratados y acuerdos internacionales en vigor, y numerosas disposiciones de la Unión Europea una Ley de cooperación jurídica internacional interna debe tener carácter subsidiario.'

[26] 'Cualquier decisión adoptada por un órgano jurisdiccional de un Estado, con independencia de su denominación, incluida la resolución por la cual el secretario judicial o autoridad similar liquide las costas del proceso.'

[27] Calvo Caravaca and Carrascosa González (n 1) 912–13.

[28] In the same vein than Arts 3 and 11 of HCCH 19.

[29] inter alia, Auto del Tribunal Supremo, 16 of October 1961.

Question 2. Procedure

a) Circumstances of Recognition and Enforcement

According to the Spanish Act 29/2015, the recognition proceedings could seek either the recognition of foreign non-EU judgments (Article 42(1)), the anti-recognition of foreign non-EU judgments (Article 42(2)), or the incidental recognition of foreign non-EU judgments (Article 44(2)).

The enforcement of foreign non-EU judgments in Spain requires their prior recognition by the competent judicial authority. This contrasts to the provisions of the EU regulations, but it is considered appropriate by the Spanish authorities since this legal regime applies to foreign judgments from non-EU countries. The proceeding for declaring the recognition of a foreign judgment and authorising its enforcement in Spain is known as the *exequatur*. The *exequatur* proceeding is always subsidiary to special international and internal rules, provided that this is a residual general regulation, any bilateral treaties between Spain and third states governing the recognition and/or enforcement of judgments issued by their respective national courts will prevail.

There is also a specific regime applied to the recognition of judgments which have a non-contested jurisdiction nature (according to Act 15/2015 on non-contested jurisdiction).[30] They will be recognised thus, once the Spanish court examine that these resolutions comply with the conditions set out in the rules of the Ley 15/2015.

b) Procedural Steps

1. Scope and Procedure of the Recognition

Under Spanish rules of recognition, this proceeding is mainly devoted to recognising final and enforceable foreign judgments, rather than provisional resolutions. However, following the tendency of the European recognition rules tendency, it is also possible to seek the recognition of non-final judgments.

By virtue of the recognition, the foreign judgment shall produce in Spain the same effects as in the state of origin. If the foreign judgment contains a measure unknown for the Spanish legal system, it shall be adapted to a known measure with equivalent effects and similar purpose under Spanish law (Article 44(2) of the Spanish Act 29/2015).[31]

Once the application is declared admissible by the court and served to the party opposing the recognition, the opposing party may file its opposition within 30 days. Once the opposition has been filed (or the time limit for filing has expired without it having been lodged), the court shall render its decision within the term of 10 days, allowing or denying the recognition. During the *exequatur* proceeding, the parties may request the adoption of precautionary measures to ensure the effectiveness of the

[30] Ley 15/2015, de la Jurisdicción Voluntaria of 2 July 2015, *Official State Gazette* 158 [BOE].

[31] Order of the Provincial Court of Bizkaia, 22 December 2021, Secc 4, no 1968/2021 (ECLI:ES:APBI:2021:1895A).

judicial protection sought, ie, the subsequent enforcement of the foreign judgment to be previously recognised.

The parties must be represented by a Spain-qualified court representative ('*procurador*') and assisted by a Spain-qualified lawyer ('*abogado*'). In addition, the public prosecutor ('*Ministerio fiscal*') will appear in the *exequatur* proceeding.

A recognised judgment may be modified by the Spanish courts when it relates to matters which are subject to modification. This possibility does not preclude a new claim before the Spanish courts in such cases, allowing the interested party to choose between the modification of the foreign judgment or the commencement of new Spanish declaratory proceedings (examples of these resolutions are usually alimony regimes or patrimonial measures).

In the same vein of Article 36(3) of the Brussels Ia Regulation, it is allowed to request the incidental and partial recognition of non-final or final judgments.

2. *Scope and Procedure of the Enforcement*

The foreign judgment may be enforced like any other Spanish enforceable final decision after its recognition. The proceeding for the enforcement shall not commence until the recognition has not been rendered on its enforceability, by means of an *exequatur*, which starts with a specific application (Articles 42 and 50(1) of the Spanish Act 29/2015).

This proceeding is governed by some provisions of the Spanish Civil Procedure Act (Article 50(2) of the Spanish Act 29/2015). It is also possible to request a partial enforcement of a judgment that previously obtained an *exequatur* (Article 50(3)). Usually, foreign judgments that are enforceable in the state of origin shall be enforceable in Spain when the recognition through the *exequatur* has been obtained and they comply with the positive and negative requirements of the Spanish Act 29/2015, as explained above.[32]

Once the application is declared admissible by the court and served to the party opposing the recognition, this party has 30 days to formalise an opposition (if any). In the event that the party does not enter an appearance the proceeding will continue by default (Article 46(1)(b) of the Spanish Act 29/2015).

The reference to the SCPA forces to consider a five-year time limitation of the enforcement actions (ie Article 518 SCPA). Some judicial precedents set out that such time limitation starts when the judgment is rendered by the court of origin,[33] other precedents establish that it begins when the Spanish competent court renders the final recognition resolution.[34] This contrasts with the provisions of the EU regulations, but is considered appropriate by the Spanish authorities since this legal regime applies to foreign judgments from countries with which there is no legal link. It is unclear and disputed among case law whether a five-year time limitation, since the judgment is rendered in the state of origin, is applicable to the recognition action in Spain. Spanish academic voices also

[32] See Question 2 b) 2.

[33] For instance, Judgment of the Spanish Supreme Court, Civil Section, 16 October 2014, no 4838/2014 (ECLI:ES:TS:2014:4838).

[34] Judgment of the Provincial Court of Málaga, Secc 7, 27 January 2021, no 21/21 (ECLI:ES:APML:2021:149A); Order of the Provincial Court of Valencia, Secc 8, no 118/2019, 1 April 2019 (ECLI:ES:APV:2019:2002A).

strongly contest this time limitation of five years. It adds a procedural requirement in the Spanish enforcement procedure under the SCPA which it is not found in other European and/or international enforcement rules. It is said that this five-year limitation creates a lack of preclusive effects of the enforced resolution while in its country of origin has preclusive effects.[35] This concern is controversial as it adds an 'extra' requirement for foreign judgments which is only stated for the Spanish enforcement resolutions in enforcement proceedings. As a consequence, this limitation is a constraint for certain decisions, and will not produce effects in Spain while they are producing effects in the country of origin.[36]

2.1. Enforcement Procedure for Interim and Provisional Measures

Interim and provisional measures can be recognised when they meet the following requirements (Article 41(4) of the Spanish Act 29/2015): (i) if the refusal of their recognition by the Spanish court might infringe the *due process* rights under Spanish procedural standards; and (ii) when the counterparty had been heard prior to its adoption before the court of the country of origin according to its procedural law. This is also valid for the *inaudita parte* measures when these measures were adopted by the court of origin following its procedural rules. Yet, this requirement must be proved by the interested parties in their recognition before the Spanish courts. If parties did not successfully prove that the *inaudita parte* provisional measures issued by the foreign court were not adopted with all procedural safeguards (considering the procedural rights of both parties), those *inaudita parte* provisional measures will not be recognised.

2.2. Enforcement Procedure for Class Action Resolutions

Foreign judgments issued in proceedings arising from class actions might be recognised and enforced in Spain, but with some additional requirements (Article 47 of the Spanish Act 29/2015). On the one hand, the jurisdiction of the court of origin is subject to a stricter control: it is required that the court of origin that heard the case had international competence in a manner corresponding to one of those provided for the Spanish law. Mere similarity of the forum is not enough. On the other hand, in order to be enforceable in Spain against those individuals affected who have not expressly adhered to it, it is required that: (i) the foreign class action has been communicated or published in Spain by means equivalent to those required under Spanish law; and (ii) the parties have had equal opportunities to either participate in or disassociate themselves from the class action as those domiciled in the state of origin.

3. *Competent Authorities and Venue Jurisdiction*

Jurisdiction to hear recognition and enforcement applications is attributed to the first-instance courts, civil and commercial courts, according to the Articles 85 and 86(2) *ter* OLJ and Article 52(1)–(4) of the Spanish Act 29/2015.

[35] This procedural requirement is actually added by the rules of the SCPA (ie Spanish *lex fori*).
[36] Gascón Inchausti (n 1) 173.

The competent court will be primarily determined by the domicile of the party against whom the recognition is sought, or of the person to whom the effects of the foreign judgment are sought, or else by the place of enforcement or by the place where the judgment produces effects. Finally, if prior criteria cannot be applied, pursuant to the fundamental right to an effective judicial protection,[37] any first instance court before which the application for *exequatur* is brought shall be competent. In addition, if the party against whom the *exequatur* is sought is subject to insolvency proceedings in Spain and the foreign judgment deals with matters within the competence of the Spanish commercial court in charge of those proceedings, then these courts (Article 52(3) shall have jurisdiction to hear the application for *exequatur*.

In any case, the Spanish court will control *ex officio* its jurisdiction.

4. The Burden of Proof of the Requirements for Recognition and Enforcement

The application for recognition will be checked by the Court clerk ('*letrado de la administración de justicia*') according to the Article 54(5) and (6) of the Spanish Act 29/2015 whether;

(i) the court lacks jurisdiction;
(ii) the application is defective as to form;
(iii) the required documentation is not completed. In such cases, the party requesting recognition will be granted five procedural days to remedy the application.

Once this application is served and formalised, counterparties to the recognition may challenge, and attach, these documents referred to in the application:

(i) the authenticity of the foreign decision;
(ii) the correctness of the summons referred to the claim originating the foreign judgment; and
(iii) the fact that the foreign judgment is final and/or enforceable.

5. Appeals

There is also a possibility to appeal the refusal of recognition and enforcement, established under Article 55 of the Spanish Act 29/2015 and, once again, complemented by some provisions of the Spanish Civil Procedure Act.

Usually, the First-instance resolution granting or refusing the recognition of a foreign judgment can be appealed before the corresponding Second-instance court (Provincial Courts to hear the appeal).

The Second-instance decision might be also challenged through an extraordinary appeal before the Supreme Court ('*recurso de casación*'), which shall only be formally admitted if there is a special legal interest.

[37] For instance, Order of the Provincial Court of Salamanca no 67/2017.

Question 3. Requirements

Requirements for recognition and enforcement as well as for their refusal under the provisions of the Spanish Act 29/2015 are basically the same requirements which are listed in the EU PIL Regulations (*viz* Brussels Ia Regulation), but with some slight differences.

As previously explained, Spanish Act 29/2015 provisions have been inspired by these institutional rules as well as by other international conventions on recognition and enforcement, but they are still rules of an autonomous system which need to be drafted in a different manner, following the principles and values of the Spanish legal order.[38]

Positive requirements or grounds for recognition and enforcement are located in Article 41 of the Spanish Act 29/2015.

Requirements for the refusal of recognition, valid as grounds for refusal of enforcement proceedings are located in Article 46 ('*causas de denegación del reconocimiento*').

In the same way as Article 52 Brussels Ia Regulation is drafted, Article 48 of the Spanish Act 29/2015 prohibits to the courts to review the substance of the judgment's view of the merits.[39] In particular, according to the Spanish PIL rules, recognition may not be refused on the grounds that the foreign court has applied a different law from the one applicable.

Spanish courts are obliged to exercise the control of requirements listed in the next sub-paragraphs to all the judgments for which the rules of the Spanish Act 29/2015 are applicable. This Act follows a mandatory examination as to jurisdiction *ex officio* system (Article 52(4)), as it is based on principles of the Spanish legal order, namely on public policy reasons (procedural approach as explained in the next sub-paragraph).[40]

This list of requirements is a closed list (*numerus clausus*), which means that if it is not clear that a foreign resolution does not comply with any of the requirements, then it will be recognised.[41]

a) Jurisdiction of the Court of Origin

According to Article 46(1) of the Spanish Act 29/2015, when a resolution is not recognised, this is due to Spanish courts considering the court of origin not to have competence on the subject. This ground for refusal is based on a reasonable connection

[38] With certain caveats, and differences from the EU Recognition and Enforcement rules, as the *exequatur* proceeding is still 'alive' in the provisions of the Spanish Act 29/2015.

[39] Order of the Provincial Court of Vitoria-Gasteiz, Secc 1, 3 December 2019, no 138/2019 (ECLI:ES:APVI:2019:663A).

[40] Calvo Caravaca and Carrascosa González (n 1) 937.

[41] ibid 936; JC Fernández Rozas, 'Reconocimiento de una sentencia de divorcio dictada por el Tribunal de Ghana por no concurrir ninguna de las causas de denegación contempladas en el art 46 LCJIMC (APP Barcelona 20 diciembre 2019)', Blog de José Carlos Fernández Rozas (2020), fernandezrozas.com/2020/01/29/reconocimiento-de-una-sentencia-de-divorcio-dictada-por-el-tribunal-de-ghana-por-no-concurrir-ninguna-de-las-causas-de-denegacion-contempladas-en-el-art-46-lcjimc-aap-barcelona-20-diciembre-2019; Order of the Provincial Court of Barcelona, Secc 18ª, 20 December 2019, no 10377/2019 (ECLI:APB:2019:10377A).

to the Spanish territory as it happens when Spanish courts were hearing the case, or had the exclusive jurisdiction to do so.

The jurisdiction of the court of origin lacks a reasonable connection in the two following cases:

(i) When the foreign decision has been rendered on a subject matter for which the Spanish courts have exclusive jurisdiction (Article 22 OLJ).
(ii) When the foreign court does not have international jurisdiction on similar criteria to those provided for the exclusive jurisdiction grounds (territoriality or a reasonable connection with the case). This ground for refusal was established under the Spanish system in order to avoid *exorbitant* fora.

b) Finality/Enforceability in the Country of Origin

Article 41(1) demands to prove that under the *lex fori* of the country of origin the judgment is regarded as a final and enforceable judgment (not challenged). This Article is in connection with what is considered as final judgment under Article 43(b) and the Article 207(2) SCPA.[42]

Similarly, it is also connected with the Article 525(2) SCPA, insofar it excludes the provisional enforcement of non-final foreign judgments, unless this enforcement has been foreseen in international rules.[43]

c) *Res Iudicata*

Resolutions will not be recognised or enforced when the judgment is irreconcilable with a judgment previously given in Spain (Article 46(1)(d)), or when the judgment is irreconcilable with an earlier judgment given in Spain or in a third country involving the same cause of action and between the same parties, provided that the earlier judgment fulfils the conditions necessary for its recognition in Spain (Article 41(1)(e)).

d) *Lis Pendens*

Recognition and enforcement are also excluded when proceedings are pending in Spain involving the same cause of action and between the same parties, and was

[42] Art 207 of the Spanish Civil Procedure Act: Resoluciones definitivas. Resoluciones firmes. Cosa juzgada formal (*res iudicata)*.

[43] Gascón Inchausti (n 1) 161; Art 525(2) Spanish Civil Procedure Act: Sentencias no provisionalmente ejecutables; FJ Garcimartín Alférez and M Virgós Soriano, *Derecho Procesal Civil Internacional. Litigación internacional* (Thomson Civitas, 2007) 604–05.

previously brought in the court of a third state (Article 46(1)f), in connection with the Article 39 of the Spanish Act 29/2015).[44]

e) Specific Requirements of Due Process

Defendants' knowledge of the proceedings and respect of the right of defence are paramount under the Spanish system. The appearance and declaration of default are conditions *sine qua non* to apply for this ground or requirement for refusal.

Absence of these rights during the proceedings is a valid reason for the refusal of recognition. However, according to seminal Spanish Supreme Court case law, the defendant must prove that he/she was not able to arrange his/her defence to challenge the judgment, ie when the defendant was not duly served with the writ of summons, the document which instituted the proceedings and so on.[45] If this is the case, the Spanish courts shall not refuse the recognition of the resolution.

f) Public Policy

Foreign resolutions that are manifestly contrary to Spanish international public policy will not be recognised or enforced.[46] However, this ground for refusal is a restrictive one, insofar it has to be triggered as few times as possible.[47] Resolutions must be a real threat to Spanish international public policy, otherwise, Spanish courts are likely to proceed with their recognition or/and enforcement.

An explanation of this from a *procedural approach* is that this ground can overlap with the next one listed, ie the breach of due process rights.[48] Basically, both are grounds for refusal, but they are separated in the Spanish Act 29/2015, even if the due process rights infringement is regarded as an infringement of the procedural public policy (note that under this Act there is no consideration of *procedural public policy* itself).[49] It will depend on the analysis and examination of these grounds for refusal by the Spanish courts to determine whether there was a right invocation or not, to avoid a blurry application by the legal operators at stake.

In addition, according to some Spanish case law, the public policy requirement will operate when the facts and merits of the cases show a manifest opposition with Spanish

[44] For instance, Judgment of the Spanish Supreme Court, 4 December 2024, no 1626/2024 (ECLI:ES:TS:2024:5879), Order of the Provincial Court of Oviedo, Secc 1ª, 14 February 2020, no 18/2020 (ECLI:ES:APO:2020:232A); Order of the Provincial Court of Vitoria-Gasteiz, 3 December 2019, no 138/2019 (ECLI:ES:APVI:2019:663A).

[45] Most recent case law of the Spanish Supreme Court is the Supreme Court Judgment, 14 March 2022, no 202/2022 (ECLI:ES:TS:2022:939); 6 February 2014, no 835/2013 (ECLI:ES:TS:2014:247); 6 October 2016, no 599/2016 (ECLI:ES:TS:2016:4287); 21 December 2005, no 715/1996 (ECLI:ES:TS:2005:18055A); Order of the Provincial Court of Barcelona, Secc 11, 11 January 2022, no 9/2022 (ECLI:ES:APB:2022:97A).

[46] Gascón Inchausti (n 1) 180; Order of the Provincial Court of Lugo, Secc 1ª, 9 April 2019, no 40/2019 (ECLI:ES:APLU:2019:95A).

[47] Calvo Caravaca and Carrascosa González (n 1) 945.

[48] See Preamble VIII of the Spanish Act 29/2015.

[49] Calvo Caravaca and Carrascosa González (n 1) 945.

international public policy principles.[50] Public policy is a very controversial ground. Furthermore, its content and scope are always carefully examined by the courts before being triggered as a requirement to refuse any recognition. Under the Spanish system, Courts must be sure that the resolutions are contrary to the Spanish supreme legal order principles when applying Spanish rules on recognition and enforcement.

g) Reciprocity

As noted above, the Spanish recognition system is based on a positive recognition and cooperation system.[51] Therefore, resolutions will be recognised and enforced if they comply with the Spanish Act 29/2015 requirements, regardless of the recognition system of their courts of origin. This is grounded on the protection of procedural fundamental rights, and also in political reasons. A former reciprocity requirement is considered inappropriate in a modern recognition system by the Spanish legislator.[52]

In so doing, it is also a modernisation of the former system, as the Spanish legislator now considers that a recognition system which is only based in reciprocity is obsolete, according to relevant principles such as the one of mutual recognition and others enshrined in international and European rules of recognition and enforcement.

However, and only by exception, the Spanish Government may order the suspension of cooperation with the authorities of a foreign state when there is a repeated refusal of cooperation with Spain or a legal prohibition of cooperation from the authorities of that state (Article 3(2)). This would provoke to apply temporarily a negative reciprocity for the resolutions that could come from the courts of this state. However, to date, no such order has been issued as it is regarded as an extraordinary and extreme measure.

h) Other Requirements

There are no other requirements under the Spanish Act 29/2015.

Question 4. Documents to be Produced

Article 54(4) of the Spanish Act 29/2015 demands that, to get an *exequatur*, the following documents must be provided:

(i) The original copy, or an authentic one, of the foreign decision, duly legalized or apostilled pursuant the HCCH 1961 Apostille Convention.

[50] For instance, Order of the Provincial Court of Pontevedra, 10 September 2009, no 219/2019 (ECLI:ES:APPO:2009:219A); Order of the Spanish Supreme Court, 18 April 1998, no 728/1998 (ECLI:ES:TS:1998:728A).

[51] Order of the Spanish Supreme Court, 18 April 1998, no 728/1998 (ECLI:ES:TS:1998:728A).

[52] VIII Ground of the Preamble SCPA: 'dicha normativa responde a planteamientos obsoletos y que se han visto superados por la jurisprudencia, de manera que estamos frene a un sector normativo especialmente necesitado de una regulación moderna y adaptada a las necesidades de una sociedad abierta como la española, en la que las relaciones exteriores han dejado de ser un fenómeno minoritario y excepcional'.

(ii) In case of judgment by default, the document accrediting the delivery or service of the summons or equivalent document.
(iii) Any other document proving that the foreign judgment is final and enforceable in the state of origin. Such information may be stated in the judgment itself or may be deduced from the law applied by the court of origin;
(iv) A Power of Attorney (PoA) presented by the party requesting the recognition. To this end, the Spanish consulates are authorised to grant this kind of PoA when required.
(v) Translations of all the above-mentioned documents into Spanish, according to Article 144 SCPA, as the provisions of the Spanish Act 29/2015 do not establish the translation as a requirement.[53] Under Article 144(2) SCPA, parties can provide private translations. However, the parties are highly recommended to provide official translations by a sworn translator to avoid any challenge by a counterparty regarding the accuracy of private translations.
(vi) According to Article 41(3), authentic documents will be recognised by the Spanish authorities provided that they comply with the requirements given by the Spanish law to their kind. In addition, they must be issued by official authorities or with analogous function in their country of origin and be served in a recognition and enforcement proceeding under the SCPA.[54]

Question 5. Securities, Bonds and Deposits

Under the Spanish regime, the applicant might be required to provide a deposit or security when:

(i) the recognition of the foreign judgment has been granted by the first-instance court;
(ii) the party opposing the recognition has appealed/challenged said decision; and/or
(iii) the appeal court considers that the foreign judgment might be enforced during the appeal proceeding but is subject of a security. Security may be provided in cash or by a joint and several guarantee of indefinite duration and payable on first demand issued by a financial institution, by any other means which, in the opinion of the court, guarantees the immediate availability, where appropriate, of the amount at stake.

Furthermore, both the appeals before the second-instance court and the one before the Supreme Court require providing a deposit of 50 euros. In the event that the appeal is totally or partially awarded, the deposit will be returned to the party (usually, the claimant) who pays for it.

[53] Art 144 SCPA: Documentos redactados en idioma no oficial; Gascón Inchausti (n 1) 166.
[54] On this aspect, the Spanish Act 29/2015 understands authority and public document following what was interpreted by the CJEU in the C-260/97; Gascón Inchausti (n 1) 185.

Sweden

ERIK SINANDER

Question 1. General Overview

Overall, Swedish private international law takes a negative position to recognition and enforcement of foreign judgments in civil and commercial matters. Chapter 3 Section 2 of the Swedish Enforcement Code (*utsökningsbalken* [1981:774]) states that 'Special provisions state the extent to which enforcement may take place within the Realm on the basis of a foreign enforcement title'. This requirement on the need for special provisions in order to enforce a foreign judgment sets the floor for the Swedish attitude towards foreign judgments. Even if the section only mentions enforcement, it is generally understood that recognition of foreign judgments is meant to follow the same standard.[1] In addition to the EU regulations, Swedish special provisions exist primarily due to international conventions to which Sweden is bound. In addition, there are no generally applicable rules on how to treat foreign judgments.[2]

Due to the negative attitude towards foreign judgments, a party that has won a legal dispute in a foreign court is, with one notable exception, indirectly requested to initiate new proceedings in Sweden to be able to enforce his or her rights. In this regard, it shall be mentioned that Swedish jurisdictional rules on non-EU defendants are very liberal.[3] According to the Swedish Supreme Court's case law, the only prerequisite for Swedish jurisdiction is that there is a 'Swedish interest to adjudicate the matter'. The liberal jurisdiction rules balance the restrictive recognition and enforcement rules.[4] Also, in a Swedish sequel procedure on a matter that has already been adjudicated in a foreign court, the foreign judgment may be brought as evidence.

[1] See eg M Bogdan and M Hellner, *Svensk internationell privat- och processrätt*, 9th edn (Norstedts Juridik, 2020) 115. In Swedish private international law, recognition is traditionally understood as all legal consequences stemming from a judgment; see further M Linton, *Erkännande och verkställighet av utländska domar i förmögenhetsrätt* (Norstedts Juridik, 2023) 33, 68.

[2] See eg M Linton, *Cross Border Enforcement of Monetary Claims – Interplay of Brussels I A Regulation and National Rules – National Report: Sweden* (University of Maribor Press, 2018) 36. For a more comprehensive description of Swedish law on foreign judgments (in Swedish) see Linton (n 1) 438 ff.

[3] For a description on the Swedish jurisdictional rules in cases related to non-EU defendants, see L Lundstedt's report in T Lutzi, E Piovesani and D Zgrabljić Rotar (eds), *Jurisdiction Over Non-EU Defendants – Should the Brussels Ia Regulation be Extended?* (Hart, 2023) 237–55.

[4] E Sinander, *SvJT* 2019, 941.

Question 2. Procedure

a) Circumstances of Recognition and Enforcement

De jure, one can question whether the Swedish procedure of enforcing foreign judgments really is an enforcement of a foreign judgment. Rather, it is an adaptation of the foreign judgment being transferred into a Swedish judgment. As described in section 3 below, enforcement of foreign judgments in Sweden is a case-law-made exception to the generally negative attitude towards foreign judgments. The exception is only available where the court of origin has based its jurisdiction on a *forum prorogatum* basis. In those cases, the judgment creditor must initiate new proceedings in Sweden to seek enforcement of the foreign judgment.

b) Procedural Steps

Formally, such a procedure follows the same procedural rules as any other civil law procedure. There are no explicit requirements for what documents that need to be produced for the application of the restrictive rule on enforcement of foreign judgments without explicit legislative support. Self-evidently, the judgment needs to be produced. In the legal literature, it has been noticed that it is not clear how a claim to have a foreign judgment enforced shall be formulated, or how the court shall decide in such a matter.[5] This procedure, sometimes referred to as a 'special examination procedure', has been compared to an *exequatur* procedure.[6]

Other foreign judgments are not given any legally binding effect in Sweden.[7] Still, a foreign judgment may serve as evidence in a Swedish procedure on the very same matter as the foreign judgment regarded or in another Swedish procedure as Swedish procedural law relies on free sifting of evidence.[8] Here, it shall be emphasised that this is no formal recognition, but only a matter of valuing evidence.

In a series of judgments from the late nineteenth century and the early twentieth century the Swedish Supreme Court dealt with the issue of foreign judgments as evidence.[9] It is noteworthy that these cases were rendered under the old Swedish procedural rules and that sifting of evidence was not free at the time, but something that came with the Swedish procedural reform in the 1940s.[10] Nonetheless, the presumption in older case law that a foreign judgment where a court has applied its own law has done so correctly also has bearing in a modern evidence valuing context.[11]

[5] Linton (n 1) 450 f.
[6] ibid 451.
[7] As mentioned above, the general rule on enforcement of foreign judgments is also considered to apply to recognition of foreign judgments; see n 1 above.
[8] See Ch 35 S 1 of the Swedish Procedural Code (*rättegångsbalken* [1942:740]).
[9] See Linton (n 1) 462 with references to NJA 1894, 96, NJA 1913, 326 and NJA 1935, 61.
[10] See eg the preparatory works to the procedural reform where the free sifting of evidence was described as a part of a major change, prop 1942:5, 275 f.
[11] Linton (n 1) 463 f.

A consequence of foreign judgments only being recognised as evidence in new Swedish proceedings and not given legally binding effect is that the relevance of the foreign judgment is dependent on the Swedish procedure and how the legal matter is classified in Sweden. As the foreign judgment has no legal effect, it is possible for a party to bring the case differently in the Swedish procedure compared to how it was brought in the foreign procedure. In practice this means, for example, that foreign default judgments can rarely serve as evidence for a subsequent Swedish procedure in the very same matter.[12]

Question 3. Requirements

a) Jurisdiction of the Court of Origin

The jurisdiction of the court of origin is crucial for whether a foreign judgment can be recognised and enforced in Sweden. Only if a foreign judgment has been given by a court that based its jurisdiction on an exclusive forum selection clause (*forum prorogatum*) may a foreign judgment be recognised and enforced.

Despite the explicit prerequisite demanding special provisions for a foreign judgment to be enforced or recognised, the Swedish Supreme Court has in its case law also allowed that judgments in which the court has based its jurisdiction on an exclusive forum selection clause shall have such a strong evidential effect that the foreign judgment is fully accepted. In practice, this situation is a type of *exequatur* procedure, with the formal difference that it is not the foreign judgment that formally is being enforced. Instead, the foreign judgment is transferred into a Swedish judgment.

The Supreme Court's case law allowing for this limited type of *exequatur* procedure has a long and interesting history that can be traced back to at least *NJA* 1949, 724.[13] In this judgment, an outspoken motive of keeping even pace with arbitration is the reason for accepting that a forum selection clause pointing out courts in England should be a procedural impediment for Swedish courts. The Supreme Court justice Hjalmar Karlgren, a professor who wrote books on private international law, made an amendment to the judgment with a relatively long argumentation for why arbitration and court proceedings should enjoy relatively similar procedural standards, as well as why the issues of jurisdiction and enforcement are mirroring each other. In the amendment of Karlgren, those factors as well as the respect for party autonomy in civil matters were arguments for treating a forum selection clause pointing out a foreign court as a procedural impediment for Swedish courts. As neither enforcement nor recognition of the foreign judgment were direct issues in the case, the judgment does not explicitly deal with those issues. However, the argumentation in the amendment can be said to

[12] See also ibid 462.

[13] Sometimes, the limited *exequatur* procedure for foreign judgments delivered by a court in the *forum prorogatum* is even traced all the way back to the Supreme Court's judgment *NT* 1871, 495 (see eg Linton (n 1) 446). That judgment may very well be interpreted as stating that foreign judgments delivered by a court in the *forum prorogatum* shall be recognised and enforced in Sweden. It is however unclear as the Russian judgment in the case was not enforced due to a legal issue of the succession of the forum selection clause at hand.

have paved the way for recognition and enforcement of judgments in which the foreign court has based its jurisdiction on a forum selection clause.[14]

The above-mentioned judgment was followed by another from the Supreme Court in 1973. In the judgment *NJA* 1973, 628, the main issue was whether or not a Greek judgment should be recognised and enforced in Sweden. The dispute that had been resolved by Greek courts involved a Swedish transport company and a Greek shipping company that had had a contract for the carriage of goods from Sweden to Sudan and Saudi Arabia, and concerned the issue of how much the Swedish transport company owed the Greek shipping company for the transportation. Despite the fact that there was a clear forum selection clause in the contract identifying Greek courts as having exclusive jurisdiction, the Greek shipping company offered to settle the dispute in a Swedish court. As the Swedish transport company refused, the Greek shipping company brought action in Greek courts. The Greek court communicated to the Swedish defendant that a court case was initiated, but the Swedish company did not appear in the Greek courts. In the absence of the defendant, the Greek court ordered the Swedish company to pay the Greek company. To have the Greek judgment enforced, the Greek company urged in a Swedish court that the Greek judgment should be enforced. The Supreme Court held that it was clear that the Greek court had based its jurisdiction on an exclusive jurisdiction clause. No circumstances that had occurred after the clause was entered into could question the intent of the parties. Here, the Supreme Court notes that the jurisdiction clause was entered during the Greek Junta dictatorship period. Conversely, one can probably draw the conclusion that a jurisdiction clause must not be respected if, for example, a subsequent *coup d'état* or similar radical societal transformation changes the conditions for the foreign jurisdiction. Also, the Supreme Court held that even if the Swedish defendant had been absent, the Greek courts had summoned the Swedish defendant to appear as well as having served the judgment. Further, the Supreme Court held that neither could the content of the foreign judgment nor any other circumstances brought in the case be seen as contrary to Swedish public policy. Therefore, the Greek judgment should be recognised as basis for a new Swedish (enforcement) judgment.

From the 1973 judgment one can conclude that a judgment delivered by a court that has based its jurisdiction on an exclusive forum selection clause shall be enforced in the *exequatur*-like manner so that the foreign judgment is recognised and transferred into a Swedish judgment. Also based on the judgment at hand, enforcement seems however to come with a few explicit exceptions. First, societal changes in the *forum prorogatum* subsequent to the entrance of the forum selection clause may be ground for not following the forum selection clause. Second, the foreign procedure must have met due process standards. Last, the judgment must be compatible with Swedish public policy.

The Swedish Supreme Court has been reluctant to extend the case law established rule on enforcement of foreign judgments. In the judgment *NJA* 1986, 119 the issue was

[14] The acceptance of a forum selection clause pointing out a foreign court was reiterated in the Supreme Court's judgment NJA 1969, 529. Just like in NJA 1949, 724, the court held that a forum selection clause constitutes a procedural impediment for a Swedish court, unless it can be proven that such an acceptance would lead to 'inconveniences' for one of the parties that could motivate the court to disregard the forum selection clause. The court does not elaborate what kind of inconveniences that were meant. Due process concerns could however possibly be such an inconvenience that could be taken into account.

whether the same principle should be applied for a foreign judgment in a matter where a Swedish company seemingly accepted the foreign court's jurisdiction. In other words, the question was if the principle could also be extended to cases where the foreign court has based its jurisdiction on tacit prorogation (ie the defendant's silent acceptance of the court's jurisdiction). In the reasoning of the court, tacit prorogation is not comparable with an explicit forum selection clause in this regard. One of the Supreme Court justices made an amendment to the judgment where he developed an argument that enforcement of judgments requires reciprocity, which can only be achieved by legislation.[15]

Another case testing the limits of the principle settled by the Supreme Court in the 1973 judgment is the Svea Court of Appeal's judgment of 5 November 2010, in case T 6639-09.[16] In this case, enforcement was sought in Sweden of a foreign judgment against a losing plaintiff. The background was that a Swedish inventor had filed a patent infringement claim in the United States (US). After having lost in US courts, the defendant urged that the US judgment should be enforced to make the Swedish plaintiff pay the procedural costs in line with what the US court had held. With references to the judgments of 1973 and 1986 mentioned above, the district court held in its decision that there were grounds to extend the Swedish principle on when foreign judgments should be enforced. Emphasis for this conclusion was put on the fact that the Swedish plaintiff had initiated the proceedings and consequently must also have accepted the jurisdiction of the foreign courts. The Court of Appeals came to the contrary conclusion holding that the US judgment should not be enforced. For this conclusion, the Court of Appeals made the point that the plaintiff had not necessarily accepted the jurisdiction of the foreign court by initiating a lawsuit there.

b) Finality/Enforceability in the Country of Origin

The limited case law that exists remains silent on the potential existence of such a requirement.

c) *Res Iudicata*

The limited case law that exists remains silent on the potential existence of such a requirement.

d) *Lis Pendens*

The Supreme Court's judgment *NJA* 2013, 209 dealt with parallel proceedings in the same matter. A Swedish company had first initiated a declaratory action procedure in New Jersey, US against inter alia a Swedish insurance company. In the US procedure,

[15] See the amendment by Justice Vängby to the Supreme Court's judgment *NJA* 1986, 119.
[16] For a longer discussion on this case, see Linton (n 1) 457 ff.

the Swedish plaintiff claimed that the court should declare that the insurance company was liable for paying compensation for environmental damages caused in the US. When the case was still pending for the US courts, the insurance company initiated a negative declaratory action procedure in Sweden claiming that the insurance company should not be held liable to pay the damages. Under Swedish procedural law, declaratory actions are only allowed if the legal relation is uncertain and that this is detrimental for the plaintiff.[17] The Swedish Supreme Court noted that the US judgment will not be recognised and enforced in Sweden. A plaintiff therefore has the possibility to initiate procedures in Sweden despite the fact that a parallel procedure is pending in the same matter in a foreign jurisdiction.

e) Specific Requirements of Due Process

In addition to the already restrictive rule on only enforcing foreign judgments where the court has based its jurisdiction on an exclusive forum selection clause (*forum prorogatum*), due process must be upheld when enforcing a foreign judgment in Sweden. This was indicated already in the 1973 landmark judgment by stating additional prerequisites regarding due process in the country of origin of the foreign judgment.

Since the 1973 judgment, the principles of a fair trial have been strengthened by support in Article 6 of the European Convention on Human Rights (ECHR) as well as support in EU law and the extensive case law on this right from both the Strasbourg and the Luxembourg courts.[18] As regards recognition and enforcement of foreign judgments, the ECHR requires that the state where recognition or enforcement is sought investigates that the foreign procedure met those due process standards that follow from Article 6 ECHR and that this duty is even stronger when the judgment has been made in a non ECHR-state.

Even if the Swedish Supreme Court seems (by mistake) to not have observed the ECHR standards on due process in a matter of recognition of a foreign marriage dissolution,[19] there is no doubt that Swedish courts are obliged to follow the principles established by the ECtHR on due process in the state of origin.

f) Public Policy

The restrictive approach to foreign judgments also comes with an exception for public policy. It is explicitly stated in the 1973 landmark case making it possible to enforce judgments where the court of origin has based its jurisdiction on an exclusive forum selection clause. Even if the public policy exception has not been put to the test when a foreign judgment is enforced under the restrictive case-law-based rule, public policy has been tested in relation to enforcement of foreign judgments under the Lugano Convention. In *NJA* 1998, 817, there was an issue whether a Norwegian judgment on defamation was contrary to

[17] The limitation of declaratory actions follows from Ch 13, S 2 of the Swedish Procedural Code.

[18] See eg from the European Court of Human Rights, *Dolenc v Slovenia*, judgment of 20 October 2022 (application no 20256/20) as well as *Pellegrini. Italy*, judgment of 20 July 2001 (application no 30882/96).

[19] See the Supreme Court's judgment of 5 March 2013 in case Ö 2475-12. For a comment to the case and the relevance of the ECtHR, see E Sinander, *SvJT* 2013, 807–14.

Swedish public policy. The background was that in a Norwegian documentary, comments were made on how seals were hunted in Norway. For this, Norwegian courts held that the moviemaker had defamed some fishermen. The Swedish Supreme Court held in its judgment that even if freedom of speech is strongly protected in Sweden it is not enough for considering it to be contrary to public policy per se. The restrictive application of the public policy exception means, according to the Supreme Court, that it can only be applied if the enforcement of the foreign judgment would appear to be a circumvention of the Swedish constitutional freedom of speech protection.

g) Reciprocity

As Sweden only allows enforcement and recognition of judgments in which the court has based its jurisdiction on *forum prorogatum*, reciprocity is not a relevant criterion for the enforcement of foreign judgments. In the Supreme Court judgments' reasoning, reciprocity has however been pinpointed as a *de lege ferenda* principle. In Supreme Court judgment *NJA* 1986, 119, the role of reciprocity was discussed. In the case, which concerned a German judgment, the court noted that an equivalent Swedish judgment probably would have been enforced in Germany and that it therefore would seem to be 'natural' to enforce a German judgment. However, the court continued to conclude that an *in casu* assessment of reciprocity is not a suitable task for the courts to decide. Rather, such reciprocity can be achieved primarily by international conventions or unilaterally by the legislator.

h) Other Requirements

None.

Question 4. Documents to be Produced

As there are no formal rules on how the exceptional case of enforcing foreign judgments from a *forum prorogatum*, there are no formal requirements for what documents need to be produced. As noted in the response to Question 2 b) above, however, the judgment itself necessarily needs to be produced. Additionally, the material that the foreign court based its judgment on must also be produced.[20] All documents must be translated into Swedish.[21]

Question 5. Securities, Bonds or Deposits

Not applicable.

[20] Linton (n 1) 452.
[21] ibid 452.

INDEX

www.ingramcontent.com/pod-product-compliance
Ingram Content Group UK Ltd.
Pitfield, Milton Keynes, MK11 3LW, UK
UKHW020233290926
15470UKWH00002B/521

9 781509 97937